Library of Congress Cataloging-in-Publication Data

Woods, Ron, 1943 Nov. 6-
  Social issues in sport / Ronald B. Woods. -- 2nd ed.
     p. cm.
  Includes bibliographical references and index.
  ISBN-13: 978-0-7360-8982-1 (hard cover)
  ISBN-10: 0-7360-8982-9 (hard cover)
1. Sports--Social aspects. 2. Sports--Sociological aspects. I. Title.
  GV706.5.W655 2011
  306.4'83--dc22

                         2010046523

ISBN-10: 0-7360-8982-9 (print)
ISBN-13: 978-0-7360-8982-1 (print)

Copyright © 2011, 2007 by Ronald B. Woods

Permission notices for photos reprinted in this book from other sources can be found on pages xiii - xiv.

The web addresses cited in this text were current as of January 2010, unless otherwise noted.

Acquisitions Editor: Myles Schrag; **Developmental Editor:** Amanda S. Ewing; **Assistant Editors:** Melissa Zavala, Antoinette Pomata, and Anne Rumery; **Copyeditor:** Joyce Sexton; **Indexer:** Andrea Hepner; **Permissions Manager:** Dalene Reeder; **Graphic Designer:** Nancy Rasmus; **Graphic Artist:** Dawn Sills; **Cover Designer:** Keith Blomberg; **Photographer (cover):** Gianluigi Guercia/AFP/Getty Images; **Photo Asset Manager:** Laura Fitch; **Photo Production Manager:** Jason Allen; **Art Manager:** Kelly Hendren; **Associate Art Manager:** Alan L. Wilborn; **Illustrator:** Nancy Rasmus; **Printer:** Sheridan Books

Printed in the United States of America   10 9 8 7 6 5 4 3

The paper in this book is certified under a sustainable forestry program.

Human Kinetics
Website: www.HumanKinetics.com

United States: Human Kinetics
P.O. Box 5076
Champaign, IL 61825-5076
800-747-4457
e-mail: humank@hkusa.com

Canada: Human Kinetics
475 Devonshire Road Unit 100
Windsor, ON N8Y 2L5
800-465-7301 (in Canada only)
e-mail: info@hkcanada.com

Europe: Human Kinetics
107 Bradford Road
Stanningley
Leeds LS28 6AT, United Kingdom
+44 (0) 113 255 5665
e-mail: hk@hkeurope.com

Australia: Human Kinetics
57A Price Avenue
Lower Mitcham, South Australia 5062
08 8372 0999
e-mail: info@hkaustralia.com

New Zealand: Human Kinetics
P.O. Box 80
Torrens Park, South Australia 5062
0800 222 062
e-mail: info@hknewzealand.com

E5030

Social Issues in Sport

SECOND EDITION

Ronald B. Woods, PhD

University of Tampa
University of South Florida

Human Kinetics

CONTENTS

PREFACE

This book critically and factually examines the sport of today's society, particularly in the United States. I have compared the historical development of sport with our modern sport world. As you will see, sport participation and spectatorship in America have significantly changed and now lean toward a corporate model of sport.

In the past 50 years, major changes in society spilled over into the world of sport. Racial barriers gave way to dominance by African Americans in sports like basketball and football, while Latinos now account for a third of Major League Baseball players. Women and girls participate more in sports and agitate for equal opportunities as participants and spectators. The Special Olympics and Paralympics have become major sport events for people who have mental and physical disabilities. Finally, consumer sports are accommodating a surging population of older adults who look to sport to enhance their personal fitness, quality of life, and social interaction. Each of these changes promotes new sport outlooks and strategies and offers hope for the continued expansion of sport for every person.

Methods of studying sport have become more rigorous and insightful as sport sociology has advanced as a science. University courses are plentiful for students wishing to study the sociology of modern sport, and hundreds of researchers and professors study the relevant issues. This book presents the controversies and the status of sport in a sociological construct without dwelling on the theoretical constructs. This text is a look at sport taken by a longtime sport participant, observer, fan, teacher, coach, administrator, and critic who has tried to maintain a balanced approach to sport.

Intended Audience

This is a book for people who are looking at sport objectively for the first time. It seeks to help you understand sport, its place in society, and possible changes it may need to make in order to maintain a positive future. I hope you will become better acquainted with the historical and current roles of sport in society. Regardless of your major course of study, if you are a sport participant or fan, you will find the information illuminating and in some cases surprising.

As you understand more about the sport world and its interaction with our society, you will be better equipped to decide what role sport will have in your life and within your family. Whether you are a competitive athlete, enthusiastic participant, or spectator, after reading this book you will likely enjoy sport more, appreciate the challenges sport faces, and be able to better evaluate the decisions of sport leaders. Sport can help unify or divide society, but clearly it has a better chance of helping if more people understand its value and limitations.

Although this book is based on research and reflects various social theories, it was not written for academic colleagues and does not break new theoretical ground. Rather, it is intended to encourage students to delve more deeply into the issues and contradictions that characterize what sometimes is a love–hate affair between sport and many of us.

Text Organization

Part I presents a framework for studying sport in society, defining terms and establishing the purpose and importance of sport study. It also looks at the overall field of sport science and how sport research contributes to knowledge within sport.

Part I also presents sociological methods for studying sport to help you understand how knowledge is gathered and analyzed. It describes social theories and the ways in which these theories help in the study of sport.

Part II examines the scope of modern sport and how it affects society. It clarifies the parallels and differences between sport participants and sport spectators, showing how popular sport differs between these two groups. It also examines and compares growth trends in various sports and distinguishes people who play participation or recreational sports from those who are devoted to high-performance sports. Part II also presents the business side of sport at the professional and collegiate levels and discusses the issues of spending public funds for private gain. It considers how finances affect athletes, coaches, owners, and participants individually and collectively. These discussions will help you appreciate the huge economic investments made in sport and the influence of money on sport policies and programs.

Additionally, part II outlines the powerful symbiotic relationship between media and sport. It acknowledges the influence of sport media personalities and journalism and the continuing challenges of including minorities and females more often in sport media.

Part III looks at sport as an institution and how it functions within other institutions such as colleges and the Olympics. Youth sports outside of the school setting have become an adult-organized activity for kids that permeates every community. Interscholastic sport teams continue to grow and prosper but face the challenges of integrating opportunities for girls in accordance with Title IX and constant funding pressures. Collegiate sports struggle to find their way under the economic pressure to support programs for a relatively few elite athletes who may or may not be comfortable in the academic setting.

The globalization of sport reflects our increasingly smaller world. International competition has increased as American sports have been exported around the world, and soccer has finally begun to take hold in North America. The Olympic Movement has propelled certain sports to international prominence and has taken on an originally unintended economic and political significance. Including professional athletes in the Olympic Games has changed the nature of the Games and focused world attention on developing elite athletes who can compete for a gold medal.

Part IV of this text focuses on the interaction between culture and sport. Beginning with good sporting behavior and progressing to race, ethnicity, gender, and social class, this section lays out the significance of social issues in our sport world. The changing role of women and African Americans in society has revolutionized sport, while ethnicity and social class continue to be powerful factors in who plays or watches sports, in general and in particular.

Religion and politics interact with sport today, as they have for centuries. Both have affected the growth of sport and have used sport to their advantage. Athletes use religion in their sport, and religious organizations use sport to promote their purposes. Government uses sport to promote identity and unity, social values, and nationalism.

A chapter unique to this book, "Special Populations and Sport," looks at groups who are physically disabled, mentally disabled, or aging and recognizes the effects of major societal changes regarding these populations in the past 25 years. As baby boomers age and life expectancy increases, we are seeing a significant change in our population demographics, with more of our population represented by older adults who view sports as recreation and as a tool for a healthier lifestyle. Similarly, since the Americans with Disabilities Act of 1990, people who are physically or mentally disabled have seen their sport participation opportunities expand exponentially.

A new chapter in this revised edition is "Development Through Sport." The increasing emphasis worldwide on using sport for the development of peace and understanding among people of various countries is explored, along with the emphasis on youth sport programs that seek to assist at-risk youngsters in academics, discipline, moral development, socialization, and avoiding a life of crime.

Deviant behavior in sport includes problems of violence, hazing, performance-enhancing drugs, and eating disorders. These behaviors are found among athletes of every age and affect individuals, teams, and institutions. Gambling on sport is also a growing concern despite the firm stand that organized professional and collegiate sports take against it, and unregulated Internet gambling on sport continues to be a problem.

Another chapter unique to this book, "Coaching Sport," acknowledges the influential role of coaches. As sport changed, so did the coaching profession, demanding higher standards in performance sport. Yet unsolved are the challenges of recruiting and training thousands of volunteer youth sport coaches needed each year, although some people are working to promote national and statewide standards for coaches.

The final chapter in this text looks to the future of sport in North America. Performance sport continues to compete with participation sport. Many youth have moved toward extreme sports that suit their needs better than the traditional, adult-organized sports. Older adults look to sport to enhance a longer life. American sport continues to face issues of finances, opportunities for women, and growing minority populations that are changing the face of society. The struggles among these interest groups will likely play out over the next 50 years.

Updates to the Second Edition

At the start of each chapter, this edition adds opening vignettes—a brief story or example that shows how the topics covered in a particular chapter relate to a real-life or hypothetical situation. These vignettes provide a bridge into the chapter content and help prepare the readers for what is to come.

eBook
available at
HumanKinetics.com

This new edition features updated sidebars that reflect the changes in the world of sport during the past five years. Current athletes, experts, and pop cultural trends have replaced the themes featured in the first edition. Some "Activity Time-Outs" from the first edition that have proved to be particularly popular with students have been retained, but many of these present new suggestions that will challenge you to delve further into topics presented in each chapter.

As mentioned previously, there is also a new chapter in this book—"Development Through Sport." In this chapter, readers will gain a better understanding of how sport can be used within a country to attract young people to programs that also help them build academic and social skills successfully. Another promising trend is the use of sport between countries to develop respect and empathy for people in other cultures, particularly youth.

Throughout all of the chapters, the essential statistics that enable us to analyze trends in sport participation, popularity, gender, race, and social class balance have been updated. Information on the business of sport also includes the latest available financial numbers that help us evaluate the reach and influence of sport and sport consumers.

Learning Tools

To facilitate student learning, each chapter starts with "Student Outcomes," which outline the chapter topics. Key terms are highlighted in bold-faced print and included in a glossary for easy reference. Each chapter ends with a summary of its main topics. Throughout the text, you will enjoy various sidebars:

 "In the Arena With . . . " sidebars highlight key players in sociological change in sport.

 "Pop Culture" sidebars discuss current trends in films, books, magazines, and so on that highlight sociological issues in sport.

 "Expert's View" sidebars show how experts in sport sociology interpret sport issues, and then raise discussion points for students.

 "Activity Time-Out" sidebars give students the opportunity to classify information, engage in friendly debates, or obtain interesting information.

Instructor Resources

Several instructor resources are available to facilitate using this text in your class. The instructor guide includes chapter summaries, student objectives, chapter outlines, additional student activities, and supplemental resources. The test package has more than 190 questions, including multiple-choice and essay questions. The Microsoft PowerPoint presentation package includes more than 380 slides that outline the text in a lecture-friendly format. All of these resources are available at www.HumanKinetics.com/SocialIssuesInSport.

Closing Comments

I have spent more than 40 years studying sport and applying that knowledge as a professor, a coach, and an administrator. I spent nearly 20 of those years on a college campus, teaching the psychosocial aspects of sport as well as coaching men's tennis at the Division I and II levels. Later I worked in various administrative roles for the United States Tennis Association, the governing body for tennis in the United States. I also spent eight years on the coaching committee for the United States Olympic Committee, which embraced the challenge of improving coaching in all sports in the United States. During my career, I have also been fortunate to have traveled extensively internationally (most recently to China) and in the process learned a great deal about sport in other countries. These experiences have given me a unique perspective on sport. It is my hope that you will enjoy that perspective and yet understand where it is limited.

ACKNOWLEDGMENTS

I want to express my sincere thanks to hundreds of students who sparked my interest in evaluating the information on sociology of sport. They challenged me to make the information relevant to today's world of sport. In particular, the students at the University of Tampa have provided consistent feedback and creative ideas and have clearly articulated their preferences for topics of particular interest to them using the first edition of this work.

I'm indebted to Rainer Martens, who challenged me to accept this project and had confidence in me to produce a worthwhile product. Likewise, I appreciate the work of Myles Schrag, acquisitions editor, for his guidance in the conception and shaping of the manuscript. Amanda Ewing, in her role as developmental editor, offered insightful advice, helped keep me on target, and made terrific suggestions for revision for this second edition.

Finally, my wife, Kathy, has been a tireless supporter throughout the project and encouraged me every step of the way. Without her interest, patience, and personal commitment to sport, it would have been a difficult undertaking.

PHOTO CREDITS

Studying Sport in Society

The opening chapters set the stage for studying sport from a sociological perspective by pointing out the integral relationship between sport and society in North America. The first chapter defines salient terms such as *play, games, sports,* and *work* in terms of purpose, organization, and complexity. As sport moves from *participation sport* played by amateurs to *high-performance sport* played by professional athletes, it moves away from recreation or leisure play activities and takes on the characteristics of work.

In chapter 1 we also look at why people study sport, and we review the sport sciences that form the basis for the scientific knowledge upon which coaching and training are based.

Chapter 2 presents the typical methods of studying sport. It defines several social theories and gives examples of how they might apply to sport research and interpretation. These social theories, referred to throughout the book, provide a framework for understanding different points of view relevant to the specific topics of each chapter. While sport psychology tends to focus on one individual, sport sociology looks at groups of people and how they interact and affect one another. The chapter describes the emerging field of sport sociology and provides information on tools for learning more.

What Is Sport and Why Do We Study It?

Student Outcomes

After reading this chapter, you will know the following:

- The definition of sport
- The sport pyramid
- Why you should study sport
- The subdisciplines of sport science

If you're like most college students, you probably think that sports play a significant role in your life. In fact, you may have even chosen your university partly because of the success of its athletic teams. In the United States, it's fair to say that many of us have heard of colleges simply because of their prowess in athletics even though sports play a relatively minor role in the mission and purpose of the institution. College sport teams typically enhance school spirit and are the focus of campus social life, so they must be important. But if college sports just produce more spectators—more people who watch others performing sports—we might ask whether they are really beneficial to students. Perhaps the question should be how physically active students on campus actually are in sport and other activities that contribute to their overall health and well-being.

On Thursday, April 15, 1954, I realized that baseball was important in the world. On that day Baltimore, Maryland, got its own Major League Baseball team and opened the brand-spanking new Memorial Stadium. The Orioles, spawned from the lowly St. Louis Browns franchise, marked the entry of my home city of Baltimore into the big leagues. Although just a kid, I knew that day was special since city hall closed for half the day, most businesses shut down, and best of all, school closed for the day so that everyone could enjoy the city-wide parade.

The city of Baltimore was about to embark on its golden age of sport, concurrent with my childhood. We rooted for moderately talented sport teams at first, but soon Hall of Famer Brooks Robinson led the Orioles while the magical arm of Hall of Famer Johnny Unitas guided our football team, the Colts. Having two superstars like Unitas and Robinson performing in the same city was like having current stars Peyton Manning of the Indianapolis Colts and Derek Jeter of the New York Yankees as your football and baseball heroes. I knew right then that I was falling in love with sports.

You probably have a similar story from your childhood of your introduction to sport. Once hooked, we never quite let go of our interest, loyalty, and devotion to sport and our heroes. In fact, the word "fan" derives from "fanatic," and that's just what many of us have been or continue to be.

If you're like me, studying sport is fun and can also help you expand your understanding of the place of sport in North America and the world. Imagine if all sports were banned, as they have been from time to time in certain civilizations. Our lives would change dramatically in how we spend our discretionary time, money, and emotion.

Sports affect our lives every day. Strangers on the street stop to chat about their hometown sport successes, discussing the local high school, college, or professional team. Entire cities wake up the morning after an exhilarating win by their home team and feel proud to live where they live, or wake up after a tough loss in a meaningful game and sink into mourning. Kids look up to sport heroes, memorize the lifetime statistics of each athlete, and dream of someday making it to their own fame and fortune. As they grow up, they copy the stance, mannerisms, and dress of their heroes.

Sports also affect the cultures, traditions, and values of our society. Stories in the sport world help us clarify our stance on issues such as racial equality, gender opportunity, rights of citizens with disabilities and senior citizens, class mobility, youth development through physical activity, and creating a better standard of health and fitness for everyone. We will examine these issues and more in the succeeding chapters. For now, let's focus on what sport is and how it differs from play and games.

Sport Through the Ages

Before we can analyze the effect of sport on society (and vice versa), we need to know what sport is and why we should study it. *Sport* is derived from the Latin root *desporto*, which means "to carry away." The term *sport* has been used throughout the ages to refer to physical activities that are competitive and organized and that divert people from everyday activities producing economic gain or sustaining life.

Sport and games have fulfilled various roles in societies throughout the centuries. The early Greek civilization used sport and games in celebrations, to honor the gods, or as part of funeral ceremonies. The great Greek poet Homer described sport in his *Iliad* and *Odyssey*. Typical contests of physical prowess included running races, chariot races, wrestling, boxing, and leaping. Hunting was also a sport of the ancient Greeks. In the ancient city-state of Sparta, sport and games helped young men refine their wartime skills. In contrast to Sparta, the city-state of Athens educated young men in grammar, music, and gymnastics to fully develop their physical and mental capacities. The difference between Sparta and Athens in the approach to sport was the beneficiary of the sporting skill: In Sparta the state benefited, while in Athens, sport aided the perfection of the individual man.

Other ancient civilizations showed evidence of the role of sport and games through paintings, carvings, and other historical documents. Running, swimming, and jumping have been part of every culture. Combat activities like boxing, wrestling, and other martial arts such as those originating in the Far East are part of every culture's history. Games with a ball were popular in diverse civilizations, including the Egyptians and the American and Canadian Indians, and various forms of football can be traced to ancient China.

Sport and games are still used today as celebrations and as examples of athletic prowess. But what is sport?

Definition of Sport

The **sport pyramid** is a helpful way to think of sports (see figure 1.1 on page 6). The pyramid contains four elements of human activity—play, games, sport, and work. These terms are often confused because of the interchange and overlap of ideas. Let's look at each element individually and then examine the interrelationships.

Play

Play forms the base of the pyramid since it is the physical activity of childhood and continues throughout life in various forms. Play is a free activity that involves exploration, self-expression, dreaming, and pretending. Play has no firm rules and can take place anywhere. Other than giving pleasure, the outcome of play is unimportant. Over the years, many people have postulated theories of play, including Dutch historian Johan Huizinga (1950), who described play as free of form, separate from ordinary life, and with no specific purpose. He considered games and sport to be specialized forms of play, with more formal rules and purposes and an emphasis on the outcome.

Games

Games are an aspect of play that have greater structure and are competitive. Games have clear participation goals that are mental, physical, or a combination of both; are governed by informal or

Sport was an important part of many ancient civilizations, including that of the Romans. This Roman mosaic shows two female athletes, one with hand weights and the other with a discus.

formal rules; involve competition; have outcomes determined by luck, strategy, skill, or a combination thereof; and result in prestige or status. Inactive games include board games like Monopoly, card games like hearts or Texas hold 'em poker, and video games like Madden NFL or Halo. Active games include kickball, Ultimate Frisbee, paintball, touch football, and street hockey. But as these "games" have become more mainstream, naturally there has been movement to organize them with national rules and competitive events, and they have taken on the characteristics of a sport. What were once informal neighborhood or schoolyard games or activities have changed.

Complicating our understanding of "games" is the rise in the past 15 years of the X Games, a commercial sport event put on by ESPN that features extreme action sports. In fact, these "games," such as skateboarding, snowboarding, motocross, and in-line skating, are actually sports rather than games.

The category of games is broader than the category of sport (described next), and actual sporting events such as a football or hockey game are often described as games. Taken by itself, a football game is a game, but when it is part of a league with rules, standings, and sponsors, as a college football game is, it becomes sport.

An example of the variation in games is the work of Dale Le Fevre, who developed and popularized the New Games that emphasize cooperation, participation, creativity, and personal expression rather than competition. New Games are being used in physical education classes, in youth camps, by religious groups, and by businesses to teach team building. Le Fevre's book, *Best New Games* (2002), is popular around the world. In many of his workshops, traditionally adversarial groups have successfully come together to play and have fun: Arabs and Israelis in the Middle East; Catholics and Protestants in Northern Ireland; mixed races in South Africa; and Serbs, Croats, and Muslims in Croatia and Serbia.

Sport

Sport can be thought of as a specialized or higher order of play or as games with certain special characteristics that set them apart. Various authors have defined sport over the years, and generally their ideas point to certain characteristics (Coakley 2004; Leonard 1980; Sage 1998; VanderZwaag and Sheehan 1978). The first and perhaps most critical is that sport must involve a physical component. Unlike play or games, which may or may not be physical, sport must include physical movement and skill. Sport typically involves physical coordination, strength, speed, endurance, and flexibility. According to this definition, a game of chess cannot be a sport, whereas games such as billiards and darts can be classified as sports although the physical skill required is fairly limited to eye–hand coordination.

The second common characteristic of sport is that it is competitive, with outcomes that are important to those involved and often to others such as families, fans, sponsoring organizations, and the media. Winning and losing are a critical part of competition and powerfully motivate participants to train faithfully and compete using their best effort.

The third common characteristic of sport is that it involves institutionalized games. Sports are governed by an outside group or institution that oversees conduct and results and enforces rules. In the United States, the National Football League (NFL) governs professional football, the National Collegiate Athletic Association (NCAA) governs collegiate sports, and local Game and Wildlife

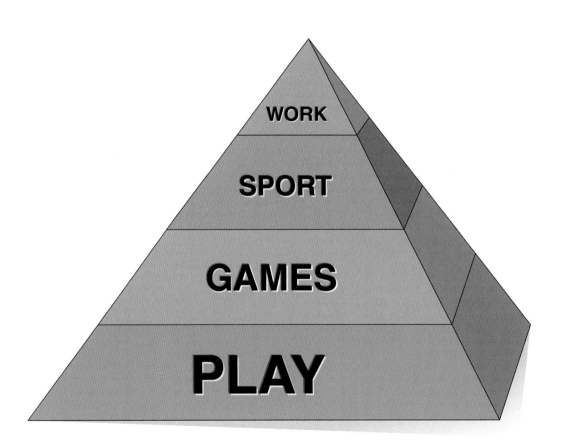

█ Figure 1.1 The sport pyramid.

POP CULTURE

Video Games

For the current generation of youth, video games are a major part of their day. Some studies have shown that the average amount of time spent on electronic video games exceeds five hours per day. Many of those video games do not include any physical activity and therefore seem to be adding to the lack of physical activity of kids. But there are some significant exceptions to this trend.

Various video games include physical activity. The Wii, for example, offers players a chance to play tennis, golf, baseball, and bowling. Dance Dance Revolution helps participants actively burn calories through vigorous dance moves, and other more adventure-based video games include prompts for players to jump, dodge obstacles, run, and balance their body. In fact, some physical education programs have experimented with developing physical activity and exercise routines using video games in the hopes of attracting kids who otherwise seem to shun more traditional sports and games. Do you know what the latest video game is that includes physical activity?

Commissions set the rules for hunting and fishing. So a pickup baseball game at a local park is just a game, but a Little League baseball game with rules, customs, standards for play, officials, coaches, and records of wins and losses is a sport.

The fourth common characteristic of sport is that it almost always requires specialized facilities and equipment. While this may be less true of sports such as cross country running or distance swimming across a natural body of water, most sports require a field with set boundaries, a pool, a gymnasium, a court, a golf course, or a similar facility. Equipment becomes particularly important at the professional level where athletes critically depend on the quality of their sled, skates, vaulting pole, tennis racket, golf clubs, or baseball bat.

Sport, then, is typically defined in North America as institutionalized competitive activity that involves physical skill and specialized facilities or equipment and is conducted according to an accepted set of rules to determine a winner.

The definition of sport in a given society reflects the culture, beliefs, and attitudes of that culture toward warfare, manhood, survival, and honoring the gods. In a society emphasizing cooperation more than competition, sports would differ from those in North American society. In fact, the rise of alternative sports among our youth (see chapter 6 on youth sport) demonstrates the changing definition of sport within a given culture.

For most people, attaining high performance and a professional career in sport is not an option. Instead, we play sports for the love of the game, as a hobby; we play as **amateurs**—the word stems from the Latin word for love. We gain intrinsic sat-

isfaction in competing to improve our fitness, refine our physical skills, work in a team, or embrace the challenge and excitement of testing our skill against nature or other competitors. For amateur athletes, participation rather than the outcome is the key. Sport participation is recreation that differs greatly from work. We participate to rejuvenate our spirit, without needing extrinsic rewards.

Sport can vary to accommodate people with physical or sensory impairments. Program directors who value the inclusion of people with disabilities use modified sports such as wheelchair basketball, tennis, soccer, and volleyball to blend those with disabilities and those without disabilities in sport competition. We'll look at sport for people with disabilities in chapter 14.

Work

Work is purposeful activity that may include physical or mental effort to perform a task, overcome an obstacle, or achieve a desired outcome. Often, people earn their living through work by trading it for compensation that provides for existence. Work appears at the top of the pyramid in figure 1.1 because sport can take on the characteristics of work at the professional level. Professional athletes are paid to perform work by training their physical skills to the highest level for competition with other elite athletes. Although all professional athletes begin their lives with childhood play and then participate in games and eventually sports, they may begin to regard sport as work after many years of facing competitive pressure, fighting through injuries, and living up to the expectations of their employer, their fans, and the media.

ACTIVITY TIME-OUT

Sport or Game?

Would you classify each of the following activities as a game or a sport? Test your understanding of the differences between sports and games and then compare your answers with those of other students. Mark S for sports and G for games:

_____ Flying a kite   _____ Jumping rope

_____ Street hockey   _____ Jogging

_____ Bocce   _____ Juggling

_____ Throwing a Frisbee   _____ Fishing

_____ Weightlifting   _____ Bowling

_____ Tap dancing   _____ Skateboarding

_____ Ballroom dancing   _____ Riflery

_____ Cheerleading   _____ Bicycling

_____ Roulette

If you had trouble classifying some of the activities, it may be that they fit neither sports nor games. They may involve physical activity, but their primary purpose is for entertainment. For example, professional wrestling involves two people who perform carefully choreographed moves that may appear to be competitive but in fact are pure entertainment. A Broadway show may entertain you with skillful dancing and singing, but that does not qualify the dancing as a sport. Evaluate the activity against all the classification criteria before judging whether it fits the definition of sport.

At the highest level of organized sport, athletes and coaches may earn millions of dollars for their performance, along with endorsement fees for the use of their appearance or name to promote particular products. Once they accept financial remuneration for their athletic skills, they are deemed professional athletes, hired to perform in their sport.

Athletes of any age who aspire to become professional athletes may be described as **high-performance athletes**. They develop their composite athletic skill so they can perform at the highest level possible and perhaps earn a living doing so. Children as young as age 10 may decide to follow their dream of becoming a star athlete and submit to a regimen of training and competition that prepares them for a professional career. Even at young ages, if the goal is a professional career, playing sports can take on the characteristics of work, which can lead to burnout and boredom for a child who is more interested in playing a sport for the fun of it.

Given the discussion on sport and work, we might represent the top levels of the sport pyramid as shown in figure 1.2.

The reality of the pyramid as shown in figure 1.2 is that much of the attention on sport in North America is focused on the highest level of sport performance. Professional sport is a business, and decisions at this level often reflect the goal of earning money. The line between professional and amateur becomes blurred at the highest levels of collegiate sport where universities commit large sums of money to support their athletic teams even though the players can receive only scholarships in return for their services. Similarly, even some youth programs take on the characteristics of professional sport by requiring kids to train year round, specialize in one sport at a young age, and perhaps risk a career-threatening injury in the heat of competition.

Only a small percentage of athletes can ever hope to reach the professional level. The health and welfare of society are clearly affected by the amount of its exercise and activity, yet the attention in sport is

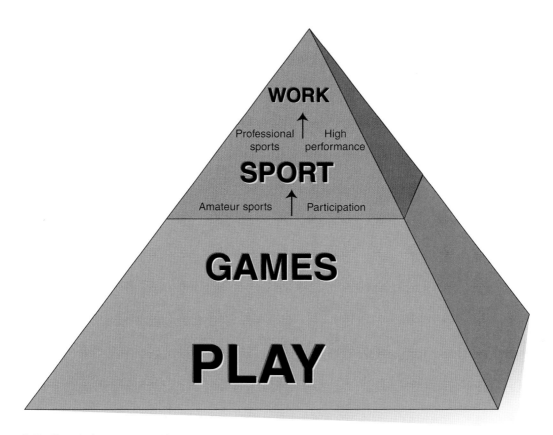

Figure 1.2 Detailed sport pyramid.

typically on the gifted few. As our population ages, obesity increases, and physical fitness becomes a national concern, perhaps participation in sport by the masses will command more attention, funding, and publicity.

It is only in the United States that amateur and professional are defined so specifically. This delineation is largely due to the unique presence of thousands of collegiate sport teams that have maintained an amateur label. In the rest of the world, this distinction is unnecessary because universities generally do not field sport teams or offer athletic scholarships. In European countries and in China, Russia, or Africa, children as young as age 10 may sign professional contracts and deals (with parental consent) that provide coaching and training expense money from a sporting goods manufacturer or from government sport agencies. In the United States, people would say that these athletes had "turned pro," while in their country no such distinction is even considered.

Two notable American athletes turned pro at young ages. Freddy Adu debuted in his professional career in 2004 at age 14, playing for Major League Soccer franchise D.C. United. He is the youngest professional player in modern team sport history and carries the burden of America's hopes for an international soccer star. Although Adu has played several international matches for the United States, he was not selected for the 30-man U.S. World Cup team for 2010 at the age of 20. Golfer Michelle Wie turned professional in 2005 just days before her 16th birthday. She immediately became the world's highest-paid female golfer, with a reported $8 million in endorsement fees. Wie was named Ladies Professional Golf Association rookie of the year in 2009. At age 20 in 2010, she is a student at Stanford University and a player who has reached a top-10 ranking on the women's golf tour. Because of their decision to become professional, these young athletes are not eligible to participate in college athletics in their sport, but for these exceptional athletes this is not a severe consequence. The athletes who do suffer from the eligibility rules are borderline professionals who may wish to someday go to college. In the United States, this demarcation between amateur and professional can have far-reaching consequences for young athletes who are uninformed.

IN THE ARENA WITH . . .

Sam Bradford

In collegiate football, players are not allowed to accept money for their play or use their athletic fame for financial profit. Just about the only tangible benefit for college athletes in the United States is an athletic scholarship to the school that pays all their expenses. That amount may be worth $10,000 per year up to more than $50,000 per year at some private schools. Yet even that compensation pales in comparison with the revenue that high-profile athletes may generate for their schools and coaches.

During the three years that Sam Bradford played quarterback at the University of Oklahoma, he set numerous school records including the NCAA record for touchdown passes by a freshman. He also led his team to three conference titles, three bowl games including the Bowl Championship Subdivision (BCS) title game in 2008-2009. Bradford won the Heisman Trophy in 2008, only the second sophomore in history to do so.

Meanwhile, his coach, Bob Stoops, earned a salary of $3.9 million per year and the university earned more than $120 million during Bradford's career against expenses of only $57 million for a profit of $63 million. Every home game was a sellout and the local economic impact of each game during the time Sam was at Oklahoma was $114.4 million (Fish 2009b). Add in the extensive publicity for Bradford and the football team, and you begin to see the impact of the Bradford years. Yet because Sam was an "amateur," he could not personally benefit. Admittedly he was not a one-man team, yet he was the inspirational leader and on-field general. There are those who believe major college football players are indeed entitled to share in the financial bonanza they generate. What do you think?

By the way, Bradford did end up being the number one draft pick overall in the 2010 NFL draft and signed a six-year contract worth $78 million dollars, the largest contract ever for a NFL rookie.

Study of Sport

Now that we know what sport is (physical competition according to a set of rules that determines a winner), we can look at why studying it is worthwhile. There are three main reasons why people learn about sport and physical activity:

- Personal development
- Scholarly study
- Professional practice

Many people enjoy learning about the science of sport and physical activity because they are attracted to sport and are intrigued enough to want to expand their understanding. There are millions of sport fans in any country, many of whom are experts at sport trivia; but there are few who truly understand sport from a scientific viewpoint.

According to Hoffman (2009), over 600 colleges and universities in the United States, along with many others worldwide, have academic programs for the study of physical activity. The growth of interest in sport study is evident in the remarkable explosion in the number of scholarly sport journals and societies that has occurred since 1960; the number of journals has multiplied about eight times, and the number of societies has grown fourfold (Hoffman 2009).

Much of the study of sport occurs in universities, where you can find departments devoted to specific sport sciences or to the overall field of kinesiology or physical education. At the undergraduate level, most students acquire a general overview of the field. At the graduate level, students seeking a master's or doctoral degree often concentrate their studies in one or two of the field's subdisciplines (discussed later in this chapter on page 12).

Professional practice within sport and physical activity has grown and developed over the years to serve others through sports. Many students study the generic field of kinesiology in college and later fashion a career by specializing in a subdiscipline or its application in everyday living. Often competency or certification tests are required for legitimately practicing within a specialty. Career options can be grouped as the following:

- Teaching or coaching
- Sport management
- Sport research
- Program directing
- Sport promotion and publicity

- Recreation and leisure
- Therapeutic exercise
- Sport business
- Health and fitness

Sport Sciences

In the past in the United States, the study of physical activity was typically labeled *physical education*, and the major goal of colleges offering majors in physical education was to prepare teachers and coaches. In recent years, labels such as *exercise and sport science*, *health and human performance*, *movement science*, and *sport and leisure studies* have been adopted to more accurately describe the study and function of physical activity.

Happily, many universities have adopted the term *kinesiology*, leading the trend toward greater unanimity in labeling the field of study of physical activity. After extensive study and debate, additional support for using the term kinesiology came from prestigious academic associations such as the American Academy of Physical Education. Although you may not include the term *kinesiology*

in your typical daily language, you should understand who studies physical activity and where to seek information about it. Sports are a part of physical activity, although many other forms of movement are included within the field of kinesiology.

During the last 40 years, the study of sport has changed remarkably as scientific study has expanded its base of knowledge. Sport study has been divided into subdisciplines, each with its own devotees, researchers, and practitioners. The emerging subdisciplines, based on scientific inquiry, slowly changed the perception of sport and physical activity and gave rise to a broader, more concrete overall discipline. It will help you to understand each of these subdisciplines, how they relate to each other, and how to integrate the information they comprise. The subdisciplines of sport science are typically divided into three domains:

- Biophysical
- Psychosocial
- Sociocultural

Let's look at each of the sport sciences.

At the turn of the 20th century, research in exercise physiology led to advances in training devices, such as the sliding practice seats used to train these rowing athletes in 1910.

Biophysical Domain

The **biophysical domain** focuses on physical activity from the viewpoint of the sciences of biomechanics, physiology, and medicine. Areas of study within this domain include the following:

- **Biomechanics** is the study of the structure and function of biological systems through application of principles of physics to human motion to understand how the body uses gravity, inertia, balance, force, or motion to produce speed, power, or distance.

- **Exercise physiology** is the study of human systems to enhance strength, speed, and endurance in performance toward the Olympic ideal of higher, faster, and stronger.

- **Nutrition** is sometimes studied as part of physiology to understand how food and drink affect performance. An athlete's diet and hydration habits under varied climates, contest durations, and environmental conditions are investigated.

- **Sports medicine** examines the prevention, care, and rehabilitation of injuries caused by participation in physical activity and sport. Research in sports medicine may also affect recommendations for training.

Psychosocial Domain

The **psychosocial domain** focuses on physical activity from the standpoint of the science of psychology. Areas of study within this domain include the following:

- **Sport psychology** is the study of human behavior in sport, including enhancing performance and treating disorders that affect optimal performance.

- **Motor learning and behavior** is the study of relatively permanent changes in motor behavior that result from practice or experience. It focuses on how people learn to perform motor skills and patterns efficiently and retain that ability even under pressure.

- **Pedagogy** is the study of the art and science of teaching. It focuses on the teacher or coach who creates the learning environment and assists the learning of sport skills.

Sociocultural Domain

The **sociocultural domain** focuses on physical activity from the perspectives of the sciences of history, philosophy, and sociology. Areas of study within this domain include the following:

- **Sport history** is the study of the tradition and practices of physical activity and sport over time and within different countries, cultures, and civilizations.

- **Philosophy of sport** examines the definition, value, and meaning of sport. Understanding your philosophy of physical activity will help you create your coaching style or prescription for sport participation.

- **Sport sociology** is the study of sport and physical activity within the context of the social

EXPERT'S VIEW

Sport Science on the Tube

Did you know that sport science is a regular feature on television? Both ESPN and Fox Sports have developed award-winning shows that feature the world's top athletes, using cutting-edge technology to analyze their performances. Topics range from measuring the reaction time of top athletes to measuring the impact force of being hit by a linebacker or a hockey puck. The beauty of these shows is that they present science in a fascinating way that appeals to coaches, sport fans, and athletes and debunk many of the popular assumptions and myths about athlete performance in sport.

The lead engineer for the Sport Science series has been Dr. Cynthia Bir, professor of biomedical engineering at Wayne State University in Detroit, Michigan. Using primarily the sport science of biomechanics, the show's host, John Brenkus, presents the inside scientific basis for things like how to succeed in the home run derby in baseball. Turns out that the secret is simply bat speed and the angle of upward swing needed to hit the ball over the fence (ESPN 2010d). The show was nominated for four Emmy Awards in 2008 and five in 2009 and settled many disputes about sports from argumentative bar patrons. Why not tune in and see how science can truly help our understanding of sport performance?

ACTIVITY TIME-OUT

Effects of Physical Activity

Since sports are a physical activity, they can affect the physical well-being of the population. Physical health has grown more important as our population ages and continues to live longer. Let's look at some alarming statistics from the President's Council on Physical Fitness and Sports (2010).

- Heart disease is the leading cause of death among men and women in the United States. Physically inactive people are twice as likely to develop coronary heart disease as regularly active people. Poor diet and inactivity can lead to overweight or obesity, which increases the risk of high blood pressure, type 2 diabetes, coronary heart disease, stroke, gallbladder disease, osteoarthritis, sleep apnea, respiratory problems, and some types of cancer.

- Nearly 60 million adult Americans are obese. More than 108 million adults are either obese or overweight. This means that three out of every five Americans carry an unhealthy amount of weight.

- The number of overweight children (ages 6-19) has tripled in the past 30 years and has reached 20% among African American, Hispanic, and Native American children.

- Requirements for daily physical education in schools have been drastically reduced so that only 28% of students in grades 9 through 12 get daily physical education, compared to a percentage of 42% in 1991.

- Less than one-third or 3 in 10 adult Americans meet the federal recommendations to engage in at least 30 minutes of moderate physical activity at least five days a week, while 40% of adults engage in no leisure activity at all.

Given the statistics, it makes sense to evaluate the promise of sport as a physical activity that could ameliorate such health concerns.

---

conditions and culture in which people live. Since this book focuses on the sociology of sport, it can help you identify the role of sport in your society and world. Whether you are an elite athlete, a recreational athlete, a prospective coach, a prospective athletic trainer, or a sport fan, you can deepen your understanding of the issues and possibilities in the sport world. Studying sport sociology may help you determine what role you want sports to play in your life, your family, and your community. Once you clearly understand that role, you can create a positive force for change, growth, and continuing prosperity for sports.

Sociology is the study of a society, its institutions, and its relationships. It relies on a systematic study of the development, structure, interaction, and collective behavior of a group of human beings (*Merriam-Webster's* 2001). Mature societies are likely to be more complex. In a modern society like ours, sociological analysis of sport is broad and deep, since its focus ranges from families to sport

participants to sport spectators to even those who gamble on sport. Sociology provides us with the tools to better understand sports as they exist in our lives. Analyzing institutions such as schools, colleges, clubs, churches, youth sport organizations, and professional sport organizations, and studying social processes such as commercialization, institutionalization, mass communication, conflict, and change, are essential for a thorough understanding of the dynamics of how sport operates.

Growth in Sport Sciences

Now that you better understand the overall field of sport science and its subdisciplines, you may suspect their influence on the field's recent growth in volume and complexity. More importantly, the explosion of knowledge in the sport sciences has improved the average citizen's experience of sport and physical activity. The knowledge acquired through the sport sciences allows us to do the following:

- Understand the historical precedents in sport and fitness, avoid mistakes of the past, and plan a healthier future
- Enhance competition performance through better training methods and produce record-setting performances that challenge us all
- Provide better motivation for citizens through understanding of the value of physical activity and help citizens plan for physical development
- Teach people new activity skills faster and more efficiently and thus convince them of their ability to successfully perform an activity
- Prevent physical injuries and speed up the recovery process following injury
- Understand the influence of sport on our culture and use sport and activity to promote equality, fairness, and success for all citizens
- Help people deal with stress and anxiety through sport
- Promote good health at all ages that allows people to function with high energy
- Understand how training for sport expands and challenges our physical systems and strengthens them to deal with emergencies
- Provide healthy activity for youth that enhances their maturation into productive adults
- Offer a better quality of life in later years as the life expectancy extends

You can see the many ways the sport sciences can positively influence our lives. You can see why their growth affects the expansion of sport and physical activity. There is a slight risk that people will use information from the sport sciences out of context because looking at the complete picture is too time-consuming or daunting. However, the knowledge gained in all of the sport sciences needs to be integrated to achieve the best understanding of sport and physical activity.

Chapter Summary

The sport pyramid is a good way to look at sport. The pyramid starts with play, which is informal, free activity that begins in childhood and continues throughout life. The second level of the pyramid is games, which are more structured than play and have specific goals and outcomes through competition. Sport is a higher order of games and has specific characteristics. The characteristics of sport include (1) a physical component, (2) competition to determine a winner and loser, (3) an outside group or institution that governs the conduct and results of the sport and enforces its rules, and (4) specialized facilities and equipment.

Sports can be further defined as professional sports that focus on the high performance of athletes who are rewarded extrinsically with money, fame, and prestige and as amateur sports in which people compete for the love of the game and value their participation for the excitement, physical exertion, test of skill, or benefits to their personal health.

Research from the sport sciences that extols the benefits of a healthy lifestyle can help motivate people to be more physically active.

Sport is studied for personal development, scholarly understanding, and professional practice. Through studying sport we can recognize historical precedents in sport, health, and physical activity and can advocate changes in the society around us. The 10 individual sport sciences belong to three domains: (1) biophysical, (2) psychosocial, and (3) sociocultural. Integrating the knowledge from the different sport sciences allows us to better interpret their collective information.

How Do We Study Sport?

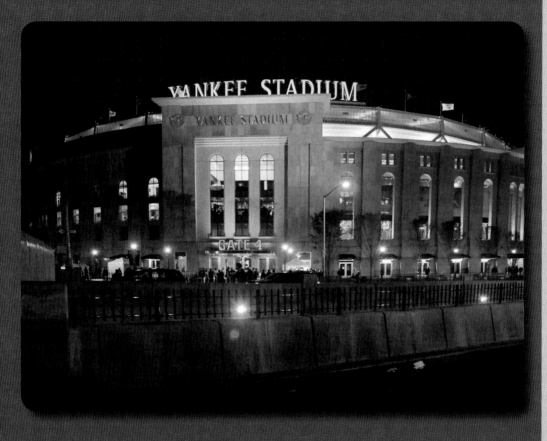

After reading this chapter, you will know the following:

- Types of research methods and data
- Sociology theories used to analyze sport
- How sociology theories apply to the study of sport
- How to use theories to interpret sport and decide on necessary changes in sport

Most sport fans have strong opinions about their favorite team, players, and sport in general. Sport talk radio shows have grown in popularity, and fans often exchange their opinions with passion and emotion. But when people discuss the burning issues in sport, how many of them have solid evidence to back up their position? Chances are, multiple research projects have investigated just about any hypothesis you might have and could help support your opinions and impressions. For example, is it true that owners of sport teams actually lose money as they often claim? Should taxpayers support using public funds to build a new stadium for the home team because the owner cannot afford the expense? Before you form an opinion, it might be best to take a hard analytical look at the cost versus benefits of owning a team franchise and decide whether you want to have your tax dollars spent to enhance the value of a franchise that the owner will likely sell sometime for a healthy profit. Once you understand the types of research that can be done and how it can be interpreted, you'll be in a much better position to make the call.

You may have watched, read about, and played a lot of sports during your lifetime. You probably know what it means to be a participant or spectator in a sport setting. But you may not know that you have been asking the same questions sport sociologists have asked for years. When your high school athletic program was in danger of losing district funding and you defended it on the grounds that sport teaches a strong work ethic, did you know you were speaking as a functionalist? Or did you know you were a critical theorist when you suggested that intercollegiate athletes be compensated as workers for the millions of dollars they bring to their universities? That you might be considered a feminist when you argued that female tennis pros winning a grand slam final should be paid the same as the men who win? These and many other examples show how sociocultural issues pervade the sport world, both locally and globally.

From chapter 1, we know that sports are physical competitions that follow a set of rules to determine a winner. We also know that we should study sport so we can recognize trends and apply that information to the current world. But how do we study sport? First, we collect data through research. Then we analyze the collected data using different social theories, all of which view the world differently.

Research Methods

In order to study sport or physical activity, the research scientist must have tools for collecting data that can be organized and analyzed. Many times a researcher will use more than one tool at a time. The sport sociologist generally uses two types of tools: **quantifiable data**, producing facts and figures that can be counted and analyzed statistically, and **qualitative data**, collected through interviews and observations of individuals or groups or through analysis of societal characteristics and trends. The following are examples of different research methods.

- **Survey research** through questionnaires is popular for determining sport participation and comparing spectator habits. With this method large quantities of data can be collected, analyzed for trends, and then generalized to the entire population if random sampling is used. However, this approach relies on self-reports by athletes or spectators that may or may not be accurate. Furthermore, unless the data are discrete enough that responses from different groups of people can be segregated, they may be misleading. For example, large surveys often combine all age groups to determine trends when separation by age might produce very different responses. Similarly, not accounting for race, gender, ethnic group, or income level may affect data interpretation. Surveys can also limit the choice of responses and thus miss the true feelings of respondents.

- **Interviews** with individuals or small groups (called **focus groups**) use more in-depth questioning and can elicit unexpected answers from open-ended questions. When designed correctly with sampling from various ethnic groups, geographical locations, income levels, genders, and other variables, an interview can provide a deeper analysis. However, interviews are time-consuming and expensive, and for these reasons they often rely on small sample sizes.

- **Content research** involves collecting information or pictures from articles, magazines, and TV programs and assigning the data to categories around a particular theme. For example, in content research, the ideal feminine body type for sport could be inferred from the frequency of photos of various body types appearing in the major sport pages. A drawback is that information is not provided directly by athletes, but rather by others reporting on them. Content research has been useful, however, in assessing the amount of coverage the media give to females in sport over a specified duration.

• **Ethnography**, which is based on observation, involves data collected by researchers who immerse themselves in an environment and keep recorded conversations or notes. Topics such as "life on the pro tour" or "life in the minor leagues" lend themselves to ethnography. Researchers use detailed notes of their observations, personal interviews, and other sources of data to gather a full picture of their subject. The obvious weakness in this approach is the time and cost required for a complete analysis. Yet some of the most interesting and helpful studies in sport have used this method to provide an inside view of a particular sport or class of athletes.

• **Historical research** involves looking at trends in sport over time. Often, the value of such research is that it can be used to compare trends in sport with trends in society. For example, the changes in female participation in sport during the second half of the 20th century closely paralleled the push for equality and women's rights in the United States. While historical research is helpful, it is usually limited to large societal trends.

• **Societal analysis** uses social theories (described in the next section) to examine life from a social point of view. For example, a researcher can apply a critical feminist model to professional sport to compare the opportunities for women and men who are professional athletes, including financial compensation for similar work.

The risk of using only one theory is overlooking other salient facts such as race, income level, and historical precedent (Hoffman 2009).

Regardless of the research method, once the data are collected, they need to be analyzed. Several social theories can be used to analyze data.

Social Theories

Social theories are used to compare the trends in sport with an overall social theory and thus allow conclusions about whether sport reflects the larger existing culture or acts as a change agent. Theories of sport sociology help organize our thoughts about a particular issue. They involve describing existing social situations, analyzing them from various perspectives, and formulating certain beliefs based on the findings. A theory can be explained to others, who can compare it to their analyses. As theories gain acceptance, they may become the basis for predicting the future or for calling for change within sport.

Analyzing sport with a social theory helps us consider the larger picture of how sport exists throughout

EXPERT'S VIEW

The Institute for Diversity and Ethics in Sports

Richard Lapchick, of the University of Central Florida's Institute for Diversity and Ethics in Sport (TIDES), conducts annual "quantitative" research on the issues of gender and racial diversity for collegiate and professional sports. His work is widely quoted in the news media as the authoritative source for statistics such as the percentage of players of various racial groups in every collegiate sport and major professional sports. If the Black Coaches Association makes headlines decrying the number of African American football coaches at major colleges, it uses—and the media publish—the actual count from Lapchick's work. Recent research has revealed that the percentage of African Americans in professional baseball has fallen to less than 10% in the major leagues while the percentage of Latinos has risen to around 30%. This research has helped us understand the changing face of race in baseball and spurred Major League Baseball to develop programs to promote baseball in cities with significant numbers of young African American athletes. Another contribution of the Institute is to annually show the percentages of females at every level of sport competition along with coaching positions, athletic directors, and other sports leadership positions. Do you believe that girls and women now have equal opportunities in sports as their male counterparts? To be well-informed and accurate, you will need to analyze the most recent data available from TIDES before you state your position.

ACTIVITY TIME-OUT

Using Research Methods

Imagine you are part of a research team looking at trends in youth sport participation in rural communities. Which research methods would you use to collect data? If you were looking at trends in youth sport participation in inner cities or suburbs, would your research methods change? Explain your answers.

society. It forces us to examine all aspects of the sport experience, including the seat of power within a sport, the values that are embraced, and the interaction of various groups involved. Sports become much more than a competitive season with a beginning and an end when examined within the context of larger social issues. Most social theories are rooted in the concept of enhancing and preserving the status quo or looking at the need for change. Table 2.1 lists the six theories considered in this chapter; let's discuss each of them now.

Functionalist Theory

Functionalist theory looks at sport as a social institution that reinforces the current value system in a society. Sports are seen as maintaining the status quo by positively benefiting a community or nation striving to work and play together. The traditional American values of hard work, discipline, and competition are perpetuated through sport and reinforced as the path to success.

Functionalist theorists see sport as contributing to the smooth functioning of a society by helping people promote common values, which in turn leads to stability within communities and the nation. At the same time, as social changes occur, sport can take a leading role in promoting those changes and thereby reinforce the dominant social value system.

The weakness of functionalist theory is that what is good for the architects of sport, who are often the economically or culturally privileged few, may not benefit society at large. Further, sport may positively benefit the average citizen while it discriminates against other groups (such as women, Hispanics, or people who have physical disabilities) that are typically underrepresented in sport.

A proponent of functionalist theory may embrace the traditional American emphasis of winning at all costs in sport. Americans celebrate winners and reward them lavishly until the next great team or player knocks them out of the winner's circle. In

professional sport, the emphasis on winning reflects the business approach to competition. However, when the preoccupation with winning seeps down to collegiate, scholastic, and youth sport programs, the results can be damaging. The overinvolvement of parents in youth sport is one recurring result that has been well documented through the headlines on the sport pages.

Sports that emphasize high achievement tend to dominate the American culture, attract media coverage, and attract live spectators and TV viewers. However, the majority of Americans who are involved in sport spend most of their time participating in recreational sport rather than seeking high performance. When the values of high performance are applied to the recreational setting, confusion and conflict are certain to occur among players, coaches, and officials (Leonard 1980; Loy and Booth 2004).

Conflict Theory

Conflict theory rejects the status quo as it exists in capitalistic societies such as the United States. Conflict theory is based on the theories of Karl Marx and views sport as built on the foundation of economic power. In a capitalistic society such as that in the United States, it is easy to point to the owners of sport teams, who benefit financially at the expense of athletes, coaches, and spectators. Likewise, many view bureaucratic organizations that operate sport like the National Collegiate Athletic Association (NCAA), governing bodies of sport, and the International Olympic Committee (IOC) as promoting sport to gain power, status, and money. Conflict arises when sport participants or spectators resist the apparent domination of controlling individuals or groups.

Unlike the functionalist theories that are based on societal imbalances, conflict theories focus on the disruptive forces that produce instability and disorganization. Sports are looked at in relation to changes in society. Nothing is as certain in life as

TABLE 2.1 Social Theories for the Study of Sport

Theory	How it looks at the world	Preferred method of research	Major concerns as it looks at sport	Shortcomings
Functionalist theory	Emphasizes maintenance of the status quo and equilibrium.	Quantitative survey research	Sport is a valuable social institution that helps build character and instill values. Competition is valuable, and high performance is a critical outcome of sport participation.	Tends to overemphasize the positive consequences of sport while ignoring those who are disenfranchised or overlooked such as women, people who are economically poor, certain racial groups, and people who have physical disabilities.
Conflict theory	Sees economic interests as shaping the world. Those who have power exploit those who do not. Change is inevitable, and struggle on the part of repressed classes is expected.	Societal analysis	Sport benefits the individuals and organizations in power to the detriment of the participants and working class. Athletes should have more control over their sport destiny and quality of experience.	Relies too heavily on economic factors and ignores the importance of race, ethnicity, gender, and age. Underestimates the effect of groups that empower individuals in a capitalist society. Tends to overlook participation and recreational sport for healthy living.
Critical theory	Views life as complex and diverse. Order is obtained through struggles over ideology and power. A better life for all citizens is the goal. Sports do not simply mirror society; they provide opportunity to change society.	Societal analysis	Sport must change to be fair to everyone, more democratic, and sensitive to diversity. Sport can help us improve our outlook toward gender, physical or mental disability, sexual orientation, and physical talent.	Critical theories are varied and sometimes confusing. They tend to encourage resistance against the status quo to protect special interests even when doing so is not advisable. They work better for specific cases than for forming an overall ideology.
Feminist theory	Views social life as based on a patriarchal ideology and controlled by men in powerful positions. Argues that feminine virtues are ignored or undervalued.	Quantifiable questionnaires, societal analysis, ethnography, and content research	Females lack equal opportunity in sport. There is a lack of women in coaching and leadership positions. Traditional masculine traits of competitiveness and aggressiveness conflict with traditional feminine traits like sensitivity and nurturing.	Feminist theory has weaknesses similar to those of other critical theories. It is also weak in addressing other categories that are connected to gender such as age, race, social class, and disability.
Interactionist theory	Views the world from the bottom up rather than from the top down. Focuses on social relationships between people. People make conscious decisions on how to respond and act toward the outside world.	Qualitative ethnographic research	People choose to participate in sport in various ways, and the quality of the experience for the athlete is important. Sport organizations should be open and democratic. Youth sport should fit the needs and desires of kids.	Focuses on the individual to the exclusion of the overall structure of sport. Does not address issues of power in sport as critical theories do.
Figurational theory	Emphasizes the connections between people and their interdependence. Views change that occurs over time.	Historical research	Sport exists as a part of society viewed historically and over the long term. Sport tends to focus on masculinity and male power. Developments in sport are seen in the context of global processes.	Devotes little attention to current issues by focusing on the long-term picture. Reduces the urgency to press for changes. Tends to emphasize the male power in societies.

In many youth sports, the focus is often on encouraging fair play, giving every athlete a chance to play, and not keeping score. A critical theorist would say these are all good things. What do you think?

the constant change produced by struggles between groups of different interests. In the middle of the 20th century, many sport sociologists moved toward the conflict theory approach and away from the more traditional functionalist point of view that tended to simply reinforce the existing status quo.

Much of conflict theory is directed at the dominant spectator sports. Advocates of this theory would place more influence in the hands of sport participants and promote sport at the local community level so that it benefits all classes of people rather than the elite few. The working class would have more influence over sport than the rich have. Conflict theorists favor player unions that confront owners, and support other organizations that guard against using public monies to build luxurious stadiums that benefit owners of professional teams.

Conflict theorists also campaign for athlete representation at all levels of decision making in sport organizations. Olympians would vote on policy questions concerning the staging of the Olympic Games. Student-athletes would help their colleges in coaching searches, and even athletes in youth sport would provide input into decisions made by league officials and coaches (Leonard 1980; Rigauer 2004).

Critical Theory

Sociologists refer to theories that evaluate culture and determine the source of authority one group has over another as **critical theories**. These theories examine how a culture operates and its struggles in the search for a better life for all citizens. A critical theorist is especially attuned to combating structural conditions in a society that lead to exploitation, oppression, or social injustice. Rather than shifting power to sport participants as conflict

 IN THE ARENA WITH . . .

Functionalism and Football Bowl Games

The traditional end-of-season bowl games for the highest level of Division I (FBS) college football continues to be a hot topic of conversation and debate. Critics believe that a "true champion" can be determined only by a play-off system that relies on head-to-head competition between contending teams, rather than the current bowl system that may or may not match the two best teams. Although many alternative formats have been proposed and debated, the inertia to change may be simply the tradition of collegiate bowl games. The root of the debate is money, since all the teams who compete earn income for their conference and school. But beyond that is a reluctance to change something that has been part of college football for generations. In spite of the fact that every level of college football except the top Division I has adopted a play-off system to determine the national champion, traditionalists continue to resist. Following the functionalist point of view, there is no reason to tinker with success.

POP CULTURE

The Blind Side

The Blind Side was a 2009 movie that chronicled the amazing life and sport career of Michael Oher, an offensive lineman who plays for the Baltimore Ravens of the NFL. The film, based on the book by Michael Lewis, traces the life of Oher from his impoverished upbringing. He lives with a succession of foster parents until he is taken in by a privileged family who enroll him in a small private Christian high school. There he finally learns to read as he is tutored in academics, plays on the football and basketball teams, and draws attention for his potential ability to protect the "blind side" of quarterbacks from his position as left offensive tackle. Eventually, he becomes one of the most highly recruited college athletes and chooses to play at the University of Mississippi, having reached the entrance requirement of a 2.5 grade point average. Michael goes on to college stardom and is eventually drafted by Baltimore in the NFL. This is a good example of a sport movie, combining a compelling story line, great acting, and a realistic look at how difficult it is to rise from a disadvantaged background to success as an athlete at the elite level. The point of the movie for critical theorists is that given the necessary economic and emotional support, many children from disadvantaged environments can be successful if we give them a chance.

theorists do, devotees of critical theories agitate to effect change where it is warranted.

Critical theorists conclude that sports do not simply mirror a society (as the functionalists or conflict theorists believe) but instead offer the opportunity to create society by affecting how people think and feel about social conditions. For example, it is possible that eventually people will understand the far-reaching benefits of regular physical activity in improving quality of life well into older ages. In America's recent history, physical activity has often been relegated to the role of fun and recreation, a worthy use of leisure time. However, the evidence keeps mounting that sport and activity should in fact be a regular part of life in order to maximize disease resistance, maintain energy, control body weight, improve appearance, and reduce the costs for health care.

One critical theory of interest is **hegemony theory**, which is largely based on the ideas of Italian political theorist Antonio Gramsci. Hegemony theory focuses on dominance, which is the power that one individual or group has over others. Coaches may fit into hegemony theory style. In professional sport where the goal is winning above all else, the authoritarian coach can usually survive so long as the team makes the play-offs. Bill Parcells, former coach of the New England Patriots, the New York Giants, and the Dallas Cowboys, is one example of a strong, authoritarian coach who survived because of his strong record of success.

Analyzing sport with critical theories may lead us to new ways of looking at our sport and our role

within sport. It should also help us understand the plight of others whose sport opportunities may differ from those we have. The goal of critical analysis is to make sport more democratic and sensitive to diversity and to provide access to anyone regardless of ethnic background, social class, or financial status. Sport can lead us to new understanding of gender, sexual orientation, and physical talent.

Critical theories take a more objective view of the conventional wisdom about sport in American society. Using critical thought, we challenge the status quo, analyze its effects on society, and propose beneficial changes. At the same time, we look objectively at the weaknesses of our current economic system, including how we treat people who are poorer or socially disadvantaged (Hargreaves and McDonald 2004; Sage 1998).

Feminist Theory

Feminist theories evolved from dissatisfaction with cultural traditions that emphasize males and either ignore females or reduce them to a subservient role. A feminist analysis of sport forces us to confront our sexuality and define our expectations of males and females and to openly discuss homophobia.

Feminist theories force us to analyze the status of women in sport. In American society, people may rejoice in the gains yet acknowledge the remaining work needed to ensure equal opportunities for both genders. For example, the dearth of women in coaching deprives half of our youth sport population of role models. A lack of women in leadership

ACTIVITY TIME-OUT

Female Athletes and the Media

Using the "content research" method, buy a local newspaper or *USA Today* for one week or check your hometown newspaper online. Note the number of articles in the sport pages that feature male versus female athletes. Calculate the percentage for one week and be prepared to share with your classmates. Discuss in class whether you believe your findings are representative of a typical week in a year or were influenced by certain sport events. If you were a feminist theorist, would you be content with your findings or would you propose some action?

positions in sport organizations affects decisions made in sport by disenfranchising a majority of our population.

An obvious weakness in analyzing sport with feminist theories is the tendency to overlook the influence of other factors such as race, religion, ethnicity, and economic class. Clearly these factors can be equally powerful; when we ignore them, we are doomed to an inadequate evaluation of sport (Birrell 2004; Coakley 2004; Sage 1998).

Interactionist Theory

Those who subscribe to **interactionist theories** view society from the bottom up rather than the top down. They focus on the social interactions among people that are based on the reality people choose to accept. Rather than simply responding to our world, we make conscious choices about how we will behave based on the effect our actions will have on ourselves, other people, and our society.

Research by interactionists involves extensive interviewing and ethnography to elicit how athletes think and feel about their sport participation. This approach helps us understand how people choose sports and how they define themselves as athletes within the culture of a particular sport. Interactionists create sport experiences that focus on the athlete rather than the business, institution, or leaders. Interactionists put kids' needs first in youth sport rather than allowing sport to be defined by adults who think they know what kids need.

Interactionists focus on the human experience of African American athletes rather than on their athletic performance. Interactionists would confront the exploitation of college athletes who never earn a degree but serve the university's purpose as an athlete for hire; they would encourage women who seek to develop traditional masculine and athletic virtues such as aggressiveness that conflict with traditional feminine values.

Interactionist theorists rely on the methods of psychology by probing the feelings and understandings of the individual rather than looking at the structured world outside. They also study subcultures within sport such as those reported in a classic text by Ball and Loy (1975), which devotes chapters to the subcultures of college coaches, professional baseball players, hockey players, and wrestlers.

Since the 1990s, the interactionist approach has become more popular and productive among sport sociologists because of the rich in-depth analyses it favors. For example, survey research has long established that more males than females are involved in sport and physical activity, but it was left to the researcher to speculate on why this was true. When research was refocused through ethnographic observations, the reasons behind the trends became more understandable (Donnelly 2004).

Figurational Theory

Figurational theories are rooted in Europe, particularly England, but are rarely used in North America. They emphasize interconnections between people that are called figurations. The crux of these theories is that we are all connected by networks of people who are interdependent on one another by nature, through education, and through socialization. Over time, the interconnections change as we mature, move in different circles, and absorb more information. While looking at sport from this perspective, figurational theorists study the historical processes through which people change.

The interrelationships in our life are dynamic and change frequently. Figurational theories require a long-term analysis for a complete understanding of social influences. If we are fully engaged in changes in our culture, our perspectives, including those on sport, change as we age. For example, consider the warm camaraderie among senior athletes who compete furiously but also view the game differently from the way the youthful athlete views it.

Figurational theories have helped researchers study the amazing rise of soccer in Europe and around the world. The rise of violence on the part of players and spectators has been instructive from this perspective; and in the early 2000s, figurational theory was used to view the reports of officials who had taken bribes to influence the outcomes of soccer matches.

Perhaps the most critical contribution of figurational theories has been a fuller understanding of the global processes at work in a shrinking world. As the connections between people and between nations strengthened worldwide, sports prospered in unimaginable ways through international training, competition, and coaching courses.

A weakness of figurational theory is that it tends to reduce the urgency for change. Since social problems are viewed over the long term, there is little chance to confront social problems within sport in a timely manner. By the time we understand what has happened and perhaps why it happened, new changes have taken place (Murphy, Sheard, and Waddington 2004).

Summary of Theories

After reviewing these six theories, you may wonder how they all fit into the sociology of sport. Each theoretical approach was developed over time and has helped sport sociology develop as a legitimate academic discipline with a discrete body of knowledge. Each of these theories has contributed to our understanding of the world of sport and exercise as it presently exists. Some generalizations may help you absorb the significance of each theory:

• Most people who extol the virtues of sport as it has existed traditionally use the *functionalist* approach. While this approach may have been useful in the past, it does not help identify existing social issues or provide any hope of solutions. People who work within existing sport organizations may adopt this approach in the interest of maintaining the status quo.

• *Conflict theories* have impressed upon us the influence of social class and the power structure

While figurational theorists have helped study the rise in popularity of soccer, they aren't always as helpful in finding solutions to social problems.

within sport. These theories have pointed out conflict within sport and have often led to dramatic proposals for change.

• Since the 1970s, *critical theories* have been the most helpful in clarifying the challenges of making sport more accessible to people from all backgrounds and abilities. One specific critical theory, *feminist theory,* has enabled us to understand the issues that women faced before Title IX (see chapter 12 for an in-depth discussion about Title IX) and their ongoing struggle to claim a share of the sporting world and make it people oriented rather than male oriented.

• *Interactionist theories* allow us to look in depth at sport from the athlete's point of view and to add a qualitative bent to our analysis. Since the 1990s, North American researchers have adopted this approach more than any other.

• *Figurational theories* have been especially helpful in Europe in long-term analyses of sporting subcultures and in understanding global expansion of sport.

Current Status of Sport Sociology

Although the study of sociology as a discipline became popular around the turn of the century, sociology was not applied to sport for another 50 years. In 1964 the International Committee for Sport Sociology was created as an outgrowth of the International Council of Sport and Physical Education and the International Sociological Association of UNESCO. This organization (presently named the International Sociology of Sport Association) has published the *International Review of Sport Sociology* annually since 1966, meets every year, and attracts scholars from around the world.

The second major organization for sport sociology is the North American Society for the Sociology of Sport. Founded in 1978, it holds annual conferences and since 1984 has published the *Sociology of Sport Journal*. The third group, the Sport Sociology Academy, is more casually organized as a unit of the National Association for Sport and Physical Education (NASPE), which falls under a large parent organization, the American Alliance for Health, Physical Education, Recreation and Dance (AAHPERD), located in Washington, DC. This large organization includes teachers, researchers, and professional practitioners of all fields relating to health, fitness, and sport. At the annual meeting, research papers are presented in the field of sport sociology.

As the popularity of sport increases, more researchers are drawn to the interrelationships between sport and society. Most large and many small universities now offer courses such as Sport and Society, Sport Sociology, Social Science of Sport, and Social Issues in Sport. Students from different fields of study are drawn to such a course as an elective because of their interest in sport.

The media rely on research in sport sociology for articles and features on athletes or a particular sport. Along with reporting current events, the media provide color commentary to help people understand the underlying causes of the behavior, attitudes, and struggles of their sport heroes. Without solid grounding through sociological research, much of their writing would be limited to their own experience, knowledge, and bias.

Chapter Summary

In this chapter we laid out the plan for looking at sport through sociology, using its methods and theories. Methods for collecting data include interviews, surveys, content research, historical research, and ethnography. Once the data are collected, they can be analyzed with functionalist theories, conflict theories, critical theories, feminist theories, interactionist theories, and figurational theories. We've presented the essential elements of each of these theories, compared them, and suggested how each is applied to the world of sport.

The researcher can analyze the data and interpret the resulting evidence within the context of the theories. Doing so organizes large amounts of data that can be examined in detail and from an overall perspective. Using scientific methodology reduces the influence of our own bias and preconceived notions about sport.

An interactionist theorist would argue that collegiate athletes deserve to be paid, especially those who play sports such as football and basketball that generate enormous revenue for universities. A functionalist theorist would maintain that we should do what has always been done—not pay college athletes. Who is correct?

PART II

Scope and Effect
of Sport on Society

This part begins in chapter 3 by distinguishing between sport participants and sport spectators. Since the two groups overlap, combining them to assess the popularity of particular sports leads to faulty assumptions. Those who participate in a particular sport are also likely to be spectators, but those who are spectators often are not participants. Think of the millions of National League Football and college football fans who watch football but do not play it.

A further distinction is made between people who participate in sport as recreation and those who strive for high performance. High-performance or elite athletes are usually younger athletes, while older adults participate primarily in recreational sports. However, increasing numbers of youth are also turning toward recreational models of sport.

Marketing opportunities through sport are presented and examined to discern trends. Chapter 4 evaluates sport as a corporate venture and also looks at how sport affects the national economy. The chapter documents the benefits to owners of professional sport teams and discusses the questionable value of financing sport stadiums with public monies. In addition, we look at the laws that allow sport leagues to operate as virtual monopolies and examine the way colleges and universities may profit from sport. We also take a realistic look at the earning power and job conditions of athletes who play corporate sports.

Finally, in chapter 5, we look at the close relationship between the media and sport. Television continues to bring sport entertainment to our homes through ever-increasing hours of sport broadcasts. Sport pages are a critical part of daily print media, although print media still cover more elite male sports than women's sports or local sports. Worldwide access to the Internet has changed the delivery of sport and will continue to affect the delivery of spectator sport. New in this decade is the explosion of social media and opportunities to link sport tracking and reporting through Facebook, MySpace, Twitter, YouTube, and blogs. Athletes are able to more directly connect with fans, and fans can connect instantly with each other.

We examine how sport and the media affect each other and how sport influences societal ideology and values through the media. Careers in sport journalism are described, as well as the substantial challenge of increasing access for women in the sport media and the way in which the imbalance between males and females affects decisions in sport media.

Participants Versus Spectators

You may still be a bit confused about what "sport" is, especially as you begin to learn about the popularity of various sports. It may be helpful for you to think about all types of "physical activity" that are voluntary movements and goal oriented. For most of us, this includes physical activities that have some alliance with good health and well-being. Generally, we should be thinking about sports or the broader categories of "exercise" or "skilled movement."

When you look at sports within this context, you'll quickly see that some sports involve more exercise while others feature skilled movement. Some of the research on sport participation, like that in this chapter, often combines these two categories and thus confuses the issue. Further, some activities can simply be informal exercise, such as walking, or can be classified as a sport at the highest level of Olympic competition. Your cue to understand this chapter is to realize that the terms physical activity, sport, and exercise are often used interchangeably even though technically there are some clear distinctions between them.

Participating in sports is quite different from watching sports. Yet in sport studies, these two activities are often lumped together statistically and anecdotally. Combining them only adds to the confusion of the value of each, leads to suspect conclusions, and interferes with the assessment of the overall influence of sport. For example, many people would rate tackle football as the most popular sport in the United States. Based on spectator interest, this is a reasonable conclusion. But if we look at participation, football is popular only through high school and only with boys. Beyond age 18, tackle football is not a reasonable option due to the number of players required, lack of equipment, and risk of injury. Thus it is more accurate to say that football is the most popular spectator sport in the United States but rates far down the list in participation.

Some evidence supports the claim that watching sports and playing sports significantly interact. Young people are often attracted to sport participation because they see famous athletes on television or perhaps in live action (Harris 2004). Youth who participate in a sport are more likely to watch that sport in later years because they understand it (Kretchmar 1994). Without question, many people who play a sport also watch that same sport and in fact are likely to watch other sports as well. Their experience as an athlete helps them empathize with competitors in other sport activities. Common athletic skills and strategies that exist across sports are fun for the sport competitor to observe and admire.

The argument has been made for years that spectators who watch favorite performers in sport are more motivated to participate in sport than those who are not fans. Particularly young people seem to naturally imitate their sport heroes in a pickup game, on the playground, or in the gym. Many sports without the role models of elite athletes languish and have low participation.

Sport Participants

An understanding of **sport participation** requires that we look closely at the characteristics of sport participants, their motivation, and the outside factors that influence their decisions.

High-Performance Versus Participation Athletes

As we introduced in the sport pyramid in figure 1.1 (see chapter 1), people who play sports can be classified as high-performance athletes or as participation athletes. The differences in motivation, training, and attitudes toward competition are marked for these two groups of athletes, no matter their age. Athletes who seek high performance (as characterized by the Olympic motto of "Faster, Higher, Stronger") train intensively, compete aggressively, and aspire to a professional career that brings **extrinsic rewards** such as money and fame. Athletes who value participation are motivated by **intrinsic rewards** such as fun and fitness. They use sport as recreation to enhance their quality of life, escape from work responsibilities, and socialize with family and friends.

About 65% of all Americans have integrated participant sport or physical activity into their lifestyle (Centers for Disease Control and Prevention 2010), thus making recreational sport or exercise the overwhelming dominant group within sport in our society. However, the human preoccupation with excellence, competition, and performance has vaulted high-performance sports to dizzying heights of popularity, fueled by business interests and the media, even though a relatively few athletes are elite. Of course, spectator sport feeds off the popularity of high-performance sport, as people enjoy watching exceptional performers match skill, wit, and courage.

We can also classify athletes by age, keeping in mind the two tracks they may follow toward high performance or recreation. At times these two paths overlap, providing some confusion for athletes, coaches, parents, and sponsoring organizations.

Youth Sport Athletes

Youth sport athletes typically fall between ages 4 and 13. Participation opportunities are usually community driven and seasonal, with an emphasis on team sports. Parents encourage their children to play so they can learn the skills of a particular sport, socialize with other children, and experience physical activity. Many parents are involved as team coaches, chauffeurs, and fans. Most youth sports encourage participation by everyone regardless of skill and strive to offer low-key competition and to generate an interest in sport that will last a lifetime.

Some parents, however, may push their children into sports, hoping that their child will be the next youth superstar. Children as young as 10 may join specialized high-performance programs that emphasize competition, rankings, traveling teams, national events, and specialization in one sport year round. These programs are clearly dedicated to developing elite athletes (youth sport is covered in chapter 6).

High School Varsity Athletes

Athletes at this level may still participate for reasons similar to those of youth sport athletes—they like to socialize with their peers and want to continue to improve in their sport. The choice to participate is usually made by the athlete rather than the parents. Participation can also be motivated by a desire to receive a college athletic scholarship for one or a few sports or to progress directly into professional play. (For further discussion about high school sports, see chapter 7.)

By definition, high school varsity sports sponsor competition against other schools. Most teams are limited in size, so the majority of high school students do not play varsity sports and must rely on intramural or community-based sports. Some high school sports, such as football, basketball, and baseball, may be high-performance programs that truly prepare athletes for college sports. In other sports, particularly Olympic and individual sports, high school teams are more recreational, and elite athletes must look outside the school setting to private

High school student athletes compete in sports for many of the same reasons as youth sport athletes—to socialize with friends and improve their game.

development programs and competition sponsored by the national governing body of that sport.

College Varsity Athletes

College athletes are an even more select group than are high school athletes. High school varsity athletes numbered 7.5 million in 2008-2009 while the number of college varsity athletes was just 418,000 (National Collegiate Athletic Associations [NCAA] 2008a; National Federation of State High School Associations 2008-2009). Competition for positions on collegiate varsity teams is intense, especially at large institutions. Most high school athletes face the fact that they are not good enough to play at the intercollegiate level, and join campus intramural programs or club teams that offer more recreational competition. (For further discussion of college sports, see chapter 7.)

The most intense high-performance programs are found at the large universities that are categorized as Division I by the National Collegiate Athletic Association (NCAA). Most of their athletes receive a full or partial athletic scholarship and are expected to produce athletically to justify the expense to the university. Other colleges compete at the lower divisions of II or III where the competition is less intense, the commitment to athletics is more modest, and the financial investment by the institutions is lower.

Many college students who have grown up playing sports find themselves shut out of sport opportunities simply due to the competition. They may turn to the on-campus intramural teams and sport clubs, and many turn to community-based sport in their hometowns during the summer to satisfy their competitive and recreational urges.

Professional Athletes

Professional athletes compete in sport for the extrinsic financial rewards offered to them such as salaries, prize money, or product endorsements. Virtually every sport holds professional tournaments and leagues somewhere in the world, including the Olympic Games. While professional athletes may compete in their sport because they enjoy it, the longer they compete at the professional level, under pressure to perform, the closer sport moves toward work.

Except for a few sport prodigies, most athletes do not qualify for professional sport until they are young adults. Professional careers have limited duration because of the exceptional physical skills they demand. As their physical skills decline in the late 20s and 30s, most professional athletes are forced to retire from competition.

Master Athletes

While older competitors typically cannot compete with younger competitors who are at the height of their physical prowess, master athletes may be focused on the highest level of performance within their prescribed age group. Competition is staged in categories beginning as young as 35 and ending up as old as (in some sports) 90 and above. The competition is intense; the athletes train year round, and often sport events are staged at local, national, and even international levels. As health, training regimens, and medical care advance, master ath-

 POP CULTURE

Popularity of Extreme Sports

Extreme sports are nontraditional sports that incorporate athletic skills with some degree of pronounced risk to competitors. Since the 1970s, extreme sports have gained in popularity primarily due to the almost cult status afforded heroes Tony Hawk and Bam Margera. Television coverage of the "X Games" and the Winter Olympics of 2010 continued to help popularize extreme sports.

Sometimes called "action sport or adventure sport," extreme sports often involve speed, height, high levels of physical exertion, highly specialized equipment, and spectacular stunts. Rock climbing and marathon running were probably the first to be identified as extreme sports. Within a few years, sports such as skiing, snowboarding, skydiving, skateboarding, surfing, Motocross, and BMX racing joined the new category of sports. Innovative sports that combine several sports continue to emerge, such as sky surfing, which combines skydiving and snowboarding.

The lure of extreme sports is that youth can take full responsibility for their participation; there are typically no coaches to cramp their style, and competition is against nature and environmental obstacles as well as fellow competitors. Extreme sports are typically not sanctioned or sponsored by schools because of the risk (Browne 2004).

letes continue to break records and grow in number. The difference between master athletes and their professional counterparts is that generally their financial rewards are modest. While some sports offer prize money, most offer only good competition, an opportunity to travel, and an expanded social network.

Adult Recreational or Participation Athletes

At every age, beginning with youth sport, some participants play simply for fun. They enjoy socializing with friends, being physically active, and playing the game. But they may not have the physical or psychological attributes needed to compete at high levels. We often spend our childhood years testing our physical limits; and by the time we reach adulthood, very few of us can compete at the elite levels of sport. Yet more than half of the U.S. population still enjoys playing sports. As we age, we tend to move away from collision sports such as football, soccer, wrestling, or boxing and toward sports that offer less risk of physical injury or stress on the body. Team sports become more difficult to organize in an adult world, and so many people turn to sports for individuals or a smaller number of contestants.

Participation athletes spend a relatively smaller amount of time practicing and training for competition. Since their time is limited by work and family commitments, most recreational athletes just play when they can. Winning or losing does not affect their life as much as it might have at a younger age or affect their reputation within their occupation.

Factors Affecting Sport Participation

Now that we have an idea of who participates in sport, let's look at the factors that influence participation as well as the conflicts between the different levels of participants.

Pursuit of Excellence

The attitudes of some youthful competitors who may be encouraged by their parents and coaches are oriented toward producing the best physical performance possible. It could be argued that youth sports in general discover the best potential competitors through a progression of competitions promoting survival of the fittest. Athletes who do well at a young age play on all-star teams, are exposed to advanced training and coaching, and sometimes

Don't let the age fool you! Master athletes are just as competitive—and accomplished—in their chosen sport as are younger athletes.

even compete at international or national competitions. Because of their early success, these athletes often have sport experiences that help them increase their edge over other kids their age.

One of the difficulties with designating *elite athletes* at a young age is that their dominance may simply result from maturing early. Once their peers catch up with them physically, they lose confidence and motivation quickly as kids they used to defeat routinely overtake them.

Of course, the American preoccupation with high achievement spills over into youth sport. Parents hope their child will be chosen for the elite, select, or traveling team. In many sports, the number of youngsters chosen for these teams may amount to as many as 30% of the participants in order to cast a wide net for future superstars. After several years in these high-performance programs, it becomes clear that only about 5% of the athletes will emerge at the top of their competitive level (NCAA 2009a).

Schools, businesses, sponsors, and the media often focus on the quest for high performance in sport. This quest reinforces the pioneering spirit of humans to break barriers of human existence and performance. Schools and colleges spend huge sums of money to support athletic teams whose primary purpose is to defeat their rivals.

Money, fame, media attention, and hero worship are part of the reward to athletes who sacrifice to perform at the highest level. Commercial sponsors, professional teams, college teams, and Olympic organizations all support athletes dedicated to excellence in sport.

Recreation Through Sport

A different attitude toward sport is that participating for recreation is the ultimate goal regardless of the level of skill or achievement. This approach is more suited to the masses since by definition very few can truly reach elite levels. Sport participation is founded on the principle that people need diversion from their work, and recreation provides this

diversion and recharges their natural energies. In many instances, what we call *participation sports* are commonly called *recreational sports*.

Participation in sports emphasizes their social side. People enjoy a friendly game of golf, tennis, or volleyball or going fishing as a way to spend time with family and friends. While high-performance athletes aim to defeat one another, participation athletes typically root for each other and help out whenever they can.

Commercial sponsors of sport who operate facilities, sell sport clothing and equipment, or run sport associations realize that participation athletes far outnumber those dedicated to high performance. To attract average people to sport participation, these commercial groups modify their sport to make it friendly to players of all ages, skills, and income levels. Here are a few examples:

• Golf is one of the few sports in which players of different skill levels can enjoy competing against each other by altering the scoring system. Participants may play a scramble format or award points for each hole depending on which player reaches the green first or holes out first.

• Tennis has been adjusted to local recreational situations through altered lengths of play. The winner may be declared after a certain time limit to accommodate indoor play. Shortened sets have also become popular and include using tiebreaks at the end of a set instead of playing a traditional third set.

• Recreational volleyball and softball leagues sponsor coed teams that require a set number of females to field a team. Spiked shoes are banned from softball, and sliding into bases is prohibited to reduce injuries.

• Soccer is played by smaller teams, such as teams of three, so that each player gets more action and the game can be played on a smaller field.

High-Performance and Participation Tug-of-War

There seems to be a perpetual tug-of-war between the supporters of high-performance participation and those of recreational participation. National

Battling the elements and conquering nature motivates some people to be active just as trying to win a competition motivates others.

associations and governing bodies often pour their financial reserves into developing high-performance athletes, to the detriment of the average sport participant. Debates rage about the percentage of resources that ought to be expended for either purpose.

Consider the **Amateur Sports Act of the United States** of 1978, in which the U.S. Congress established the United States Olympic Committee (USOC) and outlined its responsibilities. The act listed the 12 purposes of the USOC numerically. Approximately half of the list addresses the issue of amateur sport participation. The sixth purpose is "To promote and encourage physical fitness and public participation in amateur athletic activities." The law was amended in 1998 to become the Olympic and Amateur Sports Act. The internal changes in the act particularly addressed the needs of elite Paralympic athletes. The proportion of time, effort, or budget dedicated to the various purposes is not prescribed by the U.S. Congress but left to the USOC board of directors (Stevens 2005).

Likewise, rules, boundaries, equipment, and clothing are often debated from two different points of view. New equipment may allow ordinary performers the thrill of better performance and keep them hooked on the sport. But that equipment may be illegal for high-performance athletes who must compete in stadiums of a certain size and within international rules.

Professional baseball players are not allowed to use aluminum bats, while amateur college players are. The pro golf tour has considered using a special tour ball that is less lively than current golf balls to put more of a premium on accuracy as opposed to power and distance. Golf legends like Jack Nicklaus and Arnold Palmer support such a move, as they believe the game has developed into a power game with less emphasis on accuracy and skill. Yet the average weekend player thrills to the whack of a golf ball that flies farther than he ever thought possible.

Attitudes toward sport at the youth and high school level can tilt heavily toward high-performance or participation depending on the leaders of the school or league. It becomes self-defeating to lean too heavily toward the high-performance model, since doing so limits the number of participants.

It is often suggested that sport participation improves quality of life, helps fight obesity, and keeps people stronger and healthier. As health concerns rise and the population ages, the balance of spending and publicity may tip more toward sport participation. Support for emphasizing sport participation is emerging from the health community, sport organization leaders, organizations that advocate for the aging, and youth sport organizations. Comments and position statements consistent with the sixth purpose stated in the Olympic and Amateur Sports Act are beginning to appear in the media and invade the public consciousness.

The conflict between performance sport and participation sport is not unique to America. The ninth World Sports for All Congress (2002) held in the Netherlands was devoted to this topic. Close to 450 participants from 95 countries attended and after much debate concluded that it is in the interest of both participation and performance sport to cooperate to enhance a lifetime of sport and physical activity so that individuals can be physically active and participate in sport at their own levels, from recreational to elite. Rather than compete for time, facilities, and money, the two camps of sport should become complementary to better serve all citizens.

Social Influences on Sport Participation

People of all ages consciously decide to participate in sport or not. If they choose to participate, they must make another decision, conscious or unconscious, about whether to continue their participation or to drop out. If they decide to continue, they must

ACTIVITY TIME-OUT

Performance Versus Participation Sport

As you examine the potential for conflict between performance and participation sport, do you think it is possible to support both? If you were responsible for a budget for youth sport in a community, what proportions of funding would you allocate to high-performance and participation sport? Justify your answer and give specific examples. In making your recommendation, consider that approximately 5% of the population qualify for high-performance sport while the other 95% are relegated to participation sport.

decide on their dedication and performance intensity. These decisions about whether to participate for fun or for high performance are heavily influenced by outside factors and people, combined with internal feelings, thoughts, and aspirations. The interaction of external and internal forces helps us come to our current decision, although we may certainly change our minds as we develop or the external conditions change.

When we are young, our families influence us more than outsiders do. If your parents played sports, took you to sporting contests, helped you learn basic sport skills, and encouraged you to participate, chances are you gave sport a try. In some cases, other family members such as grandparents, aunts, uncles, or older siblings may have encouraged you in sport. Once you tried sports, the critical factors that influenced your continued participation may have been whether you felt comfortable in the environment created by the coach and other athletes. Your own success or failure in competition certainly helped shape your attitude about sport. Teachers, camp counselors, coaches, and older children can powerfully influence us as we try to figure out what is important in our lives.

Your environment also influences your choice of sport. For example, certain choices are a natural part of city life. Recreational facilities need to be accessible, affordable, and comfortable. Climate, tradition, and even your neighborhood will help determine the available choices. Your parents and siblings affect your earliest choices and continue to affect whether or not you sustain those interests. A pervasive influence, however, is your peers, especially as you mature and depend less on your family for decisions and support.

Once you are involved in sport, key factors that affect your decision to continue include your aptitude and the reinforcement you receive from coaches and friends. Athletes who experience success are more likely to crave that emotional support and rely on it. Heroes and role models may help kids socially adjust to sports. By watching heroes and imitating their behavior, work ethic, and love for sport, kids learn what is expected of athletes. They often imitate their role models to see if a role fits them.

Children who struggle in sports often reject them. Who wants to play right field, bat last, be picked last, or ride the bench as a substitute? Coaches may make insensitive remarks, encourage rough play, or otherwise make the experience unpleasant. Even talented athletes often withdraw from the sport scene if they do not measure up to expectations or, in the case of high-performance programs, lack the drive and intensity that are expected.

As we mature, new factors affect our sport participation. Other facets of life interfere, friends drop out of sport, social cliques develop within and outside of sport, and economic costs of continued participation drain resources. Adults have the added burden of work responsibilities, less discretionary time, anxiety about their abilities, and difficulty in finding playing partners.

Geography, Age, Gender, and Social Class

In addition to family, friends, and coaches, other factors that affect our sport participation include the geography of the area where we live and what sports are available. Winter sports are most popular in the northern reaches of the country, and water sports thrive in areas near lakes, rivers, or oceans. Interestingly, not all intuitive patterns based on geography and weather hold true. For example, the highest participation rate in tennis does not occur in Florida, Texas, or California, the three U.S. states most often guessed. The highest rate actually occurs in New York City and its surrounding counties—Westchester County in New York and counties in northern New Jersey and southern Connecticut. The reason for the greater rate is economic affluence. There is a higher correlation between economic level and tennis participation than there is between weather and tennis participation.

Age also affects sport participation. As we age, the demands of many traditional sports become daunting. Loss of flexibility, strength, and endurance along with weight gain affects most adults as they age. Only those who devote hours to training are able to ward off the physical effects of aging. Sports that are popular with young people such as gymnastics, figure skating, wrestling, tackle football, lacrosse, and track and field simply are not easy to sustain after the teenage years. The stress on the body is too debilitating for most people.

Popular youth sports tend to be team sports. Team sports present a special problem for adults who are unable to arrange their schedules around work for practice or competition. Individual sports begin to attract more participants simply because they are easier to organize and schedule. Football, soccer, basketball, and baseball participation rates drop sharply after people leave their 20s and naturally move into lifetime sports such as golf, tennis, and swimming.

Gender affects sport participation due to tradition, interest, and sometimes body structure. Girls generally do not play tackle football, rugby, or other collision sports. Some athletes in boxing, wrestling, and weightlifting have broken down traditional barriers. Now even women engage in these sports in the Olympic Games, although the contestants are admittedly few.

The Title IX legislation in 1972 opened up female participation in many sports that were traditionally male oriented. Soccer, basketball, cross country, and lacrosse are now seen as equally accessible for males and females. Spirit squads, which were formerly called cheerleading squads, now include both boys and girls, although the majority of participants are still female.

Perhaps no factor influences sport participation more powerfully than social or economic class. Some traditions of participation are based on custom and accessibility while others are simply a matter of economics. There are always exceptions to the overall trends, but there are some sport favorites by economic class (Coakley and Donnelly 1999; Eitzen 2003; Gruneau 1999).

People with a high income, high education, and high-status occupation tend to participate in individual sports such as golf, tennis, sailing, and skiing. They are able to arrange their schedule to play and can afford the cost of club memberships, travel, and equipment or clothing.

People in the middle-income group focus on sports that are publicly accessible at modest cost, are school or community sponsored, and do not require memberships in expensive clubs. Families of skilled workers often choose sports that tend toward competition, power, and machismo. The working class supports sports such as football, wrestling, auto racing, and boxing.

People who struggle to make a living tend to have little time for sport or recreation. Often their work involves physical labor, so they have little energy left for physical games. Their discretionary time and income are the lowest of those in society, and so they find it difficult to choose any recreational activity.

One of the ironies of elite competition, particularly in individual sports and many Olympic sports, is that athletes tend to come from upper middle-class backgrounds (Coakley 2004). The financial sacrifices required to fund a young athlete's development, particularly for sports like sailing, tennis, gymnastics, equestrian events, and skiing, which are not offered in public schools, are simply beyond the reach of the average family. Team sports that are offered in public schools at little cost to participants are financially feasible for average families, and thus you see athletes of all social classes competing in track and field, soccer, basketball, baseball, wrestling, and similar sports.

 EXPERT'S VIEW

The Sporting Goods Manufacturers Association

A number of sport marketing firms compile data on sport participation, but none offers a more comprehensive and detailed analysis of sport and fitness activities in the United States than the Sporting Goods Manufacturers Association (SGMA). The SGMA is a premier trade association for sporting goods manufacturers, retailers, and marketers in the sport products industry. Its purpose is to serve its members by providing information and conducting research to ensure industry vitality and promote sport, fitness, and an active lifestyle. The sport products industry generates over $60 billion in the United States and $15 billion in international revenue.

SGMA offers annual participation surveys of all sports and fitness activities that enable sports organizations, industry business leaders, and government officials to analyze trends annually and over several years. For example, a one-year high percentage of growth for a sport may be an anomaly, but strong growth over seven years is clearly a trend. Additionally, the researchers contracted by SGMA conduct follow-up interviews and focus groups to determine the causes of various trends such as the recent decline in team sports participation by youth in an attempt to analyze the reasons for the decline. You might be surprised by the significant increase in tennis participation by 43% since 2000; tennis has been the only traditional American sport to show such an increase. What do you think is drawing more people to the tennis courts?

The research presented in this chapter on sport and fitness activity participation by Americans is from SGMA; it includes actual numbers, a comparison of increase or decrease from the previous year, and the trends over a seven-year time period. To visit the SGMA website, go to www.sgma.com.

Trends in Sport Participation

Trends in sport participation change over time, and the research methodology used to study these trends has become more sophisticated and accurate in recent years. Table 3.1 summarizes the most exhaustive and up-to-date information on sport participation based on data collected in 2007 by the Sporting Goods Manufacturers Association (SGMA 2008c). You should note that the numbers reported include participants of all ages from 6 on.

TABLE 3.1   Trends in Sport Participation

Activity	Total participation trend				
	2008	2009	2000	1-year change	9-year change
AEROBIC ACTIVITIES					
Aerobics (high impact)	12,272	13,269	11,790	8.1%	12.5%
Aerobics (low impact)	24,168	25,685	21,384	6.3%	20.1%
Aerobics (step)	10,318	10,784	10,867	4.5%	−0.8%
Aquatic exercise	9,267	8,662	9,303	−6.5%	−6.9%
Cardio kickboxing	4,997	6,002	8,765	20.1%	−31.5%
Elliptical motion trainer	25,284	26,521	7,371	4.9%	259.8.0%
Running and jogging	41,130	43,892	31,398	6.7%	39.8%
Stair climbing machine	14,204	13,101	15,282	−7.8%	−14.3%
Stationary cycling (recumbent)	11,389	11,208	8,810	−1.6%	27.2%
Stationary cycling (group)	6,693	6,831	4,709	2.1%	45.1%
Stationary cycling (upright)	25,304	24,528	27,159	−3.1%	−9.7%
Swimming (fitness or competition)	19,041	17,443	16,144	−8.4%	8.0%
Treadmill	49,371	51,418	37,287	4.1%	37.9%
Walking for fitness	111,668	110,095	90,982	−1.4%	21.0%
CONDITIONING ACTIVITIES					
Abdominal machine	19,917	19,465	21,354	−2.3%	−8.8%
Calisthenics	9,147	9,106	7,758	−0.4%	17.4%
Pilates	8,886	8,653	1,556	−2.6%	456.2%
Rowing machine	9,021	9,174	9,407	1.7%	−2.5%
Stretching	36,288	36,310	24,613	0.1%	47.5%
Tai Chi	3,424	3,205	n/a	−6.4%	n/a
Yoga	17,758	20,109	n/a	13.2%	n/a
STRENGTH ACTIVITIES					
Free weights (barbells)	26,142	27,048	24,800	3.5%	9.1%
Free weights (dumbbells)	34,391	35,744	27,470	3.9%	30.1%
Free weights (hand weights)	42,997	45,934	33,784	6.8%	36.0%
Home gym exercise	24,514	24,762	20,626	1.0%	20.1%
Weight and resistance machines	38,397	39,752	32,144	3.5%	23.7%
INDIVIDUAL SPORTS					
Adventure racing	920	1,089	n/a	18.4%	n/a
Archery	6,409	6,326	6,285	−1.3%	0.6%
Billiards (e.g., pool)	49,018	43,005	46,336	−12.3%	−7.2%
Bowling	58,650	57,293	51,938	−2.3%	10.3%
Boxing	2,755	2,932	4,084	6.4%	−28.2%
Golf	28,567	27,103	28,844	−5.1%	−6.0%
Horseback riding	10,816	9,755	n/a	−9.8%	n/a
Martial arts	6,770	6,516	6,161	−3.8%	5.8%

Activity	Total participation trend				
	2008	**2009**	**2000**	**1-year change**	**9-year change**
INDIVIDUAL SPORTS					
Roller skating (2×2 wheels)	7,855	8,147	7,746	3.7%	5.2%
Roller skating (inline wheels)	9,608	8,276	21,912	−13.9%	−62.2%
Scooter riding (nonmotorized)	6,394	5,064	6,161	−20.8%	−49.2%
Skateboarding	7,807	7,352	9,859	−5.8%	−25.4%
Trail running	4,857	4,833	4,167	−0.5%	16.0%
Triathlon (off road)	602	666	n/a	10.6%	n/a
Triathlon (road)	1,087	1,208	n/a	11.1%	n/a
RACKET SPORTS					
Badminton	7,239	7,699	8,769	6.4%	−12.2%
Racquetball	4,993	4,575	4,475	−8.4%	2.2%
Squash	706	885	n/a	25.4%	n/a
Table tennis	17,201	19,301	12,712	12.2%	51.8%
Tennis	18,558	18,534	12,974	−0.1%	42.9%
TEAM SPORTS					
Baseball	15,020	13,837	15,848	−7.9%	−12.7%
Basketball	26,254	24,007	26,215	−8.6%	−8.4%
Cheerleading	3,104	3,036	2,634	−2.2%	15.2%
Field hockey	1,118	1,066	n/a	−4.7%	n/a
Football (flag)	7,310	6,553	n/a	−10.4%	n/a
Football (tackle)	7,692	6,794	8,229	−11.7%	−17.4%
Football (touch)	10,493	8,959	n/a	−14.6%	n/a
Gymnastics	3,883	4,021	4,876	3.6%	−17.5%
Ice hockey	1,902	2,134	2,432	12.2%	−12.3%
Lacrosse	1,127	1,197	518	6.2%	131.1%
Paintball	4,857	4,552	3,615	−6.3%	25.9%
Roller hockey	1,456	1,397	3,888	−4.1%	−64.1%
Rugby	690	750	n/a	8.7%	n/a
Soccer (indoor)	4,737	4,913	n/a	3.7%	n/a
Soccer (outdoor)	14,233	13,691	n/a	−3.7%	n/a
Softball (fast pitch)	2,316	2,636	2,693	13.8%	−2.1%
Softball (slow pitch)	9,835	8,525	13,577	−3.7%	−37.2%
Track and field	4,516	4,443	n/a	−1.6%	n/a
Ultimate Frisbee	4,879	4,392	n/a	−10.0%	n/a
Volleyball (beach)	4,171	4,476	5,248	7.3%	−14.7%
Volleyball (court)	8,190	7,283	n/a	−11.1%	n/a
Volleyball (grass)	5,086	4,853	n/a	−4.6%	n/a
Wrestling	3,358	2,982	3,743	−11.2%	−20.3%
WATER SPORTS					
Boardsailing and windsurfing	1,307	1,128	1,739	−13.7%	−35.1%
Jet skiing	7,815	7,724	9,475	−1.2%	−18.5%
Rafting	4,651	4,318	5,259	−7.2%	−17.9%
Sailing	4,226	4,342	4,405	2.7%	−1.4%
Scuba diving	3,216	2,723	4,305	−15.3%	−36.7%
Snorkeling	10,296	9,358	10,302	−9.1%	−9.2%
Surfing	2,607	2,403	2,191	−7.8%	9.7%
Wakeboarding	3,544	3,577	4,558	0.9%	−21.5%
Water skiing	5,593	4,862	8,765	−13.1%	−44.5%

The activities are divided into categories for ease of comparison. You should also note that all numbers reflect *millions of participants* out of a total U.S. population of 276,796,000 over age 6. The total panel of respondents has over 1 million members and is representative of the U.S. population including gender, age, income, household size, region, and population density.

A closer look at the information in table 3.1 will reveal that many of the "sport" activities are actually "fitness" activities and that in fact many of those activities are the fastest growing. Two factors are driving this participation in fitness activities: In the past 15 years, memberships at health and fitness clubs have *doubled* from 20 million to over 40 million today, and more than 25 million Americans use home gym equipment (SGMA 2009a). A second factor is the explosion of adults over the age of 50, often referred to as "baby boomers," who are keenly interested in their physical health and fitness. The AARP reports that according to population projections, by 2015 those over 50 years of age will represent 45% of the U.S. population.

Unlike previous generations who looked forward to a life of ease and relaxation in retirement, current older adults realize they may expect to live another 20 to 30 years past retirement, and trends show that many of them will continue working (at least part-time) several more years to secure their financial solvency and to feel useful and engaged in society. They believe that by improving their personal health and fitness they can expect a better quality of life in their later years, with more energy and fewer health concerns.

The following are the activities that have shown the greatest statistical growth since 2000; you can see that 7 out of the 10 are fitness activities (SGMA 2009a).

Sport	Percentage of growth
1. Pilates training	456%
2. Elliptical trainer	259%
3. Lacrosse	131%
4. Table tennis	52%
5. Stretching	48%
6. Spinning	45%
7. Tennis	43%
8. Running/jogging	40%
9. Treadmill	38%
10. Other exercise to music	37%

Since 2008, six other activities have had statistically significant, double-digit growth in participation. They are cardio tennis (42%), cardio kickboxing (20%), snowshoeing (17%), bow hunting (14%), yoga (13%), and table tennis (12%).

If we look at the trends for more traditional sports that fit the definition of sport we used in chapter 1, these are the top 10 (SGMA 2008c):

Sport	Total participants
1. Basketball	25,961
2. Soccer	17,945
3. Tennis	16,940
4. Baseball	16,058
5. Volleyball (all types)	15,844
6. Football (touch)	12,988
7. Softball (fast and slow pitch)	11,850
8. Football (tackle)	7,939
9. Paintball	5,476
10. Track and field	4,691

ACTIVITY TIME-OUT

Trends in Sport and Exercise Participation

Study the chart on sport and fitness participation for 2010 as shown in table 3.1 and develop at least *five general trends* about participation in the United States. You should particularly note changes that have occurred over seven years rather than a one-year change that could be an aberration. You may want to combine some activities into one larger category, such as using free weights of various types. Finally, suggest some possible factors that may have affected the changes in popularity of certain activities, such as aging of the adult population, the possible effect of the economy, or the popularity of new exercise equipment not previously widely available.

IN THE ARENA WITH . . .

Zumba Is Hot

Zumba is a relatively new dance–fitness activity that is sweeping the country and in fact the world. Fusing Latin rhythms and international music with dance in a way that makes exercise fun, Zumba was founded by dancer–choreographer Alberto Perez in Colombia in the 1990s. Zumba classes are now offered by licensed instructors in more than 60,000 fitness centers in 105 countries, with over seven and a half million participants. Its appeal is primarily to females who enjoy a vigorous, fun workout in one hour that is aerobic, toning, and body sculpting. Classes and instructional DVDs are available worldwide, featuring music based on salsa, merengue, cumbia, reggae, samba, hip-hop, belly dancing, flamenco, mambo, and tango. Along with Pilates and yoga, Zumba is proving to be a mainstay program for fitness centers around the world.

If we combine baseball and softball, which are similar games, the total of 27,888 participants vaults them to first place. Similarly, if we combine touch and tackle football for a total of 20,927 participants, football moves up to third place. The new order would then be baseball/softball, basketball, football, soccer, tennis. Note also the rise of the nontraditional sport of paintball into the top 10.

In spite of the growth of organized sport for children and high school sport participation, there are warning signs about total physical activity for youth. In July 2008, the *Journal of the American Medical Association* published the results of a six-year study showing that exercise patterns of American youth were declining, especially during the teen years (SGMA 2008b). Sporting Good Manufacturers Association studies referred to previously confirmed this disturbing trend; these also pointed to the impact of encouraging youth athletes to specialize in one sport at an early age and the emphasis on elite or travel teams. For example, at age 10, 49% of all kids are frequent participants in at least one sport, but by age 18 that percentage falls to 30%. Another study from the National Institutes of Health (NIH) showed that at age 9, children averaged roughly three hours of moderate to vigorous physical activity on weekdays and weekends. But by age 15, they average only 49 minutes per weekday and 35 minutes on weekends (NIH 2008).

Statistics show that sports such as soccer have peak participation at age 7, baseball at age 8, and softball at ages 9 and 10. As you might suspect, these sports show low participation percentages after age 16. In contrast, basketball peaks at age 13 and football at age 15. After age 16, basketball continues to attract nearly a fourth of its players, while most other sports fall to a single-digit percentage (SGMA 2009b).

Various researchers and scholars blame the decline in youth physical activity on the time spent watching television, as well as the rise of video games and computer use, which by some accounts averages over five and a half hours per day (Cauchon 2005). In addition, it is a fact that many schools have eliminated recess time and reduced or eliminated physical education classes. But equally significant factors that have contributed to the decline in participation are the sharp reduction over the past 20 years in "pickup games," the emphasis in youth sport on elite players, and the practice of parents or coaches (or both) to encourage kids to specialize in one sport at an early age. Basketball and touch football are the leading sports in unorganized or "pickup" play. All you need is a ball, some buddies, and a place to play. Let's look at some statistics that back up these trends, as shown in table 3.2 on page 42 (SGMA 2009c).

While traditional "pickup" games and sports have declined, there has been a rise in a new category called "extreme sports," which are also referred to as "action sports" or "adventure sports." Generally these sports involve some amount of perceived danger to the participant through activities that may involve speed, height, high exertion, or spectacular stunts. Extreme sports are usually the purview of relatively younger participants rather than adults. The competitions are somewhat uncontrolled due to environmental variables such as weather, terrain, wind, snow, water, and mountains. Popularized by television and other media sources, the first X Games were held in the United States in 1995. Their attraction for most youth participants is that

TABLE 3.2 Percentage of Play in "Organized Sports" Versus "Pickup" Games by Sport

Sport	Organized	Unorganized	Other
Baseball	52%	44%	4%
Basketball	36%	60%	4%
Ice hockey	48%	46%	6%
Football (touch)	19%	77%	4%
Football (tackle)	49%	49%	2%
Football (flag)	48%	48%	4%
Soccer (indoor)	70%	27%	3%
Soccer (outdoor)	60%	36%	4%
Softball (slow)	62%	35%	3%
Softball (fast)	76%	19%	5%

Reprinted, by permission, from Sporting Goods Manufacturers Association, 2009, *Organized sport play dominates team sport market*. Available: www.sgma.com/press/153_Organized-Sport-Play-Dominates-Team-Sports-Market.

they are typically individual competition and athletes rarely are restricted to following the rules and directions of a coach.

Sport Spectators

Watching sports has become part of the American way of life. Since the 1920s, commercial sports have steadily attracted more and more **sport spectators** primarily because people have more leisure time and more money to spend. The number of people who watch sports rises each year, and the money generated from sport spectators, sponsorships, advertising, and products has increased dramatically.

Unlike participating in sport, watching or listening to sport doesn't take much effort or talent. It is a form of entertainment that appeals to millions of people for a variety of reasons. A spectator may enjoy the particular sport itself, may formerly have played or currently play the sport, or may simply enjoy the competition and drama of superior athletes demonstrating their prowess.

While the number of spectators who watch live events continues to increase, the most significant growth results from the availability of sport on television and on the Internet. Televised sports began in the late 1940s when there were fewer than 190,000 TV sets in the country. NBC broadcast the World Series of baseball, heavyweight boxing matches, and the Army–Navy football game. In the early years of TV sports, spectator growth was enormous, and as television improved the technical presentation, the popularity of sports continued to

explode. As more people watched, advertisers spent huge amounts of money to reach a sport audience that was primarily younger men. Great moments in sports were shared with millions of viewers and became the topic of discussion at work. Televised sports not only promoted sport viewing but also helped the TV industry grow to heights not even imagined in the early days.

In the last two decades, viewing of network sports has generally declined, as cable and all-sport channels offer more choices and interest has expanded to a wider variety of sports. Despite the sharp drop in baseball viewing and the relatively flat viewing statistics for football, overall sport entertainment on TV continues to thrive. College sports, high school sports, and even some youth sports are now televised nationally. Fans can tune in to a variety of sporting events at almost any hour or check up-to-the-minute scores on the Internet. As the sport audience grows, so does the willingness of commercial sponsors to pay for an advertisement during events such as the Super Bowl. For the 2010 Super Bowl, the average price for a 30-second commercial was between $2.5 million and $2.8 million. That was actually a drop from an average of $3.0 million for 2009, the first time ever the price for advertising decreased from a previous year (CBS News 2010). A 30-second commercial during the 2011 Super Bowl cost up to $3 million depending on placement during the game.

Social class and economic status affect spectatorship as they do participation. Most white-collar workers are college graduates and therefore are natural supporters of college sport teams. Long

Early sport broadcasts reached a very limited audience. Today, a single sporting event can reach millions of people through TV and Internet viewership.

after graduation, they assiduously follow their college team, donate money to athletic programs, and buy season tickets to major sport events. In contrast, people who do not attend college have little affinity for college sports and focus instead on professional sports.

The most affluent spectators, besides watching college sports, identify with sports like polo, yachting, sailing, sport car racing, and thoroughbred racing. The upper-middle class tends to enjoy tennis, golf, sailing, and skiing. The working class leans toward auto racing, wrestling, bowling, pool, boxing, demolition derby, and roller derby.

The relatively high cost of attending many popular sporting events discourages families with modest means from attending more than once a year. Consider that the expense for a family of four (two parents, two children) to attend a major professional game will likely include four moderately priced tickets, four soft drinks, two beers, four hot dogs, two programs, parking, and two adult-sized caps. If we total up the cost of these items, National Football League (NFL) games are by far the most expensive at $396.36 per family. Similar figures can be estimated for the National Basketball Associa-

tion (NBA) at $291.93 and National Hockey League (NHL) at 288.23. Interestingly, Major League Baseball (MLB) cost estimates are only $196.89, a real bargain compared to other sports (Team Marketing Report 2008).

Interestingly, professional baseball, usually thought of as a working man's game, attracts spectators from all social classes. Perhaps its mass appeal has contributed to its long-held reputation as America's national pastime. Likewise, professional football attracts spectators of all incomes.

Perhaps the fact that baseball and football stadiums can accommodate fans of all economic levels adds to their appeal. Affluent spectators may ply their guests with food and drink in luxury suites that cost thousands of dollars for one game, or they might sit right by the action, at field level behind home plate or on the 50-yard line. Meanwhile, at the same game, the less affluent can save up for the more modest price for seats in the bleachers, the end zone, or the upper rows of the stadium.

The general socioeconomic trends just described are based on live attendance at sporting events. If you factor in watching sport on television, which mitigates the expense of sport viewing for most people, spectators choose their sports by interest, history, and familiarity rather than by expense. People watch sports they identify with through previous participation or watch performers with whom they feel a connection. Television has brought spectator sports and the performances of the world's finest athletes to every home in the United States. Today commercial sponsors reach audiences of rich or poor, male or female, young or old.

The interest girls and women have recently shown in watching sport caused a major shift in the cross section of sport spectators. The tremendous change in female sport participation due to Title IX has produced a new generation of women who enjoy watching sport, can identify with the athletes, and include sport in their life. Gone are the days when the men retired to the den to watch sport while the women retired to the kitchen or living room.

The women's movement in the 1970s improved the place of women in the workforce and politics and changed the traditional feminine role. Traits such as vigor, strength, competitiveness, and poise under pressure were added to the more traditional feminine traits of nurturance and support. The feminist movement reveled in seeing women display athleticism, grit, and courage in competitive sport on television. Hundreds of thousands of women donned sneakers and workout clothes to exercise, sweat, and improve their body images and athletic skills, modeling the exceptional athletes they admired on television.

Racial background influences spectators. Certain races have traditionally participated in particular sports that produce heroes with whom other members of their race can identify. For example, Hispanics are proud of their superstars in boxing and MLB, while African Americans love to see their heroes dominate in professional basketball and football. Of course, sometimes nontraditional heroes emerge, such as Tiger Woods in golf or the Williams sisters in tennis, attracting nontraditional spectators wanting to follow their struggles and achievements.

Trends in Spectator Sports

Spectator sports can be divided into two major categories: those watched live and those followed through media such as TV, Internet, and radio. Accurately counting the total number of viewers of a sport is somewhat difficult compared to tracking the attendance at a sport event, particularly a

professional event. Amateur sports such as youth sports and most high school sports do not charge admission and therefore cannot provide attendance records.

One overall statistic is clear: Sport watching has grown steadily over the years, and the availability of sports on television has contributed to that growth. Certain sports have enjoyed a recent boost in popularity, including figure skating and women's college basketball. Of course, the televised Olympics, alternating Summer and Winter Games every two years, clearly boosts sport interest.

Let's take a look at some trends in spectator sports. Keep in mind when reviewing the lists that follow that these percentages are based on in-person spectators and television and Internet spectators combined.

In terms of the most popular viewed sports, more Americans are fans of pro football than any other sport (Gallup Poll 2005):

Percentage of Americans Who Are Fans of Various Sports

Professional football	64%
College football	54%
Professional baseball	52%
Figure skating	41%
College basketball	41%
Professional basketball	38%
Auto racing	30%
Professional golf	30%
Professional tennis	24%
Professional ice hockey	23%
Professional wrestling	10%

Interestingly, most sports have shown a decline in fan base since the entire list of sports was last asked about in 2001. The two exceptions are professional and college football, which have had their fan base hold steady. Auto racing and figure skating have each dropped 9 points while ice hockey has dropped 8 points.

We can also rank differences in what is being watched by gender (see table 3.3).

A quick look at table 3.4 shows that the number of people attending major sporting events in person continues to climb. Since 1985, most sports have nearly doubled their attendance levels. Of course, women's college basketball has shown phenomenal growth by increasing attendance figures five times over. If you study the table closely, you might think that baseball clearly has the most spectators annu-

TABLE 3.3 **Percentage of Americans by Gender Who Are Fans of Various Sports**

Men		Women	
Professional football	77%	Figure skating	60%
College football	70%	Professional football	60%
Professional baseball	58%	Professional baseball	46%
College basketball	49%	College football	39%
Professional basketball	42%	Professional basketball	36%
Professional golf	40%	College basketball	32%
Auto racing	39%	Professional tennis	25%
Professional ice hockey	28%	Auto racing	22%
Professional tennis	24%	Professional golf	20%
Figure skating	21%	Professional ice hockey	18%
Professional wrestling	14%	Professional wrestling	7%

Reprinted from Gallup. Available: http://gallup.com/poll/14812/Six-Americans-Pro-Football-Fans.aspx

TABLE 3.4 **Trends in In-Person Attendance at Spectator Sports**

Sport	1990	1994	2001	2007	2008
Baseball (MLB)	55.5	71.2	73.2	80.8	79.9
Football (NFL)	17.6	14.8	20.5	22.2	21.8
Football (college)	35.3	36.5	40.4	48.7	48.8
Basketball (NBA and WNBA)	18.5	19.3	21.4	23.6	21.9
Basketball (college men)	28.8	28.3	28.9	32.8	33.3
Basketball (college women)	2.8	4.6	8.8	10.8	11.1
Ice hockey (NHL)	12.3	15.7	20.3	20.8	21.2

Data do not include TV viewers. Numbers represent millions of in-person attendees.

U.S. Census Bureau 2009.

ally, but consider that professional baseball relies on a schedule of 162 games per year per team. In contrast, college football typically is limited to 11 or 12 games per year, but attendance at the high-prestige football programs averages over 100,000 fans per game. While professional football is the most popular with fans overall, in-game attendance at college football is clearly more robust, partially because it includes over 100 major college programs and many more Division II and III programs. In the southern region of the United States, the popularity of big-time college football is dominant over all of professional football.

Marketing to Participants and Spectators

The business of sport generates significant income for educational institutions, the USOC, the assigned national governing bodies of each sport, television, and corporate sponsors. Cities pour millions of dollars into facilities for professional teams as well as facilities used by their residents. Manufacturers of sporting goods produce equipment, uniforms, and footwear. The clothing industry designs casual apparel that can be worn on the street and is acceptable for physical activity.

All of these groups have a strong interest in promoting their products and services to sport participants, spectators, or both. The dollars they spend on marketing have increased exponentially over the years as sport popularity has ballooned. Universities now offer degrees in the business of sport and emphasize sport marketing as a career path.

Sport marketing must adapt as various sports rise or fall in popularity, new classes of potential participants or spectators emerge, and demographic patterns shift. One example of the changing marketplace is the opportunity to globalize

■ Subway receives great advertising through its use of signage in baseball stadiums.

sport marketing. Soccer is the most popular sport worldwide, with tennis next in popularity. The global reach of these sports exposes the products of their sponsors worldwide. Likewise, American sports such as football, basketball, and baseball have worked hard to expand into overseas markets to increase revenue. Satellite television and the Internet have allowed events to be seen around the world, have helped popularize sports and their athletes, and have attracted huge sponsorship dollars.

Organizations intending to market their sport or product to sport participants need to carefully research the historical perspective of potential participants, identify potential customers, and launch marketing campaigns specifically targeting those audiences. For example, not long ago many sport advertisements featured male athletes. Organizations wanting to attract potential female consumers had to change the advertising by presenting female athletes as role models. Female athletes such as Danica Patrick, Venus and Serena Williams, Michelle Kwan, Michelle Wie, Candace Parker, Misty May-Treanor, Natalie Gulbis, Maria Sharapova, and Swin Cash now appear in commercials. Professional athletes who are at the top of their sport earn more money from commercial endorsements than they do from playing. Sport icons such as Tiger Woods, Michael Jordan, and Andre Agassi,

who have represented clothing companies like Nike, earn millions a year in endorsement fees. In fact, some athletes became more famous from their commercial endorsements than they did from playing, including Joe DiMaggio for endorsing Mr. Coffee machines, Jim Palmer for endorsing men's underwear, and Rafael Palmeiro for endorsing Viagra.

Another example of the changes in sport marketing is the impetus for sports like tennis and golf to reach out to African Americans. The success of Tiger Woods and Serena and Venus Williams provided the perfect opportunity for these sports to demonstrate openness to people of all racial backgrounds and to actively recruit them for advertising. In a former generation, Zina Garrison, who ranked number four in women's tennis, couldn't command a clothing endorsement contract for most of her career. Instead she chose to wear fellow player Martina Navratilova's signature line until eventually Reebok offered her a contract near the end of her career. Twenty years ago, companies saw little value in Zina as a role model for advertising their clothes since few African Americans were interested in tennis.

Sponsors support the sports that attract participants or spectators who most closely parallel the consumers of their product. Thus Mercedes or Lincoln luxury cars sponsor professional tennis, Chevrolet trucks sponsor auto racing, and Miller or Budweiser beers sponsor professional football. Manufacturers of women's products naturally select women's sports to reach their market. At the same time, advertising in sports like football that attract a strong male audience tends to use attractive women in sexually suggestive ads that might pique the attention of male viewers.

Sports, trying to present an inclusive environment, are careful to design ads with pictures of all ethnic and racial groups, both genders, and all ages. Showing this variety is tricky in the advertising business, as visual images of one or two athletes are more powerful than a collage of smaller images.

Similarly, on television, ads for sport products use music and speech patterns that match those of the potential customer. An ad targeting youth uses styles, sounds, and performers the youthful audience recognizes and admires.

If marketing for fitness activities desires to reach out to people age 50, the models in the ads must look like the people in this audience, or at least look how the audience would like to look. Watching a buff model who is 25 years younger does nothing to attract an older person.

Chapter Summary

Sport participants range from youth league athletes to Olympic athletes. People at each level of play participate for different reasons. In spite of the fact that the overwhelming number of participants play simply to have fun, the majority of attention and funding is lavished on the small number of athletes who make it in high-performance sport.

Trends in adult sport participation show that fitness-oriented activities are now more popular than competition activities. Trends in youth sport participation show that a significant number of youth drop out of sport by their teenage years, and the trends also show an increased participation in extreme sports. For most sports, organized play attracts more participants than casual pickup games that are unorganized.

Sport spectators come from all ages, races, and economic backgrounds. College graduates are more likely to support their college teams, while those who did not attend college tend to support professional teams. Working-class spectators often enjoy the more violent sports, and people with higher incomes are drawn to sports that are traditionally supported at private clubs and are more expensive to watch or play.

Trends in sport spectators show that professional and college football are the top sports in America for spectators. Baseball is next in popularity, and basketball trails these sports by a significant margin. If we separate fans by gender, women rank figure skating as their top spectator sport, followed closely by professional and college football. In the past 20 years, the number of Americans who are sport spectators has nearly doubled in many sports; but in the past five years the numbers have been stable while even showing some declines likely due to economic circumstances. Finally, trends in sport marketing are based on the changing demographics in society, sport preferences, and the separation between marketing to potential participants and marketing to potential spectators.

Business of Sport

4

Would you like to own a National Football League team? Are you kidding? The average NFL team is now worth over $1 billion, according to *Forbes* magazine. Ten years ago when *Forbes* first valued NFL teams, the average franchise was worth "only $288 million." The average value in 2008 was $1.04 billion, with the Dallas Cowboys at $1.6 billion, the Washington Redskins at $1.5 billion, and the New England Patriots at $1.3 billion as the highest valued (Klayman 2008). Do you know of any other financial venture in which you could essentially triple your money, especially during an uncertain economic period? The NFL is our most popular sport league with strong television contracts, rabid fan support, and a plethora of new stadiums designed to maximize on-site profits. Following the philosophy set by former commissioner Pete Rozelle, the NFL has used revenue sharing as the basis for ensuring success for every team and hope for fans in every city that next year could be "their year."

Sport is big business in the United States and around the world. In 2007, Americans spent over $25 billion on spectator sports. And the business of sports is "entertainment." We pay for the right to watch sports, root for our team, forget about work or other more weighty matters, and just enjoy life. Some of us directly participate in sport, and sporting goods manufacturers value our support for their products, venues, and programs. Others simply observe athletes performing, and most of us thrill to see compelling athletic feats especially in the midst of pressurized competition like the Super Bowl, the World Series, or the Olympic Games (Quinn 2009).

By every measure, the money generated by sport events, spent by consumers, and allocated for sport sponsorship has increased dramatically to multibillion dollar levels in recent years. Of course, the amount of money spent on recreational sport is modest compared with the amount generated by professional sport. For that reason, most of this chapter focuses on the business of professional sport, sometimes referred to as **corporate sport**. We'll also look at career opportunities recently produced by the rapid economic growth of sport.

If you recall the detailed sport pyramid (figure 1.2) that shows the progression of play, games, sport, and work, you know that within the category of sport are different levels. For example, while college athletics are reputedly an amateur venture, the business aspects of collegiate athletics at large Division I universities are undeniable. In this chapter, we'll also look at the business of college sports.

Sport and the Economy

Entertaining people during their time off from work has always been a primary role of both participation and spectator sport. Although in the past, sport entertainment was usually casual and relaxed, today's sport is often organized, mechanized, marketed, and administered as a business. Commercial interests influence virtually every decision in collegiate and professional sport. Events are rated by television audience share, ticket sales, website hits, concession sales, sponsor revenue, and media coverage. Wins and losses are important because they influence all of these standards of measurement.

How did this happen? When did commercialization begin to take over sport?

In the 19th century, almost 90% of working Americans were farmers or workers in skilled trades. As our society became industrialized, many workers quit self-employment to join larger companies. The worker became one piece of the larger machine, helping to produce whatever goods or services the company provided (Leonard 1980; Rice, Hutchinson, and Lee 1958; Spears and Swanson 1978). In other words, the worker fit into the overall hierarchy of the larger corporation.

As sport grew more businesslike, the corporate model crept into the organization of every sport franchise and governing body. Athletes were encouraged to provide their services for the good of the larger entity, to contribute to the bottom line, and to share in the profits at the end of the year with the head or owner of their sport organization. Coaches became the supervisors of athletes who were sometimes asked to go against their personal choices for the good of the team or organization. Players who demonstrated a good work ethic, exemplary moral character, and a willingness to sacrifice for the good of the team were admired and held up as role models. Those who deviated from that path were labeled malcontents and given limited playing time or cut from the team.

As the sport industry grew in economic power, it attracted commercial interests that could benefit from that power by influencing its organization.

As the industry developed, the role of the athlete became that of serving the organization. But the growth of commercial sport would not have occurred without other conditions supporting rapid expansion:

- People need time away from work to participate in or watch sports. The life of a farmer left little time for activities outside of work, but industrialization changed the worker's opportunity for leisure time.

- People also need money to spend on sport. A society has to generate an economic level at which the majority of its people can afford to be sport consumers.

- People must live in concentrated areas so that they can use sport facilities, travel to sport events, and identify with a local professional sport team. Small cities and rural areas can rarely support professional teams and rely instead on local college or high school sports.

- Media such as newspapers, radio, and television must provide access to sport and athletes in order to sustain the interest in professional sports.

- Facilities that can present professional sports must be constructed, financed, and refurbished to maintain the sport revenue stream.

Athletes such as Frank Gilhooley of the 1913 New York Yankees played baseball during a time that coincided with a shift toward more industry in the United States.

Ownership of Professional Sports

For the most part, professional sport franchises are owned by extremely wealthy Americans (overwhelmingly male) who benefit from ownership personally and financially. They may use their teams to increase their personal wealth or to serve as a tax advantage to offset other business gains.

Originally, owners of professional sport teams were people who loved the game. They spent much of their personal time and money promoting the game and strengthening their teams and the leagues as a profitable business. The next wave of owners were men like Tom Yawkey of the Boston Red Sox (owner from 1933 to 1976), Phil Wrigley of the Chicago Cubs (owner from 1932 to 1977), and Augie Busch Jr. of the St. Louis Cardinals (owner from 1952 to 1989). Their dedication to baseball was genuine, and they did not use their professional team to promote their other businesses. As this generation of owners died off, a new breed of ownership began to emerge.

Growing numbers of owners are corporate conglomerates that purchase sport franchises to help market and promote their other products. Some organizations, such as the Green Bay Packers football team, are owned by the general public, who hold shares in the team. Club owners have evolved into corporate managers who may or may not consider the welfare of the team or the host city in their decisions, which they make with the bottom line in mind. Player depreciation, capital gains tax laws, and potential income are guiding forces behind ownership decisions. In 1984 the Baltimore Colts, a storied, proud franchise, was surreptitiously moved to Indianapolis to benefit the owner, Robert Irsay, with financial inducements and a new stadium. In 1996, 12 years later, Baltimore retaliated by enticing Art Modell and the Cleveland Browns to forsake Cleveland and move to Baltimore to become the Baltimore Ravens.

Individual club owners sometimes own a professional sport franchise to find fun and excitement, boost the ego, or gain a sense of power. Others enjoy being around famous athletes. Some owners are actively involved in the day-to-day operations, standing on the field with the athletes and consulting with coaches on decisions. Others leave the sport to the professional coaches and managers and stick to the business side of the franchise.

Making Money From Professional Sports

Let's look at the ways an owner might make an investment in a sport franchise worthwhile. Not all team owners take advantage of all of these factors, but many do.

Investment

Professional team franchises **appreciate**, growing in value every year. Clubs that were once purchased for hundreds of thousands dollars are now bought for hundreds of millions. No owner has ever lost money on the initial capital investment, and putting money into a professional team has always paid off in the long run. And, if an owner is able to construct a new stadium with sources of income other than his own, he can automatically increase the value of the franchise by $30 to $40 million.

To give you some idea of the value of an NFL franchise, consider that between 1993 and 1997, seven teams were sold in the price range of $158 to $212 million. In the years since then, the average selling price for a franchise has shot up to $578 million, topped by the $800 million Daniel Snyder paid for the Washington Redskins (*Wall Street Journal* 2004a).

By 2008, the average value of the 32 NFL teams was $1.04 billion. Just 10 years earlier, that figure was estimated by *Forbes* to be only $288 million on average. At that rate, you can see just how good a financial investment it is to own an NFL franchise whether you make money each year or not (Klayman 2008).

Taxes

While some owners may show a loss in their franchise's bottom line at the end of the year, they usually go into the year expecting that outcome. In fact, they may balance those losses against significant profits made in their other businesses, thereby saving money by reducing their overall tax liability. For example, if an owner earns a profit of $1 million in another business such as a manufacturing company, he can subtract the losses from his sport franchise from the $1 million in other profits and only pay tax on the remainder. The resulting tax savings could be significant. While losing money

IN THE ARENA WITH . . .

Jerry Jones

The Dallas Cowboys were lauded as NFL's Team of the Decade for the 1990s, during which time they won three Super Bowls in four years. Acting as team general manager as well as owner, Jerry Jones has been a hands-on presence since 1989 when he took over the Cowboys. During his leadership time, the Cowboys have drafted 17 different players who have gone on to appear in a combined total of 63 Pro Bowls.

Though a proud and storied franchise under previous owners and Hall of Fame coach Tom Landry, Jerry Jones has clearly made his own indelible imprint on the Cowboys' history. He has also been a visible leader among league owners to ensure the long-term viability of the NFL, and fought many battles both privately and publicly to raise the profile of the league in general and yet protect the rights and profits of individual club owners.

One of Jones' proudest achievements is the completion of the new Cowboys stadium in 2008 at a cost of over a billion dollars and the awarding of the 2011 Super Bowl to the stadium and the fans. In a typical independent decision, Jones decided not to sell "naming rights" to the new stadium but rather simply call it "Cowboys Stadium." In this day of overcommercialized sport and revenue schemes, that decision has impressed many observers.

Like most NFL owners, Jones has been an active supporter of youth sport; his family charity will donate $16.5 million to youth sport in the city of Arlington, Texas, over the next 33 years. Jones and his wife also received the Evangeline Booth Award in 1999 from the Salvation Army for their leadership in that organization. In addition, they are major donors to Boys and Girls Clubs, the National Multiple Sclerosis Society, and a host of other local charitable organizations.

each year to gain tax write-offs may seem like bad business, remember that the value of the franchise steadily increases each year, and once the owner sells, he will see significant profits. Don't be fooled by owners who claim they are losing money with their team. If they really see the team as a loss, they'll sell.

Here is an example involving the New York Yankees. According to *New York Magazine*, the Yankees lost about $28 million in 2006, yet the value of the team rose $200 million and was worth about $1.2 billion in 2007. Table 4.1 shows a breakdown of the Yankees' revenue and costs for 2006.

Depreciation

Depreciation has always been a mainstay of American business. Assets such as equipment, tools, and athletes (in sport) have a life expectancy. Their annually decreasing value is referred to as *depreciation*. American tax laws allow businesses to reduce the book values of their capital assets each year, so businesses can show depreciation as a loss against their profits and again reduce their tax liability even if the actual values of the **capital assets** have increased. Depreciation may be one of the least understood characteristics of owning a

TABLE 4.1   Yankees 2006 Revenue and Costs

Revenue	
Tickets	$117 million
Local TV	$60 million
MLB TV and licensing	$30 million
Sponsorship-advertising	$30 million
Premium seating	$27 million
Local radio	$13 million
Concessions	$10 million
Catering	$5 million
Other	$10 million
Total	**$272 million**
Costs	
Player salaries	$195 million
Revenue sharing	$70 million
Luxury tax	$25 million
Stadium operations	$20 million
Travel and training	$20 million
Total	**$330 million**

Reprinted from "New York Yankee$$$" St. Petersburg Times. 6-14-2007 Section 2C.

professional sport franchise. The players who are under contract to the team are valued at a certain level each year. Because their values decrease over time as they age and their careers wind down, federal laws allow clubs to annually depreciate the value of their stable of players.

Here's how an owner may depreciate players for tax benefits. Suppose a sport franchise breaks even in yearly income versus yearly expenses, but the owner can depreciate the value of his players by $1 million. If his other businesses show a profit of $2 million, he can apply the depreciation of $1 million against that profit and pay tax only on the remaining million.

Revenue Sharing

There is a sharp distinction between the NFL and Major League Baseball (MLB) in the structure and amount of money that is shared among the league teams. Although the total annual revenues for baseball ($6 billion) and football ($7 billion) are comparable, the sharing formula is not. More than 80% of the NFL revenue is divided evenly between all 32 teams. As a result, market size has little to do with the revenue base of a football franchise.

However, in contrast, MLB teams share less than 25% of their total revenue. This means that more than three-quarters of the revenue generated locally stays there, with the bulk of the money going to teams in large markets with a history of strong brand and competitive success. From year to year the finances of the team can be dramatically affected due to winning or losing that affects attendance, ticket prices, luxury suite rentals, and local broadcast ratings. Consider the example of the New York Yankees, who generated nearly $400 million in 2007 while their division rival Tampa Bay Rays made barely $100 million and yet had to compete to pay players (Dubner 2007).

At the risk of oversimplifying the situation, it appears that the NFL is a national league with power held by the owners and shared revenue from national broadcast television rights, while MLB suffers from more revenue risk, depending on the local market, but pays the players better.

In the past few years, there have been some changes to the NFL revenue-sharing plan that may sow the seeds of discontent among smaller-market teams. The newly constructed stadiums have large box seats that are leased to corporations, and that revenue is not shared. Nor are revenues from naming rights for stadiums or a team's own licensed product sales. Other stadium revenues brought in by concerts, restaurants, and special events are also not shared.

The NFL salary cap is calculated as a percentage of total revenue by all league teams. Teams in the top-third NFL markets, such as Boston, Washington, Dallas, Philadelphia, Chicago, and New York, generate revenues averaging $256 million; teams in the lower third of NFL markets such as Cincinnati, Minneapolis, Jacksonville, and Buffalo generate about $177 million. The difference in revenue between some large and small markets is nearly $100 million. The problem is that once the salary cap is determined based on all teams' revenue, the small-market teams simply do not have the cash to spend up to the cap because they have less unshared revenue from luxury boxes, stadium naming rights, local media, and local sponsorships. Large-market teams are paying an average of 47% of their revenue to players, while small-market teams like the Cincinnati Bengals are paying 68% of their revenue (Curnutte 2007).

Ticket Sales

The money people pay for seats (an average of about $2.5 million per NFL game) is split between the home and visiting team 60-40, with the visiting team getting 40% of the gate. Total ticket sales are affected by the seating capacity of the stadium, the prices set for each level of seating, and the attendance at each game. Many NFL teams with winning traditions routinely sell out their seating and have a waiting list of customers wanting to purchase season tickets.

In MLB a game rarely sells out, simply because a baseball team plays 162 games per year, compared to a football team that plays only 16 games a season. Baseball's national broadcasts generate just 20% of overall sales, with the largest amount of other revenue coming from revenue at the ballpark and via local broadcasts. Some teams have stakes in their own cable networks such as the Yankees, Mets, and Red Sox; in each case the teams earn huge revenues that they do not need to share league wide (Jacobson 2007).

Stadium Revenues

Stadium revenues include income from luxury boxes, concessions, and parking. Most recently built stadiums include luxury boxes that are typically the most expensive seats available. They often include food service, have private restrooms, and feature televisions showing the game in progress. Most

▌ Concession sales are just one way stadiums can increase their revenue and generate profits.

luxury boxes are bought by corporations and are deducted as a business expense since the corporations use them to entertain clients.

The food and souvenir concessions at most ballparks and arenas also generate significant profits for the local team. Most venues ban outside food and drink, forcing fans who wish to eat or drink to patronize the concession stands during the game. Parking also produces revenue since most fans drive to the venue and like to park near the facility. In the NFL, the league-wide stadium revenue is estimated at $1 billion, or 21% of total league revenues (Bell 2004). The local franchise typically retains these stadium revenues, but in the case of publicly financed stadiums, the sponsoring agency such as the city may share in these revenues in return for financing the stadium in the first place.

Media Revenues

Media revenues include income from radio, TV, cable, and pay-per-view broadcasts. They account for the largest single source of income for the NFL and were estimated at 52% of total NFL revenue for 2004. Happily for most NFL franchises, that revenue is shared equally by all 32 teams. **Revenue sharing** among teams in the league enhances their total bargaining power and helps balance the differences in various markets due to size, tradition, and competition from other recreational activities.

Whereas television income generates nearly 60% of each NFL team's revenue, in other sports that percentage may be as low as 15% (Sage 1998). Income from television accounts for less than 20% of revenue for National Hockey League (NHL) owners since their product cannot command the same level of compensation as professional football can (Bell 2004).

Licensing Fees on Team Merchandise

Professional sport teams sell team jerseys, caps, T-shirts, and every imaginable souvenir. The NFL became the leader in capitalizing on such merchandise by establishing NFL Properties to market the league and license merchandise. The revenue from these sales is shared equally among all NFL teams. Some team owners balked at this arrangement, particularly if their team traditionally generated more sales than other, less popular teams did.

The amounts of these revenue streams vary greatly from team to team, city to city, and sport to sport. Some leagues, such as the NFL, mandate revenue sharing among all teams, while others allow each franchise to keep what it generates or caps earnings and penalizes franchises for exceeding the cap. The NFL and its franchises generate about $7 billion annually and share roughly 80% of that amount equally. In contrast, MLB teams share less than 25% of their total revenue (Dubner 2007). So in baseball, the large-market franchises in New York, Los Angeles, Atlanta, Houston, and Chicago fare better than their counterparts in smaller cities like Tampa Bay, Milwaukee, Miami, or Kansas City. This is one factor that tilts the competitive advantage toward a team like the Yankees that can spend more each year on player salaries and also afford the resulting penalty.

Naming Rights

Another major source of income for cities or teams is the selling of the **naming rights** to their stadium. In the past, stadiums were named after former owners, celebrities, or the local city. For example, Joe Robbie Stadium in Miami, which honored the former owner, and Connie Mack Stadium, former manager of the Philadelphia Athletics, have been replaced by Pro Player Stadium and Lincoln Financial Stadium, respectively. Now we are accustomed to names like Raymond James Stadium, American Airlines Arena, Pepsi Center, Tropicana Field, Safeco Field, and Ericsson Stadium. The largest stadium naming rights are shown in table 4.2.

A new or refurbished stadium increases the value of a professional sport franchise. As mentioned earlier, an owner may see his franchise appreciate by $30 or $40 million without spending a dime if

TABLE 4.2 Largest Annual Naming Rights

Stadium name	Sponsor	Home teams	Dollars per year
Reliant Stadium	Reliant Energy	Houston Texans	$10 million
Phillips Arena	Royal Phillips Electronics	Atlanta Hawks, Thrashers	$9.3 million
FedEx Field	Federal Express	Washington Redskins	$7.6 million
Bank of America Stadium	Bank of America	Carolina Panthers	$7 million
American Airlines Center	American Airlines	Dallas Mavericks, Stars	$6.5 million

Adapted from ESPN Sport Business.

outside public or private funding finances a new stadium. The owner then pockets the increased value when he decides to sell.

Stadium Financing

Financing of stadiums or playing arenas has been under public debate for years, and the discussion is sure to continue. Because of the need for constant refurbishing, upgrading, and redesign, constructing a new facility is often a better option than remodeling an old one. The cost of a new facility easily exceeds several hundred million dollars, and thus the source of that funding is a point of debate. Many creative minds have developed various financial packages to support these new facilities. Let's look at some of the packages.

The percentage of **public** and **private funds** used for construction varies in each situation. The 15 MLB parks constructed since 1991 on average received 75% of their financing from public funds. During a similar time frame, professional football stadiums averaged about 65% of public financing (Sage 1998). Since 2000, 28 new major league stadiums have been built at a cost of over $9 billion, with more than half—over $5 billion—of the costs from public dollars. Public sources include sales taxes, proximity and beneficiary taxes, general obligation and revenue bonds, and tax increment financing. Private sources include owner contributions, league contributions, bank loans, loans from local businesses, and personal seat licenses (Wilhelm 2008).

The majority of stadiums are publicly owned by local governments or by special stadium or sport authorities. These groups oversee the operation of the facility, negotiate leases with the sport teams that use it, and may also supervise nearby ancillary construction such as shops, restaurants, and other amenities. A few stadiums such as Bank of America and Gillette were privately financed and are privately owned. The Bank of America Stadium, home of Carolina Panthers football, was completed in 1996 at a cost of $248 million (Ballparks 2006a). Gillette Stadium in Foxboro, Massachusetts, has been home to the New England Patriots since 2002 and was funded entirely by owner Robert Kraft at a price of $325 million (Ballparks 2006b). The inducement for the owner to fund the facility is the ability to depreciate the asset. Over several years, the tax savings from such depreciation can be significant.

For years, Florida has assessed a **bed tax** on hotel guests who are from out of state. For every room night, $1.00 goes into a special fund to help finance public sport stadiums around the state. The state government decides which sport in which city is due for support and allocates a portion of the bed tax revenue for that project. As you might suspect, football, basketball, baseball, tennis, and other sports lobby heavily for access to these funds. The beauty of this plan is that residents are mollified regarding the use of public money since it comes from the pockets of tourists or out-of-state businesspeople. Of course, some people might wonder what other uses the money could be put to, such as education, housing for the poor, hurricane relief, or coastline refurbishing.

Personal seat licenses (PSLs) are an interesting financing option in which fans pay for the right to purchase specific seats in a stadium. If the owner of a seat decides not to purchase the seat for a particular game, the seat can be sold to the general public. This plan has been popular and has raised significant capital in cities like San Francisco ($55 million), Chicago ($70 million), Green Bay ($92 million), and Charlotte ($122 million) (Steeves 2003). More recently, the Dallas Cowboys offered what they call "seat options" in their new stadium in Arlington at a cost between $16,000 and $150,000 per year for 30 years, depending on the location of the seats. These fees are by far the most expensive in sport history. Add in the actual cost of a ticket at roughly $350 per seat per game, and you begin to see the expense to the fan (Marta 2008).

Public tax funds provide funding for construction and maintenance of most professional sport stadiums. These publicly financed stadiums may be financed by tax-free public bonds, thereby depriving the government of a source of revenue that critics of such financing argue could be better applied toward improved living conditions for residents, especially the most needy. In many cases, the city may tax ticket sales, refreshment sales, and parking fees, although each of these items depends on the negotiated agreement with the sport franchise. Most cities also charge the team a rental fee that may range from several hundred thousand dollars a year to a nominal $1.00. The fee depends on the negotiation between the professional sport franchise and the current city officials.

You might wonder how cities or states justify spending public funds to build stadiums and arenas that clearly benefit the team owners. Here are the major justifications that are typically presented to the taxpayers:

• The general public will benefit from the presence of professional sport teams because the area will be regarded as major league, real estate values

Tourists to Florida may not realize it, but the money they spend on hotels while on vacation helps to support the financing of public sport stadiums throughout Florida.

will increase, and residents will take pride in their team identity and enjoy the recreational value of following the team.

• The city will see revenue from tourists who attend the games; restaurants and hotels will see increased traffic; and the city government will realize tax revenue on all the money spent locally, which will go back into city coffers.

• The city and region will see priceless publicity that will attract potential residents, especially potential businesses looking to relocate offices and groups of employees or new businesses that provide jobs for local residents.

• National media attention will attract tourism, and local businesses will flourish because of exposure and a chance to sell their products nationally or at least regionally.

• Special events like play-offs and championships may prove an added benefit. They provide added exposure, and the revenue generated from just one such event can easily be $50 million or more.

• The sport franchise creates jobs and income for local people who work directly or indirectly for the team. Ushers, ticket takers, refreshment stand workers, cleanup crews, and maintenance workers all derive income from the facility.

Detractors of public financing for these facilities argue just as vehemently that these benefits are modest when compared to the actual costs to the cities and their taxpayers. Over the years, various opposing groups have mounted campaigns to block public financing by drawing attention to alternative fund uses that might better improve the quality of life for a city's residents. Housing for the poor, educational services, public infrastructure improvements, medical research and care, and many other services are offered as reasonable alternatives.

Who wins the debate usually depends on the amount of money spent on the campaign for public support. The owners of sport teams expend significant amounts to hire the best "spin doctors" to present their case to the public. Local politicians, business leaders, and media often happily support the new proposal by reporting its positive benefits to the public. Opposition forces, on the other hand, are often a small group of local citizens with limited financial resources to publicize their point of view.

EXPERT'S VIEW

Andrew Zimbalist

Andrew Zimbalist is the Robert A. Woods professor of economics at Smith College and one of the most prominent sport economists in the world. He has published 18 books, written countless articles, and appeared regularly on television and radio, sharing his view of the business side of sports. Holder of a PhD from Harvard University, Zimbalist has also consulted widely with players' associations, teams, cities, companies, and sport leagues. He is equally conversant in the details of big-time collegiate sport and professional sport. His most recent book is *Circling the Bases: Essays on the Challenges and Prospects of the Sports Business* (2010).

One topic that puzzles many people is whether there is value in hosting the Olympic Games and why countries get so energized about that possibility. The sobering view presented by Professor Zimbalist is that the indirect benefits of hosting the Games, while difficult to quantify, are probably more valuable than the apparent direct economic benefits. There is too much financial uncertainty; there are also heavy costs that always exceed budget projections, and almost certainly unanticipated expenses before, during, and even after the Games. While new athletic facilities that are constructed for various competitions may be a boon to the local community, they more often become a drain on taxpayers for years afterward due to minimal use, high cost of land use, and ongoing operating expenses.

From the viewpoint of a developing country, hosting a major sporting event can serve as a catalyst for construction of modern transportation system, communication, and sport infrastructure. But for countries that are already developed and modernized, hosting athletic games is typically a costly expense. Yet Zimbalist counsels each country and city to "think, before you bid" on major sporting events to be sure the goals of hosting will promote long-term development (Zimbalist 2010).

Sport owners may also subtly or not so subtly threaten to simply move their team to another city if the residents don't want the team badly enough to finance it. Although such threats are a form of blackmail, they have carried the day in many cities around the country. The actions of Art Modell in Cleveland, Robert Irsay in Baltimore, and Al Davis in Oakland have proven that such a threat is not just idle chatter (Turco and Ostrosky 1997).

Organizations as Owners

Many sporting events and even some professional sport teams, such as the Green Bay Packers, are owned by a group or organization. The dynamics of group ownership significantly differ from those of individual ownership, since decisions have to be made by group members or at least by the elected governing board of directors. If the group is a public corporation, its financial records are open to public scrutiny—an unpalatable prospect for professional sport leagues that would prefer to keep their finances private.

One of the most successful group ownerships of a professional sport event is the United States Open tennis championships at Flushing Meadows, New York. The annual tennis tournament is owned and operated by the United States Tennis Association (USTA), the appointed national governing body (NGB) for tennis in the United States. As the NGB for tennis, the USTA was granted that right by the U.S. Olympics Committee, which based its decision on the Amateur Sports Act of the U.S. Congress. The USTA has a membership of approximately 700,000 people who pay a modest yearly dues of around $35.00. But the real moneymaker for the USTA is the U.S. Open. About 85% of the annual revenue for the USTA comes from that two-week tournament. In spite of a challenging economy in 2009, the U.S. Open grossed roughly $200 million in revenue and earned profits estimated to be between $110 and $115 million (*SportsBusiness Daily* 2009).

By constitution and bylaws, the USTA is a not-for-profit organization that must spend the money it takes in each year to promote tennis. It does so by operating tennis leagues for adults and kids, developing community tennis programs, supporting elite junior players who promise to be successful professionals, and fulfilling its traditional role as a tournament organizer for every possible age group, ability level, and gender.

In the late 1990s, the facilities at the National Tennis Center in New York, the home of the U.S. Open, received a total face-lift at a cost exceeding $250 million. The USTA bore the total cost of that expense, with no expenditure of public funding. Compared to other sport owners who have their facilities built for them, the USTA stands alone as self-supporting.

The only New York team that earns more money than the U.S. Open is the New York Yankees, and they accumulate their earnings over a season of 81 home games. During its two-week tournament, the U.S. Open earns more than the Jets, Giants, Knicks, Rangers, or Islanders. How does the USTA do it?

The U.S. Open derives its income about equally from three sources: ticket, food, beverage, and merchandise sales; corporate sponsors; and television rights worldwide. Other professional tennis events around the country operate similarly, although on a much smaller scale. Some of them are owned by organizations such as the International Management Group, the sport organization founded by Mark McCormick that represents players and also owns tennis events. Other tournaments are owned by individuals or local sporting groups that secure

the sanction of the men's or women's professional tour to ensure that their date is not set on that of another event.

Sport as a Monopoly

Some people argue that professional sports in America are unique in that they are clearly a monopoly. No other business in the United States operates under the same favorable set of rules. Let's examine this argument, beginning with a review of history.

In the 1890s, President Grover Cleveland became concerned about the influence of the Standard Oil Company on the economy and influenced the U.S. Congress to pass the Sherman Antitrust Act, which made illegal "every contract, combination in the form of trust or otherwise, or conspiracy in restraint of trade or commerce among the several states or with foreign nations" (Michener 1987, p. 386). Although this bill did not directly target baseball, it significantly affected the sport. Professional baseball was conducting interstate commerce and restrained trade, since players couldn't move from one team

While professional leagues often use the Sherman Act to their advantage by making it nearly impossible for expansion teams to gain footing, some teams win big after only a few years. The Arizona Diamondbacks were founded in 1998 and won the World Series in 2001.

to another and the owners conspired to keep players' salaries at their desired level. Over the next 30 years, various interests challenged the Sherman Antitrust legislation; and in 1922, Supreme Court Justice Oliver Wendell Holmes declared that baseball was not in violation of the Sherman Antitrust laws. Numerous court suits have been filed since, with minor changes to this momentous decision. Naturally, other professional sports fell into the same favorable position due to the similarity of their businesses.

How have professional sports used this favorable ruling to operate as a monopoly? Let's look at a few of the ways:

• Team owners formed leagues like the NFL to control how teams compete against each other for fans, players, media revenues, sales of licensed merchandise, and sponsorships.

• The leagues, including the MLB, National Basketball Association (NBA), NFL, and NHL, also work together to eliminate competition from new leagues that try to cash in on their sport.

• Using a draft system for hiring players, owners force players to negotiate only with the team that drafts them, thereby keeping the prices for athletes down.

• New or expansion teams cannot join the league without paying substantial fees to all the other owners, and one owner cannot relocate his team to another city without the approval of the other owners.

• Owners of individual teams cannot sell merchandise from their team. In professional football, NFL Properties markets all the business properties of the NFL as a unit. NFL Properties has been wildly successful in negotiating sponsorships, licensing agreements, and television contracts. However, Jerry Jones of the Dallas Cowboys, the most popular team in America, wanted to merchandise Cowboy paraphernalia himself. He didn't see why he should support other franchises with sales of Cowboys hats, jerseys, and so on. Jones forced the NFL to modify the monopolistic stance it had operated under for years, although the league still retains the majority of its power.

Television revenue is a huge source of income for most sport teams, but the potential revenue for each team depends on the size of its market. The NFL restricts individual teams from negotiating local TV contracts, but the MLB does not. Hence, the New York Yankees can sell their local TV rights for $75 million a year, while a team like the former Montreal Expos was lucky to command $1 million.

Among other things, this inequity in potential income helped convince the Expos to relocate to Washington, DC, in 2005. You can see the disparity that different markets create between teams, which throws the teams' power and competitiveness off balance. The NFL remains a true monopoly by negotiating as one entity.

Management Versus Labor

Team owners restrict the options available to the workforce in their sports. First, they limit the choice of teams a player can sign with. Each league conducts an annual draft, and players are assigned teams based on their selection by a team. A player who grew up in California and thrives in warm weather may be drafted by the Green Bay Packers and has no choice but to go to Green Bay if he wishes to play professionally in his sport. Also, by assigning players to teams, leagues reduce the players' negotiating leverage and therefore limit players' salaries.

Imagine if a young lawyer just out of school was drafted by a law firm and assigned to work there regardless of her preferences and the salary offered. That's how professional athletes go into their work. Those who support athletes' rights would say that athletes who spend their whole lives preparing to play professionally ought to have the rights of other citizens who can offer their services to the highest bidder. Team owners argue that a league draft fairly distributes sport talent and allows every team a shot at signing the best players. Since the draft begins with the team that had the worst record the previous year, the theory is that the team can strengthen itself by hiring the best new talent. This argument may be more fitting for basketball, where one 7-foot (2.1 meter) player can dominate the court, than for other sports.

Second, team owners used to own the services of their athletes for life if they wished. Curt Flood in baseball was the first to challenge this reserve clause, and at great sacrifice to his personal career he changed baseball forever. Now baseball players can become free agents after a certain amount of time and can bargain with other teams for their services. Football and basketball have at various times used an *option clause*, which requires a player to play one more year after his contract expires, typically at 90% of his previous year's salary, before he becomes a free agent able to sell his services to another team. Each new collective bargaining agreement between owners and the player's union sets the terms of option clauses during the length of the agreement. Of course, when a player and his agent negotiate a contract, they also have the right to agree to an option clause in exchange for other favorable provisions such as a sizable signing bonus. Many teams try to trade a player once he announces he is playing out his option, as they figure it is better to get something in return than to lose a player's services without any compensation at all. A trade gives the player's current team some value in return compared to losing him with nothing to show for it once his obligation is satisfied and he is free to negotiate with any other team. Thus you see established players with significant careers traded for fringe players, future draft choices, or the famous "player to be named later."

Over the years, strong leadership from union officials and former athletes with backing from the player union have effected some favorable changes for athletes. Minimum pay levels have been established for rookies and veterans, options set for players who cannot agree with the team that drafts them on a contract, and freedom established for players who have fulfilled their original contract to negotiate with other teams for their services.

The owners gave in grudgingly to each of these player demands, arguing that allowing players to sign with the highest bidder at any time would upset the balance of competitiveness. Large-market teams like the Yankees would pay the highest salaries, attract the best players, and have the best teams year in and year out. Small-market teams left with poorer players would see fan attendance tumble and be at economic risk. The final irony would be that the large-market teams with deep pockets would eventually have no other teams to play and the sport would put itself out of business.

The Yankees already contend for the championship every year, beating up on their competition. In 2010, the Yankees' total payroll was listed at $206,738,389, the highest in MLB. In contrast, division rival Tampa Bay Rays were ranked 19th in payroll total at $72,323,471. Interestingly, New York paid just three players (Alex Rodriguez, CC Sabathia, and Derek Jeter) more than the total payroll of the Tampa team (ESPN 2010c).

Player Compensation

Let's look at the yearly compensation of all athletes in the United States. Keep in mind that the following statistics include all sports and all athletes, even those in so-called minor leagues. According to the U.S. Bureau of Labor Statistics (2009), in 2006 the median annual earnings of athletes were $41,060, although of course many of the highest-paid athletes earn significantly more. Statistics

Tina Charles, no. 31, was the number one 2010 WNBA draft pick. Did she have a choice to play for the Connecticut Sun?

also show that there are only about 21,000 jobs in total for all levels of professional sport athletes in the United States. While you read about the multimillion-dollar contracts of top athletes in the news, hundreds more are struggling to make ends meet in the minor leagues, hoping for a chance at the big leagues. The competition to reach the highest levels of any professional sport is intense, and the length of a career overall is only about three and a half years due to debilitating injuries and age.

Once athletes in major sports such as baseball, football, or basketball reach a certain level of performance, they are rewarded with a contract that may extend for several years or, in the case of superstars, up to 8 to 10 years. Since these athletes typically are in a high tax bracket, federal, state, and local taxes take a big chunk out of these earnings. Many athletes are required to pay state taxes in the state where their team is based and in states where their

Michael Jordan successfully made the transition from former athlete to a new career as owner of the Charlotte Bobcats. Not all former athletes are able to make such a successful transition.

our craft, and perhaps seeking additional education, professional athletes focus completely on their athletic careers.

Professional athletes face extreme competition to make it as an athlete, and that competitiveness rarely goes away. In some sports like professional tennis or golf, players earn prize money in tournaments. If they don't play well or suffer an injury, their income stops while their expenses continue. There are no guarantees in professional tennis or golf, so athletes have to prove themselves at every event, year after year.

The day-to-day work of a professional athlete is extremely demanding, even in the off-season. Athletes are constantly challenged at their physical and mental limits. They often travel extensively and spend long times away from spouses and children. If their team trades them, they are forced to uproot their families and start life in a new city.

Media coverage of athletes is very intense, and sports writers often criticize performances they judge as wanting. Very few occupations and performances are reviewed publicly, especially on a daily basis. Athletes must develop a tough skin to deal with the constant criticism and scrutiny.

Table 4.3 shows the top wage earners in football, baseball, and basketball, while the top wage earners in all sports are shown in table 4.4. Although these salaries are extremely generous when compared to the median household income (the average household size is 2.6 people) in the United States ($50,007 in 2007) (United States Census Bureau 2005-2007), athletes are not ordinary people. Their athletic talents are extraordinary; and if they can combine that talent with good business sense, they may earn double and triple their salary in endorsements, appearances, and other activities. Tiger Woods continues to be sport's highest earner with an income two and a half times higher than that of his closest competitor. Woods has topped the list for eight straight years.

The average Joe Fan may get disgusted with the exorbitant pay of top athletes, particularly when the athletes don't play up to expectations. However, a fair way to look at their compensation is to regard them as entertainers in the sport industry. When compared to earnings of entertainers in music, stage, and film, their wages are not so amazing—Oprah Winfrey easily out-earns most of the top athletes. Following is a list of the top 10

team competes, even if their residence is in a different state. The task of accounting and filing returns in a dozen states is daunting.

Even in a relatively safe sport such as tennis, the average career length is only about seven years. Most athletes need the income they earn in these years to last a lifetime, so they must invest their money wisely to grow their nest egg. You might argue that athletes can find other jobs once their career ends. However, professional athletes often fall victim to relying on their athletic prowess and have no other marketable skills. Sport-related jobs like officiating, coaching, scouting, and working in the front office are limited and demand training and experience. The income potential for those jobs is very modest, much less than what the athlete has learned to live on. Some of the most successful athletes move into television reporting and broadcast work. These careers can be very lucrative; but the competition for these spots is intense, and sustaining these jobs requires excellent skills. During the 20s and early 30s, when most of us are carving a niche for ourselves in our chosen profession, honing

TABLE 4.3 Top Wage Earners in Football, Baseball, and Basketball

Athlete	Team	Earnings (in U.S. millions)
PRO FOOTBALL (2008)		
Ben Roethlis-berger	Pittsburg Steelers	$27,701,920
Jared Allen	Minnesota Vikings	$21,119,256
Larry Fitzgerald	Arizona Cardinals	$17,103,480
JaMarcus Russell	Oakland Raiders	$16,872,400
Michael Turner	Atlanta Falcons	$16,003,840
PRO BASEBALL (2009)		
Alex Rodriguez	New York Yankees	$33,000,000
Manny Ramirez	Los Angeles Dodgers	$23,854,494
Derek Jeter	New York Yankees	$21,600,000
Mark Teixeira	New York Yankees	$20,625,000
Carlos Beltran	New York Mets	$19,243,682
PRO BASKETBALL (2008-2009)		
Kevin Garnett	Boston Celtics	$24,751,934
Jason Kidd	Dallas Mavericks	$21,372,000
Jermaine O'Neal	Toronto Raptors	$21,372,000
Kobe Bryant	Los Angeles Lakers	$21,262,500
Allen Iverson	Detroit Pistons	$20,840,625

Data from USA Today.

celebrities, including athletes, ranked by earnings (Forbes 2009):

1. Oprah Winfrey — $275 million
2. George Lucas — $170 million
3. Steven Spielberg — $150 million
4. Madonna — $110 million
5. Tiger Woods — $110 million
6. Jerry Bruckheimer — $100 million
7. Beyonce Knowles — $87 million
8. Jerry Seinfeld — $85 million
9. Dr. Phil McGraw — $80 million
10. Simon Cowell — $75 million

TABLE 4.4 World's Highest-Paid Athletes for 2008

Rank	Sport	Name	Earnings (in U.S. millions)
1	Golf	Tiger Woods	110
2	NBA	Kobe Bryant	45
3	NBA	Michael Jordan	45
4	F1	Kimi Raikkonen	45
5	Soccer	David Beckham	42
6	NBA	LeBron James	40
7	Golf	Phil Mickelson	40
8	Boxing	M. Pacquiao	40
9	Motorcycle	Val Rossi	35
10	NASCAR	Dale Earnhardt Jr.	34
11	Tennis	Roger Federer	33
12	NBA	Shaquille O'Neal	33
13	Boxing	Oscar de la Hoya	32
14	F1	Lewis Hamilton	32
15	Baseball	Alex Rodriguez	32
16	Golf	Vijay Singh	31
17	NBA	Kevin Garnett	30
18	NASCAR	Jeff Gordon	30
19	Baseball	Derek Jeter	30
20	Soccer	Ronaldinho	30

Based on Forbes.com 2009. Available: http://www.forbes.com/2009/06/17/top-earning-athletes-business-soports-top-earning-athletes

Limits on Athlete Earnings

After years of wildly escalating salaries, professional sport owners decided to set a **total salary cap** on the amount each team could spend on player salaries in order to save money and ensure competitive balance in the league. The NFL enforces the toughest version of this cap, while baseball allows some wiggle room. When a baseball team exceeds the total cap, it has to pay a luxury tax on the amount of money it pays over the cap. As already mentioned, the New York Yankees do exceed the cap most years and pay the fine.

Because of the salary cap, every team employs experts who figure out the implications of every player contract and how it will affect the team cap in the years ahead. Veteran players sometimes agree to renegotiate their contract and postpone earnings in order to free cap space so the team can sign a desirable free agent who might help the team win now. In other cases, a team may retire a veteran

IN THE ARENA WITH . . .

Tiger Woods

The rankings of athlete earnings show clearly that the top earner in all sports is Tiger Woods due to his multiple sponsorship deals with various corporations. No other athlete in history has averaged over 100 million per year in endorsement income as Tiger has. Yet, when the news of his extramarital affairs broke in 2009, many of his endorsement relationships were severed by companies that believed his association with them had become a negative force rather than a positive one. While he continued to be a terrific golfer, perhaps the finest in history, his personal conduct became a liability in terms of his attractiveness as a spokesperson for businesses. In fact, some of his top endorsement deals appeared to cause the stock of those companies to actually decline due to the negative association with his name, a figure said to be as much as $14 billion (BBC News 2009). Companies that either dropped Woods or at least loosened their ties to him include AT&T, consulting firm Accenture, razor maker Gillette, watchmaker Tag Heuer, and Gatorade sport drinks.

player with a contract in order to avoid having to count his entire salary in the cap totals.

Team administrators compile all the available data, scout for the best players, sign them to contracts while staying under the cap, and try to keep everybody happy. Making everyone happy doesn't happen very often due to the competitiveness of the athletes, their agents, and the team officials.

Collegiate Sports as Moneymakers

Let's step down from professional sports and look at intercollegiate sports. Born out of student activities, college sports have evolved into big business on many university campuses. Particularly in major or **revenue-producing sports** like football and basketball, the amount of money major universities earn and spend makes operation of the athletic department a business proposition. While the specific purpose of an athletic program may not be to make money, it certainly is clear that the department cannot lose money. Amateur sport has become big business for several reasons:

- The student body enjoys having high-profile athletic teams on campus for entertainment and recreation.

- The university administration recognizes the power of the free publicity that schools competing at high levels receive in the sport pages of newspapers and periodicals.

- Sport publicity helps universities recruit applicants. Receiving more applications

raises the competition for admission and improves the quality of students that schools attract.

- Alumni enjoy identifying with their alma mater through sport, especially if they take pride in the athletic achievements of their schools' teams. They are also more likely to return to campus to attend athletic events.

- Alumni are more likely to donate significant sums of money to their university. Some restrict their gifts to the athletic program; some donate to the general fund used at the administration's discretion; and others earmark their money for specific campus projects.

- Revenue from a high-profile sport like football can support a complete athletic program with a full complement of offerings for both men and women.

The University of Connecticut (UConn), a small regional university that was not even widely regarded as the best university in New England, moved into national prominence by dominating college basketball. The state of Connecticut invested a billion dollars over five years to refurbish the campus, build new facilities, and generally upgrade the school environment. Both the men's and women's basketball teams aided the emergence of UConn as a nationally competitive university. During the late 1990s, both teams steadily garnered titles, including a national championship. But in 2004, both teams won the national championship in basketball, making UConn the first university to achieve that feat. Afterward, the number of applications for admission continued to explode, the standards for admission were upgraded, and pride among alumni and students soared.

College athletics collects revenue from myriad sources. Big universities sell tickets to football games in stadiums that seat more than 100,000 fans. They add to their income through parking fees, concessions, souvenirs, and the luxury boxes that come with substantial fees for alumni or businesspeople who want to entertain clients.

Television rights can be a bonanza, provided the team is good enough. Notre Dame has been so well known in football for so long that it negotiates its own football package with TV and refuses to join a league and share its profit with other football teams. Most schools benefit from league membership and receive revenue from all televised league games. Play-offs or bowl games are another income source for the schools that earn those trips.

Most colleges charge every student an athletic fee that helps support the sport program. Athletic departments also charge many of their expenses to other university programs, budgets, or cost centers, making it difficult to track the actual cost for university athletics. For example, a new weight training facility may be built as part of a general fitness facility and not charged directly to athletic programs. Football stadiums and basketball arenas at large state universities are often financed with public funds or tax-free bonds available for public purchase.

Corporate sponsors also contribute significantly to big-time college sports with cash or with donations of clothing, equipment, and services. Local physicians often donate medical services in return for the publicity they receive as the team doctor.

Licensing fees on merchandise can also be a major source of income, particularly if athletic teams are successful. College bookstores that are allegedly filled with books for students are now often filled with sweats, caps, shirts, running gear, souvenirs, and any imaginable item with the university name or mascot on it. The books are often an afterthought, located in the back of the store.

High-profile athletic programs receive so much publicity that many people assume they are typical of universities. But a close look at the statistics reveals that a relatively small number of college athletic programs operate as high-profile programs. Recent figures showed that only about 30% of all Division I men's football and 26% of basketball programs reported revenue in excess of expenditures. Less than 20% of most sports, including Division I women's sports, reported that they actually made money (Parker 2004). Of course, when we consider *entire* sport programs, only 19 of the 119 Football Bowl Subdivision (FBS) institutions had positive net revenue, and all the rest showed negative net revenue. In fact, the median net loss for all 119 FBS programs in 2006 was $7.2 million (Inside Higher Ed 2008; NCAA 2010b).

Annual budgets for college athletics vary from a couple hundred thousand dollars to over $100 million. Highly competitive athletic programs are designated as Division I, while less competitive programs fall into Division II or III. Of the 1,051 active NCAA member collegiate institutions in the United States in 2009, only 331 met the qualifications for

ACTIVITY TIME-OUT

Should College Athletes Be Paid to Play?

A growing number of observers of collegiate sports, particularly the revenue-producing sports of basketball and football, believe college athletes should share in the revenues produced by their play. In fact, they believe that the players are being exploited by universities while the school pockets the money. Of course, athletes on full scholarships receive a four-year education that may be worth upward of $50,000 per year at the high end. Athletes are prohibited from part-time work to earn money because all their time is spent training for their sport.

On the other side of the argument is the statement by the National Collegiate Athletic Association (NCAA) on why student-athletes are not paid. Go to www.ncaa.org and look under "Key Issues" to see the NCAA statement (NCAA 2010d).

Consider the two perspectives and develop your position for or against pay for play for student-athletes. You might also consider a position that would pay athletes in only certain sports and not others. Share your conclusions with your classmates.

Division I. Those 331 are further subdivided: 119 schools have FBS football programs; 119 schools have Football Championship Subdivision programs that are smaller based on stadium size and average attendance; and 93 schools without football have Division I programs that concentrate on basketball (NCAA 2009d).

The top 10 athletic programs in terms of spending are at schools familiar to sport fans (see table 4.5). The only way to generate these budgets is to have a top-grade football program that makes more than half of the total revenue by itself. The top five schools in 2007 in terms of profit from their

football teams were, in order, Texas, Notre Dame, Georgia, Florida, and Auburn. Equally enlightening is the percentage of growth of each of these athletic budgets since 1999. The average growth of the top 10 schools is 113%, which is unheard of in business. Equally amazing is the fact that in 2007, the Florida Gator program reported revenue of nearly $59 million, but expenses of just $38 million—a profit margin of 65% (Gaul 2009). However, with the press of more recent difficult economic times since 2007, many schools have been forced to trim their athletic budgets, just as overall college budgets have been stretched significantly.

A lot of money is invested in college sports. Large programs offer athletic scholarships to attract the best athletes in the hopes of producing winning teams that will please the students, fans, alumni, and administration. However, not all college athletic programs fit the high-profile model, and we must clarify the levels of athletic program and commitment before lumping all college sports together.

There are hundreds of colleges where sports are simply a diversion from studies, and they attract athletes who play for the fun and experience. One such school, Swarthmore College, a highly selective liberal arts school in Pennsylvania founded by Quakers and renowned for academics, even made it a point of pride when their football program lost game after game. Their losses symbolized to their students that football was not overemphasized on their campus. Of course, the players on that team did not have much fun or a positive experience. Losing year after year makes a player wonder if the effort is worth it.

We'll look more at collegiate sports in chapter 7. We have mentioned them here since some major athletic programs truly are big business.

TABLE 4.5 Top 10 Athletic Programs

Rank	School	2007 spending	% of growth
1	Ohio State	$109,382,222	50
2	Florida	$107,781,004	101
3	Texas	$105,048,632	87
4	Tennessee	$95,401,868	85
5	Michigan	$89,079,982	105
6	Notre Dame	$83,586,903	120
7	Wisconsin	$82,579,472	94
8	Alabama	$81,946,464	153
9	Auburn	$81,696,758	186
10	Iowa	$80,203,645	144
Total		**$916,706,950**	**113**

Adapted from Washington Post. Available: http://voices.washingtonpost.com/washintonpostinvestigations/2009/01/today_post_investigations_debu_html.

 ACTIVITY TIME-OUT

Are College Coaches' Salaries Out of Control?

You probably read about but gloss over the amount of money being paid to high-profile football or basketball coaches at major Division I Bowl Championship Series (BCS) schools. With an increasing number of coaches hitting the $3 to $4 million a year range with increases built in and bonuses for performance, many supporters of athletic programs, college students, and parents are questioning the idea of paying such exorbitant salaries to coaches at what is touted to be an academic institution. Coaches' salaries not only dwarf those of professors, but even those of the college presidents. What is your opinion and why? Should there be a cap or limit on the salaries of coaches at universities? Should it be left to each school to make its own decision? Justify your answer.

Recreational Sport as a Business

Recreational sport measures its economic effects through the sales of sport equipment like golf clubs, tennis rackets, balls, boats, and fishing rods. Sales also include athletic footwear and clothing that often serve the dual purposes of active wear for sport participation and leisure wear. The Sporting Goods Manufacturers Association estimates annual U.S. expenditures on sport clothing and equipment at upward of $50 billion (Sporting Goods Manufacturers Association 2004).

Another way to measure the expenditures for sport recreation is to tally the amount of land in natural settings for boating and fishing, sport fields, public parks, and private sport facilities throughout the country. As the national economy advances, people have more discretionary income to spend on recreation, and facilities must be constructed or maintained to meet this demand. Every community spends a portion of its annual budget maintaining public recreational areas, often at significant expense to its citizens.

Even public facilities often charge a user fee to help cover the cost of operating. As municipal budgets are squeezed, recreational services are often among the first to be reduced and replaced with fees to support facility maintenance and operation. Golf courses, whether public or private, charge greens fees and cart fees and sell golf merchandise to help support their operations. Many public park systems have managed to remain solvent by treating their operations like businesses, including leasing out facilities to private contractors who guarantee an agreed-upon rate of return.

Tied in with local recreational activities are youth sports and the facilities needed for youth soccer, swimming, tennis, football, basketball, and so on. Virtually every town maintains community facilities to allow its kids to play sports for modest user fees. Arguments occasionally spring up about the priorities for creating playing fields for kids or undisturbed, passive parkland for nature lovers; but essentially the public foots the bill for either choice. As kids join school sports in middle and high school, the sport facilities in some towns appear as miniature versions of professional complexes.

▎ How much money has this hiker contributed to the business of sport?

ACTIVITY TIME-OUT

How Much Do I Spend?

List the approximate costs of all sport equipment, memberships, fees, shoes, and clothing and of all tickets to sport events that you have purchased in the past year. Total the figures and compare your total with those of at least two other students. Judge whether you are about average, high, or low in your economic support of sports. Are you surprised by the result? Why or why not? Multiply your total by 280 million people. This grand total estimates what U.S. residents spend annually on sports, assuming that you are a somewhat average consumer. What proportion of the gross national product is your projected sport expenditure?

Astroturf football fields with lights and commodious grandstands are common in football-crazy towns. Immaculate playing fields grace many suburban communities, and school-based athletic facilities may support community sport programs in the summer.

Let's look at how the individual consumer might contribute to the business of sport. I recall getting my first baseball glove, smacking it to build the pocket, oiling it to make the leather supple, and sleeping with it just to get used to the feel of it. Next came my very own baseball bat, a football, a basketball, a soccer ball, uniforms, sneakers, a bicycle, roller skates, a Wiffle ball and bat, swim gear like flippers and a mask, soccer and baseball shoes with spikes, a tennis racket, and finally golf clubs. Children of families with at least modest incomes go through a similar progression of sport equipment, and over a lifetime a family may expend thousands of dollars on toys for sport and recreation.

Recreational sports generate revenues through the services they provide to people of all ages, incomes, and skill levels. Program administrators and coaches can earn a living through using their services to organize and implement recreational sport programs. Fees from renting sport facilities or equipment are collected at the community level to maintain current facilities and in some cases to build new ones.

Sport clubs and other commercial sport facilities charge fees for use by recreational participants. Golf courses, tennis clubs or centers, bowling alleys, fitness clubs, shooting ranges, swimming pools, equestrian facilities, skating rinks, and country clubs represent millions of dollars spent for recreational sport and are a source of employment and income for the people who work in them.

Chapter Summary

In this chapter we looked at the economics of sport in our society. We learned that owners of professional sport franchises tend to be wealthy people who have been successful in another business and purchase a team to minimize their tax liability, to associate with athletes, and to enjoy the excitement and high visibility of ownership. Some sport teams are owned by groups, conglomerates, or, in the case of the Green Bay Packers, the public. Franchise owners will often tell the public that their team "loses money" in a given year, when in fact just the increase in value of the franchise will compensate the owner handsomely if he ever sells the team.

To ensure the quality of the facility in which their team competes, franchise owners often upgrade or replace the facility to create a state-of-the-art stadium. Public funds are often a major source of stadium financing, though the public may receive little direct benefit from the deal. The value of a franchise increases significantly with a new stadium, making the franchise a solid investment. Some organizations, like the United States Tennis Association, own and operate professional sport events.

We reviewed the tenuous relationship between sport management and labor and concluded that owners seem to wield most of the leverage. In recent years, athletes have acquired some control over their professional sport careers. We also looked at player compensation and compared it with that of others in the workforce in terms of longevity and earnings spread over a lifetime. We looked at the working conditions of professional athletes and the odds of making it to the big leagues. While a career in sport is very attractive to young people, the odds of cashing in on a big sport contract are long indeed.

Collegiate sports at the major institutions classified as Division I BCS operate as another form of professional sport, except that they do not pay athletes for participation except through athletic scholarships. Only about 100 schools out of over 2,500 colleges operate their athletic program as a big business. However, these schools get the media attention and the notoriety.

Finally, we saw that the amount spent on recreational sport has escalated rapidly in recent years as more people participate in athletic activities. Annual purchase of sporting goods has exceeded $50 billion in the past few years. Millions more are spent in providing facilities and services to average citizens who participate in sport for leisure.

Media and Sport

5

Student Outcomes

After reading this chapter, you will know the following:

- The evolution of media in presenting sport
- How the media affect sport and how sport affects the media
- How sport affects ideology
- Careers in sport media

It doesn't matter whether you were actually at the game or not. I bet you still depend on the media to present the game. Even if we've seen a game with our own eyes, we're curious about what others think, how they saw the same plays, and what it all meant. After the game, have you ever turned on the postgame summary to see and hear what actually happened? Watched replays of key plays or events? Listened to coaches' or other experts' opinions about the game? Read about the game the next day in the newspaper or on ESPN? Checked Twitter to see what your friends thought and what they are feeling? Read personal blogs of athletes in the game? There, you see, maybe a sporting event doesn't even exist unless the media reports it.

It is natural to follow a discussion on the business of sport (chapter 4) with an analysis of the role that mass media play in sport. The media have a tremendous influence on sport in terms of creating revenue by supplying free publicity and advertisements. Equally substantial is the influence of sport programming on the media—it is the reason many media outlets exist and is a healthy source of revenue for all media outlets. Clearly, the economic effects of this interrelationship are significant in the overall business of sport.

Sport media fulfill a number of functions for consumers of sport:

• The media help create excitement about sport events leading up to the contest, describe the action during the event, and offer analyses and criticism at the conclusion of the event.

• The media convey to fans the significance of the game, players, history, and individual matchups. We rely on the media to give us the information that makes each of us a quasi-expert on the game, able to discuss it with friends and strangers who also are quasi-experts with their own opinions.

• Personal emotional attachments are developed through media features on athletes, coaches, and teams leading up to seasons or specific contests. We pick our favorite performers based on our own biases and experiences. Athletes with compelling personal stories, such as struggles to overcome injuries, often capture the imagination of fans and develop large fan clubs. Underdogs are always favorites, as are rookies, aging veterans, and athletes who have a knack for delivering peak performances under pressure.

• Preoccupation with sport is a healthy form of recreation and entertainment for many people and helps them escape from everyday life. Rooting for their favorite team or players often provides emotional excitement and drama.

The media that cover sport usually fit into two broad categories: the print media and the electronic media. **Print media** include newspapers, magazines, and books. More pervasive in modern society, **electronic media** are led by television, radio, and the Internet. The Internet does not just mean the web, since that is just one kind of Internet traffic. More important because of rapid growth and expanding options is peer-to-peer communication using the Internet. Access to the Internet is not limited to being at a desktop computer but is also available through cell phones and personal digital assistants. Each of us has a bias toward certain media that we enjoy and feel comfortable with, but all of us are exposed to sport coverage in all types of media as technological advances encourage integration across media types. In the 1920s and 1930s, print media and radio delivered sport news. In the 1950s, television began to dominate sport delivery and maintained that position through the end of the century. At the end of the 20th century, the Internet began to open up new ways to relay sport news, and it now seems clear that the Internet along with the various social media sites will become the primary delivery system for sport around the world. As a harbinger of things to come, the 2010 World Cup was the first international event to use Twitter to keep the world informed of goals scored in real time. As consumers of professional sport, we can be categorized as either *direct* or *indirect* spectators. **Direct spectators** attend live sporting events at a stadium, an arena, or some other venue. **Indirect spectators** listen to or watch sport through radio, television, or the Internet. Although direct spectators continue to increase in record numbers, the increase is relatively modest compared with that of indirect spectators.

Electronic coverage, particularly television, has opened up sport viewing to millions of fans around the world. Major sporting events are now broadcast live across time zones and to diverse cultures that often rearrange their sleep patterns or daily activities to catch a live telecast of events like the Super Bowl or Olympic Games. Consider, for example, the power of the 2010 Super Bowl, which attracted roughly 74,059 direct spectators but more than 106.5 million indirect spectators, making it the most watched television show in U.S. television history—surpassing the former record holder, which was the 1983 finale of *M*A*S*H*. (It should be noted that while the 2010 Super Bowl broke the record for the top network telecast in terms of the total number of viewers, it still fell short of the *M*A*S*H* finale in terms of the percentage of households who watched those two events: 60.2% of U.S. households watched the *M*A*S*H* finale in 1983 compared with only 45% for Super Bowl 2010.) Overall, Super Bowls account for 8 of the top 10 telecasts of all time (see table 5.1; ABC News 2010).

Sport and large corporations are inextricably linked through the media since television stations are owned by corporations. The complex interrelationships that sprung up as a result of this link influence the decisions about which sports and events attract support and how they are presented. In this chapter, we'll look at these interrelationships and how the media affect sport and how sport affects the media. We'll conclude the chapter by examining careers in sport media and some of the challenges that women in particular face in this field.

Evolution of Sport Media

Growing up in the 1950s, I relied on news of professional sport from two major sources: newspapers and radio. A few times a year, I convinced my dad to purchase tickets to a live game and thrilled at seeing my favorite players in person. Nothing compared to seeing a game in person; but most of the year, I was entertained by poring over the daily sport pages for game results, writers' opinions, and team or individual statistics. Games were broadcast regularly on radio, and families or groups of fans gathered around to listen to the play-by-play. I spent many nights alone in my room, listening to radio broadcasts of an endless season of baseball games through the spring, summer, and fall.

Without the radio or newspaper, few of my generation would have become avid sport fans. These media provided our link to each game, stimulated our dreams and conversations, and helped form our attitudes toward sport and life. Professional sport boomed in popularity through exposure and an expansive fan base, and advertisers took advantage of that popularity to sell their wares through newspapers and radio.

Radio transmissions of sport events began in the 1920s, which just happened to be the golden age of sport, and eventually sport helped make the late 1920s and early 1930s the golden age of radio. By the end of the 20th century, radio stations in the United States broadcast over half a million hours of sport events annually. Many stations converted to an all-sport format, and by 1998, there were 160 such stations. In addition to broadcasting live action, sport stations began to provide talk shows that sparked exchanges of opinions, particularly about local teams or well-known athletes (Sage 1998).

The first sport pages appeared sporadically in the second half of the 19th century in the big-city dailies. William Randolph Hearst, publisher of the *New York Journal*, is credited with establishing the

TABLE 5.1 Top 10 Network Telecasts (Nielsen Media Research)

Program and rank	Date	Network	No. of households
1. Super Bowl XLIV, Colts vs. Saints	2/7/2010	CBS	51.7 million
2. *M*A*S*H* finale	2/28/1983	CBS	50.2 million
3. Super Bowl XLII, Giants vs. Patriots	2/03/2008	FOX	48.7 million
4. Super Bowl XLIII, Steelers vs. Cardinals	2/01/2009	NBC	48.1 million
5. Super Bowl XLI, Colts vs. Bears	2/04/2007	CBS	47.5 million
6. Super Bowl XL, Steelers vs. Seahawks	2/05/2006	ABA	45.9 million
7. XVII Winter Olympics	2/23/1994	CBS	45.7 million
8. Super Bowl XXXIX, Patriots vs. Eagles	2/06/2005	Fox	45.1 million
9. Super Bowl XXXVIII, Panthers vs. Patriots	2/01/2004	CBS	45 million
10. Super Bowl XXX, Cowboys vs. Steelers	1/28/1996	NBC	44.2 million

*Note: Other than *M*A*S*H*, the only program to break into the top 10 was the 1994 Winter Olympics. Viewer interest was keen to follow the controversy between figure skaters Nancy Kerrigan and Tonya Harding. Kerrigan eventually won a silver medal while Harding finished in eighth place and was later banned by U.S. Figure Skating.

Adapted from Nielsenwire 2008. http://blog.nielsen.com/nielsenwire/consumer/tops-in-2008-top-tv-programs-single-telecasts/#.

In 1936, most people received their sporting news from newspapers and radio. What do you think this New York City teenager is reading about?

live-action sport. The end of the 1950s was marked by what many consider the "greatest game ever played," the 1958 National Football League (NFL) championship between the Baltimore Colts and the New York Giants. It was the first overtime championship in the NFL, and the dramatic win by the Colts propelled professional football to an unprecedented run of popularity that has endured for almost 50 years.

Television networks latched on to sport to fill up weekends with programming that they did not have to invent or stage. Workers and their families who were looking for entertainment and relaxation sat down in front of the TV. Advertisers lined up to sponsor sport events to reach the attractive audience of males who were often decision makers for their families and businesses. It seemed that television couldn't broadcast enough sport events to satisfy the demand until finally, in 1979, ESPN (Entertainment and Sports Programming Network) was born as the first full-time sport station. All day, every day, sport events are available on ESPN, which has expanded with ESPN2. Newer all-sport networks include Fox Sports and regional networks such as Madison Square Garden and Sun Sports. Over the next several decades, stations devoted to a single sport such as golf or tennis came on the air and promoted their sport to their niche audience.

Mass media disseminate information to large numbers of geographically dispersed people. Through television, people across the country and around the world can view sport contests in real time. They learn about the sport, the specific game, and the players through the live telecast; the announcers who provide play-by-play descriptions; and the color commentators who point out highlights and background information.

Just as television changed the way families in the 1950s interacted with sport, the Internet has given fans yet another way to experience sport. The Internet gives sport fans virtual access to sport in real time and on demand and allows them to create personal, specific methods of interaction. By 2009, three out of four Americans had home access to the Internet, while 63% of those now have broadband Internet connections at home, a 15% increase from the previous year (PewInternet.org 2009).

first modern sport section. As Hearst acquired newspapers in other cities, he spread the sport section to Los Angeles, San Francisco, Boston, and Chicago. Sport pages in newspapers thrived during the 1920s. As professional baseball and football rose in popularity, as horse racing and boxing thrived, and as golf and tennis gained an audience, the public thirst for sport news demanded more and more information. Today, virtually every major newspaper boasts a significant sport section staffed by a small army of researchers, beat writers, columnists, feature editors, photographers, and design editors.

By the end of the 1950s, television had become a fact of life in homes throughout the United States. In 1955, 67% of American homes had a television set. Just five years later that figure jumped to 87%, and by 2000 it had risen to 98% (Neuman 2005). With the single invention of TV, sport in America changed forever. The indirect consumer of sport via television gradually became king of the fans. Millions of fanatics sat glued to their TV sets, watching

The business model for television has been to schedule programs and events at certain times and expect a mass audience to view them. However, the advances in technology in the last 10 years allow people to record any program and replay it at their convenience using TiVo or similar technology. Of course, people can also skip the advertisements if they wish, fracturing the business model that has been in place for over 50 years.

The plethora of cable channels, specialized sport networks, and sport packages has also contributed to a diffusion of the television audience. For those who want to watch sports all day, there are channels and programs available 24/7. Some of us use the Internet to supplement televised sport and newspaper accounts, but for the majority of younger folks, the Internet has become the primary source for news generally and sports specifically. **Social media** such as Facebook, MySpace, Twitter, YouTube, Flickr, and blogs have opened up other possibilities for sport news and discussion. Beyond simply reporting the news, social networking sites have the ability to link sport fans with each other and with professional athletes to share ideas, discussions, opinions, and photos with lightning speed around the world. The Internet can also present a wide variety of programming by video streaming in real time so that people can watch their alma mater play a football game in another time zone or follow their daughter's college volleyball game.

Major League Baseball (MLB) established its Advanced Media (MLBAM) site in 2000, and the result has been an entity that generated $380 million in 2007 and continues to grow at about 30% a year. MLB.com now boasts up to 8 million unique visitors per day during the season and offers team news, merchandise, and ticket sales (Jacobson 2007).

For the National Collegiate Athletic Association (NCAA) men's basketball tournament, CBS Sports and the NCAA offered an "on-demand" website; on the first day of the 2010 tournament, the website had the largest single day of traffic for a live sport event on the Internet with 3.4 million hours of live video and audio streaming consumed by 3 million unique website visitors. One of the "hit features" of the website seemed to be the "boss button." If your boss at work is nearing your desk, you simply hit the button. On the first day, the button was hit an astounding 1.7 million times. Of course, the challenge for the future for networks is to correctly balance coverage between the three types of screens—television, computer, and mobile phones (Osbourne 2010).

If you search for "sports" or "athletes" on YouTube, you'll bring up more than 884,000 photos and 31,700 videos, including sport blooper videos, various commercials and athlete interviews, videos of women in sport, and profiles of athletes at every level of competition.

We visit the websites of favorite teams, check for scores, listen to games in progress, order tickets, browse for stories, read sport blogs, or enter chat rooms to discuss the latest event results. We can track the progress of sport events anywhere in the world. Stories by sports writers are published on the Internet so that we have access to perspectives from sport newsrooms around the country.

Even sport events that are only "pretend" have cornered a significant share of the marketplace on the Internet. According to a survey from the Fantasy Sports Trade Association (FSTA), an industry organization that represents more than 110 companies, an estimated 27 million American adults play fantasy sports, translating into revenue of nearly a billion dollars per year. About 85% of gamers play fantasy football and 40% play fantasy baseball. The typical player is male, between the ages of 18 and 49 with above-average income and education, a marketer's dream. The average cost to the player per year is about $150.00 for a subscription to play. Fantasy sports are not regulated by gambling rules since the outcome of games has been judged to be based more on skill or knowledge of participants than on chance (Ankeny 2009).

The rise of the Internet is likely one of the causes for the declining circulation of major newspapers. Newspaper circulation has been slowly falling since the 1980s, but recently that descent seems to be accelerating. According to the Audit Bureau of Circulations (Bloomberg 2009), average weekday circulation for U.S. newspapers fell 7.1% during the six-month period from October 2008 to March 2009 compared to a 3.6% drop in the previous year. Among the top 20 selling newspapers, only the *Wall Street Journal* posted an increase, of 0.6%, in the Audit Bureau's report, while all other papers posted decreases. Even *USA Today*, the nation's largest newspaper, posted a loss of 7.5%, and the *New York Times* posted a loss of 3.6%. One of the key reasons given in the report for the decline is the increasing consumer interest in getting news from the Internet. In fact, some newspaper executives are buoyed by the expanded audience they are reaching by combining their print and Internet readers together. In spite of that optimistic view, the key problem is that most newspapers do not charge for their online editions, and advertising for online

Handheld personal devices, such as cell phones, have changed the way the sport media disseminates information and the way sports fans receive that information.

editions is difficult to sell. *USA Today* is one of the first newspapers to offer subscriptions to readers for its online edition, which replicates the print version.

As technology improves and access to the Internet increases, websites will fight to win consumers. Media corporations will enter the fray and try to entice consumers by offering exclusive data and entertainment on their sites. Eventually, Internet access may allow us to design our own sport entertainment by giving us access to novel event presentations with unique camera angles, favorite announcers, instant replay on demand, and player or coach interviews. The interactive nature of such experiences will draw us closer to the action and make us more involved than the average spectator.

Interplay of Sport and Media

Professional spectator sports depend on the media for survival. Ticket sales to live events simply cannot generate enough money to make profes-

sional events profitable without media support. The overwhelming bulk of revenue that sport generates from the media comes from television fees. For example, the New York Yankees generated over $100 million in dividends on top of their $84 million rights fees from their regional sport network, YES. Those figures are on top of the league-wide television revenue earned by MLB and shared by all clubs. When you consider the Yankees' annual payroll, which exceeds $200 million, you can see how important television fees are to them (Forbes. com 2010).

Other media forms, including print media, help support professional sport, but not by providing guaranteed income.

Amateur sport has a much more casual link with the media. For the most part, the media restrict their attention to occasionally featuring certain amateur events, particularly events that provide a public service, or to reporting on local amateur sport events to encourage local readership.

Let's look at the ways sport and media affect each other.

How Television Affects Sport

In his seminal book titled *Sports in America* (1987), James Michener estimated that television expended over $200 million on sport. That amount seemed unbelievable then, but the current annual rights fees swamp that figure. The NFL negotiated agreements with ESPN, NBC, CBS, Fox, DIRECTV, and its own NFL Network for the 2010 seasons that in total are worth $3.7 billion to the league. That total by far dwarfs the contracts of all other major American sports, none of which exceed $1 billion for a year. Major League Baseball's current contract is with Fox, TBS, and ESPN, dividing up the season and play-offs based on the rights fees they are willing to pay. Virtually every major sport relies on television contracts for the majority of its income, far surpassing ticket sales revenue from people who attend their contests.

Television viewing can expand dramatically through better marketing, presentation of the event, outreach to new audiences, expansion to include more female fans, and general worldwide expansion as American sports gain popularity in other parts of the world and internationally popular sports are broadcast in North America. Technology has helped expose American sports in other countries and has fueled the expansion of the uniquely American sports of baseball, basketball, and football. The major professional leagues have been able to expand to Europe and other countries as the popularity of the sports has grown.

The Olympic Games have grown into a huge moneymaker for the International Olympic Committee (IOC) through expanding television coverage around the world. In 1980, the broadcast rights for the Summer Olympic Games in Moscow cost $87 million, which grew to $793 million for the Athens Games in 2004. NBC was awarded the rights for the 2010 Winter Games in Vancouver and the Summer Games in London for a total fee of $2.2 billion. This represented a 33% increase in fees from the 2006-2008 Games. These are broadcast rights fees just for the United States; the IOC also collects fees from every other major country televising the Olympic Games (*USA Today* 2003).

Perhaps the most important factor affecting income for professional sport is the potential marketplace that televised sport provides. There is a limit to the number of spectators who can attend any given event, and there is a limit to the amount ticket prices can increase without cutting into demand. Let's review what television means to sport:

- Television networks pay significant broadcast rights fees to professional sport leagues, organizations, and franchises.
- Advertisers pay for rights to advertise their products to viewers during sport events.
- Sport owners or leagues can afford to pay athletes huge salaries due to the guaranteed income from television.
- Ticket sales and other game-day revenues pale in comparison with the income derived from television rights.
- Money is the most significant link between the media and professional sport. As rights fees increase, professional sports rely more heavily on television for their revenue stream. Television's influence over sport grows, and TV increasingly affects how sport events are presented to viewers.

How Media Affect Sport

Few people would dispute that the media can positively affect sport (aside from guaranteeing income through television rights). The media can

- affect the popularity of sport,
- provide free publicity for local teams, and
- present player personalities and build fan allegiance to teams and individual players.

The popularity of collegiate and professional sport exploded as more and more American homes gained access to television. People who had little or no interest in sport couldn't help but catch bits of games as they surfed the channels. They didn't even have to leave their chairs to see the games. Sport announcers hyped each contest to draw viewers in, and once they caught the viewers' attention, they enthusiastically and concisely described the game, making it exciting to watch.

Expert commentators work hard to educate viewers who know little about the sport without insulting die-hard fans. For people who enjoy history, statistics, individual matchups, and record-setting performances, TV presentations offer all that and more. You don't need to lift a finger to find out more about a particular event than you ever wanted to know. You can just sit back, relax, and let the game come to you. With options such as DVR now available for viewing games on your own schedule, you can even decide when you want to spend time watching sport. The media expanded the popularity of sport by making sport spectatorship easily accessible, fun, and convenient for all.

ESPN's Game Day provides publicity to the school where each broadcast is held, such as this game at the University of Texas. This is an example of how the media can affect sport.

Free publicity for the local professional team is a major contribution from all media outlets, both print and electronic. Imagine what it would cost team owners to purchase all the publicity they receive from the local newspapers, news broadcasts, magazines, and radio. The larger the market, the more media outlets there are. Local businesses also help publicize sport by advertising their support of the local teams in hopes of attracting customers who are fans.

Players depend on the media for publicity. Star players are given a public face in their community, receiving recognition for their sport performances and perhaps also kudos for visiting local schools or supporting local charities. Fans develop heroes, seek their autographs or pictures, follow their careers, join their fan clubs, and wear their jersey numbers. Kids imitate their style of play. The star player's lifestyle is often scrutinized, and athletes dedicated to their family are praised and held up as role models. Of course, for those who appear in the news for less attractive reasons, the media can also be harsh critics. Without the media's presentation of athletes, though, fans would have little opportunity to relate to them; uniforms tend to make one player look like all the rest.

In newspapers across the country, local headlines feature the fortunes of the local team on the front page. Local radio talk shows invite callers to comment on the home team. Interviews with coaches and top athletes on television help local fans understand a team's attitudes toward a game before, during, and after play. The local media, unabashedly rooting for the home team, nourish hometown pride and spirit.

But the media can negatively affect sport, too, by changing the way sports are presented to the audience. Traditionalists generally oppose any change in sport, claiming that changes ruin the integrity of the game. Depending on your point of view, you may see these changes in sport as negative developments or simply signs of progress. Let's look at the way sport has changed over the last 25 years.

Rule Changes

Sport events that are unpredictable in length wreak havoc with station schedules. Television has pressured sports to revise their format to ensure that contests finish in a predictable amount of time. In response, collegiate football instituted overtime formats in which teams try to score from the opposition's 25-yard line and the other team is allotted an opportunity to match that score. The excitement generated by this approach has been a pleasant by-product of the attempt to regulate game times.

The NFL has adopted instant replay to ensure that officials' calls are correct, and although each coach is limited to two challenges, the time spent reviewing the plays for the challenges has lengthened NFL games. College football has also begun to use instant replay, although on a limited basis. Halftimes have been modified to keep the viewer glued to the game by including game summaries, features, and analyses rather than the traditional marching bands that lose much of their entertainment value on television.

Tennis instituted the tiebreak in which the first player to win 7 points and be ahead by 2 points wins the set. This change ensured that a set would end after the equivalent of 13 games rather than last the 20 to 22 games a set could expand to under the old rules. The tiebreak at least contributes to the predictability of match lengths, which helps television producers plan their programming accordingly. Of course, the excitement generated by the critical tiebreak turned out to be a positive thing for the sport from the spectator's point of view.

Golf has moved almost exclusively to medal play, which means that the golfer with the lowest score wins, rather than match play with each hole counting for 1 point for the winner of that hole. The difference between the two systems is that the outcome is in doubt longer with medal play and may not be decided until the final hole.

The 3-point shot in basketball was adopted to put more emphasis on long-range shooting and reduce the dependence on large bodies pounding the ball inside to score. Additionally, the size of the lane or key under the basket was expanded to help push big players out from the basket, which opens up the game scoring to more athletic moves. A shot clock was also instituted to ensure that a team had to shoot the ball within the prescribed amount of time and to prevent the time-honored tactic of one team freezing the ball when ahead near the end of a game. These changes help make a basketball game more exciting and action packed for audiences who love watching great players and dramatic action.

Major League Baseball revised the strike zone and instituted the designated hitter for the American League in order to add more offense to the game. While purists contend they enjoy low-scoring

NASCAR is implementing many new rule changes in an effort to combat falling TV ratings. What additional changes could NASCAR face in an effort to bolster ratings?

pitcher duels, the average television fan is more interested in hitting and a barrage of home runs.

Perhaps the most annoying changes for television viewers are the numerous time-outs that allow for commercial breaks. Rallies are interrupted, momentum is lost, and needed rest is given because the station is obliged to fulfill its promise to commercial sponsors. Watching football sometimes seems like watching a series of time-outs with some action squeezed in between. However, when you calculate the financial benefit of commercial time-outs, you can see why they have become standard practice. During the 2009 Super Bowl, a 30-second time-out cost commercial sponsors an all-time high of $3 million, although by 2010, prices had dropped a bit for the first time in history (CBS News 2010). Of course, normal NFL games do not produce that kind of income, but they still generate critical revenue.

Attendance Declines Due to Televised Sport

In some markets, the presentation of games on television has affected attendance in the stadium. As a result, many professional football teams have adopted a blackout rule, meaning that the game cannot be broadcast within a range of roughly 150 miles (241 kilometers) of the stadium unless all tickets are sold. The owners contend that without this rule, many fans would simply stay home to watch games on television rather than buy a ticket. Of course, when the game is blacked out, free access is denied to the millions of fans who cannot afford to buy tickets or who prefer not to deal with the hassles of parking, uncertain weather, traffic, and so on. Die-hard fans get around blackouts by purchasing games on a pay-per-view basis, which still creates revenue for the media and teams, or by signing up for satellite programs that provide access to all NFL games on a given day.

Professional sports are so accessible on television that fans become spoiled watching superior athletes and often lose interest in the athletes on local minor league, college, or high school teams. A case in point is the demise of Minor League Baseball. In 1939, attendance at Minor League Baseball games exceeded that of MLB games, with 15 million for the minors and 11 million for the majors. Lots of medium-sized cities across the country sponsored local teams, and local fans supported them. Then came television, and it became easy to watch the top players in the country. Attendance dropped quickly for Minor League franchises, and the number of Minor League Baseball teams fell from nearly 500 around 1950 to about 150 teams 25 years later.

Eventually, the role of player development traditionally assigned to Minor League Baseball teams was filled by collegiate teams, who stepped up as the training ground for aspiring players (Leonard 1980).

Of course, Minor League Baseball was not the only victim of televised sport. Local college and high school sports also suffer when pitted against a professional team on television. The relatively few colleges with big-time football teams that are broadcast on TV often draw fans away from the hundreds of other colleges that offer smaller football programs. High school games have avoided some of the conflict by scheduling football games on weeknights and Friday nights, times that do not conflict with professional sport and maximize the opportunity for fans to attend games in person.

Conflicts With Scheduling

The interests of television rather than the interests of players or spectators often determine the scheduling of games. Let's look at a couple of examples.

• World Series games are typically scheduled on October nights so as to attract the maximum television audience on both coasts. Selling out the ballpark for a World Series game is not a problem since only about 45,000 fans are needed; the largest fan base and income potential is the television audience. Night baseball is not popular with most players, but they are accustomed to such games throughout the regular season. Late starting times on the East Coast mean that many potential fans, particularly children, are unable to watch because they have to go to bed. The late start allows people on the West Coast to get home from work or school to watch the game, which balances the loss of fans on the East Coast.

• Monday Night Football suffers from the same dilemma—the second half starts after bedtime for many East Coast fans, but starting late does allow many fans on the West Coast to watch the game.

• The NCAA basketball championships start after 9 p.m. on the East Coast, thus shutting out young people and many adults as well.

• The U.S. Open schedules tennis matches through negotiations between four main parties: tournament officials, representatives of the men's and women's tours, and television. Guess who has the most leverage in deciding which match to feature at what time? Players' preferences are largely ignored, and tournament officials know that the money from the TV rights pays their bills. A match featuring a well-known American player is likely to be set in a prime-time spot instead of a matchup of two lesser-known international players—that's just the logical schedule for television programming.

• Olympic telecasts are a critical source of income for the IOC, and thus events are broadcast in order to attract maximum audiences in various countries. Featured events such as gymnastics, swimming, and track and field, and recently women's team sports such as soccer and basketball get the prime spots in the United States. In recent years, when the Olympic Games are broadcast from other parts of the world, U.S. broadcasts are typically tape-delay broadcast in prime U.S. time. Eager fans who use the Internet or other social media sites to follow the progress of certain events or athletes already know the results before television can catch up.

Gambling

Gambling has always been part of the sport world. The posting of odds on each game in newspapers and on television increases the interest in winners and losers, point spreads, and possible upsets. There is no way to tell how much local betting occurs between neighbors and friends, at bars, or in office pools. At play-off time, it's rare for an office not to have at least one betting pool.

More serious betting is aided by the media reports on odds set in Las Vegas by bookmakers, picks by experts on television shows, injury and status reports of players in daily papers, and articles online predicting outcomes. Those who worry about the unhealthy influence of gambling in society wish the media did less to accommodate those who gamble (Brown 2000; Jenkins 2000). We'll consider sport gambling in chapter 18.

Free Publicity for Some Universities

Big-time college football on television and the endless publicity the media give the top schools with rankings, bowl speculation, and awards for best performances raise the public's awareness of a relatively few colleges based on their football success. Free publicity for those colleges typically means more student applications the next year, which allows them to be more selective in their admissions. Although football success is unrelated to academic excellence and a host of other factors that are important when choosing a college, there is no question that the publicity helps universities with top-ranked football teams. During a televised game, the two competing schools get a spot on television to trumpet their virtues. They also get appearance money for being on TV, which is often split with the other teams in their conference. Games are scheduled according to TV commitments and are often changed to accommodate TV networks.

As the competition for television dollars mounts for big-time college football, we have witnessed a continual realignment of leagues in an effort to generate the maximum profit from television rights for each league school. No longer are traditional rivalries or geography the key to league alignment; instead it's a question of the size of the television market a school brings to a league. The realignment of the Big Ten, Pacific Ten, and Big Twelve that occurred during 2010 is an example of the push by collegiate leagues to seek to maximize their television contracted earnings.

How Sport Affects the Media

The previous section documented how the media have been a primary support for the rapid expansion of big-time college and professional sport. However, this has not been a one-way street. Sport has provided the media with enormous, predictable

ACTIVITY TIME-OUT

Advertising to the Target Audience

If you were in charge of soliciting advertising for the sport section of a metropolitan newspaper, what products would you seek for advertising? Remember, the typical reader is a male between the ages of 25 and 50 who has an above-average income. List at least 10 products you believe would interest this demographic. Next, visit the online edition of the newspaper and also the online edition of *USA Today*. Review the advertising in the sport sections of both newspapers. Did the ads match the categories you suggested? Did any surprise you?

audiences that are attractive to advertisers both in the United States and around the world. The revenue from sport coverage has been a major source of income for various media, but particularly for newspapers, television, and specialty magazines. Let's consider each in turn.

Newspapers have thrived on comprehensive sport sections for more than a century. For many readers, reading the sport pages is the first priority and may be the primary reason for purchasing the paper. Even though they watch the sport contests in person or on television, most fans love to read the accounts in the next day's paper, evaluate the opinions of the sports writers and compare them to their own, and search for inside information they might not otherwise have access to.

Most major newspapers in North America devote more space to sport than any other topic, including business, politics, and world news. They have found that formula to be popular with readers and therefore attractive to advertisers. The primary audience for the sport pages has typically been males between the ages of 25 and 50 who have an above-average income (Coakley 2004). Advertisers for products targeted to that demographic have seized the opportunity to reach their potential customers through appearing in sport sections.

Newspapers also publicize local professional teams. Although newspapers might not derive advertising income directly from the publicity they offer, the number of readers they attract is heavily influenced by the public's interest in the local team. It is one way to guarantee a core group of faithful readers.

Printing stories on social concerns related to sport helps attract readers, stimulating their thinking and maintaining interest in lively debates. Sport pages that simply print event results and basic accounts of contests may not hold readers' interests, particularly as more people turn to the Internet or television to learn results. Social issues that are debated in the newspapers include

- racism among coaches, players, or organizations;
- economics of sport, including owner profits, union demands, club-versus-club payrolls, extravagant player compensation, and public financing of facilities;
- moral issues such as gambling on sport events, fan behavior at events, beer and cigarette sponsorship, and athletes as role models;

- gender bias, equal pay for women, appropriate attire for women, and attitudes of female athletes toward competition;
- changes in technology, such as improved surfaces, equipment, and apparel, and their effect on the integrity of the sport;
- training regimens and equipment and the effect of training on injury prevention; and
- use of ergogenic aids, drugs, drug testing, and penalties for those who fail drug tests.

While television thrives on live game-day action, newspapers are more suited to in-depth analysis of social topics that require significant research, clear presentation, and a slant that will challenge the reader to think.

Magazines that cover sport have responded to growing interest in specific sports. Most general news magazines rarely cover sport unless a major human interest story is involved. Publishers of magazines have found that appealing to fans of a specific sport guarantees a more stable audience of subscribers who are likely to support that magazine for a length of time. A quick check of www.magsonthenet.com reveals over 200 specific-sport magazines offered for subscription. General sport magazines such as *Sports Illustrated*, *SportingNews*, or *ESPN The Magazine* seek to attract the committed fan. These magazines rely on major sports for their bread and butter but include some stories on less popular sports for interest and to broaden the exposure of their readers. Of course, particular sports such as golf and tennis have their own specific readership that is loyal to *Golf Digest* or *TENNIS* magazine. The growing general interest in overall health and fitness has also spurred the growth of *Men's Health* and of *SELF*, which is targeted to females.

Because magazines are published monthly or several times a year, they lend themselves to stories that take time to develop. Stories that examine trends in sport or the social issues listed previously are prime fodder for monthlies. The in-depth analysis that is typical of a sport monthly magazine cannot be easily adapted to the Internet, just because of the background research that must occur before the writer weaves her story. On the other hand, because of their infrequent publication and lead time of several months, magazines are poor sources of information for up-to-the-minute news. By the time the reader receives the magazine in the mail, the news it contains may be out of date. Players have been traded, franchises remade, predic-

POP CULTURE

Sports Illustrated

First published in 1954, *Sports Illustrated* has been one of the most treasured possessions of American male sport fans. Owned by Time Warmer, with a current circulation of over 3 million subscribers, *SI* is published weekly. Henry Luce, *TIME* visionary leader, wanted a general sport magazine that would attract a national following. Happily, his entry into the market coincided with a boom in sport spectatorship in the United States primarily due to good economic times and the exploding popularity of sport on television.

In the early years, the magazine tended to be directed at sporting activities such as yachting, polo, and safari, but eventually the focus became clear. To attract large numbers of readers, the Olympic Games and the major American sports of football, baseball, and basketball had to be the primary focus. In addition to this change came the brilliant idea of creating an annual Swimsuit Edition featuring comely half-dressed females, which became and continues to be the single most popular issue each year. Liberal early use of color photography set *SI* apart from competitors, and by the mid-1980s, *SI* became the first American full-color newsweekly.

As the magazine is now more than 50 years old, the times have changed around it. Competitors such as *ESPN The Magazine* have challenged *SI* to get with the times. As the mission to sell copies grew, it seemed to some observers that the style and substance of *SI* had changed, not for the better. Sport journalism is so ubiquitous today that its presence on the Internet and television is nearly unavoidable. No need to wait for a weekly magazine now. But the thoughtful, in-depth pieces that so characterized *SI* through the years have fallen prey to the "fast food" era of superficial sports news coverage lacking in research, depth, or controversy. Thorough research based on investigative reporting and developing issues in sport still ought to be the *SI* edge. What about women's sports, drugs, violence, gambling, gene doping, and a host of other contemporary topics? It will be interesting to watch in coming years to see if the legacy *SI* has built will sustain it for the next generation.

Information from Levin 2007 and Fleder 2005.

---

tions proved false, and players released or injured. Keeping the readers happy under these conditions requires an astute editorial staff.

Of course, no media form has been affected by sport more than television. From its beginnings in the 1950s, television has included sport coverage as a critical part of programming. Although the camera angles were crude and replay did not exist, and many sports had not yet adjusted to television, the base was set for a happy and profitable relationship.

Television executives figured out that fans would watch TV on weekends when looking for some relaxation and diversion. Hours of ready-made weekend programming could be had by securing the rights to sport events paid for by corporate sponsors. Television executives learned that sport events minimized production costs, came with predictable ratings, and could be used to advertise the next event to the target audience. Soon televised sport included Monday Night Football; college football on Saturdays; and special events like the Olympics,

tennis tournaments, golf tournaments, and NCAA basketball championships.

In the United States, sport has typically dominated all other types of programming, especially on weekends, since the invention of television. In 2008, 9 out of 10 of the largest TV audiences were for sporting events, with only the Academy Awards show sneaking into the top 10 at number 7 (see table 5.2 on page 84). As is typical, professional football took the top sport spots, and the Olympic Games scored well in a year of the Summer Games.

It may seem surprising, but the largest television audience in the world has been for World Cup soccer. When you consider that soccer is easily the most popular sport worldwide, however, that statistic begins to make sense. Nations of every continent and fans of every economic level flock to live soccer games and follow them on television.

In the United States, the popularity of soccer was fueled by the rapid growth of youth, high school, and college soccer in response to Title IX requiring

TABLE 5.2 Top 10 U.S. Television Programs in 2008—Single Telecast

Telecast	Network	% of homes in U.S.
1. Fox Super Bowl XLII	Fox	43.1
2. Fox Super Bowl Postgame	Fox	30.1
3. NFC Championship	Fox	29.0
4. Summer Olympics Tuesday, August 12	NBC	20.0
5. Fox NFC Play-Off PST Sunday	Fox	18.8
6. Summer Olympics Opening Ceremony	NBC	18.8
7. Academy Awards	ABC	18.7
8. Summer Olympics Sunday, August 10	NBC	18.1
9. AFC Divisional Play-Off	CBS	17.9
10. Summer Olympics Thursday August 14	NBC	17.9

Adapted from Nielsenwire 2008. http://blog.nielsen.com/nielsenwire/consumer/tops-in-2008-top-tv-programs-single-telecasts/#.

equal sport opportunities for males and females. Girls and young women flocked to the sport, and the U.S. women's team first captured the imagination of the whole country by winning the gold medal in the 1996 Olympics and following that up with a 1999 victory in the World Cup. Superstars on the team included Mia Hamm, Brandi Chastain, and Kristine Lilly among others, and they were outstanding role models for aspiring female athletes.

It has taken longer for men's soccer to flourish in the United States, but the U.S. national team has begun to become a factor in world competition. The inspiring play of the U.S. men's team in the 2010 World Cup captured the attention of American sport fans for the first time. Having earned first place in their group, the U.S. team moved through to round 16 with high hopes but lost in that round to Ghana. They had not won a game in a World Cup for the previous eight years, and their top group finish was their first since the original World Cup in 1930! What's more, Landon Donovan, Clint Dempsey, and goaltender Tim Howard emerged as legitimate stars on the world soccer stage.

As a result of the strong U.S. showing in the World Cup, the entire tournament attracted an estimated 111.6 million U.S. viewers, which was a 22% increase over the previous finals for the 2006 World Cup (see table 5.3). Interestingly, 57% of the audience was male compared to 43% female, and almost half (49%) of viewers were between the ages of 18 and 49 (Nielsen Media Research 2010). In the United States, 19.4 million people watched the U.S.A.'s loss to Ghana, and the television audience for the Cup finals pitting Spain against the Netherlands attracted 25 million viewers. Worldwide, the global audience for the finals between eventual winner Spain and runner-up The Netherlands was

reported at 700 million, outpacing that for the 2006 final game. By way of comparison, the event most watched in recent years was the opening ceremony for the 2008 Beijing Olympic Games, which drew 600 million worldwide viewers (*New York Post* 2010; Sandomir 2010)

As we've seen, the more people watch sports, the more the media cover sports. This includes women's sports as well, and the media has slowly begun to reach out to female viewers. For decades, sports were a man's world, and television presentations showed a strong bias toward the male viewer. Once the networks realized more than half the population was female and many females were embracing sports, sports that were most popular with women, such as figure skating, gymnastics, tennis, and women's soccer, began to claim more programming hours. Female announcers gradually were included in the broadcast teams, and efforts were made to present sport in a style that was friendlier to female viewers. Gratuitous shots of female cheerleaders, sexist beer commercials, and commercials for pickup trucks were toned down, although not eliminated. Women's golf and tennis were featured at prime-time hours to attract larger audiences.

As more women's sports appeared on television, young girls in youth sport began to identify with their athletic heroes and copy their behavior. Women's soccer helped grow women's collegiate soccer and youth soccer. The emergence of Venus and Serena Williams in tennis opened up the sport to a new generation of black females who might never have considered giving tennis a try. Inner-city high schools with predominantly African American populations suddenly had 50 girls trying out for the tennis team. Michelle Wie, who at 14 years of age

TABLE 5.3 Top 10 Worldwide Sporting Events of 2006

Rank	Event	Average audience (millions)	Total audience (millions)
1	FIFA World Cup Final (France-Italy)	260	603
2	Super Bowl (Seahawks-Steelers)	98	151
3	Turin Games Opening Ceremony	87	249
4	UEFA Champions League Final (Barcelona-Arsenal)	86	209
5	Brazilian Grand Prix	83	154
6	Daytona 500	20	47
7	World Series Game Five (Tigers-Cardinals)	19	55
8	Wimbledon Men's Final (Federer-Nadal)	17	69
9	The Masters (Final Round)	17	59
10	NBA Finals Game Six (Heat-Mavericks)	17	48

Adapted, by permission, from SportsBusiness Daily 2007.

was competing in selected professional golf events for men, suddenly became a constant story on sport pages. Not only was her success among women in professional golf amazing; her challenge to qualify for male events also made her story riveting. It will be interesting to see if her success increases the popularity of golf among young girls.

Ideology of Sport Through the Media

The media emphasize certain sport-related behaviors that affect the next generation of athletes and spectators. The presentation of sport in the media tends to emphasize behaviors that include certain values, attitudes, and beliefs that mirror the history of sport and maintain the status quo. Generally, sport media are owned and operated by large conglomerates such as the following (Sage 1998):

- Disney (e.g., ABC, ESPN)
- General Electric (e.g., NBC, MSNBC, CNBC, Telemundo)
- Time Warner (e.g., *Sports Illustrated*, CNN, HBO, TNT)
- News Corporation (e.g., Fox, Fox Sports, Madison Square Garden, Sunshine Network)
- Viacom (e.g., CBS, MTV, BET, Comedy Central)
- Bertelsmann (various European television networks)

These conglomerates are dedicated to maintaining their powerful position and are unwilling to venture into controversial positions. Some

conglomerates have bought and many have sold professional sport franchises. There was a time in the 1990s when it made sense for companies that owned television networks to buy sport franchises to ensure available programming and the synergy between the two ventures. However, in more recent years that trend has been reversed, with most corporations selling off franchise ownership to individuals.

In order to appeal to mass audiences, the sport media tend to reflect the opinions of the majority of Americans to curry their support. Social scientists would classify the media approach to sport as *functionalism* (as described in chapter 2). The media tend to reinforce commonly held values. Controversy, cutting-edge opinions, and creating discussion are typically not part of mainstream media productions.

A few significant ideologies that pervade North American sport are worth pointing out. For example, winning is worshipped in the sport media, and all the excitement they generate is toward that objective. Athletes who advance to the finals of a championship event only to lose are regarded as losers. Consider that in the U.S. Open tennis championships, 128 men and 128 women start out contending for first place. Of these players, 127 men and 127 women are destined to be losers, according to the media, and all attention is focused on the one winner.

Professional football teams or coaches who reach the Super Bowl, even several times, are branded as losers until they win the big game. The effect on youth sport, future athletes, and armchair quarterbacks is predictable; kids may give up and drop out of a sport when they realize they are not going to win the big game.

ACTIVITY TIME-OUT

Winners or Chokers?

The NFL Buffalo Bills football team had an amazing run as they played in four successive Super Bowls from 1991 to 1994, but they failed to win any of these games. Despite the able leadership of coach Marv Levy and quarterback Jim Kelly, the Bills just couldn't seem to perform at the championship level.

It became a running joke in the media and with fans that the Bills were chokers and simply couldn't win big games. During that same time, most of the other teams in the league were wallowing in mediocrity, yet they earned no such label. Levy, however, was inducted into the Pro Football Hall of Fame in 2001 based on his overall successful career. Simply because they reached the Super Bowl, some people think that the Buffalo Bills team should have been revered rather than shunned as also-rans. What do you think?

Athletes who are cooperative team players receive reinforcement from the media and are praised as leaders and role models. Individual athletes who deliver clutch performances are idolized and revered for their fortitude and success under pressure. On the other side, the press criticizes athletes who question coaching decisions, celebrate individual achievements over team performance, or do not cooperate with the press.

The history, traditions, and past heroes of the game are revered by the media. Coaches emphasize hard work and discipline, and the media reinforce those values. Players who persevere and play even while injured are labeled courageous and team players. For example, Terrence Owens was praised for his rapid comeback from serious injury to play effectively in the 2005 Super Bowl for the Philadelphia Eagles. However, a few months later he was crucified in the press and by fans for criticizing teammate Donovan McNabb and trying to renegotiate his contract. Athletes who appear cocky, self-absorbed, or selfish get less favorable attention. Owens' image as a spoiled player was so disruptive to the team that he was suspended for the second half of the 2005 season despite his courageous performance the previous year. There are no long-term guarantees as to how a player will be portrayed by the media. After those years, Owens played three years for the Dallas Cowboys and one year for the Buffalo Bills—durations that were marked by similar incidents. Although Owens was selected to the Pro Bowl six times and has been a clearly successful player, his personal conduct and judgment have colored his success along the way.

Some cultural values of media executives, team owners, and league administrators clash with those of athletes. Issues of race, gender, and sexual preferences are often at the root of different attitudes toward sport and life; but the media realize that their audience and benefactors have fairly mainstream values, so they tend to present and reinforce those same values. Let's look at some of the general themes about sport delivered by the media.

Participation in Sport and Physical Activity

The importance of physical activity for everyone is well documented. With the alarming increases in obesity recently reported in the media for both youth and adults, you might guess that the media would take a strong stance regarding sport participation as an antidote for excess body weight.

Research to date has not supported the conclusion that watching sport on television affects sport participation one way or the other. Evidence is mixed: On the one hand, many people who are already active report that their interest is heightened by watching great athletes perform, and many young people want to emulate their sport heroes on the playground or ball field. On the other hand, most adults who watch sport on television do not exercise regularly and have no plans to do so (Coakley 2004; Sage 1998). In fact, the amount of time spent in front of the television is often cited as a primary reason for inactivity.

Traditional Values

Certain traditional values have become part of our culture. Americans generally believe in the ideal of individualism, that one person can make a difference. Even team achievements are traced back to the success or failure of key players. We also expect players to work cooperatively, and we extol the virtues of team chemistry and working cohesively as a unit. Players who put their own welfare first quickly fall out of favor with owners, coaches, and fans. At times, individual achievement and teamwork clash, creating conflict for players.

Harry Edwards, an influential critic of sport and a prominent sport sociologist in the 1970s, reviewed various publications in the media and organized the dominant social values attributed to sport. His work listed the following key values:

- Character building
- Religiosity
- Nationalism
- Discipline
- Mental fitness
- Competition
- Physical fitness

The place of each of these values in North American sport has been discussed since the 1970s, and generally these values have stood the test of time. Other behaviors that are more specific have been added over the years by other researchers, but Edwards' classic list covers the broad categories (Edwards 1973).

Winners and Losers

American society looks for winners, builds them up, showers them with praise for at least a day, and then looks to the next year. Fame is fickle. The message is clear—if you haven't won the big one, you don't count for much in sport. Historically, some of our greatest athletes and coaches have failed to win the ultimate contest and so are considered failures. Other athletes who are less talented and productive over their careers have been considered successful because they won a big game. The win may have been due to luck, teammates, or inferior opponents, but they won. Super Bowl heroes never heard from before or after their one shining moment go down as winners in history.

For some fans, the preoccupation with winners grows tiresome. Veteran fans prefer to watch a well-played or exciting contest. One-sided games, predictable outcomes, defensive struggles, and sloppy play are all reasons for discontent. Television

When Landon Donovan scored a game-winning goal against Algeria in a 2010 World Cup match, he was instantly heralded as a soccer idol in the U.S. media.

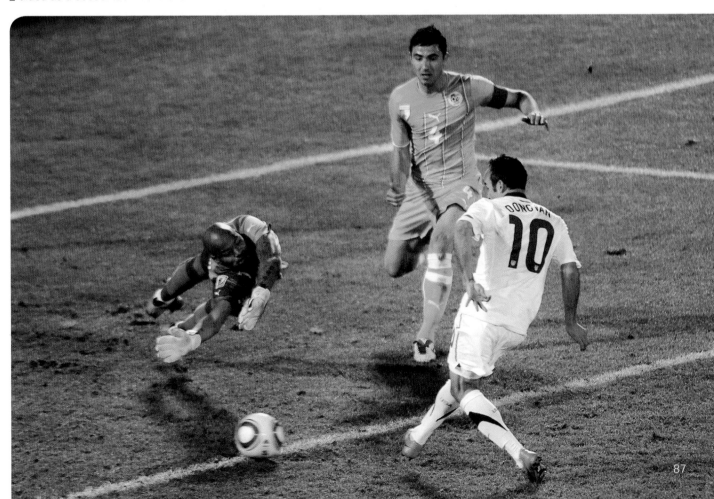

producers look for ways to minimize the chances for such disappointment by emphasizing possible upsets, possible rallies by the losing player or team, and possible contests that will end in tiebreakers.

Yet the beat goes on. Even athletes who deliver an illegal hit are lionized for their competitive spirit as long as they are not caught or the penalty is a minor inconvenience to their team. Other athletes who reenter a game after a painful injury, concussion, or exhaustion are lauded for their courage. Young people watching professional sport may start to believe that winning a contest is more critical than good health or common sense.

Gender

Predominantly hegemonic masculinity has been portrayed by the media in sport. Power, dominance, and violence are male characteristics that have been reinforced and admired. This is not surprising considering that male athletics predated the rise of female athletics; but as women's sport gained a foothold in the 1970s and has continued to grow since then, you might have expected a change in the traditional sport media worship of everything male.

Outside of the Olympic Games, women's sports have taken a backseat to media coverage of men's sports. While socially acceptable women's sports like gymnastics, figure skating, tennis, and golf have continued to get media attention, recent attention to women's soccer and basketball has begun to tip the balance slightly toward more equal media attention to female and male athletes. Yet the statistics on the imbalance that still exists between coverage of men and women in sport are revealing.

Since 2000, television coverage of women's sport overall has declined. The percentage of stories and airtime devoted to women's sport is nearly as low as it was in 1990, when women's sport received approximately 5% of the coverage. In 1999, the coverage reached 8.7%, but in 2004, the percentage had declined to 6.3% (Duncan and Messner 2005). A 20-year study released in 2010 by University of Southern California and Purdue sociologists Michael Messner and Cheryl Cooky reported that men received 96% of all sport news coverage in 2009. Women's sport actually accounted for less than 2% of network news and ESPN SportsCenter. These figures seem most surprising when you realize that women's sport participation overall has actually exploded during the past 20 years (Jenkins 2010).

To be fair, ESPN does fill airtime on its ancillary networks such as ESPNU with plenty of live coverage of women's sport—more than 1,300 hours

What will it take to make women's football a socially acceptable, and financially strong, sport?

this past year. In fact, it showed all 48 games of the women's collegiate basketball tournament. The 12 women's tournament games aired on ESPN's main outlet averaged 1.6 million viewers in 2010, and the title game between UConn and Stanford drew an average of 3.5 million viewers, up 32% from the previous year (Jenkins 2010).

Recent attention to collegiate women's basketball and televised games throughout the NCAA women's Division I tournament demonstrate at least a small shift in emphasis. The scheduling and availability of games for women have essentially mirrored the attention given the men, although reading the media accounts in most daily newspapers, you might believe the women's games held little interest for readers. In spite of the apparent equality with men in television time, women's games still command significantly little attention in many newspapers.

Professional women's tennis has been well established for some years, and the televising of the women's matches versus men's matches at Grand Slam events is nearly identical. Other sports can claim no such parity. Women's soccer, professional basketball, golf, and softball are televised only sporadically in comparison to men's. Similarly, women in the sport media are vastly underrepresented as discussed in the section on careers that follows.

Race and Ethnicity

Viewers' ideas about race and ethnicity can be influenced depending on what the viewers see and hear. Most sport journalists are careful to avoid language that could be interpreted as racist, and the few incidents that have occurred have been dealt with quickly. Yet some feel that racism in the media exists in less overt ways. For example, they feel that stories about black athletes focus too often on their rise from poverty to wealth.

Historically, many black athletes have felt belittled by the media's constant portrayal of them as physically talented while their white teammates are praised for their cool, strategic play. Those stereotypes have diminished, yet many black quarterbacks in the NFL resent the emphasis on their running ability and want to be recognized for their leadership, courage in standing in the pocket, and coolness under fire like their white counterparts. Examples of NFL quarterbacks who have intimated such feelings include Randall Cunningham and Donovan McNabb, who both played for the Philadelphia Eagles; Kordell Stewart of the Pittsburgh Steelers; Michael Vick of the Atlanta Falcons; and Vince Young of the Tennessee Titans. In more recent

years, there have been significantly more African American quarterbacks in major college football yet few who have made it to the NFL on the basis of their ability to run the ball. Perhaps it is the fear of injury that prevents NFL teams from allowing talented runners a free rein.

The dominance of black athletes in the NFL and NBA has given rise to discussions of their influence on the younger generation. While it is fine to be represented in sport, some African Americans cringe at the thought of so many young black people believing that sport is their cultural destiny. We'll look at this issue and others concerning race in chapter 11.

Ethnic insensitivities have always existed in sport, and while many have been eliminated, some persist. The use of Native American nicknames, chants, and cheers in violent ways in sport has become more offensive to the general population. Stereotypes of Asians abound in descriptions of athletes such as Michelle Kwan (figure skating), Yao Ming (basketball), Michelle Wie (golf), Ichiro Suzuki and Daisuke Matsuzaka (baseball), and others. Americans often stereotype Asians as smart competitors but don't typically regard them as superior athletes in spite of their achievements. Instead, comments are often made about their self-discipline, intelligence, and methodical approach to sport even though such descriptions do not necessarily apply to all Asian athletes.

Finally, racial overtones are contained in the media's consistent coverage of African Americans as violent. The sport media have done much to portray the violent athlete in football and basketball. Stories about domestic beatings, drugs, and arrests at nightclubs after a fight often feature black athletes. The public's impression is that black men are to be feared or avoided. We'll talk more about race and deviance in chapter 18.

Careers in Sport Media

Sport journalists may specialize in either print media or electronic media. Although the roles are similar in content, the method of communication is quite different. **Sports writers** tend to develop in-depth stories about athletic events or players. Their goal is to give readers as detailed a picture as they can within their space limits based on extensive research, personal observations, and interviews. Their focus is often the lifestyles, backgrounds, and personal situations of well-known athletes, with this information presented in a way that makes fans yearn to know the players better. The research can be a laborious process, and articles may take months to complete. Journalists who weave some controversial material into their stories are the most popular, provided they avoid straying too far from acceptable standards.

Sport announcers on radio or television have a much different role that requires different skills. Their job is to excite listeners or viewers through their description of the game. Although they need to report play-by-play information, setting the viewers up for what they will be seeing or hearing is critical, as is a quick analysis after the play. Energy, wit, and a thorough understanding of the game are critical for sport announcers.

Many networks hire former athletes as announcers to establish the credibility of their comments. The public expects a former player in the sport to understand the game, the athletes' struggles, and the significance of the ebb and flow of the game. Some athletes have done remarkably well even with little training as sportscasters. Another fertile ground for sport announcers is former coaches. Ostensibly, these coaches have an expert viewpoint to share, and their communication skills are often better than those of well-known athletes simply because of years of practice.

There is also a breed of professional sport announcers who have simply developed the skills of the craft, paid their dues with modest assignments, and risen to the top of sport announcing. These people, mostly males, often make their reputation in one sport and then branch out to others. Howard Cosell, Brent Musburger, Dick Enberg, Jim Nance, and Bob Costas all made their mark in sport announcing. Although their personalities and styles vary, all professional announcers study sport and thoroughly prepare before the event so that they can convey the complete package to viewers.

A few sport announcers command a substantial salary because they are on the national stage broadcasting major events. But the average sport anchor on the local television station earns an average salary of about $50,600 per year, with a range of $30,000 up to $70,000. Interestingly 94% of those roles are taken by men, 6% by women.

This average is less than the $69,800 average salary of news anchors and just a little less than the $54,000 average salary of weathercasters. Salaries of course are somewhat dependent on credentials and years of experience, and jobs pay better in larger metropolitan markets (Payscale 2010). Radio announcers typically earn even less than their colleagues on television, although they often have an exceptional ability to describe the action so that the listener can picture it in the "mind's eye" (Journalism Jobs 2002).

There is a certain tension between sport journalists and the athletes they cover. Because they are looking for a story, many journalists will probe the personal life of an athlete and sometimes share the less flattering aspects. Other journalists tend to be critical of teams, owners, coaches, and players in order to stimulate readership. This situation often causes athletes to mistrust the press and resort to stock answers when queried. Consider how many clichés you've heard from athletes during interviews:

- It's just another game to us.
- We play them one game at a time.
- We're focused on the next game, not our record or the play-offs.
- My teammates made this all possible.
- We just didn't get it done.
- We came out a little flat and just never recovered.
- We need to get everyone on the same page.
- My serve let me down today.
- You've got to give them credit for their performance today.
- We've all got a job to do.

 EXPERT'S VIEW

Lesley Visser

Lesley Visser is the number-one female sportscaster, according to the American Sportscasters Association. Her advice to aspiring female sportscasters is this: "There are two kinds of women who do this: there are women who love sports and end up in TV, and there are women who want to be in TV and end up in sports. My advice is the same for men and women: Knowing the game and having a passion for sports are really non-negotiable for a long career. If you want to have decades, then those two are non-negotiable: knowledge and passion" (AWSM 2009).

- We beat a great team today.
- No one player was responsible for the loss.

As women's sport has risen dramatically in participation and publicity, you might expect there to be a concomitant growth in the number of women reporting on sport. Between 1994 and 2000, the Association for Women in Sports Media (AWSM) more than doubled its membership from 400 to over 850 (AWSM 2000). Likewise, within months of its founding, the Female Athletic Media Executives (FAME) organization claimed over 200 members (College Sports Information Directors of America 2001). In spite of these advances, the percentage of women in sport media remains alarmingly small.

The authors of the 2008 Racial and Gender Report Card of the Associated Press Sports Editors (APSE) calculated the number of females employed at APSE websites and newspapers (Lapchick et al. 2008). As the main finding of the report, ASPE newspapers and websites were given a grade of "F" for gender hiring practices in the key positions covered in the study. Richard Lapchick, founder of the Institute for Diversity and Ethics in Sport (TIDES), stated in the report, "Our media clearly neither reflects America's workforce nor the competitors in the world of sports." Lapchick and his coauthors went on to say that in 2008, males made up 94% of sport editors, 90% of assistant sport editors, 94% of sport columnists, 91% of reporters, and 84% of copy editors and designers.

The report revealed that the percentage of female sport editors and copy editors and designers had increased since 2006 (from 5.0% to 6.5%) while at the same time the percentage of female assistant sport editors and staff/clerks had decreased, each dropping by 2%. Women made up 11.5% of APSE staffs in 2008, compared to the higher percentage of 12.6% in 2006. Sport editors who were women increased to 6.5% in 2008, up from 5.0% in 2006 (Lapchick et al. 2008).

For many years, female reporters were banned from male locker rooms, and once they did gain access, they were mercilessly taunted and ridiculed for their efforts. Perhaps the most well-known case of sexual discrimination involved reporter Lisa Olson, who was sexually harassed by three New England Patriot football players during the 1990s. Adding insult to injury, *Playboy* magazine not only carried a story on Olson's experience but also offered her a pictorial layout in the magazine.

The typical experience of female sportscasters in male locker rooms gained widespread publicity with the publication of "Never Let the Bastards See You Cry" by Toni Bruce (2000). Bruce's narrative is a fictional account of a female sportswriter's treatment by male athletes who taunt her, make lewd comments, and caution her against any "feminist crap."

Not only do women often find it difficult to secure positions in sport journalism; if they do manage to break down the barriers and get in, the challenge is not over. Once they are hired, they may face harassment or isolation in a sport environment populated mostly by males. They often are compensated at a lower rate than male colleagues and may find it difficult to secure promotions. Eventually, they may turn to other journalistic fields where the odds for advancement and success are more favorable (Dodds 2000). Johnette Howard, a *Newsday* sport columnist, observed, "I used to get mail saying 'You're a dumb broad and you don't know anything about sports.' Now they just say, 'You're a dumb broad.' I'd say that's progress" (McNamara 2000).

In spite of the barriers, there is a growing class of female television reporters who have earned respect in recent years for covering a wide variety of both male and female sports. In 2009, the American Sportscasters Association voted Lesley Visser, veteran CBS sportscaster, the number-one female sportscaster of all time. Others on the list in order of selection are shown in table 5.4.

TABLE 5.4 All-Time Female Sportscasters

Name	Network
1. Lesley Visser	CBS
2. Andrea Kremer	NBC
3. Robin Roberts	ABC/ESPN
4. Michele Tafoya	ESPN
5. Hannah Storm	ESPN
6. Mary Carillo	HBO
7. Linda Kohn	ESPN
8. Andrea Joyce	ABC/ESPN
9. Suzy Kolber	ABC/ESPN
10. Phyllis George	CBS
11. Bonnie Bernstein	ESPN
12. Pam Oliver	FOX
13. Donna de Varona	ABC
14. Judy Rankin	ABC/ESPN
15. Ann Meyers-Drysdale	NBC

Adapted from American Sportscasters Association 2009.

IN THE ARENA WITH . . .

Erin Andrews

Erin Andrews is a sideline reporter for ESPN who has gained recognition for her versatility in sport reporting of baseball, hockey, football, and college basketball and baseball, among other assignments. Voted "America's sexiest sportscaster" in 2007 and 2008 by *Playboy* magazine, her public profile was expanded after a successful run to the finals of the popular television show *Dancing With the Stars* in 2010.

Andrews grew up in Tampa, Florida, and graduated from the University of Florida with a degree in telecommunications. While in college, she was also a member of the Dazzlers, the Gator basketball dance team, for several years.

In 2009, Andrews was identified in a video posted on the Internet, showing her in a state of undress, that had been shot surreptitiously through a hotel peephole. The incident was immediately picked up by the press and garnered major publicity for months until the FBI arrested the perpetrator, Michael Barrett, who was eventually sentenced to 30 months in prison and ordered to register as a sex offender. Andrews recalls the entire unfortunate experience as "a nightmare," and along with a series of death threats she has dealt with a loss of privacy.

Happily, with those bad times behind her and her success on *Dancing with the Stars*, Andrews seems poised to expand her media career, since she has had multiple offers from both sport and entertainment shows. Her own comments, however, indicate that she still believes her professional career will include sport in some way (*USA Today* 2010, ESPN 2010b).

Chapter Summary

In this chapter we examined how both the print and electronic media affect sport fans by increasing their knowledge, excitement, and interest in sport at all levels, but particularly professional sport. It is clear that the media and big-time sport are inextricably intertwined and interdependent in their interrelationships.

We examined the effect of the media on sport, from the free publicity they generate for teams and athletes to how they affect the popularity of specific sports or athletes. Similarly, the sport media have forced some dramatic changes in the presentation of sport, particularly on television, since that is a major revenue source for professional sport.

Next, we looked at the relationship from the opposite point of view: how sports have affected the media. Both print media and the electronic media have turned to sport because it is guaranteed to produce interest and revenue. Millions of people worldwide thirst for the instant gratification of watching professional sport on television, and most of them enjoy reading about what they watched a day or week later in print. Of course, the print media have the disadvantage of timing, but they make up for that by having time to set the angle, tenor, and facts of their story before delivery.

Sport and the sport media have the potential to affect the ideology of a society in the way they present key values. We've looked at the effect of spectatorship on participation levels and attitudes toward gender, sexuality, and racial and ethnic groups. Since sport and the sport media have been almost exclusively the domains of white males, not surprisingly the values presented in the media have typically been oriented toward white males and have not provided fair treatment for minority athletes or females. Although minorities and women have seen rapid gains as athletes in the past 50 years, their treatment by the media has lagged depressingly behind.

Finally, we looked at the careers within sport journalism and its status as a profession. It has become clear that changes in the composition of sport staffs are occurring slowly. Women lag far behind their male cohorts in sport journalism opportunities.

PART III

Sport as an Institution

We begin in chapter 6 by looking at the trends that show a steady increase in organized youth programs over the past 20 years. Of particular note is the rapid growth in participation by females since the passage of Title IX. Yet as organized youth sport grows, informal sports and games that have been popular in other generations have declined dramatically due to transportation issues, safety issues, and competition from sedentary activities. The chapter examines the positives and negatives of youth sport programs that are organized by adults and presents several problem areas, such as the lack of well-trained volunteer coaches, along with potential solutions.

As shown in chapter 7, sport within the educational system in North America has developed differently than in any other place in the world. Although sports are designated as an extracurricular activity, they often serve their schools or colleges by unifying students, alumni, and fans. At universities they help attract more applicants, encourage alumni to donate funds, and generate lots of publicity for the school.

Interscholastic and collegiate sports have traditionally been extolled for their virtues, although many of these claims are not based on solid research. The percentage of students who actually make high school or college teams is relatively small, while the cost to the institution per student is significant.

Title IX has affected high school and college sport by requiring equal opportunities for females and males. The result has been a vast improvement in sport opportunities for girls. At the same time, budget allocations continue to be a source of debate and agony, especially escalating costs as schools try to offer equal opportunities to both genders.

Chapter 8 examines sport from an international perspective and shows how sports are expanding worldwide. As communication and the media help shrink the world, sports spread quickly from one country to another. Favorite American sports such as football, basketball, and baseball have gained popularity throughout the world such that the United States no longer dominates world competition in basketball or baseball. Soccer is finally beginning to gain a toehold in the United States after several decades of rapid growth in youth soccer, especially among females. The most popular sports worldwide will surprise you, and the chapter will help you understand the reasons for the popularity of each sport.

The opportunity to use sport competition to further relationships between countries has always been touted. Evidence suggests that athlete exchange programs between nations, world amateur competitions, and professional leagues that span the globe do help promote international understanding. However, claims that globalization through sport may alter political processes or governments seem to be more about wishful thinking than reality.

No other sporting event has had a worldwide effect comparable to that of the Olympic Games, discussed in chapter 9. Steeped in the tradition of amateur athletes competing for the love of sport, the Olympics has evolved into big business. Including professional athletes has helped the Games popularize the events and attract huge amounts of television coverage and commercial sponsorship. The nationalism that has characterized the Games for the last 50 years is giving way to an economic model of competition.

All countries that compete seriously in the Olympic Games have organized national programs to help their best athletes. The United States Olympic Committee has recently struggled with its role. Unlike programs in several other countries, it receives no government funding and instead relies on private sponsors and donations. A by-product of strong Olympic development programs with government funding in many countries has been that Olympic sports are affordable and accessible for any talented athlete.

6

Youth Sport

Student Outcomes

After reading this chapter, you will know the following:

- The history of youth sport
- Current status of organization of youth sport and participation in youth sport
- The distinction between athlete-organized sport and adult-organized sport
- Reasons why young people play sports
- Future modifications that may benefit youth sport

Did you grow up in a household like this? Your mom, like other moms in your neighborhood, spent a large portion of her day driving you and your brother and sister to various youth sports. Among the three of you kids during the ages from about 6 to 13, someone was always in soccer, Little League, swim lessons, tennis, or dance. It was up to Mom to coordinate the sports schedules for practices and games every day while Dad pitched in on weekends. Dinners as a family were few and far between since there were few nights when everyone was home at the same time. Snacks and reheated dinners were normal, followed by homework. Your mom became known as a "soccer mom," a term that became popular in the 1990s and even became a voting demographic for politicians like Bill Clinton and Bob Dole as they were trolling for votes in the presidential election of 1996. The *Wall Street Journal* described soccer moms as the key swing consumer in the marketplace, and the key swing voter who would decide the (presidential) election. According to other major newspapers, soccer moms lived in the suburbs; were swing voters; were busy, harried, and stressed out; worked outside the home; drove a minivan or sport utility vehicle; were middle class; and were married and white. As you read through this chapter you'll see that these soccer moms typify the mothers of the majority of kids who actually play youth sports.

How did our American culture move from one in which parents said to kids between the ages of 8 and 12 "Go out and play but be sure to be back by 6:00 for dinner" to one in which sports and activities for children became such an organized affair? Adult-organized sports for kids have exploded in the past 20 years for a variety of reasons that we'll consider in this chapter. There are those critics who lament the more casual days of the past, but the popularity of youth sport programs and the demand for them seem to continue to grow.

Youth sport significantly affects the development of young people simply because of the large amount of time they spend playing sports. Whether they choose to play informal games with their peers or join an organized program, almost all children experiment with different sports between the ages of 6 and 12. Those who are successful may continue with their sport through the teenage years; others may try other sport activities or drop out of sport completely.

Recent trends in youth sport participation have shown that the number of young people who play in organized programs continues to grow, and girls' participation especially is showing large increases compared to 20 years ago. The advent of both parents working outside the home has created a need for scheduled, supervised children's activities that keep kids after school. Sport has emerged as a natural child care activity and has the added advantage of delivering several benefits, such as increasing physical activity and fitness, learning physical skills, and socializing with peers.

Lest we congratulate ourselves on the continuous growth of organized youth sport, a closer look reveals a steep decline in youth sports (particularly team sports) that are not organized at school or in the community (Sporting Goods Manufacturers Association [SGMA] 2009d). Kids no longer leave the house to spend the day playing pickup games in neighborhood parks or on school playing fields as they once did. Some pundits attribute the decline to parents' hesitancy to allow their children freedom to roam unsupervised, while others point the finger at video games, the Internet, and television (Cauchon 2005). As adult-organized youth sport has grown, so too have criticisms of programs that emphasize winning, emphasize specialization in one sport, overschedule kids' time, overinvolve adults in structuring the program, and have a high cost. It's time to look closely at the current organization of youth sport and consider what changes should be made to enhance the role of youth sport in the development of young people.

Popular opinion concerning youth sport varies and depends somewhat on the influence of the media. While the media criticize excesses in youth sport, they also celebrate the successful performances of local teams and broadcast the Little League World Series into every home. Parents decry the negative influences of some coaches, but training and certification standards for youth coaches are nonexistent and it has been difficult to demand certification without enthusiastic support from parents. Organizers often recruit young people to play and stress how much fun they will have, but then structure the experience to teach conformity to rules and coaching directions and reward winning teams and athletes for exceptional performances.

A Youth Sports National Report Card was released for 2005 by the Citizenship Through Sports Alliance, a national coalition of sport organizations that includes, among others, the four major professional leagues in the United States (baseball, basketball, football, and ice hockey), the National Collegiate Athletic Association (NCAA), and the United States Olympic Committee (USOC). The report card reflected some harsh criticism of youth sport. Grades were given from A to F in five categories:

Child-centered philosophy	D
Coaching	C−
Health and safety	C+
Officiating	B−
Parental behavior	D

The ratings, given by youth sport experts from across the country, focused on community-based sport for children aged 6 to 14. Some specific findings of the report were that youth sport has lost its focus on the child; suffers from the actions of overinvested parents; fails to recruit and train quality coaches; focuses too much on early sport specialization; and fails to listen to the voice of the child who wants to play sports for fun, friendships, fitness, and skill development.

In the past, children would spend hours outdoors playing youth-organized games and sports. Now, most sports are adult-organized. What has led to this change?

History of Youth Sport

Youth sport programs became a huge factor in American society during the past 50 years. Before then, few programs existed and most children organized their own games. Children who grew up in cities spent hours playing different variations of baseball, such as stickball, wireball, and Wiffle ball. They filled in the time by jumping rope, playing hopscotch, and shooting baskets. Those who lived in rural areas were more likely to choose recreational sports that took advantage of the woods, lakes, mountains, and back roads of their environment. Hunting, fishing, boating, hiking, mountain climbing, bicycling, and running were popular outdoor pursuits.

Youth sport programs in the years following World War II were dominated by Little League Baseball, which was founded in 1939 in Williamsport, Pennsylvania. It was a community-based program in which each team was funded by local businesses.

Along with teaching baseball skills and strategy, Little League was looked upon by parents and organizers as a way to teach young boys life skills, proper values, discipline, and adherence to rules. Along with the Boy Scouts, youth sport programs were invested in training the boys of America for adulthood (Little League 2005).

Youth sport in the 1950s and 1960s was primarily for boys and was heartily endorsed by most people, particularly those in the middle class, as a worthy use of time to learn athletic and social skills. Community leaders asserted that young men would learn the lessons of life on the ball field during competition.

Perhaps the most dramatic change in youth sport programs in the last 25 years has been the explosion of opportunities for girls that came with the passage of Title IX in 1972. Before Title IX, girls

POP CULTURE

Stickball: The Crown Jewel of American Urban Sports Culture

With a broom handle, a rubber ball, a bunch of guys, and a street, you could play all day in a respectable city game that felt a lot like real baseball. Manhole covers became bases, cars and walls became foul lines and roofs of houses served as bleacher seats. Stickball thrived in large urban environments, mostly in working class neighborhoods filled with kids who needed a diversion long before the days of television and the Internet. Irish, Italian, Jewish, and Puerto Rican kids in inner cities from the 19th century up through the 1980s thrived on some form of stickball. The balls used might be a pinky, a spalden, a pimple ball, or a tennis ball.

Three main types of stickball were played depending on the local tradition (Streetplay 2010; New York Street Games 2010). First there was fast-pitch, where there was usually a wall or fence on which a rectangular strike zone was drawn. If a ball hit inside the strike zone with no swing from the batter, the result was a strike. Most games allowed two or three strikes before you were out. A second style was slow-pitch, in which the pitcher stood about 40 feet away from the batter and delivered a lob that the batter tried to clobber after it bounced once. After you hit the ball, you ran the bases. Fielders could get you out by throwing and hitting you with the ball if you were not on a base. The third variation of stickball was fungo, where you would actually toss the ball up, let it bounce, and then strike it yourself. Rules varied by neighborhood, but if you hit a ball on the roof, porch, or broke a window it could have been a home run, an out, or game over depending on the neighbors and the police. The best thing about stickball may not have been the entertainment and physical activity for kids right at home, but the sense of community it spawned within neighborhoods that cannot be reclaimed in these days of adult-organized sports and indoor diversions.

were cheerleaders, pom-pom girls, or majorettes or participated in a few ladylike sports such as gymnastics, figure skating, equestrian, swimming, and tennis. Once Title IX was passed, girls showed up in record numbers at softball fields, basketball courts, field hockey and lacrosse fields, and soccer fields.

Since the 1970s, family life in North America has endured many changes. A significant change has been the increase in the number of mothers working outside the home, from 40% of mothers in the 1970s to 71% of mothers with children under age 18 in 2008 (Bureau of Labor Statistics 2009). As mentioned previously, this change meant that kids needed someplace safe to go after school. Sport filled that void with the added bonus that kids were getting exercise and improving self-confidence, along with getting life lessons in winning and losing and good sporting behavior.

A second factor has been the increase in child abductions and sexual predators that frighten parents and make them fear for their children's safety (Cauchon 2005). With their children actively engaged under adult supervision in a sport program,

parents can feel some comfort that their children are safe.

A third factor has been the belief, particularly in areas of high crime, that children are more likely to stay out of trouble if they are in an organized sport program. Before the age of 10, many children are exposed to drugs, sex, and crime on the streets. In a safe haven after school, children who live in dangerous neighborhoods can play sport free of worry, and in many programs they spend time completing homework assignments as well.

Finally, the emergence of specialized training for high sport performance at very young ages has encouraged parents to sacrifice their time and money to give their children a chance to become a great athlete. Kids are encouraged at early ages to commit completely to one sport, train hard every day, and focus on that one sport year round. Parents feel a sense of guilt if they do not support their child's one chance to be famous and make millions, so they sacrifice money, time, and sometimes even family happiness in the pursuit of athletic excellence.

Sponsors of Youth Sport

The rise in youth sport occurred in large part because certain organizations lent their support. In broad categories, these are the groups that sponsored youth sport:

- Public community or parks programs
- Community organizations such as the YMCA or YWCA, Police Athletic League, Boys and Girls Clubs, and church organizations like the Catholic Youth Organization
- Nonprofit sport organizations such as Little League, Pop Warner football, United States Tennis Association, Amateur Athletic Union, and Youth Soccer
- Corporate sponsors of youth sport including national, regional, and local businesses
- Commercial sport or fitness clubs

One of the questions often raised is who should pay for youth sport. Once schools disengaged from sponsoring sport programs for young children, communities looked for other sources. One solution has been to use public funds to support community sport programs, often through local parks or playgrounds. The rationale is that taxpayer money is well spent if it keeps children busy, out of trouble, and physically active. Most of these programs are available in the summer when school is not in session. Programs are often free or a nominal charge

Thirteen-year-old pitching phenom Chelsea Baker has been recognized by the National Baseball Hall of Fame for pitching two perfect games—against boys no less! She honed her pitching skills through a Florida Little League team.

 EXPERT'S VIEW

A Long-Term Athlete Development Plan

National Olympic Committees and national sports governing bodies have wrestled for years to create a sport development model that would maximize their results in international competition and help produce a citizenry that is committed to life-long physical activity. One such plan, the Long-Term Athlete Development (LTAD) plan, is a training, competition, and recovery program based on each athlete's developmental age—the maturation level of an individual—rather than chronological age. It is athlete centered, coach driven, and supported by sport administrators, sport science experts, and sponsors. Athletes are guided to develop an individual plan that is specific to their unique development needs. "Following this LTAD guide will ensure that children develop physical literacy, which is the development of fundamental movement and fundamental sport skills that permits them to move confidently and with control in a wide range of physical activity, rhythmic (dance), and sport situations. Physical literacy also includes the ability to read what is going on in an activity setting and react appropriately to those events. The goal of physical literacy in all children, from early childhood to late adolescence, is quality daily physical activity and a coordinated approach to developing physical abilities" (Robinson 2010, p. 189).

The model is divided into stages with rough chronological age guidelines, although children will differ in the rate they move through the stages. A brief summary of the stages relevant to youth sport is presented in table 6.1 on page 100. Analyze the plan and compare it to your progression through youth sport. Is it similar or quite different? Be specific in your comments and share with classmates.

TABLE 6.1 Stages in the LTAD Plan

1. FUNdamentals stage	2. Learning to train stage
Chronological age	**Chronological/developmental age**
• Males, 6-9	• Males, 9-12
• Females, 6-8	• Females, 8-11
Characteristics	**Characteristics**
• Fun and participation	• Overall sport skills development
• Learn overall movement skills	• Major skill learning stage
• Integrate mental, cognitive, and emotional development	• Integrate mental, cognitive, and emotional development
• Develop locomotor skill	• Introduction to mental preparation
• Develop general motor ability	• Talent identification
• Introduce basic sport skills	• Single or double periodization
• Introduce basic rules of ethics	• Sport-specific training three times per week
• Daily physical activity	• Other sport participation three times per week
3. Training to train stage	**4. Training to compete stage**
Chronological/developmental age	**Chronological/developmental age**
• Males, 12-16	• Males, 16-23
• Females, 11-15	• Females, 15-21+/−
Characteristics	**Characteristics**
• Specific sport skill development	• Sport-, event-, position-specific physical conditioning
• Major fitness development stage	• Sport-, event-, position-specific tactical preparation
• Integrated mental, cognitive, and emotional development	• Sport-, event-, position-specific technical and playing skills under competitive conditions
• Develop mental preparation	• Integrated mental, cognitive, and emotional development
• Introduce strength training	• Advanced mental preparation
• Develop ancillary capacities	• Develop ancillary capacities
• Selection	• Specialization
• Single or double periodization	• Single, double, or triple periodization
• Sport-specific training six to nine times per week including complementary sports	• Sport-specific technical, tactical, and fitness training 9 to 12 times per week

Based on Balyi et al. 2005.

is assessed. Sport programs under this model tend to be introductory, recreational, and moderately organized.

When public funds are not available, other organizations such as YMCAs and YWCAs, Boys and Girls Clubs, and churches step in to fill the void. Funds are raised from public or private sources, memberships are established for modest fees, and donations are solicited. Youth sport programs clearly have a social component and are often targeted toward populations at risk. In some programs, tutoring and academic enrichment are combined with athletic activity.

Nonprofit sport organizations also began sponsoring youth programs to expose kids to their sport, build a solid base of fans, scout talent, and help develop elite players who might one day play professionally. These organizations largely finance youth leagues but also charge participants a modest

fee to help cover the costs. Programs operated by these organizations tend to lean more toward skill instruction, greater emphasis on winning and losing, and development of elite performers.

Commercial sponsors of youth sports saw an opportunity to influence children and their families about their products. Local businesses know that sponsoring a team promotes goodwill in the community and at the same time allows them to advertise their business on the uniforms of players and on signs at ballparks. A few national sponsors latched onto programs such as the Punt, Pass, and Kick program.

Finally, commercial sport clubs have become a mainstay of the youth sport market. Local clubs offer swimming, tennis, soccer, basketball, and so on at prices that are typically affordable only to the middle and upper classes. Programs are oriented toward high performance for serious young athletes who at the very least have a college scholarship as their goal if not a professional career. Summer camps specialize in one or two sports and draw thousands of youngsters from families who can afford to send their children to camp for weeks or even entire summers. The camps mix traditional camp activities with a heavy dose of sport instruction, drilling, and supervised play.

Depending on the organization that sponsors a youth sport program, the philosophy and expected outcomes vary. In general, the more intensive competitive programs are also more costly. The result is that kids of modest financial backgrounds often have limited opportunities to develop their natural talent without financial help or scholarships.

Current Status of Youth Sport

With participation in youth sport at an all-time high, it would appear that things are rosy in the sporting world of kids. In 2000, the number of American youth who played on at least one organized sport team was found to be 54% of kids between ages 6 and 17 (American Sports Data, Inc. 2005). A similar study five years later showed that among a slightly older age group of 10- to 17-year-olds, sport participation had jumped to 59% (National Survey of Children's Health 2005).

A related study produced a mixture of good and bad news. It revealed that team sport participation peaks at age 11, basketball remains the most popular team sport, and participation in sport by girls has never been better—but frequent participation by both boys and girls in team sports is declining. A closer look, however, reveals a host of problems. Perhaps the most alarming statistic is that by some estimates, over 70% of participants drop out of youth sport programs along the way to high school. Speculation is rampant as to the cause, but no clear pattern has yet emerged. Possible causes of youth dropouts in sport include the following (Cary 2004):

- Overemphasis on winning as the objective with resulting increases in pressure to win and achieve
- Stress on high performance that translates into longer hours of practice, longer seasons, and specialization in one sport at an early age

- Expenses of participation, traveling teams, sport camps, sport academies, coaching, and equipment that are out of reach of middle-class families
- Increased injury incidence due to inordinate demands on young bodies
- Increased participation in alternative sports by young people who are turned off by traditional adult-organized programs
- Lack of training for youth coaches and the resulting frustration of kids who take orders from well-intentioned but misguided coaches
- Earlier starts in youth sport (sometimes as young as 3 or 4 years of age); children simply grow bored with a sport after a number of years

What will it take to keep this young girl involved in sport and physical activity throughout her life?

A more recent study sponsored by the Women's Sports Foundation (2008) investigated the participation of American youth in exercise and organized team sports. The findings were that 72% were participating or had participated in a sport during the past 12 months, while 12% had dropped out of sport and 15% had never played sports. Perhaps more revealing were the statistics showing that gender, race, and location of kids significantly affected their likely sport participation.

Comparing gender, boys were more likely to be involved in sport at every age and more likely to play multiple sports, and a higher percentage of boys tended to be avid sport participants. Girls tended to enter sport later than boys (7.4 years compared to 6.8 years for boys), and girls also dropped out sooner and in greater numbers. Interestingly, girls were more likely than boys to take part in a wide array of sports including cheerleading, dance, competitive rope jumping, and volleyball while boys tended to stick with more traditional sports.

In suburban communities, participation rates between boys and girls are comparable, but in rural and urban communities, girls fall far behind boys. One telling statistic is that 84% of urban and 68% of rural girls have no physical education classes at all in 11th and 12th grade, compared with only 48% of girls in suburban schools who do not participate in physical education.

Youth sports are racially and ethnically diverse and in fact at many ages, boys of color tend to have higher participation rates in sport than Caucasians. However, the picture for girls of color is not encouraging. They seem to be hit by both gender and skin color discrimination, and their participation levels fall significantly below those of Caucasian girls. The reasons for this are a combination of culture, family responsibilities, income level, and living locations (Women's Sports Foundation 2008).

Let's take a closer look at some trends in youth sport.

If you had asked someone in 1975 which sports were most popular with youth, it is likely that the answer would have included traditional boys' sports like basketball, football, baseball, track, swimming, and perhaps skiing, wrestling, bowling, and gymnastics. Now that girls are much more involved in sport, the types of sport activities have broadened to include sports such as volleyball, soccer, cycling, lacrosse, field hockey, ultimate Frisbee, cheerleading, double Dutch, and stepping. Table 6.2 shows the most frequent physical activities by gender (Women's Sports Foundation 2008).

TABLE 6.2 Most Frequent Physical Activities (Girls)

Physical activity	% participation
GIRLS	
Dancing	61
Swimming/diving	56
Basketball	55
Jogging/running	53
Volleyball	47
Bowling	47
Soccer	40
Baseball/softball	38
In-line skating	33
Camping/hiking	29
Ultimate Frisbee	29
BOYS	
Basketball	71
Football	65
Soccer	51
Jogging/running	49
Swimming/diving	48
Baseball/softball	48
Bowling	48
Weight training	42
Cycling/mountain biking	33
Skateboarding	29
Ultimate Frisbee	29

Dropping out of youth sport and physical activity continues to be a concern, especially since a majority of youths seem to withdraw during the middle school years. The structure, emphasis on competitive results, length of season, and commitment, along with boredom, are typically cited as primary reasons. A section later in this chapter, Why Kids Play—and Stop Playing—Sports, looks at specific reasons kids give for dropping out of organized sports (see page 110).

Decreased Physical Activity

USA Today ran a front-page story titled "Childhood Pastimes Are Increasingly Moving Indoors" that set off alarm bells among parents, teachers, and sport administrators (Cauchon 2005). It seems that the typical child spends more time indoors today than ever before, watching television, playing video

ACTIVITY TIME-OUT

Burning Issues in Youth Sport

Visit the websites of three of the organizations listed here and see what catches your eye about the issues that most concern those who offer these sites. Make a list of at least five different topics that are discussed on more than one site, and give a brief summary in one paragraph on each topic. Be sure to cite the website and article from which you gleaned your information. You may also use other organizations of your choosing in addition to the ones listed.

- www.nays.org—site for National Alliance for Youth Sports, a nonprofit organization that emphasizes making sport safe and positive for young people
- http://ed-web3.educ.msu.edu/ysi/—site for the Institute for the Study of Youth Sports at Michigan State University, which sponsors research on youth sport and offers other educational materials
- www.momsteam.com—site that is the premier online youth sport information gateway for over 90 million parents of youth sport participants
- www.asep.com—site for the American Sport Education Program, a division of Human Kinetics; a premier coaching education site for coaches of youth sport
- www.sportsdonerightmaine.org—site for the youth sport initiative of the state of Maine
- www.ncys.org—National Council on Youth Sports (NCYS); comprises the "who's who" in the youth sport industry; its memberships represent more than 185 organizations and corporations serving 60 million registered participants

games, or browsing the Internet. According to research by the Kaiser Family Foundation and the Centers for Disease Control and Prevention cited in the article, youths spend their recreational time each day in the following ways:

Watching television	4 hours, 10 minutes
Playing video games	1 hour, 5 minutes
Recreational computer use	37 minutes
Total time	5 hours, 52 minutes

Gone are the days of children leaving early in the day for outside play with the only requirement that they return in time for dinner. Suburban living has divided kids by miles, and parents fear for their children's safety. Air conditioning in most homes negates the need to head for the local swimming spot to cool off in the heat of summer.

According to the Sporting Goods Manufacturers' Association (SGMA 2009d), overall participation numbers in team sports are simply not as strong as they once were. There seem to be several factors driving this trend:

- The struggling U.S. economy has affected the number of families who can afford to pay the fees for their children to play in local leagues, especially the more expensive travel teams.
- The increased popularity of developing sports like lacrosse, rugby, paintball, ultimate Frisbee, and of course extreme sports has siphoned off kids who might have once played traditional team sports.
- Pickup or sandlot play has continued to decline. But although there has been a significant decline overall, certain sports have actually increased in pickup play while losing organized sport players. The sports that are flourishing as pickup games are basketball, ice hockey, field hockey, touch football, lacrosse, and grass and beach volleyball.
- Athletes who play multiple team sports are a fading breed. Most youth now specialize at young ages in one sport in hopes of becoming successful in that sport, but miss out on the variety of experiences of other sports. Pressure from coaches and parents to focus on one sport year round may backfire as

kids tire of the sport and lose enthusiasm for it over time.

Increase in Overweight and Obesity

Nearly one-third (31.7%) of American children are either overweight or obese, and during the past two decades the prevalence of obesity has climbed from 10.5% to 18% of adolescents between ages 12 and 19. Among African American youth ages 2 to 19, an overall percentage of 35.9% were overweight or obese. The statistics were particularly alarming for African American adolescent girls, who showed a 29.2% prevalence of obesity—the highest of any age group by gender, race, or ethnicity. In comparison, fewer than one in five Hispanic or white adolescent girls were obese (Leadership for Healthy Communities 2010).

Diet and exercise are clearly the primary factors to combat these disturbing trends, although it appears that certain cultures and communities are affected by economic conditions, family traditions, and recreational opportunities or the lack thereof, including lack of physical education and athletic facilities. Living location also has been clearly identified as having a correlation with lack of physical activity in both urban and rural settings (Lee, McAlexander, and Banda 2011).

Explosion of Extreme Sport

Recent studies by SGMA and the National Sporting Goods Association (NSGA) show a dramatic shift in participation among teens and preteens from mainstream sports such as basketball and football to extreme or action sports (see table 6.3). In the 15 years between 1990 and 2005, participation in football, baseball, and basketball among 6- to 17-year-olds was down more than 30%, while participation in action sports like snowboarding, skateboarding, and in-line skating showed increases in excess of 600% (SGMA 2005a). More recent research by SGMA in 2008 concluded that extreme sports were not a temporary fad, but now are clearly established options particularly among youth in the United States. Here are some additional facts on the growth of extreme sports (SGMA 2008a):

- In-line skating by itself boasted more participants in total than any other sport with the exceptions of basketball, baseball, soccer, and touch football.
- Paintball participation has exploded more than 50% since 2000.
- More than 3.8 million skateboarders participate 25 or more days per year.
- Mountain/rock climbing participation grew by 30% from 2006 to 2007.

TABLE 6.3 Most Popular Extreme Sports in the United States in 2007

Extreme sport	No. of participants (at least once in 2007)
1. In-line skating	10,814,000
2. Skateboarding	8,429,000
3. Mountain biking	6,892,000
4. Snowboarding	6,841,000
5. Paintball	5,476,000
6. Cardio kickboxing	4,812,000
7. Climbing (indoor, sport, boulder)	4,514,000
8. Trail running	4,216,000
9. Ultimate Frisbee	4,038,000
10. Wakeboarding	3,521,000
11. Mountain/rock climbing	2,062,000
12. BMX bicycling	1,887,000
13. Roller hockey	1,847,000
14. Boardsailing/windsurfing	1,118,000

Participants are 6 or older.

Reprinted, by permission, from Sporting Goods Manufacturers Association, 2008, *Extreme sports: An ever-popular attraction.* Available: http://sgma.com/press/2_Extreme-Sports:-An-Ever-Popular-Attraction.

- Ultimate Frisbee is more popular than lacrosse, wrestling, beach volleyball, fast-pitch softball, rugby, field hockey, and roller hockey.

By now you may be curious about the sudden shift toward action or extreme sport. Skateboarding legend Tony Hawk, a promoter of the X Games, says, "Kids like the freedom of what we do, no strict practice regimen, no coaches and it's an artistic pursuit as much as sport. It has constant action, no standing in the outfield waiting for something to happen" (Scheiber 2005, p. C8). A decade ago there were approximately 100 skate parks, according to Ryan Clements, general manager of the Skate Park of Tampa. "Skateboarding used to be punk. Now it's normal" (Scheiber 2005, p. C8). The summer of 2005 marked the 11th anniversary of the X Games, which are no longer a novelty but part of mainstream youth culture. The X Games are even featured on ESPN. Another breakthrough was the agreement by NBC Sports and USA Network to televise 32 hours of the 2005 Dew Tour, an action sports tour—the first season-long professional competition involving action sport.

The X Games feature wakeboarding, which evolved from waterskiing and surfing; motocross, which came from motorcycles and cross country running; surfing; BMX or bicycle motocross, which includes racing and jumps; and skateboarding. Things all these sports have in common are racing, jumps, their own lingo, and an emphasis on creativity and athleticism. Action sports were once viewed as pursuits for outsiders, rebels, and geeks, but all that has changed; they're mainstream sports now. Participants say they pursue these sports for fun and because they like the fashion and lifestyle and just want to express themselves (Scheiber 2005).

Changes in Sport Preference

Over the past decade, several changes have occurred in the sports that youths prefer to play. As discussed earlier, baseball and football used to be the most popular sports. While they are still popular, other sports have made more dramatic gains in participants. For example, you may be surprised at the sports that have grown the most during the period from 2000 to 2007. With a growth rate of 104%, lacrosse has become the leader, followed by paintball at 51%. Two racket sports, tennis and table tennis, are next with 30% and 25% gains, respectively (SGMA 2008). Several developing sports, such as court volleyball (up 17.2%), beach volleyball (up 7.5%), rugby (up 11.8%), and indoor soccer (up 11.8%), have also shown impressive gains and no doubt affected the popularity of more traditional team sports (SGMA 2009c).

However, the most popular sports today are basketball and soccer, primarily due to the explosion of female participants in these sports. Football is also near the top of the list but traditionally attracts only boys, although some girls play flag football.

Basketball

Statistics for youth basketball show that it has become the most popular team sport for kids, with over 10 million participants (SGMA 2009c). Basketball appeals to both genders and is hugely popular as a recreational or pickup sport. Courts are accessible, particularly in urban settings where space is at a premium, and costs are minimal for players. Interestingly, basketball peaks in popularity at age 13 and continues to be strong throughout the teenage years compared to baseball and soccer, in which participation peaks at age 7 or 8. In fact, basketball has the most number of high school teams of any sport for both boys and girls. In contrast, tackle football rates only fourth in number of high school teams, although football ranks number one in number of participants for boys due to the large number of players required to form a team (National Federation of State High School Associations 2008-2009). Heroes like Michael Jordan, Dwayne Wade, Kobe Bryant, and LeBron James have inspired a generation of players. As women's college and professional basketball has gained a

ACTIVITY TIME-OUT

Extreme Kids

Locate at least three kids who have participated in an alternative sport and interview them to determine the reasons they chose that activity, why they like it, their expectations for their future in the sport, and how they think their sport compares with more traditional sports. Share your findings with others in class and discuss the implications for the future of youth sport.

solid foothold, players such as Lisa Leslie, Candace Parker, Diana Taurasi, and Sue Bird have become role models for younger female athletes.

Soccer

Soccer has grown at unprecedented rates in the past 20 years in the United States and is second only to basketball in participation, especially for younger children. Although soccer participation peaks at the relatively young age of 8, by high school it still attracts the fifth highest number of participants of all sports, spread evenly between girls and boys. Since 2007, indoor soccer participation has increased by 11.8% (SGMA 2009c). The major impetus has come from community-based programs that are affiliated with the U.S. Youth Soccer Association, as well as the dual influence of Title IX and the liberation of girls to play soccer. That happy circumstance led to the success in world competition of the U.S. women's national team led by Mia Hamm, Kristine Lilly, Brandi Chastain, and a core group of others who have starred at the professional level for over a decade. Young girls have role models to emulate, and these women have been outstanding citizens, athletes, and promoters of their sport.

After the 2010 World Cup, America found a new soccer hero in Landon Donovan. He emerged as a strong team leader by scoring critical goals throughout the competition. Landon is not physically imposing at a height of 5 feet, 7 inches (1.7 m) and playing weight of 157 pounds (71 kg), but he is recognized as one of the most competent and dangerous players in the world.

Soccer has some built-in advantages over other sports. No one body type is required for success; size is not a prerequisite; and the necessary skills to play are somewhat modest. Other popular American sports such as basketball (height) and football (height and weight) do put a premium on physical size, thus eliminating most aspiring young athletes from higher levels of play. Although youth soccer is marked by a swarm of players all moving toward the ball, players get good exercise; learn basic balance, running, and kicking skills; and enjoy the camaraderie with teammates. The cost per player is modest, since 22 kids on one field is a cost-effective use of space and personnel.

Soccer programs start as early as ages 4 and 5, snatching up kids before other sports have a chance to recruit them. Kids need only to be able to run and kick a ball to begin soccer play compared to more complicated skills required for many other sports. Recreational leagues that compete within their own league structure are plentiful, and traveling teams, a next step up in competition, are offered in most communities. Up to 30% of participants are identified as elite players and offered advanced training and coaching. Although we know that number is inflated, at a young age many players show potential to develop and parents eagerly support their children's talent.

Baseball

Participation in baseball has declined in recent years, particularly in urban settings and among African Americans. The number of players declined 26% during the 1990s, although the number who played frequently (at least 52 times per year) remained unchanged at 3.2 million (SGMA 2005b). However, since 2000, participation numbers have remained stable and resisted further decline (SGMA 2008b). A game that was once America's pastime has begun to play a much more modest role. A litany of reasons has been suggested, with no clear answers. Some people blame the decline on the bitter feuds between professional players and owners that resulted in various strikes or lockouts. Others say the game is too slow and boring. Also, the steroid controversy and the exposure of many professional stars as users of illegal substances continue to generate a lot of negative publicity (see chapter 18).

At the youth level, baseball more than any other sport has relied on parents as coaches and team administrators. In many families, both parents are in the workforce and have less time to devote to such activities. Fields are expensive to develop and maintain, particularly in urban settings. Scandal has also touched youth baseball, with several cases of players lying about their age to compete in divisions for which they were too old. However, if you combine all participants in baseball, fast-pitch softball, and slow-pitch softball, the total exceeds that of every other sport, including basketball.

Individual Sports

Participation in individual sports like figure skating, skiing, golf, and gymnastics has held steady but has shown little growth. The primary obstacle for all of these sports is the expense of practice and play. While some community programs are available for young people just starting out, elite programs are mandatory for athletes aspiring to higher performance. Various families have estimated that it costs them between $20,000 and $25,000 per year to support one child in an elite program, depending on the sport and the amount of travel required. That figure includes expenses for coaching, equipment, and travel to competition for both the child and a parent chaperone.

IMG Sports Academies

Located in Bradenton on the west coast of Florida is one of the most famous youth sport academies in the world. It began over 30 years ago as the Nick Bollettieri Tennis Academy and has since expanded to include more than a dozen sports. Young people of all ages can come for weekend training or summer camps or can become full-time residents in a variety of sports. The sports currently offered are tennis, golf, soccer, basketball, football, baseball, softball, swimming, and lacrosse. Residents train in their sport every day under the watchful eye of expert coaches and have access to regular competitive play, as well as advice from various sport science experts and performance trainers including sport psychologists. A typical day at the academy is divided into two parts; approximately half the day is spent in academic schooling at the on-site private school, and the other half is spent in sport training.

Young players who aspire to play at a high college level or eventually turn professional are the primary customers for this commercial enterprise. Approximately 80% of academy graduates go on to play collegiate sports, the majority with the aid of an athletic scholarship. The academy helps students locate colleges that would be a good fit, tailored to them and their athletic ability.

Cost to attend the academies averages approximately $1,500 to $2,000 per week for training camps, depending on how many extras players want to tack on. For individual coaching, athletic training, and work with a private sport psychologist, extra fees are added.

Full-time resident boarding students can expect to pay between $42,000 and $53,000 for the sport training and room and board for a school year. School tuition is an additional expense and public schools are not an option, so IMG students must attend a private school or have at-home schooling arranged by their family. Private school tuition is approximately an additional $16,000. The bottom line is you can expect to pay more than $60,000 for the school year to attend the IMG Academies. That price tag exceeds the costs for even the most expensive colleges in the United States. Of course, there are some opportunities for financial aid through scholarships, but it is risky to count on them.

For those select few who choose to attend a sport academy away from home, the tab can come to over $60,000 a year when you add the expenses of room, board, and schooling to the expenses already mentioned. These costs are out of reach for the average family, and only a select few can afford these high-performance programs without risking the family finances (see chapter 13). Some parents are so consumed by the possible pot of gold in professional sport that they are willing to risk everything in hopes that their child will reach payday. Just imagine the pressure children feel when the family finances depend on them (IMG Academies 2010).

A corollary to the dilemma of the finances of high-performance sport programs is that minority and middle-class families are typically underrepresented just because of the cost. That fact tends to produce artificial social environments for players who associate only with other players from families like their own.

Organized Youth Sport

Sport at the youth level is organized by one of two groups: the youths themselves or adults. Both types of organization have shown growth in recent years, and the question is whether one will dominate the other over time.

There are significant differences in the intent of the sport, the application of traditions and rules, the social influences, and the cost depending on which group is organizing the sport. Sports that are organized by adults seem to be more reflective of adult and professional models of sport. They offer kids a glimpse into the adult world of sport and socialize young people into a system that prepares them for continued play in high school, college, and beyond. Sport programs that are organized by young people, on the other hand, are accepted as an end in themselves, offering an opportunity to have fun, enjoy competition, and control the level of involvement, dedication, and control.

Athlete-Organized Sport

Athlete-organized sports include sports and games that developed naturally over the years as children went outside to play. Free from school, parents, and other adult supervision, children choose an activity, agree on the rules, and settle disputes among themselves. Games begin and end by mutual agreement or when the child who provided the equipment decides to go home.

Natural leaders who are often the best players or the oldest kids choose sides. The hurt feelings of those chosen last are ignored, and kids learn where they stand in the evaluation of their peers. The most popular games provide lots of action for every player and flexible rules to mitigate imbalances due to size, age, or experience. For example, younger children who might often strike out in baseball-type games are often given a chance to bat until they actually hit the ball.

Disputes are creatively solved by one side's giving in, negotiating between team leaders, or allowing a certain number of "gimmees" or do-overs during a game. In playground basketball, for example, the team with the ball can often call a foul on the opposing team without the foul's being open to question. Rules are agreed upon before play begins but may be changed by agreement during play. They also often change from game to game depending on the participants. Some sandlot football games are tackle, some are touch, some are two-hand touch, and some are flag. In some pickup basketball games the winners take the ball, while other games give the ball to the loser of the last basket.

The problem of uneven numbers between teams is often solved by having one player serve both teams as pitcher, catcher, or some other position. Girls are accepted as part of games but typically are treated no better or worse than their male counterparts. More skilled athletes typically choose the most active positions crucial to the game such as pitcher, shortstop, quarterback, receiver, goalkeeper, or point guard. Positions are shifted during the game to balance out the action.

The advantages of youth-controlled activity are that young people learn how to work within group dynamics, make decisions, and get along with their peers. As players come and go, lopsided scores develop, or bad feelings arise, players are forced to be creative and flexible if the game is to go on.

As discussed earlier, a more recent trend toward athlete-centered sport has been the rapid rise of alternative sport, including in-line skating, snowboarding, and so on (see page 104 in this chapter). One appeal of these activities is limited adult supervision. Although there are some inherent dangers in these sports, young people are flocking to them as an alternative to traditional sport.

Adult-Organized Sport

At about age 6, many children begin playing soccer, munchkin tennis, T-ball or biddy ball, or flag football in adult-organized programs. Often parents are heavily involved in the practices and games, serving as coaches, partners, pitchers, or base coaches. The rules are modified to suit the ability of the players so that their introduction to the sport is successful. Rules are established to protect the safety of each child, ensure fairness of playing time, and control the length of games.

Since physical development proceeds at different rates, many children are not ready or able to perform precise skills when they enter an organized sport program. Frustration and lack of confidence can easily turn off children for life when pushy parents force them into a no-win situation too early. We often read about champion athletes who started in their sport at age 3 or 4, but clearly they are the exceptions. Plus, who knows what their beginnings in their sport were like? They may have been simply hitting a tennis ball against a wall or playing a game of catch with parents or peers.

Adult-organized sports are primarily concerned with teaching kids the following:

- Skills of the game
- Rules of the game
- Proper playing of positions
- Importance of following adult directions, strategy, and training methods

Adult coaches and parents are usually the key figures who determine the success of the experience. They set the tone and the level of competitiveness, arbitrate rule infractions, determine who plays where and when, and offer encouragement or disapproval. Since their role is so important, several national organizations (e.g., National Alliance for Youth Sports, American Sport Education Program, Institute for the Study of Youth Sports) have been established to offer training for coaches or parents involved in youth sport. The challenge is great since there is a new crop of adults every season to train and educate.

When coaches or parents are not trained, the risk to athletes is great. Lack of knowledge of safety in sport, of healthy competition, and of the emotional needs of children can do real harm. Inability to teach sport-specific skills can slow down the learning process and lead to frustration for the aspiring players. Great strides in coach and parent education have been made, but the task is daunting—nothing is more crucial to ensure a positive experience for kids in adult-controlled youth sport.

Since kids are used to adult instruction and judgment at home and at school, the athletic field seems little different. To be successful, they need to please the adults, conform to the rules of the game, stay in position, and follow the strategy set by the coaches. Failure to do these things usually results in punishment, reprimands, or benching.

Spending time with friends is a key part of youth sport. Trips for pizza or ice cream are often more important than the game results for some kids. Celebrating success with friends produces enthusiasm and reinforcement that keep players coming back. On the other hand, a team that rarely wins a contest needs a wise, creative leader to salve wounded egos and maintain a healthy approach to competition.

If Pete Rozelle, the former commissioner of the NFL, were around to share his wisdom, he would probably advise youth sport leaders to design the competitive balance between teams as he did in the NFL so that every team contends for honors until the end of the season. Parity among teams produces some wins and losses for every team and helps kids learn to deal with both scenarios. Too much winning often produces cockiness and unrealistic expectations. Too much losing undermines confidence, encourages placing blame, and may sustain a self-fulfilling prophecy or defeatist attitude.

Key Role of Parents

Youth sport has the potential to become a terrific, positive influence on family life or a divisive, painful experience for all. Parents need to do some reading, attend orientation sessions, and talk to other parents in order to understand the sport philosophy, policies, and expectations of local sport programs before their children are old enough to participate in sport. That way, when their children come home and say they want to sign up for soccer because their friends are doing so, the parents are armed with information.

If parents get involved as coaches, league officials, or chaperones, chances are they will get a better picture of the experience and be prepared to counsel their child when problems arise. However, once a practice or game is over, parents need to

The most effective coaches at the youth sport level are those who are strong leaders and who have completed training to be a youth sport coach.

let it go and resume normal family life. Kids don't need to feel constant pressure from family about their performance on the ball field. Attending home games as fans, providing transportation to away games, and joining in team celebrations deliver a message of strong parental interest and support. Plus, parents get to meet their child's friends, the team's coaches, and the parents of other kids.

Watching kids play their chosen sport gives parents insight into the type of child they have raised. Rarely do they get to watch their children at school, but on the athletic field they see their children in their peer environment. Many opportunities arise for reinforcing children's attitudes toward teammates, opponents, and adult coaches and officials, as well as good sporting behavior.

If there is more than one child in the family, time and money must be balanced so that each one gets a fair share. By nature, some activities are more expensive than others, but kids need to understand the general expense and appreciate the family commitment.

Parents who take a relaxed view of the importance of competition can relieve the pressure on kids. Parents need to set expectations for good effort, improvement in skill or strategy, healthy physical activity, and cooperation with coaches and teammates. By reinforcing positive actions in these areas, they send a powerful message about what is important in sport and in life.

Finally, most parents whose children have been through the experience of youth sport would counsel parents approaching those years to have fun with them. Before they know it, those precious hours of growth and challenge will be gone for their kids, and they won't get the chance for a do-over.

Why Kids Play—and Stop Playing—Sports

Most kids are first attracted to sport because their friends are involved. The chance to spend time with peers, make new friends, and escape from the adult world (and maybe school or boredom) all factor into the attraction of sport. In addition, kids seem to enjoy the physical challenge of games and activity. In the typical suburban household, friends are separated by geography, and sport offers friends an opportunity to spend time together. There is little

doubt that if children's parents have a favorable attitude toward sport, as most parents do, they are more likely to be encouraged to join a team or a program (SGMA 2001).

Virtually every survey that investigates why kids play sport reveals that they say they enjoy it, especially if they get to play regularly and not sit on the bench. In fact, they would rather play for a team that loses most games if they get to play than be on a team that wins a championship but they don't play much (Harris Interactive 2004). In 1990, the largest study of youths' feelings about sport (over 10,000 students age 10 to 18) was sponsored by the Athletic Footwear Association and conducted by the Youth Sport Institute of Michigan State University. The results showed that the number-one reason young people play sport is to have fun. The top 10

Why do kids like to play sports? Because it's fun!

reasons also included to improve skills, to stay in shape, to do something they're good at, to enjoy the excitement of competition, to be part of a team, and to enjoy the challenge of competition. For many, these reasons are also part of the fun (Ewing and Seefeldt 1990).

Another study suggests that other benefits of participation include growth and maturation effects, increased fitness, improved self-worth, increased social competence, and enhanced moral development (Malina and Cumming 2003).

When sport ceases to be fun, youths are likely to drop out. But what does fun mean to the typical kid? Adults ascribe all types of motivations to young people and tend to try to convince them that having fun means playing like the pros with sharp uniforms, hard work, dedication, and a commitment to success. Conversations with young people, on the other hand, reveal that they are more likely to describe fun as the result of the challenge of the game, the skills they learn, the exercise they get, the time they have to be with friends, and the excitement of competition (Ewing and Seefeldt 1990).

There are also deeper reasons for sport participation other than fun. Gould (1993) suggested that young athletes' perception of their own competence or ability is crucial. If they see their own competence at a low level in comparison to their peers, they tend to become discouraged and drop out of sport.

The most critical time for youth in relation to dropping out of sport is the onset of adolescence at age 11 or 12. By then, they have evaluated their own skill competence and decided whether the activity is fun and how they respond to competition and coaching. The major reasons they drop out of sport are changing interests, interest in another activity, feeling that the sport is no longer fun, or feeling that the coach is a poor teacher or plays favorites (Seefeldt, Ewing, and Walk 1992). Here are some of the key reasons kids stop playing sports (Women's Sports Foundation 2008):

38%	I was not having fun
31%	I wanted to focus more on studying or grades
28%	I had health problems or injury
20%	I did not like or get along with the coach
19%	I wanted to focus more on other clubs or activities
17%	I did not like or get along with other players on the team
16%	I was not a good enough player

13%	My family worried about me getting
13%	hurt or injured while playing sports
12%	I had a job
11%	I had a problem traveling to practices
10%	I had to care for younger brothers or sisters
	My mother or father said I could not play

Young people also reported a variety of negative experiences in sport at the hands of coaches, parents, or teammates (Harris Interactive 2004):

Which of the following experiences have you had during your participation in youth sport?

31%	Saw parents yelling at or arguing with umpires, referees, or officials
30%	Didn't get to play as much as I wanted
28%	Saw parents yelling at or arguing with coaches
27%	Heard coaches or parents use bad language
23%	Had coaches who were too focused on winning
21%	Had teammates who insulted me
18%	Had too many practices
15%	Felt sports were too competitive for me
14%	Felt pressure to play when I was hurt
11%	Had coaches who insulted me
9%	Felt pressure to focus on only one sport
9%	Too much travel to get to games
2%	Was physically hit by an adult

Burnout in Youth Sport

Burnout is simply a natural reaction to chronic stress in young athletes. Kids who have burned out seek to reduce the stress by withdrawing from the sport. If they know that their parents and coaches will be disappointed in them, the stress is simply heightened and they may feel forced to take drastic measures such as faking an injury or illness. In fact, the pressure they feel may actually produce an illness.

Stress isn't all bad; we often learn valuable life lessons from dealing with stressful situations. Consider the stress of being the last batter in a baseball game when your team is down in the score, there are runners on base, and there are two outs. Sure, the batter and pitcher feel stress, but the one who

ACTIVITY TIME-OUT

Keeping Kids in the Game

While it would seem that in the United States we are enticing the majority of youth to at least try youth sports, we are not very successful in keeping most of them active through their teenage years and beyond. It seems that only the most intense and dedicated kids stick with sport as they get older. What strategies can you suggest that might keep kids physically active or involved in sport (or both) throughout their teenage years and early adulthood?

comes out on top gains confidence. The one who suffers in this situation may learn from his mistake, and at least he'll know that his friends, teammates, and coaches still value him as a player if they are smart.

Still, too much stress can creep into youth sport and may eventually lead to burning out and then dropping out. Athletes who worry too much about outcomes of games, have performance anxiety or low self-esteem, or believe that their parents attach too much importance to games may be at risk for burnout. Year-round sport programs, specializing in one sport at a young age, overdoing physical training, long practices, too many games without days off, and overemphasis on winning all contribute to feelings that sport is no longer fun.

Parents and coaches need to learn how to listen to kids and address potential burnout symptoms before they are irreversible. According to Waldron (2000), the signs include feelings, thoughts, behaviors, and physical symptoms. Specifically, observers may notice that players feel anxious or moody; often mention thoughts about mental errors or lack of attention; cry easily or bite their nails; or experience physical symptoms like headaches, upset stomachs, or a racing pulse.

Youth sport organizers and coaches must become sensitive to signs of burnout by learning about the effects of stress on youngsters and must be prepared to deal with the causes or refer the athletes to others with more training. The scars from a negative sport experience can turn happy, well-adjusted kids into withdrawn, unhappy kids. Parents also need to learn to recognize when kids are showing signs of burnout, which may include avoiding practice or games, never smiling, frequent physical ailments, lack of caring about performance, emotional outbursts, or other behavior that is atypical for that child. Once burnout is suspected, intervention by trained professionals may be necessary to plot a path back to normalcy that may or may not include the particular sport.

Sport psychologists who are trained in dealing with youth sport problems are likely the best source of help. They may be able to teach athletes, parents, and coaches specific strategies to combat the feelings of burnout if the damage is not too extensive. Certainly they will be able to help young athletes reassess their reasons for playing their sport and work toward a healthier approach that includes physical activity and perhaps other sports (Gould 1993; Smith 1986; Weinberg and Gould 2005).

Dropping Out Due to Burnout

Burnout can often lead young athletes to drop out of sport. According to Ronald Smith, professor of psychology at the University of Washington, "The No. 1 reason kids drop out of sports is: It's not fun. The next five reasons all have to do with parents' or coaches' behaviors" (Condor 2004, p. 2). Drawing from the sources cited previously in this chapter, here are a few common mistakes parents make that lead children to burn out and potentially drop out of sport:

- Choosing a sport that they like rather than allowing the child to decide after trying several activities.

- Insisting that a child follow one sport season with another, when the child may just want a little free time for a change.

- Putting too much emphasis on the results of competition. For example, the first thing parents often ask is "Did you win?" That question conveys the message to their child that winning is the most important thing.

- Forcing a child to compete even at the risk of physical injury from overuse of certain parts of the body.

- Becoming overinvolved in the game or team. When parents say "*We've* got a game tomorrow," they're too wrapped up in the child's sport.
- Arguing with officials, parents from opposing teams, or coaches.
- Not reinforcing the positive experiences children are looking for from sport, such as learning new skills, staying active, being with friends, achieving independence, and improving self-confidence.
- Pushing children to the next level of competition even when they resist.

Coaches of youth sport may be parents, volunteers, or paid professionals. One major concern with youth coaching is the lack of standardized training; a second concern is the rapid turnover of coaches and the continual need for training of new coaches. Based on the recommendations of the American Sport Education Program and other youth sport organizations such as the Youth Sports Institute of Michigan State, here are some of the common mistakes youth coaches need to avoid:

- Emphasizing winning rather than building skills and improving performance
- Spending more time on and allocating more playing time to more skilled athletes at the expense of average or below-average players
- Expecting kids to absorb rules and strategy that may be too advanced for their level of development in terms of understanding or skill
- Using physical punishment as discipline
- Arguing with officials or parents in inappropriate ways
- Neglecting to create an atmosphere of fun for practices or games
- Expecting families to sacrifice time, money, and priorities for the sport team
- Encouraging kids to specialize in one sport at an early age to the exclusion of other sports or school-related activities
- Using an authoritarian coaching style or imitating the coaching style of coaches of professional athletes

In addition to coaches, youth sport administrators include league organizers, publicity staff, governing board members, officials, and sponsors. All have an important role to play for a youth sport league to be successful, and they can even have a detrimental effect if their vision is not clear and the league policies are not set in writing for anyone to examine. According to the experts cited previously (Ewing and Seefeldt 1990; Weinberg and Gould 2005), typical issues concerning league-affiliated adults include the following:

- Failing to establish a philosophy for the league from which policies naturally follow
- Failing to communicate the philosophy and policies to parents, coaches, and players through training days, newsletters, and websites
- Putting too much emphasis on winning, play-offs, and all-star squads rather than a healthy program for all kids
- Requiring an unrealistic financial commitment from families, particularly those who have several children competing at the same time
- Extending seasons by having preseason, postseason, and off-season programs that force kids to choose between one sport and other activities
- Lacking proper safety procedures, training for coaches, and support from medical personnel to deal with emergencies and chronic health problems of players
- Failing to provide safe, clean, and attractive facilities for practices and games
- Adopting a casual attitude toward the hiring and training of league coaches and officials
- Failing to balance the level of competition between teams to facilitate excitement

Elite Teams and Burnout

An article that appeared on June 7, 2004, in *U.S. News and World Report* was titled "Fixing Kids' Sports: Rescuing Children's Games from Crazed Coaches and Parents" (Cary 2004). The article relied heavily on an interview with Fred Engh, the founder of the National Alliance for Youth Sports, who has spent a lifetime trying to educate youth sport leaders on the need to make team sport "less pressurized, safer, and more child friendly." He created a training manual for coaches, and his organization has certified over 2.1 million volunteer coaches. But Engh realizes his accomplishments aren't enough. He extols the virtues of training everyone involved, including parents, administrators, and officials.

One of the major problems described in the article is the phenomenon of so-called travel teams, in which kids who are judged to be above average are placed on club, select, or elite teams to travel to nearby towns for tournaments or games. These teams often practice twice a week, play two games a week, and absorb participants' time every weekend. Parents usually provide the transportation by car pooling.

The pitch to families is that if kids don't join one of these elite teams, their chances of making high school varsity teams is diminished considerably. If they fall behind their peers in skill development, they'll never catch up. Of course, Michael Jordan and many more like him have proved that you don't even have to make your high school team to go on to play professionally. Jordan got cut from his high school team in ninth grade!

Too much emphasis on playing just one sport can lead to miserable kids. In the misguided attempt by league officials and parents to make their kids more competitive, traditional seasons are extended into year-round programs. Baseball is extended into fall and winter seasons in warm climates; basketball is year round; tennis and golf are stocked with one-sport athletes; and swimmers hit the pool for workouts regardless of the month on the calendar. The potential results of this overspecialization at a young age include the following (Wendel 2005):

- Kids lose interest and playing is no longer fun, simply due to overexposure.
- When kids hit a performance barrier in their sport of choice, there are no other sports to turn to for activity.
- Friends tend to be limited to those they associate with on a daily basis in their sport.
- Complementary athletic skills that might be developed by cross-training in other sports are neglected.

One way to prevent burnout in youth sport athletes is to encourage them to try many different sports rather than focusing exclusively on just one sport.

- Kids are not exposed to a variety of coaching and training methods.
- Overuse injuries occur due to repeated stress demands of one sport.

Pressure builds on kids and families to commit time, money, and long seasons and off-seasons to one sport. Private instruction and summer sport camps add to the expense and pressure. If more than one sibling is involved, families are forced to juggle time, transportation, and finances.

Some parents justify their actions by saying, "I know the chances of my kid making the pros are small, I just want to give them a chance to earn a college scholarship." However, if you pay between $10,000 and $20,000 per year, as many families do, for one child in swimming, tennis, skating, or another sport, wouldn't it make a lot more sense to invest that money in a college savings plan? There's no guarantee that athletic scholarships will even be available in the sport in the next 10 years as colleges trim budgets and support scholarships only for revenue-producing sports.

Reforms for Youth Sport

Now that we have traced the history of youth sport and considered some of the current issues, perhaps you believe changes should be made. It's natural to try to improve an experience for children, whether it involves education or recreation. Kids need to be able to adjust to the world they will live in, not the one we lived in the past. Different skills are needed, new experiences should be embraced, and opportunities for positive social experiences through sport activity should be eagerly sought.

A society's core values tend to endure, and those for youth sport are no exception. Kids want to participate in sport programs that are designed to be a fun, positive experience and those in which they can invest energy and enthusiasm. In 1979, two leaders in youth sport training, Rainer Martens and Vern Seefeldt, developed the Bill of Rights for Young Athletes (see figure 6.1 on page 116) in response to growing concern about abuse of young athletes (Martens and Seefeldt 1979). This seminal work is still used and is available from many sport organizations.

Based on the bill of rights in figure 6.1, it is clear that there are some concerns that must be addressed in youth sport. Earlier in the chapter, we outlined some of the typical characteristics of adult-controlled youth sport, which obviously conflict with some of the rights listed here. It is likely that many local community programs do not exhibit all the characteristics of adult-centered sport or all those of athlete-centered sport but fall somewhere in between. If the athlete's bill of rights is accepted and implemented, the experience of youth sport will be enhanced for all children.

The keen interest in youth sport in the United States has spawned various organizations to provide educational services to coaches, parents, and officials. Perhaps the most inclusive organization is the National Council of Youth Sports (NCYS), a multisport corporation established to foster the continued education of youth sport administrators and to support the growth and development of young people through participation in organized youth sport. The NCYS represents more than 185 organizations and corporations and 60 million registered participants, or over 44 million actual boys and girls. By its estimates, the total number of coaches involved in youth sport is 2.4 million, and the number of volunteers has ballooned to 7.6 million. When added together, over 55 million kids and adults are involved together in youth sport programs (National Council of Youth Sports 2010).

Building on past work, the National Alliance for Youth Sports developed National Standards for Youth Sports (www.nays.org). These standards are available nationally for all youth sport program, parents, and participants. They address the most timely topics that affect the delivery of youth sport programs. These are the nine standards:

- Quality sport environment
- Sport participation should be fun and a portion of a child's life
- Training and accountability
- Screening process
- Parents' commitment
- Sportsmanship
- Safe playing environment
- Equal play opportunity
- Drug, tobacco, alcohol, and performance enhancer–free environment

Finally, you should be aware of the American Sport Education Program (ASEP), which was established in 1981 and has focused on the development and implementation of coaching education courses and resources. The program's leadership in offering online educational courses and certification for coaches provides a delivery system that reaches nationally to all youth sport programs and coaches (www.asep.com).

Athletes' Bill of Rights

1. Right to participate in sports.

2. Right to participate at a level commensurate with each child's maturity and ability.

3. Right to have qualified adult leadership.

4. Right to play as a child and not as an adult.

5. Right of children to share in the leadership and decision making of their sport participation.

6. Right to participate in safe and healthy environments.

7. Right to proper preparation for participation in sports.

8. Right to an equal opportunity to strive for success.

9. Right to be treated with dignity.

10. Right to have fun in sports.

Figure 6.1 Bill of rights for young athletes.

Guidelines for children's sports, 1979, reprinted with permission from the National Association for Sport and Physical Education (NASPE), 1900 Association Drive, Reston, VA, 20191-1599.

Based on the research on the current issues in youth sport, here are some modifications that could be considered:

- Increase public funding of open fields and other facilities to support youth sport activities.

- Use community funding to supplement organizations that sponsor youth sport to provide after-school programs that are safe, affordable, and supervised by knowledgeable adults.

- Limit specialization in one sport at an early age, and encourage kids to sample several sports when they are young, in order to broaden their athletic development and choice of activities as they mature.

- Insist on continuous coaching certification programs for volunteer and paid coaches alike.

- Offer and support sport programs at various levels of skill, commitment, and intensity, allowing parents and children to choose the level that fits the child.

- Offer affordable high-performance programs to kids who demonstrate the athletic talent and desire a more intense program. Currently, these programs seem to be limited to athletes from more affluent families.

- Provide funding to make sport programs available to children of all economic, racial, and ethnic backgrounds.
- Ensure equal opportunities for both girls and boys.

Recent news decries the lack of physical activity and the increasing rise in obesity among people of all ages. Although we seem to be getting many children started in the right direction of fitness for life, we shut down their progress just as they enter adolescence. Youth sport seems to be more of an elimination process, selecting the most talented kids for later sport participation in high school and banning those with less talent, motivation, and drive to a life without organized sport.

Should we be organizing and promoting community-based activities that attract youths who do not play interscholastic sport? Should these programs be oriented toward lifetime activities such as self-defense or martial arts, tennis, volleyball, aerobic fitness, golf, and swimming? Offering these sports as coed activities would certainly increase the appeal.

Chapter Summary

In this chapter we looked at the relatively recent historical development of youth sport and examined the reasons for growth. We also considered the current status of youth sport in terms of participation and popularity. The organizations that sponsor youth sport were identified and differences in program emphasis were considered.

The characteristics and popularity of sport programs that are organized by adults compared with those organized by the athletes themselves were described and analyzed. Regardless of who organizes sport programs, it is clear that many programs have problems and shortcomings that need to be dealt with. The recent rapid rise in alternative sport was noted and reasons for that phenomenon were explored.

Differences among various sports were described, and the relative popularity trends for each sport were examined. Although overall participation continues to increase, there are troubling questions about affordability, time requirements, dropout rates, and coaches' training in youth sport.

We spent time discussing what kids say they want out of sport programs and comparing their needs to the offerings of adult-designed programs. One major theme that emerged from kids is that they want sport to be fun. However, it seems that *fun* can mean quite different things to different people depending on their motivation for participation and their individual needs.

Finally, we considered whether changes to youth sport are needed and what the likely challenges are for the future. Issues were identified and possible solutions suggested. Overall, youth sport programs seem to receive the approval of most parents, coaches, and players. However, this does not mean that significant improvements cannot be made, starting with the needs and rights of children for healthy physical activity and recreation.

7

Interscholastic and Intercollegiate Sport

Student Outcomes

After reading this chapter, you will know the following:

- The connection between sport and education at the high school and college levels
- The trends of interscholastic sport, including positive and negative effects
- The trends of intercollegiate sport, including positive and negative effects
- Challenges facing sport in educational settings and possible changes

Friday nights are crazy in the state of Texas. That's when students, athletes, parents, and entire communities gather in anticipation of their high school football teams competing for pride and boasting rights for their town. No other state has a tradition quite like it, with folks of every age knowledgeable and passionate about their high school sports. Although Texas high school football stadiums would be the envy of most schools around the country, near the end of seasons and for play-offs, most games are played in college or professional stadiums simply because of the size of the crowd. Can you believe that the top 10 high school football games in Texas history range in figures for fans of 36,000 to over 50,000? In fact, in 2006, Southlake Carroll edged out Euless Trinity 22-21 with an announced crowd of 43,339 looking on, although observers put the crowd at over 60,000 strong midway through the third quarter (McMurray 2010).

Texas high school football was vividly shared with the rest of the country with the publication of a novel by H.G. Bissinger titled *Friday Night Lights*. The book traced the football season of 1988 of the Odessa Permian Panthers and the effect of the football team on the entire population of Odessa. The success of the book led to a popular movie released in 2004 and a television series which began in 2006, both with the same name.

Perhaps Texas is indeed a bit different from other parts of the country, but high school sports all over the United States continue to grow and expand. And the best performers go on to big-time collegiate programs to showcase their skills and hope eventually to earn millions of dollars in the professional ranks. It all starts in youth leagues and continues in high school, in college, and onward.

In the last century, sport has become an important fixture in virtually all high schools and colleges. Conventional wisdom is that sport helps complete the education of young people by emphasizing the development of physical talents, a healthy work ethic, and a moral code and attitude that conform to the expectations of society.

College athletics had a modest start with a rowing contest between students from Harvard and Yale in 1852. At first, sports were run entirely by students for their entertainment and benefit. As years went by, that system became supplanted by one that seems to benefit the school, alumni, and student body at large, with questionable benefits for some of the high-profile athletes.

Interscholastic sport soon followed the trend set by college sport programs. Leaders in high school education supported sport programs as a means of raising youth fitness levels, which were judged to be alarmingly low during World War I. They also felt that students would learn the value of hard work, citizenship, and good sporting behavior.

School-based sport became so popular that athletes were the most admired students in school. One might think that in an educational setting, those who performed best in academic work would be the most admired. However, various replicated studies have shown that athletes were most popular with peers while bright students who were nonathletes ranked ahead of students who were both bright and studious (Eitzen and Sage 1978; Hechinger 1980). Apparently it is acceptable to be a brilliant student as long as you don't work at it; conversely, athletes are admired for talent and their work ethic.

Perhaps the difference is that athletic success benefits the team, and indirectly the whole school, while academic success seems more self-centered. Another factor is that major athletic events are often key social occasions at which students congregate, flirt with one another, discuss life, and rally around their school's team. Particularly for boys who play highly visible sports like football and basketball, performance enhances status.

Student culture at the typical American high school values athletic achievement and usually confers status on successful athletes as admired members of the "in group." Likewise, popular students are usually members of an exclusive clique that may be based on economic status, appearance, and dress or possession of material things such as a cool car. Academic standouts are often the butt of jokes and left out of the social group.

In the last 25 years, the status of athletes has changed dramatically with the entry of girls into the athletic arena. Many of the most successful athletes are also top students and popular with their peers. These changes have affected the prescription for social success for girls in high school from one that emphasized femininity, cheerleading, domestic aptness, and appearance to one

■ Why do you think athletic success is viewed as better for a school than academic success?

that supports girls as students, athletes, and all-around achievers.

Intercollegiate athletics presents a different picture from that of the typical high school. First, the number of students who qualify for athletic teams in college dwindles dramatically compared to those who can play on high school teams. Second, the type of school and the way the institution views the athletic program have a huge impact on the philosophy and conduct of college sport. Big-time athletic programs labeled as Division I by the National Collegiate Athletic Association (NCAA) emphasize winning, entertainment, and revenue-producing sports. These programs make little apology for appearing to operate more as a professional sport model than an educational one. Conversely, hundreds of smaller colleges' athletic teams purport to offer students an opportunity to develop their physical skills just as other students develop their skills in drama, music, art, and other extracurricular activities.

Sport in the educational setting is a phenomenon that is stronger in the United States than in any other country in the world. Most other countries offer sport programs that are community based and supported by sport clubs in towns and cities. Education is seen as a separate endeavor, and athletics are not intertwined with education. The American trend has likely produced both positive and negative consequences for society, depending on your point of view.

Interscholastic Sport

For the purpose of this discussion, high school sport covers grades 9 through 12, although in many schools gifted athletes in seventh or eighth grade are eligible to play on high school teams. At the national level, the National Federation of State High School Associations (NFHS) provides education; publishes rules for sport competition, information, and research; and provides guidance to the state associations (www.nfhs.org). Sport at both public and private schools is typically governed by local leagues and the state association to which they pay dues. They adhere to the rules established by the state association and therefore are eligible for regional and state play-offs. Some states separate public and private schools at state competitions, especially when private schools have consistently won state titles.

In this section, we'll take a look at trends in high school sport participation, reasons high school athletes choose to participate as well as reasons they stop participating, how high school sport and community-sponsored sport interact, and some positive and negative aspects of high school athletics.

Participation Trends

According to the NFHS, the number of students participating in high school athletics has increased for 20 consecutive years (see figure 7.1), and in 2008-2009 participation reached an all-time high. The total number of students who participated in 2008-2009 was 7,536,753. That number represents 55.2% of the total enrollment in schools that play varsity sports (NFHS 2009b). In addition, boys' and girls' participation figures reached all-time highs, with 3,114,091 girls and 4,422,662 boys participating in 2008-2009. The girls' and boys' figures surpassed their highest participation totals set in the previous year. The state of Texas has more athletes competing in high school sports than any other state, with 781,000 participants. Surprisingly, Texas edged out California for the top spot in spite of the fact that California has a total population of approximately 12 million more citizens than Texas. In third place was New York, followed by Illinois, Ohio, Pennsylvania, Michigan, and New Jersey rounding out the top states (SGMAb).

Consider that in 1971-1972, only 294,015 girls played high school sports compared with 3,666,917 boys. Following the passage of Title IX and its mandatory rules for providing equal opportunity for both genders, girls flocked to the fields and courts. Today the balance is toward boys, but it reflects tremendous growth for girls.

The largest gains in 2008-2009 for girls and boys combined was in swimming and diving, with an increase of 29,987 participants, followed by outdoor track and field with 19,396 and cross country with an additional 18,193 participants. Lacrosse, one of the emerging sports in recent years, had an additional 9,579 participants.

The most popular sports as measured by the number of teams rather than participants show some interesting results. The top five sports for boys in order of popularity are basketball, track and field, baseball, football and cross country. For girls, the top five in order are basketball, track and field, fast-pitch softball, volleyball, and cross country. Soccer is seventh in popularity for boys while continuing to gain popularity among girls, having moved into sixth place for girls.

In terms of actual number of participants, the most popular sport for boys continues to be 11-player football, followed by track and field, basketball, baseball, and soccer. Keep in mind that football teams typically attract and accommodate much larger numbers of participants than a sport such as basketball. For girls, track and field took over the top spot from basketball, followed in order by volleyball, fast-pitch softball, and soccer.

According to the NFHS, the most popular sports for high school students in number of participants in 2008-2009 were as follows (NFHS 2009b):

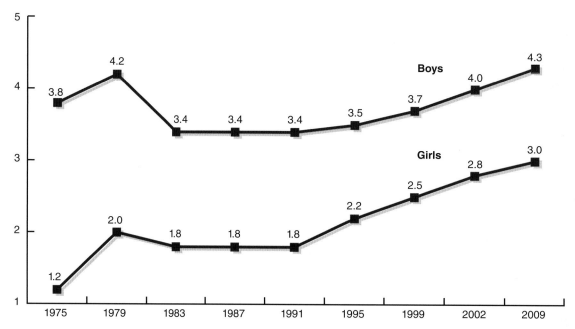

Figure 7.1 Boys and girls participating in high school varsity sport from 1975 through 2009. Numbers are shown in millions of participants.

Data from NFHS 2008-2009.

Girls

1. Track and field (outdoor) — 457,732
2. Basketball — 444,809
3. Volleyball — 404,243
4. Softball (fast pitch) — 368,921
5. Soccer — 344,634
6. Cross country — 198,199
7. Tennis — 177,593
8. Swimming and diving — 158,876
9. Competitive spirit squads — 117,793
10. Golf — 69,223

Boys

1. Football (11 player) — 1,112,303
2. Track and field (outdoor) — 558,007
3. Basketball — 545,145
4. Baseball — 473,184
5. Soccer — 383,824
6. Wrestling — 267,376
7. Cross country — 231,452
8. Tennis — 157,165
9. Golf — 157,062
10. Swimming and diving — 130,182

It is interesting to note that if you eliminated over a million boys who play football, the overall numbers for boys and girls would be about equal. This issue has been a consistent point of debate, in both high school and college, in terms of interpreting the intentions of Title IX. We will revisit this point in chapter 12, which deals with gender and sport.

Another factor to consider when evaluating participation levels is that many sports by definition require fewer athletes to field a team. In many schools, numbers are limited to reduce expenses of playing space, uniforms, games, and coaches. Large squads are necessary for sports like track and field, soccer, swimming, and football. Smaller squads are required for cross country, golf, tennis, basketball, and volleyball. Most schools limit the number of participants in these sports. However, there may have been great interest on the part of more athletes to play those sports had there been room.

Reasons for Sport Participation

In the landmark survey American Youth and Sports Participation (Ewing and Seefeldt 1990) cited in the previous chapter on youth sport, a sampling of approximately 4,000 students in grades 7 to 12 reported the reasons they played their best school sport:

Boys

1. To have fun
2. To improve skills
3. For the excitement of competition
4. To do something I'm good at
5. To stay in shape
6. For the challenge of competition
7. To be part of a team
8. To win
9. To go to a higher level of competition
10. To get exercise
11. To learn new skills
12. For the team spirit

Girls

1. To have fun
2. To stay in shape
3. To get exercise
4. To improve skills
5. To do something I'm good at
6. To be part of a team
7. For the excitement of competition
8. To learn new skills
9. For the team spirit
10. For the challenge of competition
11. To go to a higher level of competition
12. To win

In the same study, a sample of 5,800 athletes in grades 7 to 12 who had recently stopped playing a school sport or a nonschool sport admitted they would play again if the following conditions were met:

1. If practices were more fun
2. If I could play more
3. If coaches understood players better
4. If there was no conflict with studies
5. If there was no conflict with social life
6. If coaches were better teachers

Although these generalizations are important for school officials, parents, and coaches to consider, not all students have the same motivations for playing sports in school. The study divided athletes into three groups based on their motivation.

- *Reluctant participants.* Approximately 25% felt they had to be in sport because of outside pressure. They joined because of current friends and in hopes of making new friends. They were less willing to play and practice hard. They were likely candidates to drop out along the way.

- *Image-conscious socializers.* This group represents about 40% of athletes and includes many good athletes. These athletes draw motivation from rewards or the approval of others. They like being perceived as good athletes, feeling important, winning trophies, being popular, staying in shape, and looking good. They may stick with school sports but are unlikely to be lifelong athletes.

- *Competence oriented.* Athletes in this group love playing sports and are likely to continue after their school days are over. They work hard, practice intensely, and play hard to improve their skills. Sport provides a means of self-achievement that they enjoy.

Partnerships With Community-Based Programs

Most communities whose high school varsity teams have enjoyed success can point with pride to a community program that feeds their athletic teams. The wise coach who aspires to build a dynasty and ensure the popularity of a sport will get involved in youth sport programs to make sure that kids are introduced to the sport in their formative years. As young people enter high school, the coach then has the luxury of selecting athletes who have a strong background in the skills and strategies of the sport rather than having to teach them as beginning players.

In the summer, many community programs hire high school varsity athletes as coaches of youth sport programs. This helps strengthen the link between the high school and the community program. The varsity athletes act as role models for

Many studies have supported the theory that high school athletics are a positive force in students' lives. What benefits do you see to high school athletics?

younger children and can motivate them to try to achieve varsity status as they mature.

Many towns across the United States consistently produce generations of high-performing athletes in certain sports. The tradition often starts with an enthusiastic high school coach who establishes and supports a community youth sport program. Year after year, kids graduate from the youth program and fill positions when players are lost to graduation. The head coach looks like a genius, but the key to success was simply giving time and effort to young participants in the sport.

Positive and Negative Effects of Interscholastic Sport

A host of studies have supported the positive benefits of high school sport. Typically these studies have been conducted by school systems or other organizations such as the NFHS. Relying on data collected from athletes, principals, and parents, the studies make the case for the value of athletics as an educational endeavor.

The NFHS has summarized this research on its website in "The Case for High School Activities" (NFHS 2004). The site quotes research that supports the value of athletics in promoting academic performance, moral development, good citizenship, graduation rates, success in college, better attendance and graduation rates, fewer behavioral problems, higher achievement motivation, and resistance to drug and alcohol abuse. Leadership skills, decision making, social integration, and improved self-image are also mentioned as positive outcomes.

Some of the studies cited in the NFHS summary offered the following conclusions. Over two-thirds of parents support the value of cocurricular activities, including sport, according to the 29th annual Phi Delta Kappa–Gallup Poll of the Public's Attitudes Toward Public Schools. The Women's Sports Foundation has consistently supported the benefits of high school sport for young women, including physical fitness, resistance to eating disorders, social acceptance, and academic success. Finally, more than three-quarters of high school principals are strong supporters of high school athletics, according to a study supported by a grant from the Lilly Endowment of Indianapolis and conducted by Indiana University in cooperation with the Association of Secondary School Principals. Both of these conclusions are cited in an NFHS summary (NFHS 2004).

Influence of Athletics on Academic Performance

High school students who participate in athletics tend to have higher grade point averages, better attendance records, and lower dropout rates than the general student body. This conclusion has been drawn in various studies by the Women's Sports Foundation (1989); NFHS (2004); and the states of Wyoming, North Carolina, Colorado, and New Mexico (Texas University Interscholastic League 1998).

Clearly there is strong support for interscholastic athletics from virtually every segment of the U.S. population. Sport as an educational experience continues to be a critical factor in the personal development of young people, and coaches must not lose sight of that goal if they hope to retain broad support of their programs.

However, a fair and comprehensive analysis of high school sport reveals both positive and negative effects of participation. One negative effect (which we'll discuss later in this chapter) is the possibility of creating disunity within the student body when athletes form cliques. Cocurricular sport is not for every student, although for some, it may be a critical factor in self-confidence, social acceptance, and physical development. High school athletics also have an influence on peer groups and the functioning of the student body, and hard choices often have to be made about how to finance athletic programs.

Character Development Through Athletic Participation

Supporters of high school sport have trumpeted its value in helping young people develop a strong work ethic, good moral behavior, healthy attitudes toward fitness, and improved academic performance. Let's see if those claims have been backed up by research.

Studies such as those by Dworkin, Larson, and Hansen (2003) and Gibbons, Ebbeck, and Weiss (1995) often compare the performance and attitudes of high school athletes to those of nonathletes and purport to demonstrate that athletes are superior to nonathletes in the traits just mentioned. However, what is not clear from the research is whether athletes already possessed these traits due to other influences in their life or if in fact athletics was a major contributing factor. Simply reporting that athletes appear to have higher levels of physical, social, or moral development compared to nonathletes does not prove that there is a cause-and-effect relationship between athletes' experience in sport and their academic performance, attitude toward fitness, moral behavior, and work ethic.

It is possible that athletes already display more progress toward a higher standard in these traits, and this progress helps them to perform successfully on athletic teams. Studies such as those by Fejgin (1994) and Rees and Miracle (2004) have followed students over time and measured student performance. Generally, these studies showed that athletes are more likely to come from economically privileged backgrounds and have above-average cognitive skills, self-esteem, and academic performance. Of course it is also possible that students who are less privileged or weak in cognitive skills withdraw from sport or are excluded because of poor grades, thus affecting the results of such studies. These results are not that different from research findings on all students who participate in extracurricular activities in school. In general, students who choose to join musical groups, drama, debate clubs, school newspapers, and so on also show higher levels of development than the bulk of the student body.

Adults who have gone on to success in business or a profession often attribute their success to lessons they learned on the playing field. From their point of view, sport participation is vital for success in later life. A 1987 survey of individuals at the level of executive vice president or above in Fortune 500 companies indicated that 95% had participated in high school sport while 54% were involved in student government, 43% in the National Honor Society, 37% in music, and 18% in their school's publications. It is possible that those people would have been successful regardless of their sport experience, but their personal belief and testimony can be a powerful argument (Texas University Interscholastic League 1998).

Female business executives have been particularly influenced by their sport participation. Two-thirds of them report that they exercise regularly, which is almost double the percentage of women in the general population. More than four out of five (82%) female business executives played sports growing up—and the vast majority of them say lessons learned on the playing field have helped them succeed in business. The following are some specific examples as of this writing (Jones 2002):

- eBay CEO Meg Whitman played lacrosse and squash at Princeton.

- Mrs. Field's Cookies founder Debbi Fields is an avid equestrian.

- Spherion CEO Cinda Hallman, one of only six females who are CEOs of Fortune 500 companies, was a basketball guard in high school in Arkansas.

- Sue Wellington, president of Gatorade division of Quaker Oats, was captain of Yale's swim team.

- Melissa Payner, CEO of Spiegel Catalog, was a collegiate gymnast.

Most studies of high school students in sport have focused on the years of their participation. However, a comprehensive study by Carlson and Scott (2005) tracked over 25,000 high school athletes eight years after their senior year to see if sport participation had had any lasting effects. The results showed that high school athletes are more likely than nonathletes to participate in physical fitness activities or recreational sport, graduate from college, be employed full-time, and earn a higher salary and are less likely to be smokers. The most

 POP CULTURE

Television Show "Glee" Hits the Mark

Fox network's musical comedy "Glee" was the most popular new show on television for the 2009-2010 season. Along the way the show has earned four Emmy awards and numerous other plaudits while drawing a television audience of 13.6 million in April of 2010. "Glee" features cheerleading coach Sue Sylvester who is in a constant battle with the Glee Club for school funding and priority. She uses her cheerleading students to harass and bully various glee club members, particularly Rachel. Rachel joins the Glee club to improve her popularity and soon finds herself dating the quarterback of the football team. Before long, she's subjected to bullying tactics by members of the football team along with various cheerleaders. Although the music on the show makes attractive viewing, it's likely the typical social tug-of-war that we all experienced in high school really helps this show work (Fox News 2010c; *New York Daily News* 2010).

glaring negative factor associated with athletic participation was a tendency toward binge drinking. These results confirmed the conclusions of earlier studies (Barber, Eccles, and Stone 2001) showing higher rates of drinking and binge drinking among athletes compared to nonathletes.

Social Effects on the Student Body

In thousands of high schools, sport promotes school spirit; creates an "us against them" mentality; and offers natural social gatherings at pep rallies, sport events, and ceremonies. Attendance at sport events to root for friends and acquaintances strengthens the bonds between groups of students. Athletic teams often support each other by visiting each other's practices or games and cheering each other on.

Educators would point out that athletics are not the only school activity that has positive effects like these. In fact, the NFHS, mentioned previously, does not concern itself solely with interscholastic sport but also includes all cocurricular activities. Its website devotes significant space to reasons to support all school-based cocurricular activities. For example, music and drama organizations often perform similar functions in after-school settings. Altogether, school activities outside of the academic curriculum cost an average of 1% to 3% of the overall school budget, according to the NFHS (2004). However, across the United States, parents and communities have supported athletics more generously than any other school activity simply because of the number of students involved, the number of games, and the travel expenses incurred (Brady and Giler 2004b).

The social fabric of a school can also be negatively affected by the division between students who play sports and those who do not. Because athletes spend so much time together, are admired by other students, and receive plaudits from the community and media, they tend to socialize together, sometimes to the exclusion of other students. When the jock culture separates itself from the student body at large, envy and mistrust often set in. Some misguided athletes interpret their social standing to mean that deviant behavior on their part is acceptable, and various offenses by prominent athletes often hit the front pages of local newspapers with tales of poor judgment and errant behavior.

When a school is faced with a budget crunch, is it fair to make students pay to play? What if a family can't afford this expense? What is the solution?

Since many students envy athletes, particularly males, the emphasis on academic performance may suffer somewhat for all students. In spite of the fact that athletes seem to be on average better students than the norm, students who excel in the classroom are regarded as nerds in social circles. Fortunately, there are many examples of students who do well both in academics and athletics. This has been particularly true of female athletes.

Gender equity has transformed the scene in local high schools by including girls in the athletic culture. Young women now have many of the same opportunities for self-development, competitive training, recognition, and college athletic scholarships that formerly were restricted to young men. Girls have to learn to balance academics, sport, and their social life in a way that didn't exist before the passage of Title IX in the 1970s. Conflicts between generations, tradition, and a society that used to encourage women solely toward a nurturing role in

life have been inevitable. Girls are faced with acting as gutsy, tough competitors on the athletic field and then resuming a more traditional feminine role in their social environment where they are supposed to focus on clothes, personal appearance, and boys. For some girls, the challenge is intimidating; and they often lack role models in teachers or parents because earlier generations simply did not have the same experiences.

Financial Issues

In recent years, as school districts faced mounting budget crises, they often offered interscholastic sport and other extracurricular activities as areas to be cut, eliminated, or subsidized with user fees. An article by Brady and Giler in *USA Today* (2004a) recounted the dilemma in Fairfield, Ohio, where voters were asked to approve a higher tax levy with a budget increase that would support extracurricular activities, including sport. The tax levy was voted down, and fees for all after-school activities were put in place. A parents' group was organized to raise money to help support the activities, but they are having a tough time meeting the costs of the programs. Kids who choose a sport or other cocurricular activity have to pay a participation fee ranging from $100 to over $1,000 for some sports.

Fairfield's experience is not unique. The *USA Today* survey of states revealed that schools in 34 states charge for after-school activities, including sport (Brady and Giler 2004a). By 2009, the number of states that reported at least some schools charging fees was 33 compared to 18 in which schools charged no fees (NFHS 2009a). The numbers increased during the 1980s and 1990s as school budgets became tighter. Most often, the fees are levied in suburban towns where parents are used to paying for their children to play youth sport. Most schools that charge fees have waivers for those who can demonstrate an inability to pay.

It is easy to see that a family with several children who want to play multiple sports in public schools could easily be faced with a bill of several thousand dollars a year. The reality of this prospect is that eventually only middle- and upper-class students would be able to play sports. In many schools that charge fees for participation in sport, the number of athletes has dropped as much as 30% (Brady and Giler 2004b). This certainly conflicts with the prevailing educational policy for public schools of providing equal opportunity for children from all income levels in the United States.

Funding for cocurricular activities typically consumes only 1% to 3% of the total education budget.

In the city of Chicago, that figure is even smaller. In 1999, the Chicago Board of Education had a total budget of $2.6 billion, and activity programs cost $2.9 million, or a miniscule one-tenth of 1% (.001) (NFHS 2004). At the risk of seeming cynical, one could suspect that school officials and politicians often use sport as a bargaining chip in order to convince the public to vote for more money for public schools. They cut athletics first, and when the predictable public outcry materializes, the politicians respond with the solution: Vote for the increase to save school sport. Sometimes this strategy works, but it often fails and sport programs are reduced, eliminated, or offered on a fee system.

Another effect of money on high school sport is that in affluent, suburban communities the athletic programs are typically more extensive, have better facilities, have more qualified coaches, and contend for state championships year after year. These communities spend more on facilities and teams, a key factor in the programs' success. Another key factor is that most kids grow up playing organized youth sport and taking lessons in various sports like tennis, golf, and sailing.

As a result of a growing demand for sport programs in high schools, school boards and administrators faced tough economic challenges during the economic recession that began in 2007-2008. Their solutions to budget crises have been on two fronts:

- Impose user fees on kids who do play sports to generate new revenue. Typical charges are $100 up to several hundred dollars for one season in one sport. Discounts are often available for families with more than one child participating at a time or with one child participating in more than one sport season, as well as scholarships for athletes with limited family income.

- The alternative strategy has been to decrease costs of programs. Since salaries are fixed and often negotiated, they are difficult to reduce. However, many schools have frozen coaching salaries at current levels. Significant cost savings are being made in transportation costs by reducing travel, using school buses instead of private buses, combining several teams on one bus, and eliminating long trips. Some states and many communities have also reduced or eliminated middle school programs and junior varsity programs and reduced the number of contests scheduled or the length of seasons.

Across the country, it is fair to say that most school districts have adopted several of these strategies, depending on their local situation. What is clear is that in tough economic times, all public

ACTIVITY TIME-OUT

Who Should Pay for High School Sports?

In the face of continuing economic challenges, describe how you believe high schools should deal with the daunting task of paying for high school sports. Would you favor charging user fees, reducing costs in current programs, or eliminating certain sport programs? Assume that you are a taxpayer and a parent of three children in middle or high school who play or would like to play high school sports. Present your case in a three- to five-minute oral report or in a written position paper limited to three pages.

programs that depend on tax revenue are forced to cut back on expenses, and high school sports are no exception.

Collegiate Sport

College sport has shown tremendous growth in the past 100 years. The NCAA was officially founded in 1910, spurred on by the debate over safety in collegiate football, in which the "flying wedge" was a popular offensive weapon. Numerous injuries and some deaths had occurred, and most observers demanded reform or abolition of college football as too dangerous. The first national championship of the NCAA was held in 1921 in the sport of track and field. The first collegiate football game had been staged in 1869 between local rivals Rutgers and Princeton in New Brunswick, New Jersey.

Compared to the early days of student-supported athletic teams who played other local colleges, college athletics today is more diverse and offers opportunities for both men and women. Since the 1970s we've seen the following changes:

- Gender equity in response to Title IX, opening up doors for women including athletic scholarships

- Refinement of competitive divisions within the NCAA to Divisions I, II, and III, along with similar divisions of play within the other organizations (National Association of Intercollegiate Athletics and National Junior College Athletic Association)

- Support of championships for more sports for both men and women at all levels

- Separation of big-time college programs from the majority, which are more modest in expectation and expense and are closer to the original educational mission

Sport pages abound with stories on college athletics, football factories, athlete abuse, coaching indiscretions, behavioral problems and deviance on the part of athletes, and racial exploitation. Most criticism is directed at and emanates from big-time college programs; that's where the juicy stories that attract attention come from. Clearly, the vast majority of colleges do not run big-time athletic programs or suffer from the same problems to the same degree. Particularly in Ivy League and Division III schools, athletic programs are more likely to maintain high academic standards, minimize expenses, compete locally rather than nationally, limit recruiting, and resemble the original educational mission of athletics. The original mission of college athletics was to support and enhance the educational and academic mission of universities. However, the influence of these schools at the NCAA level is modest since the larger Division I schools heavily influence much of the decision making.

Typically, the larger state universities that were land-grant institutions are the ones that dominate college football. Federal legislation required every state to set aside land for an educational institution. Thus, state-supported universities were founded in the late 1800s, and in the next century many established athletic programs. The size of their budgets, facilities, available land, and geographic location were all positive factors. Typically located in geographically isolated spots, such as Gainesville, Florida, or Lincoln, Nebraska, college teams offered the only big-time sport in the area. Without competition from professional teams, university football teams became almost like a religion in the regions. In contrast, university-sponsored teams in cities typically have not flourished and just can't compete with the local professional franchise in terms of attracting fans, coverage by the media, or revenue.

Championships have grown in number and athlete participation over the past 20 years. The data show that in the past 10 years alone, the number of participants has doubled. Women's programs have begun to rival men's in some sports, particularly basketball and soccer (NCAA 2008a). NCAA Division II began staging a championship festival program by combining spring national championships at one location in an Olympic-type setting once every four years. Capitalizing on the economy of scale, media coverage, and the synergy of many sports in one locale makes the experience for athletes a memorable one. The inaugural event was held in 2004 to rave reviews. After that, a festival for fall sports was held in 2006; a second festival was held in 2008 for spring sports; and most recently, the first-ever festival for winter sports was held in March of 2009 in Houston, Texas. The 2009 festival attracted more than 900 athletes vying for five team championships and 80 individual championships in the sports of men's and women's track and field, men's and women's swimming and diving, and wrestling.

For the purposes of this discussion, collegiate sport refers to those athletic programs at four-year institutions that are members of the NCAA, by far the largest and most influential organization for college sport. Rules for conducting college sport are determined by NCAA member schools and enforced by their professional staffs. There are 1,288 member institutions that represent approximately 418,000 student-athletes who participate in varsity intercollegiate sport. Approximately 44,000 athletes participate in 88 different NCAA championship events in 23 sports (NCAA 2008a). The National Association of Intercollegiate Athletics (NAIA) includes about 300 smaller schools, mainly in the South, and offers national championships. Membership has declined as the NCAA has offered more opportunities for small schools. Over 100 Christian colleges also maintain membership in the National Christian College Athletic Association (NCCAA), although most have a dual membership in the NCAA. Two-year schools are governed by the National Junior College Athletic Association, which has 550 member institutions. All of these organizations have limited budgets, staff, and influence compared with the NCAA, which essentially controls the majority of college athletics.

In the following sections, we'll look at some participation trends in collegiate sport, the struggle for control of women's athletic programs, distinctions between different divisions, positive and negative effects of intercollegiate sport, and potential changes for the future.

Participation

Participation in NCAA college athletics grew from a total of 231,445 students in 1981-1982 to 418,000 in 2007-2008 in sports for which the NCAA conducts championships. The most eye-popping figure is that women's participation ballooned from 64,390 in 1981-1982 to 178,084, while men's participation was up from 167,055 to 240,261 (NCAA 2008a). Equally impressive is the growth in the number of students who participated in NCAA championships: 21,904 students participated in 1992-1993 compared with 54,000 in 88 championship events in 2008 in 23 sports across three divisions (NCAA 2008a). That increase is primarily the result of an expansion of play-offs in all divisions of competition.

The number of women's championship sport teams has increased each year for 26 years, while the number of men's teams has decreased in four of the last 10 years. That number, however, has been on the upswing since 2003-2004, hitting a record high in 2007-2008. There are more men's and women's teams in basketball than in any other sport (NCAA 2008a). The top sports in number of teams are as follows:

Men

1. Basketball
2. Cross country
3. Baseball
4. Golf
5. Soccer
6. Tennis
7. Track and field (outdoor)
8. Football

Women

1. Basketball
2. Volleyball
3. Cross country
4. Soccer
5. Softball
6. Tennis
7. Track and field (outdoor)
8. Track and field (indoor)

It is interesting to compare this list with the next one, which reveals which sports serve the most participants. Of course, many sports are limited to smaller numbers by the required facility space.

These are the top sports in terms of number of participants:

Men

1. Football
2. Baseball
3. Track (outdoor)
4. Soccer
5. Track (indoor)
6. Basketball
7. Cross country
8. Lacrosse
9. Swimming/diving
10. Golf

Women

1. Soccer
2. Track (outdoor)
3. Track (indoor)
4. Softball
5. Basketball
6. Volleyball
7. Cross country
8. Swimming/diving
9. Tennis
10. Rowing

The average NCAA university sponsors approximately 17 teams, 8 for men and 9 for women. The trend of more teams for women began in 1997 and has continued to the present day. The sport with the most new teams added since 1988 is women's soccer, with 551 new programs. In 2007-2008, the sport with the highest number of teams added was lacrosse with 17, followed by outdoor track and field and indoor track and field. For men, the highest number of teams added was outdoor track and field with 17, followed by indoor track and field, lacrosse, and cross country. Interestingly, the sport with the most teams dropped in 2007-2008 also was indoor track and field, with 15 for men and 10 for women eliminated (NCAA 2008a).

Since 1988-1989, there has been a net gain of 234 men's teams and 2,342 women's teams. Most of these changes have occurred in Division I, where since 1988-1989 the net loss for men's teams has been nearly 300 squads while the women have added over 700 teams. Clearly these results show an attempt to expand opportunities for female student-athletes in response to the requirements of Title IX (NCAA 2008a).

There have also been trends in the number of athletes participating who are from different ethnic backgrounds (see table 7.1). Notably, both male and female black athletes have steadily increased their participation percentage in basketball, and male black athletes have done the same in football.

Control of Women's Collegiate Athletics

In the 1960s, women in college athletics were governed by the Division of Girls and Women in Sport (DGWS) of the American Alliance for Health, Physical Education and Dance, which had taken the position of supporting low-key competition for women.

TABLE 7.1 Student-Athlete Ethnicity Percentages for 2007-2008

	White	African American	Latino	American Indian and Alaskan Native	Asian	Other
All sports: male	64.3%	25%	3.9%	.4%	1.5%	4.3%
All sports: female	71.9%	15.9%	3.7%	.4%	2.5%	5.2%
Men's football	46.6%	46.4%	2.4%	.4%	.9%	2.3%
Men's basketball	32.6%	60.4%	1.8%	.1%`	.4%	4.2%
Men's baseball	84.4%	6.0%	5.5%	.4%	1.1%	2.3%
Women's basketball	42.6%	50.1%	1.3%	.03%	1.1%	3.9%
Women's track and field	60.2%	29.5%	3.4%	.4%	1.4%	4.7%
Women's softball	78.5%	7.7%	7.2%	.8%	2.0%	2.7%

This table reflects Division I teams. Historically black institutions and data for Native Hawaiian-Pacific Islander and "two more races" excluded. Only athletes receiving financial aid are included in this table.

Data from Lapchick 2009b.

ACTIVITY TIME-OUT

Racial Groups in Sport Participation

Review the percentages in table 7.1 by racial groups and compare them to the percentages of racial groups in the United States according to the U.S. Census. Are some racial groups overrepresented in collegiate sport overall or just certain sports? If that is the case, what might be an explanation for the deviation from the overall averages?

Wary of the abuses and negative publicity (such as recruiting scandals, gambling on game outcomes, and paying of athletes with improper inducements) that had befallen men's programs, leaders in women's sport were determined to avoid the pitfalls. As the women's movement gained steam in the early 1970s, pressure began to build to offer intercollegiate competition for women similar to that enjoyed by men. A national organization, the Association for Intercollegiate Athletics for Women (AIAW), was founded in 1972, including charter membership to 276 institutions. Within the next 10 years, AIAW boasted 971 member institutions and sponsored 42 national championships in 19 sports.

The AIAW was run by female administrators and coaches who were dedicated to an education-based model of competitive athletics. The goal was to create student-athletes with an emphasis on the sport experience rather than the scoreboard. Athletic scholarships were virtually nonexistent, although a television contract with NBC to show women's sports was negotiated and implemented. The leaders of the AIAW were determined to forge their own path to benefit collegiate women and avoid the potential traps of men's collegiate athletics, including commercialism, sponsorships, competitive obsessions with winning, and devaluation of scholarship (Hawes 1999, 2001; Holway 2005; Katz 2005).

After just 10 short years, the AIAW went out of business, in 1981, and merged with the NCAA, yielding to the pressure to embrace equal opportunities for women to compete for national championships and athletic scholarships as the men had long done. The leaders of the NCAA realized the potential benefits of including women's athletics within their umbrella, such as sponsorship recruitment. Suddenly, the future of women's sport changed dramatically and moved significantly toward the male model of college sport. Many female leaders lost their influential roles and were replaced by male administrators, although they did fight for representation on committees, on boards, and in athletic departments.

The merger of the AIAW with the NCAA heralded progress for women, but at a cost. While opportunities for women expanded, the philosophy of women's sport was sacrificed and replaced by one similar to that of men's sport. Women lost the power to set their own philosophy, rules, and agenda as they were absorbed into the powerful male-dominated NCAA. Yet as a social movement, the merger was a crucial step to help create a better collegiate athletic environment for all athletes regardless of gender.

With the adoption of Title IX and the eventual takeover of women's collegiate sport by the NCAA, athletic programs for both genders began on a path of equality. As new leadership, which now included some males, took over women's sport, female athletes demanded equal rights, pay, and playing opportunities. Many men jumped at opportunities to coach women's sports and helped lead the charge toward equality.

Initially, women who had been in charge of women's athletics at their institution typically lost their power and were forced to serve under male athletic directors. It took several decades, but gradually, leaders in the athletic departments of many institutions included women in influential positions, and eventually pioneering women at various institutions took over full control of both men's and women's sports.

Divisions of Collegiate Athletic Programs

Fifty years ago, the NCAA divided all colleges into just two divisions, university and college, and championships were conducted at those two levels. In 1973, membership was divided into three categories; and in recent years, those divisions have been refined to include five. They include three at Division I: Football Bowl Subdivision (I-FBS), which includes 119 schools with big-time football programs; Football Championship Subdivision (I-FCS), which includes 119 schools with smaller football programs based on stadium size and average game attendance; and other Division I programs, which include 93 schools without football teams.

Colleges determine the level at which they will compete provided they meet the requirements of that level. For example, a school that chooses to compete in Division I-FBS must schedule other Division I-FBS opponents and support at least seven sports for men and seven for women (or six for men and eight for women). For a college to participate in Division I-FBS football, attendance must average at least 15,000 at home games, and the college must have a stadium with permanent seats for 30,000.

Division II has 291 members, and Division III has 429 members. Members of these divisions offer less ambitious athletic programs. Division III schools do not offer athletic scholarships, although they do permit grants based on financial need. Both divisions offer championships against other teams in the division, although in some smaller sports the divisions are combined (NCAA 2009c).

Cost of Collegiate Athletic Programs

The enormous salaries being paid to football and basketball coaches at colleges with prominent athletic programs, along with the economic challenges faced by higher education in general, have sparked more study and analysis of the expense of college athletics than ever before. What's clear is that no matter the level, sport programs are very likely to cost a school a lot of money with just a few exceptions. What is alarming is that expenses seem to be accelerating faster than revenues each year.

In an effort to present a more realistic and clear picture of their members' athletic programs, the NCAA began a move in 2006 to improve the transparency of college sport finances. The first step was to require that each college have an independent third-party review of its athletic program and submit the results to the NCAA for publication of its finances using a procedure followed by all schools. Second, revenues were separated into two categories. One is "generated revenues," such as ticket sales and television proceeds. The other is "allocated revenues," such as direct institutional aid, student athletic fees, indirect institutional support like payment of utilities, maintenance or support salaries, and direct governmental support that is designated for athletics. In the past, many universities that claimed their athletic programs made money simply ignored the extent of the university subsidy for sport, including construction of stadiums and other first-rate sport venues (NCAA 2008b).

The latest research by the NCAA covering the years 2004-2006 shows that athletics' reliance on institutional subsidy to balance their budgets is growing. In 2006, the proportion of revenue derived from institutions (not athletic department revenues) was 25% for the FBS. In the FCS that number is 75%, and for Division I schools without football the percentage is almost 80%.

You may be somewhat shocked to learn that only 19 FBS schools out of the total of 119 institutions at that level generated revenues that exceeded their athletic expenses in 2006. The median positive net revenue for all the other institutions in FBS was $4.3 million compared to the median negative revenue of about $8.9 million (see table 7.2). The bottom line is that most large athletic departments are being significantly subsidized by their institutions, and that $13 million difference appears to indicate a widening gap between the "haves" and "have-nots" in big-time college football.

What is equally disturbing is that during the two years (2004-2006) reported on, overall athletic expenses grew by 23% while revenues rose by only 16%. That meant colleges had to subsidize athletic programs to account for the difference of 7%. If that trend continues as it promises to, the challenge to balance athletic budgets will persist, or more universities will simply have to absorb more of the expense. The revenue that is generated is essentially due to just three sports: football, men's

TABLE 7.2 Revenue and Expenditures by Division I Subdivision

	Median total revenues	Median generated revenues	Median total expense	Median net revenue or deficit
FBS	$35,400,000	$26,342,000	$35,756,000	–$7,265,000
FCS	$9,642,000	$2,345,000	$9,485,000	–$7,121,000
No Football	$8,771,000	$1,828,000	$8,918,000	–$6,607,000

Reprinted from Ledman 2008.

basketball, and women's basketball. Here are some salient facts:

- Between 50% and 60% of FBS football and men's basketball programs actually reported a net income against expenses.
- In the FCS division, only 4% of football programs and 8% of men's basketball programs reported net revenue, and that was minimal.
- For Division I programs without football, about 10% of men's basketball programs generated net revenue.
- At Division II and III, virtually no institutions generate revenue that exceeds expenses.

The sport media like to announce the seemingly exorbitant salaries of high-profile college coaches, and indeed several coaches are currently being paid over $3 million dollars per year. The median salary for men's basketball coaches at FBS institutions was $611,900 in 2006, while their football counterparts showed a median salary of $855,500. Since 2006, these salaries have escalated dramatically, at least in the highest-profile sport programs. Those in the public who raise questions usually compare these coaches' salaries to those of the college presidents they serve and those of other distinguished faculty, which are typically much more modest.

Scholarships for Division I and II Schools

Many parents dream that their children will earn an athletic scholarship to pay for part or all of their college education. The reality is that a very small percentage of all children who start out in youth sport end up with college scholarships. However, athletic scholarships are not out of reach, especially if the child is in the right sport, is a good student, and is open to any school that offers financial aid. Many athletic scholarships go unclaimed each year, primarily for women, from colleges that are less known and less popular choices.

The number of athletic grants-in-aid rose from a total of 58,398 in 1992 to more than 126,000 full or partial scholarships in 2008. The total amount of money granted by Division I and II schools surpasses a billion dollars. Division III institutions do not award any athletic scholarships. The largest change over that period of time was the proportion awarded to women. In 1992, only 33% of grants-in-aid were awarded to women, while by 2005-2006, 45% of grants-in-aid were allocated to women, mirroring their proportion of total athletes in Division I overall (NCAA 2008c).

Rules for scholarship limits are set by the NCAA for each sport in order to level the playing field. The number of scholarships is determined as a ratio of the number of starting players needed to field a team. Of course, the limits for football are by far the largest because schools claim that due to the violent nature of the game, schools need more athletes in a backup role. When schools award more than 80 scholarships for men in football, you can see how many spots for women in other sports are necessary to match that number. Sports like tennis, golf, and archery may allow only eight scholarships. Thus the battle for equal distribution of scholarships for women and men is affected in a major way by football.

A particularly thorny issue in some sports, such as track and field, tennis, swimming, soccer, and even basketball, is the recruiting of international athletes and awarding them full athletic scholarships. The result in collegiate tennis has been an almost compete domination of the top 50 players in the collegiate rankings by players from other countries. American families who have spent thousands of dollars on their child's tennis development feel betrayed by a system that awards scholarships, often using public funds, to support foreign athletes rather than their children. Legal challenges have not held up in court, and the issue persists.

You might ask why international athletes are chosen over their American counterparts. Most of the answer lies in the fact that in other countries

ACTIVITY TIME-OUT

Are the Costs of Collegiate Athletics Worth It?

Now that you've seen the analysis of the increasing crisis in finances of collegiate athletic programs, would you propose changes to the programs? If so, what changes would you suggest? It may be interesting for you to consider that, as mentioned in an earlier section in this chapter, the costs for high school athletics range from 1% to 3% of the total school budgets. In collegiate institutions, the average costs are about 5%. Keep in mind that high school sports boast 7,535,753 participants compared with only 418,000 who play collegiate sports. Does this fact affect your argument?

EXPERT'S VIEW

What Student-Athletes Say About Their Experiences

Josephine Potuto and James O'Hanlon at the University of Nebraska surveyed more than 800 student-athletes at 18 NCAA Division (FBS) schools, those that have big-time football programs (Potuto and O'Hanlon 2006). The athletes surveyed included both males and females, athletes in all sports, and athletes across all ethnic groups. Their goal was to ascertain the educational experience these athletes experienced and identify any tradeoffs they had to make in order to compete at that level. An overwhelming number (more than 90%) were satisfied with their educational experience, felt positive about the overall education they received, and felt well-prepared for life after graduation. In addition, they believed that athletics instilled values independent of those derived from other aspects of college life.

In their role as student-athletes, some felt that it was an advantage with some professors who favored them but a distinct disadvantage with others. More than 65% say their grade point average would have been higher had they not played a sport and had more time for studies. They also reported that spending a year abroad or fulfilling an internship was very difficult for them as an athlete.

It is pretty clear from the survey response that athletes feel their social life is inhibited by the time spent on athletics, and they regret not getting to spend much time with other students who are not athletes. Extracurricular activities are nearly impossible due to time restraints. Male athletes tend to spend more time on athletic-related activities than female athletes do. In general, female athletes seem to be more interested in nonathletic aspects of college life than males, who are more singularly focused on their sport.

Athletes in team sports, particularly those who played revenue-producing sports such as football and basketball, were more likely to see themselves as "athletes first, students second" while individual sport athletes and nonrevenue sport athletes were just the opposite. In general, student-athletes are satisfied with their overall college experience and clearly contradict the claim by some critics that athletics are harmful to the education of those who choose to become student-athletes.

there is no such thing as an amateur player, and many tennis players accept money, play professional events, and have racket and clothing sponsors from a young age. Their experience, training, and financial support are limited only by their performance. American children, on the other hand, are not allowed to accept prize money or endorsements if they want to maintain their amateur status to be eligible for college athletics. The issue of international athletes in American colleges is complex, and a solution doesn't seem to be in sight.

Positive and Negative Effects of Intercollegiate Sport

As we've seen, it is impossible to lump all college athletic programs together since they vary widely. For the purpose of this section, we will divide our analysis into two primary groups: colleges offering athletic programs that are modest in expense and intensity, representing around 800 colleges and universities, versus the group of roughly 300 highly competitive programs at schools where athletics follows a corporate structure, classified as Division I-FBS or I-FCS by the NCAA.

Pressure to Generate Income for the University

Major college sport programs are run as corporate businesses that pay no taxes. Typically, the university expects them to at least be revenue neutral, or break even. Of course, that means many schools have to secure an invitation to postseason play in order to earn the dollars guaranteed from bowl games or basketball play-offs to achieve a balanced budget.

Whether the budget is actually balanced is a source of discussion at many schools. It is often difficult to calculate the total expense for the athletic program when administrators assign various costs to other units of the college. For example, facilities are often charged to the state or other building funds; student activity fees support fitness and weight rooms; and stadiums are built or renovated using other development funds.

ACTIVITY TIME-OUT

Top 10 in Football or Basketball

Without consulting any rankings or results, see if you can name at least 10 institutions that typically have successful football and 10 that have successful basketball programs. Once you have your list, compare it with the lists of classmates and develop a composite list that includes the schools that were most often represented. Are there some institutions that you included on both lists? Discuss the publicity benefits to these universities of their competitive results. Do the benefits justify the expenditures to support a top-level athletic program?

Whatever the cost, the expectations over the years at many notable universities have included outstanding athletic teams, particularly in the major sports. You only have to check the last few years' football bowl games and NCAA basketball tournaments to compose a list of the top 50 schools that traditionally vie for national recognition.

Schools that support Division I athletic programs either at the FBS or FCS level often justify their expenditures by pointing out that high-profile winning programs generate volumes of publicity for the university, contribute to school spirit among students, and increase donations from alumni and other prominent supporters.

Taking this one step further, some schools claim that based on the success of their athletic teams, more students apply for admission, allowing them to select the very best of prospective applicants. In other words, successful sport teams also improve the academic level of the school.

Although several studies reviewed by Frank (2004) suggest that these results are not likely, most of us know that generally people are drawn to winning programs. (See the next section on athlete recruitment for more on this study.) We also can point to examples such as the University of Connecticut. In the mid-1990s, the University of Connecticut (UConn) was a modest regional institution that sought to be the finest university in New England. Not content with that modest goal, a few visionaries set higher standards to raise the profile of UConn to a nationally recognized university. The state legislature funded over $1 billion in new construction, transforming a utilitarian state university into an attractive modern campus. Next came success in men's and women's basketball, culminating in a national championship for both teams in 2004. UConn was on the map, and everyone in the country knew where it was. The football team upgraded to Division I-BCS and in 2004 received its

first postseason bowl bid to the Motor City Bowl in Detroit, where it defeated the University of Toledo to conclude with a record of 8-4.

You might wonder if there is a correlation between all of this campus improvement, publicity, and sport success. The SAT scores for admission at UConn have increased steadily in recent years. What used to be a safety school for state residents suddenly became the place to go. Can you think of other schools where a similar phenomenon has occurred? A few examples come to mind of schools that were virtually unknown before the exploits of one of their athletic teams thrust them into the public spotlight, if only briefly. Consider schools like Boise State, Gonzaga, University of South Florida, and University of Nevada at Las Vegas. An upset win on the football field or in the NCAA basketball tournament suddenly pushes schools onto the national stage.

Athlete Recruitment

William Bowen, former president of Princeton University, and Sarah Levin published a book, *Reclaiming the Game* (2003), in which they document the results of athletic recruitment and college outcomes of athletes compared to nonathletes at 33 highly selective academic institutions. Relying on data from Ivy League schools, Seven Sister colleges, and other prestigious universities, Bowen and Levin expose the negative sides of college sport at schools that do not even offer athletic scholarships.

Some of the negative findings include the fact that athletes are four times as likely to gain admission to college as other students with comparable academic credentials. The data also showed that athletes are substantially more likely to be in the bottom third of their college class than students who do not play sports. Recruited athletes also tend to underperform academically in college compared to the predictions based on their test scores and high school grades. Of course, these are not the schools we think of when we think big-time college sport. It is rare when a team from Princeton, Harvard, or Yale contends at the national level.

In 2004, Robert Frank of Cornell presented a report to the prestigious Knight Commission on Intercollegiate Athletics. The report included an assessment of the effect of winning teams on applicants and on alumni donations. Citing a review of six studies conducted between 1987 and 2003, Frank reported that although there appeared to be several instances of small gains in admissions as measured by higher SAT scores, the increases were minor and not statistically significant. He also mentioned the popular example of Boston College reporting a 12% gain in applicants after Doug Flutie chucked a miracle pass to win the 1984 Orange Bowl.

Frank also reviewed more than a dozen studies that measured the effect of athletic success on alumni donations. Although most studies showed little effect at statistically significant levels, one study did show that appearances at football bowl games and basketball tournaments do positively affect donations. Frank's conclusion, however, was that there is little empirical evidence to support the contention that it takes a winning team or program to secure alumni donations.

Intercollegiate Athletics Reform

Historically, the Carnegie Commission for the Advancement of Teaching warned of the abuses in college athletics back in 1929. The commission cited corrupt recruiting practices, professionalism of athletes, commercialism, and neglected education. Sadly, those same issues are being debated today in spite of numerous efforts to reform college sport.

One of the most comprehensive analyses of intercollegiate sport was conducted by the Knight Commission on Intercollegiate Athletics (2001) beginning in the early 1990s. The analysis was conducted because the foundation's board of trustees felt that athletics were threatening the integrity of higher education. Some of the problems the commission cited as justification for its research were as follows:

When a program is investigated for potential recruitment violations by a coach who has since moved on, such as former Tennessee coach Lane Kiffin, is it fair that the new coach must deal with the punishments?

- In the 1980s, 109 colleges were censured or put on probation by the NCAA. That included more than half of the Division I-FBS schools, or 57 out of 106.

- Nearly a third of present and former professional football players said they had accepted illicit payments while in college, and more than half said they saw nothing wrong with this.

- Of the 106 institutions in Division I-FBS, 48 had graduation rates under 30% for male basketball players, and 19 had the same low rate for football players.

It seems there is a new scandal involving big-time sport programs nearly every month. Football and men's basketball are the magnets for most of the scrutiny and deservedly so. They're the big-money sports, and temptations loom for athletes, coaches, and administrators.

The work of the Knight Commission, an independent group of college presidents, university trustees, and former collegiate athletes, continued through the 1990s, and the effect of that work is ongoing. Various reports on the study have been widely circulated in the media and pressed into the hands of college presidents and boards of trustees. Essentially, the Knight Commission advocated a one-plus-three model for reform that requires presidential control directed toward academic integrity, financial integrity, and independent certification that universities are meeting the standards set for athletic programs. The commission's view was that reform of college sport will never be achieved to everyone's satisfaction; it is an ongoing process that needs continuous work.

Although the Knight Commission has no formal authority, by 2003 the NCAA had adopted almost two-thirds of its recommendations. Most notable was the overhaul of the governance structure of the NCAA, which put college presidents in charge rather than athletic directors. That way, if reform initiatives were to fail, it would be patently clear who should shoulder the blame.

The conclusion of the commission is that in spite of the changes to rules, the enforcement efforts of the NCAA, and the leadership of college presidents, the threat of college athletics operating without supervision or accountability to university leaders has increased rather than diminished. The commission calls on all members of the higher education community to unite to address the problems and clean up college athletics. The Knight commission continues to monitor the troubling issues in collegiate sports and advocate for policies that are consistent with the universities' educational missions.

One reformist group that has taken up the gauntlet is the Drake Group (TDG). Based out of Drake University in Iowa, TDG is an alliance of college faculty members at various institutions who propose seven reforms (Drake Group 2009):

1. Athletes must maintain a cumulative 2.0 grade point average each semester.

2. Institute a one-year residency requirement before an athlete can participate in college athletics (no freshman eligibility).

3. Replace one-year renewable scholarships with need-based financial aid or with multi-year athletic scholarships that extend to graduation (five years maximum).

4. Establish university policies that emphasize the importance of class attendance for all students and ensure that the scheduling of athletics contests does not conflict with class attendance.

5. Retire the term "student-athlete."

6. Make the location and control of academic counseling and support services for athletes the same as for all students.

7. Ensure that universities provide accountability of trustees, administrators, and faculty by public disclosure of such things as a student's academic major, academic adviser, courses listed by academic major, general education requirements, electives, course GPA, and instructor.

Interestingly, TDG has spent relatively little time working on college campuses mobilizing faculty members but instead has spent much of its time and resources lobbying members of Congress, pursuing court cases in support of whistle-blowers, and trying to affect the general public's perception of college athletics.

A different organization, the Coalition on Intercollegiate Athletics (COIA), has taken a much different approach although its aims are similar to those of TDG. Born out of faculty senates, COIA has worked closely with the NCAA and college establishment groups to promote reform from within the college athletics family. COIA is an alliance of 52 Division I-FBS university faculty senates whose aim is to reform collegiate sports.

In response to the work of these two faculty groups, NCAA president Myles Brand in 2005 established a 50-member task force composed primarily of Division I university presidents and chancellors to lead college sport into its second century. One of the initial conclusions of that group was that collegiate sport reform, though it needs national leadership, ultimately must be implemented at the local campus level. Further, there must be leadership from the college president at the campus level and institutional accountability for the conduct of intercollegiate athletics there.

Since then, subcommittees have presented working papers on the topics of general information, fiscal responsibility, academic values and standards, relationships with internal and external constituencies, and student-athlete well-being.

As these various groups press on to consider reform in intercollegiate athletics, other factors have recently come into play. The economic crisis beginning in 2007 has exposed the problems of ever-escalating costs of all intercollegiate programs and forced some degree of fiscal sanity. It is likely that these discussions for reform will continue as long as intercollegiate athletics exist. The road to this point has been arduous and is likely to continue to be paved with criticism, second-guessing, and "Monday morning quarterbacking."

Although there is not at this time a full-scale reform movement that is well organized or funded, the signs of a gathering storm are there. In general, the fight is against an increasingly commercialized and professional monopoly of college sport. As a training ground for a small proportion of eventual professional athletes, big-time college sport is simply a minor league.

Critics of the NCAA assert that while it talks about cleaning up college sport abuses, it simply goes about its business, perpetuating the status quo (Splitt 2004). It thus falls to various reform groups to pressure college presidents, boards of trustees, the public, and the media to call for reform (Lipsyte 2003).

Perhaps the most important step is simply to educate everyone on the facts of the matter. One group, founded by Richard Lapchick at Northeastern University, is the Institute for the Study of Sport and Society. Lapchick has now moved on to the University of Central Florida and has established a similar center there. His contribution has been to publish statistics on the graduation rates of college athletes, on race and correlates with graduation, on minority coach proportions, and on gender equity issues (Lapchick 2008).

College as a Training Ground for Professional Athletes

Undoubtedly, one of the major factors that affect the academic performance and graduation rate of athletes in Division I-FBS or I-FCS universities is that some athletes may have little or no interest or ability in school. Their motivation for going to college is to continue their training to become a professional athlete, and colleges offer the next step of training at no charge.

Division I-FBS college teams function like a minor league, or a development league, in football and men's basketball, the two big revenue-producing sports. Neither the National Basketball Association nor the National Football League has player development systems of its own. Virtually all their player development occurs at the collegiate level, at no expense to them. Neither professional sport league contributes a penny to college basketball or football.

These two sports are unlike baseball, which has had its own minor league system for development of young players for many years although the number of minor league baseball teams has declined in recent years. Unfortunately, the odds of athletes making it from high school to top-level colleges to the professional ranks are extremely long. Consider table 7.3, which shows statistics published by the NCAA.

TABLE 7.3 Professional Career Probability

	Men's basketball (%)	Women's basketball (%)	Football (%)	Baseball (%)	Men's soccer (%)	Men's ice hockey (%)
High school to NCAA	3.1	3.5	5.8	6.3	5.6	11.0
NCAA to professional	1.2	0.9	1.7	9.1	1.6	3.6
High school to professional	.03	.03	.08	.44	.07	.31

Estimated by percentage of students moving from one level to the next.

Data from National Collegiate Athletic Association 2010.

Out of approximately half a million boys and half a million girls who play high school basketball, only about 5,000 boys and 5,000 girls will play at a Division I institution. Those 5,000 boys will vie for 350 roster spots in professional basketball while the girls duke it out for only 168 spots. Of course, that includes beating out seasoned veterans who are already there.

The sad fact is, many young people, particularly from lower socioeconomic backgrounds, pin all their hopes on a successful career as a professional athlete. When that dream doesn't materialize, their absence of preparation for life through academics catches up with them. With limited skills and no college degree, their options are severely limited. We look more closely at this issue in chapters 11 and 13.

Social Issues and College Athletics

A number of social issues are constantly under scrutiny regarding college athletic programs, including the following (Splitt 2004):

- The differing standards for admission at many schools for athletes compared to other applicants. Although athletes must meet minimum requirements, at all types of institutions, including Ivy League schools, coaches often can recommend admission for a limited number of athletes who meet the minimum standard but not the average of other students who are offered admission.

- The recruiting practices to attract athletes to big-time programs, including lavish entertainment, parties, escorts, and other questionable practices. The University of Colorado made headlines in 2003 and 2004 with the exposure of problems such as alleged football recruiting violations, including use of sex, alcohol, and drugs to entice potential recruits; cases of sexual assault; binge drinking; and maintenance of an athletic slush fund.

- Once student-athletes are on campus, some schools continue to provide improper benefits to them. The University of Southern California received harsh penalties in 2010 from the NCAA for major violations in men's football and basketball. The football team was banned from bowl games in 2010 and 2011 and was forced to forfeit all games in which Reggie Bush (Heisman Trophy winner in 2005) had played beginning in 2004, including the Orange Bowl victory that earned a national championship in January 2005. Basketball player O.J. Mayo, who played only one year for the Trojans,

violated the NCAA amateur rules. Ironically, the coaches of both the football and basketball teams (Pete Carroll and Tim Floyd) had already left the university and moved on to other jobs with no penalties. It's the new coaches and current players who were not involved in the scandal that will absorb the punishment (Zinser 2010).

- The separation of athletes from the social fabric of campus life by having them live together in dormitories, eat together, attend required study sessions as a group, and work out in the weight room to the exclusion of a normal college life. The sense of entitlement that many athletes enjoy is only heightened in college, which may lead young men and women to act in socially unacceptable ways, sometimes even breaking laws.

- The encouragement by coaches or others for athletes to take minimum academic loads or less rigorous courses to ensure eligibility.

- The lack of female administrators and coaches in women's sports.

- The lack of coaches from minority groups except at historically black colleges.

- Spotty attendance at classes due to frequent and sometimes sustained travel to compete in the sport.

- The constant battle to meet the requirements of Title IX to ensure equal opportunity for sport participation for both men and women.

- The use of sport events by students as opportunities for binge drinking, wild parties, and rowdy behavior. When teams win or lose big games, it is not uncommon for students to get out of control on the field or in the community.

All of these issues have been addressed by the NCAA, various athletic conferences, and individual schools. Some progress has been made, but vigilance must be consistent to prevent abuses (Brand 2004).

Equity Between Men's and Women's Sport

The rise in women's opportunities since the passage of Title IX in 1972 has still not resulted in equality between men and women. Fewer women play college sport than men, and advocates for women contend it simply isn't true that women choose not to play.

An unintended consequence of the enforcement of Title IX has led many colleges to drop men's sports that don't produce revenue in order to beef up their offerings for women. Cancellation of men's programs such as wrestling, swimming, and tennis has raised the hackles of alumni, coaches, and governing bodies of those sports. For some Olympic sports, college provided the coaching and training for these athletes, and the loss of programs hurts the United States' prospects in international competition.

Since 1988-1989, there have been 2,947 men's teams added compared with 4,282 women's teams. The women's sport that has been most often added is soccer (617 new teams); other sports that have added large numbers of teams, in order, are golf, indoor track and field, cross country, outdoor track and field, and softball. For men, the sport with most teams added is track and field (317 new teams), followed by cross country, golf, outdoor track and field, rowing, and tennis.

In nine of the last 21 years, men's teams showed a net loss, while in all but one year there was a net gain of women's teams. Historically, the women's team with the greatest net gain is soccer (517 teams), followed by golf, softball, indoor track and field, and cross country. For men, the greatest net

gain is indoor track and field (104 teams) followed by golf and lacrosse. If we turn to net loss of teams for women, the leaders were fencing, skiing, gymnastics, and equestrian. For men, the sports with the largest net loss were wrestling (106), followed in order by tennis, rifle, gymnastics, fencing, water polo, skiing, and swimming and diving (NCAA 2008a).

The crux of the matter is football. The expense and the huge number of athletic scholarships required make football difficult to offset with comparable women's sports. Some athletic leaders contend that if football were left out of the equation in enforcing Title IX, the sport opportunities would be quite comparable. Of course, keep in mind that only about 100 out of 1,200 colleges sponsor big-time football, and only half of those make money for the institution.

The process of integrating equal opportunity for women into college athletics is long and slow. No easy solution appears imminent; but public pressure, legal battles, and changing expectations for girls starting in youth sport and high school sport may force gradual change as society changes. More on this issue will be discussed in chapter 12.

While the number of black head coaches is on the rise, there is still a disparity between the number of white head coaches and black head coaches at FBS schools.

Issues for Discussion and Possible Changes in College Sport

Changes in college athletics have been called for since 1929 when the Carnegie Report on Big Ten athletics was published in the *Chicago Tribune* (Splitt 2004). In fact, many changes have been made over the years. Enforcement by the NCAA has been strengthened, and college coaches are required to understand and abide by the prescribed rules when they are hired. Yet with the pressure to succeed, some coaches ignore the rules or bend them, especially when encouraged to do so by alumni or athletic boosters.

The infractions and failures of athletic programs and individual athletes make headlines in the sport pages with appropriate hand-wringing by college officials, coaches, and sports writers. Yet the abuses go on and seem to move from conference to conference and school to school. Perhaps the solution does not lie in setting more rules and stepping up enforcement, but in reevaluating the value of college athletics, establishing the role of sport within an educational setting, and modifying policies to reflect that consensus.

The money that is at stake is enormous. As we have seen, big-time college sport, particularly football and basketball, is big business. Imagine the pressure on those who suggest changes that might affect the status quo.

Here are some of the most compelling issues that face college sport. Consider them and spend some time discussing with your classmates the possible changes to the current situation. If you were to prioritize change, what issues would be highest on your list? Would you start with the most difficult problems, or with smaller issues that hold promise for change in the shorter term?

- *Money.* Supporting college athletic teams is expensive, and it seems that many institutions are operating their athletic department as a corporate business rather than an educational endeavor. Decisions are often made with the bottom line in mind rather than the welfare of the athletes.

- *Gender equity.* Although females outnumber males on college campuses 53% to 47%, male athletes outnumber female athletes 57% to 43%. In dollar allocation, the scales tip more heavily toward males in that recruiting money, operating budgets, and coaching salaries award two-thirds of the money to men's sport and only a third to women's sport (Suggs 2002). Thirty years after the adoption of Title IX, equality of opportunity for males and females has not yet been achieved.

- *Negative effect on academics.* Particularly in big-time programs, athletes are expected to put athletic performance first. School dropout and graduation rates in men's football and basketball programs are well above and below general student averages, respectively.

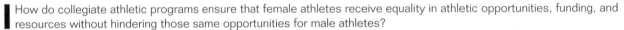

How do collegiate athletic programs ensure that female athletes receive equality in athletic opportunities, funding, and resources without hindering those same opportunities for male athletes?

- *Racial bias.* Black athletes are often recruited for their ability to earn money and fame for the institution. However, they may be unprepared academically for college, and little effort is made to remedy that gap. Some accuse college athletic programs of simply using black athletes and then discarding them before graduation.

- *Athlete rights.* Most athletic departments keep a close rein on their athletes by limiting their free time, expecting them to perform for the university almost as professionals without the accompanying financial rewards.

- *Conflict with educational goals.* Although athletic departments extol the virtues of sport for building character, independence, good decision making, and mental toughness, their practices and policies often stunt the development of these traits.

Athletes are expected to follow arbitrary rules and sacrifice their individual growth for the welfare of the team. While these practices may build character in a sense, perhaps the military is a more appropriate place to learn these life lessons than a college campus.

You may want to add issues according to your own research and experience. In any case, the question posed to all of us is, What can we do about these problems? Take some time to discuss possible solutions with your classmates and with athletes, coaches, and administrators.

Chapter Summary

This chapter looked at sport programs sponsored by high schools and universities. The major question considered at both levels was whether athletics is compatible with the educational goals of the institutions that sponsor them.

Evidence from research shows both positive and negative influences of athletics on the schools, the social structure, and the athletes themselves. Issues were presented with the hope that solutions can be found to preserve the best aspects of school-sponsored sport and mitigate some of the negative ones.

Over the past 20 years, participation in both high school and college athletics has increased, primarily due to a dramatic rise in participation by female athletes as a result of Title IX. Although opportunities for males and females are not yet equitable, they have moved significantly in that direction. As a result of new opportunities for girls, new problems have arisen, mostly centered on funding women's sport without paring back men's sport.

The issue of financial support for school-based sport was examined from a number of angles. In high school, while the proportion of total budget allocated for sport is modest, sport is often one of the first activities to be cut when schools face a budget crisis. The trend toward charging user fees for athletics threatens to put the sport experience out of reach for many students who come from modest economic backgrounds.

College sport was considered according to level of competition. The problems and publicity that make the sport pages typically involve abuses, cheating, and behavioral problems of athletes in Division I programs that are essentially businesses. Most collegiate athletic programs operate at a more modest level, suffer fewer problems of abuse, and more closely approximate the educational experience. However, those same schools wrestle with budget issues, gender equity, and racial imbalances.

At both the high school and college levels, the myth of the dumb jock has been discredited, although there are warning signs that some institutions encourage some athletes to emphasize athletic participation while allowing academic performance to lag behind. Socially, athletes are much admired by their peers, and their egos are sometimes inflated by adulation and praise from peers, coaches, and administrators. At some schools, the jock culture has become exclusionary and causes splits within the student body.

On balance, athletics in the educational setting are worth saving if educators and the public set clear goals, establish limits, and enforce standards for operation of sport programs within an agreed-upon framework and philosophy. Changes are likely to be gradual and will adjust to and reflect other societal trends, including higher expectations from our educational system, eliminating racial and gender bias, and escalating costs of sponsoring athletic teams out of university budgets.

International Sport

After reading this chapter, you will know the following:

- How and why sports have expanded globally
- How American sports, the Olympic Games, and nationalism affect worldwide sport
- How the media affect global sport expansion
- The roles of athletes and coaches as migrant workers in the sport world
- How sport affects the world at large

The interplay between sport and society is magnified when we look at it globally rather than restrict our view to the United States. Do you think sport helps shape societies around the world, or does sport simply reflect the societies that have evolved? Consider that in the past 100 years, the modern Olympic Games have become the most significant worldwide athletic competition, embraced by virtually every nation in interest, investment of funds, and the fielding of a team of athletes. At the same time, soccer (or football as it is known worldwide) has clearly dominated the world as the most popular game of all for both participants and spectators. American-invented sports such as baseball, football, and basketball have grown into a multibillion-dollar business at home but have yet to make a significant impact worldwide in either participation or spectatorship. *Functional theorists* would point out the unifying trends that sport can bring to all cultures by promoting the "modern" ideals of industrialism and capitalism, thus improving the status of less developed nations in sport that carries over to their culture. One example of this would be the inclusion of opportunities for women and girls to play and watch sport in cultures where they have traditionally been excluded because of religious or cultural tradition. On the other hand, there are those who lean toward *critical theories* of sport that would resist the movement toward one restrictive view of the value of sport in affecting culture. They would argue that citizens in developing countries need to integrate sport into their culture in a way that enhances the quality of life for their citizens as people, rather than exploit them as pawns in a capitalistic society.

Although we have mostly focused on sport in North America and the United States, it would be a mistake not to consider the international role of sport. Competition between athletes from different countries has pushed every athlete to improve performance. The media revolution allows us to follow sports around the world and promotes sports in countries where they were once unknown. International travel by athletes, coaches, and others has helped us to learn about and appreciate different cultures and to forge ways of working together toward common goals.

As our world changes, it seems to shrink through technology connections and economic and political interdependency, and the sport world reflects our increasing globalization. Among the reasons for this trend in sport are the following:

- The media explosion that connects countries through the Internet, television, film, newspapers, magazines, and satellite transmission
- Marketing and retailing of sport equipment, clothing, shoes, and casual wear among countries
- The migration from country to country of athletes, coaches, officials, and sport administrators
- Exchange of values that reflect various cultures, attitudes toward competition, personal achievement, and socialization

Globalization of Modern Sport

The Greeks originated many of the athletic traditions practiced today. Most of the terms we use to refer to sport come from Greek words such as *athlos*, from which *athletics* is derived. Other words, such as *gymnasium*, *stadium*, and *pentathlon*, also are rooted in Greek.

Perhaps the most important contribution of ancient Greece was incorporating sport into its culture—a culture that has shaped much of Western thought (Spears and Swanson 1978).

While modern sport is commonly traced to the Greeks, Great Britain had a huge hand in increasing the global popularity of sport. Great Britain had colonies in Africa, India, Singapore, Hong Kong, Australia, Canada, and the United States; and during the height of its influence in the 19th and early 20th centuries, "the sun never set" on the British Empire. Countries of the British Empire accounted for a quarter of the world's population. The British exported their language, customs, education systems, and law to their colonies. Each country belonging to the British Commonwealth was introduced to traditional English sports, and its citizens were encouraged to participate in sport as part of the preferred way of life. Competitions held within the British colonies attractively rewarded skilled athletes to further their ambition under the British flag (Maguire et al. 2002).

During the 17th and 18th centuries, the English developed the popular pastimes of the privileged, such as cricket, fox hunting, horse racing, and boxing, into sports and spread them to their colonies. During the 19th century, soccer (known worldwide as football), rugby, tennis, and track and field emerged as the next wave of popular sports. In the 20th century, the sport system of the British Empire emerged as the dominant structure in worldwide sport competition. This system was founded on sports and games, highly skilled performers, and popularity with both participants and spectators (Elias and Dunning 1986).

Nationalism helped develop sport in countries whose popular sports were strongly rooted in their culture and stoked the competitive fires between nations seeking to demonstrate the athletic superiority of their citizens. Nations established sport competitions to promote their national spirit and pride. Geography influenced the national sports adopted by various countries as colder-climate countries naturally gravitated toward winter sports while more moderate-climate countries embraced warm-weather sports. Indoor sport arenas were constructed in more developed countries as a wider economic base encouraged sports based in indoor venues.

The Germans, Swedes, and Danish influenced gymnastics, while Norway helped develop winter sports such as skating and skiing. However, no country influenced modern sport as much as Great Britain did through its worldwide network of colonies and territories. Wherever the British went, they brought their sports and games, which took root along with their government, law, and culture (Maguire 1999).

When the United States emerged as a world power, American sports began creeping onto the world stage. American football, baseball, basketball, volleyball, and lacrosse were uniquely American, while professional ice hockey flourished in Canada and then spread to the United States. Interchange among athletes, coaches, and officials of these sports and of traditional English sports promoted the globalization of both English and American sports. The influence of Western culture on world sport mirrored the political and economic dominance of the West. As the Communist world grew in

▌ The power of the Norwegian speedskating team can be partially attributed to the geography of their country.

importance, so did its influence on sport worldwide. During the Cold War years, Communist countries poured resources into high-performance athletes who captured global attention as the governments claimed that their athletes' success was rooted in their culture and political philosophies. Of course, the Western countries fought back to prove the superiority of their way of life.

Islamic and African countries have influenced worldwide sport the least. Generally, sports were incompatible with their culture, economic resources, religion, or attitudes toward gender roles. Efforts by international sport bodies to introduce sports in these countries have seen slow growth and isolated pockets of success. Track stars from Kenya and Ethiopia are examples of a changing view of sport in Africa, and the growth of soccer in some countries has been significant.

In the last 20 years, the balance of power in worldwide sport has begun to shift. England has faded from contention on the international stage; and African, Asian, and South American countries have begun to dominate their former British mentors in sports like soccer, cricket, table tennis, and track and field. The Pacific Rim countries have emerged as a formidable force and fertile ground for development due to their population size, economic influence, and rising political power.

The selection of Beijing, China, as host of the 2008 Olympic Games was a remarkable departure from the norm. It was controversial because of China's history of Communism and because many people question China's record on human rights. Those concerns were balanced by recognition that China is a world power, home to nearly 20% of the world population and a huge engine in the world economy. Television broadcast rights were attractive, and advertisers and sponsors eagerly entered what was a relatively new market for them. Four years after the 2008 Olympics, the Games will revert to a more traditional host, as London, England, won the bid to host the 2012 Summer Games.

The 2008 Olympic Games in Beijing were a spectacular success by almost any yardstick. In spite of the immense pressure of a worldwide audience, the local organizing authorities dealt with every contingency in an efficient and effective manner. Security was airtight, events were staged in modernistic venues, arrangements for athletes and attendees were top rate, and even the feared smog and pollution was controlled during the Games.

Perhaps the major impact of these Games will be the growing reputation of China as a sporting nation. China's athletes earned the highest total of gold medals of any nation in history with 51, ahead of the second-place United States with 36. When all medals were counted, the United States edged out China with 110 overall medals to China's 100. The message was clear that as a nation, China takes sport seriously and promises to contend on the world stage for years to come.

Global Consumption of Sport

The worldwide emergence of companies such as Nike, Adidas, Puma, and Reebok has modified attitudes toward world consumers. Manufacturing of soccer shoes, balls, tennis rackets, sport uniforms, and so on has become a worldwide effort. Nike pushed the envelope by paying workers in developing countries 20 to 30 cents an hour to produce sport clothing (Kidd and Donnelly 2000). China, Indonesia, Thailand, and South Korea virtually

ACTIVITY TIME-OUT

Ping-Pong: The National Sport of China?

Chinese table tennis players boast six of the top ten players in both the men's and the women's categories and won all gold medals at the 2008 Olympic Games in Beijing. There are professional table tennis leagues in China, and many players continue to play into middle age. World-class players hit the ball at 80 miles per hour, applying spins that make 100 rotations per second and thus give their opponents less than one-half of a second to anticipate, react, and make a shot.

You've probably heard of the success of Chinese players in table tennis winning world titles and gold medals in the Olympic Games. What lies behind their success? How did table tennis become the most popular sport in China? While millions of American kids aspire to become famous football or basketball players, Chinese children pin their hopes on a sport like table tennis. During your research, take note of the term "ping-pong diplomacy" and find out the origin of the term and the significance of this historic mixing of international politics and sport.

cornered the market on manufacturing by supplying cheap labor and producing products at a fraction of the cost they could be produced for in other countries. Multinational companies rushed to manufacture their products through these factories, added their markups, and sold their goods in developed countries at premium prices (Kidd and Donnelly 2000). As information leaked about the exploitation and low wages of these workers, especially children, Nike and other companies modified their practices to mitigate the resulting international outrage.

Sport clothing, starting with athletic shoes and eventually moving into casual wear, became a wardrobe staple in many societies. Starting with the young, people began wearing athletic clothing at almost any occasion. It's not uncommon to see retirees wear tracksuits in airports, malls, or anywhere else in public. The casual-dress industry has captured the clothing market by focusing on comfort and encouraging a relaxed yet active lifestyle.

The impact of sport shoes on the business of sport is a fascinating story. It began with two brothers, Adi and Rudi Dassler, who started their shoe business in their mother's laundry room in the little town of Herzogenaurach, Germany, in the 1920s. Who could have predicted that their efforts were to set off a chain of events that would eventually lead to an explosion of marketing and sales of sport shoes? Over the next 50 years, that is what happened, changing the face of the sporting world forever.

The "coming-out" party for the Dassler brothers would be the 1936 Olympic Games held in Berlin, just after Adolph Hitler had risen to power. Hitler's belief in the power of sport to bolster the young men in Germany into a dominating army fueled the sport explosion in the country. The Dassler boys capitalized by putting their shoes on the feet of the German athletes along with the Games' ultimate hero, American Jesse Owens, who captured four gold medals in the Games.

▌ Jesse Owens was one of the first athletes to wear the new adidas apparel at the 1936 Olympic Games.

The honeymoon was short-lived, as the Dassler brothers soon began a bitter feud and parted ways in their sport shoes business just as it was exploding. The result was that Adi Dassler soon christened his shoes under the brand name "adidas" while his brother moved across the river to establish his brand, "Puma."

Originally focused on producing "soccer boots," the adidas and Puma brands soon branched out into track and field. But the battles between the brands in the early years after the fall of the Nazi empire played out on the soccer pitches in Europe. A stunning victory by the German team in 1954 over a favored Hungarian squad featured the new soccer shoes with adjustable cleats, made to perform in any weather, with the adidas logo.

The next generation of the Dassler family, Adi's son Horst Dassler, made his mark early as a 20-year-old at the Olympic Games in Australia in 1954. He masterminded a scheme to have adidas shoes given out free to Olympic athletes and at the same time blocked the entrance of Puma shoes into the country. For years afterward, the practice of giving shoes to world-class athletes as free advertisement and boasting rights became a scramble to get the finest athletes into their adidas shoes. Although it was a questionable practice that just skirted the rules for amateur athletes at the time, it became the custom in the sport world (Smit 2008).

By the time the Olympic Games were staged in Mexico City in 1968, the competition for top athletes who would wear their adidas brand led to under-the-table cash payments to supposedly amateur athletes. Within a few years, actual contracts were forged with top soccer players, led by Puma's landing the famous Brazilian Pele for $25,000 for the 1970 World Cup in Mexico and another $100,000 for the next four years plus royalties of 10% of all Puma boots sold with his name on them. Before long, athletes such as Joe Namath in football, basketball players Walt Frazier and Kareem Abdul-Jabbar, tennis player Stan Smith, and a multitude of sport stars would sign with either adidas or Puma and shatter the dominance of Converse shoes in the United States.

As the shoe battle heated up, both Puma and adidas suffered some setbacks but still grew in reputation and dominance in sport shoes. In the 1970s, a small-time operation called Blue Ribbon Sports, based in Oregon, had begun to edge into the American market. Its product was the Nike shoe, a running shoe designed by former coach Bill Bowerman in his kitchen just as the jogging boom swept the United States. The Olympic Games in Los Angeles in 1984 marked the showcasing of the Nike brand, and a few years later Nike signed a young basketball phenom named Michael Jordan for a fee of about $2.5 million royalties on shoes and garments with his name on them. Adidas retaliated by bestowing a similar deal on Patrick Ewing of the New York Knicks, but Ewing's career, while a great one, never reached the influence of Air Jordan's (Smit 2008).

In the late 1970s, while Nike was dominating adidas and Puma in the United States, yet another fledgling company entered the scene. A small-time entrepreneur in Boston, Paul Fireman, gained the U.S. rights for Reebok, a British company that had been in existence since the early 1900s but had fallen on hard times. Fireman looked to the hottest sport market at the time, which was called "aerobics." From global sales of just $300,000 in 1980, Reebok had exploded to $12.8 million by 1983, an unprecedented growth.

The sport shoe industry was changed forever, with the four top brands, Nike, Reebok, adidas, and Puma, set to compete for the next several decades for world dominance. Since 2000, Nike has been the dominant seller of athletic footwear, capturing a market share of 36% in the United States and 33% worldwide. Reebok is next with a 12% U.S. share and 9% worldwide. Surprisingly, New Balance is third, with adidas fourth on the strength of a more varied product line while Puma has fallen out of the running. The merger between Reebok and adidas in 2006 resulted in a new alliance valued at $12 billion, very close to the $14 billion Nike is worth and vaulting the U.S. market share of Reebok/adidas to 21% compared to Nike at 36% (Tufts University 2006).

In some instances, economics may replace nationalism as the basis for choosing which teams and athletes to support, especially among people who profit from the success of sport clothing companies. Phil Knight, the founder and longtime president of Nike, admitted after stepping down in December of 2004 that he rooted for sport teams that wore Nike. Rather than cheering for the Americans in World Cup soccer in 1999, Knight picked his favorite teams by the uniforms they wore. Rather than look at the competition as the United States versus Brazil, he saw it as adidas versus Nike (Coakley 2004).

The United States Olympic Committee (USOC) accepts money from corporate sponsors to support the training and competition of American athletes. In return, U.S. athletes must wear the logo and warm-up apparel of the chosen USOC sponsor when competing in the Olympic Games. Imagine the outrage when a company like Nike, which paid millions to sponsor an athlete like Andre Agassi for years, found out that during the Olympics Andre had to shed Nike for the USOC brand.

Corporate sponsors also partially control the televised exposure of international sport. If the sponsors can promote their products by televising the sport, the sport gains terrific exposure in countries where the sponsor wants to advertise its product. If televising a sport doesn't benefit sponsors economically, spectators may have to find other media sources for following an international sport.

Popularity of Various Sports Worldwide

According to IPSOS World Monitor, a German sport research firm, the most popular sport worldwide in 2002 in both participation and spectatorship was soccer (or football, as it is called in other countries). That is no surprise to anyone who has traveled the world and observed kids practicing their skills with the soccer ball, fields covered with players of all ages, and newspaper and television coverage of soccer games. World Cup soccer is the most-watched international sporting event in the world. For the 2010 World Cup finals held in South Africa, the entire tournament drew an estimated 111.6 million U.S. viewers, which was an increase of 22% over the 2006 World Cup. Additionally, the U.S. loss to Ghana was seen by a total of 19.4 million viewers in a Saturday afternoon time slot. Overall, the U.S. television audience was up 50% from the 2006 event. It is interesting to compare the World Cup finals' television audience of more than 700 million with the 2010 Super Bowl audience of 106 million. The championship game, which pitted the Netherlands against Spain, drew a global audience of more than 700 million, exceeding the previous largest audience of 600 million for the opening ceremonies of the Olympic Games in Beijing in 2008. FIFA, the world governing body for soccer, reported more than 250 million people engaged online with FIFA.com during the 31 days of the event, another record shattered. Total television audience worldwide is difficult to estimate because of the necessary reliance on viewer reports that are less accurate than the standards we expect in the United States (*New York Post* 2010; Sandomir 2010).

People living in the United States may find the soccer frenzy puzzling because they are used to American sports. Only in the last 25 years has soccer taken the United States by storm, particularly in the youth market, and it now ranks second only to basketball among U.S. youth (see chapter 6). In Latin America, soccer is part of the culture and boasts huge numbers of participants and spectators who embrace it with passion.

The rest of the top 10 of most popular sports (after soccer) in the world might surprise you. Keep in mind that the raw numbers of people who play or watch sports in any country are hugely influenced by the size of the population of that country, the sport tradition there, the climate, and economic status. You should also realize that there is no precise way to measure actual numbers; rather, researchers are forced to rely on sampling of various populations and self-reported estimates of sport organizations.

According to Quinn (2007), these are the most popular sports around the world for both playing and watching combined:

1.	Soccer	3.5 billion
2.	Cricket	3 billion
3.	Field hockey	2 billion
4.	Tennis	1 billion
5.	Volleyball	900 million
6.	Table tennis	900 million
7.	Basketball	240 million
8.	Baseball	230 million
9.	Rugby football	200 million
10.	Golf	Just under 200 million

ACTIVITY TIME-OUT

What Is Behind the Popularity of Sports Worldwide?

If you're like most people, the list of most popular sports is a surprise. Many people know soccer is number one worldwide, but why are cricket and field hockey so high in the rankings? The answer lies in the country of origin of each of these sports. You'll note that some sports that were invented in America make the list while one very prominent American sport (football) is nowhere to be found. Do a little research and see if you can develop a theory that generally explains the popularity of the sports in the top 10 worldwide.

There are now professional basketball leagues in Europe, and an increasing number of star athletes from countries other than the United States are now starting in the National Basketball Association (NBA). During the 2008-2009 NBA season, there were 77 international players from 32 different countries on rosters led by stars such as Yao Ming of China, Tony Parker of France, Pau Gasol of Spain, and Dirk Nowitzki of Germany (NBA 2009). Critics of American players point to the players' playground origin, their preoccupation with individual play, and their lack of fundamental skills and team play. In international competition, American dominance has receded in recent years, and even when so-called American dream teams compete internationally, the outcomes of their games are in doubt.

Another American sport that has made international inroads is baseball. In Japan, 9 in 10 sport spectators watch baseball, and in South Korea that figure is 7 in 10. Central American countries send a steady stream of athletes to the major leagues in America, and 29% of players in Major League Baseball are international athletes.

Most Americans are shocked that American football is not even in the top 10 in popularity worldwide—football so dominates the American culture at both the college and professional level, especially as a spectator sport. Further, we know that the Super Bowl is beamed around the world to huge audiences; but for most of the world, it's only a curiosity and once-a-year event. The fact that few females participate in football also naturally cuts the potential participation numbers in half.

Tennis is played in more countries than any other sport except soccer, and it continues to grow in undeveloped nations due to sustained support from the International Tennis Federation. The Grand Slam tournaments, Wimbledon and the Australian, French, and U.S. Opens, have supported tennis in developing nations for years. Ironically, athletes from some of those nations emerge to defeat players from the countries that have provided this support.

Golf, baseball, and tennis appeal to higher economic groups worldwide. That makes them prime targets for corporate advertisers hoping to reach an audience with discretionary income. Golf attracts older participants and along with tennis and track and field relies on an older viewing audience as well. Soccer and basketball attract a younger population.

American Influence on World Sport

While soccer has gained a huge foothold in America among youth in high school and college, American sports have had their own effect on the world. Professional leagues that thrive in the United States include American football, baseball, basketball, and ice hockey. The best players around the world come to the United States to compete and test their skills against homegrown American players. International athletes have affected every American sport except football.

Ice hockey in the United States has been dominated for years by Canadians and a few great players

EXPERT'S VIEW

"Grobalization" of American Sport in Latin America

George Ritzer (2004) coined the term "grobalization" to represent the increasing profit-driven capitalist development, Americanization, or McDonalization of sports in other countries. The word is a combination of "growth" and "globalization" of sports. Indigenous sports of the local culture are replaced with modern corporate and commercialized sports. American sports, most notably major league baseball, has to some extent Americanized baseball in countries like the Dominican Republic in order to draw inexpensive new talent to MLB. Alan Klein (1991) has written of the resistance of the people of the Dominican Republic to the practice of MLB actively developing and recruiting young baseball prospects to play in the United States. The Dominican people resent the interference of MLB with their winter leagues and the draining of their best players to a foreign country. Other countries in Latin America such as Venezuela, Cuba, and Nicaragua face the same conflicts of pride in their homegrown talent that is then transplanted to the United States to seek fame and riches in another land. Given the MLB's success in developing talent overseas, other major American sports such as basketball have taken up the practice with the result that many of the finest basketball players worldwide now play in the National Basketball Association while other countries' professional teams are relegated to the minor leagues.

from other countries. Some of Japan's finest baseball athletes have migrated to the United States to share in the wealth garnered by our Major League Baseball stars. Although Japanese baseball has lost some of its superstars, Japanese interest in American baseball skyrockets when one of Japan's players competes in the play-offs or World Series. In Little League, international baseball teams are so successful that organizers divide the competition into two divisions to ensure Americans a place in the final rounds. Without the division, American teams would likely be eliminated early in the tournament, which would also eliminate potential interest and TV revenue.

Latin Americans have loved American baseball for years, and the proof of their talent is the high percentage of major league players emerging from Latin America. In 2008, Latinos made up 27% of all Major League Baseball compared with their proportion of the United States population of 14% (Lapchick 2008-2009). While Latinos have always made their mark in baseball, the plethora of talent and all-star players in recent years has solidified their influence.

Sports such as tennis that are no longer typical American powerhouse sports struggle to produce American players who can compete on the world stage. Yet the United States offers some of the most prestigious tournaments and biggest prize money.

Although the sport of tennis has grown significantly in participation in the past 10 years, television viewership of the U.S. Open championships in America has steadily fallen. In 1999 when Serena Williams and Andre Agassi claimed the title, the television audience was 4.4 million viewers compared to the 2008 championships won by Roger Federer and Serena Williams which produced only 2.2 million viewers. The fact that no American male, with the one-time exception of Andy Roddick in 2003, has won in recent years, combined with the fact that Roger Federer of Switzerland won six consecutive men's finals, have sorely affected the number of television viewers of tennis in the United States. As in most countries, fans turn out to watch their local heroes compete.

In the sport of golf, while participation has slumped badly in recent years, the phenomenon of Tiger Woods continues to carry the popularity of the sport. CBS has enjoyed an average of 11.9 million viewers in each of Woods' four wins at the Masters Tournament in Augusta, Georgia. When Tiger doesn't win, the television audience falls 20% to 9.5 million viewers (Weekley 2009). Following Woods' fall from grace and popularity resulting from his social behavior and marital difficulties, it will be interesting to watch to see if his domination of golf continues or tails off.

Olympic Games

Perhaps no event has promoted sport around the world more than the Olympic Games. The Winter and Summer Games attract huge audiences from virtually every country and are a huge international event. Based on the original Olympic Games born in Athens, Greece, the modern Olympic Games were resurrected by Baron Pierre de Coubertin in 1896 (Henry and Yeomans 1984). Along with other organizers, Coubertin hoped that athletes competing on a world stage would open up communication among people of all nations, show that friendly competition could be exhilarating, promote understanding of different cultures and traditions, and serve as a model for nations working together. Those lofty goals remain a challenge, although it cannot be disputed that Olympic competition has promoted sport around the world.

The Olympic Games helped standardize rules for competition in all sports. Each sport has a designated international organization that determines the rules of play, stages world championships, records competitive records, sets drug-testing protocols, and helps conduct the Olympic events. National governing bodies in each sport take their cues from the international groups so that all countries play by the same rules of competition. For example, standards for the field of play, equipment limitations, and even scoring procedures are set by the international bodies to ensure consistency across countries. We will focus on the Olympic Games in chapter 9.

Effect of Media on the Globalization of Sport

We cannot ignore the media's role in expanding sport worldwide. Perhaps no other factor was more influential in spreading sporting events around the world and reducing former geographical and time constraints.

As discussed in chapter 5, sport and the media exist in a symbiotic relationship. Sporting events are a staple of both printed and electronic media. On the other side, sports receive millions of dollars in free publicity for their products, teams, and athletes. Sports are in the enviable position of being able to count on extensive media coverage without paying advertising fees.

Technological advances have opened up sport on television through satellite and dish broadcasting. DIRECTV and the Dish network, the top two satellite networks in the United States, allow viewers to watch sport events from any American city and an increasing number of international sites. People who wish to watch soccer matches from other countries have immediate real-time access. Pay-per-view opens up a wide world of special sporting events.

The Internet allows us to visit favorite team websites, learn about games and players, and listen to interviews. Fans can listen to a game in progress that may not be accessible on television and can check the latest scores of games from anyplace in the world. As online newspapers continue to develop, we can read about games and events within a few hours of their completion to see what sports writers think of the results. Additionally, the potential for immediate interaction with friends through social networking sites worldwide brings athletic contests to us in real time, no matter where they are held in the world. Friends and family in South Africa for

the 2010 World Cup communicated by social media sources back to family in the United States during the games most exciting to them, mostly involving the United States, of course. (See chapter 5 for more on social networking and sport.)

In addition to freely covering sport, the media pay huge amounts in broadcast rights to events such as the Olympics and National Football League (NFL) football, both of which have worldwide appeal. The Olympic Games rely on television rights as the major source of funding. NBC paid $456 million to broadcast the Atlanta Games, $715 million for the Sydney Games, $545 million for the Salt Lake City Games, $793 million for the Athens Games, $614 million for the Turin Games, and $894 million for the Beijing Games. By 2010, the television rights for NBC to broadcast the Winter Games in Vancouver were awarded for $820 million, those for the 2012 Summer Games in London for $1.18 billion (Martzke 2003).

This revenue goes to the International Olympic Committee and all the national Olympic Committees that help train and support athletes. NBC made an estimated $75 million net profit in ad revenue from the Athens Games. The television coverage in the United States was 198 million, meaning that roughly 71% of the American population watched some part of those Olympic Games (McCarthy 2004). However, the 2006 Winter Games from Turin, Italy, saw a 37% decline from the viewing population of the Salt Lake City Games and finished no better than fourth in the weekly ratings behind *American Idol* on Wednesday, *American Idol* on Tuesday, and *Dancing With the Stars* on Sunday, according to the Nielsen ratings. In 2008, the Beijing Games grabbed four out of the top 10 spots for the year and claimed a 20% share of U.S. homes on Tuesday night prime time. Only football drew a greater television audience. The Vancouver Olympics in 2010 amazingly ended *American Idol*'s string of six unbeaten years in audience share on a Wednesday night when the Games drew 30.1 million Americans, compared with only 18.4 million for *American Idol* in the same time slot (*Vancouver Sun* 2010).

The NFL may be the most successful sport at attracting television sponsorship. In 1998, the NFL secured a $17.6 billion contract with several TV networks wanting to televise its games. Every team in the NFL received in excess of $70 million,

The IOC makes huge amounts of money by selling the broadcast rights to televise the Olympic Games. Televising the Games enables sport to reach a global audience.

or what amounts to nearly 65% of their total revenue (Miller and Associates 2005). The television networks in turn sell sponsorship time during the broadcast to recoup their expenditures. With Super Bowl advertising spots commanding more than $3 million for a 30-second advertisement, you can see how networks generate their revenue from corporate sponsors.

Events such as the NFL Super Bowl are routinely broadcast around the world to more than 200 countries. That publicity helps spread the popularity of the sport, promotes football players, and increases the sale of NFL merchandise. Due to the technological advances of delayed broadcast, satellites, and improved product delivery, fans across the globe can share in the drama and excitement of an American event. In the 10 countries IPSOS surveyed in 2002, American football ranked third in percentage of viewers, behind only soccer and baseball, even though American football is not even played in 8 of the 10 countries surveyed.

The relationship between TV and sport becomes more intertwined when you realize that if sports expect to command big bucks from television, they must be sensitive to the needs of the networks. Starting times are set to attract the largest audience; rules are modified to create drama; and coaches and athletes must make themselves available for interviews before, during, and after games.

Naturally the sports that command the most attention receive the widest TV distribution worldwide. Once networks choose their events, they do everything they can to advertise the event and increase their audience. Sharing international competition ensures viewership from the athletes' home countries, and the Olympic Games capitalize on the natural rivalries between fans from opposing nations.

American soccer can point to the broadcast of the World Cup for helping to popularize soccer in the United States, particularly among women. The success of the American team in the 1990s provided role models for girls and encouraged them to explore their own athletic prowess. The 2010 World Cup for men seemed to awaken the American public to the importance of soccer worldwide as they rooted for the American team that moved into the elimination round of the final 16 countries. Without the contributions of the media to publicizing soccer by televising games, selling soccer to the American public had been slow going and seemed destined for failure.

The emerging world markets are ripe for sport expansion. The percent of the population that watches sport on television in the following countries is high—greater than 50% in each (IPSOS 2002):

Brazil	75%
Japan	84%
China	88%
Mexico	78%
France	57%
South Korea	66%
Germany	77%
United Kingdom	70%
Italy	65%
United States	65%

As countries such as China, Japan, and Mexico increase their participation in the global economy, the rise in sport involvement seems to indicate greater emphasis on personal lifestyle and leisure. In developed countries like the United Kingdom and the United States, growth potential appears smaller because the population is satisfied with its sport involvement, and involvement has reached its peak. This is why marketing sport to emerging new markets is so critical to continued growth in sport popularity and revenue.

Sports that are truly international at the professional level, such as golf and tennis, rely on television coverage because their events are staged in different parts of the world every week. The top competitors represent many nationalities, and world interest changes depending on the performance of favorite players. The four major world championships in professional tennis are referred to as the *Grand Slam tournaments*. They are played in Australia, France, England, and the United States. Worldwide coverage is critical to their success, and the television contracts are complicated multinational ones.

Nationalism Versus Economics

During the middle of the 20th century, international sporting competition was buoyed by strong feelings of nationalism. From Adolph Hitler's mission to create a superrace in Germany to the nationalistic tenor of the 1936 Olympic Games staged in Berlin, countries around the world used sports as a rallying cry of patriotism. Perhaps more than any other event, the Olympic Games thrived on the inherent nationalism built into their structure, publicity, and team medal count.

With the rise of Communism and the Cold War between the Soviet Union and its allies and the West, including Europe and the United States, athletic competition became about more than who had the best athletes. Fueled by rhetoric from sport leaders and politicians, many people began to see sport contests as a validation of a more democratic or socialistic society. When high-profile athletes won medals at the Olympic Games, their country burst with pride at the confirmation of their political ideology.

At the Olympic Games, the medals won by each country were totaled and a winning nation was declared. That tradition faded significantly with the change in government in the Soviet Union, but medal count by country still gets some play. Of course, winning gold medals in worldwide competition depends on many factors, including national sport tradition, economics, and support for athlete development.

As the Cold War faded and tension between the West and the former Eastern European Communist countries eased, the attitude in the sport world also changed. An **economic model** began to replace a nationalistic one in the Olympics and most other international sport events. The key factor in selecting a site for the Olympics is the financial package offered to support the Games, including the construction of millions of dollars worth of athletic venues and supporting transportation between sites. Choosing a site takes years; the 2016 Summer Olympics were awarded to Rio de Janeiro in Brazil in October of 2009 after a three-year process of vetting bids from around the world by the International Olympic Committee. From the beginning of a proposal, the process lasts approximately 10 years before the Games begin. Brazil is the first South American country to host the Games.

A city's potential attractiveness to corporate sponsors is also a key factor along with the proposed television package for broadcasting the Games. Consider, for example, the staging of the 1996 Olympic Games in Atlanta, home of Coca-Cola. Corporate sponsors like Coke seize the opportunity to sell their product around the world by advertising through the Olympic Games. In recent years, McDonald's has provided food in the Olympic Village for athletes, and Mars candy bars is a major sponsor with the goal of selling snacks and candy bars to a sporting public.

The economic model for international sport can also be illustrated by the fact that Roots, a Canadian clothing company, outfitted the 2004 U.S. Olympic team with warm-ups through a corporate sponsorship. Most sponsors of sporting events are large multinational corporations dedicated to growing their business in as many markets as possible. Rather than be seen as provincial, these corporations seek to portray a global image. Because their sponsorship dollars have fueled the rapid economic expansion in sport, the sporting world depends on them to survive as a business.

Athletes and Coaches as Migrant Workers

People who make their living from sport include athletes, coaches, officials, agents, and organization officials and staff. Depending on the sport, they

POP CULTURE

Michael Jordan as an International Brand

Despite the fact that basketball is only the seventh most popular sport worldwide, Michael Jordan became a global sport star recognized by billions of people around the world. How did that happen? It wasn't just his athletic prowess, which was considerable, but perhaps more importantly his partnership with Nike, which made him the focus of the company's worldwide marketing strategy. The expansion of the global media assisted in creating Jordan as an international hero who helped to create new markets and increase profits for Nike products.

The "Air Jordan" Nike shoe was popularized worldwide and made the Nike "swoosh" one of the most well-known company logos, rivaling those of other giants, such as McDonald's golden arches. Jordan played the role of the ideal superathlete, without strong opinions on current events or even about his apparent "blackness." His role was to be a sport superstar imbued with the qualities of motivation, integrity, and success. He modeled the "American dream" as a kid who didn't even make his high school basketball team but went on to star in college and professional basketball at the highest level (Nixon 2008).

travel around the globe as a natural part of their employment. Most often, they are employed by specific sport organizations that rely on international exposure and operation. Of course, sports indigenous to one country or region of the world do not rely on international operation.

Athletes seek the highest level of competition and coaching in order to maximize their talent and earning power. They likely begin sport instruction near their home, but as they progress, they often travel to secure specialized coaching and train with other elite athletes. If their country offers a national program in their sport, they may attend a special school where training and academic education are combined. Some athletes living where their sport is not as popular or available may seek training in another country.

Athletes who train in the United States often become comfortable living there and eventually make it their home base. This is also true for their coaches, who travel with them. In sports like tennis and golf, in which world tours are the only way to make a living, both athletes and coaches are more like gypsies on the road. They move from city to city almost every week and live in hotels and out of suitcases. The cultural experience is unparalleled, and the excitement of visiting great cities on every continent is exhilarating.

But the endless travel and lack of contact with family and friends can be lonely. Maintaining friendships outside of the sport world is very difficult, and developing romantic liaisons can be a perplexing problem. Also, if athletes spend too much time sightseeing to the detriment of their competitive performance, their earning power and career are threatened.

Coaches in individual sports must also be flexible and frequent travelers, and they often switch athletes as fortunes wane or players retire. Coaching on the road makes a family life difficult, and solitary nights spent in hotel rooms challenge most people, who crave relationships.

Coaches of international sport teams also find opportunities in various countries. Many undeveloped countries hire coaches from more developed nations to build their systems in sports like soccer, basketball, swimming, and track and field. Even among developed countries, coaches often move from one to another. In 1999, England hired Patrice Hagelauer of France to head the performance development program for tennis and has since followed up by hiring, at various times, Peter Lundgren of Sweden, Louis Cayer of Canada, and Americans

Brad Gilbert and Paul Annacone. In spite of spending huge sums of money to recruit coaches from other countries, British tennis is still mired at the lowest level of performance even though it boasts the most famous tournament of all at Wimbledon. Many of the leading tennis coaches in the United States originate from other countries. People are often intrigued by different coaching approaches and reach out to international coaches who offer alternative methods and perspectives.

Officials and administrators of world sporting events also travel and often reside in foreign countries. They typically follow the world competition from venue to venue, although they may enjoy more time at home than athletes do. World championships, the Olympic Games, and similar events are not as frequent as the regular-season or tour events and are separated by weeks or months. Agents, on the other hand, usually travel constantly to attend events their athletes compete in. Since they typically handle more than one athlete, they can spend endless weeks on the road serving their clients and scouting for new talent to sign.

The result of all this global travel is that athletes, coaches, and officials become ambassadors for their home nation, learn about other cultures, and tend to develop a more comprehensive worldview. They probably do little to directly influence the countries where they travel; but as they develop followings, strong links may be created. Particular athletes may adopt or become fascinated with other cultures. Language barriers are reduced as people use more foreign phrases and expressions just to survive.

As professional athletes or coaches mature and start families, they often arrange for their loved ones to travel with them. Imagine the experience of such a family. The educational experience for kids from this background is priceless.

The countries of origin are not always happy when their athletes leave home to play professionally in another country. As already mentioned, American baseball has increasingly attracted players from Latin American countries, as well as some of the best-known Japanese players. The countries that lose the athletes lose some of their most charismatic and exciting competitors and see reduced interest in local baseball.

Over the past two to three decades in many European countries, sport leagues in soccer, ice hockey, and basketball have increasingly recruited players from other countries. The motivation is to find the best available players in the world to play for local clubs or teams. Some observers say

IN THE ARENA WITH . . .

American Basketball Players

Brandon Jennings is the first American basketball player to choose to go to Europe to play professional basketball rather than U.S. college basketball. He signed a contract in 2008 with Virtus Roma of the Italian League for a reported salary of $600,000. Of course, in American college basketball he was limited to receiving a full college scholarship and received no money. And there was the inconvenience of attending class, taking exams, and other distractions. Jennings admittedly was not a strong student academically (Zegers 2008).

A year later, basketball prodigy Jeremy Tyler dropped out of his high school in San Diego, California, to sign a professional contract with a pro team in Israel. Tyler figured he might as well get the best competition available (and get paid for it) during the two years before he was eligible for the NBA draft. Unfortunately, he lasted only three months and 10 games before leaving Israel to return home (Thamel 2010).

It would seem that these American players are seeking to compete with international players like Spain's Ricky Rubio, who turned professional at age 14 and by age 17 was starting for the Spanish Olympic team. Eventually, Rubio signed with the NBA's Minnesota Timberwolves in 2008 for a handsome contract.

One of the major factors in these recent cases is the NBA rule that says players must either be 19 years old or have completed one year of college to be eligible for the NBA draft. The idea is to ensure that NBA players are mature enough physically, mentally, and emotionally to compete. But the reality is that most phenoms attend college for just one year and leave the school high and dry, or they opt for playing overseas for pay waiting to be eligible for the NBA draft.

that this recruiting hinders the development of young athletes in the home country, who see spots taken by athletes from other nations. Leagues take away jobs from home-country athletes in the hope of producing a winning team (Maguire et al. 2002).

A parallel situation exists in many American colleges and universities. Once the top American athletes are signed to scholarships, the schools that didn't sign them recruit the best overseas athletes in hopes of competing with the leading American schools. Sports like swimming, track and field, soccer, and tennis have been particularly affected by this growing trend. Efforts to limit the number of international players have been struck down in the courts, and American families cry foul when their kids are denied athletic scholarships in favor of international players.

International competition in sport can provide a terrific opportunity for athletes, coaches, and others. On the other hand, complications in personal and family lives, burnout, and cultural shock also occur. Surviving this unusual life experience boils down to how grounded people are in their fundamental values and relationships.

Using Sport for Better World Understanding

In an ideal world, international competition would be an opportunity for those involved to learn about each other and to connect on a personal level. Once people understand and appreciate the society and culture of others, the stage is set for people to live and work together. This valued outcome does happen in world competition, although it does not happen without dedication and effort on the part of those involved.

Athletes of all ages may compete internationally if they earn a top ranking in their own country. World competitions for athletes 12 and under are staged in various sports, and athletes in their 50s and 60s also have their own competitions. College athletes in many sports have also benefited from traveling abroad to compete. For many athletes, these experiences are eye-opening cultural excursions to countries they would not normally visit. Meeting athletes from around the world helps them appreciate the humanity of all cultures and may urge them to train harder to be the best in the world.

Some international competition balances sport and travel. High school students can sign up for tours of other countries during which they also compete at arranged sites along the way. Young people who take advantage of these tours may be sponsored by sport organizations, organizations promoting international understanding, or their families. Countries often establish exchange programs for young athletes. It is exhilarating for people who struggle to communicate to find a common bond in the language of sport.

The United States is a popular destination, and most people who qualify to visit for a sport event seize the opportunity. In virtually every sport, young athletes from other countries visit and compete against U.S. kids while sightseeing and learning about American life.

Athletic coaches also have numerous opportunities to travel internationally. Most sports hold worldwide coaching conferences, and each participating nation may designate several coaches as representatives. The concept of sharing coaching philosophies is not new, and coaches from countries that lead the world competition are in demand as speakers and teachers. Along the way, coaches from different societies interact and broaden their outlook toward the world.

The value of international sport competition may be narrowed if coaches and leaders focus entirely on their athletes' performance, losing the opportunity to learn about others. Coaches personally benefiting from international travel may view competition as more than what happens on the playing field.

People who schedule trips find that sightseeing is best left to the end of the trip when competition is completed and they can relax their single-minded focus on their sport.

Sports offer potential for understanding the larger world, but this opportunity may be lost unless we structure the experience with that goal in mind. We make a mockery of one of the values we often trumpet to support sport participation if we do not establish international appreciation through competition.

Chapter Summary

The English system of sports and games had the most dominant effect on the development of international sport. For centuries, Great Britain influenced countless countries to adopt its sports. In the last 50 years, other Western countries including the United States have added their influence. As the world population changes and countries like China embrace world sport, influence is likely to shift again.

Sports have become a global enterprise by standardizing rules, staging world competitions for athletes of all ages and abilities, and covering those contests through the media. Technological advancements have made sport events immediately available to fans worldwide.

Participation sport is historically popular in its nation of origin. The most popular sport worldwide by far is soccer, followed by cricket, field hockey, tennis, and volleyball in the top five. Interestingly, American football does not even rate in the top 10.

The modern Olympic Games have helped significantly in developing sport worldwide. Most nations support the training and coaching of their athletes to ensure success in international competition. Extending the length and pageantry of the Games has attracted television viewers worldwide and generated millions of dollars for organizers and sponsors.

As multinational corporations realized the possibilities of advertising through international sport, they reached out to new audiences. Sport equipment and clothing companies discovered cheap labor in undeveloped countries and millions of consumers in developed countries.

The economics of international sport began to replace the nationalism that was the hallmark of competition during the Cold War. Olympic venues are now chosen by the potential revenue that can be generated. Athletes from competing countries are on the same team, in a sense, as they ply their trade with the backing of Nike, adidas, Reebok, and others.

Opportunities for world travel, cultural study, and personal relationships with people of other countries have expanded for athletes and coaches. However, using sport to promote cultural understanding and harmony must be a valued goal if it is to progress. Focusing exclusively on competition may improve performance but shortchange the travel experience for athletes.

9

Olympic Movement

After reading this chapter, you will know the following:

- A brief history of the Olympic Games
- The role of the modern Olympics in our global society
- How nationalism, economics, and politics influence the Olympics
- The role of the United States Olympic Committee
- How the Olympic Movement has affected athlete development and coaching and training methods in the United States

The Olympic Creed states, "The most important thing in the Olympic Games is not to win but to take part, just as the most important thing in life is not the triumph, but the struggle. The essential thing is not to have conquered but to have fought well." The Olympic Creed is attributed to Baron Pierre de Coubertin, the founder of the modern Olympic Games. Athletes are reminded of the Creed by their coaches, organizers, and fellow competitors since it expresses the philosophy upon which the Games were conceived and have been conducted since 1896.

Another important symbol of the Olympics is the five interlocked rings, which represent the union of the five original major continents (Africa, America, Asia, Australia, and Europe) and the meeting of the athletes from the world at the Games. The five colors of the rings from left to right are blue, black, and red across the top and yellow and green along the bottom. These colors were chosen because at least one of these colors can be found in the flag of every nation. The Olympic Rings are a carefully guarded logo property of the International Olympic Committee and the National Olympic Committees of each country and can only be used with permission. Corporate sponsors are given permission to use the Olympic logo on their advertising in return for the millions of dollars of financial support they provide.

No other sporting event in the last 100 years has had the widespread effects of the Olympic Games. Along with providing a venue for the finest athletes from a variety of sports, the Games provide opportunities for spectators to enjoy international competition in virtually every world nation. Through the years, nationalism developed in the Olympics as every nation took pride in its athletes and created heroes for youth to emulate.

In the more recent past, the fierce nationalism has been pushed aside by the economic effects of the Olympic Games for national Olympic organizations, corporate sponsors, and host cities. What was once an amateur competition has unabashedly morphed into a competition for the world's best professional athletes, many of whom financially capitalize on Olympic success.

By now most nations have established Olympic organizations, often under a governmental agency such as a Ministry of Sport. Relying on government funds and private donations, national Olympic organizations support the development of the country's Olympic candidates in hopes of boosting their performance as they return to the Games every four years. Sport in many countries has grown and flourished simply because of Olympic development programs that encourage young athletes.

History of the Olympics

The ancient Olympics were founded as a festival to honor the king of the Greek gods, Zeus. The Games were held every four years for more than 1,000 years, from 776 B.C. to A.D. 393. Only Greeks were allowed to compete, although athletes from Greek colonies in countries that are now Spain, Italy, Libya, Egypt, Ukraine, and Turkey gave the Olympics an international flavor (Henry and Yeomans 1984).

Although the origin of the Olympics is in dispute because of the plethora of unsubstantiated accounts of its beginnings, some general facts are known. At the height of their popularity, the Games represented the culture that made Greece the undisputed mistress of the Mediterranean. Emerging from a religious festival that lasted one day, the Games developed into a seven-day extravaganza that riveted the attention of the people of Greece and its colonies. Common men competed against soldiers and royalty for the glory of winning the coveted olive wreath symbolizing victory.

The original Games featured just one event, a footrace down the length of the stadium of about 200 yards (183 meters). At the behest of the city-state of Sparta, more events were added, and the 18th Olympic Games featured a pentathlon that consisted of a long jump, spear throw, sprint, discus throw, and wrestling match. In succeeding years, boxing, chariot racing, footraces of varying lengths, and a *pankration*, a combination of boxing and wrestling, were added (Henry and Yeomans 1984; Leonard 1980; Rice, Hutchinson, and Lee 1958).

Even as the Games expanded their physical contests and gained popularity, religious ceremonies were not forgotten. Religious ceremonies were always critical to the celebrations to honor the gods. Arts, including poetry recitations, singing, and dramatic productions, were also a vital part of the week-long celebration. Every four years, the Games turned a mosaic of religion, athletics, and arts into a national festival (Scheiber 2004).

As years went by, traditional Greek religion faded and the Games lost their significance. The decline of the Games has been blamed on the corruption of politicians and the wealthy. Athletes focused more on the prize money they could earn than on the honor of competing for the olive wreath. The rich history of morality and competing for the love of the contest was lost.

The last Games were held in A.D. 393, after which the Christian emperor of Rome, Theodosius I, banned pagan worship. The Olympic Games are one of the enduring contributions of Greek civilization. In addition to fostering a strong belief in the value of athletics, the Games produced notable works of art, music, and culture and celebrated individual achievement. Those characteristics sparked the rebirth of the Olympics more than a thousand years later, in 1896. The Games began again in Athens, with just 14 countries competing in nine sports: track and field, cycling, fencing, gymnastics, wrestling, swimming, weightlifting, tennis, and shooting. These modern Olympic Games have continued through political conflicts, world wars, and the passing of generations (Henry and Yeomans 1984).

The modern Olympic Games were revived by Baron Pierre de Coubertin, a French educator. His vision was to replicate worldwide the positive effects of the original Greek Olympics founded in Athens. According to the Olympic Charter, "Olympism is a philosophy of life, exalting and combining in a balanced whole the qualities of body, will, and mind. Blending sport with culture and education, Olympism seeks to create a way of life based on the joy found in effort, the educational value of good example and respect for universal fundamental ethical principles" (Olympic Charter 2004, p. 9).

Drawing from the holistic Athenian philosophy of a sound mind in a sound body, the Olympic Movement wanted to help people understand and appreciate their differences through competition in sport. The hope was that by establishing a community of athletes, coaches, and organizers from every country in the world, international understanding and goodwill would be promoted (Henry and Yeomans 1984).

Effect of the Olympic Games

The Games profoundly affect their host city, the media that cover the contests, and the athletes who compete. This effect is felt in the years leading to the competition as well as during the staging of the

The ancient Olympic Games included many events, such as the fierce race.

competition, and in many cases it lasts for years afterward. Most Olympic competitors devote their early years to development and training in the hope of someday qualifying for the Olympics. Once they finally realize their dream, it becomes the defining factor in their life and sets the path for the years ahead. Many trade on their Olympic success as they move on to other professions.

Host City

Cities from around the world compete furiously to host the Olympic Games because of the potential prestige and financial benefits they offer. Sport venues are created or refurbished and endure once the Olympics end, used by athletes from the host country. Yet the costs of hosting can be daunting. The 2004 Athens Games cost an estimated $14.6 billion, when the Greek government had originally budgeted $5.9 billion based on previous Olympic Games. (For example, the Sydney Games cost $1.5

billion and the Atlanta Games $1.7 billion.) But the challenges in readying the venue, construction snafus, and an unrealistic deadline, along with increased security spurred by recent terrorist activities, all jacked up the costs (Jenkins 2004).

The Beijing Olympics are reported to have cost more than $43 billion—three times more than any other Olympic Games in history. To understand how costs reach such once-unimaginable heights, you have to look at the three general categories of spending (Cummings 2009):

- The first is the direct operating expenses such as the athletes' village, transportation, security, and ceremonies. The average budget for this category is around $3 billion and is usually covered by television, tourism, and ticket revenues.

- The second category is for general infrastructure improvements in the city, which even if expensive, typically bring lasting benefits to the city. These costs often include removing decaying housing or slums, planting vegetation, building roads, and constructing new high-rise structures.

- The third category of expense is the one that is most troublesome once the Games are over—the expense to build modern state-of-the-art sport facilities that are used only during the Games. They include extravagant stadiums that seat around 100,000 spectators, natatoriums, and other similar projects. After the Games, most cities are stuck paying off the debt for constructing these venues, and in most cases the facility is no longer of practical use.

In spite of the huge financial risks, the race among potential host cities has only heated up. Leading contenders for the 2016 Summer Olympics were Chicago, Madrid, Tokyo, and Rio de Janeiro. The Brazilian city won the bid, making it the first country in South America to host the Games. The contending cities underwent rigorous vetting and presented their plans to the International Olympic Committee in 500-page tomes boasting their assets and the benefits of awarding the bid to them. Past issues of bribery and lavish entertainment of decision makers resulted in a carefully monitored bid review and a transparency of process that had been recently lacking.

New stadiums and athletic facilities are required for every Olympic Games. The host city begins by assessing the current facilities that are suitable and then constructs needed arenas, pools, and so on. The funding becomes complicated as various groups pitch in money in return for use or ownership of the facility long after the Games end.

The 1996 Olympic Games in Atlanta, Georgia, significantly affected the long-term economics of the city and state. These Olympic legacies can be grouped into three categories: (1) the creation of world-class facilities; (2) the national and international recognition of the city through extensive media exposure; and (3) community benefits such as local volunteerism, job creation and training, youth programs, and funding for community development projects.

World-class athletic facilities from the Atlanta Games include the $189 million Olympic Stadium, the Georgia International Horse Park, the $17 million Wolf Creek Shooting Range, the tennis facility at Stone Mountain, and the $10 million Lake Lanier Rowing Center. New dormitories costing $47 million were built at the Georgia Institute of Technology (Georgia Tech) and Georgia State University to create an Olympic village to house athletes and coaches. An additional $24 million was spent to build a new aquatic center on Georgia Tech's campus, and $1.5 million was used to renovate the coliseum on campus to host the boxing events (Humphreys and Plummer 1996).

Media Effects

NBC committed to a $2 billion rights package to televise the Winter Games from Vancouver (2010) and the Summer Games from London (2012) to the U.S. audience. The combined bid for the Winter and Summer Games is a 46% increase from the previous Games in 2006-2008 (Martzke 2003). The rationale from the network was that the Olympics, unlike any other event, can attract whole families to TV watching. The Olympics create a unique audience for sponsors to sell to. Unlike the Super Bowl, which lasts a few hours, the Olympic Games extend over 17 days, providing multiple time slots for advertising. As you will notice from table 9.1, the revenue impact of the Olympic Games has steadily increased since 1992. Keep in mind that these rights fees are only for the United States. Other countries negotiate separately for their television contracts.

You may wonder how television networks could commit to such large fees to televise the Games. The secret is that while NBC paid $894 million to broadcast the Beijing Games, it also attracted over $1 billion in advertising revenue that offset the cost.

The 2008 Summer Olympic Games in Beijing set a record for the most-watched Olympics ever with a cumulative TV audience of 4.4 billion, which is almost two-thirds of the world population. Compare this result with a total TV audience of 3.6 billion for the Sydney Games in 2000 and 3.9 billion for the

Athens Games in 2004. Not surprisingly, China led all countries in number of television viewers, with 94% of its population tuning in, followed by South Korea at 94% and Mexico with 93%. In the United States, approximately two-thirds of the population watched at least some of the Games (Nielsen Media Research 2008).

The Winter Olympic Games are smaller in size and scope and draw a relatively smaller television audience. At the Vancouver Games, the worldwide audience was reported to be 3.5 billion viewers, while the United States had 190 million viewers over the 17 days of broadcast. You may be interested to learn that in the United States, the Winter Games drew a higher number of female than male viewers (56% female) and a predominately older audience. The most-watched event was the gold medal men's hockey game between host Canada and the United States, which drew 27.6 million viewers (Beikoff 2010a).

Competing networks get into the action by inviting Olympic athletes onto talk shows, showing clips of their performances, and promoting their sponsors. Magazines and newspaper dailies devote pages to stories about Olympic athletes and coaches and the surrounding subplots of drug testing, romance, athletes' earnings, and judging controversies.

It seems that every two years, when either the Winter or Summer Games takes the stage, the world steps back from other events to focus on the competition. That was the original idea of the Olympic Games, and it has endured for all these centuries.

TABLE 9.1 U.S. Olympics Television Rights Fees

SUMMER GAMES			WINTER GAMES		
Year	Host city	Fee	Year	Host city	Fee
1992	Barcelona	$401M	1992	Albertville	$234M
1996	Atlanta	$456M	1994	Lillehammer	$300M
2000	Sydney	$705M	1998	Nagano	$375M
2004	Athens	$793M	2002	Salt Lake City	$545M
2008	Beijing	$894M	2006	Torino	$613M
2012	London	$1.1B	2010	Vancouver	$820M

Data from Martzke 2003.

 POP CULTURE

American Women Love the Olympic Games!

You may be surprised to learn that there are only three sporting events that draw a larger female than male television audience: the Summer Olympics, the Winter Olympics, and the Kentucky Derby. In fact, since the 1996 Olympic Games in Atlanta, more women than men have tuned in. The Games in Vancouver in 2010 drew an audience that was 56% women versus 44% men. That's just the reverse of the Super Bowl audience, which was 54% males versus 46% females in the same year (Hogan 2008).

Some observers think that women have become tired of the traditional male sports of football, basketball, and baseball dominating television coverage and long to see more female athletes in action. Olympic sports such as gymnastics, swimming, track and field, and figure skating typically show great female athletes competing internationally. Male sports are also popular with women viewers, especially some of the more unfamiliar sports that are rarely portrayed on television. Some female viewers like the "human stories" of the athletes, which are inspirational as well as entertaining. Without the success of American women in recent Olympic Games, the number of medals won would be significantly lower, and female viewers like winners as much as men do.

Female viewers also have a lot of influence on the type of ads shown during Olympic broadcasts. More than 100 advertisers spend more than $1 billion to push their product to the audience, and their marketing savvy is reflected in the types of ads produced. Women love Olympic-themed ads like the spot featuring U.S. speedskater Dan Jansen, which earned a likeability rating three times greater than the average commercial (Nielsen Company 2010).

Michael Phelps is considered one of the greatest Olympic athletes of all time winning eight gold medals in Beijing in 2008.

Elite Performance Athletes

The motto of the Olympic Games is "Citius, Altius, Fortius," which is Latin that translates to "faster, higher, braver" but is universally accepted as meaning "swifter, higher, and stronger." These are worthy goals for every aspiring Olympian who measures success by the winning of gold, silver, or bronze medals. Of the athletes who compete, few come away with a medal, but most treasure the experience of competing with the world's best in their respective sports. Hundreds of thousands of aspiring youth around the world train and test their abilities in hopes of someday becoming an Olympian.

World championships are held in many sports under the aegis of the given sport's international governing body, yet it is at the Olympic Games that almost all sports come together to stage a unique celebration of athletic competition that is the most comprehensive and lavish yet conceived. The world attends to the Games, with audiences glued to their televisions for more than two weeks. The media have latched onto the Olympics as a significant world event that can attract huge audiences and hence hundreds of millions of dollars in corporate sponsorship. The Olympics have become the largest and most successful economic engine in the sport world.

The excitement of the Olympic Games focuses the world on the best performances of elite athletes in every Olympic sport. Winning a medal at the Olympics has achieved an almost mystical status among athletes. Rising to the occasion to win a medal or set a world record is the dream of every athlete. By comparison, success at a world championship, while certainly notable, does not generate nearly the media attention or sponsorship opportunities as does an Olympic medal. The focus of world sport fans on the Olympic Games adds pressure along with conferring instant fame on athletes who offer up a performance of a lifetime.

Famous athletes in their sport jockey for opportunities to rub elbows with athletes from other sports whom they admire. Olympic athletes are clearly not inured to the celebrity factor. They are sport fans who enjoy watching performers in other sports rise to greatness.

The emphasis on winning at the Games has become a double-edged sword. Successful medal winners are heroes, and those who enter and come up short are labeled failures. In some countries like the United States, debate rages over whether athletes who qualify for the Games but are unlikely to challenge for a medal should be supported financially by their home country. In the United States, the goal of the United States Olympic Committee (USOC) is to accumulate the most medals possible in a particular event. Athletes who qualify but are unlikely to win a medal become something of a second-class citizen, and many people believe USOC resources are wasted on them. On the opposing side are those who believe that just competing in the Olympic Games is a right they have earned. Isn't competing to compete the point of it all?

The fascination with winning medals has produced an incentive plan for athletes, backed by governments and National Olympic Committees, in which they receive cash awards for each medal won. Proponents of this plan believe that cash will encourage athletes to work harder; and in smaller countries where athletes have fewer opportunities to capitalize on their success as an athlete, the awards in some cases are over $100,000.

In more developed countries like the United States, the opportunities for athletes are more

ACTIVITY TIME-OUT

Who Gets the Money?

If you were in charge of the American Olympic team, with a goal of producing as many medals as possible but with a limited budget, would you restrict your financial support to athletes with a realistic shot at a medal? If so, how would you determine an athlete's odds at success? Which sports award the highest number of medals, making them a more logical choice for a larger proportion of financial support? Or would you support any athlete qualifying for the Games according to the world standards? Justify your answer.

plentiful, so those countries typically award lower bonuses. In the more high-profile sports, the bonuses for professional athletes, the relatively modest reward of $25,000 to $50,000, is insignificant compared to their annual earnings. Most donate the proceeds to a charitable organization.

The public acceptance of winning as the primary goal of Olympic athletes has fueled the concentration on elite athletic competition. Kids are steered into elite development programs and encouraged to focus on preparing for a run at an Olympic medal. While some sport leaders believe it is healthy for kids to aspire to greatness, participation for fun may suffer, which may lead to the high dropout rate in youth sport mentioned in chapter 5. Once kids realize high performance is not within their reach, they often give up competition and turn to other activities. Another by-product of the emphasis on winning is the increasing use of performance-enhancing drugs, which has resulted in stepped-up testing of winning athletes, both in and out of competition. Heading into the 2004 Olympic Games in Athens, speculations about which athletes were using illegal substances garnered as much media attention as predictions of athletic accomplishments. We'll spend more time on performance enhancement through drugs in chapter 18.

The demand to produce elite athletes who might someday compete for Olympic medals has spawned ambitious talent scouting in many countries. Children younger than age 6 have been tested for their athletic potential and offered government-funded training opportunities in the sport that seems to suit their body type, athletic skill, and temperament. These state schools produced many champion athletes in East Germany and Russia during the Cold War, when countries dedicated state monies to train athletes so they could prove the superiority of their culture.

The recent success of athletes from China in the Olympics can be directly tied to a national system of training in sport schools. In the Seoul Olympics in 1988, China earned just five gold medals and a total of 12 medals. Compare that to 2008, when Chinese athletes earned 51 gold and 100 overall. They must surely be doing something right.

Under the Russian model of a tight-knit system of sport training schools, children train hard for up to five hours per day even at young ages. They do also spend time in academics, although that is clearly a secondary occupation. For these kids, the dream of becoming a champion is the goal and the promise of a better life economically. Especially children from modest-income homes see athletic success if they work hard at sport. Unlike children in Western countries, Chinese youngsters don't have to pay for or search for the best coaches, trainers, facilities, sponsorship, equipment, food, or lodging. All of that and more is provided by the government as long as they demonstrate their athletic prowess and follow the rules.

Some sport observers question these methods and criticize China for exploiting children and separating them from their families; and there are those who claim that the children are abused if their performances do not measure up. But if we step back for a bit, we might ask who can criticize a government that provides opportunity to those with talent to chase their dreams (MacLeod 2007).

Shift From Amateurs to Professionals

During the last 50 years, the Olympics shifted away from the idealistic notion that world-class athletes could compete solely for the love of the game and thus be dubbed *amateur athletes*. Juan Antonio Samaranch of Spain, president of the International Olympic Committee from 1980 to 2001, made it clear that his mission for the Olympic Games was to attract the best athletes in the world. Their standing as amateur or professional performers was irrelevant to him.

EXPERT'S VIEW

The World Anti-Doping Agency

The World Anti-Doping Agency (WADA) was established in 1999 to set standards for anti-doping work and coordinate the efforts of sport organizations and public authorities. The International Olympic Committee provided the impetus by convening the First World Conference on Doping in Sport in Lausanne, Switzerland.

In the Athens Games, some 3,000 drug tests were administered; and four years later in Beijing, that number had jumped by 50% to 4,500 tests. In spite of increased testing, at the Beijing Games only five athletes tested positive; the IOC had previously disqualified nine athletes for doping before the Games began. In addition, there were six doping cases involving horses in the equestrian competition. Also, an undetermined number of athletes had been eliminated along the way by their own national governing bodies. As of 2008, these are the sports that have registered the most failed drug tests:

Cycling	45
Swimming	26
Track and field	19
Rugby	12
Wrestling	11

Of course, the number of positive tests does not tell the whole story. Those athletes and coaches who are determined to cheat will continue to look for doping methods that are beyond the reach of the current testing protocols. But in sum, the coordinated approach of the sporting world under the leadership of WADA has swung the pendulum back in favor of drug-free competition for now (WADA 2010; Wilson 2010).

During the first half of the 20th century, sports were still supposed to be played for enjoyment, with no thought of financial reward. Only the economically well off could afford the time and expense of playing, so sport was limited to the privileged class. As interest in watching sport grew, spectators became willing to pay admission fees, and money became available to athletes. Commercial sponsors and television rights added to the available financial resources. Yet the athletes who performed often received a relatively small portion of this revenue.

American fans loved the idea of amateur athletes struggling to train and then succeeding on the world stage. But the amateur status was a front. College athletes received scholarships; athletes appeared in advertisements or were hired as spokespeople or consultants. Americans pointed to other countries, particularly Eastern European Communist countries, as ignoring the rules of amateurism, as the International Olympic Committee allowed each nation to determine what constituted amateur status.

The only athletes clearly excluded from the Olympic Games were professional athletes in basketball, tennis, ice hockey, and baseball who earned their living playing their sport. Rather than sending professionals, the United States sent college kids to compete in the Olympic Games. For some years, doing that worked, since the United States dominated world competition anyway. But as other nations began challenging U.S. dominance, to keep winning the United States had to change its definition of amateur, or the Olympics had to change its rules or open up competition to anyone—pro or amateur.

Over the last 25 years, all pretense of sending amateur athletes to the Olympics has been set aside. Now Olympic athletes include primarily professional athletes, and in fact Olympic stars are expected to promote the Games and their sport for compensation. Stars from professional teams, leagues, and tours are welcomed into the Games.

The continuing stumbling block in the United States is the stance of the National Collegiate Athletic Association (NCAA) toward professionalism. The NCAA continues to define college athletes as amateurs, though college athletes receive athletic scholarships and other benefits. It requires young athletes hoping to qualify for athletic scholarships to remain amateurs before attending college. This rule exists only in the United States, and it severely limits the ability of athletes in expensive Olympic sports to secure financial backers when they are young. The NCAA has an impossible task on its hands of regulating corporate sponsorship or support from organizations for young athletes. Supposed amateur athletes in youth sport cannot afford to compete unless their family has significant resources or unless they secure sponsorship of some kind. Fortunately, high school sports like basketball and American football provide development opportunities for younger athletes. But athletes in skating, equestrian, tennis, golf, gymnastics, and other Olympic sports have no such viable opportunity through the school system.

Nationalism and the Olympic Movement

Within the International Olympic Committee (IOC) there are currently 202 National Olympic Committees (NOCs) over five continents. These national committees promote the principles of Olympism within their country, support their athletes, and send athletes to participate in the Games. Modern Olympic Games have seen an increasingly nationalistic flavor, no doubt partly due to the fact that only NOCs are allowed to select and send athletes to the Olympic Games. Thus athletes feel, rightly so, that they are representing their country.

Team sports heighten the nationalism. At the Olympics, the German team competes against the British team and so on. When athletes or teams win medals, they are presented the medal while their country's flag waves and their national anthem plays. The media show these ceremonies and note the tears of successful athletes who are testimony of their country's success.

The opening ceremonies of the Games include a huge procession, with every athlete and coach marching into the Olympic stadium as part of a team representing their homeland. Usually their dress highlights their country's traditional garb or colors. Regardless of their competitive standing, medal chances, and financial status, athletes from one country march together.

Martin (1996) suggests that nationalism was catapulted into prominence by Adolf Hitler, who used the Olympic Games in Berlin as a propaganda show for Nazi Germany. Hitler's constant reference to the human *superrace* of white athletes was damaged by the heroic achievements of American sprinter Jesse Owens, a black athlete who won four medals and dominated the competition in track and field.

After World War II and the Korean War, the world settled into 35 years of what was dubbed the *Cold War*. Essentially, the Cold War was a clash of cultures and ideas of governance between the Russian Federation and the United States. Although war was never declared between these two superpowers, it was always a threat, and the tension was great. It was during the Cold War that nationalism peaked in the Olympic Games.

The two countries dominating the Olympic Games from 1948 to today have been Russia and the United States (see table 9.2). No other nation has finished as the top medal winner in all that time. Since the breakup of the Soviet Union, the United States has won the medal race in three consecutive Summer Games. However, Asian countries are beginning to assert themselves. Winning 32 gold medals in Athens, China trailed the United States in the race for gold by just three medals. Japan, Korea, Thailand, and Indonesia became significant factors in the medal race for the first time. In the Beijing Olympics in 2008, China finally surpassed the United States in number of gold by winning 51 to the United States' 36. However, in the total medal count, the United States came out on top by earning 110 overall medals compared to 100 for the Chinese team (see table 9.3 on page 170). Clearly there has been a changing of the guard in the scramble to earn the most Olympic medals.

TABLE 9.2 Top 10 Countries in Gold Medals Since 1948

Country	Total gold medals
United States	677
Russia	658
Germany	364
China	172
Italy	171
France	126
Australia	123
Hungary	116
Japan	105
Sweden	103

Includes both Summer and Winter Games through Vancouver in 2010.

Data from International Olympic Committee.

TABLE 9.3 Final Medal Count From the 2008 Summer Olympics for the Top 10 Countries

Country	Gold	Silver	Bronze	Total
United States	36	38	36	110
People's Republic of China	51	21	28	100
Russian Federation	23	21	28	72
Great Britain	19	13	15	47
Australia	14	15	17	46
Germany	16	10	15	41
France	7	16	17	40
Korea	13	10	8	31
Italy	8	10	10	28
Japan	9	6	10	25

Data from International Olympic Committee.

Interestingly, there is some controversy over whether to report all medals won in comparisons of the performances of competing countries. The U.S. press generally reports all medals—gold, silver, and bronze—while the IOC and most other countries around the world report and emphasize gold medals only. The argument is that there is only one winner and by definition the silver and bronze medalists have lost the competition. In contrast, most of us in the U.S. view any athlete who medals as a winner.

Nationalism peaked with the use by politicians of success in the Olympic Games as an endorsement of a country's society and system of government. When the Russians topped the standings, they crowed about the superiority of the Communist system. When U.S. fortunes rose, the United States trumpeted the ideals of democracy. Most of the hype was not about developing athletes but was merely boasting that conflicted with good sporting behavior.

As you might suspect, the Olympic Games have seen their share of politics. The following are some instances of use of the Olympic Games for political purposes:

- World War II interrupted the Olympics in 1940 to 1944.
- Israel was excluded after a threat of an Arab boycott in 1948.
- In 1954 the IOC invited both China and Taiwan to enter the Games, but both nations claimed to represent China. In response, China boycotted those Games.
- In 1960, the IOC told North and South Korea to compete as one team. North Korea refused. Nationalist China was forced to compete under the name of Taiwan.
- In 1964, South Africa was banned for apartheid.
- In 1968 in Mexico City, South Africa was banned again. American sprinters Tommie Smith and John Carlos raised a Black Power salute during the American anthem and were banned for life from future Olympics.
- In 1972 in Munich, Palestinians murdered 11 Israeli athletes.
- In 1980, some 60 nations boycotted the Games in protest of the Soviet Union's invasion of Afghanistan.

Although people the world over decry the politics in the Olympic Games, sport cannot be separated from the world at large. In order for countries to come together peacefully, there must be at least some political cooperation between nations. The athletes are the ones who suffer when their countries withdraw and eliminate a lifelong dream they have trained for years to reach.

Transcending the nationalism were performances by exceptional athletes who achieved historic results and became part of Olympic folklore. These included Jesse Owens' four gold medals in Berlin in 1936; Emil Zatopek's triple victory in the 5,000 meter, 10,000 meter, and marathon in Helsinki in 1952; Bob Beamon's leap of 29 feet, 2 1/2 inches (8.90 meters) in Mexico in 1968; swimmer Mark Spitz's seven gold medals in Munich in 1972; and gymnast Nadia Comaneci's seven perfect 10s in Montreal in 1976. In Beijing in 2008, swimmer Michael Phelps earned the most gold medals in history at one Games with eight gold, including seven world records. When these are added to the six gold medals he earned in Athens in 2004, that's a total of 14 gold medals for Phelps.

Observers of the Olympic Games have written for years about the negative influence of nationalism on the spirit and purpose of the Games. If the competition is about athletes, their country of origin should not matter. Critics have suggested eliminating team sports to reduce the natural nationalistic fever. They suggest removing the flags, anthems, and opening ceremony march by nations and having an international body select athletes.

Over the past several Olympic Games, the debate over nationalism has been replaced by the debate over money. The economics of staging these massive events necessitate corporate sponsors and television

IN THE ARENA WITH . . .

Jesse Owens

The Olympic feats of Jesse Owens are almost unparalleled. No individual ever dominated the sprint races as he did. At the time of the 1936 Olympic Games in Berlin, Nazi Germany had just taken control of the government. One Nazi tenet was the superiority of the white race over others, particularly black races. Owens, a black man from the United States, did more than any other athlete to disprove the German hypothesis. He broke the world record in the 100 meters, although it was disallowed because of wind; set a new world record in the 200 meters; broad jumped more than 26 feet (7.92 meters) for the first time in Olympic history; and anchored the 400-meter relay team, which also set a world record. Owens' four gold medals took the wind out of the sails of the Nazis' racist propaganda (Henry and Yeomans 1984).

for cash. The Games have become large and lavish, and viewers have come to expect that. Decisions are made to accommodate television broadcasting, with recognition of the importance of attracting millions of viewers that in turn can translate into lucrative sponsorships.

United States Olympic Committee

In 1978, the U.S. Congress passed the Amateur Sports Act as federal law. The act appointed the United States Olympic Committee as the coordinating body for all Olympic-related athletic activity in the United States. The vision of the USOC as stated on its website is "to assist in finding opportunities for every American to participate in sport, regardless of gender, race, age, geography, or physical ability" (USOC 2010).

The Amateur Sports Act also designated the national governing body (NGB) for each sport in the United States. Each NGB supports its athletes, sets the rules for competition, stages competitions, and selects athletes to compete in world championships and the Olympic Games.

The USOC is headquartered in Colorado Springs, Colorado, on land donated by the U.S. government that was formerly a military base. Over the years, state-of-the-art training facilities were constructed along with new offices for staff and housing for athletes. The weather and altitude, however, forced the USOC to also develop other training venues: Lake Placid, New York, for winter sports and Chula Vista, California, for summer sports.

USOC Funding

Unlike many other governments, the U.S. government does not help fund the Olympic Movement or its athletes. Honoring its tradition of private enterprise, the United States has designated the USOC as its keeper of the Olympic flame.

The USOC relies wholly on private donations from Americans and sponsorships from corporations. The annual budget for the USOC has hovered near $100 million for some time, a modest amount in relation to its mission. Part of those funds supports the NGBs that develop athletes in specific sports. The formula for how much funding each NGB receives is complicated and always a bone of contention. National governing bodies that do well financially on their own like the U.S. Tennis Association, which has an annual budget that surpasses the total USOC budget for all sports, still claim their share of Olympic funds.

The USOC has realized the value of the five rings Olympic logo as a trademark that can be loaned to corporations in return for financial support. Likewise, merchandise sales of goods labeled with the Olympic logo are a consistent source of USOC income.

USOC Membership

USOC members are organizations from the following categories:

- National governing bodies such as USA Baseball, USA Gymnastics, and USA Swimming
- Paralympic Sports Organizations (PSOs), a new category with membership still to be

ACTIVITY TIME-OUT

Should the U.S. Government Back Olympic Athletes?

The governments of virtually every country in the world support their Olympic athletes through the process of identification, training, and competitions world-wide. The United States has taken a different path by relying on private citizen donations, corporate sponsors, and revenue from television. As the prospects for the United States hosting another Olympic Games in the near future dim for a variety of reasons, television income and corporate sponsorships are likely to be reduced. Is it time for the U.S. government to step in to at least partially fund Olympians in order to stay competitive with other countries around the world?

determined, for organizations that represent athletes who are hearing impaired, mentally disabled, or users of wheelchairs

- Affiliated sport organizations such as the U.S. Squash Racquets Association, U.S. Orienteering Federation, U.S. Trampoline and Tumbling Association, and Triathlon Federation USA

- Community-based multisport organizations such as the Amateur Athletic Union; American Alliance of Health, Physical Education, Recreation and Dance; Boys and Girls Clubs of America; YMCA and YWCA; and Native American Sports Council

Governance

Until 2004, the USOC was governed by a board of directors of over 100 members representing the various organizations belonging to the USOC. Another significant group within the board was the Athletes' Advisory Council, which protected the interests of all Olympic athletes. An elected executive committee of approximately a dozen board members monitored the professional staff activity, oversaw the budget, and acted on behalf of the board between meetings. All of these representatives were volunteers, leaders in their sport that were either appointed or elected to serve on the USOC board.

Over the last 20 years, a series of volunteer and staff conflicts, conflicts of interest among board members, and staff turnovers drew criticism from many different people, who pointed out that the USOC had morphed into an unwieldy bureaucracy that served no one, including the athletes. Pressure from the U.S. Congress in 2003 led to serious USOC self-evaluation, which in turn led the USOC

to streamline its committees, policies, and board of directors. Essentially the reforms reduced the board to a size similar to that of the former executive committee and established four standing committees, annual reporting requirements, regular self-review, and whistle-blower mechanisms beginning in 2004 (Borzilleri 2003; *SportingNews* 2003a).

The conflict between professional staff and volunteer board members or committee chairs has been an issue at the USOC just as it has been in many NGBs. Arising from different goals and styles of operation, the USOC volunteer–staff confrontations are like those in many not-for-profit organizations. Lines of reporting are blurred, personalities clash, and frequent changes in volunteer leadership and direction frustrate staff professionals who believe their careers are being affected by people consumed with the privileges and perks of their position. The recent changes in USOC governance place the staff supervision with the chief operating officer, separating it from volunteer leaders.

The role of the professional staff, which has exceeded 500 employees, is to provide athletes access to elite training programs, assist in training programs for potential Olympic athletes, and support athletes at Olympic events. Often the staff works closely with each NGB. Latest training methods, advances in sports medicine, and equipment research are all provided at Olympic training centers for use by NGB athletes; and the results of the research with elite athletes is published and available. Along with funding, NGBs need advice on hosting competitions, training coaches, identifying athlete talent, and preparing athletes for world competition. The USOC acts as a clearinghouse for information on all these topics, identifies experts for consultation, and produces educational materials that can be applied to multiple sports.

Pursuit of Medals

It may seem that the United States is in good shape to maintain dominance in Olympic competition. However, in-depth analysis reveals the challenges that lie ahead. Since the breakup of the Soviet Union, dozens of medals have gone to smaller nations once counted with Russia. In spite of that loss, Russia continues to snap at the heels of the United States.

The nation to watch now is China, along with Japan, Korea, and other Asian countries. China is the most populous nation on the planet and from its exceptional showing at the Games in 2008 has a strong stake in setting new records. China has more than tripled its gold medal production since returning to the Games in 1984. Asian governments are pouring resources into athlete training as they never have before and are likely to see the results for years to come.

The United States continues to be strong in swimming, led by Michael Phelps' record-setting eight gold medals. But the United States is weakening in many other areas, notably track and field, in which botched handoffs sunk the U.S. hopes in several relay events that it expected to dominate. U.S. boxing has fallen on hard times and had its worst Olympics in more than 60 years in 2004.

In 2008, U.S. volleyball did well with gold medal performances from both men and women in beach volleyball and silver for both men and women indoors. In team sports, the United States fared well overall by winning medals in 9 out of the 11 team sport competitions. Only men's soccer and women's field hockey were denied medals. Regrettably, however, both baseball and softball have been eliminated from future Olympic programs; these were two sports that the United States might expect to dominate.

Interestingly, if winning medals is the goal, then the smart strategy is to assess medal potential sport by sport and spend the money where it can do the most good. Some sports, such as tennis, offer only a few medals. Men's and women's singles and doubles are the only events offered, for a total of 12 potential medals. Other sports like swimming, track and field,

Misty-May Treanor and Kerry Walsh are leading the way for U.S. volleyball. They won gold at both the Athens and Beijing Olympic Games.

and gymnastics offer multiple medals for individual and team events. To win more medals, the USOC should perhaps emphasize sports that have greater medal potential and already have a strong base of athletic development within the country.

Athlete Development

Since success is the goal of the USOC, it would seem that resources should be spent on developing American athletes. There are many factors the USOC must consider to maximize this development.

Talent Identification

National governing bodies must take responsibility for recruiting large numbers of kids into their sport, offering strong competitive events for every age, and assisting with training. By casting a wide net to find potential athletes, the NGBs increase their odds that talented athletes will emerge.

No one system of identifying future star athletes has been accepted in the sporting world. Certain athlete attributes have been identified as being critical in particular sports, but the many exceptions confound the experts. Maturation produces performance gains that simply cannot be predicted. Michael Jordan was cut from his high school basketball team and yet went on to become the finest basketball player in the world.

The key to talent identification as it stands today is to gather young athletes who exhibit the best potential in their sport; encourage them; and provide competition, including international competition, expert coaching, and financial support. Once the children develop, experts assess the natural talent and sport progress and predict future success.

Training

Training young American athletes is a crazy patchwork quilt of tradition, expediency, and entrepreneurship. The public schools offer sophisticated athletic programs in sports that are affordable and geographically accessible to any potential athlete. Other sports do not have interscholastic teams or are conducted more as recreational activities.

Community-based programs in many sports get kids started and provide excellent early training. By the time some athletes reach the critical age of 12 or so, they may have outgrown the local competition and coaching expertise and may need to travel or move to continue their athletic development. Here is where family income becomes a limitation.

The USOC has experimented with the idea of establishing mini-centers to offer training in several Olympic sports in major metropolitan areas. The jury is still out on the viability of this approach, and funding the centers continues to be an issue. The geographical size of the United States makes competition between athletes from different regions expensive.

As athletes advance to within a few years of potential Olympic competition, they need to gather with the best athletes in their sport to train, compete, and focus on their goal. Many NGBs do not have the facilities, money, or even the commitment to provide this opportunity. Some sports rely on private training academies to provide this service, although money can still be a limiting factor. Other sports have located such programs at the Olympic Training Centers in California, Lake Placid, and Colorado Springs. Through economy of scale, these multisport facilities may offer more affordable operations, and athletes may interact with kids in other sports who might be easier to befriend than the ones they compete with every day.

Coaching

Although we will examine coaching in chapter 19, we will look at it briefly here, as it is essential to athlete development. Coaching is typically the key to the optimal development of any athlete. Most successful athletes are affected along the way by several coaches with different strengths. Coaches of introductory programs must understand youth, make sport fun, teach the fundamentals, and be willing to let go. Coaches of young athletes growing more dedicated to their sport must guide their development of competitive and physical skill, help them adjust to a changing physical body, offer a comprehensive training program, and recommend a coach for the next phase. Coaches of elite athletes aiming for world competition must understand that competitive world, capitalize on the athlete's strengths while minimizing weaknesses, tap into resources like specialists in sport science or advanced coaching as needed, and be sensitive to the total makeup of the athlete as it relates to athletic performance.

While serving on the USOC Coaching Committee for two quadrennials, I helped study the challenges the U.S. coaching profession faces. During the eight years I served, from 1992 to 2000, we set the following goals, which were then transferred to the NGBs to implement within their sport:

- Improve the status and recognition of the coaching profession

- Ensure the competency of coaches at every level by encouraging each sport to develop desired coaching competencies and help its coaches acquire them
- Help the coaches desiring to research and apply sport sciences to formulate training and development programs

The USOC has continued to provide direction, materials, workshops, and consultants to NGBs wanting to improve their coaching performance. Results have varied widely, depending on the sport, its traditions, available funds, and the quality of coaching opportunities.

Chapter Summary

The modern Olympic Games have been a wildly successful international sporting event over the past 100 years. No other worldwide sporting event captures the same public interest, with the possible exception of the World Cup in soccer, which involves only one sport and sees fading interest in each country eliminated. At the Olympic Games, every country watches multiple athletes perform in multiple events lasting for more than a fortnight.

The Olympics have sparked athlete development programs in virtually all of the 202 nations that compete. Training elite athletes has become big business and is often supported by government funding. Athletes no longer need to be amateurs who compete for the love of the sport. In fact, success at the Olympic Games ensures most athletes financial bonanzas, particularly if corporate sponsors choose them as spokespeople.

During the Cold War, a nationalistic spirit dominated the Games as countries vied for athletic supremacy to symbolically validate the superiority of their way of life. Gradually, the nationalistic fervor faded and was replaced by an economic tenor. The cost of staging the Games, opening the Games to professionals, and the race to exceed previous Games in breadth and quality drove organizers to enlist the financial support of major worldwide corporations.

Politics intertwine with the Olympic Games, and over the years countries have used the Olympic Games for political purposes. Although many people are dismayed at the use of the Olympics for political statements, others view this as a natural way to seek world attention for issues such as apartheid and human rights that are simply incompatible with the lofty ideals of Olympism.

In the United States, the USOC has the daunting task of developing Olympic athletes. While governments of many other nations devote funding to developing their Olympic athletes, the USOC raises money from private donations and corporate support.

The organization of the USOC has been under discussion in recent years. In 2004, several bills were put forth in the U.S. Congress to streamline the USOC governance, reduce bureaucratic overlap, and simplify the daily operations of this nonprofit organization that has an annual budget of approximately $100 million.

Athletes and coaches have benefited from efforts of the Olympic Movement to provide better sport systems, talent scouting, support for potential Olympic athletes, and information and training for coaches. Through the national governing bodies, information is filtered and adapted to each sport.

PART IV

Sport and Culture

Part IV begins with a look at how moral attitudes affect sporting behavior or are developed through sport. Most people believe that moral behavior can be taught through sport; and in fact, that is true if the sport program or team and coach have a clear philosophy, provide effective leadership, and consistently enforce rules. However, the research over the past 25 years has clearly shown that the longer athletes are in sport, the less they tend to develop mature traits of moral decision making.

The next several chapters deal with the social classifications of people by race, gender, class, age, and disability. Each of these categories can have a powerful effect on sport participation. The exclusion of African Americans from the sport world mirrored the policies of segregation in the United States until the last 50 years; likewise, until Title IX was passed in the 1970s, sport opportunities for women and girls were severely limited. The inclusion of females and minorities has significantly changed the sport landscape in the United States. Participation has steadily increased, media coverage has expanded, and more money has been spent. While equal opportunities are not quite a reality, they are light-years ahead of where they were just a generation ago.

Social class tends to draw people to particular sports that fit their interests, available time, and ability to pay. Athletes who are more affluent are able to join private clubs, pay for coaching, and participate in expensive sports such as equestrian, skiing, and golf. Working- and middle-class families are forced to rely primarily on public or community programs and school athletic programs that are more affordable. Sports that include violence, such as auto racing, boxing, wrestling, and hybrids of sports such as roller derby appeal to the working class and the poor.

As baby boomers have reached retirement age, the number of people in the United States over age 50 has exceeded 80 million, or nearly one-third of the total population. For most older adults, physical activity for health and lifestyle reasons replaces interest in competitive sport, although as spectators they still retain a commitment to competition. Another special population in sport is people with physical or mental disabilities, whose opportunities in sport have expanded dramatically since passage of the Americans with Disabilities Act in 1990. Both the Special Olympics and the Paralympics have become major worldwide events involving thousands of athletes who were previously left out of sport.

No culture has ever functioned without some form of politics and religion, and both influence attitudes of people toward physical activity and sport. Early religion in North America tended to favor development of the spirit rather than the body; but in this century, organized religion has embraced sport as a worthwhile use of time and a powerful socializing agent. Politics has long recognized the influence of sport on the masses and used it to entertain the masses, socialize them toward a particular way of life, and inculcate feelings of nationalism.

New to this edition is the chapter "Development Through Sports." People have realized that along with sport competition for its own sake, there are a multitude of benefits of sport participation that have wider social impact. Programs for kids—particularly the disadvantaged—that feature sports are successfully addressing crime reduction and academic enhancement outside of school. At the international level, sports are being used increasingly to promote peace and understanding among citizens within their own countries. Citizens from different countries also use sports in the search for common understanding and cooperation between their countries.

The chapter on deviance and sport tackles some of the more unpleasant aspects of the sport world. Emotion generated in sport can contribute to deviant behavior, but the athletes who are the most egregious offenders cannot use this as an excuse. Performance enhancement through the use of illegal substances is a recurrent problem that has finally attracted the attention of sport organizations and the government, resulting in better research and more stringent rules and enforcement in every sport. Sport-related gambling continues to be a thorny issue but is gaining public support during difficult economic times owing to the allure of potential revenues to states. The chapter explores hazing in sport, eating disorders, and other aberrant behaviors, including those that may be life threatening, with a view toward how their impact in the sporting world can be eliminated.

Unlike most books of this type, the influential role of athletic coaches is acknowledged and considered. Coaches heavily influence many young people because they are often held in high esteem at a time when kids are looking for heroes other than parents. From youth sport to high school and college sport, coaches are often the adults most admired and respected by athletes. Their influence may go way beyond athletic training and extend to personal values, socialization into a group, and development of self-discipline and self-confidence.

Most coaches enter the profession because they want to lead young people, although many are not well equipped to do so. Coaching education is a major challenge, especially in youth programs where volunteer coaches are plentiful and the turnover rate is enormous.

In the concluding chapter, we explore the critical issues facing sport in view of larger social trends. An aging population and longer life spans are a reality. Many people look to sport participation and spectatorship to enhance their later years. At the same time, the population in general is facing a health crisis spurred by increases in overweight and obesity. Clearly, physical activity has to play a role in mitigating the effects of inactivity.

Attitudes toward sport participation based on race, gender, social class, disabilities, ethnicity, and sexual preference have changed. Power struggles are likely to continue between those who favor high-performance sport and those who prefer sport participation for recreation by large numbers of people.

Advances in science and technology will push the frontiers of sport performance ever higher and continue to cause records to fall. Sport will change as our society changes, and depending on which social theory you consult, those changes will come from within the sporting community or from outside, based on larger social changes reflected in government and laws. What cannot be doubted is that sport will change to reflect society.

Sporting Behavior

10

Student Outcomes

After reading this chapter, you will know the following:

- What *good sporting behavior* means
- The relationship between learned moral values and sport
- Conflicting evidence for the positive or negative effects of sport on moral behavior
- How parents, coaches, and others affect children's sporting behavior

179

Derek Jeter, New York Yankees shortstop and future Hall of Fame player, showed off his "acting" talents in a critical game against the Tampa Bay Rays in 2010 as the two teams vied for first place in their division. Jeter became the center of controversy when he was awarded first base by the umpire who thought a pitch hit Jeter's hand even though video-replay (which is not used in major league baseball for such decisions) clearly indicated the ball hit the knob of the bat and rolled into the field. The Rays wisely threw to first base and claimed Jeter should have been called out, but the umpire didn't agree. Jeter held his hand as if it hurt, drawing manager Joe Girardi and an athletic trainer to his side to evaluate the "injury." Later Jeter admitted to a bit of acting and claimed that his job was to get on base and "the umpire told me to go to first and I'm not going to tell him I'm not going" (Smith 2010). The next batter hit a home run to put the Yankees ahead temporarily, but in the end, Tampa Bay won the game 4 to 3. The question heard 'round the league was whether Jeter's actions were just smart baseball or cheating. We see soccer and basketball players flopping constantly as if they were fouled and wonder what has become of sportsmanship. Is the preoccupation with winning at the professional level infecting college, high school, and youth sports as well?

Grantland Rice, one of the preeminent sports writers of the early 20th century, was born in Tennessee in 1880 and became a pioneer in sport journalism, first in his home state and later in New York City, where he covered the exploits of Babe Ruth and Jack Dempsey and had just completed a column about Willie Mays before his death in 1954. As a Phi Beta Kappa graduate of prestigious Vanderbilt University, where he played football, basketball, and baseball, Rice sprinkled his columns liberally with poems and verses. One of the enduring quotes in the tradition of sport is from the poem "Alumnus Football" in his book, *Only the Brave and Other Poems* (Rice 1941):

> For when the One Great Scorer comes
>
> To write against your name,
>
> He marks—not that you won or lost—
>
> But how you played the game.

The term **sporting behavior** is often used to replace the traditional term "sportsmanship" to remove gender bias in referring to human behavior in sport. For example, the Colorado High School Activities Association's mission includes this bullet point: "Provide an environment that enhances personal development through sporting behavior, character education, teamwork, leadership, and citizenship while increasing values that partner the educational standards of the State of Colorado" (CHSAA 2010).

Throughout this chapter you will see "sporting behavior" and "sportsmanship" used interchangeably, depending on the source. **Sportsmanship** has been defined as "the ethical behavior exhibited by a sportsman or athlete . . . generally considered to involve participation for the pleasure gained from a fair and hard-fought contest, refusal to take unfair advantage of a situation or of an opponent, courtesy toward one's opponent, and graciousness in both winning and losing" (*Webster's Sports Dictionary* 1976).

Acceptable standards of behavior have been extolled, ignored, and given lip service by many coaches and sport participants. This chapter takes a fresh look at what good sporting behavior actually is, whether it can be taught and practiced in sport, and the attitude of our society toward its importance. We'll look at how good sporting behavior is practiced at different levels of play; how moral development influences good sporting behavior; and how the examples of coaches, parents, and other athletes influence good sporting behavior.

Sporting Behavior at Different Levels of Sport

Performance sports in which competition and winning are paramount have dramatically influenced sporting behavior in recent years. As performance expectations increase, pressure to succeed rises exponentially. The value of winning may become such a seductive goal that all thoughts of moral behavior are temporarily put aside.

Professional athletes in all sports are role models for youthful competitors whether they want to be or not. Kids note their taunting, trash talk, disrespect, cheating, and bending or ignoring of the rules. The more successful professional athletes are, the more media attention they receive, in spite of boorish behavior or illegal acts. Professional basketball player and sport commentator Charles Barkley is notable for his well-publicized quote, "I'm not a role model." Barkley's point was that the responsibility for moral upbringing lies with parents, not with professional athletes (Brennan 2001).

Others may agree with Barkley, but the weight of the evidence shows that young people look to people they admire for clues about life. Athletes who are successful and on display impress youth who do not have caring parents and coaches to help them differentiate positive and unacceptable traits of famous athletes. Research shows that when children are systematically taught about fair play and moral development, character can be enhanced through sport (Gibbons, Ebbeck, and Weiss 1995).

Professional athletes at the top of their game may have a disconcerting influence in that kids may mistakenly believe that the athletes' questionable behavior contributes to their success. Young athletes may emulate that behavior to test its effectiveness, often with sad results that affect their athletic career. Media can contribute to the misunderstandings of youth by emphasizing winning above all else. Winners almost always get more photographs, more film footage, and more copy. The next most popular media themes are money, ownership, coaching, and the skills that helped win the game. Media coverage of fairness, honesty, or consideration for other athletes is almost nonexistent, giving the impression that these traits are unimportant (Fullerton 2003).

Participation sports tend to have a more balanced approach to winning. Playing hard and fair wins admirers regardless of the outcome of the game. As athletes age, they naturally tend to shift their emphasis from high performance toward participation. As we discussed in chapter 3, people who choose participation or recreational sport are more focused on enjoying the game, socializing with friends and opponents, and exercising. For millions of people who choose participation sports, even in youth, healthy sporting behavior is more naturally part of the social expectations of the sport since the focus shifts away from winning.

Athletes who are young have a lot to absorb just to learn the game. This learning includes proper behavior toward others in the sport. These athletes may be too young to fully understand good sporting behavior, but they certainly can learn to follow coaches and officials in acceptable behavior. Then, as they mature intellectually, they

Was Michael Vick's conviction for dog fighting a good or bad example to young athletes? Does an athlete's off-field behavior influence youth athletes?

become capable of understanding moral reasoning and able to control their feelings.

Since young people, particularly young people in performance sport, are malleable in attitude and behavior, most programs for promoting good sporting behavior focus on them. These kids also deal with the greatest pressure to perform at elite levels of sport and with reconciling the conflicting behaviors of various role models. They need patience, clear guidelines, and consistent consequences for unacceptable actions.

Clinical psychologist Darrell Burnett (2005) developed the following sample guidelines for kids:

- I abide by the rules of the game.
- I try to avoid arguments.
- I share in the responsibilities of the team.
- I give everyone a chance to play according to the rules.
- I always play fair.
- I follow the directions of the coach.
- I respect the other team's effort.
- I encourage my teammates.

As athletes age, they grow in their capacity to place sport competition within a larger framework of life. The physical limitations that come with aging help older adults focus on the benefits of participation (Payne and Isaacs 2008). As they revise their goals to a realistic level of expectation, the pressure to win drops. Their reasoning ability along with social experience allows them to form a code of behavior that reflects their personal value system. In most cases, people behave in a way that is acceptable to their social group if they want to continue in that group.

Youth Attitudes

According to Michael Josephson, president of the Josephson Institute of Ethics, "the values of youth athletes are dramatically impacted by their sport experience, often for the worse." Josephson went on to report that based on his research it appeared that "many coaches, especially in football, basketball and baseball are teaching kids to cheat and cut corners" (Josephson 2007, p. 1).

A survey of 4,200 high school athletes revealed the following (Josephson 2004):

> Coaches and parents simply aren't doing enough to assure that the experience (in sports) is a positive one. Too many youngsters are confused about the meaning of fair play and sportsmanship and they have no concept of honorable competition. As a result they engage in illegal conduct and employ doubtful gamesmanship techniques to gain a

Although these athletes are demonstrating good sporting behavior, have you witnessed examples of poor sporting behavior?

competitive advantage. It appears that today's playing fields are the breeding grounds for the next generation of corporate pirates and political scoundrels.

A recent report titled "What Are Your Children Learning? The Impact of High School Sports on the Values and Ethics of High School Athletes" includes the findings of a written survey of 5,275 high school athletes administered in 2005 and 2006 (more information is available from www.charactercounts.org). The good news from the survey is that the majority of high school athletes trust and admire their coaches and are learning positive life skills and good values from them. However, the bad news is that many coaches, particularly in the high-profile sports of boys' basketball, baseball, and football, are teaching kids how to cheat and cut corners. Here are some other findings (Josephson 2007, 2008):

• Girls are more sportsmanlike than boys. On virtually every question, girl athletes expressed a deeper commitment to honesty and fair play. In contrast, boys are far more likely to exhibit cynical attitudes and engage in illegal or unsporting conduct.

• Some sports are worse than others. Boys in baseball, football, and basketball were more likely to cheat on the field and exhibit conduct to deliberately injure an opponent, intimidate, and engage in trash talk. Boys who participate in swimming, track, cross country, gymnastics, and tennis were markedly less likely to engage in this type of behavior.

• For girls, the most negative behavior was shown by basketball and softball players compared to female athletes in other sports.

• Coaches don't always set a good example. Most players felt that their coaches exhibited good sporting behavior; but when players were questioned about specific coaching actions, one-quarter to one-third of their answers revealed violations by coaches.

• Many high school athletes break rules and engage in unsporting conduct. Many think it is proper to (1) deliberately inflict pain in football to intimidate an opponent (60% males, 27% females), (2) trash talk a defender after every score (42% males, 18% females), (3) soak a football field to slow down an opponent (27% males, 12% females), or (4) throw at a batter who homered last time up (30% males, 16% females).

• Winning is more important than sportsmanship. More than 37% of males agreed that it's more important to win than to be considered a good sport. When asked, 31% of males and 25% of females said they believed their coach was more concerned with winning than with building character and life skills.

• Cheating and theft seem acceptable to high school athletes. In the past year, (1) 68% of both males and females admitted to having cheated on a test in school; (2) 26% of males and 19% of females said that they had stolen an item from a store; and (3) 43% of males and 31% of females said they had cheated or bent the rules to win.

• Hazing and bullying seem acceptable to high school athletes: 69% of males and 50% of females admitted that they had bullied, teased, or taunted someone in the past year, while 52% of males and 29% of females said they had used racial slurs or insults.

Off the playing field, it is instructive to note the moral behavior of athletes. A 2008 survey based on the responses of nearly 30,000 high school students reveals that more than a third of males (35%) and one-quarter of females (26%) admitted stealing something from a store in the past year. Students who attend private secular and religious schools, honors students, student leaders, and students involved in youth activities like the YMCA were less likely to steal. Cheating in school continues to be rampant and actually getting worse. A substantial majority (64%) admitted cheating on a test in the past year, and more than half did so two or more times. Alarmingly, these percentages have been steadily increasing. Varsity sport athletes cheat at a higher rate (65%) than nonathletes (60%) (Josephson 2008).

And yet, these student-athletes exhibit a high self-image, with 93% saying they are satisfied with their personal ethics and 77% saying they believe they are better than most people they know in terms of doing what is right.

The respondents in this study were high school athletes in a variety of sports in certain geographical locations. It is difficult to generalize these results to all athletes due to a wide variation in sport, location, coach, level of competition, and social class. Yet the results do indicate that the value systems of these high school athletes do not represent a developed sense of moral behavior.

Now that we've looked at sporting behavior at different levels of sport, we can examine how good sporting behavior develops, beginning with moral development and following up with how moral development and moral values affect sport.

IN THE ARENA WITH . . .

Central Washington Softball Players

Western Oregon University senior Sara Tucholsky had never hit a home run in her career. Central Washington University senior Mallory Holtman was already her school's career leader in home runs. But a twist of fate and a torn knee ligament created a fascinating story reported by wire services around the country. Here's the scenario:

Both schools are Division II softball programs and neither had ever reached the national tournament, but this year the two teams were separated by only one game at the top of their conference standings with a potential invitation to nationals in the balance. Western Oregon won the first game of the doubleheader 8-1 and set the stage for a pivotal second game. With two runners on base in a scoreless game, the diminutive Sara Tucholsky at 5 feet, 2 inches (1.6 meters) stroked the first home run of her career over the center field fence, although she had chalked up just three hits in 34 at-bats that season. After rounding first base, Sara collapsed as her right knee gave out while her two teammates scored. The umpires conferred and declared that the only option was for Sara to be replaced by a pinch runner and that her hit would be ruled a two-run single, not a home run. It was further ruled that any assistance from teammates or trainers while she was an active runner would result in an out.

Just then a voice belonging to Mallory Holtman of the opposing team piped up: "Would it be OK if we carried her around and she touched each bag?" After receiving an affirmative answer from the umpire, Mallory and shortstop Liz Wallace lifted Tucholsky off the ground and helped her round the bases. The fans in the stands gave all the players a standing ovation for the unusual display of good sporting behavior, and players and fans around the nation took note.

Central Washington did rally for two runs in the next inning and might have tied the game if the Tucholsky home run had been reduced to a single. But Western Oregon held on for a 4-2 win and the edge in the conference standings as Sara's unlikely home run proved to be the difference. Coach Pam Knox of Western Oregon spoke to the media after the game and pointed out the lesson they had all learned, that winning is not the only thing. Said Knox, "I will never forget this moment. It has changed me and I'm sure it has changed my players." Later that year, Tucholsky, Wallace, and Mallory were honored for winning "Best Moment in Sports" at the ESPY Awards for 2008.

Adapted, by permission, from G. Hays, 2008, *Central Washington offers the ultimate act of sportsmanship* (ESPN).

Development of Moral Values

The foundation of our behavior in sport is based on our level of moral reasoning. Many researchers have studied the development of moral values in society and have advanced various theories based on their findings. Many theories are similar while some take a slightly different view, but all link moral capacity to intellectual development. Jean Piaget, a famous Swiss psychologist, is renowned for his pioneering work in explaining the stages of mental development and later moral development. One of his devotees was Lawrence Kohlberg, who as a professor at Harvard University publicized his own theory of moral development beginning in the 1970s. Like Piaget, Kohlberg believed that children move through a series of stages before arriving at

their capacity for moral maturity. Kohlberg's theory will serve as an example of moral development for our discussion on good sporting behavior (Crain 1985; Smart and Smart 1982).

Kohlberg demonstrated through studies that people progress in their moral reasoning through a series of stages. Kohlberg asserted that moral reasoning could proceed only with intellectual development and exposure to socialization. He classified the stages into three levels, placing two stages in each level:

Preconventional

1. Punishment and obedience
2. Pleasure or pain

Conventional

3. Good boy or girl
4. Law and order

Postconventional

5. Social contract
6. Principled conscience

Let's take a closer look at each of these stages and how they influence good sporting behavior.

Preconventional Stage

The **preconventional stage** is the base for moral reasoning. The first stage of punishment and obedience is the level of moral thinking typically found in elementary school. Young students and athletes behave according to socially acceptable norms because they are told to do so by parents, teachers, or coaches. Being right simply means obeying an authority. Disobeying the dictates of the authority results in punishment. This concept is within the intellectual grasp of children, and they can understand it. Whether they follow directions depends on the timing, manner of delivery, and punishment for disobedience.

The second stage involves thinking that the reason for behavior is to get pleasure for oneself. This hedonistic approach to moral choices is very self-centered as opposed to respecting the values of a group or society. Children at this stage realize that there is not always one right answer as decided by an adult authority and test their own conclusions. They expect punishment if their actions are wrong, but unlike in stage one, they view punishment as simply a risk one takes for acting a certain way. Punishment will not necessarily follow wrong behavior.

Youth athletes in stage two may take certain actions because they have learned that doing so may be in their self-interest. They reason as an individual who is engaged in egocentric behavior rather than as a member of a group or community.

Kohlberg believed that younger children typically use the preconventional level of morality because they can process it intellectually. As children mature and begin to understand how the world works, they adopt a more relative approach that does not accept rules as absolute but as changeable if the group agrees to change them. Children tend to change in moral capacity around age 10 or 11, at the time when many kids are heavily involved in youth sport. It is a wise coach who anticipates this development and assists it rather than limiting players to simply following coaching dictates.

A good coach may enlist the help of her athletes in deciding appropriate punishment for players who break rules or behave inappropriately. When athletes participate in the process they must examine the seriousness of the offense, the number of occurrences, previous warnings, and possible sanctions or punishments. As they review the facts and consider alternatives, they establish a sense of moral decision making that will help them mature in their thinking abilities.

Unfortunately, some children get stuck in the preconventional level of moral development. They are the ones who often deviate from social norms and may end up in a correctional institution. Some adults still exhibit these lower levels of moral reasoning when justifying their actions, further confusing the young people who hear their opinions.

Conventional Stage

The **conventional stage** of moral reasoning is the level attained by most adults. The first stage in this level and the third stage of moral development is the one typically found in society. Behavior is guided by what is generally acceptable to friends, family, and community. Youth usually reach this stage in high school, and high school students often believe in good behavior that emphasizes love, caring, empathy, trust, and concern for others. They try on various behaviors to see how those around them respond and then typically either modify actions that do not conform to group standards or willingly pay the price for deviating from group standards.

The fourth stage is dubbed *law and order* because it is important to maintain laws, respect authority, and perform accepted duties so that society can function. Without the smooth functioning of a society, there would be anarchy. People need to follow the rules of society or work to change those with which they disagree.

The majority of any population falls into the two conventional categories because *conventional* categories are just that. Most of us stay at stage three or four for most of our lives.

Postconventional Stage

The **postconventional stage** is a level most of us do not reach. The fifth stage is referred to as a *social contract* because those in this stage have an interest in the welfare of others. This is an autonomous, principled stage of thinking in which people adopt certain moral principles and hold to certain behaviors regardless of social punishment or reward. The concept of inalienable human rights enters in here. So too does the idea of treating all people with dignity and respect regardless of their ethnic or racial background, economic class, or actions.

Kohlberg also postulated a sixth stage that relied heavily on humanistic principles of valuing human life and feeling right with oneself. The principles of

185

justice, fairness, and human dignity require compassion and ask us to treat all humans as individuals who deserve impartial love and concern. There are certain universal laws accepted by all religions that guide us toward appropriate actions. However, after a time, Kohlberg found so few humans he could point to who had reached this sixth level that he basically ignored it. Apart from great moral leaders such as Mahatma Gandhi, Martin Luther King Jr., or Nelson Mandela, few people reach the final level of moral development.

Barriers to Good Sporting Behavior

Because of the heavy emphasis on winning in sport competition, some athletes struggle with the choice between winning through any means and exhibiting good sporting behavior. With young children, it takes time to develop the intellectual understanding to move beyond simply playing by the rules to competing within the spirit of the game as well. With older youth and adults in the conventional stage, the barriers to good behavior may be customs within sports or the influence of coaches or spectators. Trash talk, verbally abusing opponents, and taunting have become a part of the social culture in some sports. Players who use these methods to distract their opponents may be rewarded with a victory that reinforces their actions.

Coaches or parents who understand good sporting behavior sometimes forgive athletes who offend because they want their team to win. The media's glorification of winners helps reinforce the importance of winning and gives the impression that our culture admires winners, not necessarily good sports.

Moral Values Applied to Sport

Now that we've covered the stages of moral development, let's look at how they affect sport. Sport can play a vital role in helping young people become socialized in their environment. **Socialization** is the process of interacting with other people and learning social customs, morals, and values. As we interact with others, we form opinions about what we believe and how we should act. Others do the same through their interactions with us. It is a dynamic process, and our understanding of our social world changes as we accumulate experiences.

Many of the theories we discussed in chapter 2, including functionalism, conflict, and interactionist theories, describe how socialization occurs in society. Let's look at how each of these theories influenced current understanding of the ways in which athletes become socialized in sport.

Functional theorists view socialization as the process in which we develop the social characteristics that allow us to fit into our world. Using this approach, we would study the athletes being socialized, their likely guides, such as parents and

ACTIVITY TIME-OUT

Moral Reasoning and Sport

What does Kohlberg's theory have to do with sport? Consider how you would answer the following questions on moral decision making in sport. For each question, list your answer, your justification, and the level of moral reasoning you used.

1. Assume you are a football player who runs for a touchdown on the last play of the game and scores for the margin of victory. As your coaches and teammates mob you in celebration, you are torn because you know you stepped out of bounds during the run but the referee did not see it. Should you continue celebrating or stop to talk to your coach and the referee?

2. While your softball team is playing a game, the opposing team's best hitter comes to the plate having hit a home run last time up. Your coach orders you to "brush her back" with a high inside pitch to get her to back off the plate. Should you follow the coach's directions or ignore them?

3. During basketball practice, your coach has the team practicing illegal holding on opponents to prevent them from getting rebounds from missed shots. Coach shows you the best way to avoid being caught by the officials. Even though holding is against the rules, would you follow the coach's orders and work on holding without being caught?

coaches, and the outcomes of their process. Functionalist studies such as that by Shields (2005) or Josephson (2004) elicit information from athletes about why they play sport and what changes occur as a result of their participation. Most of these studies have presented inconclusive or even contradictory evidence. It is difficult to generalize findings from a restricted sample size due to the wide variation of possible athletic experiences.

Conflict theory offers another approach to socialization. Advocates of this theory assume that people with economic influence use it to maintain their status in privileged positions within society. As described by Coakley and Dunning (2004), most research using this approach has focused on how highly organized sport programs with authoritarian leaders and coaches have helped develop athletes who conform to their system in order to be accepted within the group. Athletes who come from lower socioeconomic classes may be exploited by this system. In spite of poor academic skills, athletes may be pushed through college as long as they have eligibility remaining but may never actually graduate.

The work by Fine (1987) is an example of research that has evolved to more interactionist models for studying athlete participation. Interactionist models emphasize the mutual interaction occurring between athletes and their environment as the athletes form their traits of socialization. Typically, this research has been more clinical, based on qualitative, in-depth interviews with athletes. The goal is to accumulate information in a natural field setting in order to understand what happens to an athlete during socialization through sport. This method significantly departs from the research using large samples of people who are questioned objectively and asked to report on their experiences.

Whatever the theory, the fundamental question of this chapter is whether sport participation builds character or negatively influences character. Or perhaps it exerts little influence at all. For years, we have accepted the premise that sports build character with little evidence to support that claim. Let's look at the data that have been collected so far.

Sport as a Character Builder

Do sports build character? This question is much more difficult than it appears. Experts cannot agree on what character is; and even if they did precisely define it, it would still be difficult to measure. Some studies (Beller and Stoll 1994) have compared those who play sport with those who do not and have concluded that the positive traits exhibited by athletes prove that sports are beneficial. However, it could be that those who play sports already possess those positive traits. Likewise, those who do not play sports could certainly attain positive character traits through other experiences. A clear cause-and-effect relationship has been very difficult to confirm.

Another confounding variable is that not all sport experiences are inherently similar. They depend on whether the emphasis is on participation or competitive excellence. Sport experiences also depend on the athlete's age, ability to make moral decisions, and opportunities to make such decisions. Coaches may greatly influence moral decision making, depending on their philosophy of coaching and openness to athlete-centered activity versus coach-centered activity.

Consider the different feelings about moral behavior that could arise from teammates who play very different positions. Contrast the attitude of a defensive end who relies on aggressiveness to rush the passer, and perhaps is urged to physically hurt the opposing quarterback, with that of a reserve placekicker who rarely engages in physical contact but instead deals with constant mental pressure to focus on kicks in critical situations.

Likewise, athletes who compete in big-time sports at universities adopt a moral code of behavior that fits with their ultimate objective of competing at the highest levels of their sport. Although relatively mature intellectually, these athletes tend to embrace a simple, practical approach of playing within the rules to avoid punishment and progress to the next level of competition.

Athletes who compete for a Division III college with no scholarships have to determine the role of sport in their life and balance their time and effort with other life goals related to their studies and career. For these athletes, sport may be more social, a physical outlet, and a chance to test their skills. Moral behavior is more about comfortably fitting in with their teammates and coaches.

Table 10.1 on page 188 shows the results of a survey that questioned high school athletes about their attitudes toward sporting behavior. Although the majority of high school athletes viewed these negative behaviors as unacceptable, the fact that one-quarter to one-half of the respondents thought the behaviors were OK is significant. Apparently the athletes were simply reflecting the moral values they were taught, behaviors perhaps reinforced through sport. If we asked professional athletes the same types of questions, do you think the results would be similar? If not, how would they differ?

TABLE 10.1 High School Attitudes Toward Sporting Behavior

Question	BOYS			GIRLS		
	Proper	Improper	Not sure	Proper	Improper	Not sure
1. A coach orders a player to attack a preexisting injury of the top scorer on the other team.	29%	50%	22%	13%	66%	22%
2. In baseball, a key player for team X is hit by a pitch. In retaliation, the team X coach orders his pitcher to throw at an opposing hitter.	25%	52%	24%	9%	71%	20%
3. In football, a lineman deliberately seeks to inflict pain on an opposing player to intimidate him.	60%	19%	21%	27%	40%	34%
4. In football, a coach's team is out of time-outs in a crucial game. He instructs a player to fake an injury to get the time-out.	37%	34%	29%	20%	49%	31%
5. A basketball coach teaches players how to illegally hold and push in ways that are difficult to detect.	43%	31%	27%	22%	52%	26%
6. In softball, a pitcher deliberately throws at a batter who homered the last time up.	30%	43%	28%	16%	59%	25%
7. A player trash talks the defender after every score by demeaning the defender's skill.	42%	32%	26%	18%	56%	27%
8. In baseball, a coach instructs the groundskeeper to build up the third base foul line slightly to keep bunts fair.	26%	47%	27%	20%	49%	31%

Data from Josephson 2007.

Character Development in Sport

As we have discussed, performance sports emphasize winning, pursuit of excellence, and attaining the highest possible level of performance. Opponents are often seen as enemies to be dominated, demoralized, and defeated. Hard work, dedication, sacrifices, and physical risks are all acceptable and expected.

In contrast, participation sports emphasize game play; the enjoyment of physical movement; and connections between mind and body, between athlete and nature, or between one athlete and another. Decisions are typically made democratically, and all players regardless of ability get to participate in the action.

Performance sports clearly produce a lot more pressure on athletes and coaches. When people are stretched to their limits, their moral decisions may be affected until winning and great performance are more important than anything else. Many youth sports are conducted more like performance sports than participation sports, although in the long term the athletes may not be suited to performance sports.

Pickup games in neighborhoods have existed for generations. Kids learned to function as a group to agree on what game to play, what rules to follow, who would play what position, and how to handle disputes. The outcome of the game was less important than getting to play. If the group couldn't agree, the game simply didn't happen. Players learned to call their own fouls or risk social isolation. Players who hogged the ball were chosen last for future games. Moral codes of behavior were established and enforced by the group. Kids worked out disputes without coaches, umpires, or league organizers.

In child-initiated play, kids are able to create and adhere to their own set of rules. Do performance sports, sanctioned by adults, make the rules of the game too complicated?

Defining Character in Sports

The concept of *character* changes with the times and the society in which it exists. For America, good character tends to be based on the ideals espoused by the founders and the Puritan work ethic. People were admired for working hard to survive a life that demanded hard work. Collectively, people expected others to conform to societal customs, obey parents and leaders, exhibit self-discipline as well as loyalty toward family and friends, and respect external rewards. Those same virtues constitute good sporting behavior.

Young people should be able to transfer the life lessons they learn in sport to the workplace as they enter the adult world. Thus a major achievement of youth sport is to teach young people to act in socially acceptable ways and so those lessons hopefully carry over to their adult years. Most articles, websites, and manuals (Ariss 2000) on good sporting behavior list the following attributes as essential:

- Knowing and following the rules of the game
- Respecting teammates, opponents, officials, and coaches
- Never using or threatening physical violence
- Abstaining from taunting, bragging, or excessive celebration
- Avoiding profanity or other hurtful language
- Demonstrating honesty and resisting the temptation to cheat
- Accepting responsibility for personal actions
- Treating others as you expect to be treated

Some evidence (Stoll and Beller 2005) reveals that participating in high school sport may actually hinder the development of moral character. After compiling research over 20 years including more than 72,000 athletes, they offered the following conclusions:

- Athletes scored *lower* than nonathletes on moral development.
- Female athletes scored *significantly higher* than male athletes.
- *Female athletes' scores are dropping* at a steady rate and within five years are likely to mirror male scores.
- Male athletes in revenue-producing sports *score significantly lower* than athletes in non-revenue sports.
- The *longer athletes play competitive sport, the lower their moral reasoning* tends to be.
- *Intervention programs can have a significant positive effect* on moral reasoning and can affect that ability over the long term.

At the end of the day, the evidence on whether sports build character conflicts. The concept of character is vague, and the effect of sport participation is variable depending on the athlete's age, situation, and the social dynamics in the sport. Social psychologists Miracle and Rees (1994, p. 96) conclude, "Research does not support either position in the debate over sport building character."

It may be helpful to consider two different types of character: *social character and moral character*:

- *Social character* includes the ideas of team-work, loyalty, work ethic, and perseverance. Athletes who participate in team sports exhibited high levels of social character; individual-sport athletes were second, and nonathletes were third.

- *Moral character* includes the concepts of honesty, fairness, integrity, and responsibility. Nonathletes actually scored highest in these traits, followed by individual-sport athletes and then team sport athletes.

Powerful Influence of Coaches

By this point you may be convinced that it is overly optimistic to expect that sport will automatically build good character in athletes. On the other hand, you should also be clear that sports are a dynamic and powerful social experience that may, *under the right circumstances*, have positive benefits. According to Bredemeier and Shields (2006), if positive impact is to occur, the leadership and behavior of the coach is the key. These authors recommend a few key strategies for coaches:

- Coaches should emphasize effort and mastery of the athletic tasks rather than innate ability and competitive outcome. While athletes cannot control their genetic athleticism, they can control their effort and increase their skill with diligent work.

- Emphasize team cooperation rather than rivalry. Encourage team members to help each other and value everyone as a uniquely valuable individual.

- Help athletes appreciate the important role of mistakes as they learn and develop. Keep the atmosphere positive, focus on what athletes do right, and help them accept errors as part of the learning process.

In sum, Bredemeier and Shields believe sport can build character, but only if coaches deliberately seek to make this happen and have the skills and training to structure the situation appropriately. They believe that an emphasis on mastery of skills is a healthier and more powerful motivator of athletes than an emphasis on ego satisfaction in which the primary focus is on winning games.

Sport Ethic

A dominant sport ethic is not a new concept in sport, but it is one that constantly changes to reflect a system of values for coaches and athletes. It represents the behavior norms that are acceptable and praised within the sporting culture. Athletes who eagerly endorse the prevailing sport ethic are warmly embraced by sport owners, the media, coaches, and teammates. Those who rebel against the norms find it difficult to exist in that same world. In team sports, one generally accepted rule is that a player should not publicly criticize teammates. Terrell Owens, who is arguably one of the top five wide receivers in National Football League history, has had a propensity for insulting teammates and especially quarterbacks. While he has been a prolific receiver, his attitude, locker room explosions, and touchdown celebrations came to define his reputation. His career has spanned 14 seasons, including seven years with San Francisco, where he began his career. That was followed by brief stops in Philadelphia (two years), Dallas (three years), and Buffalo (one year) on the way to free agency (Dudley 2010).

High-performance sports tend to have more clearly defined expectations for athletes. Dedication and sacrifice are expected and required of athletes to ensure success. There is little room for athletes to question prevailing norms if they want to be respected by teammates and competitors.

Coakley (2004) analyzed the culture of high-performance sport and saw dominant themes emerge:

- Striving for excellence is the hallmark of performance athletes. Athletes are expected to compete to win, train to exhaustion, sacrifice to meet their athletic goals, and put other areas of life aside in a single-minded pursuit of excellence in sport.

- Love of the game is expected, and athletes must demonstrate it. Without a genuine love of the game, many athletes could not endure their sacrifices, hours of training, or the exclusion of other areas of life. Commitment to the team, teammates, and coaches is preached by coaches and athletes who accept that mantra and are held up as role models.

- Playing with pain and adversity is a badge of courage for an athlete. As soldiers are admired for their bravery in battle and courage in facing death, so athletes are expected to deal with physical and psychological pain as the price they pay for respect.

Athletes must decide to embrace the current sport ethic or to struggle against the system. Young athletes in particular are susceptible to the exhortations of coaches and respected teammates as they search for behavior that will earn them acceptance, praise, and respect in a world they admire. Without a strong sense of personal identity, young athletes eagerly adopt the athletic code simply because of their age and inexperience.

Those who benefit the most from the current American sport ethic are those who gain in money or reputation when their affiliated athletes succeed. Owners of teams, the media, and coaches have a stake in the performance of a team and reward those who readily accept the prevailing values system.

Players who play with pain are labeled courageous even if they risk permanent injury. Those who overtrain may be admired for their dedication until their overtraining interferes with their performance. Eating disorders, particularly among female athletes, are prevalent in certain sports in which body weight is a factor, even though these disorders may lead to death.

Physical courage is expected, particularly for males as proof of their manhood. Risk taking without regard for the consequence is admired. Players who shy away from physical danger are labeled unworthy of the fraternity of male athletes.

Unquestioned acceptance of the prevailing sport ethic sometimes is a form of deviant overconformity. Athletes may adopt behaviors that are outside the norms of society because their insulated world of sport has its own brand of ethics. The sport ethic may be reinforced by fans and the media who encourage athletes to pursue athletic excellence at any cost.

When the athletic ethic succeeds in building special bonds between teammates to the exclusion of bonds with others, the athlete's interpersonal relationships outside of sport may suffer. Marriages, families, and friends are all excluded from the special circle. Athletes may become so cocky that they believe themselves to be special and immune to rules of behavior to which others are expected to conform. The sport pages are rife with examples of athletes who expect special privileges and preferential treatment and who display a sense of entitlement. Adults and fans idolizing these athletes encourage this antisocial behavior and then wonder what went wrong when the athletes disappoint them.

Linking Good Sporting Behavior to Mental Toughness

One of the important connections made in recent years is that between emotional control and good sporting behavior. In the heat of battle, many athletes lose control of their emotions and subsequently behave poorly. They are also likely to perform poorly since highly aroused negative emotions usually harm competition.

Sport psychologists and coaches have found that teaching athletes how to control their emotions can help them compete in an ideal state of emotional arousal. In that state the athletes clearly focus on the task at hand, block out distractions, relax tense muscles, and regulate breathing. Other skills for achieving this state include rituals, positive self-talk, and visual imagery.

Since all athletes want to maximize their success, they are very receptive to learning skills to improve their mental toughness. A strong by-product of improved mental toughness may be better sporting behavior. Athletes are much more likely to ignore opponents' poor behavior and the vagaries of bad luck during play if they are under emotional control and focused on their performance.

Learning the rules of competition is still the foundation for good sporting behavior. But to develop further, athletes must understand the spirit of the rules: a commitment to fair play and socially acceptable behavior from all athletes, coaches, and fans.

Moral Values Taught Through Sport

In spite of the lack of convincing evidence, most people still assume there is value in linking good sporting behavior with competition in sport. Certainly it allows contests to exist under a common framework of rules and customs. Without those, chaos would reign.

It is also true that young people learn moral behavior as they mature. Sport can be one of the arenas that inform them of acceptable and unacceptable attitudes and behavior. As they gain intellectual maturity, their ability to process this information grows and a personal moral code emerges.

In the critical teenage years, most kids rely on their peers for guidance in acceptable behavior. Originally they rely on their parents, teachers, and other adults for that information; but as they begin the struggle into adulthood, being accepted by their peers becomes paramount. They exhibit the conventional level of "good boy or girl" or "law and order" moral reasoning.

Recognizing the powerful influence of sport on youth, many organizations have begun aggressive campaigns to promote good sporting behavior. Since 1992, the Institute for International Sport has sponsored National Sportsmanship Day on the first Tuesday in March. The celebration involves youth sport organizations, schools (elementary, middle, and high schools), and colleges in the United States totaling more than 14,000 schools and in more than 100 countries. It promotes awareness of good sporting behavior by stimulating dialogue among all those involved in sport (International Sport 2010).

By registering to participate, schools or organizations receive posters, role-playing scenarios, games, sport quotes, discussion questions, and other ideas for involving students, parents, teachers, and administrators. Some schools proudly display their banners and include good sporting behavior as a goal of their athletic teams. Outstanding high-profile athletes are carefully screened to serve as role models and make appearances on behalf of the organization. The theme of National Sportsmanship Day for 2010 was "competitive restraint," which means competing hard while maintaining one's self-control and playing within the rules. As part of the celebration, students were invited to write essays of 500 words or less which addressed the theme. The Pop Culture sidebar on page 193 provides one of the winning essays.

In Colorado, the sporting behavior program for high school athletes takes the position that sport participants are placed in a unique context of competition that can develop the values of self-respect and respect for others. The Colorado High School Activities Association lists the values as follows (CHSAA 2010):

Respect for self

Respect for others

Self-esteem

Teamwork

Discipline

Loyalty

Courage

Compassion

Responsibility

Tolerance

Integrity and honesty

Courtesy

Ethics

Fairness

Pride

Integrity

Poise

Humility

The Colorado High School Activities Association developed a guide for coaches, players, parents, and officials titled "Game Management and Sportsmanship Expectation Guide" (2009) that lays out the expectations for managing behavior during all after-school activities, including sports. For 2009-2010, one of its initiatives was to focus on eliminating tacit approval of taunting and demeaning types of behavior. The sport environment is one place where some people think it is acceptable to taunt, ridicule, heckle, or otherwise disrespect another human being. Examples are student and fan chants directed at opposing teams, such as "We can't hear you," "We've got spirit, how 'bout you," "Where's your crowd," "You got swatted," "Start the bus," and "Hey, hey good-bye." Though traditional in sport and somewhat innocuous, these chants only reinforce an attitude that is confrontational and disrespectful (CHSAA 2010).

Other organizations have similar programs to alert sport participants to the value of good sporting behavior. Almost every youth sport organization, including those of the Olympic Movement, incorporates good sporting behavior in its offerings for players and coaches.

Strategies for Good Sporting Behavior

Clearly sport can be an opportunity for youth to learn the precepts of good sporting behavior. Due to the dynamics of play and the natural situations of competition, athletes may be tested hundreds

ACTIVITY TIME-OUT

Locker Room Slogans

Make a list of at least 10 locker room slogans you have seen or read that reinforce the sport ethic. Consider the impact of those slogans and decide which ones should be banned and which ones have value. Then, come up with five new slogans that you believe would be healthier and reflect a more enlightened view of sport.

POP CULTURE

The Courage to Hold Back, by Myles Campbell, Grade 4, Englewood Cliffs, New Jersey

When I first saw the movie *The Jackie Robinson Story* and heard his discussion with the Dodgers' owner Branch Rickey about "not fighting back no matter what they do to you," I thought that Robinson was a "pussycat." I knew I wasn't like that since when my brothers start something with me, I'm very quick to return the favor.

When Sharon Robinson, Jackie's daughter, came to our school I learned that Jackie Robinson was anything but a "pussycat." Like me, he was a fierce competitor who never looked to back down from a good fight. In spite of all the terrible things that were said about him and done to him, he had the courage to control his anger. He was strong enough not to fight back because his larger goal of breaking the color barrier in baseball was more satisfying than short term revenge.

I have to wear thick glasses when I play baseball and it gets me mad when some of my classmates call me "Four Eyes." At times I have felt like getting revenge and teaching them a few moves I have recently learned in wrestling. Although I am very tempted, I have tried to channel my anger into my game. I get back at them by playing harder. I try to concentrate better, to swing a little quicker, to throw a little faster and to run a little swifter. By doing this, I keep getting better and our team now wins by more runs. I have noticed less name calling. Who knows, if I continue to have the courage to hold back, like Jackie Robinson, my classmates may someday ask to borrow my glasses.

Reprinted, by permission, from Myles Campbell, 2010, "A day to promote good sportsmanship across the USA," *USA Today*. Available: www.usatoday.com/sports/2010-02-27-sportsmanship-day_N.htm?loc=interstitialskip.

of times in a season of play and thus develop their sense of a moral code in sport. Many of their attitudes will come from early life experiences, but the ones they learn on the athletic field are just as likely to transfer off the field and become part of their moral behavior.

If we hope to positively influence good sporting behavior, we have to adopt it as a key goal of youth sport. All of the significant sporting organizations for youth have done so, but in some cases their good intentions are simply not followed up. Colorado appears to have a model program that is comprehensive in concept, clear in purpose, and practical to apply. Schools in Colorado are asked to adopt and promote the program; recognize athletes who are good models; and educate players, coaches, and parents.

Parents are usually the first to teach their children fair play. From their parents, young athletes learn to share, take turns, accept agreed-upon rules of the game, and accept winning or losing. As they join youth teams and leagues, they learn to follow directions from coaches and officials or suffer the consequences that usually mean exclusion from play. Parents continue to model good behavior during games by admiring play by both teams, controlling their emotions, and respecting decisions of coaches and officials. After the game, parents need to help the athletes focus on the good aspects of their performance and not become consumed with the outcome.

Coaching behavior powerfully influences a team of young players. Along with teaching the rules, coaches must model good sporting behavior at all times. That means they must treat everyone with respect, make fair decisions, and positively reinforce good behavior. If coaches verbally abuse the referee from the sideline, they send a clear message to their players that such behavior is OK.

Coaches also need to help players modify their behavior when it does not meet acceptable standards. Good kids sometimes are bad sports. Kids become frustrated, lose patience, get overly emotional, react to poor behavior from opponents, or allow other issues in their life to affect their decisions. A wise coach can spot the possible cause for poor decisions through insightful questioning and suggest alternative methods of dealing with the situation.

At some levels of play, the fans can also influence the atmosphere through unacceptable behavior. Small groups of fans such as parents can be cautioned that their behavior is becoming a negative influence. Larger crowds simply require crowd control

EXPERT'S VIEW

Teachers and Coaches as Leaders Demonstrating Character and Competence

Angela Lumpkin, professor at Kansas State University, quotes the United States Army leadership framework (Be...Know...Do) to emphasize the essentiality of character and competence with "be" describing character, "know" describing competence, and "do" describing action taken based on character and competence. She further shares that cadets at the United States Military Academy "are taught that leaders choose the harder right, rather than the easier wrong." She encourages a similar framework for coaches to guide their modeling and teaching efforts toward good sporting behavior. She suggests that coaches be guided in their actions as role models by the following: If an ethical dilemma causes you to have a negative, gut-level reaction, you will not take that action. Secondly, if you would feel uncomfortable if your actions were reported in the media, you will not take that action. And third, if you feel your action will violate the moral values of someone you cared about, you again will not take that action. As others have said, the challenge is to act in an ethical manner even if no one is looking (Lumpkin 2010).

to ensure safety, and disruptive fans should be forcibly removed from the scene. The effects of too much alcohol consumption before and during athletic events are well documented. Limits must be publicized and enforced to prevent alcohol from turning a fan into a disruptive, rude, or dangerous instigator.

The power of sport role models cannot be overlooked. Young athletes often model their behavior after their heroes in college and professional sport. If they see National Football League players taunting each other and celebrating excessively after a good play, you can bet that they'll imitate those actions during their Pop Warner League football game. Leaders of professional sport need to be pressured to eliminate poor sporting behavior from their games. Rule enforcement, fines, and suspensions are all actions that can gain attention and help athletes change their behavior. Generally, most sport organizations do act on bad behavior, but often not until public outcries inspire them to do so.

We can also do much by rewarding those athletes who do exhibit good sporting behavior. Most organizations and leagues seasonally recognize certain athletes for their exemplary behavior. Even in fiercely competitive professional sports there are numerous players who deserve admiration for their good sportsmanship. No young girl who has watched the last 10 years of U.S. women's soccer could come away with anything less than a healthy respect for exemplary sporting behavior.

Chapter Summary

Good sporting behavior has been defined as ethical behavior exhibited by athletes. Some studies have shown that today's athletes are confused about the meaning of fair play and sportsmanship and have no concept of honorable competition. On the other hand, there is also evidence that sports provide a fertile ground for developing good sporting behavior, provided that it is an agreed-upon outcome accepted by coaches and players. The active occasions for moral decision making in sport make sport an ideal venue for learning moral behavior.

Highly competitive sports are more likely than participation sports to produce poor behavior. Males are more likely than females to exhibit poor behavior. Violent and contact sports have a strong history of poor sporting behavior. Various research projects with youth sport athletes and high school athletes have revealed an alarming understanding of acceptable levels of moral choice and decision making.

The stages of moral development as outlined by Kohlberg give us insight into how sporting behavior develops. The relationship between moral behavior and intellectual development in sport was examined. Young people in particular can be socialized into groups through their experience in sport and adoption of acceptable moral behavior.

Because athletic situations vary widely, there is no definitive way to declare that sport teaches either positive or negative sporting behavior. However, an increasing number of youth sport programs, state athletic associations, and school districts are adopting clear statements of intent to promote good sporting behavior and following up with concrete programs that include publicity, education, enforcement, rewards, and recognition for exemplary behavior in sport.

Race, Ethnicity, and Sport

Student Outcomes

After reading this chapter, you will know the following:

- How race and ethnicity are defined
- Sport participation by various ethnic populations
- How sport is both a positive and negative force for promoting racial and ethnic equality in society
- Strategies to combat challenges to racial diversity in all levels of sport

11

Arthur Ashe Jr. was a good friend of mine. I watched a young Ashe enter the world of professional tennis, win the U.S. Open and Wimbledon, and later on captain the U.S. Davis Cup team. Some years later fate brought us together within the family of the U.S. Tennis Association when we worked together to establish the first player development program for U.S. Tennis to help develop top American players who would be successful on the world stage. John McEnroe and Jimmy Connors had retired, and Chris Evert and Martina Navratilova would shortly follow. Our task was to replace them and develop a plan to maximize the chances for young American players.

Our working relationship turned into a friendship of mutual respect, shared visions, and a shared commitment toward a better world for people of all races. You see, Arthur loved playing tennis but knew there were much more important matters for him to tend to. A student of history, Ashe penned the unique three-volume work that has become the definitive history of the black athlete in America, titled *A Hard Road to Glory*. Lest the heroic exploits of innumerable black athletes be lost forever because their performances were ignored or repressed throughout history, Ashe ensured that future generations would be able to trace their past. It took years of detailed, painstaking research, but I was there to share the satisfaction of an author who truly contributed something of value through his own insight and effort. Later, he published an autobiography, *Days of Grace*, in which he chronicled his unfortunate infection with AIDS through a blood transfusion during a heart bypass operation. It wasn't long before his health deteriorated; he suffered through brain surgery and died at the young age of 49 (Carter 2005).

We were the same age and grew up in the same era, but clearly lived in different worlds of white and black. Arthur graduated from college, became a writer, and became a leader in the black community who spoke out and acted to combat racial prejudice, South Africa's apartheid, and U.S. policy toward Haitians seeking asylum here. Yet he also moved easily in the white world of tennis and the U.S. Tennis Association. He was grateful for his own success in sport, but he hoped for so much more for the next generation of young African Americans and dedicated his life to making that happen. I am grateful for having shared a friendship with Arthur Ashe, from whom I learned some priceless life lessons.

The face of professional sport in the United States has changed dramatically in the last 50 years through the inclusion of African American, Latino, and Asian athletes and their subsequent record-setting performances and domination of certain sports and positions. Where white males once dominated sport, the balance in major team sports such as basketball and football has now shifted to dominance by black athletes. African Americans and Latinos have both increased their representation in Major League Baseball, and many have achieved superstar status.

Despite the integration of athletes of all races into sport, there are still challenges:

- Opening opportunities in all sports to people of all races and ethnic backgrounds, especially for youths

- Integrating athletes from all races and ethnic groups into the social fabric of the sport world and capitalizing on the diversity of participants

- Recruiting and training sport leaders, such as coaches, managers, and owners, of all races and ethnic backgrounds

In this chapter, we'll take a look at sport participation by various racial and ethnic groups, sport participation as both a positive and negative factor in social change, and strategies for increasing participation by minority groups at all levels of sport. Before we look at these issues surrounding race, ethnicity, and sport, let's first consider what we mean by race and ethnicity and then review some census numbers.

Classifications of Race and Ethnicity

The terms **race** and **ethnicity** are often interchanged in references to various groups of people. However, it is more accurate to use *race* when referring to attributes that are passed along genetically from generation to generation and to use *ethnicity* to refer to the cultural heritage of a group of people. All groups except whites are also referred to as **minorities** since they constitute a smaller percentage of the population in the United States than the majority group (white Americans). Although these definitions may differ slightly depending on the discussion, they are a good starting point for this chapter.

Race is not as easy to define as you might think. Due to the mixing of many generations of different races, more Americans are of a mixed racial background than an unmixed one. Historically, many people used the so-called one-drop rule when describing racial origins, meaning, for example, that those who had even one drop of blood from an African American ancestor were considered African American. Of course, in popular culture, skin color, facial features, or type of hair might define members of a minority group. Adding to the confusion is the classification by the U.S. Census of Hispanics or Latinos, who are tallied as a single group with a footnote that they may be of any race (United States Census Bureau 2008a).

The term **racism** refers to the belief that race determines human traits and characteristics and that racial differences result in the superiority of a particular race. Groups that have been victims of discrimination due to racism have typically been minorities. The dominance of white males of European origin in the early days of the United States resulted in the belief that whites were superior to people of other racial backgrounds.

The U.S. Census of the population in 1930 showed that 88.7% identified themselves as "white," while just 9.7% identified themselves as "Negro." There was no Hispanic or Latino category, but there was a category labeled "Mexican," who numbered only 1.2% of the population. Take a look at table 11.1, which shows the current percentages of racial groups as of 2008—they are markedly different from 75 years ago.

The forecast by the U.S. Census Bureau is that by 2050, Latino/Hispanic Americans will double and Asian Americans will nearly double. At the same time, the white population will drop to just 46% by 2050, the lowest percentage in the nation's history. The decline appears to be due to declining birth rates among whites and to immigration of minority groups. These eventual changes will mean that

groups who were formerly minorities in the United States will actually be in the majority.

Another striking pattern is emerging as to where minority groups choose to live in the United States. According to William Frey, demographer at the Brookings Institution in Washington, DC, "Blacks are returning to the South while Hispanics are dispersing throughout the country where there are jobs" (Frey 2010, p. 54).

In the 1990s, most Hispanic immigrants entered the country through five gateways: California, Texas, Illinois, New York, and Florida. Today, Hispanics make up at least 5% of the population in 30 states, up from 16 states in 1990. The trend is toward Hispanics dispersing to cities such as Washington, DC, and Atlanta. Riverside, California, ranked first in total Hispanic gains from 2000-2008 while metro Dallas and Houston were close behind. The Florida cities of Tampa, Orlando, Cape Coral, Lakeland, and Jacksonville each were large gainers as well. As the end of the decade approached, further expansion of Hispanics slowed somewhat due to the lack of jobs in many areas (Frey 2010).

For blacks the pattern is different, with over 17 million—almost half of all blacks—living in the 11 states that were in the Confederacy, an increase of one million since 1990. The continued shift of blacks southward has been primarily to "New South" growth centers such as Texas, North Carolina, Georgia, and Florida rather than the historic "Old South" states such as Louisiana, Mississippi, and Alabama. In fact, Atlanta more than doubled its black population to surpass Chicago with the second largest African American population in the United States.

Asians tend to concentrate more heavily in traditional immigrant magnet areas than Hispanics, with the top three areas of New York, Los Angeles, and San Francisco housing one-third of all Asians nationwide. However, similar to the Hispanic population, Asians are steadily dispersing across the country.

One other trend worth noting is that four states, Hawaii, New Mexico, Texas, and California, have minority populations that exceed 50% of their total population. This is also true for 17 large Metro areas, up from just five in 1990. Interestingly, because the younger part of our population is even more racially diverse than adults, there are already 31 Metro areas where the "minorities" are really a majority (Frey 2010).

The concentration of various minority groups in particular areas of the country will likely have an effect upon the popularity of various sports in those regions. Both in participation and in spectatorship,

TABLE 11.1 United States Population by Racial Groups 2008 and Projected for 2050

Racial group	2008	2050
White	66%	46%
Hispanic/Latino	15%	30%
African American	14%	14%
Asian American	5%	9%

United States Census 2008.

racial groups tend to favor certain sports and ignore others. An example of this effect is the heavy recruiting of football players by major colleges in the southeastern United States. Football recruiters know that since a higher percentage of blacks live in the Southeast, it makes sense to recruit there.

The size and location of minority groups are significant when we consider the numbers of minority athletes in particular sports. When compared with their percentage of the general population, minorities are heavily represented in certain sports at elite levels and are virtually absent in others. A question to consider is whether these imbalances are the result of race or simply a function of opportunity and culture. In the following sections, we'll look closely at who is participating in what sports and what factors influence that participation.

Sport Participation Among Racial and Ethnic Minorities

In this section we will consider each of the major racial groups and examine their sport participation.

As a result of the civil rights movement and elimination of many racial barriers, African American athletes have assumed a dominant place in certain sports at the college and professional levels. Yet overall, blacks are underrepresented in the vast majority of collegiate sports. The data in this section often point to the challenges and triumphs of black athletes in the last 50 years simply because their struggle has been studied and debated widely. To a lesser extent, Hispanics, Asians, and Native Americans have affected sport; however, each of these groups has always included key contributors to sport and is continuing to battle its own set of barriers.

As you read this chapter, it will be helpful to refer periodically to tables 11.2 and 11.3, which show detailed information on participation in collegiate and professional sport by racial groups. You will notice some stark differences between the percentages of participation by different racial groups at the various levels of collegiate and professional competition. It is also instructive to compare the percentage of racial groups in sport to their percentage of the U.S. population. Significant cases of overrepresentation and underrepresentation in various sports are obvious.

TABLE 11.2 Participation in Collegiate Sport by Racial Group

MALES					
Racial group	Division I, II, III	Division I	Football Div. I	Basketball Div. I	Baseball Div. I
White	72.2%	64.2%	47%	32.5%	84.5%
African American	18.3%	24.7%	45.9%	60.4%	6.0%
Latino	3.9%	3.8%	2.2%	1.8%	5.4%
Am. Indian/Alaskan Native	.3%	.4%	.4%	.4%	.4%
Asian American	1.6%	1.6%	1.6%	.4%	1.2%
Nonresident Alien	n/a	n/a	n/a	n/a	n/a
Other	n/a	5.3%	2.9%	4.7%	2.5%
FEMALES					
Racial group	Division I, II, III	Division I	Basketball	Cross country/track	Other sports
White	78.8%	72.1%	44.4%	65.5%	71.0%
African American	11.2%	15.7%	47.6%	23.7%	4.9%
Latino	3.6%	3.7%	1.8%	4.0%	2.9%
Am. Indian/Alaskan Native	.4%	.4%	.4%	.4%	.3%
Asian American	2.1%	2.3%	1.1%	1.3%	3.1%
Nonresident Alien	n/a	n/a	n/a	n/a	n/a
Other	n/a	5.8%	4.7%	4.9%	8.8%

Adapted from Lapchick 2008.

TABLE 11.3 Professional Players by Racial Group Percentage

Racial group	NFL	NBA	WNBA	MLB	MLS
White	31%	18%	21%	60.4%	59%
African American	66%	77%	65%	10.2%	22%
Latino	1%	3%	0%	27%	14%
Asian American	2%	1%	0%	2.4%	1%
Other	<1%	1%	0%	0%	3%
International	2%	18%	14%	28.7%	31%

Note: Percentages are based on 2007 for NFL and MLS, 2008 for MLB and WNBA, and 2008-2009 for NBA. WNBA international players not reported by racial group.

Adapted from Lapchick 2008-2009.

African American Athletes

A quick look at the history of sport reveals how African Americans have not only moved into prominent roles in the major American sports but have reached a point of domination. In his definitive history of the black athlete, Arthur Ashe divided history into three volumes (1988). The first volume dealt with black athletes from the 1600s up to the time of World War I. As sport entered its golden age in the United States in the 1920s and 1930s, a few black athletes made their mark, including Jesse Owens in track and field and Joe Louis in boxing. But it was not until after World War II that integration became a reality in most American sports and black athletes began to achieve a level of prominence. Most historians would agree that one of the major events in this period was the breaking of the color barrier in Major League Baseball (MLB) by Jackie Robinson.

The black athlete has been studied, written about, admired, scorned, and persecuted in American sport. Because of notable success by black athletes, a great deal of attention has been given to the reasons behind this success. Conventional wisdom ranges from "White men can't jump" (compared to black men) to "Blacks have brawn, not brains."

If you were to ask John Q. Public about black athletes, chances are he would say they dominate American sport. However, out of 35 million African Americans in the United States, nowhere near the expected percentages are involved in sport. In most sports, they are woefully underrepresented or completely missing—consider, for example, sports such as sailing, ice hockey, tennis, golf, swimming, diving, soccer, cycling, figure skating, softball, vol-leyball, water polo, and almost all winter sports. It's in the major American sports of basketball and football, along with track and field, that African American males tend to participate in large numbers. Because those sports gobble up a huge proportion of attention, money, media, and television, we assume that black athletes dominate sport.

African Americans in Professional Sport

In the early 1940s until the conclusion of World War II, there were no black athletes in MLB, professional football, or the National Basketball Association (NBA). Outstanding black athletes were relegated to playing in the Negro Leagues or other competitions organized for African Americans. In the latter part of the decade, each sport made the move to sign a black athlete, marking a change in American sport that was to have far-reaching implications for the next 50 years. For black athletes, the five years following the end of World War II were the most memorable in their sport history (Ashe 1988).

By the end of the 1950s, African Americans had moved to a percentage of participation in the major sports equal to their percentage of the national population, which was approximately 11% to 12%. The civil rights movement, which eliminated segregation in public places, schools, and the workplace, no doubt had a major effect on the phenomenal rise of the black athlete. If we fastforward to 2010, over 50 years later, the percentage of African Americans in professional sport is quite different (Lapchick 2009a).

Baseball	10.2%
Football	66%
Men's basketball	77%
Women's basketball	65%

Even sports that traditionally have not included black athletes have begun to show some signs of inclusiveness. The sport of tennis boasted its first black champion in Althea Gibson, who won Wimbledon in the 1950s. Arthur Ashe followed on the men's side, but black athletes had few other champions in the next couple of decades. The arrival of the Williams sisters, Venus and Serena, however, touched off an explosion of interest in tennis in the African American community in the late 1990s. Suddenly a sport that was traditionally for the white and privileged had a pair of role models who were from modest means. They burst onto the tennis scene without traveling the hard and expensive road of junior tennis and instead chose to vault right into professional play.

IN THE ARENA WITH . . .

Jackie Robinson

He thrilled fans with his play, shattered the color barrier in baseball, and helped change the face of sport. In 1947, segregation ruled in the United States. There were separate schools, swimming pools, drinking fountains, hotels, restaurants, and baseball leagues for blacks and whites. Jackie Robinson helped change all that by becoming the first black man to play MLB.

Branch Rickey, the owner of the Brooklyn Dodgers, chose Robinson for his amazing physical skills, his courage, and perhaps most important, his ability to turn the other cheek when faced with hateful behavior. According to a tribute by Hank Aaron, holder of the all-time home run record, Jackie had to "endure teammates who petitioned to keep him off the club, pitchers who threw at him, opponents who dug their spikes into his shin, fans who mocked with mops on their heads and death threats" (Aaron 1999, p. 2). "Robinson could hit, bunt, steal and run," says Roger Kahn in *Boys of Summer* (Schwartz 2005b, p. 2). "He passionately wanted to win, could intimidate opponents and burned with passion." Robinson's debut for the Dodgers in 1947 came a year before President Truman desegregated the military and seven years before the Supreme Court outlawed segregation in public schools.

He earned the Rookie of the Year award and two years later won the Most Valuable Player award based on a year in which he batted .342 and stole 37 bases. His lifetime batting average was .311, and he was voted into the Baseball Hall of Fame in his first year of eligibility. Robinson was dogged by diabetes and was nearly blind by middle age. He died of a heart attack at age 53 in 1972. His final request: "We ask for nothing special. We ask only to be permitted to live as you live, and as our nation's Constitution provides" (Schwartz 2005b, p. 4).

The effects of the Williams sisters success are that tennis now ranks fourth in popularity among African Americans, following only football, basketball, and baseball, and African Americans are the most avid tennis fans of any racial group. Approximately 11% of African Americans say they are avid tennis fans, nearly twice as many as whites (5.7%). That compares with 39% of African Americans who pick football, 37% who pick basketball, and 18.2% who pick baseball for their avid sport support (Lapchick 2001).

Similarly, Tiger Woods boosted the popularity of golf by 14% in the late 1990s when he began to dominate the game, and he has continued to be one of the dominant golfers. However, only 7% of African Americans describe themselves as avid golf fans (Lapchick 2001).

African Americans in Collegiate Sport

In collegiate sport, African Americans dominate National Collegiate Athletic Association (NCAA) Division I basketball for both men and women. Likewise, black men dominate football, and the next most popular sport for both male and female African Americans is track and field. A quick look at table 11.2 reveals some stark differences between Division I athletes when compared to all athletes in all divisions. The percentage of African American athletes, both male and female, drops about 10 percentage points primarily due to the lack of African Americans represented in Division III programs. Keep in mind that Division III schools are typically smaller, private schools and cannot offer athletic scholarships.

African Americans, particularly in Division I of football, basketball, and track and field, far surpass the percentage of expected participation rates based on their share of the U.S. population, which is 14%. However, when you look at all other sports at all levels of competition, African Americans are less than 5% of collegiate sport teams, far below what you might expect.

Change in collegiate sport has not come quickly, but gradually black athletes have made their presence known. The Southeastern Conference was the last major athletic conference to integrate, in 1966. In the late 1960s, there were still no black athletes at several schools in the conference, including Alabama, Auburn, Florida, Mississippi, Mississippi State, Louisiana State, and Georgia. By 1972, though, more than 100 black athletes were playing football in the conference, and by 1975 the University of Alabama started five black athletes in basketball. This fact is somewhat remarkable when you consider the attitude of former Alabama governor George Wallace, who used physical restraint to block African Americans from attending the university in 1963. Ten years later, in 1972, several teams in the Southeastern Conference even had black starting quarterbacks, an anomaly in those days.

Although African American athletes certainly have a large presence in the revenue-producing sports of football and basketball, the overall assessment of collegiate sport for racial diversity is modest. The Institute for Racial and Gender Diversity assigned a grade of "C–" to college sport for hiring. White people hold 88 out of the 97 available high-level positions in all three NCAA divisions, which includes college presidents, conference commissioners, athletic directors, head coaches, and faculty representatives. In fact, college football at the Football Bowl Subdivision (FBS) level received a grade of "F" for hiring at the head football coach position (Lapchick 2008).

Race and Athletic Dominance

Do black athletes dominate certain sports because of race? Numerous studies, such as those cited by Entine (2000, 2004), have been conducted to examine this issue from every perspective. The proportion of fast-twitch and slow-twitch muscle fibers has been used to explain the jumping ability of black athletes. Explosiveness on the track is also attributed to the muscular makeup and high proportion of fast-twitch fibers of black athletes. However, Ethiopian and Kenyan black athletes have dominated distance running for the last generation. Kenyans and other East Africans are born with a high number of slow-twitch fibers. They tend to be ectomorphs, short and slender, with a large natural lung capacity.

In contrast to East Africans, athletes of West African ancestry, including most North American, British, and Caribbean blacks, are generally poor distance runners. Rather, they tend to excel in sprinting and other sports in which explosiveness, speed, and power rule. Thus, if we simply define race according to skin color, in this case black athletes, there is significant variation between different groups of blacks (Entine 2000).

According to Price, writing in *Sports Illustrated* in 1997, "Generally accepted research has shown that African American children tend to have denser bones, narrower hips, bigger thighs, lower percentages of body fat and tests also show that they run

faster and jump higher." However, these are generalized observations that have not included extensive study of all types of black athletes at the world-class level. And there are certainly exceptions, such as former outstanding professionals like Charles Barkley and Karl Malone in basketball and Warren Sapp in football, who certainly don't have the characteristics that Price listed in his article but have been eminently successful in professional sport.

Some people believe black athletes have longer arms or reach compared with their white counterparts. Others believe that black athletes are mentally tougher and more relaxed under pressure. However, no matter how thorough the testing is, it is difficult to isolate factors and ascribe them exclusively to race. In fact, if you were to take a random sampling of youth athletes of all racial groups, it is unlikely that you would find significant differences.

A complicating factor is that within any prescribed definition of race, huge differences in variability exist because race is not a precise factor. The question of who is a black athlete is not a simple one when you realize all the possible ancestral origins of blacks and variations in skin color. The most well-known golfer today is Tiger Woods, whom many classify as a black athlete. However, Woods proclaims to be "Cablinasian," denoting his Caucasian, black, American Indian, and Asian heritage. Although many observers herald Woods' ascension to the top of golf as a landmark moment in which black athletes once again proved superiority, it seems that Woods would not attribute his success to his genetic makeup.

Another possible explanation for the dominance of black athletes in certain sports is the environment in which they grow up. Since blacks are a minority group, their choices in life may be fewer because they have fewer economic resources and less hope of landing a well-paying job as an adult. Young blacks see successful athletes and imagine following that path. A survey of 4,500 African American male youths by Assibey-Mensah (1997) showed that when asked about their role models,

- 85% of 10-year-olds and 98% of 18-year-olds picked athletes or sport figures;
- of those who picked athletes, 63% of 10-year-olds and 90% of 18-year-olds picked basketball players; and
- no child picked an educator.

A lack of role models for young black males may be due to the absence of a father or the presence of a father who is unemployed. According to the

U.S. Census (2005-2007), African American single mothers account for one-third of single-mother households in the United States. Black youths who live in inner cities may be particularly hard-pressed to find alternative role models, as successful local businesses are scarce and many potential role models have fled to the suburbs in search of a better life. Add to these complications the fact that African Americans are the racial group with the highest percentage of families below the poverty line, and you can see why young blacks would yearn for high-profile, high-paying careers in sport whether this is a realistic goal or not.

Sports like football, basketball, and baseball are relatively affordable and are usually offered by schools that provide coaching, uniforms, and equipment to athletes. Minority athletes are naturally drawn to these sports at school because they are accessible and affordable. On the opposite end of the spectrum, sports that are expensive such as skiing, water polo, and equestrian, or those offered primarily through private clubs such as golf and tennis, are often out of reach of minority athletes.

African American culture, particularly in urban settings, has drawn black youths toward the basketball court, and the draw has been reinforced by friends and heroes. Television offers plenty of opportunities to watch professional role models compete in basketball, football, and baseball. Basketball courts are plentiful, are relatively inexpensive to build, and can accommodate lots of players at a low cost. Playground basketball and recreational leagues that are free or low cost have been the training ground for thousands of city kids.

Stacking in Sport

The concept of stacking was thought up by activist Harry Edwards, who is widely recognized as a leading authority on issues of race and sport. Edwards has been a longtime professor of sociology at the University of California at Berkeley and a consultant for MLB, the Golden State Warriors, and the San Francisco 49ers on issues of racial diversity in sport. **Stacking** refers to an unusual distribution of whites and blacks in certain sport positions

Yannick Bonheur and Vanessa James made Olympic history at the 2010 Olympic Games as the first black pair to grace the rink in ice skating. Why is it that there aren't more black figure skaters?

that cannot be explained by a random distribution. For example, in football, the position of quarterback has typically been dominated by whites, while running backs and wide receivers have been predominantly black. In baseball, pitchers and catchers have been predominately white while outfielders have tended to be black. In basketball, centers and guards are more likely to be white and forwards more likely to be black. Many of these percentages have changed in recent years as the overall percentage of black athletes has risen dramatically, but there is still the historical aberration that gave rise to the suspicion that black athletes were excluded from certain positions on a team.

Various explanations have been offered for the apparent existence of stacking. One such explanation is the centrality theory, which places white athletes in the center of the lineup or the middle of the team. In baseball this means whites are pitchers, catchers, shortstops, and second basemen; in football it means whites are quarterbacks, centers, middle linebackers, and offensive guards. The idea was advanced that the so-called white positions require more thinking and decision making central to the outcome of the game while blacks are drawn to positions that require more raw physical talent.

Another theory is that blacks and whites tend to be attracted to certain positions and that children follow the lead of their role models and seek out similar positions in youth sport. A similar theory is that coaches move players into certain positions based on race where they think the athletes would be most successful. Those positions are ones that require a relatively higher level of physical talent and speed and a lesser amount of cognitive ability.

As black athletes have moved into professional sport in large numbers, the concept of stacking has received less attention and sparked fewer debates. Black quarterbacks have now led teams to Super Bowls, and blacks have become All-Stars in the positions of pitcher and catcher. The Institute for Racial and Gender Diversity reports that as of 2007, stacking in the NFL is no longer a major concern—based primarily on the near doubling of the percentage of black quarterbacks during the past 10 years. In MLB, the concern is not so much stacking as it has been the falling overall percentage of African Americans in recent years. The black athletes who do perform in MLB are overrepresented as outfielders and still underrepresented by pitchers and catchers. You may be interested in the actual percentages by position for African Americans shown in table 11.4, which presents the trends over the 10-year period from 1998 to 2008 (Lapchick 2008-2009).

TABLE 11.4 Stacking in the NFL Percentage of Black Athletes by Position

Position	1998	2003	2007
OFFENSE			
Quarterback	8%	22%	19%
Running back	87%	86%	89%
Wide receiver	92%	86%	89%
Tight end	42%	42%	42%
Offensive tackle	55%	55%	49%
Offensive guard	29%	41%	35%
Center	17%	12%	18%
DEFENSE			
Cornerback	99%	98%	97%
Safety	91%	81%	84%
Linebacker	75%	80%	71%
Defensive end	79%	77%	73%
Defensive tackle	63%	77%	76%

Note: Keep in mind that the overall percentage of African American players in the NFL is 66%.

Data from Lapchick 2008.

If black athletes are restricted from playing certain positions, then a case can be made for racism within professional sport. Such racism may result in the loss of earnings in that players in certain positions such as quarterback and pitcher tend to command greater compensation because they are so valuable to their team. Another factor is that the positions dominated by black players tend to require greater strength, speed, and explosiveness. Since those attributes are often the first to decline with age, black players may have shorter careers and thus less earning power. In fact, the positions held most often by blacks—running back, cornerback, and wide receiver—tend to have the shortest careers. Overall, it was concluded by researcher Clayton Best that "experience and career length in professional football [are] the effects of positional segregation" (Best 1987, p. 410). Consider that players who occupy positions typically held by blacks have a career expectancy of about three years in the NFL compared with four years for positions typically held by white players. That difference may seem inconsequential, but it means that black athletes may have careers that are 25% shorter on average, thus affecting their earning power.

Of course, limiting black athletes to certain positions also affects their long-term prospects for coaching or managing teams. Athletes who play in

POP CULTURE

Is Racism Still Alive for Black Quarterbacks?

The popular belief that the quarterback position in football is a thinking position that excludes African Americans has long been an example of institutional racism in the National Football League. Racism is the unequal treatment of a person or group of persons based solely on their race, which leads to prejudice and discrimination. To be clear, if a coach or owner precludes black athletes from playing certain positions such as quarterback, that is racism. The history of black athletes in the NFL shows clearly that black athletes had little chance to compete for the role of quarterback.

William Roden, eminent sports columnist for the New York Times has written a book, *Third and a Mile: From Fritz Pollard to Michael Vick – an Oral History of the Trials, Tears and Triumphs of the Black Quarterback* (2007). Using testimony from NFL greats such as Warren Moon, Doug Williams, Vince Evans, James Harris, Donovan McNabb, Daunte Culpepper, and Michael Vick, among others, Rhoden chronicles the heroic struggles of black quarterbacks to overthrow one of the sport's most confounding racial barriers. For decades, talented black athletes were told that their athleticism made them better suited to playing wide receiver or defensive back. Usually left unsaid was that in spite of a record of success at lower levels of competition, they were unlikely to be able to handle the rigors of becoming the field general of an NFL team simply because of their skin color.

In spite of the fact that African Americans dominate professional football, it has taken decades for them to rise to the quarterback position and prove their mettle. The early days for the trailblazers such as Moon and Williams were filled with suspicion, racist taunts, and critical fans and media until their performances proved they were worthy of a shot at leading a team and, in the case of Williams, winning the 1988 Super Bowl as the starting quarterback for the Washington Redskins.

In 2009, the number of black quarterbacks was 16% compared to 81% who were white in a league that is 67% black. Even more revealing is the fact that in the running back and wide receiver positions, blacks represented 87% of players compared to just 11% white players (Lapchick 2010c). Based on this information, it would seem that playing quarterback in the NFL still carries almost insurmountable odds for young aspiring African American quarterbacks. Do you agree?

the central positions that require decision making and game understanding obviously have a leg up on others. The dearth of black coaches, especially in football, has been a long-standing issue for many blacks.

Exploitation of Black Athletes

An unfortunate outcome of opening sport participation to black athletes has been the shameful way in which some schools, coaches, and universities exploit them for their athletic talent. Leaders in the black community speak out against exploitive practices, use the media to publicize infractions, and warn athletes to watch their backs. But the potential to exploit talented black athletes is often there when they are quite young.

As early as middle school, when the adolescent growth spurt is in full flower, teachers, coaches, and administrators notice the gifted athletes who demonstrate exceptional talent, size, or strength.

These athletes may be given the benefit of the doubt in the classroom in spite of lackluster academic performance because of their athletic potential or their importance to the school team. At the end of the year, they may be promoted to the next grade in spite of substandard academic performance. A few minority athletes have made it through college without ever learning to read, such as James Brooks, star running back at Auburn University, one of the most dramatic cases publicized in the media (Muse 2000).

When colleges recruit top athletes and offer them scholarships, they believe that they are entitled to protect their investment. It is normal practice at Division I institutions that compete at the national level to encourage athletes to choose relatively easy majors and courses, take a lighter academic load during the season, attend mandatory study halls, use a tutor when necessary, and delay their academic progress to gain another year of eligibility to play. All of these practices are susceptible to abuse, and coaches who are caught lose their job and reputation. However, many are not caught, and the result is the low graduation rate of minority athletes. Even those who graduate may have learned little and have no employable skills. If they don't make it as a professional athlete, their future is bleak.

On the other hand, the professional leagues have conspired to keep college-aged athletes from playing in the pros. While most athletes are not ready physically or mentally to compete at a young age, some, like LeBron James in basketball, are not only ready to play but also to be a star. Of course, colleges don't want to lose athletes in whom they have invested time and money to a professional team before the athletes' collegiate eligibility is up. So professional leagues and colleges work together to keep players in school (e.g., forcing players to wait until their class graduates to turn professional), even if the athletes have no interest in it and want to turn professional. However, the barriers have fallen in basketball, and exceptions have been made in football. Baseball has always signed young players and often encouraged them to join minor league teams rather than go on to college.

The decision to turn professional rather than play one more year of college usually has to do with the potential for a lucrative contract. If an athlete is offered millions of dollars, he takes a terrible risk if he rejects it to return to college and then sustains a serious injury. That injury may be the end of his career and long-term financial security for his family. In the end, if the deal is good enough, most athletes leave for the pros. Even if another year in college would have been good for their athletic development or academic career instead of sitting on the bench for a professional team, the temptation and security of a contract are often too great.

While athletes of all racial backgrounds are susceptible to exploitation in professional sport, because black athletes make up a large percentage of players in the major American sports they are disproportionately at risk.

Double Jeopardy for African American Female Athletes

Despite being in the majority in schools and colleges, females represent only 35% of all high school athletes and less than 34% of all college athletes. Although enormous progress has been made in the last 25 years due primarily to the passage of Title IX legislation, women still have not achieved parity in participation or resources at any level of sport.

The case of black women is doubly discouraging. They are discriminated against twice, because of gender and because of race. African American females represent less than 5% of high school athletes, less than 10% of college athletes, less than 2% of all coaches, and less than 1% of all college athletic administrators according to Donna Lopiano, PhD, former executive director of the Women's Sports Foundation (Lopiano 2001). More recent data show that the percentage of black female athletes surpassed 11% in 2008 overall and rose to 47.7% in college basketball, 23.7% in track and field, and 15.7% overall in total Division I sports (Lapchick 2008).

Lopiano says that "the African American female is a victim of sport discrimination and positional stacking within sports. She is generally restricted to basketball, track and field and the least expensive sports. (Unlike for boys, football is not an option.) Within the sports she does play, she has been historically underrepresented in the skill/outcome positions of setter in volleyball or point guard in basketball" (Lopiano 2001). In the past 10 years, African American women have excelled at the point guard position in basketball at the highest levels of competition, making that concern a relic of the past.

Elite black female athletes are offered fewer speaking engagements, endorsements, and sponsorships. They have not been at the forefront of the civil rights movement or the feminist movement because sport has been seen as trivial or reflective of a male model that should not be emulated. The two notable exceptions have been Venus and Serena Williams, who have captured huge sponsorships from Reebok and Nike, respectively. If Serena meets performance-related criteria for bonuses over eight years, she could earn upward of $55 million from her Nike deal. That is all added on to several million a year in prize money! That is an amazing achievement for a black female athlete.

Lopiano proposes a series of actions to rectify the situation of black female athletes. Using lessons learned from civil rights battles and gender equity battles already fought, she proposes collecting and maintaining accurate data on participation percentages of black females at all levels of play to be used in an annual report card. With the gathered data, she suggests using media pressure to announce and pursue a national agenda targeting specific groups such as high school athletes or coaches, as well as to demand that sport organizations and associations take action to fulfill their public responsibilities with regard to equal opportunity in sport for everyone regardless of race or gender (Sabo et al. 2004).

Latinos and Hispanics

Hispanic is used to describe all people whose ethnic heritage can be traced to Spanish-speaking countries. *Latino* typically refers to people of Latin America, including Central and South America and the Caribbean. This is a diverse group in ancestry and language, and their skin color may be black or white. As noted previously, Hispanics and Latinos have recently nudged ahead of African Americans as a percentage of the U.S. population, and the forecast is for the percentage to increase steadily over the next few decades.

When asked to think of athletes who are Latinos, most Americans think of baseball first. In recent years, Latinos have claimed a higher percentage of major league players than African Americans and seem to be on an upward trend. Of the 833 players on Opening Day of the 2010 season, 23.7% of the players had been born outside the 50 American states and represented 14 different countries and territories. Besides the United States, the country that has the most major leaguers is the Dominican Republic with 86, followed by Venezuela with 58. Other countries or territories with high numbers include Puerto Rico with 21, Mexico with 12, Cuba with 7, and Panama with 5. As a team, the Mets have the most foreign-born players with 18 who represent seven different countries and territories (Major League Baseball 2010).

As more players find success in MLB, young Latinos look up to them as role models and pour their energies into honing their baseball skills. Young men from modest economic backgrounds can see few opportunities to achieve success and economic security for their family more attractive than becoming a star baseball player.

Major League Baseball has established baseball academies in many Central American countries and made top coaches and competition available to promising prospects. While the vast majority of Latinos who have made it to the major leagues in baseball are from Central American countries, their successes have attracted a huge following of American Latinos who identify with their origins.

The Dominican Republic has a long tradition of sending players to the major leagues, as illustrated by their lock on half of the spots on the All-Time Latino Team. The team was announced during the 2005 World Series after selection by fans. Voting was sponsored by MLB for 60 players from seven different countries and territories. The final selections included 12 players, one at each infield posi-

While Hispanic athletes are common in soccer and baseball, many athletes have also competed in tennis, golf, boxing, and running. Scott Gomez, who is of both Mexican and Columbian descent, currently plays hockey for the Montreal Canadiens.

tion, three outfielders, three starting pitchers, and one relief pitcher. These were the players on the team (Sanchez 2005):

Ivan Rodriguez, Puerto Rico, catcher

Albert Pujols, Dominican Republic, first base

Rod Carew, Panama, second base

Edgar Martinez, Puerto Rico, third base

Alex Rodriguez, Dominican Republic, shortstop

Roberto Clemente, Puerto Rico, outfielder

Manny Ramirez, Dominican Republic, outfielder

Vladimir Guerrero, Dominican Republic, outfielder

Pedro Martinez, Dominican Republic, starting pitcher

Juan Marichal, Dominican Republic, starting pitcher

Fernando Valenzuela, Mexico, starting pitcher

Mariano Rivera, Panama, relief pitcher

The Chicago White Sox, World Series champions in 2005, claim a Latino as their manager, Ozzie Guillen. A three-time All-Star player, Guillen spent most of his 16-year career as a shortstop for the White Sox. He is the first native of Venezuela to manage in the big leagues. Latino managers at the start of the 2010 season in addition to Guillen were Manny Acta (Washington Nationals), Fredi Gonzalez (Florida Marlins), and Lou Piniella (Chicago Cubs) (Lapchick 2010a).

Soccer is the most popular sport in the world and clearly king of sports among Latinos. But Major League Soccer (MLS) in the United States has been a tough sell. Unlike American football, basketball, and baseball, American soccer is not the best in the world. According to some estimates, it may be the 10th best league in the world, well behind European, South American, and Latin American leagues. A quarter of its spectators are Latino, and in 2001 almost 25% of players were Latino as well. That number fell in 2010 to just 14% (Lapchick 2010b). Part of the reason is the cap of five foreign players on any one team.

Soccer is clearly the choice of Latinos. A miniseries titled *Raices (Roots)* aired in July of 2005 on the History Channel. The six-part series was hosted by Pablo Mastroeni, a member of the 2004 MLS All-Star team and a native of Argentina. The series highlights the greats of the game from Brazil, Mexico, Argentina, Uruguay, and Colombia, including players such as Pelé, Garrincha, Romario, Ronaldo, and Alfredo di Stefano. As the Latino population grows in the United States, the owners and organizers of professional soccer plan to market American soccer to them.

In March 2006, the first National Hispanic Games for recreational athletes was staged in Tucson, Arizona. More than 2,000 athletes competed in an Olympic-style tournament featuring the sports of basketball, soccer, baseball, and boxing (Tornoe 2005). Even the sport of NASCAR is moving full throttle into the Latino market. Led by youngster Carlos Contreras and racing legend Adrian Fernandez of Mexico, the sport is reaching out to the growing Latino market through marketing initiatives. Presently, Latinos account for close to 9% of NASCAR's fan base, and between 1999 and 2002 their number increased at a rate of 23%. NASCAR has founded the Drive for Diversity (D4D) program to train and encourage female and minority drivers. Cuban-born Armando Fitz owns Fitz-Bradshaw Racing along with his wife, Mimi, and Hall of Fame football player Terry Bradshaw. Although it is the only present Hispanic-owned NASCAR team, the future promises more to come.

Interestingly, according to NCAA statistics, Hispanics are underrepresented in virtually all sports at the college level with the lone exception of men's volleyball. That may be due to the heavy concentration of Hispanics in California, where volleyball is a popular sport. However, in 2008, the percentage of Hispanics increased overall in participation in college sports and in Division I athletics as well (Lapchick 2008).

Asian Americans

Asian Americans along with Latinos are the fastest-growing minority population in the United States, but their participation in sport has been slow to develop. Compared with other racial groups, famous athletes of Asian descent are relatively few, and participation in sport generally has been lower than that of other groups. It is difficult to generalize about the sport participation of Asian Americans due to their varied countries and backgrounds. Many came to the United States already highly educated and in the middle or upper-middle class. They did not reach out to sport as a means to greater economic, social, or educational goals. The goal of becoming a doctor, lawyer, scientist, or other professional is instilled in their youth by their parents and culture rather than that of becoming a sport hero, according to Central Florida professor Yun-Oh Whang, a native Korean (Lapchick 2003). Recent census data support the notion that Asian Americans have a higher household income and

| Apolo Anton Ohno, with his eight Olympic medals, is the most decorated American Winter Olympic medalist of all time.

Amy Chow, gymnastics

Se Ri Pak, golf

Kristi Yamaguchi, figure skating

Apolo Anton Ohno, speed skating

Jim Paek, hockey

Michelle Kwan, figure skating

Yao Ming, basketball

Hideo Nomo, baseball

Vijay Singh, golf

Michelle Wie, golf

According to the NCAA (2002), just half of 1% of all Asian or Pacific Islander students were also athletes in college, compared to nearly 6% for African American students and 2.6% for white students. But in large population centers where there are usually more Asian Americans, the anecdotal evidence suggests that Asian American children are becoming more interested in sport both as spectators and as participants.

Compared to the overall percentage of Asian Americans in the population at large (4.1%), Asian Americans are overrepresented in collegiate sport at Divisions I, II, and III in women's archery, women's badminton, men's and women's fencing, men's and women's gymnastics, women's soccer, women's squash, men's and women's water polo, and men's and women's tennis. Most of these sports do not require a large physique, and they put a premium on skill; perhaps they are more suited to the traditional body types of Asians.

Asians also tend to be attracted to martial arts because such sports are part of their cultural heritage. Martial arts have been some of the fastest-growing activities among the general population in recent years. Participation in yoga and tai chi increased 134% between 1987 and 2003, while martial arts, such as judo, taekwondo, and karate, grew by 28% (Sporting Goods Manufacturers Association 2004).

Native Americans

Native Americans and Alaska Natives made up .9% of the U.S. population in 2003 with just over 2.7 million people. With this relatively small percentage of the population, you would not expect them as a group to have had much of an impact on sport, but they have produced some notable athletes over the years.

The Olympic Games have produced several sport heroes for Native Americans. Probably the most famous is Jim Thorpe, a Potawatomi Indian,

higher graduation rate in high school and college than any other group, including whites. However, Asians and Asian Americans can boast a number of star athletes in a variety of sports:

Sammy Lee, diving

Ichiro Suzuki, baseball

Michael Chang, tennis

Tiger Woods, golf

who won two Olympic gold medals, played professional baseball and football, and became the first president of the league that would become the NFL. His Olympic medals in 1912 were earned in the pentathlon and the decathlon, and Thorpe's records in these events stood for decades. In 1950 he was named the greatest overall male athlete for the first half of the 20th century by the Associated Press, and few years later ABC's Wide World of Sports named him the athlete of the century.

In the Tokyo Olympic Games in 1964, Billy Mills won the gold medal in the 10,000-meter race. A fellow Olympian in the Games at Tokyo was Ben Nighthorse Campbell, who captained the U.S. judo team and had been the U.S. champion in judo three times. Campbell later went on to the serve in the U.S. House of Representatives and the U.S. Senate. Altogether since 1904, there have been 14 Native American Olympians (Native American Sports Council [NASC] 2009).

By 2005, Native American professional athletes actively engaged in their sport numbered about 20 (NASC 2009). Their sports range from the traditional American sports like baseball (five players) to the less traditional sports like the Iditarod (five competitors). Other sports include speed skating, golf, bowling, ice dancing, rodeo, and auto racing. None of these athletes has achieved wide acclaim, but all make their living in professional sport.

The Native American Sports Council (NASC) is part of the Olympic Movement, an affiliated organization of the USOC, and conducts community-based sport programs for Native Americans to encourage community participation. It also provides financial assistance for Native American Olympic hopefuls.

The North American Indigenous Games are a celebration of sport and culture for aboriginal peoples of Canada and the United States. In 2002, 6,136 athletes and 1,233 coaches participated in the games held in Winnipeg, Canada (NASC 2009). The following sports were included:

Archery	Lacrosse
Athletics	Riflery
Badminton	Soccer
Baseball	Softball
Basketball	Swimming
Boxing	Taekwondo
Canoeing	Volleyball
Golf	Wrestling

Subsequent games were held in Denver, Colorado, in 2006 and Duncan, British Columbia, in 2008. The games in Denver attracted approximately 10,000 athletes, with more than 1,000 tribes represented. The 2011 games are scheduled to be held in Milwaukee, Wisconsin. In the United States,

Jim Thorpe is one of the most well-known Native American athletes.

the National Native American Games have been held in the state of Arizona, drawing over 1,000 participants in the inaugural year of 2003. The competition is open to all tribes, and athletes must be one-quarter Native American to compete. Sports include basketball, cross country, adult softball, track and field, and volleyball.

Sport participation has not been easy for many Native Americans in today's world. Poverty rates are nearly 50% on many reservations and in many urban areas where Native Americans live. Time, money, and access to sport are limited, and the cultures also limit assimilation into the American sport scene. Discrimination against Native Americans is widespread, and the athletic field is often just another battle for respect and acceptance. Native Americans have been stereotyped, displaced from their land, restricted to reservations, and saddled with poor economic status (King and Fruehling 2001).

Coaches have expressed frustration with Native Americans who have been enculturated to cooperate rather than compete with each other. Many Native Americans simply are not comfortable with the "winning is everything" mentality and may withdraw rather than try to change their beliefs. White coaches who have worked with Native Americans have been frustrated with the attitude of their players toward the importance of winning athletic contests (Bloom 2000).

Legacy of Lacrosse

There is no more significant Native American contribution to sport than the game of lacrosse. Considered America's first sport, lacrosse was created by North American Indians and embraced by non-Native Americans and Canadians alike. Lacrosse is a combination of basketball, soccer, and hockey that rewards skill, speed, and agility rather than brawn.

Since 1994, lacrosse has been growing at an average rate of over 10% nationally. US Lacrosse chapters have been established in 39 states that in 2008 boasted more than 500,000 members on organized teams compared to just over 250,000 in 2001 (United States Lacrosse Association 2009). Table 11.5 shows how participation grew from 2004 to 2009.

At the college level, lacrosse has grown by 39.5% for men and women in the past 10 years. In high schools, the growth rate has been an astounding 200% for boys and girls. Traditional hotbeds for lacrosse such as Long Island, Baltimore, and Phila-

TABLE 11.5 US Lacrosse Participation Rates

Level	2004	2009	% 1-year growth
Youth	186,048	297,271	12.1
High school	133,857	227,624	4.0
College	23,162	31,614	6.0
Professional	150	180	−40
Postcollegiate	8,635	11,342	12.6
Total	351,852	568,021	8.4

Adapted from United States Lacrosse Association 2009.

delphia are now being challenged by teams from other areas of the country (United States Lacrosse Association 2009).

Native American Mascots

In recent years, the use of Native American mascots by professional teams and by schools has come under scrutiny. The complaint is that the use of stereotypical team names, mascots, and logos perpetuates an ideology that dehumanizes and demeans the cultures of Native Americans. Students of American history will recall that Native American tribes were settled in North America long before the Europeans "discovered" America. As more Europeans came to the "new world," Native American tribes had their lands taken and their lives changed irreparably by these new settlers. Many Native Americans paid with their lives to defend their land, civilization, and culture. Years later, Euro-Americans labeled their athletic teams at schools, at universities, and in professional sports with Native American logos, names, cheers, and mascots. Defenders of such names and mascots claim that these actions were and are meant to honor the legacy of Native Americans and perpetuate memories of brave and heroic warriors. However, those who object to Native American mascots and symbols in American sport argue that they blatantly stereotype the Indian persona; ignore racist attitudes and displacement of populations of Native Americans; and encourage white Euro-Americans to arbitrarily define the Native American culture and experience and in some cases even claim to be part of that heritage (King 2004).

In 2001 the U.S. Commission on Civil Rights, an independent bipartisan federal agency, called for an end to the use of Native American images and team names by non-Native schools. By 2006, the NCAA issued a policy advising schools to specifically forbid the displaying of hostile and abusive racial, ethnic, or national-origin mascots, nicknames, or imagery. Moreover, some 19 schools with team names such as the Braves, Redskins, Indians, Tribe, and Savages were put on notice to make changes. The changes these schools make will be the result of self-study to ensure their use of mascots does not violate the hostile or abusive standard as judged by the NCAA. For example, schools that use the generic term Warriors without referring to Native American culture have been deemed as meeting the compliance standard. As of 2007, 11 schools had changed their nickname, mascot, or imagery; five schools were declared exempt from the policy; and three were determined to be subject to the policy. The NCAA has clarified that schools that violate the policy cannot host NCAA championships and cannot participate in championships if their uniforms violate the policy (NCAA 2007b).

The NCAA relied on its core principles regarding diversity and inclusion in making the recommendation to eliminate nicknames that may be considered abusive or hostile. Following the action of the NCAA may take some time and courage for other athletic bodies, but the trend is growing. Publicity and pressure from a variety of sources have focused on this issue; and scholars, journalists, and leaders against discrimination in any form have joined forces. Progress is being made slowly but surely.

Sport and Promoting Equality

Although you have just read about the roles of minorities in sport, the more important question may be whether sport participation is a negative or a positive force for those groups in achieving racial equality. Let's look at both sides of the issue.

Negative: Sport as an Unrealistic Dream in the Black Community

In spite of the relatively high percentage of black athletes in the professional sports of basketball, football, and baseball, the odds of making it to the professional level are exceedingly small. (See chapter 7 and table 7.3 for the specific odds of transitioning from youth sport to the pros.) Regardless of the odds of success, young black athletes still dream of being professional athletes.

In the words of William Ellerbee, basketball coach at powerhouse Simon Gratz High School in Philadelphia, "Suburban kids tend to play for the fun of it. Inner city kids look at basketball as a matter of life and death" (Price 1997). Professional sport seems like a way out of a life marked by economic struggle, educational challenges, and poor prospects for a successful career. Sport is something young people can understand, relate to, and almost taste. The problem is that there are just not enough spots to fulfill all the dreams.

In 1990, blacks made up about 9% of all professional athletes, while there were nearly three times more black physicians than athletes. A decade later, the percentage of black professional athletes had jumped to approximately 20%; however, the number of doctors had also risen to twice the number of black athletes. Of course, that's just one profession, and there are many more possible choices. Many black youngsters are just not as tuned in to the possibilities of other careers.

Leaders in the black community such as Arthur Ashe, former U.S. Open and Wimbledon champion, have spoken out about the need to keep black children interested in school and committed to attending college. However, a survey by Indiana University researchers of more than 1,000 black teens found that the majority of athletes chose their university not for the academics but to increase their chances of being drafted by the pros. They admitted that they would do only the minimum required to stay eligible in school and if drafted would leave before graduating (Hutchinson 2004).

The historical graduation rates of black athletes at most Division I institutions reflect the apparent determination of many black athletes to use college as a training ground for a professional career. Graduation rates posted by the NCAA on its website for 1994 to 1995 showed that overall, male students graduated at a rate of 54% and student-athletes at a rate of 51%, but African American student-athletes graduated at a rate of only 42%. The results were significantly better for females. Women graduated at a rate of 59% while female student-athletes graduated at a rate of 69%. African American female student-athletes graduated at a rate of 59%. A more recent study conclusively shows a marked improvement in graduation rates for both male and female student-athletes.

EXPERT'S VIEW

"Blacks Are Retreating From Athletics"

Shaun Powell, author of the provocative book *Souled Out*, makes this surprising claim based on the rise of the black middle class. He points out that in the early 1980s, children of the Civil Rights era became adults blessed with college degrees and helped by affirmative action and a more tolerant white society. Rather than repeat the vicious poverty cycle of their parents and grandparents, they aspired to become typical middle-class Americans who could provide their children with lives previously thought impossible—filled with education, professional success, appreciation for art, culture, and a wide variety of sport experiences. Their children are more likely to succeed in school, join the debate team, play a musical instrument, do social work, or learn the family business. This suburbanization of black kids has not increased black participation in sport and in fact has decreased the pool of young black athletes.

Yet Powell goes on to point out that the apparent domination of football and basketball by blacks is not due to natural athleticism but rather simply to what is available within their environment. Since young men have not previously been lucky enough to have role models of dentists, doctors, administrators, TV producers, computer analysts, and university professors, they tend to gravitate toward what they do see. Poor black kids turn to basketball because it is available in every park, playground, and school in America. Similarly, football teams attract huge numbers of kids and reward those who work hardest to excel at the sport (Powell 2008).

In fact, African American college athletes graduate at a higher rate than African American students as a whole by an 8% margin (53% vs. 45%). African American male athletes graduated at a rate of 48% versus 38% for all male African Americans, while African American female athletes posted a 66% rate of graduation versus 50% for all female African Americans. It appears that being a student-athlete tends to be a positive factor for females and a negative factor for males (Lapchick 2009a). Table 11.6 shows good news in increases in graduation rates for African American athletes comparing 2006 to 2009.

In spite of the trend of improvements, there are still some particularly negative statistics that are hidden in the overall percentages. In the 2009 NCAA men's basketball tournament, a number of high-profile teams showed some embarrassing off-court performances. UConn players posted a graduation rate of only 22% for African American players and only 33% for the whole team. Similarly, Missouri had a 25% rate for African Americans and 36% overall (Lapchick 2009a).

Ten years ago, the top 16 seeded teams had an overall graduation rate of 44%, but in 2009 that number jumped to 64%. That is testimony to schools such as North Carolina, Pittsburg, Duke, Villanova, Xavier, and Wake Forest, a nice mixture

TABLE 11.6 Graduation Rates for African American Athletes

	2006	2009
African American men's basketball	49%	54%
African American men's football (I-A)	54%	58%
African American women's basketball	71%	76%
African American student-athletes	59%	62%
African American male student-athletes	54%	57%
African American female student-athletes	73%	76%

Reprinted from Lapchick 2009.

of public and private colleges. However, the bad news is that while overall the top 16 rates have improved, half of those schools had only a 32% graduation rate for their African American players. This group of schools included five of the top eight seeds: UConn, Louisville, Oklahoma, Michigan State, and Memphis (Lapchick 2009a).

Universities needn't shoulder all the blame. Arthur Ashe toured predominately black high schools in the late 1980s and early 1990s as he was gathering information for his three-volume history of the black athlete, *A Hard Road to Glory*. Ashe reported that he was "thunderstruck" by the emphasis placed on sport at the schools he visited.

He went to on to report, "Black families are eight times more likely to push youngsters into athletics than are white families. The disparity is glaring, if you think of the Black parents' involvement at a sporting event compared to participation in a PTA meeting. We need to turn that around" (*Houston Chronicle* 2004).

Similarly, former NBA player Charles Barkley has said, "Sports are a detriment to Blacks . . . not a positive. You have a society now where every Black kid in the country thinks the only way he can be successful is through athletics. People look at athletes and entertainers as the sum total of Black America. That is a terrible, terrible thing, because that ain't even one-tenth of what we are" (Shields 2002).

Barkley has used his platform as a former basketball star to get the attention of the black community. His message is echoed by Gary Sailes, a sport sociologist at Indiana University who provides life skills training to high school and college athletes. Says Sailes, "About 95% of NBA players need to find a job after their careers end and about 81% of those players are bankrupt when they retire from the sport." In spite of the millions of dollars commanded by superstars, not all professional players make that kind of money, and the temptation to spend lavishly is often hard to resist (Sleek 2004).

Positive: Sport as a Force for Racial Equality

Sport at every level of competition can have a positive effect on the quest for racial equality in society. The helpful outcomes of sport participation should be considered in balance to the negative effects, which are often sensationalized in the media.

Harry Edwards, who has been a racial activist for over 30 years, has a unique perspective on the value of sport for black youths. He offers the opinion that in the next 30 years, we will see a decline of black athletic participation. Edwards expects the black youth community to split into two groups, middle class and poor, with each group shying away from sport. Middle-class kids will go on to become professionals, doctors, lawyers, and businesspeople. But he believes that black youngsters from poorer communities are dropping out of society and landing in gangs, on the street, or in jail. Edwards still believes that sport offers hope for a way out of poverty, crime, and disillusionment. In his mind, sport may be the last chance to reach out to disaffected black youth (Leonard 2000).

Success in sport can have a dramatic effect on the self-image and self-confidence of young people from minority populations. Their exploits on the playing field earn them respect and admiration from peers and the community and reassure them of their worthiness as individuals.

Achievement in sport can also earn players respect and admiration from peers who are outside the minority group. Minority athletes are more easily integrated into the mainstream of their contemporaries who are members of the majority group through team membership, leadership, and the critical roles they play.

Many communities have instituted after-school sport programs to care for youths who have no parental supervision at home when school is dismissed. Kids look forward to physical activity and playing with friends after a day of inactivity in school. Adding an academic component to after-school sport programs in minority communities has encouraged kids to complete homework, learn about computers, and explore other academic interests in addition to the time allocated to playing sports. The message conveyed to these young children is that school and sport do mix and that both can help them learn skills for future application.

A number of sports have begun outreach programs to attract minority youngsters. Among them, tennis and golf have probably initiated the most ambitious programs. Traditionally, both sports have been played by affluent families, and marketing efforts have been directed toward those audiences as well as toward corporations that also seek to reach a consumer group with household incomes well above the average. However, in an effort to reach larger audiences and open the sports to a more diverse population, programs for young people have been established and subsidized to introduce them to tennis or golf.

Arthur Ashe and businessman Sheridan Snyder founded the National Junior Tennis League (NJTL) in the 1970s with a unique philosophy for tennis development. The concept, called *instant competition*, got urban youths actually playing tennis from their first day at the courts. As they tried to play and realized it took certain skills to be successful, the kids asked for help in techniques such as serves and ground strokes. This was a radical departure

School physical education classes are a great opportunity for students to be exposed to sports that they may not otherwise have a chance to play.

success is based on achievement in any field, regardless of heritage or skin color.

As a coach of tennis at a primarily white college in Pennsylvania, I consistently scheduled at least one match each spring with a historically black college during our annual trip through Virginia or the Carolinas. When our team of white players set foot on a campus of African Americans, they were curious and a bit uneasy; and when they entered the college dining room to eat, all eyes were on them. They gained a bit more empathy for the minority students back home who dared to enter a mostly white university. After our tennis match, their appreciation for the skill and competitive spirit of athletes from a different background was enhanced. The visit was often a highlight of an educational experience that offered more than simply a tennis competition.

Exceptionally talented minority athletes have opportunities for travel, educational scholarships, and experiences outside their community. These experiences open them to new possibilities and to attitudes that are characterized by hope and possibility rather than bitterness and discontent.

Kids who play sports are more likely to stay out of trouble with law enforcement and are less likely to become dependent on drugs or alcohol. Interestingly, binge drinking among college athletes generally exceeds that of nonathletes by 29% to 22%, but African American athletes, particularly women, have the lowest prevalence of binge drinking (Wechsler 2005). While athletes as a group are not immune to temptations or antisocial behavior, the time and dedication that excellence in sport requires often takes precedence over other activities that typically result in unacceptable behavior. In addition, athletes run the risk of losing the chance to play the sport they enjoy if they violate rules for conduct and behavior.

Black athletes who do beat the odds and forge successful careers in professional sport have the opportunity to better themselves financially, sometimes in amazing ways. Other opportunities as spokespersons or employees in businesses or sport organizations often materialize once their athletic

from traditional tennis instruction found in country clubs at the time. Twenty-five years later, game-based teaching became all the rage among tennis coaches, a philosophy of teaching not far from the pioneering concept of the NJTL. Perhaps the most notable characteristic of NJTL programs was the requirement that they had to be free or inexpensive so that all kids had access to tennis. Public parks, foundations, and fund-raising projects provided funding.

Interscholastic sport, supported by tax dollars from the public, offers sport opportunities for youngsters of all racial backgrounds at no charge or for modest fees. Black and Hispanic youths can play on a team, receive coaching, and have all expenses paid for, including equipment and uniforms. For those drawn to football and basketball, for example, school programs have been helpful for minority families who have modest discretionary income or none at all. Other sports that require training or competition outside of school continue to require huge financial investments from families and thus are out of reach for many black and Hispanic households.

Integration of young people from all racial and ethnic backgrounds occurs naturally in sports where teammates are forced to work together for success. Even when athletes of different races compete against each other, they learn to respect and admire competent athletic performance of opposing players. The lesson young athletes learn may be that career has ended. Upward mobility through sport has been demonstrated repeatedly by a generation of black athletes.

Once they reach the peak of athletic performance, many black athletes have used their prominence to speak out for causes they believe in. For example, improved race relations was a theme of the proposed Olympic boycott in Mexico City in 1968. When the boycott fell through, African American sprinters Tommie Smith and John Carlos instead used the award ceremony to call attention to the plight of African Americans in the United States. Although they were criticized heavily for using sport to promote their personal point of view, their actions were no different from those of many other influential people who do the same.

Michael Jordan, perhaps the greatest basketball player of all time, demonstrated the global reach of sport success through his role as a spokesperson for Nike. Kids the world over adopted the mantra "Be like Mike" and consumed Nike products from shoes to clothing in hopes of emulating Jordan's performances. He also showed how fame in one field can be transferred to the business world through ownership of a basketball franchise and through other business ventures.

Minority athletes become role models for the next generation of athletes. Their fame is not limited to children from a single racial background; children choose their heroes based on their performance, flair, and personality rather than race. Although some athletes reject their role as models for youths and simply want to be accepted as an athlete, the dynamics of the media, fans, and kids simply won't allow it. Their actions, lifestyle, and values are scrutinized and embraced or rejected simply because they are in the public spotlight. They can choose to be a positive force for improving society or a negative example of behavior that should be abhorred.

As the struggle for racial integration continues, sport offers a fertile ground for exposing the futility of erecting artificial barriers to integration, for embracing athletes from all backgrounds based on talent and conduct, and for promoting understanding and appreciation of people from all different backgrounds.

Minorities as Sport Leaders

Virtually anyone who has studied the situation of minority athletes has come away believing that leadership in sport has to change for progress to occur. The lack of minority leadership in key positions in sport is sobering and shows few signs of improving in the near future. However, change can still happen. In the following sections, we'll look at some ways to increase the presence of minority groups in all levels of sport. Most of the examples are based on African Americans since their role as athletes in certain sports has been so dominant. Increasingly, though, people are also becoming more sensitive to the need for leaders from other minority groups as well.

Minorities in Leadership Positions in Collegiate Sport

With the statistics showing the dominance of African American athletes in the collegiate and professional sports of football, men's and women's basketball, and track and field, you might expect to see similar gains in the coaching ranks and other leadership positions. However, the proportion of African American coaches is well below the proportion of African Americans in the population at large and is much lower than the proportion of African American athletes playing the major revenue sports.

Overall, college sport received a grade of "A" for race in the number of Division I men's head coaches and assistant coaches for basketball and NCAA headquarters staff (Lapchick 2008). Sadly, college sport received a grade of "F" for FBS head football coaches, sport information directors, athletic director, conference commissioner, and FBS university president. Table 11.7 on page 218 provides a look at the percentages of African Americans versus whites

ACTIVITY TIME-OUT

Is Sport Positive or Negative for Change?

Based on the information presented in this chapter, do you believe sport plays a positive role or a negative role in promoting diversity and equal opportunity? List the pros and cons of each view and then decide which list is more powerful.

in head coaching positions by NCAA division and males and females.

In the most visible sport of football at the FBS level, out of 120 head coaches, only three were African American in 2007, although that number increased to six in 2008. Mario Cristobal at Florida International University was the only Latino head coach in the FBS, while Ken Niumatalolo of the Naval Academy became the first Samoan head coach in FBS history in 2008. By the end of the year in 2009, the number of black head football coaches had increased to 10, which is the highest total ever. However, keep in mind that this number is still only 8% of the total of the 120 major head football coaching positions. This statistic is woeful when we consider that the percentage of black athletes at this level of play is listed as 45% of college football players in Division I (Watkins 2009).

In contrast to football, Division I head basketball coaches for men's teams had 22.9% African American while their female counterparts showed a percentage of 13%.

Compared with the approximately 14% of African Americans and 15% of Latinos in the U.S. population, these percentages are woeful. But if you match them with the percentage of black athletes in basketball, 60% for men and 47% for women in Division I, the results are even worse.

One popular explanation for the dearth of black coaches is the small percentage of athletic directors and other administrators in universities who are black. It has been theorized that white administrators know fewer black coaches, are less comfortable with them, and thus resist placing key programs in their hands. According to Lapchick and Mathews (1999), black athletic directors in 1996 to 1997 were present in just 3.2% of Division I institutions. The numbers were somewhat better in some administrative positions other than the head person (see table 11.8).

Minorities in Leadership Positions in Professional Sport

In professional sport, the percentage of black athletes is even higher than in college (see tables 11.2 and 11.9). Those responsible for recruiting and hiring black coaches are the owners of professional sport franchises. In 1999, according to research by Lapchick and Mathews, there were no minority owners of any professional sport franchises. There were, however, a number of limited partners in various leagues, the most notable among them Magic Johnson with the Los Angeles Lakers. Since then, Michael Jordan has joined the Washington Wizards, and Robert L. Johnson, who made millions from BET television, acquired majority ownership of the Carolina basketball franchise, an expansion team that began competing in 2004. He also owned the Charlotte Stings of the Women's National Basketball Association (WNBA), making him the first African American majority owner of a professional

TABLE 11.7 Comparing Percentages of White and African American Head College Coaches

	MEN			WOMEN		
Division	**I**	**II**	**III**	**I**	**II**	**III**
White	89.2%	88.7%	92.5%	87.7%	88.9%	91.9%
African American	7.2%	5.3%	4.0%	7.0%	5.1%	4.4%

Data from Lapchick 2008.

TABLE 11.8 Minorities in Administrative Leadership Positions

	AFRICAN AMERICAN (%)			LATINO (%)			ASIAN (%)			NATIVE AMERICAN (%)		
Position	**I**	**II**	**III**	**I**	**II**	**III**	**I**	**II**	**III**	**I**	**II**	**III**
Athletic director	7.2	3.8	1.8	1.9	3.0	0	0	.8	.7	.6	.4	.4
Assistant or associate	7.2	7.5	3.2	2.2	1.6	.4	.6	1.0	0	.1	0	0
Senior female administrator	10.2	7.8	1.9	n/a	n/a	n/a	n/a	n/a	n/a	n/a	n/a	n/a

Data from Lapchick 2008.

TABLE 11.9 African American Coaches in Professional Sport

Position	NBA (%)	NFL (%)	MLB (%)	WNBA (%)
Head coach or manager	40	19	26	46
Assistant coach or manager	42	36	33	42

Data from Lapchick 2008-2009.

sport team, although that team has since ceased operation.

By 2004, the picture had begun to change. Baseball had its first Hispanic owner, Arturo Moreno of the Anaheim Angels, and three other minorities had shares of teams. The NBA showed six minority limited partners in addition to Robert L. Johnson as a majority owner. The NFL had five minority limited partners, and the WNBA had one majority owner. Michael Jordan, former superstar NBA player, purchased the Charlotte Bobcats from Robert Johnson in 2010, making him the only African American majority owner in the NBA.

By 2008, of five professional sports that include NFL, MLB, NBA, WNBA, and MLS, there were still just two majority owners (Johnson and Moreno) of any franchises. Major League Soccer is a bit different from the others in that it is owned by a board of governors who invest in the league rather than individual franchises. There are 49 members of the board with a percentage of 18.4% people of color. Those folks were two African Americans, four Latinos, and three Asian Americans.

In the league offices of professional sports for 2008, people of color were 27% of WNBA, 35% of NBA, 31% of MLB, and 40% of MLS. The NFL did not report on its staff. The highest percentage of minority staff for both MLB and MLS were Latino.

Strategies to Promote Racial Diversity in Sport

From the discussion in the previous section, it is clear that one key strategy to promote racial diversity in sport is to improve the hiring and retention of minority coaches in both college and professional sport. Institutions must follow guidelines for affirmative action that include strategies for recruitment of minority candidates, inclusion of minorities in the hiring process, and a "good faith" effort to evaluate minority candidates objectively and fairly. Other possible strategies include the following:

- Agree on the need to improve the percentages of minorities in all sports and all sport leadership positions. Targets should be set based on percentages in the population at large and within the sport community.

- Leaders in sport must help collect data such as those provided currently by Dr. Richard Lapchick of the University of Central Florida, which detail the participation and presence of minorities at all levels of sport. Without a baseline number to work from, efforts to improve diversity will be impossible to measure. The process should be unbiased, objective, and transparent, and the results should be widely disseminated.

- Leaders in minority communities and heads of sport organizations should confront any instance of discrimination or racism when they become aware of it and take steps to rectify the situation.

- Major sport organizations, both amateur and professional, should adopt statements of inclusion of minorities for their players, coaches, and administration staff.

- Major media outlets including television, radio, magazines, and newspapers should actively recruit minorities for their staff and aggressively endorse the need for change in sport.

- All sport organizations should develop standing policies of inclusion in pictures, graphics, and media representations.

- Politicians should adopt laws to ensure that public money is used for projects and organizations that are committed to providing opportunity for all and improving minority representation.

- Prominent minority athletes must assume the responsibility to point out inconsistencies and inequities and use their popularity to improve the future for other minority athletes.

- Local communities and youth sport organizations should adopt strong policies on nondiscrimination and should actively recruit minorities to participate in sport as players, coaches, leaders, and organizers.

- Minority-owned businesses should expect action by the organizations they support financially through sponsorship and marketing.

ACTIVITY TIME-OUT

Promoting Racial Diversity

The possible strategies for promoting racial diversity listed in the text are intended to get you thinking. See if you can come up with at least a dozen new strategies for sport at any level to eliminate racism and increase the number of minorities who participate. If you prefer, you may narrow your recommendations to one sport that you are familiar with.

Chapter Summary

In this chapter, we have reviewed the meaning of racial and ethnic background in sport. The differences in physical prowess between races were examined, and the issue of whether differences were due to genetics or environment was considered. At the present time, there is no clear evidence either way, although research is ongoing. It is likely that both factors will prove to be crucial in most sports.

Participation by minority groups at various levels of sport was compared to the number of minorities in the general U.S. population. Generally, the data show that black athletes dominate major American sports such as basketball and football at both the college and professional levels. Baseball, which led professional sport in integration efforts and formerly had a significant number of African Americans, has fallen back to less than 10% while Latino players have advanced to 28% of MLB. However, in all other sports, whites overwhelmingly dominate in terms of participation at every level of play.

The history of minority athletes was briefly reviewed, and the exceptional influence of outstanding black athletes was noted. Most gains in participation by minorities have occurred since World War II when college and professional sport opened to black athletes. Latino athletes are exceedingly well represented in professional baseball, surpassing even black athletes by percentage. In other sports, Latinos are generally poorly represented, as are Asians and Native Americans.

Both the positive and negative contributions of sport to racial and ethnic equality were presented. Sport has shown the potential to be a positive force for racial integration, although progress has not always been smooth. On the other hand, we considered some of the negative aspects, including minority preoccupation with sport at the expense of schooling and alternative career choices.

The struggles of black athletes were pointed out even as these athletes dominate some college and professional sports. Their participation tends to be limited to just a few sports, and access to the majority of sports is still limited. The tendency of powerful sport institutions to exploit the physical abilities of black athletes at the expense of their potential for a fulfilling life after sport was discussed. Leadership positions in sport at all levels continue to be dominated by whites, thus affecting efforts to open opportunities for African Americans as coaches or other leaders in the sport world.

Strategies for lessening the present inequities in sport were presented, along with an opportunity for readers to add creative strategies of their own. For the progress of the last 50 years to continue at the same rate, a collective commitment to racial diversity in sport must be accepted at every level of play.

Women and Sport

Student Outcomes

After reading this chapter, you will know the following:

- The historical roles of women in and out of sport
- How Title IX affected women's sport participation
- How increased sport participation by females affected society
- Current challenges in women's sports

Children who participate in exercise and athletics are generally seen as an asset for American families, both dual-parent and single-parent families. Not only do sports provide social support for kids, but they often bring children into closer contact and communication with parents. And while research reveals that mothers and fathers provide similar levels of encouragement and support for both their daughters and sons, there is also evidence that girls are being short-changed by dads who may spend more time in sport with their sons. Most dads today would probably say they support the athletic exploits of both sons and daughters; the facts are that boys ranked fathers as number one on their list of mentors who "taught them the most" about sport, while girls ranked their dads in the number three spot, behind their coaches and physical education teachers. Girls ranked their mother in fifth place while boys ranked their mother in sixth place. If parents, particularly dads, don't encourage girls to enter sport when they are young, there is a risk it won't happen, especially with the elimination of so many physical education programs in recent years (Women's Sports Foundation 2008).

One of the most consistent forms of discrimination is the social role forced upon women throughout history. From the time of the ancient Greeks to the present day, societies have relegated females to subservient roles revolving around child rearing, family, and sex. Changes in American society in the last 35 years have dramatically altered the roles for women, but the quest for equalizing women's opportunity in society is still short of its goal.

A majority of women in the United States are now in the workforce. According to the U.S. Census 2006-2008 Community Survey, 67.9% of women are employed compared to 77.9% of men (United States Census Bureau 2006-2008). In 1960, the percentage of working women was just 36%. By the fall of 2009, women were poised to overtake men in sheer numbers in the workforce by claiming 49.83% of the workforce. This history-making change in employment patterns is the result of the economic depression and the resulting loss of jobs by men, particularly in construction and manufacturing industries. However, women overall in the workforce hold more part-time jobs, work fewer hours than men, and earn only 77% of what males earn. Men still dominate the higher-paying executive jobs. The result of this shift in the workforce is that women are now shouldering a large burden to seek and keep their jobs, ensure health care for their families, and still serve as the primary caregiver in most families (Cauchon 2009).

Along with decades of fighting for greater equality in employment opportunities, women have campaigned for and significantly progressed in admission to institutions of higher education, rights in marriage, roles in the armed forces, and opportunities for sport participation. The sporting world changed greatly with the passing of Title IX, which granted females equal participation in sport. With this foray into the sporting world, however, females faced new forms of discrimination.

In this chapter, we'll look at the factors that have affected women's participation in sport, the sweeping changes that have occurred in sport over the past 35 years, and the challenges women in sport still confront.

Historical Role of Women

To understand the magnitude of the first female breakthroughs in sport, you need to appreciate the context in which these pioneering women accomplished them. Since the times of the ancient Greeks and Romans, the family was based on a patriarchal model wherein the male was the absolute ruler. He alone could own property and enter into business contracts, and if his wife violated social customs or his wishes, he could punish her. In many societies, if a husband determined that his wife was guilty of infidelity, he could have her put to death.

The institutions of society reinforced the subjugated role of women throughout history. Even the church made it clear that the male was the head of the family and often portrayed the female as an agent of the devil whose role was to tempt the male. Women could not act as clergy and were expected to adhere to the teachings of men.

The prescribed role for women stayed the same for centuries. The male was always the leader, the provider for the family, and the center of power. The female was the child bearer and nurturer and keeper of the home. Females were not allowed physical exercise other than that required by their domestic roles. They were expected to look attractive to men, dress prettily, and be well mannered. Women were expected to depend on the men.

Women and Sport Before Title IX

Sports have reflected the limited role of women by excluding them from participation for centuries and resisting change to include them. Girls were ignored, ridiculed, and disciplined for their efforts to compete in sports (Rice, Hutchinson, and Lee 1958; Spears and Swanson 1978). It wasn't until the mid-1800s that women even ventured into physical activity programs founded at colleges such as Mount Holyoke and Vassar. Medical doctors dedicated to improving the health and fitness of students typically led the early programs of physical education. Exercise for girls was carefully controlled and emphasized graceful, ladylike movements. Competitive sports were ruled out as simply inappropriate for women.

A few women dared to participate in individual sports such as tennis and golf. Figure skating, gymnastics, and swimming, considered more feminine sports requiring grace, beauty, and coordination, were gradually accepted for women. Power and strength sports were deemed inappropriate, and even the Olympic Games banned women from most track and field events. Running, jumping, and throwing heavy objects were not consistent with the social view of the female. In the modern Olympic Games that began in 1896, women were not allowed to compete. In 1920, the Olympics invited only 64 women, compared with more than 2,500 men. In the Berlin Games in 1936, the number of female participants swelled to 328 while male participants boosted their number to 3,738 (Fanbay.net 2005).

A few female athletes gained fame during the 1920s and '30s.

Glenna Collett Vare was a remarkable amateur golfer who won the U.S. Open Amateur Championships six times between 1922 and 1935. Helen Wills Moody dominated women's tennis in the '20s and '30s by winning eight Wimbledon titles, eight U.S. national titles, and every set she played in competition between 1927 and 1932. The most famous and perhaps best athlete was Mildred "Babe" Didrikson Zaharias. (In the second half of the 20th century the top female athlete, according to *Sports Illustrated for Women* in 2000, was Jackie Joyner Kersee, track and field Olympian. She was followed closely by tennis legends Billie Jean King, Chris Evert, and Martina Navratilova.) In 1950, Zaharias was voted the greatest female athlete of the first half of the century by the Associated Press. Her accomplishments included two gold medals and one silver medal in track and

Mildred "Babe" Didrikson Zaharias was a great basketball and tennis player, a three-time Olympic medal winner, and a dominant golfer.

field events at the 1932 Olympics. As a golfer, she dominated both the amateur and professional field. She was also a tennis player who could compete with the best players in the United States. Other women also made their mark in professional sport. The popular movie *A League of Their Own* chronicles the trials of the All-American Girls Professional Baseball League during World War II. You also might want to view the documentary, *Dare to Compete: The Struggle of Women in Sports*, which traces the history of women in sport.

These outstanding female athletes blazed the trail into the sport world. But their successes would not open up sport opportunities for the majority of women until society changed its general view of the woman's role. The following are some of the reasons society gave for excluding women from sport.

Females Aren't Interested

Lack of interest was in hindsight an irrational justification for excluding girls from sport. Since girls had little access to sport, few sport role models, and no encouragement to play sport by social institutions such as families, schools, and churches, of course they appeared uninterested. They were expected to become cheerleaders, pom-pom girls, and majorettes and to play in the band and fill the stands to cheer on the boys.

Physical Activity Harms the Female Body

In the last century, led by physicians and physical educators at universities across America, people gradually awakened to the positive benefits of physical activity for girls. Although limited to certain ladylike physical activities, girls were encouraged to become aware of their bodies for reasons of health and appearance. Research began to show that girls could train their bodies to become stronger and faster and endure longer without damaging their physique. It wasn't until the late 1970s that experts began to affirm the positive values of sport participation for females. In 1978, Klafs and Lyon said, "Let it be stated here, unequivocally, that there is

no reason, either psychological, physiological, or sociological, to preclude normal, healthy females from participating in strenuous physical activities, nor does such participation accentuate or develop male characteristics. Strenuous activity for the well-trained and well-conditioned female athlete results in good health and accentuates the very qualities that make her a woman" (Klafs and Lyon 1978, p. 10).

Although female leaders in sport forged a brave path toward physical activity for girls, they also held girls back. Up through the 1950s, leaders of women's sport limited the types of acceptable sport and encouraged girls not to become too competitive. Play days or sports days on college campuses were the norm in the '50s. Women from several different colleges gathered at one campus and were assigned to teams for that day. The events were largely informal and encouraged mass participation. Several sports were typically played, and competition was low-key and usually in round-robin format. The closing event was a tea or social hour when girls could talk with each other (Spears and Swanson 1978). When the National Collegiate

Early physical education classes touted the benefits of exercise for young women.

Athletic Association (NCAA) threatened to take over women's sport, the leading female coaches and administrators fought against it. They preferred the more ladylike approach to sports in which girls were athletes tempered by good manners, winning was deemphasized, and femininity was maintained.

Remnants of this ladylike approach are team monikers such as Lady Lions, Lady Vols, and Lady Tigers. Imagine if the men's teams were called Gentlemen Bears, Gentlemen Gators, or Gentlemen Warriors.

Women Cannot Compete With Men in Sport, So They Don't Deserve Equal Opportunity to Play

Objections about the relative skill and physical prowess of girls versus boys were a natural outcome of a few girls daring to compete against boys. My high school boys' tennis team competed against a young girl named Tory Fretz, who played first singles on the boys' team for Harrisburg High School and went on to a professional career. She defeated every boy in the conference, usually by lopsided scores. Her performance was an eye-opener for adolescent boys and humiliating for her victims, who endured teasing and taunting.

But unlike Tory Fretz, most girls were at a disadvantage when competing against boys once puberty set in. Before puberty, girls can compete equally with boys in any sport. But once the relative size, strength, and body proportions change, the comparative athletic ability also changes. To achieve equal opportunity in sport, women needed a whole new structure for girls' sports, starting from little history, equipment, or tradition.

Girls With Natural Talent in Sport Are Probably Lesbians

Girls who gravitated toward sport were often suspected of lesbian tendencies long before the term *lesbian* was even used in polite society. Women who liked sport and seemed to have more testosterone were looked at askance by males and females alike. The average person had little notion of the balance of testosterone and progesterone that exists in both male and female bodies. Women who were stronger and faster or could hit harder excelled in women's sports, leading some to suspect that they were really men disguised in women's bodies.

In the Olympic Games, testing for gender was an issue for years as a result of the masculine appearance of many great female athletes. **Gender verification** was required for nearly 30 years until after the 1996 Atlanta Games, when all gender verification was discontinued at the urging of virtually all professional medical associations including the American Medical Association. The extensive procedures used for verification were too complex, uncertain, and expensive. Furthermore, very few athletes actually failed the tests that were administered. With the advent of doping control policies that included voiding urine under direct supervision, it became virtually impossible for male athletes to escape detection if they tried to pose as women (Genel 2000).

But the issue of gender testing made headlines once again in 2009 when the International Association of Athletics Federations (IAAF) performed gender tests on an 18-year-old South African track star, Caster Semenya. Her amazing performances in the 800 meters at the World Championships and her masculine appearance led the IAAF to request gender verification tests. It has been reported that Semenya has no ovaries, but rather internal male testes that have not descended normally. The controversy dragged on for eleven months until July of 2010 when the International Association of Athletics Federation (IAAF), the international governing body for track and field, cleared her to resume competition including the London Olympics in 2012. IAAF refused to reveal the medical details in dispute or make any comment, so it is likely we will never know exactly why a doctor questioned her gender or why it took so long to adjudicate the issue (*Daily Mail* 2010).

Social attitudes toward women and lesbians continued from the first half of the 20th century to be heavily weighted against equal participation of women in sport. Consider this quote from Woody Hayes, a famous football coach at Ohio State (Vare 1974, p. 38):

> I hear they're even letting w-o-m-e-n in their sports program now [referring to Oberlin College]. That's your Women's Liberation, boy—bunch of goddamn lesbians. . . . You can bet your ass that if you have women around—and I've talked to psychiatrists about this—you aren't gonna be worth a damn. No sir! Man has to dominate . . . the best way to treat a woman . . . is to knock her up and hide her shoes.

Title IX

Social change throughout the 1950s and '60s helped change women's sport. The women's movement of the 1960s and organizations such as the National Organization for Women and the Women's Action Group helped further the movement for equality of men and women. In the sport world, however, it was the passage of **Title IX** that ultimately gave women an even playing field with men. (For a comprehensive work on the substance, effects, and challenges of Title IX, consult *Title IX* by Carpenter and Acosta 2005.) Title IX, passed in 1972 by the U.S. Congress, stated the following:

> No person in the United States shall, on the basis of sex, be excluded from participation in, be denied the benefits of, or be subjected to discrimination under any education program or activity receiving federal financial assistance.

When Title IX was passed, there was little immediate outcry since America was in the throes of

ensuring equal protection for all students, regardless of race or gender, in public education. Most parents agreed that their daughters should have the same right to a fine education that their sons had. It wasn't for some time that people understood that sports were included in the decree and that big changes would have to be made.

The imbalance in sport participation between boys and girls was dramatic up until the 1970s. At that time nearly 3.7 million boys were playing varsity high school sports compared with just 295,000 girls. Out of every dollar spent on sport, boys received 99 cents while girls received just 1 cent. In college, there were approximately 180,000 men playing varsity sports versus just 32,000 women.

Many questions were raised about what Title IX really meant and what specific changes had to be made. Did it mean girls had to have as many teams as boys had? Did girls get half the money spent on

 IN THE ARENA WITH . . .

Billie Jean King

Billie Jean was a champion tennis player and an outspoken advocate of gender equality in sport. Over the years, King's actions made her the center of attention in debates over the equality between the sexes, amateurism versus professionalism in sport, and gay and lesbian rights. Her crusading led *Life* magazine to recognize her in 1990 as one of the "100 Most Important Americans of the 20th Century." She was the only female athlete on the list and was one of only four athletes along with Babe Ruth, Jackie Robinson, and Muhammad Ali.

As a tennis player, Billie Jean won Wimbledon six times, won the U.S. Open four times, and was ranked number one in the world five times. In 1971, she was the first woman in any sport to earn more than $1 million in a single year. In 1972, *Sports Illustrated* named her the first Sportswoman of the Year.

Perhaps Billie Jean is most remembered for her 1973 "Battle of the Sexes" match against Bobby Riggs, a 55-year-old male tennis champion. Watched on television by nearly 50 million fans, King defeated Riggs decisively 6-4, 6-3, and 6-3 in the Houston Astrodome amid a media circus. Her victory convinced even skeptics that a female athlete can survive pressure at the highest levels and that men are just as vulnerable to nerves as women are.

During her playing career, Billie Jean in 1973 was one of the founding leaders of the Women's Tennis Association, which owns and operates the women's professional tennis tour. Upon retirement as a professional player, she continued her activism for women's sport and was the founder in 1974 of the Women's Sports Foundation, an organization that continues to promote and support physical activity and sport for girls and women. She later was the cofounder of World Team Tennis, featuring professional players on coed teams, which is still thriving today.

In the 1990s, she turned to coaching as the United States Fed Cup captain and Olympic coach. In recognition of her trailblazing leadership within the tennis world and advocacy for gender equity, King was honored in 2008 by the United States Tennis Association, which renamed the National Tennis Center the USTA Billie Jean King National Tennis Center. The center is the world's largest public tennis facility and is open to the public year round. Of course, it is also home of the U.S. Open Tennis Championships, one of tennis' four Grand Slam events. The facility also houses the largest tennis stadium in the world, named in honor of Arthur Ashe Jr. (Schwartz 2005a; World Team Tennis 2010; United States Tennis Association 2008).

ACTIVITY TIME-OUT

Equity in Athletics Is Public Information

Check out your university to see how it stacks up in equity between male and female sport teams, participants, coaches, and budgets. Visit http://ope.ed.gov/athletics/ and type in the information for your school. The key information you'll need to know is the undergraduate enrollment along with the name, state, and NCAA division of your school. Once you have studied the information, write a one-page summary of what you found, including observations, conclusions, or questions about the data.

sports, thereby reducing funding for boys? While many people thought girls should have an equal chance to play sports, few wanted to see programs for boys cut. What a dilemma!

After much debate and foot dragging, in 1975 the Office for Civil Rights published guidelines clarifying what it meant to comply with Title IX. To be eligible for federal funding, schools and colleges had to meet any of three tests:

1. Proportionality test: If a school is 50% female, then no less than 45% of its athletes should be female. The 5% deviation was deemed the allowable margin.

2. History of progress test: A school demonstrates progress toward expanding women's programs, particularly over the last three years.

3. Accommodation of interest test: A school shows that it has fully accommodated the interests and needs of the underrepresented (female) sex. Inequality exists due to lack of interest or to the inability to field additional teams for athletic competition.

As these clarifications were issued, female athletes and their advocates began filing legal suits. In one of the lawsuits, the U.S. Supreme Court surprisingly ruled that Title IX did not apply to sports since sports were not supported by federal funds. Three years later the U.S. Congress overturned this decision by passing the Civil Rights Restoration Act, clarifying that it did indeed intend Title IX to apply to sport. President Reagan vetoed the law, but Congress overrode his veto.

Massive changes in high school and college sport began shortly after the passage of Title IX. While most schools and colleges were slow to respond, the process had nevertheless begun. Supporters of male athletics initiated numerous lawsuits to delay the inevitable, but gradually women began to assert their rights and demand sport opportunities at every level.

Women and Sport After Title IX

In the 30 years following Title IX legislation, the numbers of girls and women playing sport changed dramatically:

• More than half of all frequent (100 or more times annually) fitness participants are female. Females make up at least 45% to more than 50% of all tennis players, bowlers, and hikers. Women represent 91% of step exercisers, 73% of aerobic exercisers, 71% of kickboxers, 62% of exercise walkers, 62% of ice skaters, 58% of traditional roller skaters, 58% of badminton players, 54% of swimmers, 53% of volleyball players, 52% of in-line skaters, and 52% of people exercising with equipment (Hoffman 2009, p. 195).

• Women showed remarkable gains in participation in high school and college sports and in the Olympic Games. Look at tables 12.1 to 12.4 on page 228 to see their progress. In the past 30 years, women's participation in U.S. teams has drawn nearly equal to that of men.

• Olympic performances by women improved dramatically as training intensified and the pool of competing athletes enlarged. Joan Benoit Samuelson's time for the marathon in Los Angeles in 1984 was faster than all men's times before 1956. In Olympic swimming, the women's record in the 100-meter freestyle, set in 1992, was faster than all men's times before 1964. In cross-country skiing, the Olympic record for women in the 15-kilometer race, set in 1994, was faster than all men's records before 1992.

TABLE 12.1 High School Sport Participation by Gender

Year	Boys	Girls
1971	1 out of 2	1 out of 27
2008	1 out of 1.7	1 out of 2.4

Data compiled by Women's Sports Foundation based on NFHS and Department of Education statistics, 2009.

TABLE 12.2 College Sport Participation by Gender

Year	Men	Women
1981-1982	167,055	64,390
2008-2009	240,822	180,347

Adapted from NCAA Participation Study, 1981-1982 to 2008-2009.

TABLE 12.3 Women in the Summer Olympic Games

Year	Percentage of participants who were female
1900	1.6
1960	11.5
1984	23
1996	34
2000	38
2004	40.7
2008	42

Data from The Beijing Organizing Committee 2008.

TABLE 12.4 American Women in the Olympic Games

Olympic year	Total on U.S. team	Number of U.S. female athletes	Female percentage of U.S. athletes
1972	428	90	21.0%
1992	619	203	35.1%
2008	596	286	48.0%

Data from Women's Sports Foundation 2009.

The following are several outcomes resulting from the increased presence of females in sport and physical activity.

Women as Sport Fans

As women's participation in sport exploded, females also became avid sport fans. Many females began watching sport to track the performances of their favorites and appreciate the contest not just as spectators but as fellow participants.

- You may be surprised to learn that 62% of women say they watch sports on TV regularly or occasionally. That compares with only 42% who watch soap operas on TV regularly or occasionally (Gumpel 2009).

- There are three major sporting events for which female viewers outnumber males: the Kentucky Derby, the Winter Olympic Games, and the Summer Olympic Games. The Olympic Games has traditionally catered to a female audience, and much of the airtime is taken up with women's gymnastics, figure skating, and beach volleyball (*Orlando Sentinel* 2010).

- NASCAR is the second most-watched sport on TV after the National Football League (NFL), and 40% of the viewers are female (Thibaut 2009).

- Women make up 47% of Major League Soccer (MLS) fans, 46% of Major League Baseball (MLB) fans, 45% of NFL fans, 40% of National Hockey League fans, and 46% of National Basketball Association (NBA) fans (Women's Sports Foundation 2009, p. 46).

- Over the Atlanta, Barcelona, and Seoul Olympic Games (1988-1996), viewership among women increased more than it did among men across all age groups, especially in the 18 to 34 age group (39%). However, the 2008 Olympic Games in Beijing saw an increase among men in all age groups and among older women in age groups 25 to 54 and 35 to 64, while the numbers of female viewers in the age groups 12 to 17 and 18 to 34 both decreased. Overall, women 18 and older made up the largest percentage of viewers for the Beijing Games, with 49% of the audience compared to men 18 and older (42%) (McCarthy 2008).

Perhaps because of their increasing interest in sport both as participants and as spectators, women have become powerful consumers of athletic apparel. According to the Sporting Goods Manufacturers Association, women buy 81% of all athletic apparel, including 91% of sport clothing for children and 50% of sport apparel for men (Women's Sports Foundation 2009, p. 46). From 1992 to 1999, sales in women's athletic footwear increased by 37%, while sales in men's footwear increased just 5%. *SELF* magazine reported that 88% of its readers indicated it is very important or important in their purchase decision that a company provide a product or service that supports girls and women in sport and fitness activities (Women's Sports Foundation 2007).

Popularity of Women's Sports

Women's sports at every level of competition have begun to attract large numbers of spectators. Here are some landmark attendance figures:

• In 1973, at the height of the women's movement, Billie Jean King defeated Bobby Riggs to win the "Battle of the Sexes" before 30,472 fans, a record for the largest crowd to attend any tennis match that stood until 2010 (Women's Sports Foundation 2009). Interestingly, the match that broke the record was an exhibition match between Serena Williams and Kim Clijsters in the summer of 2010 in the tiny European country of Belgium. That match, staged in the city of Brussels, set the new attendance record of 35,681.

• The 2001 U.S. Open singles final featuring Venus Williams versus Serena Williams drew a 6.8 television rating on CBS. The prime-time final outscored NBC's Notre Dame versus Nebraska football game, which recorded a 4.8 rating (Women's Sports Foundation 2009, p. 45).

• More than 4.8 million people attended Women's Tennis Association (WTA) events in 2008.

Women's collegiate sports have exploded, and schools with successful women's teams enjoy stellar attendance. Some college women's teams, such as the women's basketball team at the University of Connecticut, even have lucrative cable television contracts for the broadcast rights to their games. Here are some of the most remarkable collegiate viewership statistics as compiled by the Women's Sports Foundation (2009, p. 41).

• Women's basketball set an all-time high with more than 11 million fans in the 2007-2008 season, an increase of more than one million from two years earlier.

• Television ratings on ESPN and ESPN2 rose 37% and 26%, respectively, during the 2008 NCAA Women's Collegiate Championship tournament.

• The University of Tennessee's Lady Vols led the nation in women's basketball total attendance at 232,646 and averaged 15,510 fans per game for 2000 to 2001.

• The NCAA Division I women's college basketball championship game between Connecticut and Tennessee received a rating of 4.3, making it the most-watched women's basketball game in ESPN's history.

• The University of Utah's women's gymnastics team has consistently averaged more than 10,000 fans per meet since 1992 and is the only revenue-producing women's sport on campus.

POP CULTURE

Danica Patrick—Life on the Fast Track

It is one thing to compete against other women in traditional women's sports but quite another to take on the boys. Danica Patrick is an American auto racing driver who competes in both the IndyCar Series and the NASCAR Nationwide Series, along with work as a model and advertising spokeswoman. She was named Rookie of the Year for the 2005 Indianapolis 500 and has placed as high as third in the event (2009), the highest finish by a woman in the event's history. Although several other women have tried to compete in this aggressively male-dominated sport over the past 30 years, none had ever actually won a race until Patrick accomplished that feat by winning the Indy Japan 300 in Motegi, Japan, in 2008.

She has been criticized by some for capitalizing on her good looks to garner contracts to advertise products. Patrick also posed for the *Sports Illustrated* Swimsuit Edition in 2008, taking advantage of her physical appearance. Yet there is no denying her positive impact on the sport of auto racing, which has been slipping in popularity in recent years.

In the first race following her victory in Indy Japan, Patrick helped draw 1.1 million viewers—an increase of 191% over the previous year's race. Her online store (danicaracingstore.com) outsells those of all her male colleagues combined by a factor of 10. Yet her most significant contribution to the sport is the legions of new fans of the sport, from curious males to women who want to see her best the men to young girls who see her as a role model (Jensen 2008).

- The 2003 Women's National Basketball Association (WNBA) championship game between the Detroit Shock and the Los Angeles Sparks drew a record crowd of 22,076.

You probably won't be surprised by the spectator figures for women's soccer given its huge popularity since the 1980s. More than 650,000 tickets to the 1999 women's World Cup were sold. The final match drew a women's sport record of 90,185 to the Rose Bowl in California. The same World Cup final between the United States and China earned an 11.4 Nielsen rating, with 11,307,000 households, or a 31% market share, watching. This was the most-watched soccer game (male or female) in U.S. television history, with more than 40 million viewers tuning in (Women's Sports Foundation (2009, p. 45).

Men as Fans of Women's Sports

Men deserve some credit for contributing to spectatorship in women's sport. According to the Harris Poll in 2001, the following percentages of fans watching women's sports were male (Harris Interactive 2001):

WNBA	47%
Ladies Professional Golf Association (LPGA)	58%
Women's soccer	66%
Women's tennis	42%
Women's college basketball	56%

For the 1999 women's World Cup mentioned in the previous section, 49% of those viewing the final game were adult men, compared with 36% who were adult women and 15% who were children under 18 (Women's Sports Foundation 2007). Men enjoy watching women compete for a variety of reasons. Some like the novelty of women competing; some like to root for the underdog (such as professional golfer Annika Sorenstam when she competes against men on the pro golf tour); and others enjoy watching fit, attractive women in action. Some men, particularly as they age, relate better to the level of athleticism of women in a sport like basketball, where men's play is dominated by athletes who appear as giants to most of us. Women's tennis tends to produce longer rallies than those found in men's tennis, just as does the sport many of us play.

The style of play can also attract male viewers. Women's basketball tends to feature more passing and teamwork than its male version does. This style appeals to basketball purists who appreciate a game built on teamwork over the modern male version that emphasizes individual play and slam dunks.

There is no substitute for results. The U.S. women's soccer team garnered a large audience, both male and female, simply because of their excellence of play over 10 years. Their capture of Olympic gold medals and the World Cup championship thrilled us and inspired patriotic pride. We loved watching star players such as Mia Hamm, Brandi Chastain, Kristine Lilly, and Michele Akers. Men's soccer may be more popular worldwide, but in the United States no soccer team had ever captured the attention of the nation as these women did. The media declared the 1996 Olympic Games in Atlanta the "Year of the Women" (NewsSmith 1996). Female athletes reached the pinnacle of participation: 3,800 female athletes from around the world competed. Women represented 34% of all the athletes in the Games, and for the first time women contributed more than a third of the participants. Just eight years later, that percentage rose 44%, and female participants are rapidly approaching a number equal to that of men.

Fine performances by American female Olympians also captured the attention of the media and spectators. The American team won gold medals in the Olympic debut of softball and soccer in the 1996 Olympic Games. Female gymnasts and the American women in both singles and doubles tennis also claimed the gold in the 1996 Games. Swimmer Amy Van Dyken became the first American woman to win four gold medals in a single Games, and the women's basketball team also captured the gold medal.

Social Issues in Women's Sport

As sport opportunities and fitness activities for women have increased, so, too, have unique social issues. Prior to women's participation in sport and physical activity, issues such as women's health and fitness and clothing designed specifically for a woman's body weren't topics that warranted study and attention. In this section, we'll explore several social issues that have emerged as women have entered the playing field.

Women's Health

Donna Lopiano (1994) of the Women's Sports Foundation has summarized the benefits that women's sport advocates claim sports and physical activity can have for females. Psychosocial, physical, behavioral, and emotional benefits have been identified and substantiated. Research has shown that introducing girls to sport and physical activity early is essential for them in making exercise a lifelong habit. In fact, Linda Bunker of the University of Virginia asserted that if a girl does not participate in sport by the time she is 10, there is only a 10% chance she will participate when she is 25 (Women's Sports Foundation 2007).

The amount of physical activity that a young girl gets relates to her race and culture and the influence of those who surround her. White girls (with 59% participation) are more likely than black (47%) or Hispanic (49%) girls to participate in sport (Centers for Disease Control and Prevention 2000). Girls who come from middle- and upper-middle-class homes are also more likely to participate in vigorous physical activity. Girls who grow up in a culture that ascribes relatively narrow female roles oriented toward childbearing and families value the sport experience differently. Likewise, families who are struggling economically are more likely to encourage girls to spend time helping in the home and caring for younger siblings. Girls who grow up in poor urban settings may face daunting barriers to sport participation. See chapter 13 for more information on the specific challenges.

Research has shown that teenage female athletes are less likely than nonathletes to use illicit drugs (marijuana, cocaine, or others), to be suicidal, or to smoke and are more likely than nonathletes to have positive body images (Women's Sports Foundation 2009). These results mirror those for male athletes and speak to the value of encouraging young people to take better care of their bodies and develop a strong self-concept that helps them resist peer pressure.

Teenage female athletes are less likely to get pregnant, more likely to abstain from sexual intercourse, and more likely to experience sexual intercourse at a later age (Women's Sports Foundation 1998). One might wonder if the lack of sport participation among economically disadvantaged girls correlates with their significantly higher rate of teenage pregnancy.

Women who are active in sport as girls feel greater confidence and pride in their physical and social selves than do women who are sedentary as kids (United States Department of Health and Human Services 1997). Sport and exercise reduce the incidence of osteoporosis, breast cancer, and stroke. According to data in a special issue of the *American Journal of Health Promotion* (Anspaugh, Hunter, and Digman 1996), exercise lowers blood pressure, blood sugar, and cholesterol. Furthermore,

Many health issues—such as osteoporosis, breast cancer, and heart disease—can be combated by engaging in physical activity. What must society do to help encourage young women to become, and stay, physically active?

231

exercising women report that they feel happier, have more energy, and feel healthier. Exercisers also missed fewer days of work. The only potentially negative influence of sport participation is the possible exacerbation of eating disorders or exercise addictions that develop in some girls.

As our culture has begun to encourage women to join the workforce and even contend for leadership roles in society, the lessons of the playing field appear to be just as helpful to girls as they are to boys. Experiences in leading, dealing with pressure, taking pride in accomplishment, and working on a team equip women with some of the critical skills needed for successful careers. Linda Bunker (1988) found that 80% of women identified as key leaders in Fortune 500 companies participated in sport during their childhood. Another similar study reported that more than four out of five executive businesswomen played sports growing up, and the majority claimed that lessons learned on the playing field contributed to their business success (Game Face 2002).

The evidence overwhelmingly shows that exercise and sport participation are good for women and girls. This may make you wonder why it took so long for society to realize this fact and encourage healthy activity for the female sex. To learn additional information and the latest facts and figures on women in sports, visit the website of the Women's Sports Foundation: Women's Sports Facts & Statistics at www.womenssportsfoundation.org.

Lesbian Athletes

While the stereotype that all strong, female athletes must be lesbians is false, it is true that athletes who are lesbians still face misunderstanding and discrimination in the sporting world. Some famous female athletes, such as Billie Jean King and later Amelie Mauresmo of France, have been frank with the media about their sexual orientation. Billie Jean was a founder of the Women's Sports Foundation, an icon for women's liberation, and a role model for many in spite of her bisexuality. While she is popular with women, her fan base among men is much smaller. In 2005, some fans were stunned when Sheryl Swoopes, three-time Most Valuable Player for the WNBA, revealed her homosexuality. Although she was previously married and has a son, Swoopes told the world that she currently has a female life partner.

Pat Griffin was a pioneer in exposing and clarifying the issues surrounding lesbian athletes. Pat has been a top athlete, coach, and spokesperson against prejudice and homophobia in sports. In her book

Strong Women, Deep Closets, she analyzed the lesbian experience in the sport world. In it she admitted to once dating a male wrestling coach to cover up her lesbianism and save her coaching job. Strong leaders like Pat Griffin have given voice to the conflicted lesbian athletes who fear showing their homosexuality will damage their career (Griffin 1998).

Not all discrimination against lesbian athletes comes from outside women's sport. This fact was highlighted at Penn State University in the early 1990s when women's basketball coach Rene Portland created a furor by stating in the press that she did not recruit or allow lesbians on her team. The controversy escalated in 2005 when a former player, Jennifer Harris, filed a federal discrimination lawsuit. Attempts to mediate the situation were unsuccessful; and an internal investigation by the university fined Portland $10,000, ordered her to take professional development courses devoted to diversity and inclusiveness, and warned she would be dismissed for any future violations (Associated Press 2006b, 2006c). Portland resigned her position in 2007 after 27 years as women's basketball coach. In spite of growing acceptance in society at large, lesbian athletes are still at risk for harassment, exclusion, or perhaps expulsion if their coaches or teammates disapprove of their lifestyle.

Sportswear

As girls and women moved into sport, they sparked changes in sport clothing as they demanded clothing that fit their unique needs. Apparel companies raced to design sport clothing for women, and marketing campaigns followed to attract buyers of athletic gear designed specifically for women. The economy of sport business was affected, along with cultural attitudes toward females in sports. Let's look at two significant developments in sport clothing.

Sports Bra

The sports bra was invented in 1977 to give women playing sport the same kind of physical support that men had enjoyed for years. Hinda Miller and Lisa Lindahl created a prototype for the sports bra by imitating the male athletic supporter that "pulled the body parts closer to the body" (Sharp 1994). Eventually their idea was labeled the Jogbra, and females quickly adopted it for comfort and safety and as a way to limit embarrassment and perform uninhibitedly during vigorous activity.

It wasn't long before clothing companies began marketing versions of the sports bra that not only facilitated physical activity but also looked attractive. Women began wearing sports bras under their jerseys, but soon they shed their jerseys in the gyms, on the courts, and on the fields. Female athletes found the comfort and freedom exhilarating.

When Brandi Chastain ripped off her jersey to celebrate the 1999 U.S. women's victory in the World Cup soccer championship, it was a seminal moment in sport. Her action was captured on film and her image was viewed round the world. Brandi's sports bra somehow symbolized to different people all that was right or wrong with women in sport.

Brandi Chastain's disrobing was accepted by many as an expression of pure joy at victory. After all, the gesture had been made previously by male soccer players and tennis players, notably Andre Agassi and Andy Roddick of the United States. Yet her action also ignited a storm of criticism.

Some saw Chastain's act as a striptease, as if she were offering her body to male viewers. Others thought her action was calculated to draw attention. Still others simply saw it as a celebration of a strong, muscular woman proud of her body. Whatever the opinion, her act stimulated debate and exposed the conflict in both male and female opinions about women's bodies and their acceptability in public view.

Athletic Shoes

As girls and women flocked to sport participation in the past 30 years, improper athletic footwear was a recurrent issue. Forced to wear sneakers designed for the male foot, female athletes suffered in silence until the 1990s when athletic shoe companies began designing and marketing shoes specifically designed for the female foot. Female basketball players, who typically are well above average in size, had previously been forced to wear men's sneakers for basketball. The women complained of the heaviness, bulk, and width of the male shoe (Brown 2001). Basketball player Sheryl Swoopes became the first woman to endorse her "Air Swoopes" during the Atlanta Olympics in 1996. By 2001, at the inaugural WNBA All-Star Game with the best female basketball players in the world gathered, the game became a celebration of how far women in sport had come. Five of the All-Stars wore basketball shoes designed specifically for them.

▌ Is the amount of skin shown by women wearing sports bras any different than the amount of skin shown by cheerleaders? Why is one more socially acceptable than the other?

On average, the female foot is narrower and thinner than a male foot. Although foot shape varies from one female to another, generally a woman's foot has a wider forefoot and narrower heel than a male's foot. Orthopedists have attributed the high incidence of sport injuries in women and girls, particularly in the knee, ankle, and lower leg, to poorly fitting shoes (Sports Doctor 2000).

Modern athletic shoe development, led by Nike, Reebok, and adidas, has introduced the public to terms such as *pronation, stability,* and *motion control*. New concepts in design have helped absorb shock, stabilize the foot, and reduce injuries in high-performance athletes as well as casual recreational athletes (Pribut and Richie 2002). Shoes are made to accommodate the differences between the feet of male and female athletes.

The athletic shoe industry has benefited significantly from the increase of women and girls in fitness and sport activities. In 2009, women purchased 55.2% of all sport footwear and at the same time tended toward more expensive, high-performance footwear as opposed to the fashion look. Women also purchased 56% of home fitness equipment compared to only 36.6% purchased by men (National Sporting Goods Association 2009).

But the shoe industry for women still has a way to go. The feet of females are getting bigger . . . but not the shoes. That was the gist of an article originally published in the *Wall Street Journal* (2004b). Sports were cited as a reason for increased sizes of feet: "The biggest single contributor to the big-foot phenomenon may be the rise in participation in girls' sports since Title IX 32 years ago." As girls walk, run, and play sports, their feet become larger, stronger, and more muscular.

The average foot size has jumped from an American size 7 or 8 to an 8 or a 9 (European sizes would be 37, 38, and 39). According to Marshal Cohen, senior analyst for the NPD Group, more than 33% of women now wear a size 9 or larger, compared with just 11% in 1987. A survey by Carol Fry at the University of California at Los Angeles showed that 10% of high school girls now wear shoes larger than size 10. The population is generally increasing in size. Also, the baby boomer generation is aging, and with age the feet tend to enlarge as ligaments stretch and feet flatten out (*Wall Street Journal* 2004b).

Shoe manufacturers have not yet adjusted to the need for larger shoes and are still making the bulk of their shoes in an "average" size that's now outdated. Many women squeeze their feet into shoes that are simply too small. The resulting poor fit causes foot problems, and eventually pain spreads throughout the body.

The problem for manufacturers is that producing larger shoe sizes means creating new molds and using more goods in each shoe, both of which will drive prices up. Manufacturers are hesitant to begin producing larger shoes, waiting for the market to prove substantial enough to warrant such production. Since many manufacturers are located overseas where people tend to be smaller, the demand for larger sizes is unusual for them.

Objectification of Female Athletes

As strong, independent women delve into the sport world, they attract many types of attention. The female athlete's strong and agile body, with defined musculature and muscles, is a magnet for thousands of viewers. As clothing trends changed, women moved from dowdy dresses, boxy pinnies, and kilted skirts to form-fitting swimsuits, gymnastics leotards, and skimpy outfits on the tennis court. And, although the sports bra was a technical improvement for women and serves a utilitarian purpose that allows them to move freely, it has symbolized the duplicity of society's view of women as strong athletes and also sex objects for men (Schultz 2004).

Female athletes may be looked at as sex objects, whether they want to be seen that way or not. Successful female athletes are often judged more by their appearance than their athletic success. Jan Stephenson was more famous for her physical attractiveness than for her golf game, even though she was a fine golfer. Similarly, Anna Kournikova long held the title of sexiest female tennis player but was roundly criticized because of her popularity given that she never won a singles tournament in her career. She was in fact ranked among the top 10 players, but that did not mollify critics who believed she capitalized on her looks rather than her talent.

But are female athletes partially to blame for this objectification?

Every Olympic Games, there is a rush to promote the Games and focus on attractive female athletes. While the men get most of their attention for their athletic success and odds of winning a medal, there is a whole other culture built around women who are both good athletes and sexy. In fact, *Playboy* magazine's "Women of the Olympics" Issue rivals the annual *Sports Illustrated* Swimsuit Edition as eye candy for primarily male readers. Female athletes such as Amanda Beard (swimming), Jennie Finch (softball), Paula Creamer (golf), Maria Sharapova (tennis), Swin Cash (basketball), Lindsey Vonn (skiing), and Danica Patrick (auto racing) virtually have a second career that highlights their physical attractiveness. No doubt these and other women know that publicity shots and features can only help their career and indirectly promote their sport. And who is to say what is appropriate for an attractive athlete who is blessed with natural beauty that she enhances through physical training?

Many female athletes are conflicted about posing to show off their bodies. Some favor it, believing that it helps promote their sport through publicity, while others think it dispels the notion that you can't be sexy if you're an athlete (Topkin 2004). When female athletes do intentionally display their bodies, some people may question whether such images are appropriate for public viewing, especially by younger children. Suggestive images of both male and female athletes can be controlled and standards of decorum can be established, but only if the market demands it. The cutting-edge advertising agency will do whatever attracts attention and gains publicity, as it was hired to do.

Consider this advice from the Women's Sports Foundation in "Media—Images and Words in Women's Sports: The Foundation Position" (1995). This document was reviewed by more than 50 of the nation's most highly visible champion female athletes.

"Women are no different from men athletes in the skill, dedication and courage they bring to their sports. Sports commentary and reporting, like the use of the English language in general, should reflect the fundamental equality of women and men, both on and off the field. There is nothing wrong with women wanting to look feminine/ attractive from a traditional perspective. However, female athletes deserve the same respect for their athletic abilities as is afforded male athletes. When a female athlete appears in a sport publication or advertisement to promote her sport or fitness product, she should be portrayed respectfully as is her male counterpart . . . as a skilled athlete.

Some specific guidelines for media images of female athletes are suggested:

- Female athletes should look like athletes shown doing a skill they do well.
- A female athlete's clothing should be authentic for her sport.
- She should have all of her appropriate clothes on and she should not be dressing or undressing.
- Certain body parts (breasts or buttocks) should not be the focus, nor should the image be a sexual one.
- Her pose or movements should be authentic, not appear dainty, shy, or seductive. Nor should she be gazing adoringly at men either in the photo or at male consumers viewing the ad.
- Photos and captions should go together; the caption should not undermine the image.
- Young female athletes should not be portrayed as older than they are.
- The final image should be something any woman could feel proud of as a current or future athlete.

Do you think this photo of Amanda Beard adheres to the Women's Sports Foundation in Media's guidelines for how women should be portrayed in sport publications and advertisements?

- What if the woman or girl in the photo was your daughter, your mom, or a female friend?

Global Status of Women in Sport

While the numbers of women in sport continue to rise in the United States, that trend is not typical around the world. The social system in many countries, particularly Arab countries, discourages women from sport participation. Their adherence to the traditional role of women as subservient to men and focused on the home does not allow girls to explore their physical side through sport and activity.

As shown in table 12.3 on page 228, the percentage of women in the Summer Olympics increased steadily, from 34% in 1996 to 42% in 2008. At the 2000 Olympic Games, 36 countries, or almost 30% of the 123 participating nations, sent no female athletes. By 2008, the number of countries entering an all-male team was only five. Female participation rates have not universally grown in all countries, especially in those countries where women's rights in general lag behind those of men. In countries where poverty, famine, political instability, and religion dominate, females are virtually excluded from participation in sport. Countries such as Ethiopia, Saudi Arabia, Algeria, Kenya, and Nigeria are beset with wider social problems than women in sport. Followers of Islam are blocked from participation because of a decree that women should be covered in public, and wearing this covering makes it difficult if not impossible to play sports. Women who seek to participate in sport are seen as threats to the social, moral, and religious codes of their societies and as repudiating their culture in favor of the Western influence. Saudi Arabia is the only country in the world that completely bars women from any sport activity (Al-Ahmed 2008).

The success of Sania Mirza of India in women's professional tennis holds promise for other Muslim women. She skyrocketed from a virtual unknown to a world ranking of 31 in her first year in 2005 on the professional tour. She earned her highest world ranking, number 27, in 2007 and became the first Indian female tennis player to earn a Grand Slam title by winning the mixed doubles at the Australian in 2009. While wearing traditional tennis clothing that exposes her arms and legs, she retains her spiritual values by praying up to five times a day. She is an example of a modern Indian woman who stands for progressive thinking while respecting her religious background. In 2010 she married Shoaib Malik, a Pakistan citizen, garnering critical media headlines in her home country. Her success is the antithesis of the strait-laced image of a backward, illiterate, conservative Muslim woman hidden behind a veil (Bahri 2005).

Similarly, swimmer Rubab Raza, then 13 years old, was the first female swimmer from Pakistan to represent her country in the Olympic Games by competing in Athens in 2004. Recent advances in full-body swimsuit design promise to enhance swimming efficiency by imitating the skin of a shark. They may also allow Muslim women to jump into the pool, something they have not been able to do because of the requirement to keep their bodies covered.

In the 2000 Sydney Olympics, more than 110,000 people saw Nouria Merah-Benida win the 1,500 meters, following up on the 1992 Olympic championship performance of her Algerian countrywoman Hassiba Boulmerka. These two runners have sparked debate about whether women may break out of the mold of Arab tradition and enjoy athletic success. Indeed, by the 2008 Beijing Olympics, of the 958 medals given out at the games, 60 went to citizens of Muslim majority countries—44 to men and a mere 15 to women and one to open/mixed competitors (Amr 2008).

Worldwide, the story in developed nations mirrors that in the United States. White women from middle-class backgrounds are most likely to be supported by their families and communities to participate in sport, strive for excellence, and embrace physical activity. Enhanced self-image, better health, and greater resistance to disease through sport should be available for all women, but some must still fight against the repressive customs of their society to enjoy these benefits.

Barriers for Women in Sport

Learning about the rapid gains of women in sport during the last 30 years may lead you to think there is not much more for these women to accomplish. But a closer look reveals changes that must still come to truly create an equality of opportunity in sport for females. We review these changes in this section. Perhaps progress will come from outside the sport world as women gain power and influence in business and affect more of what is portrayed in the media. As society changes, so do women's sports.

Yet sport can also be a catalyst for change led by confident, determined females who have a public stage on which to share their beliefs and dreams.

Title IX Challenges

The most perplexing question facing Title IX enforcement on college campuses focuses on American football and the 85 athletic scholarships for football awarded at most Division I schools. These schools must provide 85 women's scholarships just to match the football total. Once the 85 men's and 85 women's scholarships have been awarded, a university then decides how many other scholarships it can afford for other sports.

Many athletic directors have completely dropped less popular, non-revenue-producing men's sports like wrestling, tennis, golf, gymnastics, and swimming. Programs rich in tradition, some of which earned national championships, have suddenly disappeared from college athletic programs. The governing bodies for these sports, such as wrestling and tennis, have mounted campaigns to reinstate those sports. Although they are careful not to criticize Title IX, the underlying mumbling blames women. Dropped sports are called *unintended consequences*, with the recognition that the authors of Title IX never intended to harm men's sports by opening up women's sports (National Women's Law Center 2002).

"Where is the money going to come from?" That's the plea of every athletic director and college president faced with Title IX compliance. We've taken their athletic budget, which was largely devoted to men's sports, and asked them to split it down the middle for men and women. On top of that, they are unwilling to reduce support for football, the main revenue sport at 131 Division I institutions and the source of publicity, pride, recruiting, and alumni donations. It would simply be unthinkable to reduce the number of football scholarships, even though some may ask why, if it

takes only 22 men to play football, 11 on offense and 11 on defense, 85 scholarships are needed.

The football picture at the high school level may be very similar, although athletic scholarships are not a factor. Instead, the focus is on budgets for uniforms, equipment, fields, coaching salaries, and publicity. In every category, football is still a huge expense.

Physical Activity Participation

Physical activity participation among women reveals some interesting statistics when compared with that of men. In the age groups of 18 to 24 and 75 and over, men showed a significantly higher percentage of engaging in vigorous leisure-time activity. However, in the 25- to 64-year age group, women actually exceeded the percentage of men by a small margin, and they were nearly equal to males in the 65 to 74 age group (Women's Sports Foundation 2009).

- Females over the age of 7 reported their most favorite physical activities as exercise walking (56.1 million), swimming (28.4 million), and exercising with equipment (27 million).

- According to the Sporting Goods Manufacturers Association's 2007 Annual Fitness Survey, females account for a minimum of 50% of total participants in 15 of the leading fitness activities (Women's Sports Foundation 2009, p. 36). These activities include walking for fitness, aerobics, running, treadmill running, Pilates, yoga/tai chi, stair climbing, and elliptical training machines.

- Boys are more likely than girls are to regularly watch televised sports (33% boys vs. 7% girls). Girls are more than twice as likely to watch talk shows (25% vs. 10%).

- Ninety percent of U.S. boys regularly or often watch televised sports with a fundamentally male cast of players, coaches, and

ACTIVITY TIME-OUT

Football and Title IX

Some people have proposed that colleges leave football out of Title IX compliance. In other words, equalize the number of scholarships for men and women, but do not include the 85 football scholarships in the mix. Is this a fair solution to the issue of equal opportunity for females? Proponents of this view contend that football is a different animal and that there is no comparable activity for girls. At large Division I institutions where the football team actually makes money, those revenues can help support other sports.

Is leaving football out of Title IX an equitable solution? If not, what other ideas would you offer an athletic director who faces increasing costs without an increasing budget?

commentators. Commercials during these televised events tend to target the male viewer, reinforcing male stereotypes and gender roles.

Women as Leaders in Sport

Women still occupy a small percentage of leadership roles compared with their proportion of the sport or at-large population. Perhaps the most disappointing percentage is that for female coaches of collegiate women's sports. The 2007 percentage of 42.8% is close to the lowest percentage in history, and 25 years ago, women coached 90% of women's teams (Acosta and Carpenter 2009b). Here are some other percentages for women in significant leadership roles in high school, college, and Olympic sports (Acosta and Carpenter 2009b):

Coaches of collegiate women's sports	42.8%
Athletic directors at colleges	21%
College sport information directors	11.3%
Head athletic trainers at colleges	27.3%
Senior staff at NCAA	22%
Heads of state high school athletic associations	6%
Members of International Olympic Committee	14.5%
Members of United States Olympic Committee	27.2%

Additional information, including the percentages for professional sport, can be viewed in the Racial and Gender Report Card published by Richard Lapchick at the University of Central Florida (Lapchick 2008; Lapchick 2008-2009).

Equal Pay for Equal Play

The opportunities for women in professional sport have expanded significantly in tennis, golf, basketball, and soccer, where professional careers are a realistic goal. Other sports such as gymnastics, track and field, figure skating, and swimming offer prize money and endorsement possibilities since the Olympics have recently allowed professional athletes. Yet compared with men, women still struggle to make a career in professional sport because in many cases, the financial compensation barely covers their expenses.

Traditionally at the four Grand Slam events in tennis, Wimbledon and the Australian, French, and U.S. Opens, the purse of prize money for men exceeded that of women. Though all four Grand Slam events now have equal prize money for men and women, there is some pressure to reverse that decision. And, at other tennis events, men and women still receive significantly different levels of compensation. The argument against paying women the same amount as men is usually as follows:

 EXPERT'S VIEW

Why It's Nonsense-Talk That Females Prefer Male Coaches

Vivian Acosta and Linda Carpenter, professors emerita at the City University of New York's Brooklyn College and coauthors of a book on Title IX, have collected and analyzed data on women's roles in intercollegiate sports since 1977. They were outstanding college athletes at Brigham Young University, coached both men's and women's college teams, chaired departments, and have been leaders in issues that affect women in sport for decades.

They believe that one measure of equity in college sport is the opportunity for both males and females in coaching. Currently 2% of coaches of male teams are female. But even more surprising is the fact that only 42.8% of coaches of women's teams are female. Acosta and Carpenter's concern for female athletes is that they would benefit from having female coaches because the life of a college athlete is very intense and having female role models during that time is particularly valuable. But the fact is, some female athletes say they prefer male coaches.

Acosta and Carpenter point out that the studies showing that women prefer male coaches are flawed because for many women, that is all they have ever known. And if you had a good season and enjoyed your teammates, you're probably happy. But young college women need to see and know females who are capable leaders, able to make good decisions and deal with work–life balance issues. They need role models that they can identify with more closely (Pappano and Taylor 2009).

- Women don't play the same level of tennis as men. Head to head, a good collegiate men's player would defeat most women on the pro tour. (Probably true.)

- Women are not as strong, don't hit the ball as hard, and play mostly a baseline game featuring rallies rather than an exciting, power game. (True, although short points dominated by powerful serves can be boring to watch. Fans do like the rallies in women's tennis.)

- Women play only three sets in championship matches whereas men play the best of five and therefore have to work harder. (Men do play five sets, but who wants to watch a match that takes five hours between exhausted competitors? Two out of three has more excitement because every point affects the outcome of the match.)

- Fans come to see the men, and ticket revenue should be the basis of the prize money. (For years the men argued this point, until the women's game and superstar personalities started to grab the headlines. Suddenly, the men backed off this statement.)

Here are other notable facts on pay for female versus male athletes (all amounts are in U.S. dollars; Women's Sports Foundation 2009):

- In basketball, the minimum salary in 2009 for a WNBA veteran was $35,190 and the maximum salary was $99,500 while the team cap for salaries was $803,000. In contrast, for NBA players for the 2008-2009 season, the minimum salary was $442,114; the maximum salary was $13,758,000; and the team salary cap was $58,680,000 per team. Perhaps more eye-opening was that for the 2008-2009 season, the *average* NBA salary was $5.85 million per player while the WNBA *maximum* salary was $99,500. In other words, the NBA average was *59 times higher* than the WNBA's maximum.

- In soccer, a third-place finish for the women in the 2003 World Cup netted $25,000 for each team member. Players on the men's team each received $200,000 for reaching the quarterfinals.

- In golf, the average purse in the LPGA rose from just over $840,000 in 1999 to about $1.8 million in 2008. Total prize money for the 2008 LPGA tour was $62 million. Compare these figures with those for the men: The average purse in the PGA was $5.8 million for 2008, and total prize money was $214.4 million for the regular season.

- Golfer Annika Sorenstam signed a deal with Cutter and Buck that could earn her up to $600,000 per year. That figure is approximately 60% of what a male golfer can demand for a typical apparel contract.

- Although huge endorsement deals are scarce for women, tennis star Venus Williams signed a five-year, $40 million deal with Reebok. Her sister Serena topped her a year later with a contract with Nike that could make her the richest woman in sport if she gets the performance-related bonuses, with a possible net income of $55 to $60 million. Of course, this income doesn't include any of the on-court prize money both sisters are likely to win in the coming years.

- In women's sports, the big money for professional athletes is in tennis and golf. Although several female golfers have recently moved into the ranks of earning seven figures, the top female athletes overall are still tennis players. For 2008, the top four highest-paid females were Maria Sharapova ($26 million), Serena Williams ($14 million), Venus Williams ($13 million), and newly retired Justine Henin ($12.5 million).

- According to Forbes.com, in 2008 the top 50 paid athletes were all male. Males in team sports dominated the list, although golfer Tiger Woods topped all athletes.

- While the endorsement deals for female tennis players may stun the average fan, the amounts commanded by women and men still differ significantly. Although the Williams sisters and Maria Sharapova earn handsome incomes, male tennis player Roger Federer earned over $33 million in 2008 and made the Forbes Top 50 list.

Inequities still exist in college sports too.

Unlike professional sport, which determines earnings based on what the market will bear, collegiate sports are governed by Title IX restrictions, which by law ensure women and girls equality in dollars spent. In spite of significant progress toward that goal, there are still glaring inequities.

In 2004-2005 at Division I Football Bowl Subdivision schools, men's athletics accounted for 70% of overall expenses. In fact, these schools spent more overall money just on football programs ($5,740,000) than on all women's teams combined ($4,447,900).

In 2005-2006, the average amount of money spent on recruiting for Division I women's teams was $115,900 per school. More than double that was spent for men's teams, an average of $247,300 per school.

Comparing coaching salaries reveals similar advantages for coaches of men's teams compared to coaches of women's teams (although quite a few men are coaches of women's teams). On average, the 2007-2008 median salary of head coaches of men's teams was $4,957 more than that for head coaches of women's teams. This statistic did not include football, of course, since there is no comparable sport for women. The sports cited were basketball, golf, gymnastics, ice hockey, lacrosse, rowing, soccer, tennis, and volleyball.

If we isolate Division I, in 2005-2006 the salaries of head coaches of men's sports averaged $1,202,400 while head coaches of women's teams averaged $659,000. For the same year, the average salary for a Division I men's basketball head coach was $409,600 compared to only $187,300 for head coaches of women's teams (Women's Sports Foundation 2009).

Media Coverage of Women's Sports

More media coverage of women's sports would likely boost their popularity and enhance the opportunities for girls and women to see role models in action. There have been notable successes in televising women's sports. During the first quarter of 2002, the 10 highest-rated broadcasts on network television included the Winter Olympics women's figure skating long program, which ranked third behind only the Super Bowl and Super Bowl kickoff show. The Women's Final Four Championship game, featuring UConn versus Oklahoma, was the third-ranked sport broadcast on cable television. In contrast, the men's championship game of Duke versus Maryland, aired on network television, ranked only sixth (WomenSport International 2006).

At the 2006 Winter Olympic Games, NBC carried about 200 hours of live coverage; and during prime time and late-night periods, the coverage of women's sports was very similar to that for men's sports. During the day, however, the time devoted to men's sports was significantly higher.

Other than during the Olympic Games every four years, the dominant sport shown on television for women is tennis, which accounts for 42.4% of all women's sport stories on news and highlight

TABLE 12.5   Women's Sport in the Media

Sport coverage	Males	Females
ESPN, 30 days (June 2002)	778 stories	16 stories
Sports Emmy Awards (2002 and 2003)	31 nominees	0 nominees
ESPN Top 100 Athletes (20th century)	92	8
Sportscasters (2000)	335	81
Cover of *Sports Illustrated* (1997-2008)	94.4%	5.6%
Overall sport news coverage (2009)	96%	4%
Local television sport reporting (2008)	93%	7%

Data from Tuggle 2003; National Academy of TV Arts & Sciences 2003; Women's Sports Foundation 2009; Jenkins 2010; Sheffer and Schultz 2007.

programs. Women's track and field is second with 16% of the airtime.

A quick look at table 12.5 confirms that when compared to men's sports, women's sports are poorly represented in media coverage and there has been little change in the past 10 years. According to Gibbons (2003), the decisions on coverage are made in newsrooms across the country, where women in charge are in the distinct minority. Perhaps the news media will soon awaken to the opportunities to attract female sport fans. A national study from Scarborough Sports Marketing revealed that there are over 50 million female sport fans in the United States, and that percentage is growing. In 1998, the number of women over age 18 who identified themselves as very or somewhat avid sport fans was 28%. Just four years later, the number had more than doubled, reaching 58% (Gibbons 2003).

Golden Age of Sports Reborn

Perhaps in this new century we'll recreate the excitement of another "golden age of sports" that this time around includes women and girls. To reach that goal, some significant changes are still needed in the world of sport. However, changes to promote equity in sport will never occur without concomitant changes in our society. The following are some of the changes that will promote equality.

The percentage of women in the workplace is nearing that of men. But salaries for females still lag behind those of their male counterparts. The glass ceiling also prevents many women from reaching upper management. Workplaces, government agencies, and the courts, although all dominated by men, can help eliminate these discriminatory practices.

Challenging the rigid sex roles that have historically guided our society, expanding our definitions of sexuality, and accepting those who are lesbian and gay will help us all find equal places in society.

Collecting data to show inequities in all forms, particularly for women's sport activities, will keep us aware of where we need to work to reach equality. Dr. Richard Lapchick, author of the Racial and Gender Report Card, and Donna Lopiano, former executive director of the Women's Sports Foundation, have taken it upon themselves to inform the public of salient issues and statistics about racism, sexism, and other related topics.

Leaders in women's sport along with sympathetic corporate sponsors need to challenge each other to press ahead. Advocates for women's sport must aggressively recruit, train, and mentor young girls and women into key positions of influence such as coaching, officiating, administration, athletic training, marketing, and media. By taking their place in these positions, women can become a more powerful influence on the sport world.

Women must aggressively pursue leadership positions in sport organizations at every level. In 1994, Kathy Woods became the first female president of the United States Professional Tennis Association, a trade association of over 13,000 tennis teaching professionals. A few years later, Judy Levering ascended to the presidency of the United States Tennis Association, again the first woman to do so. Within a few years, two other women, Jane Brown and Lucy Garvin, followed their lead to the top job. Anita DeFrantz of the United States became the first female elected to the International Olympic Committee. These trailblazers deserve appreciation and a new succession of women to follow their lead.

Leaders in women's sport must take the initiative and look for ways to make their sports revenue producing so that men become their allies rather than remaining their competitors. A few colleges have figured out how to earn money from women's basketball and gymnastics, but other sports and schools lag behind. Professional women's sports need to build on the attractiveness of their product of athletes and strong, independent women.

Parents of girls must help them take the first step into exercise and sport at a young age, and even more critically, support them through the early teen years when they are most likely to drop out. Fathers need to step up to the plate and become advocates, role models, and mentors for their daughters as they are for their sons. Recreational community-sponsored sport teams, high school teams, and collegiate teams must lead the way to ensure equal access and encouragement for girls and women in sport. College sports need to get over their preoccupation with football and men's basketball if they are truly to serve the mission of their university rather than focusing on revenue production, creating opulent athletic stadiums and arenas, and mining alumni to donate money earmarked for athletics rather than the institutional mission overall.

Finally, we must continue to educate people about the value of sport for women. Never underestimate the power of the mind in convincing people of the need to combat sexism in sport. In the early 1980s, as a college professor at a midsize state university, I was invited to join a semester course called "How to Combat Sexism in the Classroom." Five women who knew their stuff and could argue their case taught the class on Saturdays. Although few men attended, all of us, women and men, learned strategies to combat sexism, applied them in our classes, and received feedback from students and colleagues. Our lives have never been the same. Many of the lessons I learned over 25 years ago are still a vital part of my thinking and working character.

Chapter Summary

In this chapter we looked at women in sport, beginning with ancient Greek and Rome, when women were virtually excluded from all sports including the Olympic Games. That exclusion lasted until the 1850s, when U.S. women gradually began to play selected games.

During the first half of the 20th century, physical educators encouraged women's sport and physical activity in colleges as a route to good health. However, competitive athletics were deemed too violent, competitive, and aggressive for young women. It wasn't until the late 1960s, when the women's movement took hold, that women realized that competitive athletics were another restriction to conquer.

In 1972, the U.S. Congress passed Title IX, which states that no person can be excluded from participation in sports on the basis of sex in any educational program receiving federal assistance.

Title IX set the stage for years of lobbying by those in control of men's programs who did not want to give up any of their funding or perks to women. Numerous lawsuits were filed and the law challenged, and in the end it was reaffirmed.

The next 30 years were exciting for girls and women as opportunities opened up in sport. The proportion of female athletes rose rapidly, proving that girls wanted to play sports, though some men had suggested otherwise. Women and girls became consumers of sport, bought equipment and clothing, watched sports on television, signed up for youth sport programs, and made their presence felt in high school and collegiate sport. Research has overwhelmingly attested to the benefits of physical activity for women. Numerous studies have shown improved academic performance, self-image, confidence, and physical health, all benefits similar to those enjoyed by boys for years.

Ideological roles for women had to be modified to fit their aggressive attitudes toward equal opportunity, equal pay, and equal representation as coaches, administrators, and leaders. The marketplace confirmed the popularity of female athletes as role models and awarded them multimillion-dollar endorsement deals, particularly for tennis players. The ideal woman became strong, lean, and attractive. A nurturing, caring, and passive model of women in general began to pass from the scene.

Despite all the positive changes for women in sport in the second half of the last century, women are still underrepresented as sport leaders, in sport business, and in the media. Continued progress cannot be made without persistent effort and determination on the part of women and the men they can recruit to assist them.

Social Class and Sport

Student Outcomes

After reading this chapter, you will know the following:

- The importance of social, economic, and cultural capital
- The different social classes and the typical characteristics of each
- Access or barriers that social class places on sport
- Who controls amateur and professional sport
- The opportunity for social mobility through sport

Do you really know how much your family spends on your kid sister's figure skating? You'd probably be surprised. See, the fact is most families of young figure skaters have to figure out a way to make it work if they hope to give their daughter a chance to follow her dreams. Figure skating is great for a young girl if it keeps her fit, active, strong, and confident. She may develop the attitude of a champion and know how to deal with winning and losing. These aren't just sport skills, but life skills. But how much are they worth, and can you justify the costs?

Here's what one Ice Mom shared: "I set aside a fund from my own paycheck every week to pay for my daughter's ice skating . . . my hubby doesn't really know all the costs. On the road for competitions, we share rooms with other families or use points earned to get the cheapest rate. At home we never eat out as a family and I always pack lunches for all of us. We see other families driven apart over the expenses, couples divorcing and siblings jealous of the money and attention their sister gets full-time."

Here's a post on a website, from a 12-year-old who is a novice-level competitive figure skater, inviting you to help support the expenses she faces annually (Smith 2009). Here's her accounting:

$5,000	Ice time at rink
$15,000	Coach fees
$2,600	Travel expenses to and from practice rink
$4,000	Travel expense for coach
$7,000	Lodging and food at competitions
$5,500	Off-ice training (ballet, gymnastics, etc.)
$2,400	Choreographer fees
$3,425	Skates, practice clothes, and costumes
$545	Photography, videotaping, and music
$45,470	**Total annual expense**

Maybe you've always loved sports and hope someday your kids will get the chance to become successful athletes. But you better have your eyes wide open on the financial commitments required for many sports. Parents who are savvy consumers need to explore costs for youth sports that fit within their family budget realistically. Certain sports just don't make sense for kids from all economic levels. Perhaps we wish it weren't so . . . but you'll see the reality very quickly.

"We hold these truths to be self-evident, that all men are created equal." In 1776, Thomas Jefferson penned these words as the opening of the United States Declaration of Independence. He was saying that all people are born with equal rights. A natural assumption that follows is that everyone has the freedom to get an education, find work, vote for our leaders, or even become a leader. Our society has traveled far to live up to those ideals, and yet the evidence suggests that equal opportunities do not exist for a large proportion of our population. Social class or perhaps race, gender, or disability may limit these opportunities.

Americans are divided according to economic class, with each class possessing different material goods, income levels, inheritances, educations, work descriptions, or influences over others. Regardless of how we define or divide these classes,

each experiences real differences in opportunity. In this chapter we will define **social class** as a category of people who share similar positions in society based on their economic level, education, occupation, and social interaction. Although we pride ourselves on being a classless society, our form of capitalism naturally allows for different possible levels of economic success.

Capitalism is an economic system that is based on the accumulation and investment of capital by individuals who then use it to produce goods or services (Sage 1998). We tend to downplay the idea of social classes because it conflicts with our American ideal of an equalitarian society. But we need to recognize that there are different economic classes that expand to also include our social system. The inequities in our society are obvious: power, prestige, and wealth. When we assign classes according to the levels of power, prestige, and wealth, we refer to **social stratification**. Other forms of stratification include race, gender, age, and disability, which are covered in other chapters.

Turning to the sport world, we can readily see how social class influences a family of four who decide to attend a professional football game. In 2009, the average ticket price to see a National Football League (NFL) game rose to $75. The highest ticket prices were for the Dallas Cowboys, which averaged $160. But ticket prices are not the whole story. For a family of four, the total cost of tickets in Dallas is $640. Adding in parking at $25 and refreshments at $15 per person ($60 total) means the family spends $725 in all (*USA Today* 2009).

If this family belonged economically to the upper class, they would likely contact some friends who have a skybox, inquire about availability, and end up with seats with complimentary refreshments and possibly a parking pass. A middle-class family would likely save for a once-a-year excursion, perhaps buy cheaper seats, and treat the game as a special occasion. A working-class family would likely wait for special promotions or discounted group tours, or they would opt to attend a preseason game or scrimmage.

Both social capital and economic capital help people access different levels of society. Let's define the different kinds of capital. **Economic capital** refers to the financial resources a person has or controls. People inherit, earn, invest, and spend money depending on their background and occupational status. **Social capital** depends on family, friends, and associates and includes resources based on group memberships, relationships, and both social and business networks. **Cultural capital** comprises the skills and abilities people gain from education and life experiences. Cultural capital may include attitudes, expectations, and self-confidence (Bowles and Jenson 2001).

Cultural capital affects how we see the world of sport, and sport participation offers an opportunity to develop cultural capital. For example, a young girl from the middle class may view sport as a way to be accepted into a social group. Her parents may encourage her interest in sport to promote her fitness, help her gain self-confidence, and perhaps help her earn a college scholarship. Her athletics coach will help her learn to set goals, employ self-discipline, and perform under the pressure of competition. Sports will help her form a self-concept as a skilled, fit competitor. All of these influences assist her during the confusing years of early adolescence by enhancing her cultural capital.

In America, we like to think that sport transcends social class. We believe that hard work and dedica-

tion ensure success and that failure simply results from a lack of perseverance. In the land of the free, we are all free to play and watch sports. However, our economic, social, and cultural capital defines what sports we watch and participate in and affects our chances at success.

Social Classes

Most people gain their economic capital through their annual earnings. In the United States, the average family income for 2008 was $50,303 (see figure 13.1). Asian families had the highest average income and black families the lowest average income.

Of the multitude of ways to divide people into economic classes, the *upper, upper-middle, middle,* and *lower* classes will be used in this chapter. The **upper class** makes up the top 1% of American households, and members of this class control approximately 35% of the nation's wealth. In fact, the top 10% of American households control approximately 71% of individual and family wealth. Members of this class have plenty of disposable income and many choices as consumers. Their children often attend the best private schools, their families are often members of exclusive clubs,

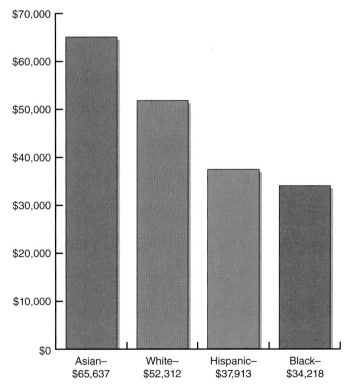

Figure 13.1 Average 2008 income for U.S. families.
U.S. Census Bureau 2008.

and their children are often expected to mature to meet the expectations of their parents. People in this economic class essentially control much of the financial world and seek to maintain their position in society.

The **upper-middle class** is composed of professionals such as physicians, attorneys, business leaders, and managers. Typically members of this class have significant amounts of discretionary income and join private clubs for social experiences. While most do not have the economic resources to exist without their earned income, as white-collar professionals they do supervise and influence others in the workplace. People in the upper-middle class often value education and strive for advanced degrees. They establish a network of contacts that serves them throughout life. They also often become leaders in government and can affect laws to maintain their position.

The **middle class** is the largest economic group in the United States. They must carefully choose their expenses for daily living and leisure spending. They often work as skilled laborers, as teachers, and in service industry positions. Their earned income provides their economic base, and many middle-class families rely on two wage earners.

The **lower class** is composed of unskilled laborers who essentially do work that is assigned and supervised by others. Their income barely meets the minimum wage standards set by the government, and they have few chances to improve their economic level. In 2008, the official poverty rate for all U.S. citizens was 13.2%, or more than 39.2 million people (United States Census 2008c). To be considered below the poverty line, annual family income must be below $22,025 for a family of four (see figure 13.2).

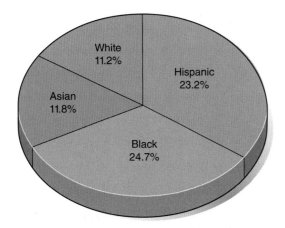

Figure 13.2 U.S. families below the poverty line.
U.S. Census Bureau 2008.

Social Class and Sport Activity

There are wide differences in general access to sport and in which sports families of the various economic classes are likely to choose. Let's look at how social class affects sport participation and spectatorship.

Social Class and Choice of Sport

Sport participation has always been more popular and accessible within the upper class due to the availability of leisure time and money. Historically, people of wealth used sport as entertainment and as a way to demonstrate their wealth. They often use sport to build social capital through networks and contacts in business. Many of today's sports, such as tennis, golf, equestrian, and sailing, were traditionally pastimes of the wealthy, and many business deals were consummated after a round of golf or a set of tennis. Our current society is similar in that people of the highest income levels typically have the highest rates of sport participation. They also are more likely to attend a sporting event, and they even watch more sports on television (Booth and Loy 1999). The upper and upper-middle classes have favored sports such as equestrian, golf, tennis, sailing, polo, and skiing that are typically performed at private clubs. Similarly, Olympic sports such as gymnastics, figure skating, swimming, riflery, and archery typically are the choice of the upper-middle class. As most of these sports are individual, they are often expensive to participate in. The facilities are often costly, the individual or family bears the training expenses, and traveling to compete consumes huge amounts of money.

The working class (lower-middle class) is more likely to choose community sports that are readily accessible and cheap. Community youth sport programs start kids in sport, and many kids go on to play on interscholastic teams that are subsidized by schools and taxpayers. Coaching and facilities are typically free, and athletes with talent can enhance their performance at a modest expense to their families. Team sports dominate this class since they are cheaper to stage, accommodate more players on a field or court, and provide a social environment as well. Sports such as basketball, football, soccer, baseball, softball, and volleyball are popular. Parents often serve as volunteer coaches or officials to stay involved with their children and keep the expenses within reason.

The poor and working classes devote so much time to earning a living and taking care of basic needs that they have little time or money left to spend on sport. As our society's standard of living has improved, blue-collar families have been able to participate in or watch certain sports that appeal to them and are readily accessible to the public, inexpensive to play, and available in public recreational facilities (Sage 1998).

Those who have higher levels of income and education and work in professional or managerial roles are the most ardent and frequent consumers of health and fitness activities and sport. They value physical fitness and enjoy leisure activity. In contrast, those who labor physically are less likely to feel the need or inclination to exercise or play sports. They are more likely to spend leisure time resting for the next day of work (Gruneau 1999).

The lower economic classes typically choose sports such as boxing, wrestling, weightlifting, auto racing, bowling, pool, and motorcycle racing. Most of these sports share the characteristics of violence and uncertainty based on physical strength and daring. They are often available at low costs and in urban areas and are accessible to all. They lean toward the masculine identity of toughness, a trait that kids from modest backgrounds may find necessary for survival (Coakley 2004). Many people at lower incomes live in rural areas, and those people favor sports that are readily accessible such as hunting and fishing.

French sociologist Loïc Wacquant (2004) joined a gym on the south side of Chicago in a predominately black neighborhood. There he learned the importance of boxing for boys from the lower socioeconomic class who are looking for a legitimate way to establish self-respect and a sense of masculinity.

The alternative to boxing for many kids in that neighborhood was "to end up in jail or dead in the streets." Boxing has traditionally appealed to the lower economic classes and to recent immigrants to the United States. Boys in the cities turned to boxing to try to escape lives marked by a lack of employment prospects. They preferred the controlled violence of the boxing ring to the random violence of the streets.

Basketball is unique in that it appeals to all classes and is popular in both the suburbs and the city. But at heart, it is a city game with its own history, hierarchy, and heroes. A driveway, an asphalt playground, or a parking lot with a hoop can provide the court. Anyone can play, and winners typically stay on the court to challenge all comers. The dream of escaping the ghetto through basketball has been the subject of articles, books, and motion pictures such as *White Men Can't Jump* and *Hoop Dreams*. A few players do make it to professional basketball, but the odds are miniscule for the millions of kids who dream of making it.

IN THE ARENA WITH . . .

Professional Wrestling

Some people think professional wrestling is a fraud and a fake. But let's take a look. Pro wrestling is entertainment, is athletic, and has a dramatic flair, with the script always leaning toward the triumph of good over evil. Some advocates say that it's the closest thing to a live sport soap opera you can find. The participants don't so much compete against each other as cooperate to produce a good show that follows the script.

With the advent of television is the 1950s, professional wrestling provided low-cost programming to local stations that became immensely popular. Always appealing to the proletariat, in the 1980s pro wrestling went after a new audience, the middle class. Cartoon television shows featuring animated drawings of professional wrestlers like Hulk Hogan helped popularize the sport for kids. The kids brought along their parents, and suddenly it became a "family activity."

As the sport faded in popularity once again, it began to seek a new audience. Perhaps not surprisingly, it went back to those kids who had once watched cartoon wrestling and were now college students. The tremendous success of wrestling websites is largely attributed to its popularity with college students (Kreit 1998). Who knew that pro wrestling would be a hot entertainment activity for the next generation of college students? Are you or is anyone you know into professional wrestling either online, on television, or even in live action?

ACTIVITY TIME-OUT

Looking Into the World of Dogfighting

Do some online research about the case of Michael Vick, All-Pro quarterback for the Atlanta Falcons who was convicted of promoting dogfighting on his personal property. His high-profile arrest and conviction opened many people's eyes to this long-practiced sport. Dogfighting is certainly nothing new to society; it has been around for generations, although often below the radar. The purpose of this assignment is for you to investigate its current status. Where does dogfighting typically occur in the United States? Who are the typical participants? Who benefits? Are there laws against it? If so, are they enforced? Do we need to do more to curb this practice?

Social Class and High-Performance Sport

Young athletes who aspire toward high-performance sports have to invest large amounts of time and money in training and competition. If their family doesn't have the resources to support their dream, their chances of success are severely curtailed. The choice of sport is critical, since the opportunities to develop within some sports depend highly on economic investment while other sports can be pursued at a more modest expense.

Young people from the upper-middle and upper classes typically do not develop strong motivation to succeed in highly competitive sport. Their exposure to a family that makes a living in business or a profession influences their interests from their earliest days. Sports are seen as more of a diversion, played for fun. Family and friends encourage these children in sports such as golf, tennis, sailing, and skiing so that they can acquit themselves admirably on social occasions. Many friendships are developed and business deals consummated on the golf course or tennis court. Family vacations often include these sports. A certain level of skill and understanding of such sports is expected, just as good table manners and other social graces are expected.

Young men from the middle class often see sport as a way to establish their masculinity and to gain social capital by acceptance in their peer group. Combined with the cultural capital instilled by their parents of self-discipline, hard work, and focus on achievement, middle-class youth often become high achievers in sport. Coaches of youth sports tend to reward the work ethic and reinforce the behavior of high-achieving athletes.

Families tend to support their kids' quest for excellence and often will sacrifice financially to support training costs. It is not unheard of for families to move to another part of the country to train with a better coach or better competition. In sports like tennis and golf, families with exceptionally talented kids often move to warm climates where the competition is strongest and academies are typically located. At the extreme, families even split apart, one parent moving with the talented athlete and the other staying behind because of a job or other siblings.

Male athletes from lower classes also link sport to masculinity because sports provide a chance to exhibit fearlessness and aggressiveness. Since they often can't compete with young men from higher classes in school or in material possessions, their sport success becomes the badge of courage that defines them (Messner 2002).

Olympic Sports

Olympic sports were historically dominated by the upper classes, and many sports in the Olympic Games (both Summer and Winter) reflect that tendency. The leaders of the Olympic Movement were typically males from well-to-do backgrounds. They promoted the sports indigenous to their social class and for years limited participation to amateurs. By excluding professionals, they restricted participation to athletes from their social class, since athletes with limited resources couldn't afford to train as amateurs. In fact, early definitions of *amateur* were based on social class, and athletes from lower economic classes were categorized as nonamateurs.

The problem with limiting the Olympics to amateurs was simply that doing so excluded some of the best athletes. Furthermore, there were extensive reports of athletes who violated the rules and secretly accepted money for training expenses. Some countries established free training schools that prepared their young athletes for the Olympics, virtually making these athletes professionals. The discussion on Olympic restrictions came to a head in the 1980s; and beginning in 1988, professional athletes were admitted to the Games (Amateur Athletic Foundation Olympic Primer 2005).

Most of the recent Olympic athletes have come from working or middle-class families who sacrificed to support their child's Olympic quest. David Hemery (1986), a former Olympian, studied 63 of the top performers, who included athletes from 22 sports and 12 countries. His sample, which was relatively small and focused on the best of the best, fell into the following class distribution:

Poor	2%
Working class	26%
Middle class	44%
Upper-middle class	3%
Upper class	0%

Athletes who aspire to compete in certain sports at the Olympic Games run into special problems. Many Olympic sports are not emphasized or even offered at high schools or colleges. High-performance athletes must pursue their athletic dreams through private academies and competitions that are expensive and time-consuming.

Olympic sports that require specialized training include gymnastics, swimming, judo, weightlifting, boxing, and almost all winter sports, although a limited number of schools and colleges offer varsity programs in winter sports. Families must often move to allow their kids to train with a top coach living in another part of the country. Athletes of modest means may seek employment to help them afford competition, travel, and coaching. Some corporate sponsors of the Olympic Movement help provide jobs for prospective Olympians.

Another option for prospective Olympians is to train at one of the Olympic training centers at Colorado Springs or San Diego. Of course, athletes have to qualify for these programs, but if they do, the costs of training are generally borne by the U.S. Olympic Committee or the national governing body of the given sport. In many countries, the expense of training future Olympians is borne by the government and administered by the minister of sports. Government financial support for training has been debated in the United States for many years.

Cost of High-Performance Sport

Many people are unaware of the financial investment it takes to compete at the highest levels, whether it's the Olympics or professional sport. Here is where parents of talented kids can put their social and cultural capital to good use to help circumvent the financial challenges of elite training. Perhaps the most expensive sports involve the equestrian events. Owning and caring for a horse in competition can cost upward of $100,000 a year. Unlike athletes in other sports that entail travel expenses for the athlete and perhaps a coach, equestrians must also ship their horses to compete nationally and internationally at the highest levels (United States Equestrian Team Foundation 2010).

Let's look at the yearly expenses of a tennis player. If a tennis player attends 12 national tennis tournaments a year at a cost of $1,500 to travel to and compete in each, the player needs to budget $18,000 to start. If a parent or coach travels with the player, this expense doubles or triples, especially if the athlete pays the coach for his time. Weekly lessons, some group and some private, cost an average of $250, and athletes living in a cold climate pay more to practice on indoor courts. Then add in the expense of tennis rackets, shoes, clothing, and other incidental equipment at a cost easily greater than $2,500 a year (unless the player gets an endorsement deal with a clothing or racket company).

Many young athletes also use the services of a fitness gym or a physical trainer and perhaps a sport nutritionist or sport psychologist. Their fees can easily add several thousand dollars in expense. The total probably will exceed $25,000 a year for frugal athletes and may reach $50,000 if money is not a concern.

Families with no financial worries may send their prodigies in sports such as soccer, tennis, golf, and basketball to a live-in academy in a warm climate where they play tennis half the day and attend a private school the other half. Expense at such a facility *will likely exceed $60,000 for just the school year*, and of course if the athlete continues to train or compete during the summer months, more expenses will be added. (See chapter 6, "Youth Sport," for more description of the IMG Sports Academy.)

You can see how children of most families face limited opportunities in certain sports. As we noted earlier, the median income for all households in 2008 was $50,303.

Families whose combined annual income exceeded $100,000 ranked in the top 5% to 10% of all American families. The average family with a total income of $50,000 can't begin to afford sports like high-performance competitive tennis, and even top wage earners making six-figure salaries can't afford to expend a quarter or half of their family income on sport training for one child.

You can also see now why team sports and varsity high school teams are the most popular options

The expense of equestrian makes it a sport that is limited to the financially elite.

for most kids. The costs are reasonable, and almost every family can finance sport participation if they are creative and frugal. Of course, every other family has also figured out that team sports are more affordable, so the competition is keen. Children whose families are well off financially might find it better to develop skills in a more exclusive sport and compete for a national championship against fewer opponents.

Social Class and High School Sports

Children from lower-class families usually do not have much family support in playing sports since their families are struggling to make ends meet. Girls are expected to help out with household chores and care for younger siblings. Sport dropout rates are well over 50% for teenage girls from lower income levels (Dobie 2000). Research discussed in a *USA Today* article shows that "the most affluent high schools—those in the top quarter of the state of New Jersey—have won athletic championships at more than twice the rate of those in the bottom quarter" (groups based on the household median income of the school neighborhood and the percentage of students on federal free or reduced lunch; Brady and Sylwester 2004):

A. Top quarter = 40%

B. Upper middle = 22%

C. Lower middle = 22%

D. Bottom = 16%

Schools in wealthier neighborhoods tend to have better sport facilities, better coaches because the pay is better, money for equipment, weight rooms, and booster clubs to pay for extras. Athletes have team jackets, shirts, uniforms, banquets, rings, and other goodies that are out of reach of other schools.

The training in youth sport in affluent communities tends to be better organized. Families typically start their kids early and encourage them to attend specialized coaching camps to refine their skills. The kids might go to a summer camp for tennis, soccer, golf, swimming, or the more traditional team sports like basketball, soccer, or volleyball. At such camps they are exposed to top coaching, and rubbing elbows with other talented kids from outside their neighborhood heightens cutting-edge concepts and their expectations.

The article from *USA Today* (Brady and Sylwester 2004) also specifically dealt with the high school in Glen Rock, New Jersey. Glen Rock won 13 state titles over the five years in the 10 core sports analyzed in the article. The state titles included four in football, four in girls' track, three in girls' soccer, one in baseball, and one in boys' track. The median income in the Glen Rock neighborhood was $120,000, more than double the statewide median. Similar sport statistics abound for suburban school districts in southern Connecticut like Greenwich, New Canaan, and Westport—neighborhoods that are within easy commuting distance to New York City and have high per capita incomes. This pattern in high school sport statistics is replicated around the country in affluent, typically suburban communities.

A glaring omission from the study cited is that the only sports included were basketball, soccer, outdoor track, football, girls' volleyball, girls' softball, and baseball. What do you think the study would have shown if tennis and golf had been included? Have you ever heard of an inner-city high school winning a state championship in tennis or golf?

The lack of golfers or tennis players in urban environments is not solely due to a lack of affluent families. The accessibility to golf courses or tennis courts is limited in urban settings simply because of lack of space and the cost to build sport facilities. Renting indoor tennis courts in New York City can cost $100 an hour simply because they are so expensive to build and maintain. Golf courses, except for the few public courses in city parks, are likewise few and far between.

There are some exceptions to the general trends in high school sport statistics. Small rural communities sometimes excel in sports because their kids have few choices for entertainment and so most play sports. Some inner-city high schools have strong traditions of excellence in sports like basketball where playgrounds abound and kids follow history.

Some boys may learn that their role models in professional sport making millions of dollars came from a similar socioeconomic background. Sports give them hope and a roadmap to fulfill their dreams of upward mobility. They typically choose team sports since training can often be found close by at modest expense. As they mature, they can continue to improve their skills through high school varsity programs and eventually can win an athletic scholarship to college. Sport programs at all levels set aside funds to provide scholarships for youth from poorer families and are eager to assist deserving and talented kids.

Solutions to Financial Barriers in Sport

Access to sport has somewhat opened up in the United States through community sport programs that are available to all kids in a community. Many programs are staged at public school facilities or parks that are supported with taxpayer funds. Although programs usually charge a modest user fee, families who qualify for scholarships based on income often can still send their kids to the programs. Usually recreation departments, again funded by taxpayer funds, provide facilities, provide some equipment, and pay for coaching. Most communities typically offer team sports that can accommodate large numbers of players at modest expense. Some communities also offer swimming or tennis as after-school or summer programs.

Some sports are promoted by nonprofit community organizations established to fund and organize programs in a given sport. Often these nonprofit groups are assisted by their national governing bodies and supported financially by local donors, government grants, fund-raisers such as auctions and dinner dances, and business donors who want to help support their local community. Typically these nonprofit organizations provide programs at very modest fees and welcome every child regardless of ability to pay.

Other strong sources of youth sport programs are organizations such as the YMCA and YWCA, Boys and Girls Clubs, Catholic youth organizations, Jewish community centers, police athletic leagues, church leagues, Girl and Boy Scouts, and Big Brothers Big Sisters. All are dedicated to providing healthy recreational experiences for kids, and many concentrate in disadvantaged neighborhoods. Although their goal is not to produce high-performance athletes, if a talented child is spotted in the program there are often ways to additionally support extended training or scholarships for specialized programs.

Control of Amateur and Professional Sport

People with power in the sport world can effect significant change or prevent change. The power in sport is different at every level of competition.

In local community, high school, and recreational sport programs, a board of directors usually hires staff to administer the programs. Parents, politicians, and others in the community may join the board or exert their influence from outside the organization. Typically, those who make program decisions even at the local level are adults who have their own biases and ideas about how a sport should be presented and run.

At the national level of sport, the people who control the money make decisions on how to run the sport programs. Their economic capital is based on the organizations they head rather than on their personal wealth. However, most of the people who have a say at the national level of sport belong to the upper or upper-middle class by virtue of their income, background, and robust social and cultural capital.

BusinessWeek ranked the 100 most powerful people in sport for 2007. The criteria included how individuals were ranked by their peers; how much money they control, generate, or influence; how long they have exercised power; and how lasting their impact on a sport or the larger world of sport will be. From the list of the Top 100, here are the Top 10:

Roger Goodell, Commissioner, NFL

Tiger Woods, golfer

David Stern, Commissioner, NBA

George Bodenheimer, President, ESPN, ABC Sports, co-chair Disney Media Networks

Bud Selig, Commissioner, MLB

Brian France, Chairman, CEO NASCAR

Dick Ebersol, Chairman, NBC Universal Sports and Olympics

Phil Knight, Chairman, Nike

Sean McManus, President, CBS News and Sports

Rupert Murdoch, Chairman, CEO News Corp

The Top 10 listed represent the commissioners of the most popular professional sports; media executives or owners; one athlete; and the chairman of Nike, a sport shoe company and sponsor.

This group represents a new leadership of the sport world who replace previous generations of gentleman owners of sport franchises such as Busch, Hess, Wrigley, and even Steinbrenner. Today's leaders are business executives who are trained to make money through sport using every available tactic. The importance of the close ties between sport and the media is obvious, as they have collaborated to push the sport world into leading broadcast properties.

All of the men on the list are white males with the exception of Woods, and there are only five females ranked in the Top 100—led by Katie Bayne, Chief Marketing Officer for Coca-Cola North America, who is ranked at number 67. Another relatively recent change is that 11 athletes, led by Tiger Woods, are listed in the top 50 compared to a few years ago, when athletes were virtually nonexistent as top power brokers. Interestingly, as in the past, there are no coaches in the Top 100 in spite of their apparent prominent role in sport (Lowry and Keating 2007).

At the United States Olympic Committee, the traditional heads of the board of directors and the officers were often white males. In recent years women and blacks were gradually included in the controlling group of the USOC; and Leroy Walker, a distinguished former coach of track and field, was the first African American to serve as president, while Sandra Baldwin from swimming became the first female president.

 ACTIVITY TIME-OUT

Power at Your University

Investigate your university to assess how sport decisions are made. Who gets involved in the big decisions—the college president, the board of trustees, politicians (if yours is a state university), significant donors, coaching icons, student leaders, athletes, the media, or fans? Interview at least three people in different positions who influence the decisions and ask them to list the five most powerful people in sport at your school. (Remember to use the definition of power as the ability to effect or prevent significant change.) To help the people you interview, you might ask who would have the most influence at this university on topics such as adding or suspending a particular sport, building a new sport facility, increasing student fees to support sports, accepting a major new sport sponsor, allocating scholarships by sport, or accepting a bowl bid for the football team. Feel free to use your own examples.

EXPERT'S VIEW

Why Millionaire Athletes Go Broke

Roy Hadley, an attorney who counsels clients in legal matters associated with professional sport, shares some sobering statistics. A young National Basketball Association (NBA) or NFL athlete who signs a contract worth millions of dollars may think he is suddenly rich, but within a few years his life could be in tatters. In fact, *80% of NFL players* can expect to face bankruptcy soon after they retire; and within five years of retirement, *60% of NBA players* are broke. How could this be possible? Let's say a first-round draft pick signs for a $10 million bonus. Here's how it may very well be spent:

- First, he has to pay Uncle Sam along with state and local taxes on the money. With good legal advice, let's say he's able to limit his taxes to 45%, which is admirable. He's now down to $5.5 million.

- Second, he's got to pay his agent a percentage of the gross figure, not after taxes. At the going rate, that's probably going to cost $300,000. Now he's down to $5.2 million.

- Third, he needs somewhere to live, has lots of cash, and decides a $4 million mansion is just about right compared to his teammates' digs. He's down to $1.2 million.

- Fourth, everyone needs a car, and a nice, super-luxury vehicle might cost him $250,000. Now we're looking at a remaining $950,000.

- Finally, he needs clothes, jewelry, electronic gadgetry, gifts for family and friends, household expenses, and travel expenses that are compatible with his "new lifestyle."

- And before long, he'll have a slew of former friends and new acquaintances asking him for loans or investments in their business schemes that "can't miss," and maybe want to buy a new house for his mom.

Whew! Where did all that "guaranteed money" go? And now what does he do?

The fact is that young men who claim these exorbitant bonuses and salaries may also have a short professional career with no alternate backup plan for the rest of their lives. If our player divorces, his ex-wife will claim she and any children are entitled to be supported in the lifestyle she envisioned when he struck it rich. While these superstars temporarily have a huge income, it's probable they have had little education and no training in finance, nor have their family or friends, and they are at the mercy of business advisors (Hadley 2010).

The people who control sport in America often base their decisions on the welfare of the organizations or businesses they head. They decide what sports will receive high visibility, what image of each sport to portray, and what accompanying messages to send to the sport consumers. Of course, they need to please the customer, and for the most part that means taking a conservative, mainstream position on all issues. They can be conscious of public sentiment and media criticism, but they also have the means to influence or deflect much of that.

Perhaps the best example of the powerful control of sport is Rupert Murdoch, chairman and CEO of News Corporation, a media corporation that owns Fox, FX, Fox News, Television Games Network, part of the Golf Channel, Fox international sport channels, and cable and satellite networks around the world. The company also owns major newspapers across the country. It owns major league teams including the New York Knicks, the New York Rangers, the New York Liberty, and the Los Angeles Dodgers and several minor league teams as well. At the same time, it owns Madison Square Garden, Dodger Stadium, and Dodgertown. Fox has television contracts with every major sport and has shown remarkable growth in its coverage of NASCAR.

It is easy to see the sprawl of Murdoch's influence in sport by looking at the breadth and depth of his companies' holdings in sport organizations. His decisions can have far-reaching effects on what happens in sport on any given day and where and when it happens. For example, in the case of a national or regional disaster, such as the attack on the World Trade Center or a major earthquake, the News Corporation has considerable power over the response of the sport world, such as deciding what events to postpone or seasons to suspend.

Murdoch's purchase of the Los Angeles Dodgers was driven by his desire to create programming for his television holdings. A similar situation exists for the Atlanta Braves, owned by Time Warner; the Anaheim Angels, owned by Disney; and the Chicago Cubs, owned by the Tribune Co. In fact, 22 of the 30 Major League Baseball (MLB) teams have broadcasting deals with Fox Sports Net. The potential for conflict of interest between a media empire and baseball was illustrated during the potential baseball strike of 2002 when Rupert Murdoch could have collected $500 million in liquidated damages from his fellow baseball owners. That agreement was part of the News Corp deal for television rights to broadcast baseball games (Frankel 1998; Sandomir 1997).

Consider what might happen if Rupert Murdoch was a devoted fan of women's sport. How could he translate his cultural capital into promoting the cause? Could he forward women's sport by hiring women in prominent leadership positions within his businesses, owning women's sport franchises, or dramatically increasing the exposure of women's sport on television and in the newspapers?

Class Mobility in Sport

A part of the American dream has always been the ability to enhance your social or economic status in life through hard work and discipline. The popular corollary was that Americans who do not improve their status do not have the motivation or discipline to do so. Sports provide an opportunity to improve social and economic status through success on the playing field. Once again, the conventional wisdom is that hard work is even more important than talent in reaching the ultimate prize in a given sport.

The typical example illustrating social mobility through sport is that of football or basketball players or boxers who come from a low-income family and make their way to the professional ranks and command a huge contract. By earning millions of dollars, the athlete automatically joins the upper class, a society he may find difficult to fit into.

There are many dimensions to rising in class status through sport. The most obvious is through education that goes along with continuing a career in sport, even if a career in professional sport is not a reality. Most lower-class kids who passionately latch onto sport realize that maintaining their academic eligibility will allow them to pursue their sport. If they keep up their grades, they may also earn an athletic scholarship that opens up the possibility for higher education their parents never had. The knowledge and friends gained through their col-

 POP CULTURE

The *Rocky* Film Series

There has never been another film series quite like the six *Rocky* films, which have grossed more than $1 billion in worldwide sales. The films star Sylvester Stallone as Rocky Balboa, a small-time boxer who is clearly going nowhere in his life until his boxing career suddenly takes off through a most unlikely scenario. It's a story that has played out hundreds of times in the rough neighborhoods and streets of our largest American cities. Poor immigrant boys with little education and few prospects turn to boxing to defend themselves, prove their virility, and perhaps earn a few bucks. After a few years of mindless pummeling at the hands of sparring partners and unsympathetic opponents, many of these young men end up with brain damage and little else to show for their efforts.

The first movie, *Rocky* (1976), was set in the streets of Philadelphia and left the American public with a vision of an exultant Rocky lifting his arms in triumph on the steps of the Philadelphia Museum of Art. This first film was a critical and public success and won an Oscar for best picture. The sequels, while not as popular as the original, nevertheless kept the legend alive, and by 2006, when the latest installment in the series, *Rocky Balboa*, was released it was again hugely popular. There has even been talk of one more *Rocky* film with Stallone, but perhaps based on the sport of mixed martial arts rather than boxing (totalrocky.com 2010; rocky.com 2010).

lege education will set them up for employment opportunities beyond their social and economic class even if they never make it as a professional athlete.

Athletes who play sports in college seem to have more opportunities than nonathletes do. The reason for their success may be the sport experience, which teaches discipline, teamwork, and leadership. Of course, they may have innate capabilities that allow them to succeed in sports, and athletics may simply enhance those abilities. Sport participation may also help them build their own social and cultural capital. Their education, personal expectations, and social network surely help them in the business world. Numerous research studies have documented both male and female business leaders who participated in athletics and attribute their success at least in part to the lessons learned through sport (Acosta and Carpenter 2010; Carlson and Scott 2005).

In every sport, certain athletes stand out because they appear hungry to succeed. When these athletes come from lower socioeconomic families, people usually conclude that they are striving to escape a life of poverty. Many elite athletes on the world stage have emerged from poor countries to become international celebrities and economically wealthy compared to their countrymen.

French sociologist Loïc Wacquant, who authored *Body & Soul: Notebooks of an Apprentice Boxer* from his three years of study at a boxing gym in Chicago, quotes from some of the men he encountered there who typify the love–hate feelings they have for their sport and profession. "I wish I had been born taller, to a rich family. I wish I was smart and had the brains to go to school an' really become somebody important. For me, I can't stand the sport, I hate the sport, but it's carved inside of me so I can't let it go." More than 80% of the boxers Wacquant interviewed said they didn't want their sons to become boxers. Said

The minimum salary for a three-year WNBA player is $51,000; the minimum salary for a three-year NBA player is $826,269 (Beesley 2009). How do these numbers affect social class?

one, "No, no fighter wants his son to box…that's the reason you fight…it's too hard, jus' too damn hard" (Coakley 2004, p. 341).

How likely are young athletes to make it to the professional level? Evidence from the National Collegiate Athletic Association (2010a) suggests that a small percentage of athletes actually make it from high school to college to professional sport. The odds of a high school athlete making a collegiate team are only about 5%. That means 95% of athletes have no chance of a career in sport beyond their high school years. Only 3% of college athletes make it to the pros. So of high school athletes, roughly .2% make it to a professional career. These are small odds indeed. In spite of many inspiring biographies of athletes who moved from poverty to the professionals, the percentages are stacked against such mobility.

When we are tracking athletic success, the sports involved may affect the results. We have already seen that many sports, such as golf, tennis, swimming, and gymnastics, tend to attract athletes from upper-middle class families. Their records are often lumped in with large-scale research studies on class mobility, but their chances of achieving upward mobility are limited since they're starting from a relatively high level. Similarly, female athletes have fewer sports through which to gain upward mobility due to the dearth of professional sports for women. Women's National Basketball Association players earn a modest salary compared to the men in the NBA, and many great women athletes in track and field collect only modest prize money due to the limitations of the sport.

Understanding the limited chances for women to make it in professional sport only reinforces the amazing success of Serena and Venus Williams. Coming from Compton, California, an economically depressed area rife with crime and poverty, they have risen to the top of the sporting world in a sport usually reserved for the upper classes. Combining natural athleticism and talent with the savvy management of their parents, they managed to break into and dominate professional tennis. They accomplished all that without spending years and money in junior competition. Their simple formula was to play a few tournaments and practice under their father's tutelage until they were eligible to turn professional. The result has been Grand Slam championships for both women and record-setting endorsements, which in the case of Serena, were worth over $50 million!

The losers in the quest for upward mobility through sport are the thousands of children who have an unrealistic view of their potential and misjudge the odds of realizing their dreams. Leaders in the African American community decry the tendency of young black males to put all their hopes into a possible professional contract. Those goals are unrealistic for all but a special few, and when lower-class families emphasize sport over academics, most are setting their kids up for failure.

Arthur Ashe Jr. (featured in chapter 11) shared his views on the importance of education in a *New York Times* "Open Letter to Black Parents" (Ashe 1977). Although the statistics have changed today, the sentiments have not. "Unfortunately, our most widely recognized role models are athletes and entertainers—'runnin' and 'jumpin', 'singin' and 'dancin'. While we are 60 percent of the NBA, we are less than 4 percent of the doctors and lawyers. While we are about 35 percent of major league baseball, we are less than 2 percent of the engineers. While we are about 40 percent of the NFL, we are less than 11 percent of construction workers such as carpenters and bricklayers. Our greatest athletes have been athletes such as Jack Johnson, Joe Louis, and Muhammad Ali. These were the ways out of the ghetto. We have been on the same road—sports and entertainment—too long. We need to pull over, fill up at the library, and speed away to Congress, the Supreme Court, the unions, and the business world" (Ashe 1977).

Yet the lessons learned through sport participation are valuable for young athletes even if a pro career is not in the cards. Hard work, determination, sacrifice, and teamwork can certainly be valuable assets in their future careers. Perhaps the optimistic view of social mobility through sport makes sense when considered in this light.

Chapter Summary

Although Americans prefer not to emphasize social classes, the economic differences between families in our society are clear. People in the upper socioeconomic classes of course prefer to maintain the status quo since they are comfortable with their position. In addition to economic capital, social and cultural capital affect which sports people choose to watch and play, and through sport, people in lower classes may improve their social standing.

There are strong relationships between social class and the types of sports people tend to choose for participation or watching. People from the upper classes tend to choose individual sports and sports that are often played at private clubs not open to the public. They also choose sports that are more expensive to pursue, whether it be for recreation or high-performance training.

Most people in the middle or working class gravitate toward the team sports that are more affordable. Children can take advantage of free or low-cost programs at the community level to begin playing a traditional team sport and can continue their career in the public schools at no cost in most communities. Team sports emphasize the traditional American values of hard work, discipline, determination, and teamwork. Athletes who do well are admired for their All-American values, while those who fail are criticized for laziness or lack of effort.

The people who control sport are often the people in charge of the large media conglomerates, the heads of the professional sport leagues, the heads of the Olympic Games, and the owners of professional franchises, stadiums, and facilities. Almost without exception these leaders in sport are white males who tend to perpetuate the status quo that has clearly favored them. They have the power to make or prevent change in sport.

The odds are against social mobility through success in sport. In spite of a few poster boys and girls who have risen from poverty to great riches, the majority of athletes never play professionally. Using sport for academic motivation or funding for higher education may be the best ticket to improving social and economic class.

Special Populations and Sport

Student Outcomes

After reading this chapter, you will know the following:

- Special populations in sport and the challenges they face in sport participation
- How the Americans with Disabilities Act affected special populations
- The role of the American Association of People with Disabilities
- Sport opportunities for people who are physically or mentally challenged and for older adults
- Issues facing athletes with physical or mental disabilities and older athletes

Oscar Pistorius of South Africa is a double-amputee sprinter who has run the 400-meter sprint in the amazing time of 46.56 seconds. His prosthetic legs are blade-shaped; German sport scientists say that his legs require him to expend 25% less energy than an able-bodied runner and that the prostheses are about 30% more efficient than a normal human ankle. Oscar was originally banned from trying to qualify for the Olympic Games in Beijing, but he persevered and eventually was cleared to compete by the Court of Arbitration for Sport, if he could qualify. His reaction to the court decision: "When I found out, I cried. It is a battle that has been going on far too long. It's a great day for sport. I think this day will go down in history for equality of disabled people" (Zarda 2008).

But not everyone agrees with the court decision. Some skeptics wonder why an athlete who may gain an advantage from a prosthetic device should compete in the Olympics and suggest he may better be invited to the Paralympic Games instead. There is no disputing that Oscar is an inspirational role model to be admired, but should he be competing against able-bodied athletes? As Pistorius struggled through the courts, another South African, Natalie Du Toit, quietly qualified for the Games in the 10-kilometer swimming event. She also is an amputee but does not use a prosthesis to swim. Oh, it should be mentioned that in the end, Pistorius was not able to meet the qualifying time and did not compete in the Olympic Games. Do you believe athletes who use prosthetic devices should be eligible to compete in the Olympic Games?

This chapter covers three distinct groups of unique populations in sport: people who are physically challenged, people who are mentally challenged, and older adults. Each group faces unique circumstances and has had a different history of acceptance and accommodation within our society. Their participation in sport and recreational activities is relatively recent, and law at every level of government now supports their participation.

More than 54 million people in the United States have one or more physical or mental disabilities, and this number will increase as the average age of our population increases. According to the recent Survey of Americans with Disabilities (Harris Poll 2004), a fifth of American people have disabilities. Yet historically, people with disabilities have had few chances to pursue their American dream of equality of opportunity.

Things began to change dramatically (for example, with requirements that government buildings be accessible to those with handicaps) when the federal government started enacting legislation that addressed various issues of discrimination, such as Title V of the Rehabilitation Act of 1973, including discrimination against those with disabilities. Then in 1990, President George H.W. Bush signed the Americans with Disabilities Act (ADA), which became a landmark law and began to effectively limit long-standing discriminatory practices.

Older adults, or adults older than 50 years, are often included as people with disabilities as they begin to combat both physical and mental problems of aging. However, even for relatively fully functioning adults older than 50, the opportunities for sport participation are limited. Life expectancy has been steadily increasing, and the maturing of the baby boomers has resulted in an explosion of older adults. The number of U.S. residents older than 50 is expected to reach 100 million by 2011, which means they will comprise one-third of the total population. Further, people over 50 account for 45% of all U.S. consumer spending, or $2.1 trillion per year, and those over 55 own 77% of all financial assets in the United States (*AARP Magazine* 2008).

As the population ages and seeks a better quality of life, the focus lands on physical health and fulfilling social relationships. Sport and physical activity can contribute to a healthier lifestyle, help fight diseases, and prolong life. Sport programs and physical exercise facilities are critically adjusting marketing and programming to serve this burgeoning population.

Americans with Disabilities Act

President H.W. Bush, marking a long and tedious battle to ensure the rights of all people with disabilities, signed the **Americans with Disabilities Act (ADA)** into law in 1990. Before this act, living with a disability was characterized by discrimination and segregation. The situation was not unlike that suffered for centuries by minorities or women. The ADA has been amended several times since its pas-

The ADA requires that adequate seating is provided for spectators with disabilities.

sage and will continue to be refined as court decisions clarify and interpret the law. Unfortunately, some recent Supreme Court decisions have eroded the ADA protections for people with disabilities by placing severe restrictions on the class of people who are protected, have narrowed the remedies available to complainants, and have expanded the defenses available to employers. However, in the 2004 decision *Tennessee v. Lane*, the court ruled that the state of Tennessee must allow plaintiffs to sue for financial damages over inaccessible courthouses (United Cerebral Palsy 2004).

Let's review the history of laws preceding the ADA that removed barriers for various groups and laid the groundwork for a society that affirms the equality of people with disabilities. In the late 1960s, major civil rights legislation changed the face of America. Led by Dr. Martin Luther King Jr., who envisioned a society that was just and inclusive for all as expressed in his now-famous "I Have a Dream" speech, the civil rights movement created major changes in schools, businesses, public buildings, federal funding, transportation, and virtually every area of life.

Young people today have a hard time believing that until the 1960s, African Americans were excluded from playing intercollegiate sport in most parts of the country and that there were none in the professional sport leagues until the late 1940s. Baseball player Jackie Robinson was the first to break the color barrier in 1947, and within 30 years, black athletes dominated professional basketball and football.

In the 1970s, women's rights took the stage. Although women had the right to vote, their rights in the workplace were abysmal and their earning power was a fraction of that of males. Women began to claim an equal place in society and agitated for fairer opportunities. Title IX legislation established the equal rights of females for sport participation. Colleges, high schools, media, and the public slowly adjusted to a world in which women could be fit and competitive and become champions just like men.

In the late 1960s, the last of the major antidiscrimination statutes of the civil rights movement was passed with the enactment of the Fair Housing Act. That act did not include people with disabilities in its protected classes. Likewise, Title VII of the Civil Rights Act prohibited discrimination on the basis of race, religion, national origin, and sex in the sale and rental of housing but again offered no protection for those with disabilities.

Finally in 1988, the Fair Housing Act was amended to add the new protected classes of people with disabilities and families with children. Two years later, President H.W. Bush declared at the signing of the Americans with Disabilities Act, "This Act is powerful in its simplicity. It will ensure that people with disabilities are given the basic guarantees . . . of freedom of choice, control of their lives, the opportunity to blend fully into the mosaic of the American mainstream" (Americans Disability Technical Assistance Centers 2004, p. 9).

The ADA addressed discrimination against those with disabilities in employment, state and local government, public accommodations, telecommunications, and transportation. The purpose of the law was to provide a clear and comprehensive national mandate to eliminate discrimination against individuals with disabilities and to establish standards that are clear, strong, and enforceable. Over the past 15 years, many advances have been made as courts have upheld the law and interpreted its application and as organizations have adopted similar statements of inclusion for people with disabilities.

While reading this brief historical review, you may have noticed how recently the developments occurred for creating fairness for people with disabilities. Businesses, schools, churches, public programs, organizations, and of course governments have all adjusted their practices to conform to the law.

The current opportunities in sport participation emanate from the shift in attitude of our society. Why shouldn't people with disabilities have the same opportunities to enjoy sport and fitness activities that others in society enjoy? The challenge is to welcome their participation and accommodate their needs within the sporting world.

Although in the last decade there have been quantum leaps in improving the quality of life for people with disabilities, they still face significant inequalities in key areas of living (United States Census Bureau 2008b):

- Only 38% of people with disabilities are employed, compared with 80% of those without disabilities.
- Three times as many live in poverty, with annual household incomes below $15,000 (adjusted each year).
- They are twice as likely to drop out of high school (24% versus 11%).
- They are twice as likely to have transportation problems, and many go without needed health care.
- They are less likely to socialize, eat out, and attend religious services.
- Only 34% say they are very satisfied with life, compared to 61% of people without disabilities.

Sport and recreation opportunities are perhaps less important than issues of fair housing, access to buildings, access to schooling, fair employment opportunities, and access to health care. But sport participation, whether at the competitive or participation level, does enrich life for all of us.

American Association of People with Disabilities

The **American Association of People with Disabilities (AAPD)** was founded in 1995 as a nonprofit organization to represent all Americans with disabilities. Family members and friends are welcome to join the AAPD for an annual membership fee of $15.00. The AAPD was conceived, advised, and managed by people with disabilities for people with disabilities. It is not a government program. Although the mission of AAPD is much broader than fairness in sport, it does provide leadership and lobby to ensure that recreational opportunities exist for its constituency.

ACTIVITY TIME-OUT

Protecting Civil Rights

Develop a list of the three major legislative acts that were passed to protect the civil rights of minorities, women, and the physically or mentally disabled. Include the dates the laws were passed, the political climate preceding their passage, the short-term results, and their status today. Note the effects of each law on both sport participation and the general quality of life.

According to the AAPD, more than one in five Americans, or over 50 million people, have a disability. Nearly half of these people are of employable age, yet only one-third are employed. Government and private plans that support people with disabilities cost American taxpayers over $230 billion each year, and another $200 billion in earnings and taxes are lost because of their unemployment. The economic impact alone is striking (American Association of People with Disabilities 2005).

Many governing bodies for specific sports have expanded their programs for people with disabilities since the passage of the ADA. You may notice pictures of physically disabled athletes in their literature, videos, and materials for coaching courses. Whenever possible, athletes with disabilities are mainstreamed into regular sport programs, although athletes with severe disabilities require specialized coaching and rules for competition.

Sport Participation for Athletes With Physical Disabilities

According to the Americans with Disabilities Act, the term **disability** applies to any individual who has a physical or mental impairment that substantially limits one or more of the person's major life activities. In sport, physical disabilities can range from loss of limbs or loss of hearing or sight to physical impairment due to disease or accident. In the conduct of sport, the degree of disability is taken into account to ensure fair competition.

Paralympics

The Paralympic Games are the second largest sporting event in the world, after the Olympics. The inaugural Paralympics were staged in 1960 in Rome, Italy, and included about 400 athletes from 23 countries. Today, the Summer and Winter Games together include over 5,000 athletes representing 120 countries in the Summer events and 36 countries in the Winter events. The Paralympics feature competition in 21 sports, 18 of which are also contested in the Olympics (United States Paralympics 2005). The following sports are included in Paralympic competition:

Winter Games

Alpine skiing

Nordic skiing

Curling

Sled hockey

Summer Games

Archery

Rugby

Men's basketball

Sailing

Women's basketball

Shooting

Bocce

Soccer

Cycling

Swimming

Equestrian

Table tennis

Fencing

Tennis

Men's goalball

Track and field

Judo

Men's volleyball

Powerlifting

Women's volleyball

Many of these sports, including fencing, volleyball, basketball, rugby, and tennis, are played in wheelchairs.

The mission of the U.S. Paralympics is "To be the world leader in the Paralympic movement by developing comprehensive and sustainable elite programs for our athletes. To utilize our Olympic and Paralympic platform to promote excellence in the lives of persons with disabilities." Founded in 2001, U.S. Paralympics is a division of the United States Olympic Committee (USOC) with a focus on enhancing programs, funding, and opportunities for persons with physical disabilities to participate in sport (United States Paralympics 2005).

This is a clear statement of commitment toward producing excellence in competitive sport by athletes with physical disabilities. Because the Paralympic movement is under the aegis of the USOC, it generally follows the Olympic model for the development of athletes and applies a similar philosophy and purpose.

In order to participate in the Paralympic Games, athletes have to meet eligibility standards established by the International Paralympic Committee.

Eligible athletes include those with amputations, those who are blind or visually impaired, those with cerebral palsy, those with spinal cord injuries, those with multiple sclerosis, and those with dwarfism, along with other categories of disability.

The Paralympic division of the USOC manages 18 Paralympic sports. It also supports the programs offered by USA Curling, the U.S. Equestrian Federation, US Sailing, and U.S. Tennis Association.

Elite athletes who have qualified through competitive performance are selected for financial support, coaching assistance, and training for the next Paralympic Games. They are required to comply with the policies of the U.S. Anti-Doping Agency, including unannounced out-of-competition testing.

In 2000 the USOC put a comprehensive development plan in place to ensure that American athletes with disabilities have every chance of performing to their highest potential. Funds in excess of $23 million were committed for 2000 to 2004 for soliciting sponsors for support, educating the media, and providing coaching training and support. American Paralympic athletes finished the Games in Beijing ranked third in the world, earning 99 medals in the various competitions. In the Winter Olympics in Vancouver, the American team finished fifth, earning 13 medals overall.

State and Community Development Programs

Elite athletes don't just pop up. They develop over many years and require nurturing through expert coaching, organizational support, competitive events, and financial assistance. Grassroots programs that provide opportunities for athletes with disabilities are scattered throughout the country and depend heavily on local leaders and dedicated coaches in each community.

The Paralympic Academy is supported by the USOC and is an annual event held in each state. The academies last one or two days and are designed to introduce sports to potential Paralympic athletes aged 12 to 18. They also provide training for coaches, program administrators, families, and community leaders who are involved in local Paralympic sport programs. By attracting media attention, state academies help garner public attention and support for the mission.

It is at the community level that the real work of ensuring equal opportunities for physically disabled athletes occurs. When practicable, programs should include all young athletes, with adaptations as required for athletes with disabilities. This practice provides economy of operation and viable compe-

IN THE ARENA WITH . . .

Paralympic Athletes Go to Court

When he competed in the 1,500-meter wheelchair race in the Beijing Olympics in 2008, Tony Iniguez wore his team uniform with pride. He was also suing the USOC for discrimination along with Scot Hollonbeck and Jacob Heilveil in a case that had begun in 2003. They alleged that the USOC was underfunding American Paralympic athletes by making health care benefits available to a smaller percentage of Paralympians, giving smaller quarterly training stipends, and paying smaller financial awards for medals won at the Paralympics compared to the Olympics ($25,000 vs. $5,000 per gold medal). Some other nations, notably Canada and Great Britain, support their Paralympians virtually equally. The USOC did not dispute the claim but contended that the benefits were smaller because the USOC receives no government support. As a result, it has to rely on revenue generated by the media exposure of its athletes, and Paralympic success does not generate enough increased revenue.

The case was heard by a U.S. District Court and the U.S. Court of Appeals, which ruled that the Olympic and Paralympic programs are distinct and the USOC has the legal discretion to finance able-bodied and disabled athletes differently. However, not all the judges thought the outcome was a good one. The district court judge who ruled against Iniguez in 2006 wrote, "Do I decry a culture that relegates Paralympians to second-class status in the quantity and quality of benefits and support from the USOC? Emphatically yes." The case was appealed to the U.S. Supreme Court, which announced in September of 2008 that it would not hear the appeal. During the time the case was working its way through the court system, Olympic support of Paralympic athletes increased to $11.4 million in 2008, up from $3 million in 2004. Meanwhile the U.S. performance at the Paralympics has decreased significantly over the last 20 years. United States Paralympians won about 12% of medals in 1988 and 1992, but in 2004 won just 5.6%. Perhaps the tide is turning with the success of the U.S. team in Beijing with a third-place finish.

ACTIVITY TIME-OUT

Researching Paralympic Sport

Do some research on a Paralympic sport to see how it differs from the normal sport competition. You might be particularly fascinated by the sports that are played in wheelchairs or the design of sport wheelchairs and how they differ from traditional wheelchairs. The most popular wheelchair sports are basketball, tennis, rugby, track and field, and fencing. You might want to check out the popular prize-winning movie *Murderball*, a documentary about players who are "quads," that is, people who have lost or have at least partial impairment of all four limbs. Their sport is rugby, and the film focuses on their fierce rivalries, violent competition, intense training, and incredible personal motivation to live a "normal life."

An alternate investigation would be to learn as much as you can about "beep baseball," which has been played for more than 30 years in the United States by blind or visually impaired athletes. In normal baseball, players often complain that the umpires are blind; in this sport, it's the players who are. You'll be amazed how these athletes play baseball using their sense of sound and assistance from sighted pitchers, coaches, and umpires.

tition for athletes who may not find local events to participate in or other athletes to train with. A national program is relatively easy to put in place because of the limited number of athletes involved, whereas aggressive efforts are needed if these local programs are to flourish in every community in the country (United States Paralympics 2005).

Sport Participation for Athletes With Mental Disabilities

According to Special Olympics, people with mental disabilities include those an agency or professional has identified as having one of the following conditions: intellectual disabilities, cognitive delays, or significant learning or vocational problems due to cognitive disabilities that require specially designed instruction.

Special Olympics is an international organization, involving 185 countries and more than 1.7 million people with intellectual disabilities, that provides year-round sport training and competition. Founded in 1968 by Eunice Kennedy Shriver, Special Olympics gives people with mental disabilities opportunities to develop their full potential, develop their physical fitness, demonstrate courage, and experience joy and friendship through sport.

Since its inception, Special Olympics has helped its athletes improve fitness, develop motor skills, increase self-confidence, and enhance self-image. The same values that make sport attractive to

all athletes have also helped Special Olympians develop physically, socially, and spiritually through participation. People with profound disabilities can also participate in Special Olympics through the Motor Activities Training Program (MATP). The MATP was developed by specialists and emphasizes training and participation rather than competition.

The worldwide participation in Special Olympics can be seen in the Special Olympic World Games that are held every four years for both summer and winter events. The 2005 Special Olympic Winter Games were held in Nagano, Japan, and were the first Games held in Asia. More than 1,800 athletes from 80 countries competed in seven sports. The 2007 Special Olympics World Games were held in Shanghai, China; and the 2011 Games will be hosted by Athens, Greece (Special Olympics 2010). The 2007 Winter Special Olympics was held in Boise, Idaho, where over 100 countries and more than 2000 athletes competed. The Summer Games include aquatics, athletics, badminton, basketball, bocce, bowling, cycling, equestrian, soccer, golf, gymnastics, handball, judo, powerlifting, roller skating, sailing, softball, table tennis, tennis, and volleyball. The Winter Games include Alpine skiing, cross-country skiing, snowshoeing, figure skating, floor hockey, snowboarding, and speed skating.

Special Olympics is divided into seven world regions: Africa, Asia Pacific, East Asia, Europe and Eurasia, Latin America, Middle East and North Africa, and North America. In the North American region, most U.S. states have a Special Olympics office that offers and coordinates Special Olympics activities in all 26 sports. Funding is provided by

IN THE ARENA WITH . . .

Eunice Kennedy Shriver, 1921-2009

Born into wealth and privilege, the fifth of nine children in what some have called this country's version of a royal family, the Kennedys, Shriver chose to lobby for the powerless. Her older sister Rosemary had a "mild form of retardation" as it was called in her day. She was lobotomized in 1941 and spent most of her life in an institution until she died in 2005. While her brothers John and Robert went on to careers in politics and suffered untimely deaths, Eunice raised her own family of five children.

More than 190 million people in the world have an intellectual disability, about 7.5 million in the United States. They are at greater risk than others for virtually every medical malady, vision problems, tooth decay, and obesity, and were once locked away in institutions. They are bullied, sexually abused, ignored, and unemployed at a far greater rate than the rest of the population. Shriver's vision of athletic competition for people with intellectual disabilities helped release an entire population worldwide from a prison of ignorance and misunderstanding. She often recited the Special Olympics oath, "Let me win. But if I cannot win, let me be brave in the attempt."

Shriver's indomitable spirit carried her through the early days when the Special Olympics movement was called Camp Shriver and took place in her backyard. From there it spread nationally and eventually internationally, where it has helped change laws and attitudes in every country regarding people with intellectual disabilities. In recognition of her contributions around the world, she received many honors and awards, including the Presidential Medal of Freedom, the highest civilian award in the United States; the French Legion of Honor; induction into the National Women's Hall of Fame; the NCAA Theodore Roosevelt Award; and the International Olympic Committee Award. In addition, she received 14 honorary doctorates from prestigious universities including Yale, Princeton, and Georgetown.

the international organization along with local financial support.

The first Special Olympics was held in Chicago and attracted 1,000 athletes from the United States and Canada. The inaugural Winter Games were held in 1977 in Colorado and involved 500 athletes. By 1987, the Summer Games had grown to include over 4,700 athletes from 70 countries. A year later, the International Olympic Committee officially recognized Special Olympics. The Games continued to expand, and more than 7,000 athletes from 150 countries competed in the Special Olympics World Summer Games in 2003 in Dublin, Ireland, the first Summer Games ever held outside the United States. The Special Olympics World Summer Games in Athens, Greece, will include 7,500 athletes from 185 nations competing in 22 Olympic-type sports. From its humble beginnings as a summer camp in the backyard of founder Eunice Shriver, the organization has grown in numbers and prestige around the world (Special Olympics 2010).

Coaches, family members, and other volunteers are essential to the sport programs. Most donate their time to the athletes and are rewarded with smiles, hugs, and self-satisfaction. Hundreds of these dedicated volunteers are the lifeblood of the organization, and they allow it to offer programs and competition at no charge for participants.

State organizations in cooperation with various governing bodies in sport also train coaches and officials for the Special Olympics. Since many athletes require personal support and supervision, the demands of coaching and officiating are extremely people intensive and require adequate training.

Participation in Special Olympics is valued regardless of the participant's skill. Special Olympics offers both the performance and participation tracks; that is, events are held for highly skilled athletes, and the same events are held for those whose accomplishments are more modest (Special Olympics 2010).

Sport Participation for Older Athletes

No doubt you've heard about the aging population in the United States and its effect on health care and social security. The first "boomers" turn 65 in 2011, and that age group will be growing faster than the

U.S. population in general. Adults between the ages of 45 and 65 already number over 81 million, while those over 65 number 40 million out of an overall U.S. population of approximately 308 million. Adults over age 55 control 70% of the net worth of U.S. households at a level equal to $7 trillion and have twice the discretionary spending of younger market segments. Many industries, including sport and fitness, are just beginning to recognize the potential of the aging adult marketplace (Ambrosius 2010). The fitness industry is seeing the effects of the older population as those over age 55 make up 29% of core fitness participants (those who participate in a given activity 50 or more times per year). This group continues to drive the fitness industry, swelling membership rolls at health clubs and purchasing billions of dollars worth of home exercise equipment (Sporting Goods Manufacturers Association 2009a).

As mentioned earlier, adults older than 50 years are often included among people with disabilities due to disabilities associated with age. They also have organizations that advocate for their equal treatment. The largest and most powerful is the AARP, which has a membership of over 40 million people. AARP has a strong voice on issues such as taxes, insurance, health care, and social security that older adults often deal with as they leave the workforce. Due the wide diversity of the physical needs of its members, AARP has settled on a strategy of encouraging more Americans to get at least the minimum amount of physical activity as recommended by the U.S. surgeon general by walking several times per week or participating in other forms of moderate physical activity.

The International Council on Active Aging (ICAA) is a relatively new group that promotes quality of life, physical activity, and sport participation by older adults. It publishes a newsletter and a bimonthly magazine, *Journal on Active Aging*. The ICAA also hosts conferences to share research information and educate people on creative approaches to innovative programming, staff training, and product selection to assist in the aging process. Its more than 5,000 members include many commercial organizations and health clubs that are seeking to accommodate older adults in their programs and facilities and are looking for guidance (ICAA 2010).

Performance Sport for Older Adults

In most sport organizations, senior divisions for competition have existed for years, although most of them included adults beginning at age 35 or 40. Today, with the changes in life expectancy, 35 to 40 hardly makes an athlete a senior athlete. Senior divisions are now called masters divisions and usually begin at age 50. By that age, most athletes are unable to physically compete with younger people who are in their prime as to physical ability, and they seek competition within their own age group for social reasons as well as competitive ones.

There are a few remarkable older athletes who still compete with younger age groups such as Martina Navratilova, who turned 50 years old on October 18, 2006, and was still competing on the women's professional tennis tour at that time. The Senior Olympics, Senior PGA tour, and masters games in other sports give athletes for whom the competitive fires still burn the chance to test their skills.

In 2010, more than 15,000 athletes were expected to compete in 18 different sports at the National Summer Senior Games (Senior Olympics) to be held in Houston, Texas. The minimum age to compete is 50, and athletes are divided into five-year age groups. The National Senior Games began in 1987, and now more than 35% of the competitors are female. The Summer Games attracted over 12,000 athletes to San Francisco in 2009.

The Senior Olympics negotiated with the USOC to grandfather in the use of the Olympic name, although the senior organization as a whole is now referred to as the National Senior Games Association. The Summer Olympics includes archery,

ACTIVITY TIME-OUT

Hook Up With Special Olympics in Your Area

If you would like to experience the thrill of volunteering or coaching Special Olympians, you can locate programs in your area by going to the website, SpecialOlympics.com, and following the instructions on who to contact at the state office. The contact will be able to refer you to a program or competition in your area. You can be sure the experience will be one you will never forget!

EXPERT'S VIEW

The International Council on Active Aging

Colin Milner is the chief executive officer of the International Council on Active Aging (ICAA), a coalition of more than 8,200 organizations that manage, own, or operate more than 40,000 locations in 37 countries around the world. Milner founded the organization in 2001 to "change the way we age" by embracing the aging process in promoting good health, preventing disease, and encouraging living life to the fullest. He is recognized as one of "the most innovative and influential minds" in the world on aging-related topics.

The two initiatives of the organization that stand out among a host of strategic actions are the ICAA conference and the *Journal of Active Aging.* The annual conference brings together professionals from around the world who spend a week networking and learning from each other as well as listening to outstanding speakers and authors in the aging field. By sharing creative program approaches, practical philosophies, and innovative new products and equipment, attendees stay on the cutting edge of the aging process. *Journal on Active Aging* is published six times per year and filled with articles that help aging professionals stay current in the field, challenge their creativity, and inspire them to push forward against the inevitable obstacles they face.

The active aging philosophy of the ICAA is to change the ways we age by staying active within all areas of life: physical, spiritual, emotional, intellectual, professional, and social. The philosophy embraces a concept of "engaged in life" so that older adults can participate fully in life regardless of socioeconomic status or health conditions within the wellness dimension. For more information on the ICAA, visit their website at www.icaa.cc.

bowling, badminton, basketball, cycling, golf, horseshoes, race walking, racquetball, road racing, shuffleboard, swimming, table tennis, tennis, softball, track and field, triathlon, and volleyball.

Competitors qualify for the national events through the state games held annually in their age division. Most of these athletes have been competing all their life and have slowed down the aging process by improving their diet, working on their fitness, and keeping up with the latest advances in sport science and sports medicine (National Senior Games Association 2010).

Clearly, older adults suffer in performance results when compared with younger competitors; research has shown that physical ability declines after age 50 at just about 1% per year up to age 80, when it begins to decline more rapidly (World of Sport Science 2009). One of the constant struggles for most senior athletic competitions is whether to admit only the best elite athletes or to encourage virtually all senior athletes to compete as part of the quest for a healthier lifestyle. Like athletics at all age levels, most senior competitions have set up a logical qualifying process for progressively higher levels of competition.

Participation Sport for Older Adults

All trends point toward an explosion in physical activity for people over age 50 as in the next few decades our population tilts toward older adults. Many people now consider 50 to be middle age and expect to live another 25 or more years. They want those years to be fun, vital, and active. Their health is a major concern, and slowing the aging process is a top priority.

Recreational sports offer the best opportunity for older people to have fun, enjoy activity, test their skills, socialize with others their age, and keep fit. Every community offers free or low-cost programs for its citizens, and now more of these programs are beginning to target adults age 50 and over.

Older adults are turning to activities and sports that they can participate in for a lifetime, like swimming, walking, tennis, golf, dance, biking, skiing, bowling, yoga, and weight training. Some team sports, such as softball, basketball, and volleyball, are also thriving, using rule adjustments and age groups to equalize the competition. Sports that require maximum strength, quick bursts of energy, or body contact and carry the risk of injury tend to decline in popularity as people age.

Most people 50 and older crave the excitement of playing sports, want to stay fit, and enjoy the mental challenge of trying to outsmart an opponent. They gain confidence and still get a "high" from competing or moving vigorously. They value youthfulness, and sports help them attain that goal.

They may cut down the frequency, duration, or intensity of play that were customary in their younger days but enjoy playing even more. Rules, rankings, and awards are less important to many who achieved previously in their life, and just getting to play is its own reward.

In St. Petersburg, Florida, the legendary Kids and Kubs softball league has been around for more than 75 years. The club's 56 members gather in North Shore Park to play a doubleheader every Tuesday, Thursday, and Saturday beginning at 10:30 a.m. They divide into two teams and go at it. The minimum age is 75!

Paul Good, who was 95 at the time, said, "It adds years to your life and life to your years!" Some years ago, the club reached a landmark when George Bakewell at age 101 took the field along with his son Elton, who was 75. Ethel Lehmann broke the gender barrier in 2005 by joining the group at age 75 (*St. Petersburg Times* 2005). The Kids and Kubs pay about $75 per year to play and look forward to exhibition games against local politicians, kids, or other older players; and they travel to other states to test themselves. The annual road trip in 2008 featured a much-anticipated sojourn to Hawaii, where they competed with a Japanese team. The uniqueness of the situation was that all players were of an age at which the military combat galvanized by the bombing of Pearl Harbor by the Japanese was still a potent memory. Kids and Kubs has sent teams

to senior world championships around the country, winning the over-80 division in 1998 and finishing third in the 1999 Senior World Softball Championships. Their next step is to establish feeder leagues in nearby communities like Tampa, Sarasota, and Bradenton to start training some "youngsters" who can eventually move up to their league.

Not to be outdone, the Freedom Spirit senior women's softball team out of Clearwater, Florida, has competed in national tournaments since 1997. The team has been notably successful at the World Senior Games, where they won three straight gold medals between 2001 and 2005 competing in the 70 and older category (Page 2009).

In the sport of tennis, the United States Tennis Association holds national championships for men 90 and over and for women 85 and over. Although some seniors still play singles, most have opted for doubles play; and matches are typically just two sets with a 10-point tiebreak played instead of a third set if necessary.

Golf similarly holds tournaments by age groups and even boasts a senior professional tour that showcases some excellent golf. One concession to age for many senior players is to seek out golf courses that are considerably shorter to compensate for their diminishing power.

You may be surprised that many older people who value being physically active are heading to the gym. In fact, this age group has swelled the membership rolls of fitness clubs in recent years, participating in activities such as yoga, strength training, treadmill running, and various other group exercise programs. Interestingly, nearly 30% of all core fitness participants in 2008 (core participants are those who participate 50 or more times per year) were 55 years of age or older. Nationally, 6 of the top 10 sports and fitness activities that grew in participation

POP CULTURE

Pickleball

Pickleball has been around for about 40 years but has recently undergone a rebirth because of its popularity in active adult living communities. It's a combination of tennis, ping-pong, and badminton played on a court the size of a badminton court. Using rules similar to tennis, a wooden paddle, and a perforated plastic ball (think Wiffle ball), the game is easy to learn yet attracts skilled athletes too. The hottest spot in the country is at The Villages, an active living adult community in central Florida that boasts over 80,000 residents, 150 outdoor pickleball courts, and more than 2,000 regular players. The USA Pickleball Association sets the rules, provides information, and even stages a national championship divided by age groups. What makes it so appealing? Well, it appeals to the baby boomers who want to be physically active and socially involved but look for sports that are not quite as hard on their bodies. The game requires less running than tennis or badminton but has similar skill requirements. For more information, check out pickleball at usapa.org.

were fitness-related activities, including step aerobics, high- and low-impact aerobics, elliptical training, dumbbell usage, and walking for fitness (Sporting Goods Manufacturers Association 2009a).

Issues for Special Populations in Sport

Although many opportunities for special populations have opened up in sport, opportunities for older athletes and for athletes who are mentally or physically disabled must expand to meet the needs of this rapidly growing population. As the demographics shift to an older population, the proportion of people in these categories will increase, as will demand for the following:

- Widespread acceptance of the need for sport for special populations
- Funding support from public and private sources
- Organizational support by all sport bodies including the national governing bodies
- Programs offered at the community level through parks and recreation departments
- Training for coaches, officials, and sport administrators who understand and want to work with the target population
- Equipment and rule modifications that allow special populations to play sports
- Sport opportunities that include all athlete populations when appropriate
- Media support for publicity and information

All people should have access to participation in recreational sport regardless of their age or disability. While most acknowledge this fact, conflict arises when programs do not exist or budgets do not permit expanded activities. In some sport activities, including special populations with the general population works well, but combining all populations is not always possible. Similarly, aging can prevent players from competing with younger players in any meaningful way. Public programs in schools and recreation departments should be required to provide access for older adults and athletes with disabilities.

Sport organizations at every level should seek ways to accommodate special populations. High school and collegiate sports have barely scratched the surface of possible inclusion. For example, numerous tennis players using wheelchairs have competed on their high school varsity teams and gone on to compete in college. In 2003, a wheelchair user from Oakville High School in St. Louis, Missouri, received his varsity letter after compiling a 15-to-3 win–loss record his senior year. The only concession to wheelchair players is that they may play the ball after two bounces rather than the customary one bounce. This simple change has allowed nondisabled and physically disabled players to compete with each other, a perfect example of a policy of inclusion (Woods 2004).

Community sport programs typically cannot accommodate special populations due to a lack of participants in the age group or ability level, and need to explore creative methods of including these populations in existing programs. More and more programs for older adults are springing up due to the demand and the availability of so many older players.

Educational conferences and programs of study need to be sponsored by organizations for the physically disabled and elderly, sport organizations such as governing bodies, and colleges and universities. Coaches, officials, and sport administrators sorely need training to work with special populations. Those who have sport experience are good candidates to fill these roles, but more people are needed who have a special interest in serving these populations. Family and friends should be recruited, trained, and put to work.

Equipment advances have made sport participation possible for many physically disabled or older athletes. Sport wheelchairs that are lightweight and mobile permit athletes in chairs to play a variety of sports including basketball, tennis, fencing, volleyball, and rugby. Lighter bats, golf clubs, and rackets allow easy manipulation by athletes. Artificial prostheses allow athletes without limbs to run, jump, and play sports in ways never imagined in the past. Aids for visual or hearing impairment allow athletes to track balls, run on their own, and play multiple sports.

Finally, the media must help educate the public on the needs of special populations. Television features on older athletes and those with disabilities are a powerful tool for garnering public support for sport access for all athletes. Movies can significantly affect the general population's understanding of and empathy for special populations. In 2004, the movie *Million Dollar Baby* highlighted the effects of quadriplegia. Other films that feature people with disabilities such as *Ray*, *My Left Foot*, *The Miracle Worker*, *Johnny Belinda*, *Children of a Lesser God*, *Rain Man*, *Elephant Man*, and *A Beautiful Mind* have

Advances in equipment have made it possible for athletes with disabilities to enjoy many sports that were once unavailable to them.

typically shown people who triumph over their disability. Through these films, people became and continue to become enlightened and inspired by the challenges and successes of a population many know little about.

Chapter Summary

We identified special populations as athletes who are physically disabled or mentally disabled or are older adults. All these groups face different challenges that affect sport participation.

National laws to protect these three special populations were passed relatively recently. The Americans with Disabilities Act in 1990 spurred understanding of the need for accommodating people with special needs.

Physically disabled athletes may compete nationally and internationally under the supervision of the Paralympic Games. Much like the Olympic Games, the Paralympics are contested every four years and offer both winter and summer events. Medals are awarded in 21 sports, and more than 5,000 athletes compete in each Paralympic Games.

Mentally disabled athletes may compete through the Special Olympics, which is typically held in the United States and hosts state, national, and worldwide competition. More than 1.7 million athletes are involved in the Special Olympics movement, and that number is expected to continue to grow worldwide.

Older athletes, often referred to as **masters** athletes, also compete worldwide. Age groups up to and including athletes 90 years old ensure equitable competition in various sports that are staged by the National Senior Games Association in the United States. The achievements of these older athletes are becoming increasingly inspirational to an aging population looking for challenges in their later years.

Participation sports for older athletes or athletes with disabilities are not as well organized as performance sports but nevertheless are offered throughout the United States. Typically, schools, recreation departments, or other local sport organizations sponsor these participation sports. The emphasis is on healthy physical activity to enhance quality of life. Efforts to include people with special needs in mainstream sport programs are growing and gaining acceptance.

Key issues need to be addressed to ensure continued progress in sports for special populations. Among these are consistent funding; education of coaches, officials, and sport administrators; publicity from the media; and support from sport organizations at every level.

Religion and Sport

Student Outcomes

After reading this chapter, you will know the following:

- How religion has affected sport throughout history
- Interrelationships between sport and religion
- How athletes use religion in sport
- How institutions and organizations use both religion and sport
- How coaches and sport organizers use religion
- Conflicts between religion and sport

It's near the end of a high school basketball game with the score tied at 55-55 when a foul is called. As the player who suffered the foul steps up to the free throw line, he quickly makes the sign of the cross at his chest. Do you wonder what is going through his mind at that point? Why make the sign of the cross? Is he imploring divine intervention to ensure that his shot goes in the basket? Or is he simply performing a habit he has seen other players exhibit and developed on his own as part of his ritual preparation for every foul shot? Do you think that God notices his symbolic act and takes note? Why do players in many sports invoke religion at critical points in athletic competition? Let's take a look at the ties between religion and sport, real and perhaps imagined.

Religion is the belief in a god or supernatural force that influences human life. Humans in every society on record have created belief systems about the supernatural. Such beliefs are essential to the core structure of a society and help humans understand their purpose for living and how they should spend their days, treat others, and deal with death and the afterlife.

Religion plays a central role in helping people find purpose and meaning in life, in allaying fears of the unknown, and in providing guidelines for interacting with others. It is the basis for a moral code that keeps society functioning and respectful of all persons. Religious customs can bind people together through common acts and unite them in spirit.

Religion and sport share a common trait in that both have been labeled as an "opiate of the masses" (Hoffman 1992). In the 1800s, Karl Marx wrote in *The Communist Manifesto* that religion was an opiate used by governments to distract people from their miserable life and instead focus them on an afterlife. Similarly, people have accused political leaders of encouraging sport participation and spectatorship to distract citizens from economic or political concerns (see chapter 16).

At first blush, sport and religion may seem unrelated. But throughout history people have often linked the two and blended them into their belief systems. At times, organized religion has been at odds with sport and has viewed games as not worthy of humankind. The belief was that people live on earth to develop their spiritual side, and pursuing leisure through sport simply detracts from that mission.

One of the main reasons the Americas were explored and settled was the possibility of religious freedom. Although there have been many athletes in many sports who follow religions other than Christianity, no religion has dominated American sport as the Christian faith has. Thus, much of the information in this chapter will focus on Christianity, although there are sections dealing specifically with the Jewish and Muslim faiths. Those of the Jewish faith made up 1.2% of the population in 2008 while Muslims were .6%.

An American Religious Identification Survey (ARIS) was completed in 2008 through the collection of information by telephone interviews with 54,461 people. The results of the survey revealed that the American population self-identifies itself as primarily Christian, although America is continuing a trend toward becoming less Christian due primarily to the increase in numbers of people who now classify themselves as "Nones"—those who have no stated religious preference, atheists, and agnostics. Those categorized as "Nones" increased their percentage of the population from 8.2% in 1990 to 14.1% in 2001 and to 15% in 2008.

In 1990, 86% of Americans identified themselves as Christians, but by 2008 that percentage had fallen to 76%. The historic mainline churches and denominations have suffered the steepest declines, while nondenominational Christian churches have been trending upward. Interestingly, 38% of American adults considered themselves "Born Again or Evangelical Christians" in 2008. Table 15.1 shows a comparison for the years 1990, 2001, and 2008 of religious identification of the U.S. adult population.

In today's sport world, we may see athletes praying together before or after contests, making the sign of the cross before attempting a foul shot in basketball, crediting God for a victory, or quoting Scripture to justify their pursuit of excellence in sport. In the last century, organized religious leaders gradually embraced sport as another avenue to reach the masses and influence their behavior toward a worthy, godly existence. That change in philosophy gave rise to the interrelationship between religion and sport that exists today. This chapter looks at the interplay between religion and sport, the use of sport within religion, and the use of religion within sport.

Religion and Sport in History

The ancient Greeks mingled religion with athletics. Demonstrations of athletic prowess were a major part of their religious festivals. The Greeks portrayed their gods as perfect physical specimens who took pleasure in the pursuit of physical excellence. They held the Olympic Games and their athletic contests to honor Zeus, the king of the gods.

The Olympic Games were suspended by the Roman emperor Theodosius I, who as a Christian wanted to stamp out paganism. The Olympic Games in those days were a series of pagan rituals that featured many footraces along with some "sports" that were violent and life threatening. Chariot races in which horses and drivers risked life and limb were favorites. Also popular was the *pankration*, a no-holds-barred combat sport that melded elements of boxing, wrestling, and street fighting (Gertz 2004).

Often animal sacrifices were also a part of the pagan religious festivals.

The early Christians did not think that sport was evil, as evidenced by the apostle Paul, who wrote approvingly of physical activity. But the history of paganism surrounding sport events caused the early church to separate itself from the sports played by the pagan masses. Some church leaders felt that the body was inherently evil and should be subordinate to the spirit. Therefore time spent in exercising the body took away from time that should be devoted to the spirit.

With the Protestant Reformation in the early 16th century, the negative attitude of the church toward the body might have had a chance to wane. However, the Puritanical interpretation of religion that was eventually transported to America embraced a new asceticism that pushed the physical side even farther into the background. The Puritans believed that the only purpose for the body was to perform the physical labor necessary for survival. They thought that no time should be spent in leisure pursuits, and they viewed pursuits that involved gambling, that harmed animals as in cockfighting, or that pleased the participants as evil (Eitzen and Sage 2002).

TABLE 15.1 Religious Self-Identification of U.S. Adults

	1990		2001		2008	
	No. of people	%	No. of people	%	No. of people	%
Catholic	46,004,000	26.2	50,873,000	24.5	57,199,000	25.1
Other Christian	105,221,000	60.0	108,641,000	52.2	116,203,000	50.9
Total Christian	151,225,000	86.2	159,514,000	76.7	173,402,000	76.0
Other religions	5,853,000	3.3	7,740,000	3.7	8,796,000	3.9
Nones	14,331,000	8.2	29,481,000	14.2	34,169,000	15.0
DK/refused to answer	4,031,000	2.3	11,246,000	5.4	11,815,000	5.2
Total	175,440,000	100	207,983,000	100	228,182,000	100

Data from Kosmin and Keysar 2009.

ACTIVITY TIME-OUT

Effect of Muslim Religion on Sport

After Christianity, the Muslim religion is second in the world in popularity. Do some investigation of how sport or sport participation is affected in those countries where the Muslim population is in the majority. You might want to seek information on how it affects youth sports, school sports, elite competition in world events including the Olympic Games, participation by women and girls, and the popularity of professional sports. In Muslim countries, are sports conducted totally independently of the predominant religious view or are they closely intertwined?

By the mid-1850s, people in the United States began to change their attitude toward sport. As the population shifted from rural to urban and production shifted from manual labor to the industrial age, physical well-being became a concern. Led by physicians and, surprisingly, by ministers, the concept of a sound, healthy body through physical activity once again gained favor. Leading universities hired medical doctors to promote the health of their students, and those doctors in turn founded departments of physical education. Influential Christian men labeled *muscular Christians* extolled physical fitness as a virtue that fit well with godly behavior as a means of glorifying God by taking care of the body. The founding of the Young Men's Christian Association near the end of the century capitalized on the emerging acceptance of the positive link between body and spirit.

Although churches still battled to keep the Sabbath (Sunday) as a holy day of rest, church leaders began to accept and even promote sport as long as it did not interfere with developing the spiritual side of people. The lone holdout to this trend was the Congregational Church in New England, which in 1957 became the United Church of Christ; this church viewed sport and games as inconsistent with developing the soul.

In the 20th century, the bond between sport and religion expanded in the United States in ways never envisioned by the founding fathers. They became two institutions that often cooperated to promote a better life for their constituencies. Churches sponsored sports, and many sports promoted churches. Some people have even declared that sports are a religion, although that view is hard to substantiate.

Christian Influence on Sport

Churches realized that they could attract people to their doors by offering social occasions that involved sports. They constructed gymnasiums, sponsored basketball or softball teams, provided playing fields, and encouraged people to come to play sports and stay for Sunday services. The Catholic Church founded the Catholic Youth Organization (CYO) to organize sport leagues for young people. Protestant groups supported the Young Men's Christian Association (YMCA) and the Young Women's Christian Association (YWCA). Housed in gymnasiums around the country, Ys became a powerful force in providing organized sport for youth while espousing a broader purpose of developing their minds and spirits. The famous triangle that shows mind, body, and spirit was the hallmark of the Y movement. The YMCA even established what is now Springfield College in Springfield, Massachusetts, to train its instructors. For many years, Springfield College was the preeminent institution for studying physical education and sport.

A major contribution to American sport emanated from Springfield and the YMCA when in 1891, Canadian James Naismith invented basketball, a game that became the most-played sport in America and is now taking off worldwide. Just a few years later, William Morgan invented volleyball at the YMCA in Holyoke, Massachusetts, just a few miles away from Springfield. Thus, two popular team sports indigenous to the United States are products of the YMCA.

POP CULTURE

A Brand-New Day for YMCA

For the first time in 43 years, the YMCA has changed its brand with a new logo and a new name. From now on, YMCAs will be known simply as the "Y." They believe that the new look and name better reflect the vibrancy and diversity of today's organization. The YMCA was founded more than 160 years ago in England on Christian principles that included loving your neighbor with kindness, goodness, and gentleness. Today's focus, according to its press release on the name change, is on three key areas: youth development, healthy living, and social responsibility. Some critics fear that the name change is just another example of secularization of what was once thought of as a religious organization.

It's true that lots of folks already refer to the organizations as the "Y" because it is quicker and easier. But one group that is sorely disappointed in the name change is the Village People, the disco singing icons from the 1970s who have sold over 15 million copies around the world of their famous song, "YMCA." They vow to keep performing the song along with every other band that plays at weddings, Bar Mitzvahs, and ball games (YMCA 2010; Girard 2010).

The sport world welcomed the backing of religion since it promised to spread access to sport for the average citizen. Athletes also seized upon religion as a way of addressing their fears in the face of competition. While some athletes are simply superstitious, others use their religious beliefs to keep them safe, bring them luck, and calm their nerves. Many athletes admit to praying before important contests and to achieving focus through prayer.

Athletes also use religion to ascribe a deeper sense of purpose to their sport participation. Believing that it is God's will to develop your talent to glorify Him is a powerful motivator. Some athletes believe that God has a plan for their life and that to become a top athlete is fulfilling that plan. Others justify their consuming passion for sport by using their sport success to gain the attention of fans and witness their faith in God.

Christian athletes often quote Scripture to justify their complete dedication to sport and hard work as a way of glorifying God. A favorite verse some athletes use from I Corinthians 9:24: "Surely you know that in a race all the runners take part in it, but only one of them wins the prize. Run, then, in such a way as to win the prize." Another favorite is found in I Timothy 4:7-8: "I have fought a good fight, I have finished my course, I have kept the faith" (Deford 1976, pp. 92-99).

Coaches and owners of sport teams often promote the link between sport and religion because it reinforces a code of conduct that they prefer for their athletes. The sport pages are full of tales of professional athletes involving violence, drugs, cheating, promiscuity, and alcohol abuse. In many cases, the athletes in these stories lack a strong moral code or a personal belief in religion that might have prevented dubious choices. Rehabilitation is often linked to an acceptance of a new moral code based on religious beliefs and reinforced by teammates and friends who are fellow believers (Coakley 2004).

Protestantism has always preached an absolute belief in the value of hard work, self-discipline, and striving for success. Indeed, in the United States, those characteristics are widely considered to be all-American and the very foundation of the nation.

Athletic coaches in America endorse those values beyond all others. Even talented athletes cannot reach their potential without at least a nodding acquaintance with hard work and self-discipline. The lessons learned on the playing field and extolled in the sanctuaries of churches are often identical: Work hard, play hard, and do your best to win every day!

According to Overman (1997), traditional Catholic doctrine emphasized that the body was a "temple of the Holy Spirit" that should be kept pure rather than developed through physical activity. Protestants, on the other hand, trumpeted competition as an opportunity for people to prove their value through achievement and become the best they could be. In more recent times, both Catholicism and Protestantism have fully embraced sport as a special way of glorifying God by developing physical and competitive skill.

The belief systems of Protestantism, sport, and to some extent Catholicism are so closely intertwined that it is not surprising they have found a mutual synergy. They each reinforce the value system of the others and together help young people organize their lives and social system according to the code of church and sport. Both religion and sport often resist social change and seek to maintain the status quo that benefits both institutions.

Sport and Religions Other Than Christianity

Worldwide, religious faiths are distributed among Christianity (33%), Islam (21%), Hinduism (14%), and many others (Adherents 2005). Each religion directly affects the attitudes of its believers toward physical activity, sport, and competition and in many cases sets different standards for males and females. The result is that sport within each culture may be promoted or severely restricted according to the religious teachings.

Let's look at Judaism and Islam, which have significantly influenced North America as well as other parts of the world.

Judaism

Judaism has had a prominent role in the United States since its religious beliefs are generally consistent with a Judeo–Christian heritage. The Old Testament recounts the history of the Hebrew people, and Jesus Christ of the New Testament was a Jew. The early Christians were essentially Jews, and the religion that developed and expanded around the world had its roots in Judaism.

Jews have played a somewhat obscure role in sport, probably because they make up a relatively small proportion of the U.S. population. Yet they have affected American sport through enviable success in boxing. Many Jewish athletes have also been celebrated for their achievements in the Maccabiah Games, a unique event similar to

Hank Greenberg attracted national attention in 1934 when he refused to play baseball on Yom Kippur, the Jewish day of atonement, even though the Detroit Tigers were in the middle of a pennant race. He is considered by many to be the first Jewish baseball star.

for their teams, these principled men chose to put their beliefs before their livelihood.

Other notable Jewish athletes have included Sid Luckman, quarterback for the Chicago Bears, and Red Auerbach, a coaching legend who led the Boston Celtics when they dominated the National Basketball Association (NBA). Perhaps the most amazing achievement by any Olympic athlete was the performance by Mark Spitz, who won seven gold medals in swimming in the 1972 Olympic Games. Other Olympic champions who were Jewish include Kerri Strug, a gymnast who won a gold medal in the 1996 Atlanta Games, and Sarah Hughes, a gold medalist in figure skating at the 2002 Winter Games. Professional tennis players who left their mark were Brad Gilbert and Aaron Krickstein, as well as Eddie Dibbs and Harold Solomon, who were dubbed the "bagel twins" (Slater 2003).

The first half of the 20th century was blessed with the golden age of sport, particularly in the 1920s and 1930s. During that time, Jewish men dominated American boxing in virtually every weight class except heavyweight. Jews won more than 29 world boxing titles during that time. The most famous of these boxers were Benny Leonard and Barney Ross, who stood out in the 1930s. It may seem surprising that Jewish men pursued boxing, but they were no different from other poor immigrants in the United States who found hope through boxing. Other ethnic groups who dominated boxing at one time include the Irish and Polish, and recent champion boxers have been Puerto Rican and African American.

Jewish basketball players also flourished in inner-city basketball long before African Americans began to dominate it. During the 1940s, Jewish boys who were the sons of immigrants played street basketball in cities like New York and Chicago and laid the groundwork for the NBA. The first basket scored in the Basketball Association of America, the forerunner of the NBA, was credited to Ossie Schectman of the New York Knickerbockers in 1946.

Along with Schectman, Sonny Hertzberg, David Stern, and Red Auerbach were sources for *The First Basket*, a documentary film that explores the origin of inner-city basketball, the role of basketball in the lives of young immigrants seeking to become Americans, and the gradual decline of Jews in professional basketball through the early 1950s.

Young Jewish men in the 1940s honed their skills in synagogues and Young Men's Hebrew Associations (YMHAs) and throughout the Borscht Belt. Colleges in the cities were stocked with Jewish players, and at one time St. John's University in

the Olympics but open only to participants from a Jewish background.

Perhaps the most well-known Jewish athletes in American sport have been Hank Greenberg, a slugger for the Detroit Tigers in the 1940s, and Sandy Koufax, Hall of Fame pitcher for the Brooklyn/Los Angeles Dodgers. Shawn Green of the Los Angeles Dodgers is the most prominent Jewish baseball player since Koufax. He was number two in salary, behind only Alex Rodriguez of the New York Yankees. All of these athletes were challenged by fans and the media for their decisions not to play baseball on Yom Kippur, the holiest day of the year for Jews and a day when they atone for their sins. In spite of the pressure to play in the World Series or play-offs

New York had a team starting five Jews. Other notable Jews who made their mark in basketball were coach Larry Brown, Washington Wizards owner Abe Poling, and announcers Howard Cosell and Marv Albert (*The First Basket* 2008).

After the 1950s, as more Jewish families stabilized their economic base by establishing businesses and working in crafts, they encouraged their children, both male and female, to pursue their education to prepare for careers that were longer lasting and more socially acceptable.

Islam

Islam is second only to Christianity in world popularity and has been growing rapidly in the United States as more immigrants arrive from countries where Islam is the primary religion and as more African Americans are drawn to Islam. Muslims believe that every action they take must be to glorify Allah (God). Male Muslims have participated in sport for centuries and have had a history of success particularly in soccer and basketball. Females in Muslim cultures have largely been excluded from sport participation, primarily due to restrictions on their dress.

Perhaps one of the most well-known Muslim athletes was Muhammad Ali. Ali was recognized as the world's greatest boxer after compiling a professional career record of 56 wins, 37 by knockout, and only 5 losses. But he was renowned throughout the world for his religious beliefs and political activism. Born as Cassius Marcellus Clay Jr., he carried that name as he won an Olympic gold medal in Rome in 1960 but soon converted to the Nation of Islam and adopted his new name. He fought racism, the military draft, and war and spoke eloquently and passionately about social injustices that were not compatible with his religious beliefs. During the Vietnam war, Ali refused the draft into the army and suffered the wrath of the public as cowardly and un-American. He was stripped of his boxing championship and sentenced to five years in prison, a sentence that was overturned three years later by the U.S. Supreme Court. Eventually, Ali rejected the teaching of the nation of Islam and converted to Sunni Islam. A victim of Parkinson's disease in later life and living with obvious tremors of his limbs, he ignored the disease and became a symbol for many American sport fans, honored for his sport success and fidelity to his personal religious beliefs (Gale Group 1999).

The Islam religion makes no prohibition against sport participation. Historically, sports and games were part of the expected teachings of parents to children. Muslims have always encouraged youth to run, jump, and engage in basic physical activities. Swimming and using weapons have long been a part of Muslim tradition. However, in conservative Muslim countries, sports for women have largely been ignored; and in Saudi Arabia, women and girls are prohibited from playing sports.

In some Muslim sects, a female may not expose any skin in mixed company. Thus the clothing they wear limits or at least makes sport participation very uncomfortable. The trials of a young Muslim, Andrea Armstrong, in playing on the varsity basketball team for the University of South Florida were covered in the *St. Petersburg Times*, a daily newspaper. She sought permission from the National Collegiate Athletic Association (NCAA) to waive the uniform requirements so that she could play with a hijab (head scarf), long pants, and a long-sleeved shirt (along with her uniform) to conform to the tradition of her Muslim sect. Before the NCAA ruled on the matter, she quit the team due to the negative publicity and scorn she was exposed to when her request became public. The university and the team coach publicly supported her choice and right to apply for the clothing waiver, but some in the community and the American public clouded the issue with racist comments and derisive actions, including hate e-mails and negative comments on talk radio. Her case is not unusual for Muslim women who want to play sports in countries around the world, and keeping sport open to everyone in the United States may require accommodating women such as Armstrong (Auman 2004; Matus 2004).

Some summer sport camps for Muslim girls such as the one at Westridge School for Girls in Pasadena have sprung up in the United States. In these camps Muslim girls are free to wear what they like and learn to play all types of sports. They decide whether or not to wear a hijab. The reason these camps work so well for Muslims is that they exclude men and boys. As long as no men are around, girls can dress normally for sport (Issa 2001).

Muslim women have also made their mark on the Olympic Games. Algerian Hassiba Boulmerka was the gold medalist in the 1,500 meters at the Barcelona Games. But Muslim women have been few and far between in the sport world due to the restrictive dress code of their religion. It is estimated that more than 500 million Muslim women around the globe are essentially banned from sport participation. People attempting to change the culture and practices in conservative Islamic countries have been careful, realizing that by winning a few battles for women's rights, they may lose the larger

Female Muslim athletes are slowly starting to enter the international sport world. In 1992, Hassiba Boulmerka of Algeria won an Olympic gold medal in the 1,500 m.

war. Still, change may come slowly as courageous women and men within Muslim cultures agree to allow more choices for women in all areas of society.

Use of Religion in Sport by Athletes

Now that we've examined the major religions that influence sport in North America, we can take a closer look at how athletes balance religion and sport. Athletes in competitive sport use religion in many ways:

- To justify their commitment to high-performance competitive sport
- To reduce pressure and uncertainty
- To enhance bonds with teammates
- To guide moral decisions

Judeo–Christian teachings in recent centuries have emphasized the obligation of individuals to fully develop their talent to "glorify God." Discipline, sacrifice, intense training, and commitment to high performance are religious principles that apply well to sport competition. Personal achievement is something to be valued and encouraged, and the intense dedication to winning is honorable and pleasing to God. This is not dissimilar to the belief that in a capitalistic society, individual achievement is a mark of success and hard work and looked upon favorably by God.

Athletes use their religious beliefs to reduce the pressure they feel in competition. Some adopt the point of view that the outcome is in God's hands and so they are free to relax and focus on their own execution. Others pray before or during a contest to ask for divine guidance during play. Some also might ask specifically for a favorable outcome (Eitzen and

Sage 2002). Soccer players use religious rituals such as touching a crucifix or making the sign of the cross before attempting a penalty kick. Football players sometimes point to the sky to acknowledge their gratitude to God when they score a touchdown, or kneel in humble appreciation.

Prayer is a powerful practice in which believers communicate with their god. The three major religions, Christianity, Judaism, and Islam, endorse prayer as a central practice of their faith. In recent years, sport psychologists have explored the implications of working with athletes who believe in prayer. Athletes who do believe in prayer should be encouraged to use prayer to help deal with the pressure, uncertainty, and depression that can arise from competitive sport. There is evidence that sport psychologists would be wise to recommend the use of prayer to those who are comfortable with it. Traditionally, prayer has been used to confess sins, express adoration, petition for needs, intercede for others, and offer thanksgiving. In sport, athletes tend to use prayer for three purposes (Watson and Czech 2005):

- To cope with uncertainty and anxiety
- To put life and sport into a proper perspective
- To provide meaning to sport participation

Many athletes use religious beliefs to strengthen their bonds with their teammates. When people share their personal beliefs and discuss weighty matters like the meaning of life, they take certain risks with each other and often develop strong trust and loyalty. Members of a team who share common religious beliefs may attend study groups and religious services together, pray together, and together support youth organizations or charities that have religious affiliations. Each of these activities enhances their relationships with each other, and they hold one another accountable for actions both off and on the field.

All athletes face moral decisions in life and encounter many of these in sport. When young, people are taught to follow the rules and often do so unquestioningly. But as they grow, they examine the meaning behind moral decisions, assess what is generally acceptable in society, and often use religious teachings as their guide. Questions about cheating, breaking the law, abusing drugs, intentionally harming an opponent, or behaving after winning or losing can all be guided by religious teachings. Many athletes use the popular phrase "What would Jesus do?" for guidance in everyday decisions made on and off the athletic field.

Use of Sport by Athletes to Promote Religious Beliefs

A popular religious justification for striving so hard to win is that fame through sport performance enlarges an athlete's sphere of influence. Athletes then have the opportunity to share their religious beliefs and influence people to follow their religious path. Thus, winning glorifies God and spreads His message. Athletes who are more famous automatically command a large audience that is more than impressed when hearing how the athletes live their lives. Athletes who become role models can powerfully influence the behavior of young athletes as they struggle with growing up and making decisions in sport and life.

Athletes who come from a fundamental or evangelical religious orientation use the term *witness for Christ* to describe one of their primary responsibilities as a born-again Christian. They do not hesitate to share the specifics of their personal commitment to Christ, what that commitment means in their lives, and how important that commitment should be in others' lives. They can be powerful recruiters for Christian organizations, schools, and churches where youth can join with others committed to following their faith.

Many athletes do much more than use words to promote their beliefs. Professional athletes who want to give back to their sport, community, or society often donate money to worthwhile causes or establish a charity in their name. Some choose charities that helped them or a loved one in a time of trouble. Others choose charities that help impoverished neighborhoods where they grew up. Of course, charitable organizations that promote certain religious beliefs are attractive to athletes who subscribe to the principles of the organization.

Some athletes are also generous with their time, especially in the off-season. They talk to fans, sign autographs, and make personal appearances to promote causes they believe in, often for no remuneration. Summer camps staged by Christian organizations such as the Fellowship of Christian Athletes (FCA) are natural opportunities for athletes to contribute to the overall development of young athletes and share their faith. Specialized sport camps can also teach skills and strategy, but often the most enduring lessons come from famous athletes sharing their beliefs with aspiring youngsters.

IN THE ARENA WITH . . .

Tim Tebow

Tim Tebow was clearly one of the most successful and celebrated football players in collegiate history. His leadership, ruthless running style, and targeted passing led his Florida Gators to two national championships before his senior year, and they challenged again for the top spot in 2009, eventually finishing third in the final polls. Tebow won the 2007 Heisman Trophy, emblematic of the best collegiate football player, when he was only a sophomore. His overall record as a starting quarterback at Florida was 35 wins to 6 losses.

While in college, one of his trademarks was a Bible verse set in the eye black he wore on game day. (After Tebow graduated, the NCAA banned the display of any type of writing on eye black to avoid having to rule on the appropriateness of any words that players might choose to display.) Most of his interviews with the media included some reference to his deep religious beliefs and dedication to God. His off-seasons were spent speaking to people in prisons and doing missionary work in Asia.

Yet Tim has his critics. His evangelical conservative beliefs, marked by a strong commitment to sharing his personal faith as the "one true way" to salvation, rub many Americans the wrong way. In fact, 65% of Americans believe that many religions can lead to eternal life and in recent years have been trending toward a more ecumenical view of religion. Criticism comes from those who contend that espousing only one narrow view of religion by definition becomes critical of all other belief systems.

There is no question about Tebow's football ability, toughness, leadership qualities, or his off-the-field demeanor. The question is whether he should use his high-profile image within the sport world to promote his personal religious beliefs. What do you think?

Celebrity athletes may use their religious beliefs to guide their choices of commercial products to endorse. Many religiously conservative athletes are uncomfortable endorsing products such as beer or balk at appearing in a commercial that includes sexual innuendo or is offensive to ethnic groups, races, or gender.

Use of Religion by Coaches, Organizations, and Owners

Some athletic coaches use religion as social construct to unify their team. As pointed out in the previous section, when athletes share a belief system, this pulls the team together and the athletes will do anything to avoid letting down their teammates. Like soldiers in warfare who count on each other for support, athletes have to know they can count on each other as they enter the athletic arena for battle.

Over the years, some coaches have invited informal team chaplains to lead their team in prayer before and after games. Typically, the chaplains pray for God to bless the contest by preventing serious injuries and allowing athletes to perform at the high level that reflects their athletic talents. These prayers emotionally affect team members who are religious and consider prayer an important part of their life. These athletes do not find prayer unusual since they pray regularly in private, in church, and in group Bible studies. More than likely they also prayed more than once as a former student, asking God to help them perform well on their exams.

Athletes are much more likely to use prayer in sport if they also use prayer in their daily lives. Coaches at private church-sponsored schools are also much more likely to use prayer before games than are coaches at public schools. Students enrolling at a secondary school or college that is church related also expect prayer to be part of the school culture, whereas students in public school do not.

Coaches also know that young athletes are susceptible to temptations in their lives. Some coaches establish priorities for their athletes that place God first, family second, academics third, and commitment to teammates fourth. This guideline helps the coach influence the decisions of young athletes to keep them out of trouble. Romantic attachments and partying fall farther down the priority list, and their lower priority reduces the possibilities for poor choices.

Most coaches consider themselves role models and molders of talent in the persons they coach. They believe that if their athletes adopt a system of values centered on spirituality, work ethic, respect for family, and academic learning, they will have performed a terrific service for the young athletes. For many coaches, teaching sport skills and strategies is their least important role.

The danger of coaches advancing a particular brand of religion or Christianity with players is that it excludes those who may not choose to follow that path. Religion may promote cliques of players who rally around a set of beliefs that can isolate nonbelievers and damage a team's social fabric and unity. In fact, just such a situation was a focus of a religious discrimination lawsuit filed in New Mexico in 2006 against a football coach who labeled two Muslim players as "troublemakers" and kicked them off the team. The case was settled out of court, and the players eventually transferred to another school.

Organizers of professional sport leagues have also encouraged prayer breakfasts and Bible studies between opponents in the off-season or before or after games. The sight of a couple of dozen NFL players kneeling in prayer on the field after a football game during which they tried to annihilate each other is at once thrilling and confusing. The players point out that in the larger game of life they are all brothers striving to do God's will and that they show respect for God, the game, and their opponents by praying together.

Organizers of the Olympic Games have also provided opportunities for athletes to gather together to share their beliefs and prepare for the competition. Young men and women from a variety of backgrounds and sports find that they share a common belief in spirituality and realize that they face similar temptations, trials, and uncertainties. While not endorsed by the Olympic organizers themselves, many religious organizations capitalize on the Games by hosting events such as prayer breakfasts featuring well-known speakers and former athletes; Bible studies; and prayer groups for interested athletes, spectators, and local citizens.

An example of religious outreach at the Olympic Games is Quest Australia More Than Gold, a cooperative effort of denominational and parachurch ministries. Leading up to the 2000 Games in Sydney, their mission was to capitalize on the athletic spectacle to "reach and teach people about Jesus Christ" during the Olympic and Paralympic Games. They conducted youth sport clinics, staged 10 major evangelistic events during the Games, sponsored one citywide festival of believers, trained a mission team, and presented the gospel through creative arts at 500 performances around Sydney (*Quest* 2006).

Plans call for a Christian outreach ministry at the London 2012 Olympic Games. Lay Witnesses for Christ International (LWFCI), led by founder Dr. Sam Mings, has been a strong presence at Olympic Games, from those in Los Angeles in 1984 through Beijing in 2008. With their "Evening With the Stars" led by former Olympian Carl Lewis as a highlight, the LWFCI hopes to attract all Christian Olympians for an evening of inspiration and prayer (*Christianity Today* 2008).

Many athletic contests begin with a ceremony to mark the significance of the occasion. In the United States, the two most common inclusions to the opening ceremony are the national anthem and an invocation. In recent years, praying at public events sponsored by schools has been questioned as to its fairness to people who do not practice Christianity. Some who offer the prayers speak to the wide range of beliefs of the audience, while others offend some listeners with entreaties to "Jesus Christ, Our Savior" or similar language.

In June of 2000, the U.S. Supreme Court ruled that public schools cannot constitutionally organize school prayers at regular sporting events. At the same time, the court did reaffirm the right of players or fans to pray by themselves at such events and for students to pray together on their own accord. Separation of church and state only prohibits school officials from organizing prayer at regular school functions. For many Americans, this is a departure from a long-standing tradition of public prayer offered at official public functions of all kinds, including sport events (*Santa Fe Independent School District vs. Doe*, U.S. Supreme Court 2000).

Organizers of Minor League and some Major League Baseball teams, particularly those located in the Bible Belt, use Faith Nights to attract spectators to their games. Local churches encourage their members to attend the games, which may feature Christian singers, players who share their testimonies, and faith trivia quizzes for prizes. Sport promoters are holding dozens of Faith Nights to attract record attendance. Faith Nights have been a marketing success for Minor League Baseball teams struggling to entice fans. Game attendance is also promoted by religious organizations such as Athletes in Action and the Fellowship of Christian Athletes and is heartily endorsed by parents and community leaders. To avoid offending spectators who do not care to participate in Faith Nights, the religious events are scheduled before the game, perhaps in the parking lot. Cities involved include

ACTIVITY TIME-OUT

Should We Mix Sport With Religion?

By now, you have a pretty clear picture that sport and religion have a fairly tight relationship at almost every level of competition, from high school to the Olympic and the professional levels. On balance, do you think this is a healthy thing for sport? Consider, for example, that approximately 38% of Americans categorize themselves as evangelical Christians and that nearly all the organizations, chaplains, and sport leaders who seek to bring sport and religion closer together are of that same belief. But what about the other 62% of Americans who do not share those beliefs? Encouraging athletes with identical or similar views on religion may build team cohesiveness, but it also could drive a wedge between players who are believers and those who have a different view. Would it be appropriate for a Muslim, Jew, or Mormon to also express his faith publicly given the public stage of sports? Make a case for your position that sport should or should not be closely intertwined with religious beliefs.

Hagerstown, Maryland; Johnson City, Tennessee; Columbus, Georgia; Birmingham, Alabama; Nashville, Tennessee; Mobile, Alabama; Tulsa, Oklahoma; and Portland, Oregon. Who would have thought that giving away bobble-head dolls of Moses, Noah, and Samson could cause such a stir by attracting fans to baseball games (Cherner 2005)?

Organizations Using Sport to Promote Religion

Numerous Christian organizations have flourished in the United States over the past 50 years by combining religious teaching and sport. Perhaps the oldest and largest of these organizations that intertwine religion and sport is the FCA, established in 1954. It is still the largest interdenominational, college- and school-based Christian sport organization in the world. From its modest beginnings when founded by Don McClanen, Paul Benedum, Branch Rickey, and other Pittsburgh businessmen, in 2008 FCA reached more than 356,250 people on 7,125 campuses and worked with more than 46,000 coaches and athletes across the globe (Fellowship of Christian Athletes 2008).

The FCA was originally aimed at the major sports, and among the charter members were football great Otto Graham and baseball pitcher Carl Erskine. The FCA publishes a monthly magazine, *The Christian Athlete*, and offers study guides, videos, and materials for Bible study and huddle meetings. The organization even has commercial sponsors, which currently include Chick-fil-A, Schutt Sports, and Krystal.

The mission of FCA (2008) is "[t]o present to athletes and coaches and all whom they influence the challenge and adventure of receiving Jesus Christ as Savior and Lord, serving Him in their relationships and in the fellowship of the church."

The basic organizational unit of FCA is the local huddle, which can be established at a high school, at a college, or in a community. Team members meet regularly in the huddle to study the Bible, follow devotional guides, or discuss their issues of Christian faith or sport. Most often, the huddle advisers are coaches who assist student leaders. Local huddles distribute opportunities through FCA such as the widely held summer camps. At the camps, famous athletes dedicate their time to teach sport skills, talk about their faith, and encourage young athletes to follow the precepts of FCA: integrity, serving, teamwork, and excellence.

Tom Landry, famous coach of the Dallas Cowboys, and one of his quarterbacks, Roger Staubach, were both key figures in the FCA and other organizations promoting sport and religion. They carried impeccable sport credentials as "winners" and used that platform to testify to the importance of their faith in the "game of life." The personal dedication of these men and hundreds of others throughout the years has influenced hundreds of thousands of young people. No young person can help but be impressed by a famous athlete she looks upon as a hero.

Another Christian sport organization is Athletes in Action (AIA), a branch of Campus Crusade for Christ. Athletes in Action is a group of former college athletes who travel the country playing exhibition games against amateur teams including collegiate teams, especially early in the season.

Athletes in Action has secured approval from the NCAA to compete against NCAA members, and typically the players take advantage of the halftime and postgame to talk about their faith.

Sport missionaries like those from AIA generally try to convince young people to "follow the right path." They typically present a fundamental view of religion and rarely speak out on social issues such as discrimination against women or minorities, drug abuse, cheating, and violence in sport. They've been labeled "jocks for Jesus" or "the God squad" and tend to present God as desiring to become the master coach of the lives of all people who will let Him. Positive stories about good things that happen to Christian athletes, finding faith, and a higher reward tend to be their themes no matter the audience (Deford 1976).

There is also Pro Athletes Outreach (PAO), which sends professional athletes to meetings, camps, and events held by other organizations. At the events, pro athletes talk about sport and their faith and what faith means to everyday life.

Once limited to white, middle-class boys, these organizations have gradually included girls and some racial minorities. They tend to thrive in working-class communities among athletes playing traditional team sports. Perhaps not surprisingly, most of these religious sport organizations are strongest in the Bible Belt of the United States.

A final organization of note is the National Christian College Athletic Association (NCCAA), a national group that was founded in 1968 and now includes more than 100 colleges. It represents more than 13,000 collegiate athletes and 700 collegiate coaches and sponsors championships in 20 sports. The NCCAA divides itself into two divisions, with Division I encompassing liberal arts colleges and Division II comprising Bible colleges. Their athletic programs are dedicated to students and serve a larger purpose than simply winning athletic contests. Christian teachings are part of the total learning experience on their campuses and throughout their sport programs.

 EXPERT'S VIEW

Life as an NFL Chaplain

Father James Barniak has been chaplain for the Green Bay Packers for 13 years. On Sundays, his schedule includes holding pregame chapel services and leading the Lord's Prayer pregame in the locker room and again postgame with both teams at the 50-yard line. Every NFL team has at least one chaplain like Barniak whose primary influence may be during the week as the chaplains conduct Bible study groups, provide individual or family counseling, and try to address players' spiritual needs. They are not paid team salaries, but usually are categorized in the rubric of "player development." Athletes in Action provides chaplaincy to 11 of the 32 NFL teams.

"The popular perception of Christianity in America prior to the last 10 to 15 years, has been that being a Christian meant you were soft—you were considered weak, kind of a pushover," says Father Trapp of the Atlanta Falcons. "You're the guy who was going to turn the other cheek. But you read in the Bible that some of those guys were brash and bold and forceful but still had a heart and desire for God." Team chaplains often help players with the challenges that come from players' new money and fame.

Among pro football players, 35% to 40% are evangelical Christians compared to about 25% of the rest of America. Evangelical leaders are pleased with the opportunity presented by big-time sport for players to share their religious beliefs on a stage not available to most priests and pastors. Coaches value the work of the chaplains who may help straighten out athletes who have lost their way or simply have their priorities confused.

When a player is asked by a sport announcer, "Tell me about that catch you made to keep the drive alive on third and 10" and the player responds by saying, "First, I want to thank my Lord and Savior Jesus Christ . . . ," journalists and many of the public groan inwardly. But in general, team chaplains say that what they encourage their players to strive for is to "play with honor, play to the best of their ability, honor God in the way they play, and pray for an injury-free game." Maybe we'd all be better off with that simple focus in sport (Plotz 2000; Kelber 2009).

Using Sport to Promote Christian Colleges and Secondary Schools

Since many colleges were founded by religious organizations, it is not surprising that some use sport to promote their school. Perhaps the most well-known university in America is Notre Dame, a Roman Catholic university famous for the exploits of its football team. Notre Dame has such a large fan base throughout the United States that it negotiates multimillion-dollar agreements for the rights to televise its football games on its own rather than through a league as most colleges do. Kids grow up knowing Notre Dame is the place to go for football, and the university has been fortunate to parlay its reputation into both sport and academic excellence, with a high graduation rate for its athletes. The Notre Dame allure was burnished during the years of Knute Rockne, a football coaching legend during the 1920s. Rockne stood up staunchly to the anti-Catholicism that prevailed in the United States at the time and to criticism from the Ku Klux Klan. In fact, the "more Rockne was exposed to prejudice around him, the more he was attracted to the religiosity around him at Notre Dame" (Robinson 1999).

Many other private schools have used sport to gain publicity, swell their pool of applicants, and attract an academically better-qualified student body. Smaller schools typically put their money into basketball since basketball is less expensive than football. Small Catholic schools like St. Joseph's, LaSalle, and Immaculata (Philadelphia), St. John's (New York), Marquette (Milwaukee), Gonzaga (Spokane), Loyola (Chicago), and many others are well known in the basketball world. More recently, Oral Roberts University in Tulsa, Oklahoma, and Liberty University in Virginia have used sport promotion to get their schools early notice. Founded by Oral Roberts and Jerry Falwell, respectively, these schools find no conflict between their Christian values and winning games. In fact, winning draws more attention and allows them to spread the word of God.

Brigham Young University (BYU), founded by the Church of Jesus Christ of Latter-Day Saints (Mormons), also intertwines religion and sport, as expressed by the statement of purpose of its athletic department to "develop students academically, athletically, and spiritually." Over the past 20 years, BYU has consistently ranked in the top 25 nationally for the Director's Cup, which takes into account the overall performance of all varsity sports (Brigham Young University Athletics 2006). (Note: The Director's Cup is sponsored by the United States Sports Academy as a result of a joint effort by the National Association of Collegiate Athletic Directors and *USA Today*.)

Many private secondary schools founded as Christian schools have dedicated themselves to excellence in sport to help attract students. Since their funding relies on donations and private tuition payments, they need to show value for the money not only in academics but in all programs. They realize that top performance in sport attracts fans, builds school cohesion, and encourages boosters and donors. It is no accident that many top professional athletes have graduated from these schools over the years. Top high school athletes are recruited and often offered scholarships based on need or academic performance to gain their contribution on the field or in the gym.

Among the most well-known Catholic secondary schools are Christ the King in Queens, New York, and St. Anthony in Newark, New Jersey. These schools have been perennial basketball powers. Another famed basketball team under the guidance of Coach Morgan Wooten is that of DeMatha in Hyattsville, Maryland, just outside Washington, DC. *Sports Illustrated* ranked DeMatha number two out of 38,000 high schools nationwide for excellence in total sport programs over the past 10 years (Huff 2005; Menez and Woo 2005).

Conflict Between Sport and Religion

Common conflicts seem to arise between religious beliefs and sport. For example, how is it an act of love for fellow man to put a bone-crushing tackle on an opponent, throw at the batter's head, slide hard into second base to break up a double play, or humiliate an undermanned opponent by running up the score? These actions are not unusual in most sport settings. Athletes with well-defined religious values often draw the line at certain behaviors they deem inappropriate. However, they might overlook the actions of coaches or teammates they have no control over. Their attitude is that they are responsible only for their own behavior and for living according to their principles.

Stevenson (1997) researched the methods Christian athletes in high-performance sport use to reconcile the apparent contradictions between their religious beliefs and the demands of their sport. As mentioned earlier, some declare their sport participation to be for "the glory of God" and reason that success in sport gives them influence for spreading their Christian beliefs. According to Coakley (2004), some religious athletes also may reconcile conflict by refocusing on the ascetic aspects of sport, such as discipline and self-denial. These athletes believe that ascetic devotion morally justifies their sport experience.

Other athletes simply put their spiritual beliefs aside while playing sports. They follow the customs of their sport on the field and reengage their spiritual beliefs off the field. While this approach is common, it can certainly provoke criticism if an athlete's on-field behavior does not square with off-field pronouncements of spiritual beliefs. Some actions in sport may be legal but not ethical. Usually, these actions are difficult to evaluate as they involve intent, which is hard to determine. For example, did the defensive end maliciously slam into the opposing quarterback with the preexisting injury? Or was slamming into the quarterback a coincidence during a routine pass rush? In sports like professional boxing, the intent is more straightforward,

as the object is to win the fight by punching the opponent into submission.

Although Stevenson's (1997) study involved only 31 athletes who were also members of AIA, a third of these athletes admitted to reaching a crisis during their athletic careers in trying to reconcile the demands of their sport with their religious beliefs. Many found the question of the real value of sport difficult to answer. Even when winning trophies and recognition, they felt they were missing something more important in life. Of the 31 athletes, three eventually withdrew from elite sport, citing their inability to resolve the conflicts between the sport culture and their Christian beliefs.

These moral dilemmas are not unique to the sport world. People have fought more wars over religious differences than over any other cause. Consider the religious strife that's occurred for generations in Ireland or in the Middle East. Religions have always allowed for war against infidels. The religious justification for violence and inhuman treatment toward enemies has been a source of curiosity and confusion for people throughout the ages.

While in college, Tim Tebow (see the sidebar on page 282) wrote scripture verses on his eye black as a way to share his faith.

Chapter Summary

Religion and sport have historically interacted in both negative and positive ways. Early religious festivals beginning with the ancient Greeks featured athletic contests. Over time, many religions began considering sport and games as mundane diversions that detracted from people's spiritual development.

In the last 100 years, religion and sport have forged a mutually beneficial link, with each promoting the other. Churches have used athletes and sport to attract people, particularly youth, to their facilities and to recruit believers into their church family. Sports have used religion to justify sport competition as a worthy pursuit and to control the conduct of athletes. Coaches have promoted prayer to enhance performance and foster team togetherness. They have also reinforced religious values to encourage their athletes to work hard, show good teamwork, and commit to team goals.

Although Christianity, particularly Protestantism, has been the dominant religion in the United States, other religions such as Judaism and Islam have had an impact on the sporting world, too. In some cases, religious beliefs have interfered with an athlete's sport participation when customs or expectations of the two institutions clashed.

Various organizations have developed over the years, spurred by the link between sport and religion. The Young Men's Christian Association and Young Women's Christian Association have built sport facilities across America and have organized thousands of sport programs for all ages. The Fellowship of Christian Athletes has grown steadily over the last 25 years, now boasting more than 6,000 organized huddles and employing a national staff of more than 600.

Christian secondary schools and colleges have also used sport to gain positive publicity and attract students and donors. They make no apologies for embracing the competitive ethic of striving for excellence. Liberty University and Oral Roberts University are two examples of universities following the path first trod by Notre Dame of football fame and by Roman Catholic universities with a tradition of excellence in basketball. Secondary schools such as DeMatha, Christ the King, and St. Anthony have capitalized on outstanding athletic teams for the purpose of publicity.

Athletes may use religion by asking for God's help in their performance, focusing on the competition through pregame prayer, and justifying their dedication to excellence. Many prominent athletes have also used their success in sport as a platform to share their religious beliefs and influence young athletes to stay on the "right path."

Religion has helped Americans justify their preoccupation with sport and has joined in that preoccupation, urging the pursuit of excellence through sport and convincing athletes that their religious beliefs should accompany them to the playing field. By promoting sport and using famous athletes to deliver their message, religious leaders are able to gain the attention of young men and women. Conversely, by applying the tenets of a worthy spiritual life to sport, participants can feel a powerful endorsement for what otherwise may seem a self-indulgent pastime.

Politics and Sport

Student Outcomes

After reading this chapter, you will know the following:

- How government and sport interact internationally, nationally, and locally
- How government may interact with sport to protect the rights of all citizens
- How governments use sport to promote identity and unity among citizens
- How governments use sport to promote social values
- How sport creates nationalistic feelings that reinforce the governmental policies
- How political groups within sport organizations can direct the development and delivery of sport to consumers
- Why sport personalities, athletes, and coaches may lean toward a conservative political philosophy

On October 2, 2009, President Barack Obama flew on a 20-hour emergency mission across the ocean to convince the International Olympic Committee to award the 2016 Olympic Games to Obama's home city of Chicago. It was an unprecedented gesture by an American president to involve himself in sport to that extent. Both Vice President Joe Biden and first lady Michelle Obama had worked the phone in the weeks leading up to the vote and spent time in person with delegates hoping to convince them on the excellence of Chicago's bid. Predictably, leaders of the opposition Republican party (Michael Steele, chairman of the Republican National Convention) criticized Obama for spending time on trivial matters when he might better have spent those 20 hours on more urgent matters such as rising unemployment, soaring health care costs, winning the war in Afghanistan, and dealing with Iran's nuclear threat.

Alas, in the end Obama was unable to persuade the group, and Chicago's bid was rejected in the first round of voting. After several votes, the city of Rio de Janeiro was selected for 2016. The extraordinary insertion of an American president into lobbying for the Olympic Games may reflect Obama's personal interest in and affection for sport or may illuminate the prestige of the Games and their impact on the world stage (Baker and Zeleny 2009).

Politics is the art and science of government, of influencing governmental policy, or of holding control over a government. While there are some negative connotations of the term politics, politics is clearly a dominant component of any culture. This chapter examines the interrelationship between politics and sport from four primary perspectives.

The first perspective looks at how government uses sport to improve the quality of life for its citizens and regulates sport to protect the rights of its citizens. Currently in the United States, the government also regulates the conduct of sport, particularly when public monies and land are involved. The legislative and judicial branches also make decisions regarding antitrust issues in sport; levy taxes on the public to finance some aspects of sport; and referee the conflict among sport performers, owners, unions, and organizations.

A related area of interest is how communities build their identities through local professional sport teams, community teams, and even local university or high school teams. Political leaders may use sport to unify their citizens around a common interest such as attracting a professional franchise to their city. Rooting for the home team often links city residents who might otherwise feel isolated from government or fellow citizens. Governments also use sport to facilitate social integration. They may use sport to reduce juvenile delinquency, improve academic performance through after-school programs combining academics and sports, or encourage healthy competition between disparate ethnic or racial groups.

The second perspective examines how sport can reinforce the prevailing political structure and status quo. Political leaders often use sport to promote self-interests or support for the government they lead. Generally, sport organizations, leaders, coaches, and athletes support the establishment that serves them well.

The third perspective focuses on how nations sponsor international teams in world sporting events to promote patriotic pride. National teams that successfully compete against other nations in the Olympic Games inspire a sense of identity and pride in their fellow citizens. As mentioned before, a by-product of international competition is using success in sport to justify a particular nation's government and way of life. International sport events are also used to advance political aims when certain nations boycott events or are restricted from participating by other countries that are offended by their social practices. Sport is also a way of maintaining good relationships or building understanding among nations.

The fourth perspective explores the politics of sport institutions. Within each sport, different interests struggle over who will set the policies and procedures and who will benefit from decisions—the team owners, athletes, or spectators. As with all organizations, the people who organize and govern particular sports or leagues develop political structures within their group. People in the political structure campaign to influence policy decisions, financial commitments, and competition rules. Leaders in sport organizations often must become consummate politicians in order to convince their constituency to follow their vision for the success of the sport and its organization.

Governments around the world make it their business to ensure they have a physically fit nation. A current law in Japan levies significant financial penalties on companies and local governments that fail to meet specific waist circumference target goals in their employees.

Government in Physical Activity and Health

Governments sometimes take on responsibility of the health and welfare of their citizens. In the United States, a division of the federal Department of Health and Human Services, the Centers for Disease Control and Prevention (CDC) at Atlanta, Georgia, disseminates nationwide the latest information linking physical activity to better health. In its role of preventing and controlling disease, the CDC makes strong recommendations for every citizen to participate in physical activity.

The most recent recommendation from the U.S. government for physical activity for children is to engage in one hour or more of moderate or vigorous aerobic physical activity a day, including vigorous-intensity physical activity at least three days a week. For adults, the recommendation is for at least 150 minutes (two hours, 30 minutes) a week of moderate intensity or 75 minutes of vigorous intensity, or an equivalent combination of moderate- and vigorous-intensity aerobic activity (United States Department of Health and Human Services 2008).

The official position of the U.S. government is that regular physical activity contributes to health, promotes well-being, and reduces the costs of medical care. It is in everyone's interest to use healthy activity as a means of ensuring a higher quality of life, increasing longevity, and reducing the expense and ravages of disease.

Research demonstrating the value of exercise for slowing the aging process has been a popular topic for the CDC, particularly since the U.S. population is tending toward increased longevity. Increasing longevity significantly affects the U.S. government, since it portends increased costs for health care and a greater need for long-term care facilities and threatens the solvency of the Social Security system and Medicare.

In the 1950s, physical testing of military recruits made it clear that American youth were woefully lacking in physical fitness. Then, in a test of minimum muscular fitness developed by Hans Kraus and Sonya Weber, 56.6% of American schoolchildren failed one or more of the six tests. That percentage was compared to a failure rate of only 8.2% among schoolchildren in Austria, Italy, and Switzerland. The results became big news, and President Dwight

D. Eisenhower eventually founded the President's Council on Youth Fitness, headed by Vice President Richard Nixon. The result was a series of publicity releases touting the virtues of physical fitness (Rice, Hutchinson, and Lee 1958).

In 1961, President John F. Kennedy established the President's Council on Physical Fitness and Sports (PCPFS) to promote physical fitness and sport participation among Americans. The first recommendation from the President's Council was that all schools should provide daily a minimum of 15 minutes of vigorous exercise. At that time, 75% of America's schools had no daily class for physical education. Perhaps the most enduring contribution of the President's Council has been to develop standards of fitness for schoolchildren. These standards have been in place in schools for more than 50 years (Hackensmith 1966; Weber 1956).

In more recent years, the PCPFS has included recommendations and programs for all Americans, not just youth. One specific program, The President's Challenge, guides people through a specific physical activity program using activities of their choice that will improve their health and fitness. Awards for improvement are given to those who complete the program.

The PCPFS has numbered among its leaders Bud Wilkinson, a famous football coach, and Arnold Schwarzenegger, a bodybuilder and movie star who later became governor of California. Although the organization has helped raise public consciousness toward physical fitness, its stature and funding have limited its impact to less than what its proponents

desired. Perhaps the most effective policy of the council has been to award citations to schoolchildren who meet its standards in testing administered through the public schools.

Government in Sport

Many governments around the world, particularly those that have established a ministry of sport, aggressively promote sport participation, financially support high-performance athletes who represent their country in international competition, and help fund public athletic facilities. No such agency exists in the United States, and while some people would welcome the governmental support, most sport advocates believe that American society is better off by keeping government red tape, endless discussion, and partisan bickering out of the sport world. Some citizens might even question the Constitutional right of the U.S. government to interfere in sport.

As mentioned in chapter 9, the U.S. Congress designated the United States Olympic Committee (USOC) to develop and conduct amateur sport and to train and support Olympic and Paralympic athletes. Although the government does not directly fund the USOC, it did donate a closed military base to provide the site for the USOC Headquarters and Training Center. The USOC raises its own funds to conduct its business. Although the U.S. Congress does not normally interfere with the USOC, in 2003 it stepped in when the USOC met with scandal,

IN THE ARENA WITH . . .

Let's Move

In 2010, Michelle Obama announced a new White House campaign, "Let's Move," in partnership with Major League Baseball and the MLB Players Association. Other organization partners include the U.S. Department of Health and Human Services and the President's Council on Physical Fitness and Sports and Nutrition. The campaign is directed at American kids to help them cultivate an appreciation for nutritious food and engage in physical activity to combat the rapid rise in childhood obesity. The campaign will include 30 television and 30 radio public service announcements featuring an MLB player, one in each city that has an MLB team.

Mrs. Obama kicked off the publicity by attending a baseball game in Baltimore between the hometown Orioles and the Tampa Bay Rays. Several players from both clubs partnered with Obama as she spoke to kids at the game about the need to "get moving for at least 60 minutes every day." Major League Baseball commissioner Bud Selig said, "The health and welfare of the country's youth is a top priority for Major League Baseball and we're happy to help any way we can." It can't hurt baseball, either, to have received all the positive national and local press from the campaign while highlighting its star players in the public eye. You might describe this as a win-win situation for both the political establishment and MLB. After all, who could possibly be against this campaign (Newman 2010)?

EXPERT'S VIEW

Unintended Effects of Youth Bicycle Helmet Laws

To protect our nation's youth from potential fatalities or injuries, many states, sport organizations, and sport facilities enforce certain regulations requiring the use of certain protective equipment. To reduce head injuries, sports such as equestrian, football, baseball, and in-line skating require approved safety helmets to be worn.

Bicycling has been one of the most popular sports and means of transportation for generations of American kids. Yet it also can cause fatal or serious head injuries in the event of a crash. To date, 21 states enforce laws requiring children to wear bike helmets, and the result over the last two decades has been a reduction in fatalities by about 19%. Incidentally, states with bicycle laws are all coastal states, both east and west, with little interest shown in the midsection of the country.

Interestingly, researchers Carpenter and Stehr found in their 2009 study that while laws requiring the use of bicycle helmets have significantly reduced fatalities, in those states the requirements for helmets also reduced bicycling by about 4% to 5%. This appears to be an unintended consequence of the law just at the time government is actively encouraging youth to become more active. It was certainly not the intention of the lawmakers to discourage kids from riding their bikes, but to simply protect them better.

The researchers hypothesize that some children simply can't afford helmets, which cost between $10 and $40. However, they believe that a more potent factor is the social costs, the fact that many youths believe riding with a helmet is simply not cool. Peer pressure and taunting especially as kids age can lead to parking the bike in the garage and leaving it there. What would be interesting to learn is whether these kids then seek out other sports to play instead or whether they simply retreat to their computers and video games (Carpenter and Stehr 2009).

Is it possible that states are overreaching with laws that regulate the conduct of youth sports? Should these laws be national rather than left to the states? Another possibility is to allow sport leagues to set their own standards, but what about activities such as biking where there is no viable organization? Do you agree with government laws that protect citizens "for their own good," or do you prefer to let people make their own decisions no matter how uninformed they may be? Compare your views with those of your classmates.

breach of ethics, and internal strife. The resulting changes began to take effect in 2005, and the hopes are that the USOC will steadily progress in bringing itself under order (see chapter 9).

Safeguarding the Public

The U.S. government helps provide safety for its citizens. Sports that are dangerous or involve cruelty to animals are outlawed or discouraged. Bullfighting, cockfighting, and other so-called sports that abuse animals are punishable by fines or imprisonment. Sports that are inherently dangerous to participants, such as boxing, bungee jumping, skydiving, and auto racing, are carefully monitored and controlled by government regulations.

The U.S. government also regulates sports that may be reasonably safe within a controlled environment. Activities such as boating, fishing, hunting, using firearms, water sports, and bicycling have certain rules, require training for instructors and participants, and require certain protective equipment. The government also regulates outdoor activities that may affect the natural environment or endanger species. For example, the U.S. government regulates where, when, and how fishing can be done.

The U.S. government also strives to protect the public in sports when unruly fan behavior is a risk or when a terrorist attack threatens the staging of large events. For many Americans in my generation, the first wake-up call to terrorism in sport came in 1972 when a Palestinian terrorist group took Israeli athletes hostage during the Summer Olympics in Munich, Germany. After a daylong standoff and a failed rescue attempt, eleven Israeli athletes, one German police officer, and five of the eight kidnappers were killed (Lowitt 1999).

Nearly 25 years later, at the Atlanta Olympics, a bomb went off in the Olympic Park and killed two people while injuring over 100 others. Panic set in, events were suspended, and spectators feared for their safety. But the Games went on, and five years later the main suspect, Eric Robert Rudolph, was found hiding in the mountains of North Carolina.

The Olympics has always been a potential target for those with a political axe to grind, and as a result, more than $600 million was spent on security for the Athens Games in 2004. More than 15,000 law enforcement personnel were employed to guard against attacks along with more than 8,666 supplemental military officials (Gebicke 1996). Terrorism really hit home in America when terrorists attacked New York City and Washington, DC, on September 11, 2001. In every sporting event since that time, security plans have been a major priority.

College football stadiums filled with 100,000 fans on an autumn Saturday could be a prime target for terrorists. The Super Bowl has not only a live audience but also a worldwide television audience that could potentially witness an attack. Aircraft are routinely prohibited from flying within miles of the stadiums on game days. Bomb searches, undercover police, alarm systems, and video surveillance have become commonplace. Everyone who enters the event facility may be searched; limits on what people may carry into the facility have become strict; and people who appear suspicious are quickly moved to the side for further inspection. The costs for these precautions have driven insurance premiums to more than $1 million a year for a typical National Football League (NFL) stadium. Security precautions and insurance protection have added significantly to the expenses of sport promoters, who have passed along those increases to fans.

Protecting the Rights of Citizens

The government can play a key role in protecting the rights of its citizens in sport. As discussed in chapter 12, in 1972 the U.S. Congress passed Title IX, which declared that women and girls should have equal access to sport. Organizations that refused to meet the standards were denied federal funds of any type. In 1990, U.S. President George H.W. Bush signed the Americans with Disabilities Act (ADA), which protected the rights of athletes with physical or mental disabilities (see chapter 14). Public facilities, including sport facilities, now meet certain standards to accommodate people with physical disabilities; and the USOC provides sport competition and training for athletes with physical disabilities. Now, the Paralympics immediately

ACTIVITY TIME-OUT

Protecting Kids in Youth Sport From Criminal Coaches

Do you think the government at any level should be involved in requiring criminal background checks before someone can serve as a coach for youth sport? Investigate the issues and develop a well-reasoned argument for or against government involvement in the protection of kids in sport. Here are some of the issues. The National Amateur Athletic Union, which employs over 65,000 coaches around the country, discovered that some of its coaches had committed crimes including murder, incest, delivering drugs, and theft. In Seattle, Washington, a pilot program checked the roster of 4,236 coaches and discovered 38 felons (Willmsen 2004).

Background checks at the state level often do not ferret out infractions in other states, and coaches can simply change their name and move to a new state. Neither state nor federal name checks are sufficient; fingerprint testing is the most accurate. But the cost for such checks may be nearly $50 per coach, and the question is who is going to pay the fee. Youth sport organizations say they can't afford it, and volunteer coaches resist paying as well. Should this be a government expense?

Some state legislatures, such as Florida's, have passed bills requiring background checks, but the response from youth sport has been tepid. Most organizations are hesitant about outside (government) influence and concerned that state mandates will require background checks they can't afford (Basichis 2010).

After you have concluded your research and developed a position, summarize it in a two- to three-page paper and be ready to debate your conclusion in class.

follow the Olympic Games in the same venue with full support of the International Olympic Committee and most national governing bodies.

Civil rights acts decreed that discrimination against persons of various racial, ethnic, and class preferences is illegal by governments who support or regulate access to sport programs. Although private clubs continue to have some leeway in determining their membership, any public facility or program must provide equal access for all persons. National governing bodies for specific sports are expected to develop policies that ensure equal access to all athletes. People who take issue with the conduct of any organization or facility can seek redress in a court of law and protection from discrimination based on race, creed, national origin, religious preference, or sexual orientation (see chapters 11 through 15).

Other U.S. laws protect the rights of children through child labor laws and protect the rights of athletes to play as professionals and to represent a specific country. Some laws regulate performance-enhancing drugs in sport. In 2005, the U.S. Congress held hearings on drug use in MLB and threatened to toughen the rules unless MLB significantly changed its policies on drug testing and penalties for infractions. Both the league and the players' union quickly realized that tougher drug enforcement was necessary and approved much more stringent policies.

Protecting the Financial Interests of the Public

Sports are a huge economic engine in the United States, and the money wrapped up in sport affects every citizen either directly or indirectly. In the past, the U.S. government sometimes stepped in to direct and control the expansion of sports as they grew in power and significance. For example, in cities where proposals were advanced to use public monies to build stadiums or arenas that would benefit the owners of professional franchises, governments have stymied the proposals or put them to a public vote.

Historically, laws have been passed exempting professional sport leagues from antitrust laws (see chapter 4). Major League Baseball, the NFL, and the National Basketball Association have a virtual monopoly on their sports and wield tremendous influence over their athletes, ticket prices, television rights, and the sharing of revenue between teams and cities. The point to be taken here is that when government decides what is in the public interest, those who have economic power and influence are

more likely to affect government decisions than those who have little power or influence. Also, owners of professional sport franchises are often able to further their business interests by claiming that their success will benefit the community and other local businesses such as hotels and restaurants.

Local governments often give huge tax incentives to owners of professional franchises in order to convince them to locate or keep their franchise in a certain city. When an owner loses money due to mismanagement, excessive player contracts, or changes in the economy, he may ask the city for a better tax deal or threaten to leave town for a more attractive financial package. For example, the Oakland Raiders football team relocated to Los Angeles in 1982 only to move back to Oakland in 1995 when it could not agree on a deal for a new stadium in Los Angeles. Oakland offered the team some $63 million in up-front incentives, loans, and other benefits to return (CNN Sports Illustrated 2001).

Government in Promoting Identity and Unity Among Citizens

Local, city, and state governments have long used sport to promote pride, identity, and unity among their citizens. By attracting a professional franchise, city leaders expect to capitalize on their financial investment by providing entertainment to residents and creating a bond among people of all backgrounds forged by a common interest in the home team.

On a given Monday morning during football season, the performance of the local professional team is a hot news item. Strangers use the fortunes of their local team to break the ice in conversations with others. If the team performs beyond expectation, fans feel a little bit prouder to be a part of their city and just a bit better about life. In contrast, an entire populace can be cast into gloom due to a seemingly unimportant detail such as a flubbed field goal in the waning seconds of play.

Even very large metropolises such as New York, Chicago, and Los Angeles rally around their home team. In strikingly diverse race and ethnic groups, the city residents and suburban dwellers join to support their teams. Although most residents never actually see a professional game, they form strong opinions concerning the team's performance and learn the details through the print media, radio, and television. Team jerseys and hats appear throughout

The Dawg Pound section of the Cleveland Browns Stadium is full of zealous fans.

the city, and at every turn the team logo is displayed on billboards and auto stickers.

A particular type of fan support grows around pro teams that are cast in the image of their city and its historic ethnic groups. The Broad Street Bullies (as the Philadelphia Flyers were once known) emanated from their rough-and-tumble approach to the game of ice hockey that resulted in a world championship. The pride of the City of Brotherly Love has been the Flyers, Iggles (Eagles), and Phillies. In this city dominated by ethnic enclaves of immigrants, fans are unique in their approach to sport, fanaticism, and impatience with their heroes.

This is a city that cheered the triumph of Rocky on the steps of the Philadelphia Art Museum and booed Santa Claus at an Eagles game.

Likewise, Baltimore and Boston teams have been in a love affair with their fans for decades. Generations of families have shared a special sport fanaticism, and even when younger generations moved away they never lost their passion for their true home team. Meanwhile, teams relatively new to cities, such as teams in the Sun Belt, do not have the same hard-core fans. Some games don't even sell out on a Sunday simply due to a more modest passion for professional sport and a competition with too many other leisure activities, especially outdoor activities.

Special sporting events also can unify a city. Hosting the Super Bowl, the National Collegiate Athletic Association (NCAA) basketball play-offs, baseball's All-Star Game, the Olympic Games, the Pan American Games, various collegiate championships, and even youth national championships can draw communities together, uniting businesses, media, and fans. The economic benefits the host cities accrue often more than compensate for the expenses of staging the event. Local volunteers often spend long hours helping operate the event in exchange for perks such as access to tickets.

A notable example of a city using sport to build an identity is Indianapolis, which labels itself the "amateur sports capital of the world." Through the entrepreneurial activities of a local sport commission, the city aggressively bids to host every imaginable amateur sport championship and has staged over 250 national or international sporting events. The city is also home to collegiate sports (NCAA) and high school sports (National Federation of State High School Associations) and the American College of Sports Medicine. A dozen national sport organizations have their national headquarters located in Indianapolis. The city's business community has been steadfastly supportive, and the financial bonanza to the city's economy has enabled the government to improve the downtown and add sport and recreation facilities that are the envy of similar cities. From 1977 through 1991, the amateur sport movement pumped $1.05 billion into the local economy (Indianapolis Chamber of Commerce 2006).

Even smaller cities use sport to build unity. They may focus on a particular sporting event, on a local college, or even on the local high school. State universities located away from large metropolitan areas usually garner tremendous fan support because they have no competition from professional sport events or teams. In a state like Texas where fans take their high school football seriously, the local football team is a source of town pride.

Nationalism and Sport

Sport events are replete with patriotic symbols that unify people by encouraging them to celebrate their shared heritage and common bonds. Games open with the national anthem, the presentation of colors by a military team, a military jet flyover, or a marching band playing rousing music; and they stage halftime ceremonies that feature music and dance celebrating the nation's culture and history.

One football game in America stands out for intertwining nationalism and sport. Up to 100,000 people attend the classic Army–Navy game, usually held in Philadelphia, and the game enjoys a national television audience. Decades ago, this game not only matched the two military academies but also boasted great football players. Both teams were among the elite in college football and featured superstars such as Doc Blanchard, Pete Dawkins, and Roger Staubach. Though recent years have seen a decline in the performance level of both teams, the Army–Navy game is still a memorable occasion. The pomp and circumstance of the game, along with the heartily rooting sections of cadets and midshipmen, create an atmosphere unlike any other in college sport. As the U.S. Air Force Academy has improved its sport programs, it occasionally dominates football among the three academies, but the Army–Navy

game still has the cachet. America, soldiers, the brightest and best of the nation's youth, and an undeniable patriotic theme permeate the day and bestow significance on the game regardless of the quality of play.

Nationalism is an expression of devotion to one's country. In times of war or disasters such as the attack on the U.S. World Trade Center, expressions of nationalism take on a poignancy that unites all citizens. Shared tragedy helps create a strong bond among people of all backgrounds. When national symbols such as the American flag are displayed at sporting events and carried on live television, millions of people collectively take pride in their country in spite of their apparent differences.

As we discussed in chapter 9, perhaps no sporting event has traded on nationalistic feelings like the Olympic Games. Adolph Hitler staged the 1936 Olympics to demonstrate the superiority of the Nazi government and way of life. East Germany claimed 90 Olympic medals in the 1972 Games, more medals than any country in the world in proportion to its size; consider that East Germany is the size of California. Its 90 medals are impressive compared to the 94 medals the United States won and 125 medals the Soviet Union won.

Since 1972, the system of selection and training that produced those medals has been discredited because of the abuse of young athletes and illegal drugs fostered by the East German government. The success of East Germany's Olympic athletes was a source of national pride that, once exposed, turned into a national embarrassment.

 ACTIVITY TIME-OUT

The 1980 Boycott of the Olympic Games

President Jimmy Carter called for a boycott of the Olympic Games in Moscow in 1980 to register protest of the Soviet Union's invasion of the country of Afghanistan. The United States was joined by 64 other countries in the boycott. The losers were our best young athletes, who were torn between supporting our government in an international crisis and their own interest in participating in the Games and the culmination of an athletic career for many. For these young people, their lives had been devoted to performing at the highest level of world athletic competition, and the countless hours of training, competing, and preparation went for naught. Not surprisingly, four years later the Russians boycotted the Games in Los Angeles, robbing the events of some of the world's best athletes (Brennan 2005).

The question here for you to ponder is whether it is ever appropriate for a political leader to use competitive sport to make a political statement as Jimmy Carter did. Is it fair to the athletes, coaches, fans, and media who have long prepared for the event? Do you think it was appropriate for some 25 of the would-be Olympians to sue the United States government for loss of opportunity and eventual career earnings because they could not compete? Is it fair to the Olympic Games to affect a positive world event that has existed for over a hundred years due to political bickering between countries? Would you be in favor of a ban on such sporting events imposed by the U.S. government?

The expulsion of South Africa from the Olympics in 1964 and 1968 affected world opinion and South Africa's long-standing apartheid. No doubt the resulting publicity pressured a major reform in a government that had repressed black citizens for centuries. Similarly, the People's Republic of China was ostracized for its dismal record on human rights. In a remarkable change, Beijing was chosen as the host city for the Olympic Games in 2008. China believes that its selection shows other nations' stamp of approval on its progress to right the wrongs in the country.

Sport in Promoting Social Values

In the United States, sport is a conservative institution that promotes traditional values and can integrate people into the social construct. Generally, sport strives to maintain the status quo by teaching people mainstream values or perhaps by functioning as a distraction for people who are unsatisfied with their society or lives. Yet sport can also serve as a platform from which to point to the need for change.

In the United States, striving for excellence is a critical social value, and success is measured by achievement. Competition spurs Americans to perform to the maximum of their ability and to reach heights of excellence they may never have thought possible. The American recipe for success is to work hard, show discipline, and stay dedicated to personal goals. There is no shame in defeating or being defeated, for in striving to win against the competitor, both athletes are inspired to perform at their best.

In China, the values learned through sport can be very different. According to writers who studied Chinese attitudes toward sport in the 1970s, the prevailing attitude was not that winning is the ultimate goal. Rather, Chinese competition emphasized cooperation, working toward a group goal, friendship, and physical fitness. There was little emphasis on individual success, and athletes displayed devotion to the success of the group (Johnson 1973a, 1973b, 1973c). Some of those attitudes changed in the decades since, and China has risen to a world power in competitive sport, a power culminating in Beijing's selection to host the 2008 Summer Olympics.

Adults use competitive sport to teach kids the lessons they believe necessary for later success in life. Kids learn that by trying their best to win in sport, they will develop the life skills to compete in the world. Those skills could also be developed through academic achievement, excellence in arts, or exploration in technology and invention. Yet sports are often the first thing that comes to the minds of people wanting to teach children the right habits for future success.

Sports are used throughout the world to socially integrate people from diverse backgrounds. For example, Northern Ireland has extensively invested in sport facilities to promote constructive interaction between Protestants and Catholics. In France, sports are often seen as a way of regenerating French youth and improving social discipline. In many countries, including England and the United States, sports are used to combat urban unrest and to reduce crime and juvenile delinquency (Coakley and Dunning 2004).

Sport as an Opiate of the Masses

Various critics throughout history have charged governments with using sport to distract their citizens from the inequities in their society. These critics charged that the government used sport as an "opiate" to calm the masses, dull their senses, and distract their attention from their everyday social or economic problems. The hype given to sport puts the citizenry to sleep on matters of deeper significance. This charge has typically been leveled at authoritarian governments, especially those in countries with a large number of poor people (Eitzen 2004).

Developing countries have learned to use sport well. Powerful governments in the world's poorest nations have effectively rallied their citizens to support national teams representing their homeland. In most countries, the chosen sport is soccer, or what is referred to as *football* around the globe. Brazil is a good example of a nation that has embraced soccer as a national pastime and elevated its most famous son, Pelé, as a legendary hero. The exploits of the Brazilian soccer team have united rich and poor in a country beset with myriad social and economic tensions. Brazilian pride is stoked by every success fashioned by the national soccer team. Around the world, Brazil is respected for its tradition of excellence in world soccer competition.

Even in the United States, the charge of using sport as a distraction has been made by public figures such as Bill Bradley, a former All-American basketball player for Princeton University and later for the New York Knicks. After his basketball career,

Do you think sports enable fans to forget about reality for a while? Is it a way for citizens to ignore larger social issues?

Bradley entered politics and became a U.S. senator. He was also a presidential contender in 2000. In the early days of his political career, he referred to sport as "a temporary fix, an escape from the problems of the world such as war, racism, and poverty that distracts the minds and saps the energies of people away from the problems of the lower classes" (Hoch 1972, p. 12).

Typically, political activists seek changes in their present government by criticizing those in power for diverting attention from critical social problems. A contemporary example is Noam Chomsky, a brilliant political activist and professor of linguistics at the Massachusetts Institute of Technology. Chomsky has been acknowledged as one of the most influential voices in contemporary political discussions and is a left-wing critic of American foreign policy. He believes sport is an opiate of the masses (Tsiokos 2005):

> "Sports keeps people from worrying about things that matter to their lives. Sports is a major factor in controlling people. Workers have minds; they have to be involved in something and it's important to make sure they're involved in things that have absolutely no significance. So professional sport is perfect. It instills total passivity."

Social critics ask, How do you explain the American preoccupation with sport when the country still faces racial tensions, discrimination toward women and ethnic groups, a rising national debt, concern for long-term welfare of senior citizens on limited incomes, affordable health care, rising rates of obesity, continued assaults on the environment, and a deepening divide between the so-called red and blue states? Rather than facing a distrustful nation, the U.S. government may find it better to keep its citizens focused on the Super Bowl, the March Madness of college basketball, the start of spring training for baseball, and the next Olympic Games (Huston 2005).

Critics ask why cities spend millions to attract or retain professional sport franchises when those millions could be used to help the poor, build cheap housing, raise teachers' salaries and improve school facilities, fight crime, and provide quality health care.

It may be that people simply choose to focus their energy on more positive events. They may feel powerless or may not know how to address the issues that social critics list as important.

Sport and the Status Quo

Generally in the United States, people associated with sport are politically conservative. These people include coaches, athletes, sportscasters, and sport owners or executives. Although there are notable exceptions, athletes and coaches who are politically liberal, they stand out because they are unusual. In this context, *conservative* refers to those who adhere to traditional methods or views and generally seek to perpetuate the status quo. On the other hand, *liberal* refers to those who are not bound by authoritarianism, orthodoxy, or tradition and are open to and often seek change from the status quo (*Merriam-Webster's* 2001).

Owners of professional sport teams generally benefit from maintaining a political structure that supports them and that they have influence over. Likewise, leaders in most sport organizations have no desire to change the social standards they used to work their way into their top positions.

Coaches at every level of competition tend to have a conservative outlook. They strongly believe in the traditional values of hard work, discipline, perseverance, and respect for authority. Regarding their society, coaches often favor the status quo and resist change. In fact, coaches in the United States often play an authoritarian role (Eitzen 1992). Athletic coaches are judged publicly on their job performance after every game. They are held responsible for their team's winning or losing, and if the percentage of losses is too great, they lose their jobs without discussion. As a result, coaches tend to control their own destiny by controlling the behavior of their athletes. They have strong opinions on how athletes should dress, act, wear their hair, represent their school, and interact with the media. Coaches may also have a direct interest in an athlete's academic performance, which affects athletic eligibility; an athlete's friends, who may get the athlete into trouble; and even an athlete's boyfriend or girlfriend, who might distract from athletic performance. We'll look at coaches in more detail in chapter 19.

Athletes often follow their coaches in their political leanings. They may not question their coaches, as these athletes are typically admired by their peers, fawned over by adults, and looked upon as heroes by younger people. They enjoy a high social status, especially during their teenage years, and if they continue on to a professional career, their success explodes exponentially.

Typical athletes choose to participate in sport and submit to the direction of various coaches. They learn to push themselves physically and mentally in order to succeed and perhaps to punish their body. If they are successful, the reinforcement of winning encourages them to continue to punish their bodies so they can continue their success.

Athletes who are in the public eye are taught from an early age that they are representing their parents, peers, community, and school. Coaches warn athletes about aberrant behavior that might reflect negatively on those who rely on them. Athletes learn to act in ways that are socially acceptable and adhere to the standards of the existing community.

Particularly in team sports, team cohesion is part of the formula for success. Team members who think alike, share common goals, and are willing to sacrifice for the good of the group are popular with coaches and other athletes. Those who march to a different drummer are accepted only if their athletic contributions are exceptional. So sport encourages conformity to normal behavior (Sage 1973).

In recent years in the U.S., the Republican party has generally tended toward a more conservative platform while the Democratic party leans toward a more liberal platform. However, it would be a mistake to classify all Republicans as conservative and all Democrats as liberal; there are many shades of gray on both sides that depend on the specific issues being debated or discussed.

As the 2004 U.S. presidential election loomed, the *Yale Daily News*, a student newspaper published at Yale University, featured an article titled "Many Elis Break From Norm, Lean Right" (August 2004). Yale has a long history of being a politically left campus. However, the "Elis," or members of the Delta Kappa Epsilon fraternity, broke tradition to lean right. Many players on the football team, baseball team, and soccer team belonged to Delta Kappa Epsilon. One after the other these players said that they believed many varsity athletes on campus were politically conservative in contrast to the rest of the student body. In their view, athletes at Yale tended to vote Republican.

In a poll taken early in the year by the Yale Sports Publicity staff, 62 football players planned to vote for Republican candidate Bush, 27 planned to voted for Democratic candidate Kerry, and 11 were undecided. The conservative stance of many members of the football team might have been due to more than sport participation. In fact, 20 players were from Texas, 35% were from Southern states, and about 13% were from the Midwest, all regions that are traditionally Republican. Only four players called a northern city home. Perhaps their choice for president was not so surprising considering their origins.

In the 2008 presidential election, professional sport figures gave twice as much money to all presidential candidates combined as they had in the two previous presidential races combined. As of

August 1, 2008, several months before the election, the donations showed that sport figures had donated over a million dollars toward the candidates. As has been typical, Republicans maintained their lead in the percentage of donations, but the gap was the narrowest it had been since George Bush was first elected in 2000. Republicans donated $584,502, while Democrats coughed up $458,034. For the final two candidates, McCain and Obama, the contributions were $248,300 versus $197,034, respectively—percentages of 55.8% for McCain and 44.2% for Obama.

The choice in 2008 was between a former Navy boxer and war hero in McCain and Obama, a younger pickup hoops player. Democratic candidates in the previous two elections were never able to gain more than 16% of pro sport donations. Republican presidents have tended to leave professional sport empires alone while Democrats often have pushed for more regulations. Sport owners and leaders also tend to favor Republicans, who typically favor lower taxes for the well-to-do (Lavigne 2008).

Yet not all athletes fall neatly into the same niche. As professor William Kelly pointed out when interviewed for the *Yale Daily News* article, athletes in more individualized sports such as squash, tennis, track and field, gymnastics, and skiing are not necessarily as conservative as players in team sports. Kelly also stated that female athletes are often less conservative than male athletes, perhaps because they are less satisfied with the status quo and desire change.

Using Sport to Change Society

Is it possible to change people's attitudes, feelings, and beliefs through the sport experience? Some people may respond quickly to this question with personal examples while others may be more cautious. Over the years, sports have clearly been used to dramatize certain social inequities or injustices, racism, gender bias, and homophobia.

Champion athletes have a platform from which to share their views if they choose. Boxer Muhammad Ali spoke his mind on the draft, the war, and racial prejudice. Tennis player Arthur Ashe Jr. spoke

After their Black Power salute at the 1968 Olympics, Tommie Smith and John Carlos were subjected to abuse and even death threats.

on the same issues, though in a much different way than Ali. Olympic athletes Tommie Smith and John Carlos used their Olympic success to raise the Black Power salute during the American national anthem in 1968 in Mexico City. Tennis player Martina Navratilova was open about her lesbian lifestyle throughout her professional career and still is wildly popular. Billie Jean King preceded Martina and in some respects gave Martina the courage to affirm her lifestyle publicly. Billie Jean was also a relentless pioneer for women's rights through the Women's Sports Foundation. Curt Flood basically sacrificed his outstanding baseball career to stand up for a player's right to free agency and some degree of self-determination as a professional athlete. He abhorred the idea that athletes could be bought and sold by team owners and had no say at all in the decision.

These examples demonstrate how some athletes used sport to agitate for change in their society. Whether they succeeded is not the point. They raised consciousness and inspired others to stop and question their views. In an institution that generally preserves the status quo, these outspoken actions are all the more remarkable.

Use of Sport by Politicians

American athletes who win a Super Bowl, World Series, or other significant event can bet on receiving a congratulatory phone call from the president of the United States. In the last 50 years, virtually every U.S. president has used his image as a sport fan to link himself to Everyman. Presidents have thrown out the first ball of the baseball season, attended the U.S. Open tennis championships, and graced the opening ceremonies of the Olympic Games with their presence. President Richard Nixon even suggested certain plays he thought the Washington Redskins should use in their quest for a Super Bowl title. Nixon was perhaps the first U.S. president to use sport contacts and his keen personal interest in sport to portray himself as a regular guy (Ball and Loy 1975).

President Barack Obama leaped onto the front page of newspapers by predicting the outcome of the NCAA basketball tournament in 2009 in picking the University of North Carolina. He also shared his personal opinion with the world that the NCAA Bowl Championships in football should involve a play-off system to determine the number-one team rather than relying on polls. Even more notable was his unprecedented decision to support the bid of his hometown of Chicago to host the 2016 Olympic Games by flying to Copenhagen,

Denmark, and addressing the delegates before the vote. Unfortunately for Chicago, the International Olympic Committee chose Rio de Janeiro instead.

For athletes who achieve notable success, one of the most coveted rewards is a visit to the White House following their victory. Young athletes are impressed with the experience and tend to rank it high among their personal highlights. The president and his invited political allies use the occasion to solidify their support and demonstrate a personal admiration for winners of significant competitive events.

At the local level, state governors, members of the state legislature, mayors, and other political figures are never far from view at major sporting events in their state or city. Mayors almost routinely wager on the outcome of the contests involving their city's team, and when they lose the wager, they award a symbolic prize indigenous to their region. The media pick up the news of the wager, and the politicians manufacture a media opportunity both before and after the event.

Lest you get the impression that modern politicians invented the use of sport to enhance their image, they did not. For centuries, kings, queens, and heads of state seized upon athletic contests as opportunities for public relations. Current politicians are simply following a well-worn script.

Certain athletes have used their sport fame to propel themselves to political prominence once their playing days end. Notable examples include Jim Ryan, representative from Kansas and former Olympic distance runner; Jim Bunning, Hall of Fame pitcher for the Detroit Tigers and current senator from Kentucky; Jack Kemp, quarterback for the Buffalo Bills and former representative from New York; Bill Bradley, basketball player for the New York Knicks and former senator from New Jersey; Jesse Ventura, a professional wrestler

 POP CULTURE

Betting on College Games

The governor of Alabama, Bob Riley, bet Florida governor Charlie Christ on the outcome of the Southeastern Conference Football Championship game between the Universities of Florida and Alabama. It the Crimson Tide lost, Riley had to send ribs to Christ and if the Gators lost, Christ would send oranges to Riley. Seems harmless enough, but many Alabama citizens criticized the governor and viewed his bet as a conflict of interest. Here's why. Riley has consistently taken an anti-gambling position and in fact set up a state task force in 2009 that has been raiding illegal gambling establishments that house gambling machines. Riley learned his lesson, as just a few weeks later he declined to bet Governor Rick Perry on the national championship game between Alabama and the Texas Longhorns (Jones 2010).

who became governor of Minnesota; and Arnold Schwarzenegger, a bodybuilder who became governor of California. On the local level, celebrities such as coaches at universities and high schools parlay their name recognition to enter public roles as mayors, commissioners, and community leaders.

Politics Within Sport

Every sport is controlled internationally by a governing body that sets the rules of play, defines age groups for competition, sanctions competitions, stages world championships, administers drug tests, and promotes the sport worldwide. The organization comprises representative governing bodies from every participating nation, and organizational officials are elected from within the membership. The process of electing members to the international board of directors is clearly political and not unlike what transpires in other governmental elections. Powerful nations protect their turf and self-interests by forming liaisons with other nations, dispensing favors, and using their vast resources to advance their influence. Nations with less influence form coalitions to pressure for a place at the decision-making table.

The picture at the international level is replicated at the national level in every country. National boards wield awesome power, and aspiring leaders campaign for years to earn a place of prestige on the board. Depending on who is on the board, the mission of the organizations may tilt toward developing high-performance athletes, increasing participation by the masses, showing sensitivity to minorities, demonstrating compassion for athletes with physical disabilities, attracting more spectators, or generating more revenue through marketing the sport. In an ideal world, a national governing body would have the will and means to do all of the above and more.

Aside from national governing bodies, there are also organizations dedicated to youth sport. Some are multisport, such as the Amateur Athletic Union, while most focus on one sport. When more than one organization emerges in a single sport, such as in youth soccer, the result is a confusing war of words and political clashes over purpose, rules, and championships.

In the United States, the National Federation of State High School Associations loosely governs interscholastic sport. But as the name *federation* suggests, the organization has minimal control. It sanctions no national championships and allows each state to set its own rules of competition. The result is policies that differ widely from state to state and can be most confusing for athletes and their families, especially for those who move from one state to another.

Over the years, college athletics in the United States have endured several political battles between organizations fighting for control. The winner has been the NCAA, which claims the bulk of colleges and universities as members. The NCAA has created different levels (I, II, and III) of competition and allows schools to choose their level provided that they meet certain standards. The philosophical differences between the three levels create controversy and political horse trading. Big schools want to be free to spend their money and conduct what amounts to a quasi-professional sport program. Smaller schools where athletics are more student centered demand more accountability from institutions, stronger academic standards for athletes, and emphasis on participation rather than high performance.

In U.S. professional sport, various competing leagues spring up to challenge existing professional leagues. Some competing leagues enjoy success, such as the American Football League, which eventually merged with the established NFL. The two football leagues found that together they could be more efficient, powerful, and attractive to commercial sponsors and television stations than two competing leagues could be.

Professional tennis has suffered from being divided into two organizations, one for women and one for men. Although women and men often play at the same tournaments, their separate organizations compete for facilities (e.g., practice courts, weight room, training room, press room), courts for matches, prize money to award champions, commercial sponsors, and fan loyalty. So far, politics and distrust from both sides have blocked a beneficial merger. The result is a fractured delivery of the professional game that confuses fans around the world and limits the appeal of both men's and women's tennis to potential commercial sponsors.

Chapter Summary

In this chapter we discussed how sport and politics interact internationally, nationally, and locally. The U.S. government is responsible for protecting the rights of its citizens, and it enforces certain safeguards in sport, ensures that the rights of all citizens are respected in sport, and protects the financial interests of the public. Governments use sport to develop local, state, or national identities and promote unity among citizens. Governments and political leaders also use sport to promote dominant social values and encourage social integration of all citizens. Critics of government accuse politicians of using sport to distract citizens from other pressing issues or to reinforce the status quo. Politicians often use sport to enhance their personal image.

When athletes succeed in international competition, their excellence is often attributed to the superior way of life of their home nation. The Olympic Games have been used repeatedly to validate systems of government, generate support for political leaders, and prove the superiority of various ethnic or racial groups.

Sport events are typically staged with nationalistic displays that include the national anthem, marching bands, patriotic themes, and flag presentations. Citizens who take pride in their country are more likely to reelect current governmental leaders and feel content with their society.

In the United States, when young children are exposed to sport, they begin the socialization process of learning to respect authority, work hard, persevere, rebound from failure, and cooperate with others. Sport is just one way these traditional American values are passed to the next generation.

At times, sport can be a powerful agent in promoting change in society. The sport world constantly reminds the public, fans, and participants that changes are occurring. The emergence of the African American athlete on the public stage, and later the rise of women's sport, confirm recent landmark changes in U.S. culture.

Within sport organizations, politics influences the direction of the group and determines who leads the group. Those who advocate for radical change within a sport fight to select sympathetic leaders, while those who do not want radical change rally around their chosen candidates. Most athletic groups have gradually begun to reserve a place at their decision-making table for females, minorities, and athletes with disabilities. Through diversity, sport can grow by reaching out to new populations of participants and fans.

Finally, we looked at the tendency for coaches and athletes to be politically conservative. Their training to respect traditional values and authority figures, along with a belief in hard work, discipline, and good attitude, tends to influence their political philosophy. Those who succeed in sport or life often want to conserve the environment in which they excel.

Development Through Sport

Student Outcomes

After reading this chapter, you will know the following:

- A definition of development through sport and physical activity
- The benefits of sport that have been substantiated through research
- The distinct benefits of sport at various ages
- The four types of educational–developmental sport programs
- What sport developmental programs are like in the United States and worldwide
- Potential sources of funding for sport development programs

The varsity girls' basketball team at Friends Central High School in Philadelphia, Pennsylvania, were excited to meet their new friends from the "Katie at the Bat Team" at the Shepard Recreation Center in West Philadelphia. The varsity girls turned into instructors and cheerleaders for their younger charges, who were just learning to play basketball. Set up at stations, girls worked on their skills while having fun and making new buddies. Eventually, teams were drafted, with players from both the "student" and "coach" groups on teams for full-court scrimmages to test their newly learned skills. The girls from the Katie at the Bat Team had first linked up with their mentors when they came to watch them compete in a high school basketball game. That was the beginning of a partnership designed to expose a group of at-risk and lower-income kids to a life outside their normal sphere.

In every culture through history, sport and physical activity have been used to enhance the quality of life for participants. While sometimes the focus is on the training and competitive skills of elite athletes, there has always been an acknowledgment that all citizens can derive immediate personal benefits from participating in sport and physical activity.

In recent years, the focus of sport and physical activity for developmental purposes has become more clear, better organized, more abundantly funded, and more highly valued as a method of improving societies for people of all ages and both genders, able-bodied as well as disabled, and from all income levels.

In this chapter, we will consider exactly how sport and physical activity are used for personal and societal development, the types of programs that are available, and their potential for achieving their objectives.

We will also consider sport development programs from a worldwide perspective and their possible impact on global health issues, cultural understanding, and peace among nations. In the United States, we'll look at the potential impact of these programs on underprivileged youth and older adults, on academic performance, and on crime reduction, as well as their usefulness as a tool to fight health issues such as rising obesity and diabetes.

Benefits of Sport and Physical Activity

If you think back to chapter 1 where we defined the differences between sport, physical activity, and games, you will remember that in order for an activity to be classified as a sport, it must include physical activity, rules set by a governing body, competition, and typically specialized equipment or venues to play in. For purposes of the discussion to follow,

we will view physical activities and sport as one overall concept, similarly to the way the Sporting Goods Manufacturers Association does in its reports of sport participation (SGMA 2008c). That means that when we refer to sport in the chapter, we are including physical activities such as strength training, running, walking or swimming for recreation, Pilates, and yoga.

The benefits of sport can be placed into the following categories:

- Fun: Physical movements that are performed for recreation and are pleasurable for the participant.

- Better health: Types of physical activities that enhance physical well-being include cardio-respiratory and muscular strength, endurance, and flexibility activities. Regular sport participation promotes the functioning of all body systems and helps develop resistance to disease.

- Social integration: Sport activities promoting interpersonal interaction, cooperation, and competition affect social development and develop teamwork and social skills.

- Moral development: Sport activities can provide opportunities for developing an acceptable moral code and create situations that require moral choices by participants. A positive personal moral code includes development of honesty, integrity, fairness, and responsibility. The key to developing moral decision making is for the coach to set the program philosophy, allow players to confront moral choices, and encourage them to adopt the best course of action.

- Personal development of self-esteem and self-efficacy: Sport enhances an individual's sense of self-worth, self-concept, and feelings of adequacy. In particular, youth can experience a feeling of success through sport that improves self-confidence and promotes a positive personality.

EXPERT'S VIEW

Lisa Hoffstein

Lisa Hoffstein believes in her vision and approach to working with disenfranchised, inner-city girls. Her approach has been to use sports, particularly softball, basketball, and tennis, to attract girls to the program. Once they are in the program, the staff and volunteer mentors offer educational programs in literacy, nutrition, health, and the arts. The goal is to help improve their current life overall and enhance their prospects for the future.

A lifelong athlete and former varsity tennis player at the University of Pennsylvania, Lisa Hoffstein has dedicated her professional career to working with disenfranchised youth. You've heard, I'm sure, of the classic American poem, "Casey at the Bat"; this poem was the inspiration for Lisa's children's book for young girls titled *Katie at the Bat,* which also features illustrations by talented young artists from several Philadelphia schools. The driving force behind the book was to share the story of the heroine, who steps up to the plate with the game in the balance. The story is about believing in yourself, facing up to challenges, and expecting that anything is possible.

Using the book as a springboard, Lisa founded the Katie at the Bat Team, a nonprofit dedicated to "helping kids hit homeruns in life." The program enlists the help of local high school athletes, along with the men's and women's varsity tennis teams from the University of Pennsylvania, to mentor the younger girls. In addition, more than a dozen of the girls are bused to Bethel Academy in nearby Ardmore for academic tutoring.

The very existence of programs like this around the country is testimony to what one determined individual like Lisa Hoffstein can achieve by having a vision, commitment, and a wide network of supportive volunteers to sustain a program. Hoffstein prepped for this life work by earning both bachelor's and master's degrees in education from the University of Pennsylvania and an MBA from the Wharton School in 1988. She then began her career as a classroom teacher in the Philadelphia public schools and the Quaker schools. One of her early experiences in outreach was to design and implement the Wharton West Philadelphia Project, partnering the prestigious Wharton Business School with the urban community. She has also been national executive director of the Milken Young Entrepreneurs program (Hoffstein 2010).

• Cognitive development: Sport can improve thinking, help improve academic performance, and allow the brain to continue healthy growth even at advanced ages.

Benefits of Sport at Various Ages

While the accepted benefits of sport apply generally to participants of all ages, there are some differences in the significance of various benefits that depend on age. For example, children are in the process of growth and maturation, and physical activity can have a powerful effect on their development. Older adults, in contrast, are fully developed but typically are more focused on maintaining physical health, avoiding disease, and enhancing the quality of their daily life. Let's look at some of the key differences between age groups.

Childhood

Childhood is the time from birth through the elementary school years. It is the time of the most rapid growth and development we will ever experience physically, emotionally, cognitively, and socially. Children begin to learn about their world through movement, and by practicing fundamental movement skills they can develop the skills to explore their world. During the early years, children should learn to walk, run, skip, hop, balance, fall, catch, throw, and kick, to list just a few fundamental movements. Once these basics are under control, they are capable of learning and enjoying basic sport skills, playing games, and learning to play sports.

Children also can use sports to enhance their self-concept in its early stages of development by mastering certain physical activities and then learning new ones. They are introduced to ideas of fair play, playing by the rules, being a good sport, and cooperating with teammates.

ACTIVITY TIME-OUT

"Development" Activities

Pick a sport of your choice, either one you have played or a new sport you would enjoy exploring. See if you can determine if that sport has specific "development" programs or foundations to reach out to specific groups. You cannot assume that simply playing a sport will necessarily promote development, although it is likely to enhance physical skill. But your aim in this inquiry is to see if the sport you choose has developed a formula and process to do more through the sport than simply develop skilled players or to provide fun for participants. Report back to your class on what you discovered.

Team sports are particularly attractive to children because they introduce kids to working together for a common goal, accepting their role on a team, and learning to deal with winning and losing in competition.

Sports also fill an important role if they are fun, invigorating, and challenging for youngsters. Their attitudes and habits about lifelong physical activity are likely to be formed at this stage of life.

Youth

Youth includes youngsters in middle and high school who are in transition between childhood and the adult world. Sport and physical activity can continue to affect all dimensions of their development if they continue to be physically active. Unfortunately, the system in our culture tends to weed kids out based on their competency in sport so that during adolescence, more than half of children who were physically active have dropped out of sport. Those who have had success as children often feel lost and betrayed by the people who encouraged them in sport. It is difficult for youth to maintain or enhance self-concept when they are cut from a school team, which implies to them that they lack talent.

Puberty also affects youth in that they must deal with rapidly changing bodies that are unfamiliar to them. Growth spurts that occur before or after changes in most of their peers can cause embarrassment, self-consciousness, and social withdrawal. Interest in the opposite sex may consume thoughts and time while sport participation takes a backseat.

This is a critical time to help youth stay physically active in a way that is fun, challenging, and enjoyable. New sports and physical activities should be explored that allow participants at all levels of experience and skill to join in. Youth need

to realize and accept that their world of physical activity and sport need not revolve only around traditional team sports. The challenge is to expose them to a wide variety of physical activities that are enjoyable now and hold promise for future participation.

Adults

The adult years are consumed with discovering who we are and want to be, forming close relationships with others, challenging ourselves intellectually, and plotting a career path. Young adults tend to experiment with different behaviors, try them on, and then decide whether they fit.

The years of young adulthood usually involve some physical activity that is chosen to improve fitness, appearance, and attractiveness to others. The pressure of college, work, or young families begins to challenge a commitment to physical activity, and for some, the easy option is to reduce or drop regular physical activity. For young adults who are healthy and feeling invincible and busy, physical activity often slips as a priority.

Joining a group or team for sport or physical activity can be terrific motivation to persist and at the same time enlarge people's circle of friends and contacts. Those who choose sports or activities they can do by themselves often have the toughest time persisting in their activity.

Adults who have discovered the fun and exhilaration of sport are most likely to continue to seek that thrill as a stress reducer and respite from work. People who view physical activity as "work" often dread the "workouts" they believe they should do but don't feel like doing. The key is for them to identify what activity they would actually look forward to and never miss if they can help it.

Continued participation in some form of physical activity is imperative to ensure adults maintain a healthy weight and hopefully prevent chronic diseases.

Older Adults

Older adults who continue their patterns of physical activity are lucky in that they decided long ago it was important for them, or they simply enjoyed it so much that they made time for regular physical recreation. For those who may have slipped away during their adult years, health concerns begin to help them refocus on the importance of physical activity for fitness, good health, and resistance to disease. Plus, in the back of their minds is the question of both length of life and quality of life in the years they have left.

Older adults tend to gravitate toward physical activities that are group oriented, especially once they retire from the workforce. They treasure the social interaction and friends who share similar interests. Travel that involves sport is often attractive, and at this stage of life, people have more time and money to afford it.

As we age, most of us become concerned with the expected decline of our cognitive functions. Recent breakthroughs in research clearly show that physical activity can in fact help us continue to generate new brain cells and strengthen the connections to those we already have. Many older folks would much rather walk, swim, play golf, or play tennis

than settle for a life of crossword puzzles to keep them intellectually vibrant.

While not a topic for this chapter on development, current research and practice for communities designed for older adults always involve programs for ongoing physical activity. In fact, the term "active living" is commonly used to refer to the lifestyle promoted in various communities. It implies that people will be happier and healthier if they stay active.

Education–Development Programs for Children and Youth

Recent history has seen myriad uses of sport and physical activity to enhance the overall development of children and youth. Each program is designed to fit local needs and to complement other programs that may be available in the community. The emphasis of each program is determined by the founders and board of directors. Let's take a look at some of the most common program philosophies (American Sports Data 2005).

Stand-Alone Sport and Physical Activity Programs

Stand-alone sport and physical activity programs are typically established to teach youngsters the skills and strategies of various sports and introduce them to competition. The expectation is that they will improve their physical capabilities, test them in competition, and build a foundation for later participation as they age and improve.

Team sports are particularly popular for teaching social and moral values, good sportsmanship, and teamwork. Many individual sports place more emphasis on developing independence, self-reliance, self-discipline, and confidence. Examples are tennis, golf, martial arts, dance, swimming, wrestling, track and field, and a host of extreme sports.

Examples of stand-alone team sport programs are urban youth baseball academies in Compton, California and Hialeah, Florida. These academies have facilities and programs to introduce inner-city boys and girls to baseball and softball and renew interest in baseball in areas where baseball has become unavailable due to lack of public support, expense of maintaining fields, and lack of proper equipment. These academies are also an outreach program to African American and Hispanic youth, designed to enhance their quality of life; one of the program goals is to ensure that each child graduates from high school. Trying to counteract the image that baseball is not "cool" with inner-city youth, these urban youth academies offer programs, instruction, and competition free of charge to participants. They are supported by the major league teams in their city.

Similar to the urban youth baseball academies is another initiative of Major League Baseball, dubbed "RBI" or Reviving Baseball in Inner Cities. The youth of today may not remember great black players such as Jackie Robinson, Willie Mays, Hank Aaron, Frank Robinson, and Roberto Clemente. In fact, the percentage of black baseball players has fallen to only 8% of all players in Major League Baseball in recent years, and the lack of popularity of the sport in cities where African Americans are the majority is clearly a factor.

At-Risk Prevention Programs

Many communities have used sport as a hook to attract children and youth who are at risk of delinquency from school and running afoul of the law. The Police Athletic League (PAL) is an example of a program that includes sports among its attractions, along with other activities such as arts, crafts, and dance. The local police department contributes to funding youth programs, and many officers volunteer as leaders and coaches.

Another organization that is particularly popular across the southern part of the United States is Boys and Girls Clubs. A typical program to attract inner-city kids might be a midnight youth basketball league to encourage kids to engage in sport rather than roam the streets looking for trouble.

In the northern part of the country, YMCAs and YWCAs or Jewish Community Centers (JCC) are plentiful and offer attractive facilities along with sport programs for kids. In many cases, the Y offerings include classes and programs for the whole family, which enables these facilities to function as family recreation centers.

Another example of an at-risk prevention program is Girls in the Game, founded in 1995 by a small group of women in Chicago to ensure that girls were exposed to and participated in sport and fitness activities. The target population was specifically one we identified in chapter 11 as least likely to be physically active—inner-city minority girls. The girls in the program are divided racially as 53% African American, 24% Latino, 7% Caucasian, and 16% other. By age groups, they are 14% ages 6 to 8, 35% ages 9 and 10, 28% ages 11 and 12, 13% ages 13 and 14, and 10% ages 15-18. Research has shown that girls who are physically active and involved in healthy-lifestyle programs have higher grades; are more likely to graduate; have higher self-esteem; and are less likely to drink, use drugs, or engage in risky behaviors. Sadly, today one in every six girls is overweight compared with 1970, when only one in 21 girls was overweight. Eighty-four percent of urban 11th- and 12th-grade girls do not take a gym class, compared to 48% of boys. It wasn't long before the leaders of the program realized that their girls needed more than just sports, and the program was expanded. The girls wanted information on nutrition, health education, and leadership development; these components have now been integrated into the total program experience. Partnerships with the city of Chicago, the public schools, and public parks have provided the financial and facility support, along with the help of fund-raising and the largesse of private donors (Girls in the Game 2010).

A distinctly different program is designed to recruit coaches for Coach for America (CFA), the flagship program of Up2Us. The parent program Up2Us is a national coalition of sport-based youth development organizations. This program seeks coaches who will teach sports and nutrition to kids

Day camps that expose kids to nature are a great way to incorporate education into a physically fun-filled day.

in under-resourced communities in the hope of preventing childhood obesity. Coaches also encourage kids to stay off the streets and stay in school and help them bolster their self-esteem and self-image. Coach for America is funded by an AmeriCorps National grant from the Corporation for National and Community Service, a federal government program established by the U.S. Congress.

Academic Enrichment and Sport Programs

Academic enrichment and sport programs have spread across the country especially to serve economically disadvantaged youth. These programs typically offer a safe haven after school and include physical activity and sports along with an academic focus. Tutors are often available, and time is devoted to completing school homework assignments. Many federal and state grants have been available to establish such programs because they promise to improve the academic performance of participants, encourage good citizenship, and yet still offer fun and recreation through sport. Organizations in this category often sponsor fund-raising events along with relying on grants to provide financial support. Typically the organizations are established as nonprofit so that they can raise funds and receive

donations from businesses and individuals, and this money is tax deductible.

Golf and tennis have nationwide programs of this type called The First Tee and National Junior Tennis and Learning (NJTL), respectively. The First Tee is an initiative of the World Golf Foundation, and its stated mission is "to impact the lives of young people by providing learning facilities and educational programs that promote character-development and the life-enhancing values through the game of golf."

The nine core values that the program espouses are honesty, integrity, sportsmanship, respect, confidence, responsibility, perseverance, courtesy, and judgment (The First Tee 2009).

The NJTL was founded by professional tennis players Arthur Ashe and Charles Pasarell more than 40 years ago, when it was the first program of its kind. While these programs are sponsored by their national sport organizations, their purpose is not to develop elite athletes but to expose underserved populations to the sport in the hope that they will become lifelong participants and spectators. Because these programs are either free or very low cost to participants, funding is a local challenge even for programs that are national in scope. In most cases, costs are reduced for programs like this through recruitment of volunteer coaches, and leaders and local chapters sponsor an array of fund-raising events to sustain their operations.

Academic Development and Sport Programs

Programs that integrate sports and academics seek to attract the interest of youth by combining the two. For example, an after-school enrichment class in math could use sport statistics as a vehicle to interest kids and show practical applications. Kids can practice and improve writing skills by writing about sport situations, athletes, or events such as the Super Bowl or other national or international championships. Reading about sports can stimulate a lifelong habit of reading in youngsters who might otherwise be uninterested in reading. Even history can come alive for young people who are exposed to information about where and how sports were developed, famous champion athletes, and world record holders.

Scuba diving courses can incorporate the rudiments of marine biology or oceanography to get kids excited about the sciences of studying bodies of water and their effects on society. Similarly, sport experiences can be the vehicle through which to teach young people moral codes and decision making and enhance character development. Social development is also often demonstrated by participation in team sports and activities and will later transfer to the classroom and the workplace if the experiences are properly structured and delivered.

An appreciation of the appeal of nature is often the focus of sport or physical activity programs such as snow sports, hiking, camping, or wilderness survival. Kids can learn much about nature, geography, forestry, and the environment through outdoor activities in the mountains, on the water, in the desert, or on a trip through the Everglades. When programs expose kids to nature and teach them how to interact with the environment, a by-product is an enhanced self-confidence to deal with unfamiliar or uncertain surroundings.

What all of these various educational–sport programs have in common is that they typically fill a need for after-school care in a safe environment that kids enjoy. In our society, with women now outnumbering men in the workplace and both parents working, kids are often left to fend for themselves after school unless they are enrolled in programs like these. The importance of physical activity and sport in programs is clear for a generation of youth who get too little physical exercise, often have poor diets, and are bombarded with technology like video games that has frequently replaced physical play and exercise.

International Outreach Through Sport

Outside the United States, sport and physical activity have taken on a significant role in helping to promote better health and well-being, prevent

 IN THE ARENA WITH . . .

Outward Bound

Many of the finest schools in America have linked up with Outward Bound, an international organization that was founded in Great Britain in 1941 to give young seaman the ability to survive harsh conditions at sea. It has morphed into a nonprofit, independent outdoor education organization with approximately 200,000 yearly participants. One of its target audiences is inner-city youth at risk, who learn to make better life choices and better understand themselves and others. Participants learn wilderness skills, team skills, and leadership skills through activities such as climbing and rappelling or taking on an obstacle course using beams and cables suspended high in the sky. Other groups focus on canoeing, rafting, hiking, sailing, dog sledding, or rock climbing. In a typical class, which can last for a week or a semester, participants are divided into small groups under the watchful supervision of a highly trained instructor and given the basic outdoor and skills development training necessary. Eventually the group learns to be self-sufficient, and instructors hang back and let the group handle the challenges as a unit. Social skills and leadership skills emerge during this phase of the experience. It is telling that schools see the value of challenging youth to work together to enjoy and appreciate nature while coping with the barriers it may present. Vital survival skills learned build participants' knowledge, skills, and feelings of mastery and accomplishment (Outward Bound 2010).

diseases, and enhance the quality of life for people of all ages. The goal of the organizations that follow is to promote regular physical activity for all people all over the world.

The World Health Organization (WHO) has taken the lead in the fight against noncommunicable diseases such as cardiovascular disease, cancer, diabetes, and chronic respiratory disease. "Unhealthy diets, caloric excess, physical inactivity and obesity and associated chronic diseases are the greatest public health problem in most countries in the world" (WHO 2003).

Worldwide, more than 60% of adults do not engage in sufficient levels of physical activity. The groups most affected are women, older adults, people from lower socioeconomic groups, and people who are disabled. People are becoming more sedentary the world over, and the result is an alarming increase in obesity and the consequences of poor health. The World Health Organization believes that regular physical activity, active play, and sport can directly affect the major risks to good health such as high blood pressure, high cholesterol, obesity, tobacco use, and stress.

Overall, physical inactivity is estimated to cause 1.9 million deaths globally and about 10% to 16% of cancers (breast, colon, and rectal) and diabetes mellitus, along with 22% of ischemic heart disease.

The International Olympic Committee (IOC), although it is a sport organization that promotes the performance of elite athletes at the highest level of competition worldwide, has a different take on the value of sport for all.

The IOC believes that human development through sport is based on the three core values of the Olympic Movement. One of these values is *excellence*, which involves giving one's best; making progress toward personal goals; and benefiting from the healthy combination of a strong body, mind, and will. *Friendship* is another core value of the IOC, which encourages us to use sport to develop an understanding of people from all over the world. The final core value is *respect*, which includes respect for self, for one's body, for others, and for rules and regulations in sport. It also encompasses fair play and support for the battle against doping in sport.

The IOC believes that in addition to promoting physical wellness, sport can contribute to a safer, more prosperous, and more peaceful society. It can bridge cultural and ethnic divides, create jobs and businesses, promote tolerance and nondiscrimination, and reinforce social integration.

The Olympic Charter describes the IOC's social responsibility in this way:

"The goal of Olympism is to place sport at the service of the harmonious development of man, with a view to promoting a peaceful society concerned with the preservation of human dignity."

From the time of the revival of the Olympic Games near the end of the 19th century, founder Pierre de Coubertin, who was a French educator, believed that the Olympics should be a strong advocate of international cooperation and emphasize the social and human values of sport.

Lest you think these descriptions of the Olympic Movement are simply more esoteric philosophies than actual practice, consider that the IOC has put forth the following initiatives:

- *Bringing sport to rural and underdeveloped communities.* In cooperation with the United Nations Food and Agriculture Organization, the IOC has provided basic sport equipment and facilities to encourage people toward a lifestyle of physical activity. Nations that have benefited include Burkina Faso, Cambodia, Ecuador, Tanzania, Niger, Mauritania, Guinea, Samoa, and Laos.

- *Local economy development.* In cooperation with the International Labor Organization, the IOC has implemented a major poverty alleviation and economic development program in Mozambique. Highlights of the program include paying schools fees to enable over 600 primary school–aged children from underprivileged families to attend school. Women have received training to manufacture school uniforms and to produce groceries to be sold at market. A sport training center open to more than 1,000 children has been built, and sports and education are the key programs.

- *Rehabilitation of war victims.* In collaboration with the International Paralympics Committee, the IOC has established a project on rehabilitation of those injured by war through sports for amputees and other persons with physical disabilities. This project has begun in Angola and Portugal.

- *HIV and AIDS prevention through sport.* The IOC has partnered in the fight against HIV and AIDS with the United Nations, UNICEF, and the International Federation of Red Cross and Red Crescent Societies. The first Toolkit designed specifically for members of the sport community was jointly published by the IOC and the United Nations. It is available in five languages and provides guidance for athletes, suggestions for programs, and sources of further information. Jointly sponsored seminars by all the organizations mentioned are held regionally to discuss and develop strategies to deal with the pandemic of HIV and AIDS.

• *Bringing hope and joy to refugee camps.* Again, in cooperation with the United Nations, since 1996 the IOC has worked on sport projects for refugee camps and resettlements around the world. The effort is designed to foster hope and optimism among people who are bored by idleness and weighed down by the stress of their daily existence.

Peace Initiatives Through Sport

The Sport for Development and Peace International Working Group (SDP IWG) was created in 2004 to work with governments to develop their sport systems and at the same time initiate programs through sport that promote peace between communities, ethnic groups, and countries. At its core, this movement is dedicated to using sport and participation in physical activities to build peace throughout the world.

In order to build strong civil societies, all people must be exposed to the concepts of tolerance and friendship between disparate groups. Sport offers the opportunity to present conflict prevention measures and discourage actions that generate aggression, hatred, and fear.

While it is recognized that sport inherently promotes conflict between opposing players and teams, within the sport framework is an opportunity to engage in conflict that is constructive, healthy, and peaceful. Sports can be conducted within certain rules, traditions, and unwritten rules in the spirit of competition that allow highly contested athletic events to become a model of citizen competition and cooperation at the same time.

A strong negative outcome of conflict is violence, whether in sport or in society at large. Disagreements between groups of people cause gang-related crime, ethnical and racial conflicts, and wars within and between countries. These conflicts affect the entire society and often harm innocent bystanders who become targets or victims.

Sports can become a model to communities in conflict by demonstrating their commitment to the values of *human rights* and *democracy*. Through establishment of self-governing leagues that respect the rights of all individuals and groups and the sport tradition, participants can learn firsthand how to exist in a more peaceful environment.

These are specific ways in which sports can contribute to peace building (based on Kvalsund 2007):

• *Security:* Sport programs can provide a safe haven for children, especially those who have grown up with war and even perhaps participated in war.

• *Rebuilding economies:* Sport facilities need to be funded, constructed, and utilized by everyone. They can become a center for socialization, cultural programs, and additional education and training outside of schools.

• *Rebuilding traumatized populations:* Those who have lived with war, apartheid, genocide, human trafficking, or other heinous social disasters need to rebuild mental and emotional health. Sport can provide an outlet to heal and repair.

• *Political structure:* Sport bodies can become models of democratic functions and influence the attitude of citizens about government, encourage participation, and raise expectations about their leaders.

• *Communication:* Sport is easily communicated through radio, TV, and the Internet and can be of interest to the society at large. The demand for sport news can encourage free communication and build loyalties and pride in the performance of athletes. Sport can also provide a model of athletes from disparate backgrounds or ethnic or racial groups working as a functioning team with respect for each other.

ACTIVITY TIME-OUT

Outward Bound and Peacebuilding

One of the more recent initiatives of Outward Bound (described earlier in this chapter on page 312) is the founding of its Center for Peacebuilding, which is located in Long Island City, New York. Your assignment is to do some research online to discover the goals and methods of this center, which serves more than 30 countries worldwide. Be able to explain the uniqueness of an Outward Bound experience that is focused on peace building and how it differs from a more traditional course. Finally, after reflection on the possibilities, suggest some ways in which this initiative might be better publicized and promoted in the United States.

POP CULTURE

Invictus

Invictus tells the story of legendary leader Nelson Mandela of South Africa as he is elected the first black leader of that country. One of the tools he uses to unite the white and black populations is the remarkable success of the national rugby team, which is heavily populated by white players as they seek the World Cup. In spite of their relative underdog status, the team members rally to win the cup and the hearts and minds of all South African citizens. Mandela shrewdly uses this sporting team to build national pride, unity, and spirit in a fledgling and wobbly union.

- *Reconciling torn societies:* Sports participated in by people from conflicting sides offer opportunities for athletes to respect others as performers and come to know them as people. Once competition has ended, competitors can spend time together discussing social problems, identifying solutions, and building trust in each other.

On May 7 and 8, 2009, the first-ever International Forum on Sport, Peace and Development was broadcast live around the world from the Olympic Museum in Lausanne, Switzerland. The discussions were wide ranging but focused primarily on the overall theme of using sports to promote peace and national cohesion. This international sharing of concepts, ideas, and practical solutions has begun to open up the larger role sports can play in society beyond simply physical fitness, fun, and recreation.

Potential Funding Sources for Sport Development Programs

The ambitious ideas that have been presented in this chapter must be financially supported in order to become a reality, especially in poor and underdeveloped communities and countries. Who should we look for to provide the funds to create and sustain these programs?

International groups such as the United Nations, UNESCO, and the International Olympic Movement are just a few of those that have stepped up to support these efforts to date. In fact, there must be more international groups that have an interest in improving life for citizens of all countries even if it is also in their own self-interest.

Multinational corporations are a potential source of new funds as they expand their reach worldwide. They can't afford to simply exploit a country and its workforce without offering development opportunities to the locales where they operate. Although we could argue that they have a moral duty to do so, they are more likely to join forces as they see that it will improve their business investment to also support efforts to improve the lot of the population where they function daily.

Government groups must also bear responsibility for appropriate funding especially to be used in poorer communities and among people who are disadvantaged. Without erecting insurmountable roadblocks in the form of red tape, delay, and bureaucracy, governments must be creative in disbursing funds on a matching basis with other groups to maximize their impact.

Social organizations and institutions such as schools, community centers, recreation departments, and faith-based organizations must also pitch in by joining with others with similar goals. Repetition and separateness is not efficient, nor is duplication of effort. Coordination and cooperation are needed between the various groups who aim for sport and physical activity programs to have a broader meaning than just sport competition; they must work together to maximize their collective resources.

Finally, a message needs to be crafted and delivered to charitable organizations at every level and to charitable citizens who have the financial resources to contribute. People around the world who hope for world peace and reconciliation can grasp the opportunity through sport that could help us move in a better direction.

Chapter Summary

In this chapter we have taken a broad view of the meaning of sport for development locally, nationally, and worldwide. We have summarized the documented benefits of sport and physical activity and specifically examined how those benefits differ for folks of different ages.

We also explored the four types of educational–developmental programs that exist and detailed their differences. Some programs simply offer sports; some combine sports and education; and others use sports as a tool to prevent crime and school dropout and to build positive social characteristics in youth. Over the years, the growth and success of many of these programs have been documented; and it has been shown that they enhance the lives of youngsters, particularly those from underserved communities suffering from poverty, neglect, and lack of leadership.

Stepping out of the United States, we've looked at the role sports can play in other countries, par-

ticularly those that have been impoverished or torn apart by war from within or from without. Sports are seen as part of the solution for rebuilding and regenerating local and national pride, hope, and conciliation. Led by such prestigious organizations such as the United Nations and the IOC, the emphasis on sport is directed toward improving the health and well-being of all citizens.

Finally, we've looked at the possible funding sources for these sport development programs both in the United States and abroad. Without financial backing that is significant and long term, sport programs especially in poorer communities will fail. It is up to governments, sport organizations, and the business community to work together to ensure continuing opportunities through sport.

Deviance and Sport

Student Outcomes

After reading this chapter, you will know the following:

- Issues pertaining to rule breaking in sport
- How emotion helps create deviant behavior
- The problem of violence in sport on and off the field
- Issues relating to performance enhancements and doping
- The problems of eating disorders and hazing in sport
- The debate about sport gambling

317

Over the Thanksgiving weekend in 2009, the world that Tiger Woods had built suddenly began to crack, eventually to fall apart. One of the greatest athletes of our lifetime and certainly the biggest moneymaker in the history of sport threw away his reputation, his family, and lucrative endorsements and lost millions of fans. His off-the-golf-course behavior of infidelity was with a string of women, ranging from a young next-door neighbor to cocktail waitresses to women of questionable reputation. One by one, more than a dozen women materialized to claim having had a sexual relationship with Woods, and some media sources say the total could be over 100.

The immediate result was that Woods took some time from the golf tour and entered a rehabilitation center for sexual addiction. Within a few months, he was back on the tour but exhibiting just a shadow of his former intimidating golf skills. Perhaps his spotty play was due to the money, gone forever due to lost sponsor endorsements from AT&T, Accenture, PepsiCo Gatorade, and Proctor and Gamble Gillette totaling somewhere between $25 and $30 million. The companies themselves lost between $5 billion and $12 billion in market value for their shareholders. Woods' agent, IMG, lost between 15% and 20% of sponsor deals it would have been entitled to (Tse 2010; Marikar 2009). The most disastrous loss was of his wife Elin, who had trusted him and eventually divorced him, along with approximately $750 million in compensation to support her and their two children (Fox News 2010b). This sad story is clearly a dramatic case of deviant athlete behavior on the part of someone who seemed to have made all the right moves up to that time. Why did he throw it all away?

People in a society are expected to conform to the rules and norms of the group. People who do not conform are labeled as *deviant*. **Deviant** is an adjective that means departing from or deviating especially from an accepted norm. Deviating is not necessarily negative; it can be positive or negative. However, in U.S. popular vernacular, *deviant* is often equated with *devious*, which has a decidedly negative connotation. It is in this negative context that we will explore deviance in sport in this chapter. We will examine the relationship between sport and destructive actions such as generally breaking the rules, committing crimes, behaving violently against others, using drugs and other performance-enhancing substances, and gambling on competition outcomes.

Because there is so much publicity about the misconduct of college and professional athletes in the United States, it may seem that on the whole athletes clearly lack moral values and are out of step with mainstream America. This chapter will discuss whether that impression is justified and will compare the incidence of deviant behavior among athletes with that among others in society. We will also study the related question of whether athletics promote, encourage, or reward deviant behavior. Similarly, we will see if people who are attracted to athletics might be predisposed to deviant behavior.

Typically when we study deviant behavior, we study behavior that does not conform to standards of normal behavior owing to the person's unawareness or outright rejection of those norms. Underconformity refers to behavior that does not conform to the generally accepted rules of sport. Such behavior includes breaking team rules, school rules, and competition rules. Many athletes use profanity, haze teammates, drink alcohol, argue with others, or bet on the outcome of a sport event. It is only when that behavior reaches a point outside of accepted limits that it becomes deviant.

Another form of deviance that exists in sport is an overconformity to the expectations of high-performance sport. Examples of overconformity are drastically altering food intake to gain or lose weight or using supplements to improve strength or bulk up muscles. Many athletes may engage in similar practices, but do not carry them to the extreme that qualifies as overconformity.

Excessive conforming may manifest itself as following the rules and customs of sport too well. Particularly in high-performance training, athletes may put such a high priority on sport that they ignore or undervalue other critical areas of life. They may sacrifice friendships, ignore families, or neglect academic studies due to a single-minded dedication to sport training. In the long run, such behaviors are counterproductive.

Cheerleading in the United States is often an example of overconformity. Approximately 95,000 high school girls, along with about 2,200 boys, are high school cheerleaders, with cheerleading now recognized as a sport by the National Federation of State High School Associations (NFHS). Cheerleading has evolved from cheers aimed at raising school spirit to exhibits of great gymnastics skill and athleticism. Unfortunately, the risk involved has vaulted cheering to the most dangerous sport for girls, according to the annual report by the National Center for Catastrophic Sports Injury Research. A 2008 report showed that high school cheerleading accounted for 65.1% of all catastrophic sport injuries among high school females over the preceding 25 years. The report counted only fatal, disabling, or serious injuries. While the most common injuries from cheerleading are strains and sprains, between 1982 and 2007 there were 103 fatal, disabling, or serious injuries in girls' sports, and 67 of those were sustained by cheerleaders (LiveScience 2008).

Another example of overconformity is seen in athletes who use physical violence within the rules of the game. While these actions may be legal in the boxing ring, on the football field, or in an ice hockey rink, similar actions used by everyday citizens would lead to jail. But in sport, a vicious blow delivered to an opponent draws cheers from the crowd, admiration from teammates, and exclamations of "Attaboy!" from the coaching staff.

Rule Breaking

You have to learn the rules of the game in order to play a sport: You can't dribble with two hands in basketball, walk with the ball without dribbling, or hit the arm of an opponent who's shooting without causing a foul. You can't intentionally touch the soccer ball with your hands, run into an opponent without trying to play the ball, or commit a foul in the penalty box without giving up a penalty kick. You can't touch the tennis ball with your body or clothing, reach over the net, serve from inside the line, or throw your racket in frustration.

Sometimes rules are broken because players are unaware of them, do not understand them, or violate them accidentally. At other times, athletes may intentionally break the rules, hoping not to get caught, to interrupt the opponent's flow; or they may do so to vent their frustration and anger.

Is rule breaking today occurring more, less, or about the same as it has historically occurred in sport? Athletes cheat in scoring, modify equipment illegally, commit fouls when officials aren't looking,

In pushing the boundaries of cheerleading higher and higher, many high school girls have suffered serious injury. Do you think collegiate cheerleading competitions, such as the one shown here, are any safer?

participate in brawls, or call a phony injury timeout to get a strategic advantage. Students of sport history will remind us that such instances are not new and have always been a part of playing games. For decades, baseball players have been accused of cheating by doctoring the baseball or throwing spitters that cause pitches to break unpredictably. Ice hockey has always been notorious for its inevitable fights, and most fans are disappointed when fights don't break out. Although illegal, these examples of cheating were tolerated as part of the game unless a player was blatantly caught in the act.

Cheating in sport is nothing new nor is it linked to any one sport. The genteel game of croquet was fraught with cheating by young women who would move the balls or hide them under their skirts.

In reality, there is probably less rule breaking during modern games due to improved officiating, clearer rules, television replays, immediate media comment, and a certain maturity that has evolved in most sports over the years of competition (Dunning 1999). When athletes or coaches do break the rules today, they often do so unintentionally or because they've concluded doing so may advance them toward their ultimate goal. For example, an offensive lineman may risk a penalty for holding to keep the opposing team from flattening and possibly injuring his quarterback.

More people seem to be following the rules also because of the rapid growth of organized youth sport. A coach's primary role in youth sport is to teach her young athletes the rules of the game and expect her athletes to abide by them. Organized programs such as the Citizenship Through Sports Alliance that promote good sporting behavior have also sprung up around the country. National programs backed by universities, youth sport organizations, or national governing bodies publicize and reward players who demonstrate good behavior. Books, websites, and videos on good behavior are widely available. Coaching clinics often feature sessions on teaching good sporting behavior. These tools help coaches, parents, and sport leaders explain the differences between acceptable and unacceptable behavior and suggest alternative actions for controlling frustration or aggressiveness. Athletes who learn these lessons when young develop positive habits that last a lifetime.

Most sport programs have always offered awards for good sporting behavior, often as a second thought for athletes who are not chosen as most outstanding, most valuable player, or team captain. Recently, these standard performance-oriented awards have been supplanted with awards for team behavior, and high schools have adopted an emphasis on good sporting behavior within their athletic philosophy. Banners hung in the gym proclaim the school's stance on good sporting behavior; slogans tout good sporting behavior; and literature refers to good sporting behavior.

By the time most athletes reach high school, they have been exposed to several years of youth sports in which they learned the fundamental rules of the sport and the boundaries of acceptable behavior. As they move up in competitive level, the action becomes faster, the players become more skillful, and some rules become looser. Coaches make sure the athletes know they must abide by the rules or face disciplinary action including lost playing time.

Myriad off-field regulations ensure fair competition and protect the rights of people involved in sport. Sport administrators and coaches must learn these rules, understand how to apply them, and make sure athletes follow them carefully.

Major deterrents and punishments for breaking the rules have evolved over the years, particularly in college sports. The 2008-2009 *NCAA Division I Manual* is composed of 439 pages of rules, explanations of rules, and examples of decisions on breaking the rules. The manual devotes more than 40 pages to academic eligibility alone (National Collegiate Athletic Association [NCAA] 2009a).

The purpose of the NCAA rules is to protect the rights of athletes and coaches who are honest and to eliminate cheating. In the last 25 years, it has become the responsibility of all collegiate athletes, coaches, boosters, and athletic administrators to understand and obey the NCAA rules. Schools now hire specialists in rule enforcement to guide their athletic personnel and monitor actions to prevent unintentional or intentional rule breaking. A college that discovers rule violations is advised to turn itself in for sanctions before the NCAA finds out and comes to investigate.

The penalties for violations have been stepped up in recent years. Coaches have been fired, athletes have been punished by suspension from games or even for a season, and athletic programs have been severely hindered for years to come. When the media learn about the violation, the resulting publicity affects the reputation of the university and its people and affects admissions, fund-raising, and recruiting of future athletes. Schools also suffer huge financial penalties when banned from postseason play or bowl appearances worth millions of dollars.

In spite of the number of stories the media report on deviant acts of athletes, the percentage of athletes involved in such behavior is small when compared to the total athlete population. Rees and Miracle (2004) concluded that participating in high school sport does little to aid or harm the development of social values in adolescents. After reviewing research evidence, they also concluded that certain behaviors labeled as *delinquent* possibly represent positive deviancy within athletics. Behaviors considered deviant in other social contexts seem normal in sport. Hazing, petty theft, and drunkenness seem part of the ritualized acceptance into the sport culture.

Violence seems to be increasing in American society, and the general public believes that athletes are leading the way. The media reporting of crimes committed by high-profile athletes sensationalizes the incidents and leads readers to believe that athletes, particularly African American males, are out of control. In his article "Race, Athletes and Crime" appearing in *Sports Business Journal*, Richard Lapchick (1999) asserted that over a five-year time frame, nearly 100 athletes and coaches are arrested for assault against women. However, he goes on to point out that in a given year,

- three million American women are battered;
- one million American women are raped; and
- 1,400 American women are murdered.

These statistics may include athletes, but the problem is not in athletics. The huge problem of violence against women cuts across race, economic class, age, education, and profession. American streets are more violent than in the past. Although the National Education Association has reported that generally the U.S. public believes schools are becoming more dangerous, the evidence contradicts that belief (National Education Association 2005). School violence in public and private schools remained stable from 2002 to 2003 and continued at about half the rate reported from 1992. The Centers for Disease Control and Prevention (CDC), the Department of Education, and the Department of Justice periodically gather and analyze data to assess the extent and nature of school violence. In 2005-2006, approximately 38% of public schools reported at least one incident of violence to police. In 2005, 24% of students reported gangs at their schools, and 10% of teachers in city schools reported that they were threatened with injury by students. Students ages 12 to 18 were victims of 628,200 violent crimes at school, which included rape, both sexual and aggravated assault, and robbery (CDC 2008).

Emotion and Deviant Behavior

The human emotions that are experienced through or within sport add flavor to our world. For the most part, we are taught to keep our emotions in check during our daily life, and particularly males subvert strong emotions as a requirement of masculinity. But in sports, we are free to express emotions as long as we do so within reason.

The excitement generated by an athletic contest whose outcome lies in doubt down to the last second of play is unusual in daily life. While the excitement is energizing, it is also sometimes stressful. Nervousness, perspiration, clammy palms, headaches, and clouded thoughts can all result from the stress of the game. The more important the event seems, the more exciting and stressful it may be. Once the outcome is decided, the ecstasy of victory or the agony of defeat takes over. It may

ACTIVITY TIME-OUT

Tracking Deviant Behavior

Over the next month, pick at least one major newspaper, online source, or television source and track the stories of athletes exhibiting deviant behavior. Record the athlete's name, the infraction, whether the athlete is a repeat offender, and the punishment given. Once you have assembled your list, look for trends and summarize your impressions. Following are some examples of what to look for:

- Players charged with infractions involving alcohol
- Players charged with violent or abusive crimes against another person
- Positive drug test results
- Illegal recruiting by high schools or colleges
- Illegal actions committed during play
- Coaches cited for unethical or illegal behavior
- Official who helped fix games

be hours or even days before the strong feelings subside and equilibrium returns.

When emotion overcomes us to the point where we stop thinking clearly, deviant behavior can result. An athlete who is consumed by the moment in a game may commit an egregious foul, let loose a stream of profanities, or become violent. Later, after cooling off, the actions committed in the heat of battle may seem immature, antisocial, and despicable.

Big-time sports exploit the emotional makeup of athletes. The stage is set before the game by the coach, who often psyches up his athletes using music, pep talks, slogans, films of moments of glory, or VIPs who exhort the players to perform. As the athletes jog onto the arena, the band fills their ears with stirring music, cannons or fireworks go off, and the crowd roars for the home team.

Some sports or some athletes may not prosper if the state of arousal is too heightened. Athletes who play highly skilled sports may need to lower their arousal to achieve best performance. But most American team sports thrive on excitement and energy.

Spectators are also affected by the emotional excitement. The traditional pregame cocktail party, tailgating, and consumption of alcohol have become synonymous with sport. Students seem to view big-time college football games as an excuse for binge drinking, and by halftime some fans are barely able to function. Some families are so put off by the crude behavior exhibited at college football games or many professional sport events that they do not

feel comfortable bringing their children. Colleges and professional teams have experimented with limiting the number of drinks sold per customer, stopping sales after halftime, and restricting alcohol consumption to pregame tailgating. An increasing number of venues are banning alcohol, although some fans manage to hide their supply. The University of Florida and University of Georgia no longer want to be known for throwing the "World's Largest Outdoor Cocktail Party" at their annual football game held in Jacksonville, Florida. Fans and the media affixed the label to the game in the 1950s. In recent years, the deaths of two students involving alcohol and an emphasis on responsible use of alcohol at both universities prompted Southeast Conference commissioner Mike Slive to request that CBS and ESPN consider dropping the use of the label during telecasts (Fox Sports 2006).

Fans, plied with alcohol, boo the opposing players, taunt the officials, insult visiting fans, perform the wave, cheer their team's good plays, and try to get in front of a television camera. If the game is an important victory, a rush to pull down the goalposts often follows.

When the home team wins a championship, unruly fans often let their emotions carry over to the postgame celebration. In spite of increased security, mobs of fans sometimes get out of control, brawl, destroy property, and embarrass their city or school. Such behavior is no longer all in good fun.

Recent steps to curb student drinking at football games include a policy at the University of Minnesota that models a program at the University of

Wisconsin. The UW program requires that a student who is kicked out of a game for drunken rowdiness won't be allowed back to future games unless she passes an alcohol breath test at the gate. Students under age 21 must be completely clean to enter the stadium, while those over 21 must be below .08 blood alcohol (Associated Press 2009).

In case you think such behavior is indigenous to the United States, let's take a peek at the behavior of fans at soccer games around the world.

Soccer seems to inspire passion like no other sport, and because it is played worldwide and frequently matches country against country, the emotional investment people make in the games is huge. In countries where poorer or less educated people make up the fan base, the behavior may be even worse than anything typically seen in the United States.

Hooliganism of British soccer fans has been a tradition for several hundred years. Usually, the label *hooligan* is applied to working-class men who disrupt soccer games with their antisocial behavior. They may direct their aggression against referees, opposing players, team owners, or other spectators. They may drink excessively, exchange insults, destroy property, and interrupt the game. Fans running on the field, throwing beer cans, pitching stones, and generally frightening other spectators became so pervasive that the British government became involved in an effort to control the growing violence. Even though the British press may sensationalize the stories, violence by fans at sporting events, particularly soccer, has reached alarming levels. In fact, because soccer is played worldwide and enjoys a passionate following, the incidence of violence at soccer matches likely exceeds that for any other sport (Young 2004).

Hooliganism has morphed into a subculture of soccer in many countries and has affected attitudes about the sport. Men with little education and working-class backgrounds seem to embrace such behavior and view it as their right to misbehave even if they harm the rights of others. Aggressive, masculine behavior seems strongly connected to people who lack education, have limited choice in occupation, and lack the skills to personally compete in professional soccer (Dunning 1999).

Violence in Sport

Violence pervades some sports because of their nature and the athletes they attract. The violence that takes place during an athletic contest may carry over into violent behavior off the field, and then both athletes and society suffer the consequences. Young athletes may use the athletic arena to test their masculinity and to establish acceptance by peers.

Violence is highly visible in American sport because it is so prevalent in televised events. Violent plays are shown over and over in instant replays as the sport announcers exclaim over the hit, tackle, block, or body check. Athletes who deliver these violent acts are lionized by fans and teammates for their aggressive play. If a serious injury occurs, the tide shifts as people suspect the athlete's motives and admit that perhaps the game got out of hand.

On-Field Violence

American society seems to be confused about the place of violence in sports, particularly when the sport itself promotes aggressive play and physically abusing an opponent's body. Football is a collision sport. Wrestling, boxing, ice hockey, and lacrosse all require violence just to play the game. Even high-performance basketball involves heavy body contact and physical intimidation. Tackles, blocks, sacks,

 POP CULTURE

Green Street Hooligans

You can get a firsthand look and experience from the original *Green Street Hooligans* of 2005. The movie traces the experience of a wrongfully expelled student from Harvard who moves to London. There he is introduced to the violent underworld of football hooliganism. You may be somewhat shocked and surprised at the culture of hooliganism that has permeated football (soccer) in Great Britain and threatened British teams with disqualifications for the abhorrent behavior of their hooligan fans. The behavior, however, has spread to many other soccer-crazy nations, much to the chagrin of organizers, law enforcement, and other fans. Though American sport has its own die-hard fans in stadiums around the country, I doubt you'll ever encounter anything in the United States quite like the gangs of hooligans.

body checks, and jabs are clearly part of the culture of many sports. The place of violence becomes unclear when it involves acts prohibited by the rules of sport but often accepted by competing athletes. Examples of borderline violence include fistfights between players, hard body blocks in basketball, the brushback in baseball, and the intentional foul in basketball.

Many sports, such as golf, tennis, volleyball, swimming, skiing, equestrian, dance, and track and field, have little or no violence associated with them. These sports emphasize skill, are nonconfrontational, and lack body contact, and all these aspects factor into nonviolent activity. Add to these characteristics the tendency of these sports to be favored by participants with better education and financial resources, whose attitudes toward violence differ substantially from those of working-class athletes.

Masculinity is often rooted in bravery, willingness to risk bodily harm, toughness, and personal aggression. Boys grow up with role models who exhibit these traits. They are accepted by peers if they mimic these traits to prove their worthiness as men. Failure to do so can result in labels of "sissy," "wuss," or worse. Traditionally, sport was closely associated with warfare. Coaches who condition athletes to risk bodily harm for the good of the team often use the language and ethics of war. Think of the traditional headlines in the sport pages: "Vikings destroy Patriots," "Eagles bury Giants," "76ers blow out Nets," "Duke blitzes Wake Forest," "Gators swamp Bulldogs," "Oklahoma guns down the Longhorns, " and so on. Players give teammates the highest compliment when they say, "He's a guy you wanna go to war with."

In the hype leading up to the 2005 Super Bowl between the Philadelphia Eagles and the New England Patriots, television and newspapers featured stories on the "Hit Man," Rodney Harrison, who plays strong safety for the Patriots. Columnist Gary Shelton wrote for the *St. Petersburg Times* (2005), "This is the world of the Hit Man, the nastiest, dirtiest, most frenzied player in the NFL. If you can count on nothing else in Sunday's Super Bowl, you can count on the Patriot's strong safety to go borderline mental. He will shove and scrap, bite, and bully. If you want to wager on who gets the first 15 yard penalty, he is the easy favorite." He has been fined over $350,000 in his 11-year career, more than any other player. Yet among players, he draws respect and admiration. John Lynch, safety for the Denver Broncos, said, "He's one guy I would pay to see play" (Shelton 2005).

In a *Sports Illustrated* poll of 296 players in 2009, wide receiver Hines Ward of the Pittsburgh Steelers easily earned the title of "Dirtiest NFL Player" for the year. It is unusual for a wide receiver to be delivering blows to opponents, but Ward has long been considered an excellent blocking wide receiver. A year earlier, he received back-to-back fines of $15,000 each for hits that weren't even penalized during the game. In the same month, Ward broke the jaw of Bengals rookie linebacker Keith Rivers with a surprise downfield block that ended Rivers' season and did not draw a flag. Ward responded to the charges of dirty play by saying, "When I go across the middle, those guys aren't going to tackle me softly and lay me down to the ground. That's not football. I find it ironic that now you see a receiver delivering blows, and it's an issue. But . . . I've been doing it this way for 11 years" (Deitsch 2009).

Rodney Harrison and Hines Ward clearly overconform to the image of a rough, aggressive player who takes violence in football to the limit. Rather than exclude them from play, others in the game respect them for their physicality and fierce hits. They may leave broken bodies in their wake, but aren't they just playing the game the way it was meant to be played?

Violence in football is not limited to opponents but can also threaten teammates. Consider the 2006 case of Northern Colorado backup punter Mitchell Cozad, who brutally attacked starting punter Rafael Mendoza to gain the starting punting role. Cozad stabbed Mendoza in the knee of his kicking leg and was later found guilty of second-degree assault and sentenced to seven years in prison. That incident brought back memories of the Tonya Harding–Nancy Kerrigan incident in which Harding's hit man clubbed Kerrigan in the knee to knock her from the Olympic U.S. figure skating team (Delaney and Madigan 2009).

One of the more bizarre examples of violence in sport occurred in a boxing rematch in 1997 that became known as the "the Bite Fight" when Mike Tyson bit Evander Holyfield on one of his ears and had 2 points deducted. The referee was ready to disqualify Tyson, but Holyfield wanted to continue. Tyson then bit Holyfield on the other ear, tearing off the top and spitting it into the ring. This time Tyson was disqualified.

While some athletes push their violence to the limit, survive in the sport, and even earn respect from opponents and fans, others cross the line. In March of 2004, Canadian hockey player Steve Bertuzzi sucker punched another player from behind and was suspended for the rest of the season. In November of 2004, National Basketball Association (NBA) players led by Ron Artest of the Indiana Pacers went into the stands to attack hecklers during a game. Artest was suspended, and though this was not the first time Artest was suspended for violent behavior, it drew the toughest penalty in NBA history: suspension without pay for the season. Artest lost about $5 million of salary.

Professional ice hockey struggled with its reputation for violence for years and could not seem to reconcile stricter rules and harsher penalties with the popularity of game fights. Many hockey supporters relish the breakout of violence and anticipate the potential fights. However, for the beginning of the 2005 season, the National Hockey League (NHL) adopted new rules, three relating to violence:

- Instigation penalties: A player who instigates a fight in the final five minutes of a game will receive a game misconduct and an automatic one-game suspension. The player's coach will be fined $10,000. The suspension times and fines will double for each additional incident.

- Officiating: Zero tolerance on interference, hooking, and hold obstruction.

- Unsportsmanlike conduct: Players who dive, embellish a fall or a reaction, or fake injury in an attempt to draw penalties will be fined. Public complaints or derogatory comments toward the game will also result in fines (MSNBC 2006).

Five years later, in response to a series of serious injuries to players from blows to the head, the NHL, with the full support of the players' union, outlawed blind-side hits to the head. The rule prohibits a "lateral, back-pressure or blindside hit to an opponent where the head is targeted and/or the principal point of contact." The league has the power to review such hits and mete out discipline (Srakocic 2010).

Not to be outdone by male athletes, in a 2008 Women's National Basketball Association game between the Detroit Shock and Los Angeles Sparks, a confrontation between the Shock's Plenette Pierson and the Sparks' Candace Parker turned into a bench-clearing brawl. Five players from each team were suspended for several games, and Shock star center Cheryl Ford was lost for the season because of an anterior cruciate ligament torn while she was coming to the aid of her teammates (Voepel 2008).

As women's sports continue to become more competitive and we find female athletes imitating their male counterparts, violence among the fairer sex has escalated. In 2009, New Mexico women's soccer defender Elizabeth Lambert was suspended indefinitely for rough play, which included tripping, kicking, tackles, and a forearm shiver to the back. But the coup de grace occurred when Lambert yanked Brigham Young's forward Kassidy Shumway to the ground by pulling her ponytail violently, an image that quickly appeared on YouTube and was the most popular sport news piece for several days (ESPN 2009).

Off-Field Violence

It is not clear if on-field violent behavior leads to off-field violence. Common sense suggests that people who become accustomed to using physical intimidation and violence in sport naturally revert to those behaviors when facing conflict outside of sport. Athletes who hang out at bars, restaurants, or clubs are often targets for other tough guys, who bait them with insults and disrespect. The athlete, who feels his manhood is being challenged, may struggle not to respond with physical force. However, athletes who do respond physically may be simply reflecting cultural upbringing that was established outside of sport. Sport may not be the cause of violence, but rather a result of the athletes' upbringing or natural disposition, which led them to choose a violent sport. As we saw in chapter 13, young males from lower socioeconomic classes tend to embrace sport to prove their masculinity. Any challenge to their manliness compels them to respond or lose face in front of their peers.

Alcohol consumption and binge drinking add to the problem of violence. In chapter 7 we discussed studies showing that athletes are more likely than nonathletes to binge. Athletes who are not in full command of their faculties are more likely to lose control and commit violent acts.

A sensitive topic for many athletes is the apparent rise in violence against women among male athletes. Most men would be quick to say that they respect women and certainly don't intend women harm. Here are some statistics from the National Coalition Against Violent Athletes on its website at ncava.org:

- A three-year study showed that while male student-athletes make up 3% of the population on college campuses, they account for 19% of sexual assaults and 35% of domestic assaults on college campuses.

- Athletes commit one in three college sexual assaults.

- The general population has a conviction rate of 80% for sexual assaults, while the rate for athletes is only 38%.

These statistics were gathered from 107 cases of sexual assault reported at 30 Division I schools between 1991 and 1993 (Crosset, Benedict, and

McDonald 1995). Critics of this study say the sample size was relatively small and was not controlled for the use of alcohol, the use of tobacco, and the man's attitude toward women. Those three factors are the main predictors of a male's inclination toward gender violence. More recent studies have corroborated the study by Crosset and colleagues, and one researcher concluded that "a disproportionate number of campus gang rapes involve fraternities or athlete groups" (Simmons 2002). However, Todd Crosset (1999) reviewed the published research on violence against women by male athletes and concluded that while male athletes seem to be more frequently involved in sexual assaults than other male students, the differences between the two groups were not statistically significant.

Domestic violence is the number-one crime perpetrated by athletes (Benedict and Yaeger 1998). In almost every case, the domestic violence involves male athletes who play violent sports physically abusing wives or girlfriends. In 2010, starting running back Steve Jackson of the St. Louis Rams was accused of beating up his girlfriend while she was nine months pregnant with his child. His former girlfriend, Supriya Harris, said that Jackson "forcibly grabbed my arm, flung me against the door and repeatedly pushed me to the ground." Jackson took Harris to the hospital and told her to tell the doctors she had fallen in the shower. Ten days later, she delivered their child, but the couple separated four months later after he threatened her again (TMZ 2010).

Yet it is not clear that athletes are any more involved in serious crime than the general population is. In a follow-up study, Blumstein and Benedict (1999) showed that 23% of the males in cities with a population of 250,000 or more are arrested for a serious crime at some point in their life. That compares with the 21.4% of NFL football players who had been arrested for something more serious than a minor crime as reported in Benedict's earlier study (Benedict and Yaeger 1998). In fact, when Blumstein and Benedict compared NFL players with young men from similar racial backgrounds, they discovered that the arrest rates for NFL players were less than half that of the other group for crimes of domestic violence and nondomestic assaults. Is it difficult or nearly impossible to turn the violence off as soon as practice or the game is over? The majority of athletes who display violent on-field behavior don't continue their aggression off the field. If they did, the court records and news media would surely let us know. We simply do not have enough research to address this question, nor do we have complete data on the incidence of domestic violence by athletes. Most families prefer not to publicize such incidents until they become frequent or incapacitating, and most women do not wish to press charges.

Some athletes do develop a sense of entitlement as their fame grows (Benedict and Yaeger 1998). Whatever city they're in, male athletes are surrounded by female groupies. The athletes often treat these women with disdain and yet are still tempted

 EXPERT'S VIEW

Katherine Redmond

Katherine Redmond was raped by a varsity football player while she was a student and lacrosse player at the University of Nebraska. She sued the university and vowed to dedicate her life to preventing others from having to deal with violent acts perpetrated by athletes, founding the National Coalition Against Violent Athletes in 1998. The mission of the organization is to educate the public on issues relating to athletes and violent behavior and providing support to victims including advocacy, referrals, and research so that they can regain their sense of value and self-worth. The organization also works to ensure that athletes are held to the same standards and laws as others in society.

Through her experiences and further training, Redmond has become a national expert on athlete violence and has served as a consultant in many high-profile cases. These have included the Kobe Bryant case; a University of Colorado rape scandal; an Air Force Academy sex scandal; Title IX cases at the University of Notre Dame, University of Oklahoma, Arizona State, and the University of Washington; and many other high-profile rape and domestic violence cases. She has appeared on numerous television shows and in the print media and is a paid consultant for the NFL. She has been named an American Hero by *Reader's Digest* and was nominated for *Cosmopolitan's* Fabulous Female Award.

by their offers of sex. Wilt Chamberlain, a former great NBA player, boasted in his autobiography that he had slept with over 20,000 women . . . which, if true, shows a definite degree of deviance (ESPN 1999).

A notable case involved boxer Mike Tyson, who attacked and raped Desiree Washington, a church-going beauty queen with a squeaky-clean image. Although Tyson was convicted and sent to jail, Washington's career, psyche, and reputation were sullied forever. Typically, the male aggressor contends that his victim was "asking for it" and acting like a "slut." Tyson claimed that he did not rape Washington, but once she filed charges he became so angry that he said, "I just hate her. Now I really do want to rape her" (Rivers 2003).

More recent cases of violence or rape charges against prominent superstars such as basketball player Kobe Bryant of the Los Angeles Lakers and football player Ben Roethlisberger of the Pittsburgh Steelers illustrate just how difficult it is to evaluate the facts of the cases. While both players admitted to a consensual sexual relationship, they denied having forced themselves on the women. It is no secret that there are many cases of women who actively pursue a relationship with a famous athlete and then later renounce their responsibility for it. Although some of these cases make high-profile news reports, the legal process is often lengthy and costly and in the final analysis reveals only shades of gray in assigning blame.

Perhaps no case captured the public's attention as much as that of O.J. Simpson, who was accused but found not guilty of killing his wife Nicole in 1994. As a football player, Simpson had won the Heisman Trophy in 1968 while at the University of Southern California, and he went on to stardom in the NFL for the Buffalo Bills and then the San Francisco 49ers. Simpson followed his football career as an on-air television sportscaster and was a familiar television personality. In spite of widespread suspicion of his guilt, Simpson was acquitted of all charges. However, in 1997, he was held liable in civil court for the deaths of Nicole and her acquaintance Ron Goldman, who had been at her home. O.J.'s case is often pointed to as the ultimate example of a professional athlete who avoided punishment because of his money and fame.

Could reports of violent behavior by professional football and basketball players be rooted in the racist fears of the U.S. public? You'll recall that table 11.3 showed the percentage of African Americans in 2008 in the NFL to be 66% and in the NBA to be 77%. With such dominance also comes some jealousy and suspicion on the part of

whites about violent black men since they see violent behavior on the football field or the basketball court. According to the National Opinion Research Center survey sponsored by the National Science Foundation at the University of Chicago, 56% of Caucasian Americans believe African Americans are more violent than whites are (Lapchick 1999). Also, of the 1,600 daily newspapers published in the United States, fewer than half a dozen have African American sport editors in cities where there are pro franchises. The United States appears to have Caucasian American sport journalists writing for a Caucasian American audience that may already have prejudiced views of African American men.

While there is no question that violence occurs, when it involves football or basketball athletes it receives exhaustive media coverage. Since African American men dominate those sports, if they are involved in violent behavior it is practically guaranteed that the case will be widely publicized. African Americans such as Satch Sanders, who helped the Boston Celtics win eight world championships, are outraged by the violent portrayal of African American athletes. They point to the millions of dollars that famous athletes donate to schools, charities, and youth foundations. Most professional athletes are solid family men who respect their wives, mothers, sisters, and women in general. Joyce Williams-Mitchell is the executive director of the Massachusetts Coalition of Battered Women's Service Groups and an African American woman who hates the violent image of athletes. She says, "It is a myth! Most batterers are men who control women through their profession, and they include police officers, clergymen, dentists, and judges. Athletes get the headlines, though, and an unfair public rap. Men from every profession (regardless of race) have the potential to be batterers" (Lapchick 1999).

As already stated, we need more research before coming to any conclusions about violence and sport. Rather than rely on sensational examples from the press, we need solid data such as rates of occurrence to compare with the data for other groups of people. Drug and alcohol use should also be noted, since they and not sport may be the cause of violence. No one is helped by sensationalized reporting or hidden facts. We need to address this issue as a society and take steps to prevent violence (Hughes 2004).

Consequences of On-Field Violent Behavior

Violent acts within sport shorten careers, permanently disable people, and reduce the earning power of the victims. In professional football, spearing opponents by leading with the helmet and delivering blows to opponents' heads have drawn the most attention in recent years. Quarterbacks are particularly susceptible to a blind-side rush, and the concussions suffered by prominent quarterbacks have crippled some teams and forced great athletes like Troy Aikman of the Dallas Cowboys into premature retirement.

Most professional athletes who suffer an injury try to keep playing or return to playing too soon. Then they often suffer further injury or their body compensates for the previous injury and thus predisposes them to further problems. It's a badge of honor to play with pain and injury and something that tough guys do. The sad result is that more and more athletes live the rest of their lives with bad backs, knees, or shoulders and a host of other complaints. Football players who carry the ball are running targets, and running backs have the shortest careers in the NFL, lasting an average of three or four years.

In the 2009 collegiate football season, daily headlines across the country chronicled the progress of Heisman Trophy winner and Florida quarterback Tim Tebow after he suffered a concussion in midseason. Fortunately, his team had a "bye" the next week so he had two weeks of therapy and rest from football before he returned to action.

In a development related to Tebow's injury, Gay Culverhouse, former president of the Tampa Bay Buccaneers (owned by her father Hugh), has dedicated herself to helping former players suffering from the results of head injuries. She's reported a host of former players now in their 40s and 50s who have increasing cognitive problems, depression, dementia, and anger.

The NFL and the players union have a variety of programs to aid former players including the "88 Plan," which helps pay expenses for players with dementia. A *New York Times* analysis of 73 former NFL players in the "88 Plan" reports they are experiencing dementia at several times the national rate, although the NFL continues to discredit such studies. Fortunately, other athlete advocates have embraced the cause and begun to gather factual information that could lead to modifications in equipment, rules, medical care, and limitations on playing careers when athletes are at risk (Schwartz 2009).

Violent on-field acts can rob big-time collegiate football teams of their best players. Professional football teams invest millions of dollars in their

Concussions are a scary reality for athletes in many sports, including professional wrestling. After his death, Chris Benoit's brain was examined as part of a concussion study conducted by the NFL.

key players and have lots of money at stake. If the starting quarterback goes down, the team's fortunes are likely to plummet. League administrators are slowly realizing that protecting the players is crucial to keeping them on display and that curbing excessive violence helps the league. Likewise in the NBA, protecting players from violent fouls is crucial to the welfare of the league.

On-field violence presents a poor model to youth. Kids cannot withstand the same amount of physical abuse that adults can. Kids have less mature bones and muscles and are more susceptible to injury, including career-threatening injury. Since younger athletes reach physical maturity at different rates, games may match athletes of vastly different size and weight. In youth and high school sport, clear rules against violence are needed to ensure the health of all players.

Reducing Violence

Earlier we discussed the stringent standards professional hockey has imposed since 2004, which clearly showed that the league believed changes in athlete behavior were necessary. Violence can be significantly reduced if those in charge of the sport agree that doing so is a worthy goal. Team owners have an investment in their athletes and can't afford to lose star players. Families don't want to see their kids injured or sentenced to a life of physical disability. League officials need to protect their superstars so they can continue to market them to potential spectators. Almost everyone in sport has a financial investment in the health and productivity of athletes and stands to gain by protecting them.

What can be done? Once violent acts are clearly defined in the minds of officials and coaches, penalties can be assessed right when the acts happen. Offenders can be immediately suspended from that game and future games. Players can also be fined, but forced inactivity carries more effect for most athletes. Coaches and teams who condone violent play can also be punished until they find the risks too great to allow such play any longer (NHL rules now punish coaches when players break the rules).

Educational programs like Mentors in Violence Prevention (MVP), founded in 1992 at Northeastern University, help reduce violence. Mentors in Violence Prevention is the largest program nationally to use athletes to address violence against women (Lapchick 1999). Similar programs must be initiated in schools, churches, sport programs, and every other potential avenue. Professional sports must see it as in their self-interest to minimize violence and must become leaders in the campaign against vio-

lence rather than waiting for others to take action.

Society must also tackle violence. Violent acts in the sport world may attract the headlines, but such acts also pervade business, professions, and education. When linked to social class and race, violence raises uncomfortable discussions that some people would rather avoid. But according to the U.S. Department of Justice, African American men have a one in three chance of spending time in prison during their lifetime (Chaddock 2003). Without addressing violence in light of race, ethnicity, sexual preference, or lack of education, American society may witness antisocial actions for years to come.

Performance Enhancement Through Drugs

Perhaps no sport-related issue has received more attention in recent years than the use of drugs and performance-enhancing substances. This is not a new topic, nor is there convincing evidence that drug use is more prevalent today than in the past. The differences are in the media reporting, the increasingly aggressive drug-testing programs, and the sophisticated methods abusers use to mask their actions.

One of the earliest mentions of performance-enhancing substances was made by Galen, a Greek physician who was born in A.D. 129 and practiced sports medicine. Reports from the early Olympic Games stated that athletes used herbs, animal proteins, and mushrooms to improve their performance. In the 19th century, French athletes reportedly drank a concoction of wine and cocoa leaves to reduce sensations of fatigue and hunger.

The Winter Olympics held in Oslo in 1952 was marred by heavy use of stimulants. The use of anabolic steroids was first reported in the 1960 Rome Olympics and again at the 1964 Summer Olympics in Tokyo. From that time until the 1980s, the illegal use of doping substances increased substantially because of lack of awareness and detection. In 1983, media attention focused on illegal drug use at the Pan American Games, where 19 athletes were found in violation. When Canadian Ben Johnson, winner of the 100 meters, tested positive for steroids and was disqualified at the 1988 Seoul Olympics, the problem of doping in sport received international attention (Lajis 1996).

Modern athletes may use three distinct types of drugs. First are the **prescription** or **over-the-counter drugs** that promote healing from sickness or injury or mask pain to allow the athlete to return to competition. Although elite athletes who mask their pain to continue competing may be at risk for long-term disability, they argue that it is their personal decision whether to risk the early return. Many athletes realize that a quick return is essential to keep their place on the team. Fans and the media applaud the athlete who guts it out after an injury, even though the athlete may be masking the pain through medication. Decisions to use restorative drugs should be made with honest medical advice. Young athletes should involve their parents in the decision rather than rely on the coach, trainer, and medical staff.

Stimulants, such as caffeine, cocaine, Benzedrine, Ritalin, and Methedrine, make up the second class of drugs in sport. Stimulants have been rampantly used in professional sport for decades. Players use them to get hyped up before competition and to heighten their arousal level. Speed or amphetamines are a fact of life in professional baseball, football, and basketball; and high-performance athletes feel pressured to take these substances just to stay competitive.

The third type of drugs in sport comprises **anabolic steroids** and related substances that increase muscle size, decrease fat, and produce secondary male sex characteristics. Anabolic steroids are faster and more effective than any physical training program for increasing size, strength, and speed. Weightlifters, track and field athletes, football players, and baseball players have all witnessed miracle performances enhanced by steroids. There is evidence of chronic use of steroids by athletes in virtually every high-performance sport.

Other types of performance-enhancing substances used and abused by aspiring athletes include vitamins, health foods, human growth hormones, amino acids, and natural herbs. Athletes may also use blood doping, a technique in which oxygen-carrying red blood cells from blood previously withdrawn from an athlete are reinjected just before an event. Let's take a closer look at anabolic steroids and other performance enhancers.

Steroids

Steroids increase muscle size, speed, and power. They can also enhance masculinity, aggressiveness, sense of well-being, and sexual prowess. For decades, sports fans have dismissed reports of drug use in sport. Americans prefer to accuse Eastern Communist countries led by East Germany as the

While steroid use has been rampant in sport at higher levels, there is an alarming increase in the use of performance enhancing drugs among high school students. Should they undergo random drug testing?

main offenders in the Olympics. When evidence of illegal drug use became well publicized after the fall of the East German government, Americans merely nodded and assumed the bad guys had finally been caught.

But American Olympians had been quietly adding performance-enhancing substances to their own training regimens. In 2004, the world finally insisted on tougher drug testing before and during the Athens Olympic Games. Popular American athletes, particularly track and field athletes, were finally caught and labeled as drug cheats. Other athletes such as the premier sprinter Marion Jones and her partner, sprinter Tim Montgomery, were cast under a heavy cloud of suspicion. Montgomery was banned from the competition. Jones, along with dozens of others, was implicated in the investigation of BALCO Laboratories in California; and although she never failed a drug test, she was found guilty and sentenced to prison on the basis of information in records released from BALCO. Montgomery was banned following testimony from BALCO founder Victor Conte, who pleaded guilty to distributing steroids and was sentenced to four months in prison. Conte has also admitted supplying Jones and other Olympic and professional athletes with illegal drugs (ABC News 2004; Layden 2004).

Drug testing has evolved into random testing at any time, day or night, and when athletes least expect it. These policies are the only sure way to catch sophisticated violators who have learned how to clean out their systems before competitions or anticipated tests. The response of the International Olympic Committee (IOC) has been to step up the number of tests both before and during the Games and to keep samples for eight years, allowing the use of new testing protocols as they are developed to test samples from previous competitions. The trend of number of tests and positive results in recent years looks like this:

Recent Summer Games

- In Sydney there were 2,359 tests and 11 positives.
- In Athens there were 3,667 tests and 26 infringements.
- In Beijing there were 4,500 tests and 15 positives, including six horses in equestrian events.

Recent Winter Games

- In Salt Lake City there were 700 tests and 7 positives.

- In Turin, there were 1,200 tests with 1 positive.
- In Vancouver there were 2,100 tests with one infringement that did not result in a ban.

In London 2012, there will be a record number of drug tests. More than 5,000 blood and urine tests will be administered, and a few weeks later an additional 1,200 tests will be carried out at the Paralympics at the same venue (Beikoff 2010b).

Concurrently, professional sports in the United States are stepping up their efforts to eliminate drug use. During contract discussions with MLB and other leagues, the players' unions finally accepted significant penalties for drug use. Major League Baseball seemed to have moved beyond the "Steroid Era," which extended from the mid-1990s until the mid-2000s, when it finally instituted steroid testing. Babe Ruth's record of 60 home runs in a year stood for 34 years until Roger Maris hit 61 homers in 1961. For the next 35 years, no player hit more than 52. But between 1998 and 2006, players hit more than 60 homers six times. Mark McGwire set the record at 71 in 1998, and that was topped by Barry Bonds, who hit 73 in 2001. It wasn't until 2010 that Mark McGwire finally admitted his steroid use; the case against Bonds is still in the courts. Roger Clemens still proclaims he is innocent, and Alex Rodriguez has admitted he cheated. Since steroid testing was instituted, the rash of home runs has shown a steady decline (Fox News 2010a).

Bill Romanowski was an NFL star who won four Super Bowl rings and was named to the Pro Bowl twice. His book *Romo: My Life on the Edge—Living Dreams and Slaying Dragons* was released in 2005. According to *Publishers Weekly*, the book is about 30% football and 70% apothecary. Romanowski details his consistent drug use, which allowed him to play at a high level and return from injuries. He admits to having used ephedrine, THG, DMSO cream, prescription-strength Motrin, and Naprosyn and claims he would do it all over again. Romanowski might have been an aberration, but his open account of years of drug use has made people pay attention to drug use in professional sport (*Publishers Weekly* 2005).

Bode Miller, who won the 2004 World Cup series in skiing, has made surprising comments to the media, saying that drugs such as erythropoietin (EPO) carry minimal risk and can help skiers if taken under supervision. While EPO is usually taken to boost endurance, Miller claims that it can help athletes; it can make dangerous ski runs safer by improving instantaneous decision making (BBC Sport 2005). In the Turin Olympics, Miller won no medals and didn't seem to care. He vowed not to ski again for the U.S. team but did return finally in Vancouver as a changed man. The controversial athlete who once declared on *60 Minutes* that "it's easy to ski drunk" found a renewed sense of purpose and commitment four years later, and his reward was a bronze medal in the men's downhill event (Sappenfield 2010).

Even the American hero Lance Armstrong, who fought cancer to reclaim his place as cyclist extraordinaire, has been accused of using drugs to capture the Tour de France, one of the most grueling physical tests in sport. Armstrong appeared on the national television program *Larry King Live* in August of 2005 to deny his use of any performance-enhancing substances and to bitterly denounce the inappropriate release of data from 1999, the year of his first victory, by the French sport newspaper *L'Equipe*. Testing done six years later on the B sample taken in 1999 showed evidence of EPO, a natural hormone produced in the kidneys. Erythropoietin increases the blood's ability to absorb and carry oxygen to cells, thereby increasing stamina in endurance races like the Tour de France, which requires cyclists to cover 2,500 miles (4,023 kilometers).

Without the A sample of urine, which was used up in 1999, the testing for EPO cannot be completed. There was no viable test for EPO in 1999, and so EPO testing was started seven years later with frozen samples of urine. Armstrong has never failed a drug test and has been tested more than

any other cyclist both in and out of competition because of his prominent status and performance record. The controversy is unfortunate for both Armstrong and American sport fans, especially within a sport that has history of drug abuse. Millions of Armstrong fans are upset by the scurrilous charges brought against their hero who fought back from cancer to win a remarkable seven Tours de France (*Cycling News* 2005; *Washington Post* 2005).

In 2006, American Floyd Landis won the Tour de France but was stripped of his medal and banned from competing for two years after a failed drug test. Despite claiming his innocence for years afterward, Landis finally came forward in 2010 to admit to using drugs and charged former friend and teammate Lance Armstrong with cheating too. Landis said in television interviews that he saw Armstrong receiving blood transfusions during races. Some athletes use blood transfusions to increase their red blood cell count, which enhances their endurance. In addition, Landis said that Armstrong personally gave him testosterone patches. While the jury is still out on the accusations, one has to wonder if virtually all our athletic heroes are doping to simply keep up with their peers (Quinn and Fainaru-Wada 2008).

Responding to Doping

Virtually every sport organization has begun to clarify and enforce the rules on drug use. The Olympics defines doping as the use of "any method or substance that is harmful to athletes' health or capable of enhancing performance." That broad definition is followed by numerous descriptions

ACTIVITY TIME-OUT

Aren't Drugs the American Way?

There are people who sincerely believe it is foolish to try to ban substances. They suggest removing the rules and testing programs that don't seem to work anyway and allowing athletes to use substances with the advice of health professionals. Drug testing will never keep up with those intent on using illegal substances, and elite athletes simply can't keep up with their peers unless they level the playing field by taking banned substances.

One justification for allowing drug use in sport is that many nonathletes rely on drugs to deal with daily life. Preschoolers are put on Ritalin so they can focus. Parents take sleeping pills to sleep or tranquilizers or alcohol to relax. Other people use drugs to prevent pregnancy, cope with menopause, enhance sexual function, lower blood pressure, counter the aging process, fight migraines, and on and on. College students rely on caffeine or amphetamines to study for exams, and truck drivers take these drugs to stay awake on long hauls.

Why should athletes be any different? What do you think? Would you continue down the same path of drug testing in sport, change the approach to drug testing in sport, or eliminate drug testing altogether?

of doping methods and lists of illegal chemicals. Meanwhile, others press ahead to discover new masking agents that hide drugs and new combinations of substances that cannot be detected by current testing. As in most cases of illegal behavior, it seems the perpetrators are always just a step ahead of the enforcers.

Complicating the drug testing are debates about cold medicines that are banned but are still taken, perhaps simply by an athlete who contracts a cold just before a championship. Wouldn't the average citizen do the same if he caught a cold and needed to go to work? In Vancouver in 2010, Lubomir Visnovsky, a Slovakian ice hockey player, was reprimanded after testing positive for a common cold and allergy medication. His test showed the presence of pseudoephedrine, the main ingredient in Sudafed that can be used as a stimulant at high doses. Visnovsky told officials that he had been taking Advil Cold & Sinus medication. A Russian women's ice hockey player tested positive for tuaminoheptane before the games began, which she attributed to a cold remedy she took before the games began (Olympics Fanhouse 2010).

Other controversies surround everyday vitamins consumed by average Americans. Are such vitamins illegal for athletes? Is Gatorade sold at grocery stores to help hydration and fight heat exhaustion an illegal aid? At American health food stores, you can find and read the claims of thousands of agents that are not regulated by the U.S. Food and Drug Administration. The questions of illegal drugs are unending and sometimes so confusing that no solution seems possible. There are signs of progress in drug testing and educational programs that combat the use of performance enhancers by athletes at all levels. Even some high schools are drug testing all students in cocurricular activities.

Under pressure from the U.S. Congress, MLB took major strides in 2005 to clean professional baseball of drug use. After a series of embarrassing interviews, media leaks, and public criticism, the league and the players' union agreed to a new drug policy that increases the penalty for a failed drug test to 50 days of suspension for the first offense, 100 days for the second, and a lifetime ban (with appeal for reinstatement possible after two years) for the third (Associated Press 2006a). Major League Baseball had ignored the problems of illegal use of drugs so long; finally the exposure of so many star performers such as Barry Bonds, Manny Ramirez, Sammy Sosa, Mark McGwire, Alex Rodriguez, and Roger Clemens simply forced MLB and the players' union to toughen their policies.

But lest you get the mistaken impression that drugs have been eliminated from professional sport, consider that the NBA and NHL test only during the season, which makes their programs essentially useless. No pro sports test blood, and no pro sport uses either of the tests available to test for human growth hormone. NASCAR essentially has no testing plan at all, and the PGA is just beginning to test players, but only at tournaments.

The most hopeful sign that has emerged recently is trials of a longitudinal testing plan whereby athletes would have established certain individual blood levels of various substances and repeat testing at irregular intervals would identify any significant changes. This procedure holds much promise for identifying those athletes who still insist on circumventing the established rules (Quinn and Fainaru-Wada 2008).

The IOC now forces all international governing bodies of sport to institute effective drug testing. Although the drug testing varies in different sports, it conforms to the basic IOC-recommended format. Unannounced random testing throughout the year, mandatory testing of competition winners, and minimum standards for frequency of testing have all led to more disqualifications than in the past. Legal action such as that against the personnel at BALCO Laboratories in California has helped publicize offenses and thrown the weight of public support behind stronger enforcement.

Clearly the standard is set by the IOC, which has established doping as deviant behavior. No sporting organizations accept doping as proper and within the bounds of normal behavior (Luschen 2000). Continuing drug use in sport may lead to the following issues:

- Fans, parents, and kids will increasingly reject sport as a healthy, worthwhile activity.

- Corporations that follow public sentiment will withdraw financial support. If conventional wisdom lumps sport with other negative social activities, the benefits of being a corporate sponsor will fade quickly.

- Sport officials will accept that unless strong action is taken, athletics could be restricted to drug users, and athletes who refrain will only be also-rans.

- Drug use will affect the long-term health of former athletes long after use is discontinued. Athletes with shorter life spans and diminished quality of life will become commonplace.

- Young athletes will be enticed at an early age to follow the examples of their sport heroes.

- Female athletes who use drugs in early years may risk their ability to bear children later on.

- Genetic engineering may produce athletic capabilities only dreamed about and thus relegate performance enhancers to a thing of the past.

Resolving these drug issues lies with sport leaders working cooperatively to ensure the health and welfare of athletes. New attitudes and creative solutions to drugs must emerge in order for the sport world to avoid a rapid descent into competition dominated by chemicals. International sport bodies must work together on improving drug use in sport. Otherwise, if Americans solve some of the drug problems in their sport, they won't be able to compete with Chinese, German, or Russian athletes who may continue drug use.

The media can help by exposing doping in sport in a fair and unbiased manner. Blaming specific athletes is not useful if they are simply the victims of the situation. Coaches, sport administrators, officials, and sponsors must accept their share of the blame and accept the need for change.

Parents can band together to insist on consistent and fair policies for ensuring equal competition for their kids. Educational programs on doping should be available to families and required for sport participants.

Sport scientists can volunteer to provide guidance and recommend policies that support the philosophy of sport organizations. People who earn their living from sport or work with athletes to enhance performance can agree to a code of ethics that considers the welfare of athletes and sport in general.

Finally, sport participants can think carefully about the value of an activity that may threaten their well-being. If athletes who love sport and value fair competition join together to restrict drug use in sport, they can catalyze powerful change in the sport world. The alternative is to withdraw from high-performance sport and move toward a society that values participation in sports regardless of the level of performance (Peretti-Watel et al. 2004).

Eating Disorders in Sport

An example of overconformity in sport is the incidence of athletes who develop eating disorders caused by or related to their sport. Athletes who are highly competitive often go to extreme lengths to maximize their chance for success. In some sports, maintaining a lower body weight for either appearance or performance is clearly advantageous.

IN THE ARENA WITH . . .

Andre Agassi

Andre's recent book titled *Open* lays bare his life as a kid who hated tennis and loved it at the same time. Agassi was coaxed to swing a racket in his crib and was forced by his father to hit hundreds of balls as a kid in grade school. Not surprisingly, he resented the constant pressure even as he became a tennis prodigy, and the inner conflict stayed with him. He rose quickly to the top of professional tennis, winning eight Grand Slam titles, and was the only man to win all four Grand Slams plus an Olympic gold medal. He now admits that in midcareer as his ranking plummeted and he was forced to play in the minor leagues of tennis, he failed a drug test and lied to the ATP professional tour, saying he had accidentally drunk from a soda spiked by "Slim," his assistant. In fact he was snorting crystal meth in the hopes of recreating the energy and passion he had once brought to the court.

His relationship with Barbra Streisand and doomed marriage to Brooke Shields seemed to define him but only added to the pressure. Eventually he found love with fellow world champion Steffi Graf, settled down, and dedicated his life to a world outside of tennis. He founded the Andre Agassi Charitable Foundation and has raised more $85 million for the Andre Agassi Preparatory Academy, an acclaimed K-12 charter school for underprivileged children in his hometown of Las Vegas, Nevada, where he lives with Steffi and their two children.

A quote from Agassi: "The only perfection there is is the perfection of helping others. This is the only thing we can do that has any lasting value or meaning. This is why we're here. To make each other feel safe" (Agassi 2009).

Athletes in sports that focus on physical appearance are at high risk for developing eating disorders. These sports include gymnastics, dance, figure skating, diving, and cheerleading. Other athletes at high risk are those in sports that reward body leanness, such as cross country, wrestling, horse racing, and swimming. Power sports that rely on strength or body mass are less likely to encourage eating disorders, although there are cases of these disorders in every sport.

Most high achievers in sport are also highly disciplined and determined. They set lofty goals and spend many hours each day striving to reach them. They are rewarded for behavior that demands perfection, high motivation, attention to detail, and sometimes even obsession. If fellow athletes, coaches, and parents encourage these athletes to maintain thinness, these tendencies are only reinforced.

The three most common eating disorders found in athletes are **anorexia nervosa**, **bulimia nervosa**, and **compulsive exercise**. Anorexia is exhibited by people who starve themselves in order to maintain their perception of an ideal body weight. No matter how thin they are, they still regard themselves as fat. Bulimia is demonstrated by binge eating followed by purging. Compulsive exercise is characterized by overexercising rather than by undereating. These disorders may become so serious that they lead to death. Other, more benign behaviors that may be precursors to these eating disorders include using diuretics, taking laxatives, dieting, fasting, following rigid patterns of eating certain foods, and consuming inadequate protein; being preoccupied with food may be another precursor.

Both men and women in any sport are susceptible to these disorders. Athletes are more at risk than nonathletes are. Depending on the sample of athletes and the study methodology, research shows that the percentage of female athletes who report eating disorders ranges up to 33%. In contrast, the percentage for male athletes is typically 10% or less, and the proportion between males and females is approximately 10 women for every male. Perhaps not surprisingly, one study of college students revealed that 59% of female college athletes felt that parts of their body were too fat compared to only 20% of males (Nichols 1997; Sundgot-Borgen and Torstveit 2004; Holmes 2005).

Females clearly are more likely candidates for eating disorders. Research indicates that in the United States, 66% of high school girls and 17% of high school boys are on diets at any given time. These figures include both athletes and nonathletes.

Of course, women who have careers in the entertainment or modeling industries also have a high incidence rate due to the pressure to limit their body weight (NFHS 2000; Quinn 2005).

Females who develop an eating disorder are likely candidates for **female athlete triad**, which includes disordered eating, amenorrhea, and osteoporosis or loss of bone density. Excessive exercise and restricted eating cause an energy deficit that stresses the body and changes its levels of hormones. The female athlete triad can affect the reproductive system, which shuts down the menstrual cycle, and lack of nutrients begins to destroy bone.

Before Title IX opened up athletic opportunities for women, eating disorders were relatively rare in sport. In the past, actresses, female entertainers, and models struggled with expectations to maintain low body weights and slim figures. Now athletes also feel those expectations, combined with pressure to perform in sports. In fact, some parents and coaches may partially cause eating disorders by sending messages to young female athletes about their body weight. Some research indicates that men may be especially insensitive to the feelings of their daughters, sisters, or wives and contribute to the problem (Women's Sports Foundation 2001a, 2001b).

National organizations, health professionals, coaching educators, and parent educators have all confronted the continuing problem of eating disorders. They've helped raise public awareness, and health professionals are now trained to recognize the signs of possible eating disorders. Coaches and parents know to look for warning signs and seek help at the first indication of a developing problem.

Hazing in Sport

According to the NFHS, **hazing** is "any action or activity which inflicts physical or mental harm or anxiety, or which demeans, degrades or disgraces a person, regardless of location, intent or consent of participants" (NFHS 2006). Hazing is usually a rite of passage that must be endured to gain acceptance into a particular group like a fraternity or an athletic team. While hazing is not new, it has caught public attention as hazing practices moved from actions that were mostly annoying to actions that threatened physical or psychological harm. Activists fighting hazing liken their cause to that of sexual harassment.

The Stophazing.org website clarifies several facts about the practice, asserting that it is much more widespread than in fraternities and sororities and in fact includes the military, athletics, marching

Eating too much, as opposed to too little, is an eating disorder, too. Why do you think overeating among some athletes receives so little attention?

bands, religious groups, professional schools, and increasingly high schools. The organization believes that hazing is more than foolish pranks but actually a form of victimization that is an act of power or control over another person. It is premeditated, abusive, degrading, and often life threatening (StopHazing 2009).

If you were to judge whether certain acts are actually hazing or not, the following questions are appropriate ones to ask:

- Is alcohol involved?
- Will current members of the group participate along with new ones?
- Does the activity risk emotional or physical abuse?
- Is there a risk of injury or a question of safety?
- Would you have any reservation describing the activity to your parents, a professor, or a university official?
- Would you object to the activity being photographed for the school newspaper or filmed by the local TV news crew?

If you answer yes to any of these questions, the activity is likely hazing.

A 1999 study of 244 college campuses completed by Alfred University and the NCAA found that approximately 80% of college athletes had been subjected to hazing (Alfred University 1999a). About half of these athletes were required to participate in drinking contests, while two-thirds were subjected to humiliating behavior. In the last 10 years, the media have picked up on the story, widely reporting on hazing in colleges and high schools. In some cases legal action was initiated.

Today, both the NCAA and the NFHS have express written policies against hazing and publish literature and sponsor educational seminars on combating hazing. In 2002, ESPN ran a weeklong television series on hazing in sport and followed it up with a companion piece on the Internet.

According to the study by Alfred University (1999b), the following athletes run the greatest risk for hazing:

- Male
- Non-Greek
- Swimmers or divers

- Soccer players
- Athletes on a residential campus
- Athletes at schools in the U.S. East or South
- Athletes on a rural campus
- Lacrosse players
- Athletes in a state with no anti-hazing law

All athletes are at risk for hazing. Hazing can include excessively consuming alcohol, which is the most common behavior; enduring excessive physical punishment; acting as a personal servant to other players; going without sleep or food; engaging in or simulating sex acts; consuming disgusting food combinations; making prank phone calls; stealing or shoplifting; and being restricted from associating with certain people. More serious, life-threatening rituals include being violent toward others or being paddled, kidnapped, or abandoned. Men are much more likely to be threatened with extreme or harmful behavior than women are.

Hazing is not just something that occurs among males in team sports or in fraternities, but has spread to young female athletes as well. For women, hazing tends to include more acceptable initiation rites such as extending practice sessions, taking oaths, doing volunteer work, dressing up for team functions, or participating in other activities that build the team. In 2006, the Northwestern women's soccer team was suspended from all activities pending an investigation of an alleged hazing of team members. A website displayed pictures allegedly of soccer players in various stages of undress, some with blindfolds on and others with hands taped behind their back. It appeared that some were drinking alcohol (Brennan 2006). In 2009, East Stroudsburg University in Pennsylvania (which coincidentally is my alma mater) made headlines when its women's field hockey team was accused of hazing and suspended by the college president from competition in the league championships for which they had qualified with an exceptional season record. One of the unique issues involved in this case was the alleged involvement of the campus police who helped perpetrate the incident (Brelje & Kuhns 2009).

According to ESPN.com, since 1980, most of the reported hazing incidents have involved football players. Incidents among football players were almost three times as many as those among baseball players, who were second in hazing incidents. Athletes in sports such as track, fencing, and golf were less likely to be hazed. Athletes in cross country, basketball, rowing, and tennis were less likely to be involved with alcohol use or other unacceptable or dangerous activities (Garber 2002).

Historically, many athletes and coaches believed that hazing was a benign ritual that built team unity, created camaraderie, and helped new athletes gain acceptance. But as the seriousness of hazing escalated, athletic teams and schools stepped in to ban hazing practices. According to Stophazing.org, which monitors legal developments related to hazing, all U.S. states except Alaska, Hawaii, Montana, South Dakota, and Wyoming have banned hazing.

Some victims of hazing have died, such as Chuck Stenzel, the student at Alfred University whose death stimulated the national research on hazing. Some incidents end in lawsuits, such as one in which a California school district paid $675,000 to a Rancho Bernardo High School baseball player who was sodomized with a broom handle in the locker room after a game. Perhaps even more shocking was the 2008 incident in Las Vegas, New Mexico, in which six high school football players were accused of sodomizing six younger teammates with a broomstick during a training camp. More scandalous was the fact that coaches turned a blind eye to the hazing. Since then, the head football coach and all five assistants have resigned, and prosecutors are considering charges against the adults and players.

Other victims have dropped sport or withdrawn from school to deal with the personal trauma they experienced (Farrey 2002). The researchers who conducted the Alfred University study estimated that more than 1.5 million high school students are subjected to hazing each year. Of those, most were subjected to hazing in sport (24%). Others were hazed by peer groups or gangs (16%); in music, art, or theater (8%); or in church (7%). The number of student athletes in high school who are subjected to hazing totals 800,672 each year. Thankfully, due to media attention, comprehensive research by Alfred University, and educational programs for athletic personnel, parents, and athletes, the number of incidents seems to be decreasing. Hazing is an issue worth monitoring for the future.

Gambling and Sport

Gambling on sport activities is nothing new. Accounts of gambling on sport are centuries old. In early colonial days, gambling focused on horse racing, cockfighting, boxing, and bearbaiting (Leonard 1980). As baseball gained popularity in the 19th century, local ball clubs began to pay some players under the table, and fans began betting on games. When the National League formed near the end of the century, baseball became an openly professional game enjoyed by the masses; under-the-table payments were a thing of the past, but betting on games survived (Stephan 1994).

The general public became keenly aware of illegal sport gambling when the infamous Black Sox scandal broke in the news. In the 1919 World Series, the Cincinnati Reds beat the Chicago White Sox in a disputed set of games. Investigations revealed that eight players on the White Sox were guilty of "dumping" the series in return for a financial payoff; thus the team became known as the *Black Sox*.

College basketball suffered a similar scandal in the early 1950s when investigations revealed that eight colleges had fixed some 86 games over three years. Thirty-two players were involved in the point-shaving scandal.

Pete Rose, one of baseball's all-time greats, has been banned from the sport and the Hall of Fame because he bet on baseball during his career. He steadfastly denied the charges until it became clear he had no hope of reinstatement, at which time he admitted guilt.

Soccer scandal arose in Germany, the country that hosted the 2006 World Cup. Just a day before tickets were to be released for sale to the public for the 2006 event, a number of officials and players were implicated in a series of fixed games that had occurred in the previous year. The referees apparently made dubious calls, awarded suspect penalty shots, and conspired to change the outcome of the game (DW-World.de 2005).

In the United States, long-time NBA referee Tim Donaghy pleaded guilty to federal charges of conspiracy to engage in wire fraud and transmitting wagering information. He was sentenced to 15 months in federal prison in 2008 and served 11 months before his release to a halfway house. During the investigation it was revealed that Donaghy had a gambling problem, was in debt, and had tried to recoup his losses by more betting. In his proposed book, *Blowing the Whistle: The Culture of Fraud in the NBA*, which was later cancelled by the publisher, Donaghy chronicled his dealings with organized crime and the "underworld" and recounted how easy it was for the NBA officials to affect the outcome of games or the point spread (Fish 2009a).

The problem with gambling on sport is that it calls into question the integrity of the performances by players, officials, coaches, and others. Players standing to gain sure money can be tempted to throw a game or

The 1919 Chicago White Sox team saw eight of its members banned from baseball for life for throwing some of the World Series games. Among those banned was Shoeless Joe Jackson.

shave points. Once the public loses confidence in the integrity of the sport, its popularity is certain to decline. How many times have people watched a boxing match and been astounded at the decision, or watched international judges at the Olympic Games show clear prejudices toward athletes from certain countries?

In the United States, 48 of 50 states allow some type of legalized gambling. Utah and Hawaii do not. Nevada is the only state where sport wagering is legal, although Oregon and Delaware have ventured into controlled sport gambling. The American Gaming Association estimates that illegal wagers are about $380 billion annually, while only $2.57 billion is wagered legally in the state of Nevada. Approximately two-thirds of all sport betting in Nevada is on professional sports, not college sporting events. More bets in Nevada are placed on the Super Bowl than on any other event, approximately $92 million in 2008. However, March Madness basketball did generate legal bets in the state, of approximately $80 to $90 million in 2009 (American Gaming Association 2009).

The NCAA and the major professional sport leagues have taken a strong stand against legalizing gambling in order to preserve the integrity of their games. Colleges are particularly sensitive to sport betting, and they mete out harsh penalties to students, athletes, coaches, or administrators who violate NCAA rules. At the heart of their concern is that almost all gambling profits organized crime. Those profits are funneled into other illegal activities such as prostitution, supporting loan sharks, and selling drugs (NCAA 2007a).

In 1992 the U.S. Congress passed the Professional and Amateur Sports Protection Act to declare sport betting illegal in every state except Nevada, Oregon, and Delaware, which had preexisting laws. Though across the United States gambling has been recently legalized on riverboats and reservations, sports continue to be off-limits.

The state of Delaware formulated plans in 2009 to expand sport gambling on individual professional games and collegiate sports. However, a three-judge panel of the Third U.S. Circuit Court of Appeals said the Delaware plan violated the federal law cited earlier. All the major professional sport leagues and the NCAA challenged Delaware's plan and contended it would harm their sports. The court, however, did allow the state to continue so-called "parlay" bets, in which bettors have to select the winners of at least three separate NFL games in a single wager (CBS News 2009; Frommer 2009).

At the start of the decade in 2000, the concern of campus communities was focused on binge drinking and how binge drinking interacts with use of other drugs. However, student involvement in gambling was relatively overlooked until midway through the decade as legalized gambling grew throughout the United States. A 2004 investigation of gambling at four Connecticut state universities revealed that one out of nine students had a gambling problem that was significantly connected to substance abuse and food-related problems. Perhaps more alarming, the incidence of university gambling at 11.4% was similar to the rate previously found among Connecticut high school students, 11.3%, and both were more than double that of the general adult population at 5.4% (Engwall, Hunter, and Steinberg 2004).

College athletes have a higher rate of problem gambling than nonathletes. Athletes who are problem gamblers and in significant debt, especially to bookies and loan sharks, are particularly vulnerable when approached to shave points or fix games. According to the NCAA, in 2008 about 30% of male athletes and 7% of female athletes admitted wagering on sporting events within the past year. Students who were identified as problem gamblers, compared to other students, were significantly more likely to be heavy drinkers and be regular tobacco and marijuana users. Problem gambling was also related to binge eating and greater use of weight control efforts. Other statistics about gambling by college students include the following (Engwall, Hunter, and Steinberg 2004; Florida Council on Compulsive Gambling 2008):

- 66% of college students report gambling at least once in the past year.

- Male college students (78%) are more likely to gamble than females (60%).

- The most frequent type of gambling among college students was sports-related: 26% on professional sports, 18% on nonprofessional sports, and 18% on sport pools, for a total of 62% of gambling on campus. The next most popular form of gambling was the lottery at 39%.

- College athletes are more likely than nonathletes to bet on sports, games of skill, and card games. Nonathletes are more likely to bet at casinos, on the lottery, or using slot machines.

- College students are at risk for problem gambling at a rate that is double that of the

▌ Have you ever gambled on a sporting event?

adult population (adults = 7%, college students = 14%).

- College students who gamble also tend to show higher than normal tendencies to engage in drug and alcohol abuse, high-risk sexual behavior, eating disorders, and have grade-point averages below 2.0. Debts from gambling range from $100 to more than $5,000 and are usually spread among several credit cards.

The NCAA opposes all forms of legal and illegal sport wagering on college sports, professional sports, and amateur sports in which the association conducts championships. This includes the Football Bowl Subdivision and emerging sports for women. The NCAA believes that sport wagering has become a serious problem that threatens the well-being of student-athletes and the integrity of college sport. Here are some salient facts from NCAA (2007a):

- The Internet has made it easier than ever for student-athletes to place bets in virtual anonymity and with no supervision.
- Student-athletes are viewed by organized crime and organized gambling as easy marks.

- Student-athletes who gamble are breaking the law and jeopardizing their athletic eligibility.
- When student-athletes become indebted to bookies and can't pay their debts, they are at risk of being forced to undermine the outcome of an athletic contest or shave points.
- The NCAA has rules that prohibit athletes, athletic department staff, and all conference and national staff from engaging in any type of sport wagering.

A recent survey by the NCAA (2010c) shows that progress is being made, along with some specific areas in which more education and enforcement are needed. The survey shows a significant decrease in frequent wagering by Division I men's basketball players, one of the target groups for education. There has also been a decrease in Division I men's basketball and football players sharing information (such as injury status) with outsiders. Compared to 2004, men still greatly outnumber women as social, frequent, or heavy gamblers in all three divisions, with up to 30% of males across all divisions reporting that they gambled on sports—a violation of NCAA rules. Perhaps surprisingly, the highest incidence of gambling is by male athletes in Division III.

Among sports, men's golf is a particular problem across all three divisions, with 20% of male golfers reporting at least monthly sport wagering. In Division I, 40% reported social levels of wagering compared to just 12% of Division I male basketball players. The NCAA is taking steps to address this anomaly through aggressive education and publicity throughout the collegiate golf community (NCAA 2010c).

Not everyone believes sport gambling should be restricted. Mark Cuban, the controversial owner of the Dallas Mavericks of the NBA, has proposed a betting hedge fund. Hedge funds are loosely regulated investment funds favored by the wealthy since they typically require a significant minimum investment. Cuban compares sport betting to "betting" on the stock market. And people who buy stocks often do so knowing very little about the companies they are investing in. Cuban asserts that there is far better information about local sport teams than there is about local businesses; the local papers cover the sport teams every day (Cuban 2004). His proposal has drawn little support, and the NBA is clearly wary of introducing gambling into the sport (Cuban 2004; Hills 2004).

The strongest justification for legal sport gambling comes from those who suggest that it can provide a bailout for local and state governments, which are searching for new revenue streams. When the governments promise to follow the example of Oregon and channel the profits into education or sport programs, there are public officials and many citizens who are tempted to embrace sport wagering if a significant revenue stream can be allocated to worthy causes such as education or youth sport. Proponents point out that currently illegal profits generated by sport gambling mostly go to illegal operations and organized crime, and this money could be used for worthier causes.

Those opposed to sport gambling believe that it will corrupt youth, offer an entree to people from organized crime to become directly involved in sport, and take money from those who can't afford to lose it. They say that the benefits will go to bookies, a few gamblers, and offshore Internet betting sites. Those who will suffer include athletes who are pressured to throw games or shave a few points off the score, fans who lose faith in the legitimacy of games, gamblers who lose money, coaches who may become deceitful about their team's chances, and perhaps the American system of sports that will lose any semblance of integrity and eventually lose the fans that have made sports so successful.

A relatively recent trend in sport gambling is online betting, which so far is legal in the United States. A quick visit to the Internet reveals numerous opportunities to bet on virtually any sport. Betting begins at $5, and limits are set at $5,000 or in special circumstances up to $100,000. Online sport betting generated only $1.7 billion in 2001, but that number had more than doubled by 2005 to $4.29 billion (American Gaming Association 2009).

Fantasy football leagues have also become the rage in the United States. People select their own teams and then wager on their success each week. Fantasy team owners can select their players from any professional team, and the composite performance of their players (who play on many different teams) determines the success of their team. The future of online betting such as fantasy football is uncertain, but clearly it will become an issue as it grows in popularity and receives more publicity.

Current laws, rules, and public opinion have rejected legalizing sport gambling; but as citizens have become more tolerant of gambling at casinos, on Native American reservations, and in state lotteries, the aversion to gambling seems to be subsiding.

 ACTIVITY TIME-OUT

Should We Legalize Sport Betting?

You've read some of the arguments for and against sport wagering, along with a description of the situation that exists today. But throughout the United States, there has been a trend more favorable toward gambling partly because of the revenue it could raise to help cash-strapped states. In opposition are all professional sports and college sport organizations, fearful that legalized gambling could ruin their sport events and turn off the public to sport. Others figure that since sport gambling is already occurring, it would be better to legalize it, regulate it, and reap the financial rewards.

If you were to cast a vote on the question of legalizing sport betting in your state, how would you vote? List the pros and cons in a short, concise statement that you might share with your friends and fellow voters.

While certain spectator sports such as horse racing, auto racing, and dog racing have long depended on gambling, most sports have steered clear of it. Stay tuned for continued strong debate.

Chapter Summary

Deviance occurs in sport when athletes do not conform to accepted standards of behavior. Two distinct types of deviance were described in the chapter: one in which athletes disobey the standards and a second in which athletes carry the standards too far.

The frequency of deviance occurring among athletes and coaches was compared to that occurring among the general population. In spite of abundant media publicity that makes it appear otherwise, there is evidence that athletes generally conform to expected standards of behavior and in fact probably exceed those standards.

Behavior is sometimes affected by the energy and intensity created during play. When those emotions overtake reason and control, people may act out of character. Coaches use emotional arousal to coax exceptional performances out of their athletes. Fans use the emotional release of sport to spice up everyday life. Hooliganism in soccer is an extreme example of this behavior.

Violence committed by athletes, whether on or off the field, is an issue of much debate. Some people believe violent acts within sport contribute to violent acts outside of sport. The facts, however, show that violence occurs among a relatively small percentage of athletes and is restricted to a handful of sports.

Drug use to enhance performance appears to be increasing in spite of strong actions to eliminate this practice. Doping has become more sophisticated, and testing with penalties seems unable to keep up with the creativity of athletes driven to excel by any means. In fact, there are some who believe it would be more honest and fair to athletes to simply allow the use of performance-enhancing substances and thus even the playing field. The current situation of enforcement, which trails the ingenuity of athletes, coaches, and trainers who choose to cheat, simply rewards the cheaters in sport.

Eating disorders affect more female athletes than male athletes. People who participate in sports that emphasize physical appearance, such as gymnastics, ice skating, dance, and cheerleading, are at greatest risk for developing an eating disorder. Athletes in sports favoring leanness, such as wrestling, cross country, and swimming, are similarly at risk. The most common eating disorders are anorexia, bulimia, and compulsive exercise.

Hazing in sport has burst into prominence in the past 10 years due to widely publicized deaths, injuries, and humiliations suffered at the hands of athletic teammates. While hazing is not limited to athletes, researchers estimate that over 80% of college athletes are exposed to hazing; and in high school, nearly 25% of hazing victims are athletes. The alarming trend of growing numbers of serious incidents seems to have slowed due to wide publicity, educational programs, and state laws against hazing.

Gambling in sports is illegal in almost every U.S. state, and sport organizations at the professional and collegiate level have taken strong stands against it. Unfortunately, illegal betting on sports, encouraged by organized crime, has tarred the image of some sports in which fixed games and point shaving have occurred. Arguments for and against legalizing sport gambling continue to this day.

19

Coaching Sport

Student Outcomes

After reading this chapter, you will know the following:

- Negative and positive influences of coaches
- Current standards, certification programs, and continuing education for coaches
- Differences in coaching at different levels of sport
- Personality, social orientation, and leadership style of coaches
- Challenges for the future of coaching

John Wooden died in 2010, leaving a legacy that is unlikely ever to be matched in the world of coaching. He was the most successful coach in the history of college basketball and the first person to be elected to the Basketball Hall of Fame as both a player and coach. He retired from coaching in 1975 with a 40-year head coaching record of 885 wins and 203 losses. What was most remarkable was that during his 27 years of coaching at UCLA, his teams won 10 national championships in a 12-season stretch from 1964 to 1975. From 1971 to 1974, UCLA won 88 consecutive games, still the NCAA record.

Perhaps Coach Wooden's most enduring legacy is the lessons he taught us about coaching. His famous "Pyramid of Success" features 15 conceptual building blocks of traits like industriousness, alertness, and poise, held together by faith and patience. Long after retirement, he often gave speeches to large crowds of coaches and others featuring the concepts outlined in the pyramid. He viewed himself more as a teacher than as a coach, perhaps because he treasured a message from his father that he carried with him always: "Be true to yourself. Make each day a masterpiece. Help others. Drink deeply from good books, especially the Bible. Make friendship a fine art. Build a shelter against a rainy day. Pray for guidance, count and give thanks for your blessings every day."

Kareem Abdul-Jabbar, a 7-foot, 2-inch center who led UCLA to three national championships was quoted in the *New York Times* in 2000 as saying, "Coach always said that basketball was a simple game, but his ability to make the game simple was a part of his genius." Abdul-Jabbar added, "There was no ranting, no histrionics or theatrics. To lead the way Coach Wooden led takes a tremendous amount of faith. He enjoyed winning, but he did not put winning above everything. He was more concerned that we became successful as human beings, that we earned our degrees, that we learned to make the right choices as adults and parents. In essence, he was preparing us for life" (Litsky and Branch 2010).

Here are two of Coach Wooden's many famous quotes:

- "Success comes from knowing you did your best to become the best that you are capable of becoming."

- "Be more concerned with your character than your reputation, because your character is what you really are, while your reputation is merely what others think you are."

In looking at sport from every conceivable angle, we've examined the people who play sports and those who watch them. Now we'll examine a group that fills a critical role in sport: the coaches who provide the sport experience. No matter the level of competition, the coach significantly affects the experience of both athletes and spectators.

When you ask former athletes about their sport experience, they often mention significant coaches in their career. More than teammates, team owners, sport organizers, or parents, coaches are in the spotlight of athletic competition.

Coaches often help young people mature, set priorities, establish goals, learn sport skills, develop self-discipline, and so on. Because coaches typically work with younger athletes who are going through critical stages of personal development, they have a golden opportunity to influence young people. The fact that they are perceived as the keepers of the keys to the kingdom of athletic success doesn't hurt their potential to influence aspiring athletes.

Influence of Coaches

Tom Crawford, formerly the director of coaching education for the U.S. Olympic Committee (USOC), cited this adapted quote from Haim Ginott, a prominent psychologist and author who wrote two best-sellers, *Between Parent and Child* and *Between Parent and Teenager*, in the 1960s (Mills 1997; Crawford substituted the word "coach" for "teacher"):

"I have come to a frightening conclusion. I am the decisive element on the playing field. It is my personal approach that creates the climate. It is my daily mood that makes the weather. As a coach, I possess the tremendous power to make an athlete's life miserable or joyous. I can be the tool of torture or an instrument of inspiration. I can humiliate or humor, hurt or heal. In all situations, it is my response that decides if a crisis will be

Coaches can be one of the biggest influences in an athlete's life. What qualities do you think make for a good—or a bad—coach?

elevated or de-escalated, and an athlete humanized or dehumanized."

Those of us who have played sports would no doubt agree heartily. Coaches have been our heroes, role models, confessors, disciplinarians, mentors, teachers, leaders, and often our beloved friends. Their influence on us is incalculable, and we know how important they have been in our lives.

Like teachers, coaches have the opportunity to affect young people who are in the process of becoming adults. The uncertainty young people face opens doors for coaches to suggest appropriate behavior and attitudes. The questioning of authority figures by teenagers presents coaches with opportunities to respond with patience and reason to influence rebellious minds. The battle with emotions uncovers feelings of inadequacy and the inability to manage feelings. Coaches can help athletes embrace these challenges, and they can suggest a course of action and reinforce good decisions.

Outstanding former athletes often do not make the best coaches. They may have learned skills easily and demanded much of themselves and thus are impatient with the performance of lesser athletes. Yet the public often seeks top former athletes to coach their children even when the former athlete has little training or experience in coaching. Educating the general public is the only way to combat this mistaken bias.

Coaching awards are almost always handed out to the coaches who win championships. However, the winning coach may win because he has the best talent (in his athletes), the best facilities, or the most money. It is easier to judge winning records than the more intangible results of coaching, but this approach reinforces an unhealthy emphasis on winning.

Positive Influences

We cannot describe successful coaching without comparing the coaching results with the expectations of the position. Obviously, success is defined differently for coaches of Little League teams than for managers of Major League Baseball teams.

In the public assessment of coaching success, wins and losses are typically the yardstick used. Yet we know that the best win–loss record does not always represent the best coaching job. Let's consider the criteria by which a coach might be more fairly judged, beginning with professional and high-performance sport. Currently, event outcomes are an accepted standard of measurement. Let's

POP CULTURE

"Coach"

Craig T. Nelson starred in the television show "Coach," which aired on ABC for nine seasons from 1989 to 1997. Nelson played Hayden Fox, the head football coach of the Minnesota State Screaming Eagles, a college football program with a long history of little success on the field. Despite the questionable help of some bumbling assistant coaches and former players, he eventually turned the team into a perennial college bowl contender, and that led to an offer to coach an NFL expansion team. The show found its popularity as a sitcom with engaging characters and humorous entertainment, and it permitted a look at the life of a coach who also struggled with his private life, for which he has little time. The show is now available on DVD and you might enjoy watching a few episodes to see what all the fun was about (USA Network, 2010).

look at other standards that should be considered for coaches in these situations.

Coaching success over several years with demonstrated consistency in performance, regardless of the particular athletes participating, is a more accurate indication of coaching ability. You may have heard coaches say they were more proud of their 20-year record than the number of conference championships they won. They realize that consistency over time is the real mark of excellence in coaching.

Innovative coaches who change their sport through their training methods, strategies, or other visible influences deserve to be recognized for their contribution. Regardless of their teams' win–loss record, the results of their innovation endure.

Coaches may be ultimately judged by the loyalty of their athletes even after those athletes' careers are over. Many former athletes keep in touch with good coaches who made a difference in their life. They rely on those coaches' counsel and support.

Leadership skills are critical for coaches at every level of competition. Successful leaders learn to adapt their skills to the group of athletes on a team and to individual athletes. This means not relying on a single, fixed coaching or leadership skill, but rather on tailoring that skill to the athletes. Coaches must develop leadership ability in training athletes' physical and technical skills, applying appropriate strategy, and setting a framework for the team to operate in a way that benefits the athletes as a group and as individuals.

Coaches who use democratic methods can allow greater athlete participation in setting group goals, arranging team practices, and plotting team tactics. This approach can foster significant growth, especially with younger players. However, it involves some risk on the part of the coach, who has to allow the group to make certain decisions. Coaches of sports that require a great deal of independence in athletes can especially benefit from a more democratic approach. Team sport athletes generally seem to prefer a more autocratic approach, in part because of the nature of the sport, the complexity of player interaction, and the dynamics of group interdependency (Riemer and Chelladurai 1995).

Coaches who work within an educational setting should be measured according to their contribution to the overall education of the young people in their charge. If the school district or university has clearly delineated the expected outcomes for student-athletes, the task is much easier for the coach. Coaches can pay attention to more than athletic instruction. Their focus can be toward enhancing the self-concept, self-awareness, and personal development of all athletes. The coach fills the role of adviser and supporter as athletes explore their potential through sport. Coaches help athletes make good decisions, figure out strategies, set performance goals, and learn from their mistakes.

Coaches who have a reputation for good sporting behavior contribute to the development of integrity in athletes. These coaches point out the requirements for moral behavior, and they allow athletes to make moral decisions and analyze the results of their choices.

Negative Influences

For all the positive influence coaches can have on athletes, there is another side. Coaches who are inadequately prepared to be a coach or who coach for the wrong reasons may actually damage young lives. Terry Orlick (1974), a well-known sport psychologist, puts it this way:

EXPERT'S VIEW

A Coaching Code of Ethics

The following code was developed by the National Federation for State High School Associations (NFHS). Virtually all other sport organizations now have in place a similar code of ethics that coaches must read, understand, and abide by. You might want to check out the code of ethics for your particular sport as posted for the national governing body, or the United States Olympic Committee Coaching Ethics Code (USA Coaching 2010).

"The function of a coach is to educate students through participation in interscholastic competition. An interscholastic program should be designed to enhance academic achievement and should never interfere with opportunities for academic success. Each student-athlete should be treated as though he or she were the coaches' own, and his or her welfare should be uppermost at all times. Accordingly, the following guidelines for coaches have been adopted by the NFCA Board of Directors.

The coach shall be aware that he or she has a tremendous influence, for either good or ill, on the education of the student-athlete and, thus, shall never place the value of winning above the value of instilling the highest ideals of character.

The coach shall uphold the honor and dignity of the profession. In all personal contact with student-athletes, officials, athletic directors, school administrators, the state high school athletic association, the media, and the public, the coach shall strive to set an example of the highest ethical and moral conduct.

The coach shall take an active role in the prevention of drug, alcohol and tobacco abuse.

The coach shall avoid the use of alcohol and tobacco products when in contact with players.

The coach shall promote the entire interscholastic program of the school and direct his or her program in harmony with the total school program.

The coach shall master the contest rules and shall teach them to his or her team members. The coach shall not seek an advantage by circumvention of the spirit or letter of the rules.

The coach shall exert his or her influence to enhance sportsmanship by spectators, both directly and by working closely with cheerleaders, pep club sponsors, booster clubs, and administrators.

The coach shall respect and support contest officials. The coach shall not indulge in conduct which would incite players or spectators against the officials. Public criticism of officials or players is unethical.

The coach should meet and exchange cordial greetings with the opposing coach to set the correct tone for the event before and after the contest.

The coach shall not exert pressure on faculty members to give student-athletes special consideration.

The coach shall not scout opponents by any means other than those adopted by the league and/or state high school athletic association."

Used with permission of the National Federation of State High School Associations (NFHS).

For every positive psychological or social outcome in sports, there are possible negative outcomes. For example, sports can offer a child group membership or group exclusion, acceptance or rejection, positive feedback or negative feedback, a sense of accomplishment or a sense of failure, evidence of self-worth or lack of evidence of self-worth. Likewise, sports can develop cooperation and a concern for others, but they can also develop intense rivalry and complete lack of concern for others.

For every positive coach who sets a good example, there are coaches who provide a negative example. Many coaches negatively influence young athletes, but the reasons they do so vary considerably. For instance, volunteer coaches who have little or no training may inadvertently make

Coaching philosophies can greatly influence an athlete's enjoyment of sport. If the coach's philosophy conflicts with an athlete's reason for playing, the athlete may perceive the coach negatively.

errors in judgment due to their lack of preparation for coaching. No matter how well intentioned they are, their lack of understanding of players and the coaching process may harm their athletes. In order to minimize the risk of poor coaching due to lack of preparation, parents, players, and communities must raise the expectations for coaches who accept the challenge of working with youth. Parents have the right to expect coaches to have a basic understanding of coaching, attend training sessions, and access appropriate distance-learning coaching information online. Coaches who may be certified or have some level of experience can also create a negative environment. Perhaps the most common conflict occurs when the coaching philosophy clashes with the athletes' reasons for playing the sport. If the coach is focused on winning, some decisions will seem unfair to athletes who are more interested in the joy of playing than in winning every contest.

Another common conflict is the routine use of physical punishment to discourage bad behavior, poor performance, or lack of effort. Athletes who must suffer endless running laps or push-ups soon learn to avoid physical activity whenever they can. Coaches who instill an aversion to physical activity in young athletes are setting those children up for a lifetime of inactivity. Physicians, educators, school

boards, and sport psychologists all advise teachers and coaches to avoid using physical punishment. Instead, they recommend emphasizing what students or athletes are doing right and reinforcing that behavior. Negative feedback and punishment are generally recommended only to prevent behavior that is unsafe or emotionally abusive to others. The National Association of State Boards of Education states, "Teachers shall aim to develop students' self-confidence and maintain a safe psychological environment free of embarrassment, humiliation, shaming, taunting or harassment of any kind. Physical education staff shall not order performance of physical activity as a form of discipline or punishment" (NASBE 2008).

In youth sport, there are often conflicts between parents and the coach. The parents may misunderstand the coach's intentions and may question the coach's methods and allocation of playing time. The solution is for coaches to share their philosophy before the season starts, hold regular parent meetings to discuss issues, and try to find common ground with parents. Without the support of the parents, the coach's role is considerably more difficult and may even become impossible.

Coaches at higher levels of play may face many of the same issues as those who work with younger players. In addition, coaches whose employment depends on a winning record often make decisions that don't please every athlete on the team. Athletes who accept the competitive challenge to join a team where winning is clearly the focus must expect the coach to build a system that in the coach's judgment will produce the best results.

Because coaches are human beings with certain beliefs, prejudices, and personality quirks just like anyone else, athletes need to evaluate coaching behavior within the overall context of the situation. If the coaching philosophy and behavior are simply at odds with the athlete's reasons for playing, the athlete may prefer to change sports, schools, or private programs and find an organization in which she feels more in tune with the program and the coaching personality.

At the extreme negative end of coaching behavior, you can find verbal, physical, and psychological abuse of athletes. **Abuse** is the willful infliction of injury, pain, mental anguish, intimidation, or punishment, and it exists in the workplace, at home, in the government, and even in religious organizations. Adults who have power over younger people sometimes cannot resist the urge to use their power inappropriately.

Awareness of sexual abuse has risen, particularly with the increase of females in sport and given the fact that more than half of their coaches are males. The Women's Sports Foundation has led the way in educating coaches, players, and parents on how to minimize the chances for sexual abuse through background checks, clear policy statements that delineate unacceptable behaviors, and a process for reporting and dealing with abuse if it occurs.

USA Swimming, the national governing body for swimming in the United States, garnered national headlines in 2010 when it released a list of the names of 46 coaches who have received lifetime bans or permanently quit the organization, most for sex-related offenses. Most prominently named among the coaches was Everett Uchiyama, former director of the national team. A woman now in her mid-30s, who remains anonymous, claimed she had a relationship with Uchiyama soon after she started swimming for him when she was 14 years old. Uchiyama hastily resigned as national team director for USA Swimming on January 27, 2006 without explanation. He was permanently banned from USA Swimming on January 31, 2006, but that did not stop him from securing a job at a nearby country club. On the same day that the list was released by USA Swimming, Uchiyama also resigned from the Colorado country club where he was the aquatics director. The club said it had received a positive recommendation from USA Swimming and knew nothing about the allegations against Uchiyama. USA Swimming had come under increasing scrutiny for its handling of sexual abuse cases, with some critics charging that it covered up wrongdoing by prominent coaches. The Associated Press reported that at least four lawsuits had been filed, and the sport has been subjected to a wave of negative media reports. The posting of names was part of a response to these accusations, and USA Swimming is currently studying what it can do to prevent these situations in the future. The organization admitted that it must do more to educate athletes, parents, coaches, and club leaders on what they can do to help (ESPN 2010a).

Verbal and physical abuse have always been issues in sport, but athletes today are less tolerant of it and more likely to strike back or report it to authorities. Most educational institutions prohibit the use of degrading racial remarks, profanity, and public sanction or embarrassment, and offenders can lose their jobs.

The key to avoiding abuse and negative behaviors in coaching is for athletic organizations to delineate their expectations for coaches in writing and secure agreement from prospective coaches before hiring them. In addition, coaches should be trained in the policies and should be given specific examples of inappropriate behavior. A procedure for filing complaints against coaches should be spelled out and explained to coaches, parents, and athletes so that situations can be resolved and everyone's rights protected in the process. Finally, the consequences for a coach who exhibits abusive behavior should be spelled out and applied in situations in which the charges are clearly proven.

Status of Coaching

The number of young athletes who play sports has been estimated recently at about 40 million, which includes more than half of all kids age 5 to 10. To serve these young athletes, more than three million coaches work at all levels of ability. More than 500,000 of these coaches work in high school programs with varsity athletes. The Bureau of Labor Statistics (BLS) expects the job outlook for coaches to grow much faster than the average for all occupations through 2018 and in fact expects a percentage increase of 25% (BLS 2010-2011).

Coaches of college and professional athletes are more likely to have professional preparation for coaching than those who work with younger athletes. In most cases, they have graduated from college sport programs and served some time as an

apprentice coach with other experienced coaches. However, at the professional level, many coaches have been outstanding sport performers who have little background in coaching. Their coaching methods are more likely the result of watching former coaches and imitating qualities that they admired.

It may be helpful to separate coaching into different levels when considering its history, current status, and future needs. Coaches of high-performance athletes tend to have the most preparation for coaching. Coaching is their chosen occupation, and their career success depends on their knowledge and competency. They are highly motivated to seek every last bit of knowledge that may influence their chances for success. Because these coaches work with elite athletes, the number of positions available is limited. The vast number of athletic coaches will never coach high-performance athletes.

Coaches of athletes who are more interested in participation than performance include almost all youth sport coaches and many at the high school level. These coaches enjoy being around young people and enjoy sport. At the youth level, they are typically volunteers; at the high school level they may be paid a modest stipend. Almost all of these coaches have other sources of income from work that represents their true profession. This group also includes some individuals who work for sport organizations, private clubs, and public parks.

Admittedly, some coaches blend the goals of participation and performance when working with adolescent or adult athletes. This group is likely to have some coaching preparation, and the demands of their competitive athletes force them to continue to upgrade their coaching skills. High school coaches in highly competitive sports such as football and basketball, particularly in sport-crazy communities, usually lean toward the performance model of coaching by virtue of the demand for winning teams.

Without drawing a sharp line between the two major groups of coaches, those of performance and those of participation athletes, it may be helpful to consider the significant differences between them. As we consider various topics, keep in mind we don't want to lump the two groups together, especially where they differ in major ways.

Coaching Compensation

You read and hear about the coaches who make several million dollars a year for coaching professional players or coach at elite football or basketball programs at the college level. But those coaches are a small percentage out of the hundreds of thousands of coaches of sport. Their salaries are determined by the market for coaches at the highest-profile, most pressurized level of competition—if their teams don't win, they are gone.

Most coaches at the college level of nonrevenue sports earn modest salaries; the median income is $39,550. At the high school level, many coaches are full-time employees of the school system as teachers or in other positions. Their salaries for the school year are typically set by a union contract negotiated with the school board. If they elect to take on a coaching responsibility apart from their teaching assignment, they receive additional compensation that can range from about $1,000 for smaller sports such as cross country, golf, and tennis up to $10,000 for a large sport such as football. The level of pay depends on the geography and wealth of the school district.

Coaches who work in youth sport may be paid, or in many cases they are volunteers. Paid coaches who rely on that income are typically paid at a modest level unless they teach and coach at a private club or large public facility. Golf, tennis, ski, and swimming coaches are typically at the high end of paid coaches and may earn a solid middle-class living over their career (BLS 2010-2011).

Coaching as a Profession

Although we often refer to coaching as a profession, it is very difficult to make the case that it is indeed a profession. A profession is an occupation that does the following (Martens, Flannery, and Roetert 2002; VanderZwaag and Sheehan 1978):

- Dedicates itself to providing beneficial services to people
- Is based upon a generally accepted scientific body of knowledge
- Requires a rigorous course of study to transmit knowledge and skills
- Requires certification by demonstrating mastery of knowledge and ability to use the appropriate skills (membership is controlled by licensing after testing)
- Has an accepted public code of ethics
- Monitors itself to sanction or remove those who do not live up to the expectations of the profession
- Provides and expects continuing education of members to ensure up-to-date information and skills
- Establishes an organization to implement the standards, certification, and education of members

In general, coaching in the United States does not meet these standards. Many coaches are volunteers; they are untrained and they coach only as a hobby. The problem in requiring volunteers to submit to more rigorous standards is that their numbers may simply decline, resulting in a huge coaching shortage for youth sport programs.

Full-time professional coaches who work at their craft would likely benefit in their career and in their compensation if coaching were to become a true profession. Raising the standards for coach-

ing would likely improve the skill and knowledge of coaches and garner greater public recognition of the quality of the athletic experience. The casual, uncontrolled manner in which many coaches are hired simply does not merit public acceptance or regard for coaching as a profession when compared with law, medicine, engineering, or religion. There is no reason not to work toward making coaching a profession.

Coaching Standards

Standards for youth sport coaching are primarily set by the local community. Depending on the organizing group, coaches may be expected to have playing experience, coaching experience, or some level of coaching certification or training. On the other hand, organizations may simply require a willing volunteer. The level of expertise varies widely from sport to sport, community to community, and possibly year to year.

Because there is such a great need for youth sport coaches, most communities are only too happy to welcome volunteers and often have to persuade hesitant parents to coach. Without volunteer coaches, sport teams cannot operate and children lose a great opportunity. Parents who lack time, experience, or skill in coaching may agree to coach just to be sure that their kids can play on a team.

This situation creates two perplexing concerns. One is the lack of experience and training among coaches. The second is that even if the community sponsors coaching education or training for volunteer coaches, the turnover rate is extremely high and training has to be repeated every year. Most volunteer coaches continue only while their own children are in the program. If they want to continue to spend time with their own kids in sport, they move to a higher level or become a fan and spectator.

High school coaching standards have suffered from a similar dilemma. In the 1970s, the demand for competent high school coaches skyrocketed due to the passage of Title IX, which ensured equal opportunities for girls in sport. Suddenly, high schools were faced with a critical coaching shortage. Added to the expansion of girls' teams were declining enrollments, a depressed economy, and fewer job openings for classroom teachers who might be coaching candidates. As the teaching staff aged, many retired from coaching yet kept their teaching jobs, further complicating matters. Principals were forced to change or reduce their standards for coaches just to find available bodies to staff their athletic programs.

It wasn't until 1995 that the first set of national coaching standards for high school coaches was crafted. Led by the National Association for Sport and Physical Education (NASPE), more than 140 sport organizations have agreed that these standards, referred to as National Standards for Athletic Coaches (NSAC), represent the core body of knowledge for coaching expertise. These standards were developed through review and adaptation of scientific knowledge, practical coaching experience, and content of existing coaching education programs. Now in the second edition, the NSAC consists of 40 standards that are divided into eight domains of knowledge and competency (NASPE 2009):

- Philosophy and Ethics
- Safety and Injury Prevention
- Physical Conditioning
- Growth and Development
- Teaching and Communication
- Sport Skills and Tactics
- Organization and Administration
- Evaluation

The hope is that with these standards for coaching competency organized into one comprehensive and cohesive document, the document can serve as a blueprint for coaching education programs and certification processes. A National Federation of State High School Associations coaching education task force, along with the American Sport Education Program (ASEP), took the lead by recommending that state high school athletic associations mandate an ongoing professional development program for interscholastic coaches. By 2004, after working together since 1990, the NFHS and ASEP persuaded 35 states to offer coaching education courses. With the courses offered online, coaches could access them from virtually anywhere they could access the Internet (ASEP 2010).

The NFHS Coach Education Program was started in 2007, and more than 90,000 coaches have taken the core course, Fundamentals of Coaching. As of 2009, 44 of the 51 NFHS member state associations have adopted the course. Coaches are now able to become Level 1 certified as an Accredited Interscholastic Coach. To qualify, in addition to the Fundamentals course, they must complete NFHS First Aid for Coaches or the equivalent and one of the sport-specific courses or Teaching Sport Skills. In future years, NFHS will offer advanced certification at Level 2, Certified Interscholastic Coach, and Level 3, Master Interscholastic Coach (NFHS 2009c).

Perhaps the most important contribution of these standards is that they identify the vast breadth of knowledge that is required of competent coaches. As these standards become more publicized and more familiar to sport administrators, school personnel, parents, and the general public, it is likely

ACTIVITY TIME-OUT

Domains of Coaching Knowledge

Interview a coach of your choice. Ask the coach to rate the eight domains of coaching knowledge from the most important (with a rating of 1) to the least important (with a rating of 8). Ask why certain domains rated very high and others rated low based on the coach's practical life experience and experience in coaching. In your analysis of the coach's answers, be sure to consider the level of athletes the coach works with when evaluating the ranking of categories. Share your findings with your classmates and see what conclusions you can draw as a group from the responses you received from the interviewed coaches. The eight domains of coaching knowledge are the following (NASPE 2009):

- Philosophy and Ethics
- Safety and Injury Prevention
- Physical Conditioning
- Growth and Development
- Teaching and Communication
- Sport Skills and Tactics
- Organization and Administration
- Evaluation

that more will be expected of athletic coaches. At the same time, we can hope that as more training is required, the compensation and general status of coaching will be elevated (Brylinsky 2002).

In the last 10 years, the USOC encouraged each of its national governing bodies to identify the coaching competencies needed for its sport. National models were developed that were similar to the NASPE standards but tailored specifically to volleyball, soccer, tennis, swimming, and other Olympic sports. Information was shared between national governing bodies, and the result was a more developed model for coaching education and certification programs within the Olympic family.

Coaching Educational Expectations

There is tremendous variation in the requirements for athletic coaches in school settings. According to NASPE, 22 states require coaches to have state teaching credentials, and 6 states recommend them. Twenty-three states do not require teaching credentials. Although a teaching credential is a reasonable minimal standard, it does not include any specific knowledge or training in athletic coaching methods. Only 9 states do require specific coaching education, and half of those allow some flexibility as to the requirement. There has been a strong movement since 2006 when the National Standards for Sport Coaching were revised by NASPE and supported by dozens of other organizations to use the standards to upgrade the coaching profession at all levels. In fact, there is a national movement toward certification of high school coaches as evidenced by the fact that 40 states have adopted, recommended, or required one of two national certification programs. Those two programs are administered by the NFHS and ASEP.

Here are some key facts about the current state of coaching education in high school sports (NASPE 2008):

- The number of sport opportunities and the scope of sports in high schools are at the highest point ever, therefore creating a greater demand for quality coaching across all sports.
- Coaching education most frequently requires include a first aid course, CPR (cardiopulmonary resuscitation) training, and a fundamentals of coaching course. Some schools also require sport rules training, and sport-specific skills training is typically offered as an elective option.

- Many states are beginning to include non-education-based requirements for coaching such as background checks and health screenings.
- Coaching education courses are typically delivered through online courses, weekend workshops, and formal academic courses.
- There are few if any continuing education requirements for coaches once they meet the initial standards, so there is little incentive for coaches to update their knowledge or skills periodically.

In most colleges and universities across the United States, the minimal standard for an athletic coach is a college degree. Because coaches will be working with college athletes and operating in a college setting, most athletic directors believe that a college background is a minimum standard. Beyond that, the requirements vary widely, including experience as an athlete in the sport, coaching experience at the high school or college level, and certification by a national governing body or other agency in the sport. Some coaches work their way into college coaching by serving as volunteer assistant coaches, interns, or graduate assistants to gain experience and a foothold in the profession.

Coaching in professional sport differs markedly from coaching within the educational system. In professional sport, the required background can range from experience as a player at that level to years of successful coaching at a lower level of play. The educational requirements are typically not critical, since the emphasis of a professional team is simply to win contests. However, the lack of preparation in coaching is a heavy weight for many professional coaches who are limited by their own personal experiences in sport. For example, most coaches of professional tennis are excellent former players who rely on the coaching methods used by their coaches perhaps a decade earlier. Without any firsthand knowledge of current coaching science, they simply use coaching methods and information that are hopelessly out of date.

Coaching Certification

Now that standards for coaching have been developed, publicized, and disseminated, you might expect that there would be ways for prospective coaches to gain certification. In fact, there are at least three avenues to pursue, depending on the sport, the level of coaching, and the depth of coaching education that interests you.

A total of 179 institutions of higher education offer either an undergraduate major or minor in coaching education or a graduate degree in coaching. Most college programs are offered by state universities, although a few private colleges also offer programs. At a minimum, the typical undergraduate program requires six to eight courses, including principles of coaching, some sport science, sport-specific courses, and practical experience in coaching. Virtually every curriculum also requires a course in prevention, care, and treatment of injuries. Many students major in physical education, kinesiology, sport studies, or sport and exercise science and minor in coaching education. For prospective coaches who hope to find employment at the high school or college level, these programs are the logical track.

A second possibility for coaching certification is to investigate the requirements in the sport you are interested in. Most national governing bodies have a certification program that evaluates coaching knowledge and competency. Various levels of competency may be identified for beginning coaches, and there are opportunities to advance with more study, experience, and demonstration of higher levels of coaching expertise. These coaching certifications may be slanted toward youth coaching, private coaching, or high-performance coaching. For example, professional tennis coaches are certified as having the skills to work at tennis clubs and public facilities.

A third possibility is to seek certification through a national agency that is neither offered by an educational institution nor affiliated with a particular sport. These programs are primarily targeted toward youth coaches, high school coaches, Special Olympics coaches, or coaches of athletes with disabilities.

The American Sport Education Program was founded by Rainer Martens in 1976 and is committed to improving amateur sport by encouraging coaches, officials, administrators, parents, and athletes to embrace a philosophy of "athletes first, winning second" and by providing education to put the philosophy to work. ASEP has continued to produce training materials on coaching education, offering courses and videos. In spite of the availability of these excellent materials, the barrier for many coaches and program administrators is simply finding the time to use them. ASEP has helped solve that problem by developing online courses that can be taken at the coach's leisure. ASEP was the original coaching education provider for the NFHS, but that relationship ended in 2006. The NFHS has continued to expand its program for coaching education for high school coaches, while ASEP still works with approximately 40 states directly delivering programs for high school coaches and many youth coaching organizations.

The National Youth Sports Coaches Association (NYSCA) also offers certification to coaches by partnering with many community organizations such as the YMCA, Police Athletic League, Catholic youth organizations, Jewish community centers, Boys and Girls Clubs, and local park and recreation departments. NYSCA also offers an introductory instructional video for coaches, one-day clinics, and a web-based course.

Certification for coaches is usually awarded by organizations after the prospective coach demonstrates competency through written tests of knowledge and understanding, a face-to-face course of instruction, or evaluation of his coaching or teaching. For beginning coaches, the focus is typically on an introduction to coaching philosophy, first aid, basic coaching principles, and ethics.

Program administrators should be aware of the different standards of these certification programs, since they vary widely and typically measure only a small fraction of the competencies required for successful coaching.

Continuing Education for Coaches

Once coaches enter the profession, they have an obligation to expand their knowledge and keep up to date with new developments. Imagine how much coaching methods have changed over the last 30 years with advances in nutrition, physiology, sport psychology, sporting equipment, dealing with injuries, and performance-enhancing substances, to name just a few areas. While the strategy and tactics of most sports remain relatively constant, approaches to teaching them do not. Technique constantly changes as athletes invent new ways of performing; and for some sports, new skills are invented that were only dreamed of in the past.

Fortunately for interested coaches, many self-education resources are available. Here are a few of the options:

- Purchase books, videos, and DVDs for a personal coaching library.
- Review information online. Online courses are available, as are coaching discussion groups and networks of coaches eager to exchange ideas. Information from international groups and other countries is also often available online.

- Attend coaching conferences sponsored by national governing bodies, state high school sport associations, and college sport associations held locally or at the state or national level. Experts in every imaginable area will tutor you, and informal conversations with other coaches provide a wealth of knowledge.

- Subscribe to newsletters, periodicals, or magazines such as *Coach and Athletic Director Magazine, Scholastic Coach* magazine, or one published by a specific sport or coaching organization that delivers current coaching tips and information on a regular basis. Typically the information is screened by a panel of experts and written by experienced coaches or writers.

- Join a professional coaching organization in your sport, such as the United States Professional Tennis Association. Such organizations offer workshops, materials, and regular mailings to keep you on the cutting edge of your sport.

- Attend a coaching school offered by the national governing body in your sport for a few weeks of intensive study and practical experience.

- Volunteer to assist an expert coach whom you admire.

- Take graduate courses in coaching education at a nearby college or university.

- Take a coaching course offered by ASEP or sign up for other national programs for coaching.

- Watch sport on television, observing the coaches' behavior.

- Consult specialists in fields about which you know little. For example, a sport psychologist may be willing to help you learn about the basics of mental toughness.

- Read books that chronicle the careers of popular coaches who have had success.

- Rent movies that feature coaches, such as *Friday Night Lights, Remember the Titans, Hoosiers*, or *Glory Road*.

- Listen to interviews with coaches that you admire to see how they handle questions, criticisms, victory, and defeat.

Coaches have to work at their profession just as others work at theirs. You would be horrified if your personal physician who attended medical school 25 years ago did not keep up with advances in medicine. My personal physician just spent two weeks away from his office studying and taking examinations to renew his board certification in internal medicine. This recertification is required every five years and helps to ensure that doctors stay current with all the latest information. Not only do physicians have to give up office appointments during that time, but recertification costs them several thousand dollars out of their own pocket. Coaching should be no different and demands a lifetime of continuing education, although the expenses of continuing education are typically more modest.

How do the skills of this youth lacrosse coach need to differ from the skills needed by a collegiate lacrosse coach?

Coaching at Different Levels of Sport

It is unfair to lump all coaches together when considering what skills and competencies they ought to have. Different levels of athletes by age, skill, commitment, and sport require different coaching skills. In the following sections, we'll look closely at coaching at each level of participation and what makes a coach at that level successful.

Professional Sport

At the highest performance levels, coaches typically have a personal background of competing at that level. They also need to understand and accept the business aspect of sport, the commitment to winning that is required, and the criticism they will absorb if their team does not win. Since the athletes may be paid handsomely and may make several times more than the coach, motivation is sometimes a challenge. In addition, years of athletic training have inured some professional athletes to advice from coaches. And although these athletes are adults, they often are susceptible to lifestyle habits that interfere with their performance.

A perplexing conundrum exists in that although these athletes have reached the highest levels of sport, fundamental skills may be lacking. Coaches of professional athletes have to be skilled in teaching fundamentals to athletes who are typically resistant to change.

Finally, the length of the season, the physical injuries, and the intensity of competition all take a toll on professional athletes. Coaches need to be well versed in the mental skills and strategies that can help athletes deal with constant challenges to maintaining a healthy psyche.

High-Performance Amateur Sport

Some children begin specializing before the age of 10 with the goal of reaching the highest levels of sport—the Olympics, international competition, or professional sport. Those who coach these athletes must be able to teach fundamental skills to young athletes who will stand up against top competition as they age and gain experience.

Coaches of young athletes also need a firm understanding of the growth and development of prepubescent athletes since their charges will be going through significant physical, emotional, and mental changes as they experience puberty.

Knowledge and understanding of the mental side of performance are essential for coaches, since their athletes will be dealing with competitive pressure even at relatively young ages. Psychological skills that enhance performance must be taught and practiced along with physical skills. Burnout is common in intense competitive training, so coaches need to recognize warning signs and know how to deal with related problems.

Physical training and conditioning for elite levels of sport is quite intense and can be harmful if not properly designed and monitored. Injuries from overuse are common unless steps are taken to minimize them. Diet, nutrition, and strength training are all essential parts of high-performance training.

Finally, coaches of athletes with high aspirations must deal with parents and agents who also have opinions about the training and competitive schedule of the athletes. Their motives may be noble but they may be less informed than the coach, so it falls to coaches to provide steady, responsible guidance, relying on specific experts to bolster their position when necessary.

Intercollegiate Sport

The requirements for college coaches vary depending on the college that employs them, the level of competition (Division I, II, or III), and the sport they coach. There is a wide range of expectations, facilities, levels of athletes, and compensation depending on those factors. Many smaller colleges hire part-time athletic coaches who are paid several thousand dollars for their work during the season. In contrast, large universities with highly competitive programs employ many full-time coaches who devote their time year round to recruiting, off-season training, preseason training, and of course in-season practices and games.

The National Collegiate Athletic Association (NCAA) publishes and enforces a set of rules that college coaches must follow. Coaches must spend a significant amount of time verifying that their actions are within the rules to avoid embarrassing mistakes that could cost their employer dearly in penalties.

Building strength and endurance is also a key factor at this level because the athletes are capable of making huge gains in size, speed, and endurance. Year-round training is expected, especially for

IN THE ARENA WITH . . .

C. Vivian Stringer

Vivian Stringer was inducted into the Naismith Basketball Hall of Fame in 2009 on her record as the third winningest coach in collegiate women's basketball with an overall record of 644-199 in her 29-year career. She is the only collegiate coach (male or female) to have directed three different schools to berths in the NCAA Final Four (Cheney, Iowa, and Rutgers). She has been named Coach of the Year three times, has led her teams to 15 appearances in the NCAA Tournament, and has posted 20-plus season wins 22 times. Stringer coached the United States to a bronze medal in the Pan American Games, coached the U.S. team in Mexico, toured China as head coach of the U.S. Select Team, and coached in the World University Games.

"I grew up in a time when we didn't have organized sports for girls. Now, because of Title IX, players are able to make a million dollars playing basketball. Who would have thought they'd give you 10 cents?" says Stringer. Thirty years ago, Stringer was the women's coach and legendary coach John Chaney the men's coach at Cheyney State in Pennsylvania; he was also elected to the Hall of Fame. They shared a tiny gym—and a dream—before Chaney left for Temple and Stringer for Iowa and then Rutgers.

Stringer is an American original who has never fit into a neat box in the college sport arena. She has had a cordial but prickly relationship with the NCAA, fueled by everything from questionable tournament seedings to a feeling that certain factions within the association tried to block her success. Fortunately they were not successful.

Stringer has excelled as a full-time coach despite dealing with challenges from managing a daughter disabled by spinal meningitis to surviving breast cancer and losing her husband, Bill, who died of a heart attack on Thanksgiving Day in 1992.

As Stringer enters her 38th year of coaching, the only thing she has not achieved is a national championship. She admits winning the championship has long been her heart's desire but adds "I've come to a level of peace that if it is just not meant to be, I'm at peace" (Rhoden 2009; Women's Basketball Hall of Fame 2010).

Division I athletes, although contact with a coach is limited by the NCAA during the off-season.

High School Sport

Coaches of high school athletes need to have a wide breadth of coaching knowledge and a keen understanding of young adults. Skills and strategy expertise are a must. Athletes who have developed bad habits need special care to learn new skills. Practical sport science knowledge such as injury prevention, physical training, and sport psychology can be extremely helpful in teaching gifted athletes and dealing with psychosocial issues.

Generally, coaches of high school sport are former athletes who may also have played sports in college. They are hired to teach in the school system and offered a supplemental contract to coach after school. Young teachers may coach several seasons and thus earn supplemental pay each season. However, teaching a full day and then adding coaching duties is challenging and exhausting. Many retire from coaching as their own families mature and they no longer enjoy the fast-paced intense schedule.

Coaching education for high school coaches is spotty, and aspiring coaches must seek out coaching clinics, workshops, and conferences on their own. Some sports offer easy access to education through books, videos, and seminars while other sports are poorly organized. Few states have rigorous standards for coaching, and many athletes have suffered under the tutelage of so-called warm-body coaches who accept the job under pressure but have minimal expertise or interest.

A typical high school coach usually likes kids, knows how to organize and administer the team,

IN THE ARENA WITH . . .

Bob Hurley

Bob Hurley was inducted into the Naismith Basketball Hall of Fame in 2010, only the third high school basketball coach to be enshrined. Entering the 2010 season, Hurley is just 16 victories shy of reaching 1,000 in his 38-year career. Despite not having a gym at the school, St. Anthony High School in Jersey City, New Jersey, his teams are known for their discipline on offense and tenacity on defense and have won 24 state titles and nine Tournament of Champions crowns. His Friars have been *USA Today*'s mythical national champions three times, and he estimates that more than 150 of his former players have earned college scholarships.

Coach Hurley's story is fascinating, instructive, and inspiring. He attracts players from the streets of Jersey City and forges them into teams that dominate high school basketball at the state and national level. A former Hudson County probation officer, Hurley acts as a father figure to many of the teenagers he coaches by providing the stability and discipline they have missed at home. His rules are firm, clear, and nondebatable. His methods are sometimes unorthodox, but they seem to work.

Despite numerous offers to coach at the college level, Bob has stuck with St. Anthony. He has not only saved the basketball program, but also helped raise money to save the school when it was threatened with bankruptcy. Some coaches are blessed with great athletes for a few years and then never heard from again. But the mark of a genius is to take kids year after year and turn them into consistent high performers. In the process, Hurley has changed the lives of hundreds of kids who hung out on the mean streets of Jersey City.

St. Anthony's 2007-2008 team, which went 32-0, was featured in the documentary *The Street Stops Here*, aired nationally on PBS. To truly understand the genius of Bob Hurley, pick up a copy of the 2005 book *The Miracle of St. Anthony*, an account of one season for the St. Anthony boys' basketball team. It is a truly amazing story of the life of a coaching giant in high school sports (Wojnarowski 2005; Politi 2010; Rubin 2010).

and can be a helpful adult role model during the critical adolescent years. It is more unusual for high school coaches to have a broad and deep knowledge of coaching and their sport. If they do, greener pastures at the collegiate level often beckon.

High school coaches who are dedicated to their sport often get involved in the sport at the community level and help develop youngsters as a feeder system for the high school team. They track potential athletes from an early age, offer advice, coach them in high school, and help them choose a college. For many dedicated coaches, this is a lifelong pursuit; and they gain so many friends and supporters over the years that a run for mayor is not out of the question. I've known more than one former coach who easily "retired" to the position of mayor or council member.

As athletes enter their preteen and teenage years, their coaches need to be strong both technically and strategically. They need to empathize with kids entering puberty, and they must be sensitive to the vast physical and emotional changes that accompany this period. Discipline and hard work will enable athletes to develop their individual talents. The coach must also help the athletes balance their dedication to sport with responsibilities to family, friends, and school.

Youth Sport

When kids are young and first exposed to sport, they need coaches who understand them and also understand why they play and what they expect out of sport. Coaches who are sensitive to their needs, concerned for each child's welfare, and able to produce success for each child to some degree are worth their weight in gold. Coaches of young beginners also need to be well schooled in teaching the basic strategy and skills of the sport so that children develop sound fundamentals.

Coaches of young athletes must help them understand the rules of the game, develop good sporting behavior, learn basic skills and strategies, and have fun. If they don't make sport attractive to children, even talented athletes will drop out since they haven't yet invested much time or effort. In addition, unlike at other levels, parents may need education in the philosophy of the program. When athletes are young and malleable, parental understanding of the sport and support of the program goals are critical; and attitudes about winning and losing are particularly crucial for parents to be aware of to embrace and guide their youngsters.

A coaching personality that is fun, warm, and engaging is critical for young athletes. They want to enjoy time with their friends, test their skills, and celebrate games with a trip to the Dairy Queen regardless of whether they won or lost. Coaches should love to spend time with kids and enjoy their foibles without judging them or their parents.

Of course, at different levels of coaching even within youth sport, situations can vary. Very young high-performance athletes such as gymnasts, tennis players, swimmers, and others who compete nationally and internationally present a coaching dynamic that is very challenging. Parents sacrifice huge amounts of money, and sometimes they uproot families to seek better competition. Their kids thus feel tremendous pressure to succeed. It takes special training and a special personality to work with young athletes and their families while dealing with the pressure for immediate success against the best competition in the world.

Coaching for Male or Female Athletes

Since the passage of Title IX and the opportunities for women as coaches have expanded, most research has focused on tracking the numbers of women in coaching rather than their coaching methods. Perhaps this is partly because so many men have taken over women's teams. In any case,

female athletes agree that they prefer a coach who is a quality person and a role model, and who is assertive, cooperative, determined, respected, willing to help, dedicated, responsible, energetic, and cool under pressure. They also prefer coaches who have a great personality. Not surprisingly, these traits do not differ significantly from those valued by male athletes (Holbrook and Barr 1997).

However, there are some indications that boys and girls react differently to coaching styles and that coaches should tailor their coaching methods to maximize the athletic experience for both genders. Craig Stewart has summarized the research on the need for different approaches in coaching female and male athletes (Stewart 2005). According to Stewart, girls are more intrinsically motivated by self-improvement and goals related to team success than boys. They are also more motivated by a cooperative, caring, and sharing team environment. Some female athletes can be turned off by coaches who overemphasize winning, and they seem to approach competition somewhat differently from male athletes (Garcia 1994). For example, girls seem to place more emphasis on playing fair and tend to blame themselves for a poor performance. Boys are more likely to break rules; strive to win at any cost; and blame other people or things for their defeats such as the weather, referees, or lucky breaks. It is not clear whether these differences are the result of cultural expectations or whether they have to do with innate traits (Stewart 2005).

It is quite possible that girls who are exposed to male coaches and compete at highly competitive levels will be more likely to exhibit traits similar to those exhibited by boys simply because of their training and competitive experience. Nevertheless, it is important for coaches to recognize that differences exist and that coaching styles should fit the needs of the athletes.

ACTIVITY TIME-OUT

Females Coaching Male Teams

Since the passage of Title IX, many male coaches have moved to coaching female athletes and in fact are 58% of college coaches of women's sports. But what about women coaching male players? Is that an avenue that is becoming more accessible to female coaches? Do some research to find an example of a female coach of a male high school or college team. Find out all you can about her experience coaching boys or young men, and identify the difficulties she may have faced simply because of her gender. While there are examples of women coaching males in sports such as tennis, golf, soccer, and cross country, you may be surprised that some women have successfully negotiated the challenging role of boys' basketball or even football coach. Share your results with others in your class.

Coaching Personality

It may be unfair to lump all coaches together in a single group and attempt to describe their personalities, beliefs, and orientations. However, in every occupation, certain similarities among practitioners give the impression of a stereotype that has some basis in fact.

Coaches are not immune from stereotypes. Movies, television, and books often present coaches in a baseball cap with a whistle around their neck shouting profanities at their young charges. Of course, these representations are unfair, but they are based on years of observation by athletes, parents, and spectators.

Researchers have revealed that historically, male coaches have typically manifested certain personality traits. Sport psychologists Tom Tutko and Bruce Ogilvie and sport sociologist George Sage collected information in the 1970s suggesting that coaches tended to be moderately conservative; that is, they tended to value loyalty to tradition, respect authority, expect obedience, follow normal standards of conduct, and have a strong religious orientation. Coaches in traditional team sports in highly competitive environments still tend to exhibit these characteristics because that style of authoritarian coaching fits with the so-called professional model of coaching (Lombardo 1999; Sage 1973).

Athletic coaches tend to be more conservative on most matters than the college students they coach, a situation that has often led to conflicts. However, when compared with other adults such as businesspersons or farmers, coaches were more to the middle of the road. Compared with other teachers at both the high school and college level, coaches tend to be among the most conservative of those groups.

The historical reasons for athletic coaches tending toward a conservative personality include the following (Lombardo 1999):

- Coaches are typically former athletes who have seen their own coaches operate in a conservative atmosphere, and they tend to perpetuate that style.
- Coaches often have clear concepts of right and wrong based on strong religious and cultural backgrounds.
- Coaches often come from working-class families where traditional values are emphasized, as well as respect for authority and tradition.

- Because most coaches are held accountable for their team's performance, they like to seize control of the team even if that means coaching in an authoritarian style.
- In the past, many coaches had a strong military background that influenced their attitudes, beliefs, and habits. Since a volunteer army was instituted in the United States and fewer current coaches have had military experience, this influence may have declined.

Since this research was conducted, sport has changed. In many instances the changes mirror changes in society. Women are now fully engaged in competitive sport; significant progress has been made in racial integration within sport; and scientific research on sport has added to the existing knowledge base for coaches.

Active coaches today have certainly been affected by their own athletic experiences, mentors, and life experience. If they model their coaching behavior on the past, they will likely encounter difficulties. Young athletes today have grown up in a world much different from the one their coaches grew up in. They have more personal freedom, are more likely to question authority, make decisions without parental knowledge or support, and often rely on peers for advice and counsel. The decline of stable two-parent families has contributed to some of these changes. Other general societal trends toward a more permissive environment have aided these changes, such as the fact that many families have both parents employed outside the home, thus giving kids a lot of independence.

Young athletes expect to enjoy their sport experience and often simply withdraw if they don't. They expect coaches to be attentive and interested in them as people rather than just sport performers. Authoritarian coaches may succeed in certain situations, but generally they have been forced to modify their coaching behaviors to adjust to today's athletes. Many coaches of women's teams also have learned to adapt to the needs of their athletes that are different from the needs of male athletes.

An in-depth look at the characteristics of coaches is likely to reveal some trends that may differ from those of the past. Coaches of certain sports that are more individual may have a different view than the traditional team coach. Consider the role of a tennis or golf coach who deals with only six or eight athletes compared with a football coach who presides over a squad with well over 100 athletes.

Naturally, with such a large squad, the opportunities for close interpersonal relationships are limited and the coach may be forced to adopt a role similar to that of the CEO of a small company.

Another factor is the shifting emphasis in professional sport from autocratic coaches to those who can manage a sizable business with the acumen of a savvy businessperson. The exorbitant contracts of star players and their influence on the success of the team have also shifted the balance of power from coach to outspoken players. A case in point is the breakup of the Los Angeles Lakers dynasty after the 2004 season and the firing of Phil Jackson, one of the most celebrated coaches in recent years. Because star player Kobe Bryant was unhappy with

his role compared with that of Shaquille O'Neal, both Jackson and O'Neal were let go. Eventually, O'Neal was traded to the Miami Heat, and Jackson was rehired by the Lakers for the 2005 season. This dynamic has been repeatedly played out in the National Basketball Association when one superstar player has an inordinate amount of power and influence. Imagine the diplomatic skills required by the coach of a team with an athlete who believes he has the right to decide what is best for him and the rest of the team.

It is dangerous to generalize too much and stereotype groups of people. Athletic coaches are victims of stereotyping even though much of the conventional wisdom about coaching styles is

IN THE ARENA WITH . . .

Joe Paterno

At 83 years old, Joe Paterno was preparing for his 45th year of pacing the sidelines as head coach of the Penn State Nittany Lions football team. He is simply the winningest coach in history among major college football coaches, with a record of 394-129-3 over 44 seasons. His long-time friend and colleague Bobby Bowden of Florida State, who retired after the 2009 season, is in second place. Paterno is also the all-time leader among coaches in bowl appearances (36) and postseason triumphs (24). Additionally his coaching record includes two national championships; five undefeated, untied teams; 23 finishes in the top 10 national rankings; selection as American Football Coach Association Coach of the Year an unprecedented five times; and more than 350 former players who have signed National Football League contracts, 31 of them first-round draft choices.

"JoePa," as he's affectionately called in the Central Pennsylvania hamlet of "Happy Valley," otherwise known as State College, has fashioned a coaching career that has spanned the administrations of 13 U.S. Presidents beginning with Harry Truman. One of his trademarks as a coach was to see that his athletes attend class, devote the proper time to studies, and graduate with a meaningful degree. He often has said that he measures team success not by athletic prowess but by the number of productive citizens who make a contribution to society.

Proof of the value of Paterno's philosophy is the fact that the Nittany Lions can count 15 Hall of Fame Scholar-Athletes, 34 first-team *ESPN: The Magazine* Academic All-Americans (44 overall), and 18 NCAA Postgraduate Scholarship winners. Penn State has had at least one Academic All-American in each of the past eight years, with 10 first-team honorees over the past four years. In these days of focus on the graduation rates in major college sports, Penn State posted a record 85% graduation success rate, the highest among the 2009 AP Top 25 teams. The average among Football Bowl Subdivision teams was only 67%.

Renowned for his charitable contributions to academics at Penn State, Paterno and his wife Sue have donated over $4 million toward various departments and colleges, including gifts for the Penn State All-Sports Museum and the Pasquerilla Spiritual Center. After they helped to raise over $13.5 million for the 1997 expansion of Patee Library, the university named the expansion Paterno Library in their honor. Paterno and his wife have been very active in the Special Olympics and were inducted into the Special Olympics Pennsylvania Hall of Fame in 2008.

Joe Paterno is a bit older and wiser now, but he hasn't lost the spark for coaching. He is clearly the most successful coach in the history of college football. But more importantly, he is one of the most admired figures in college athletics, and one whose influence has extended well beyond the white chalk lines of the football field (Pennsylvania State University 2010).

outdated. In order to be successful in today's world, the majority of coaches have had to adapt their behavior to the coaching job they accept and align their coaching methods to the goals of the sponsoring organization and the expectations of the athletes entrusted to their care (Lin, Jui-Chia, and Esposito 2005; Lombardo 1999).

Coaches at other levels of competition, including nonrevenue sports at colleges, most high school sport, youth sport, and sport for athletes with disabilities and older athletes, are more likely to develop a humanistic or invitational style of coaching. They need to focus on the total development of the people they coach rather than on competition results. Coaches of sports that require independent thinking by athletes need to encourage and help players to think for themselves. Those who subscribe to the invitational style need to ensure that every aspect of their program and coaching behavior is warm and welcoming to athletes. Sport participation for these athletes is an opportunity to test their limits and realize their potential as human beings.

Many successful coaches have written an autobiography or had someone write a biography of their life and coaching career. For aspiring coaches, these can be inspiring and instructive words. The trick, though, is to sort through the lessons learned by another coach who lived in a different era and pick out those that will stand the test of time. The days of authoritarian, no-nonsense coaching are gone no matter how successful Vince Lombardi was years ago. Some coaches whose careers have stood the test of time and are worth investigating include the following:

- Football: Joe Gibbs, Don Shula, Bill Walsh, Marv Levy, Bill Parcells, Bill Belichick, Urban Meyer, Steve Spurrier, Pete Carroll, Bobby Bowden, Joe Paterno, and Eddie Robinson

- Basketball: John Wooden, Adolph Rupp, Rick Pitino, Phil Jackson, Lenny Wilkens, Mike Krzyzewski, Pat Summitt, Vivian Stringer, Geno Auriemma, John Chaney, John Thompson, Dean Smith, and Jim Valvano

- Other sports: Dick Gould, tennis; Doc Counsilman, swimming; Leroy Walker, track and field; Nick Bollettieri, tennis; Dan Gable, wrestling; Joe Torre, baseball; Earl Weaver, baseball; Billie Jean King, tennis; Tony DiCicco, soccer; and Anson Dorrance, soccer

An analysis of their lives and careers can be very instructive to aspiring coaches.

Challenges for the Future of Coaching

Coaching is difficult to describe and evaluate because it differs greatly from one situation to the next. The common identifiable theme is that coaches are part of sport to help athletes achieve their best performance and enjoy the experience. In other words, coaches are leaders of people engaged in sport participation.

The United States is different from other countries in that we have no generally accepted body of knowledge that coaches are expected to know. Most developed countries, particularly in Europe, have a coaching education plan in place that is approved by the government agency responsible for sport and typically administered by the governing body of each sport. Canada and Australia are examples of other countries that have programs. Their nationwide certification programs have five levels of coaching certification; and to reach Level 3, a coach must complete approximately 100 hours of training in theoretical, technical, and practical areas.

In the United States, there is no process for coaches to gain certification from a neutral agency that verifies their knowledge and skill. It is up to the sport consumers to demand a minimum level of expertise from their coaches and to insist on change when coaches do not measure up to these expectations.

The first step was to develop a national consensus on the NASPE national coaching standards that differentiate among the levels of coaching knowledge necessary for various athletes according to skill, age, and level of performance. These standards have been endorsed by over 140 other sport organizations and form the essential framework for certification, along with sport-specific knowledge and competency in strategy and skills of the particular sport (NASPE 2009). Now that this groundbreaking step has been taken, the next move is for each organization that has adopted the standards to figure out how to develop a delivery system that is affordable and accessible to all prospective and continuing coaches.

Enforcement of coaching certification has always been a puzzle in the United States, but those groups that do adopt at least a minimal certification requirement have taken a necessary step. Coaches who are employed by organizations, schools, and colleges should certainly be required to meet a level of certification that is appropriate for their position. In addition, the public needs better education on the importance of coaching certification so that they too demand it. Coaching organizations need to spend time and money educating the public so that they can make enlightened choices of coaches for their athletic experiences and those of their kids.

Enforcement of such standards leads to a national certification process delivered locally that enables coaches to verify their understanding and ability to apply knowledge in practical situations. At most levels, the certification process could be available through an interactive online distance-learning system to ensure the widest possible accessibility. Higher levels of certification may require additional face-to-face learning with an emphasis on applying the principles of sport science.

Finally, once coaches have achieved certification, there must be a systematic method of continuing education to keep them current with new knowledge and allow more in-depth exploration of coaching skills and competencies.

A second challenge involves recruiting, training, and supporting the army of volunteer coaches who are the backbone of most youth sport programs. Because there is such high turnover of volunteer coaches, recruiting and training processes must be streamlined, easily accessible, and inexpensive. Efforts should also be made to reduce resignations of volunteer coaches who quit as soon as their own kids graduate to another level. Perhaps a model of sharing that divided coaching responsibilities and decreased time investments would encourage more experienced coaches to continue.

A related issue that needs to be addressed is making the coaching education and certification programs relevant enough to convince sport program administrators, parents, and prospective coaches that their time will be well spent. Unrealistic expectations will doom attempts to educate and certify volunteer coaches who may simply turn down a coaching position instead; the effect would be a crisis of too few coaches available to staff youth sport programs.

A third challenge is to develop strategies for recruiting females into coaching at every level. Despite the explosion of girls' sport in the last 25 years, the number of women who coach female teams is less than one-third of all coaches. For many women, family responsibilities take priority; but in these days of shared parenting, men should accept more family responsibilities in order to help put prospective female coaches on the field. Many women could make significant contributions to coaching young people. We accept a similar role for women as teachers in schools, so why not entice them to our ball fields or gymnasiums? In addition,

when recruiting and retaining female coaches, it is necessary to make certain their compensation is equal to that of male coaches. We also need to encourage the media to promote successful female coaches as role models for aspiring coaches.

A fourth challenge is to ensure that athletes are protected from negative behavior or exploitation by athletic coaches. Background checks, credential reviews, and consistent monitoring with comprehensive performance reviews should be required by sport programs that employ coaches. Abuse of athletes by coaches must be defined, acknowledged, and eliminated so that every athlete at all levels has a healthy experience.

A fifth challenge is to develop a recognition system that is based on criteria other than just wins and losses. While the performance of their athletes is one measure of coaches' success, there are other measures that should be considered in the context of the goals of the program. If teaching fundamental skills is critical for young athletes, then coaches who are masters of skill acquisition should be widely recognized and rewarded. Volunteer coaches who invest so much discretionary time must also be rewarded through public recognition and perhaps granted incentives such as trips to the highest championships of their sport or further educational experiences at no cost to them.

A sixth challenge is to recruit and promote coaches from minority groups to provide role models for younger coaches and athletes. Lapchick's Racial and Gender Report Cards (2008 and 2008-2009) suggest that with the exception of professional basketball, very few sports have a representation of minority coaches that mirrors their presence in the population.

Chapter Summary

The influence of coaches on younger generations is enormous. Testimonials from former athletes abound with praise for their coaches as mentors, advisers, and heroes. Coaching athletes through the stress of sport links coaches and athletes together in a bond unlike other adult–child relationships.

Regrettably, there are also opportunities for coaches to have a negative impact on youths. Unrealistic demands from a coach may turn kids off of sport and activity, make them resentful of authoritarian discipline, damage their self-confidence, and confirm their worst suspicions about adults who are using them for their own self-interests.

We explored the current status of coaching in the United States and learned that standards for coaching have only recently been developed and have been accepted by over 160 different sport organizations. In spite of this landmark accomplishment, implementation of those standards is just beginning, and few general certification programs are widely available or mandated by organizations that sponsor sport programs.

Youth sport is unique in that its hundreds of thousands of coaches typically have little if any background in coaching. Perhaps more distressing is that after they learn coaching skills on the job, they often resign from coaching as soon as their own children leave the team or sport.

We examined the skills and competencies that are useful for coaches at different levels of sport. We also acknowledged that the coach's philosophy should match the level of coaching required and the athletes' expectations.

While it is difficult to generalize about such a diverse population, athletic coaches typically exhibit fairly conservative personalities, particularly in team sports and at the professional level. Coaches who work with athletes who are oriented more toward participation than toward high performance are more likely to employ a democratic model than an autocratic model of coaching. Most aspiring coaches model their behavior after former coaches and their experience as athletes, and the majority accept the values of hard work, discipline, respect for authority, and love of sport. Female coaches tend to be more committed to establishing a cooperative, caring team attitude than male coaches, who tend to focus heavily on winning or losing.

Finally, we wrapped up the chapter with a look at the challenges for coaching in the future. Unless some dramatic steps are taken in the next 25 years, it is possible that sport participation will decline as a result of dissatisfied athletes and families who expect more from coaches. While coaching does not yet merit acceptance as a profession, there is no reason we cannot work in that direction.

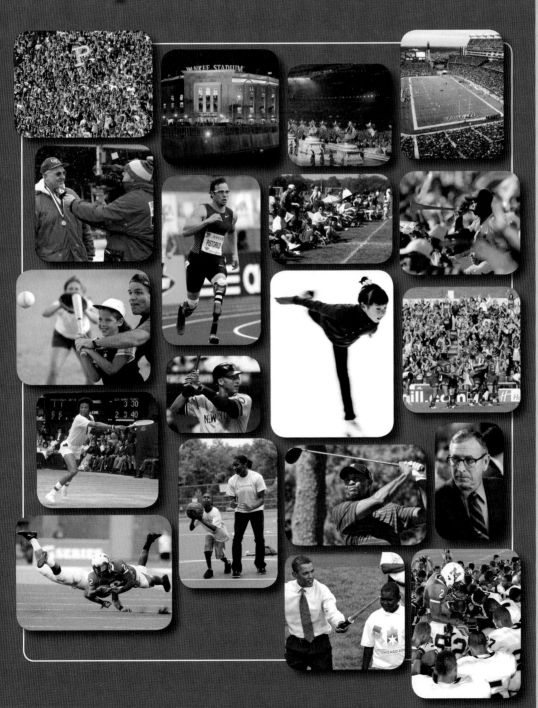

20

Future Trends in Sport

Student Outcomes

After reading this chapter, you will know the following:

- Social trends that are likely to affect sport
- The conflict between performance sport and participation sport and the effects of money, sponsorship, facilities, programs, and sport popularity
- The influence of changing attitudes toward sport participation
- How spectatorship affects sport participation
- Effects of technology on equipment, training, performance enhancers, and media support of sport
- How different social theorists would effect change in sport

It is pretty rare for people to be able to predict the future with any accuracy, but if you study the trends and analyze the odds for those trends to gain traction, stall, or disappear, you might make some educated guesses. Assuming you've absorbed the changes in sport that have occurred in the past 50 years, try to imagine some that may occur by 2025 or 2050. Here are some ideas to get your creative juices going:

- Can you envision raising the height of the basketball hoop to 12 feet to decrease the dominance of freakishly tall players with limited skills and recapture some of the magic of the skillful game of the past?

- Will advances in medicine enable injured or aging athletes to replace damaged limbs so that they can still compete at a high level with a custom-fitted prosthetic device including limbs and joints?

- Will computers replace sports writers? Rather than dispatching writers to cover games, information from box scores can be gathered over the Internet, analyzed by computer, and reported as a game summary. It is already happening.

- Will Major League Baseball finally do something about the splintering bats that endanger players and spectators? Is a composite bat the answer? Different woods?

- Is it just a matter of time before parents will be able to determine the gene mix of their offspring to maximize the child's chances to become an elite athlete?

- Will the National Basketball Association (NBA) expand internationally to take advantage of the worldwide interest in the sport and reach out to new markets like Europe and China to generate millions of fans?

Add your own predictions here, not matter how outlandish, and then consider the odds of those changes occurring.

One of my favorite professors in college, Lee "Pappy" Warren, professor of history at East Stroudsburg University, used to tell us, "There are four kinds of people in this world: Those that know, and know that they know; those that know, and don't know that they know; those that don't know, and know that they don't know; and those that don't know, and don't know that they don't know."

I've pondered those words over many years and have become convinced that Pappy was a wise man. He valued education, learning from the past, and self-study as the path toward enlightenment and a better society. After reading this book, noting current events in sport, working through the student activities, and discussing sport issues with others, you should be much closer to the first group identified in Pappy's saying—"those that know, and know that they know." Your understanding of sport in society should be light years ahead of where it was when you began your studies. Yet, the picture is not complete without a peek at the trends that are likely to carve out the future of sport. This chapter considers those trends and invites you to predict where those trends will lead. Where you find the potential trends inconsistent with your personal beliefs, you may begin to form a plan of action to influence the future of sport in a way you believe will help society.

If you and I do nothing, it is possible that events and influences in our society will shape sport participation or lack of it in ways that we find unhealthy or even harmful. Those who profit financially from sport as entertainment, promote spectatorship, and ignore participation in sport by average citizens may take complete control over the sporting world. Given the potential for sport to enhance every citizen's quality of life, such a narrow focus would be a shame.

Social Trends

Social trends are difficult to predict since we have no way of knowing how outside influences in society are likely to affect our state of mind, our economy, or our values. Certain worldwide trends such as the rise in terrorism may drastically affect our lives in ways that are difficult to predict. Likewise, the shrinking of our world into a global economy of interdependence has the potential to either bring our world closer together in cooperation or split us wider apart in conflict.

Within our own society, certain social trends seem clear. First, our population is rapidly aging, and the proportion of the populace that is older than 50 years will continue to skyrocket in the immediate future. Concerns for quality of life, health care, and productive use of leisure time after retirement will command the attention of a large proportion of the population as they age. In addition to an aging population, we are also a declining population. Forecasts for the next 50 years show that Europe will continue to have a declining population. The United States will maintain its low birth rate, but that will be offset by a continued influx of immigrants, most of whom will be of Hispanic descent (Wottenberg 2003).

Second, the rights of all people regardless of age, race, gender, sexual preference, or disability will continue to be protected, and discrimination laws are likely to be strengthened in the United States. The stage is set to not only protect the rights of every citizen, but also to enhance quality of life by opening up avenues for new experiences and adventures.

Third, those who have benefited most from supporting performance sport will fight to protect their investment in sport. Rather than just protecting the status quo, they will bring ingenuity to strategies to expand the influence of performance sport. This group will continue to strengthen the bond between big-time collegiate sport, professional sport, and the Olympic Games.

The field of sport management is growing rapidly and will continue to expand as sport organizations search for ways to enhance their bottom line by enticing and serving consumers. Education on sport management is available in many universities and includes training in sport-related event management, finance, human resources, law, marketing, public relations, and program management. People training in sport management are playing an increasingly critical role in professional sport, amateur sport, nonprofit organizations such as the YMCA or YWCA, sporting goods manufacturing, sporting events, and sport facilities (Hoffman 2009).

Fourth, the natural human tendency to push against barriers will result in development of new materials and processes to produce better sport equipment, facilities, and training regimens so that elite athletes can challenge the frontier of athletic achievements. Records will continue to be broken

As our country, and the world, faces an obesity epidemic among our youth, it's imperative that we find ways to encourage children to become and remain physically active.

as athletes benefit from scientific advances. Another key area of research will be the effort to rid sport of performance-enhancing substances that provide an unfair advantage to some athletes, create mistrust on the part of fans and the media regarding great performances, and threaten the integrity of athletic competition at every level.

POP CULTURE

Is Soccer in the Future of the United States?

In the 1960s we viewed soccer as a "foreign sport." In the '70s, the North American Soccer League brought the sport to American fans for the first time. By the '80s, youth soccer was the most popular sport for the next generation of kids, and the '90s brought two World Cups to the United States and Major League Soccer. After 2000, the media began to see the potential appeal of soccer, and nearly 17 million viewers watched the United States versus England in the 2010 World Cup, rivaling the 16.4 million average viewers for the NBA finals (Wilt 2010).

What the Brazilians have dubbed "the beautiful game" has taken a while to catch on in the United States. Critics cite low scores, ties, and general boredom. But to the rest of the world, those criticisms don't hold up. Part of the fault lies with uneducated or biased sport announcers who perpetuate these myths. But as America begins to learn how to play and watch soccer, opinions may change. Soccer is a game that revolves around human passion—with amazing heroics, both team and individual, or boneheaded plays that get the juices flowing.

The American preoccupation with "kicking and chasing" from an early age must give way to an understanding that soccer is a game of space—and the manipulation of that space. Teams that simply go for the goal can be easily defended against, but teams who hold onto the ball and show patience while looking for the best angles for a pass or a shot will be rewarded. It's true that American-style heart and hustle are admirable traits, but they are not enough when competing with the best players in the world. We need better coaches especially at the youth level to help kids learn to play a more sophisticated and clever brand of soccer (Bird 2010).

You've read throughout this book of the changing demographics of America. Indeed, minorities will soon become the majority; and if we can get Hispanics/Latinos and African Americans on the soccer field, our talent pool will immediately burgeon. Similarly, youth soccer in America draws from the upper-middle class and upper class, while in the rest of the world it is "the people's game' populated by children of the working class. History tells us that is where most of our great champions in every sport come from (Didziulis 2010).

Our most popular sports, football, baseball, and basketball, are largely intramural affairs in which we simply compete against ourselves. No other nation even takes these sports seriously with the exception of basketball. It might be fun to take on the world as underdogs in soccer and fight our way to the top. Isn't that the American way, after all?

Fifth, coaches will adapt to their athletes by increasing their coaching competency and adjusting their coaching philosophy toward meeting the needs of their athletes. At the same time, athletes will pressure coaches to endorse a certification process that indicates coaching knowledge, skill, and competency at various levels of coaching.

Conflict Between Performance Sport and Participation Sport

There has always been keen competition between performance sport and participation sport. The competition centers on publicity, funding, accessibility, cost, facilities, coaching, and recruiting players into one track or the other. During the past century, performance sport has had the edge in just about every category. But things may change in this century as a result of our changing demographics, the shift to an older population, a potential national crisis in American health care, and in some cases public lack of interest in performance sport.

However, it seems more likely that both categories of sport will grow steadily but perhaps for different reasons. Let's look at the potential for expansion of each one in turn.

Performance Sport

The institutions that support performance sport are strong, well funded, well established, and determined to perpetuate their roles. They are composed of powerful businesspersons, athletic directors, college presidents, and commercial sponsors who have joined with the media to glorify the finest athletes in the world. The emphasis on superior athletes assaulting performance barriers makes a captivating story. We love to see athletes running faster, jumping higher, hitting harder, or proving their power in sport, especially if their success can be attributed to hard work, dedication, or overcoming obstacles. Their success becomes our success, and we rejoice in it.

Performance sport at the youth level will continue to thrive as youngsters and their families follow their dreams to achieve competitive success. Youth programs will grow as parents thrust their potential prodigies into sport training before they even enter school. The major barrier for many talented kids will continue to be the expense of such training and competition. Young people from modest financial backgrounds will thus continue to gravitate toward inexpensive sports, such as those in school-based programs. Sports such as skiing, tennis, golf, and many other Olympic sports will continue to be beyond the financial reach of the working and middle classes.

High schools will continue to offer varsity programs and, particularly in affluent communities, will expect excellence from their athletic teams. The major team sports like football and basketball will continue to rely on high school programs to develop talent supplemented by off-season programs, camps, and leagues that keep kids playing one sport year round. The expense of these high-performance programs will continue to rise, and many will be forced to adopt user fees to pay for them. However, in many communities, recreation or parks programs will provide the summer and off-season programs at modest expense or offer scholarships for those who qualify on the basis of need.

Most colleges will struggle to fund their athletic programs but invest in them as a publicity and recruiting tool. College football and March Madness in basketball unite the college family like no other events. As a feeder system for professional sport, major colleges will continue to fight to retain the athletes in whom they invest time, money, and effort. The question of whether athletes should be paid to play beyond athletic scholarships will continue to be debated, and likely some compromise will occur in the not-so-distant future. Athletes who are lured by the glamour and financial reward of leaving college early to turn professional will force the issue of financial compensation for what is essentially professional play.

Professional sport will continue to thrive. The investment in football, basketball, and baseball by corporate sponsors and television will continue to grow, and advances in delivery of those sports through television will expand. As the popularity of those sports grows in other countries, gradual expansion of franchises to Europe is likely; and the potential for true world championships will emerge. It is likely that women's professional basketball will increase in popularity as more people begin to appreciate the style of basketball they play, which emphasizes teamwork and passing.

A likely change in sport in North America will be the rising popularity of soccer. As immigrants continue to enter our country and the Hispanic population grows steadily, cultural interest in soccer will follow. A sport that can accommodate both males and females as well as players of all sizes, shapes, and body types can appeal to millions of kids who lack the size or strength to compete in elite basketball or football. A new generation of Americans who played soccer as children will become adults who will likely encourage their own children to at least try the sport.

The owners of professional sport franchises and league officials will continue to convince cities to build more elaborate facilities to host their teams. City officials will scramble to attract professional franchises to their cities to enhance the economy and create fan interest. However, the trend toward publicly financed stadiums will slow due to the economic woes of recent years. Public officials are reluctant to add to the daunting financial challenges their cities face by adding long-term debt to build facilities that primarily benefit millionaire professional sport owners.

The parity of teams established by the National Football League (NFL) will continue to stir fan interest because any team will have the chance to play in the Super Bowl if they make good management decisions.

Baseball will shift toward a similar philosophy, dooming the longtime dominance of big-market teams like the New York Yankees. Professional baseball will be forced to change if it has any hope of regaining its former title as America's pastime. Otherwise the decline in youth baseball participation, particularly in urban settings, forecasts a continued decline in popularity. Baseball officials and team owners must come up with a plan to ensure that every franchise has at least a possibility to be competitive through mandatory revenue sharing more like the NFL's.

Olympic sports will continue down the path of professionalism. The finest athletes in the world will showcase their talents in bigger and better Games staged in countries that can offer the financial package to host them. Women's sport will grow in popularity through the Olympic Movement; and led by soccer and basketball, professional leagues will grow in strength and popularity. Corporate sponsors will invest huge resources to support the Olympic Games, and the emphasis will continue to shift from nationalism to corporate dominance.

The outlook for performance sport isn't all rosy. If drug testing and control of performance-enhancing substances do not improve, public disenchantment with professional sport could result as athletes continue to use illegal substances in the pursuit of exceptional performances. There has clearly been significant progress toward more comprehensive drug-testing programs in all sports led by the Olympics and more recently in Major League Baseball. Yet there will never be a drug enforcement program that will be able to completely eradicate cheating, because there will always be athletes, coaches, and others who will experiment and try to evade the reach of the testing programs.

Scientific advancements in equipment and sports medicine may enable athletes to perform at levels heretofore believed out of reach. If the public begins to see athlete performance as the result of technological achievements, it is possible that they will lose interest. The humanity of sport is a delicate balance of technology, financial interests, entertainment, and the athlete's struggle to achieve.

Youth programs will continue to struggle to provide development for superior athletes who come from modest financial circumstances. In the meantime, some parents will become frustrated with the demands made by excellence programs and coaches. Families who choose to expose their children to a wider range of activities will find themselves left out of excellence programs.

Kids who do not excel early in their sport career may become discouraged and withdraw from sport before they have a chance to blossom in it. The dropout rate for kids in performance sport will continue to be high.

Participation Sport

As Americans continue to struggle with health, people will begin to recognize how important exercise and sport are to controlling body weight, enhancing energy, resisting disease, improving physical appearance, and having a better quality of life. Leaders in the medical and health professions are doing a better job of educating the public on the value of sport and physical activity particularly to fight the alarming trends of an increasingly obese and overweight population. Even the White House under the leadership of Michelle Obama has joined the chorus to help kids eat better and move more.

Using sport as a development tool as discussed in chapter 17 will continue to be employed as a strategy to combat crime and fight physical inactivity. Sport programs for youth that combine academic enrichment and good citizenship will grow and prosper to improve the quality of life for kids in the United States and all over the world. Underdeveloped countries have only begun to explore the power of sport to attract and motivate their youth toward higher achievement. All countries will continue to explore ways to use sport to promote better understanding between nations and move us toward a more peaceful and respectful attitude worldwide.

Most youth sport programs attract large numbers of children between the ages of 6 and 8. More than half of them drop out of sport by age 14. By high school, only a fraction of those who continued in youth sport programs will make their high school varsity team. The system has a built-in rejection mechanism that forces the majority of young people to drop out of sport.

A possible solution is to expand the number of athletic teams sponsored by schools or institute a no-cut policy at least for certain sports. Different teams could have different ability levels and training intensities. This system has been used successfully for generations by private schools that require every student to devote time each day to athletics and exercise.

A variation would be to sponsor complete intramural programs within schools to attract the masses of students who do not play varsity sport. The key is to find the money and facilities to support such an expansion. Lighted athletic fields that can be used for longer hours is one way universities have solved the problem of inadequate facilities, and high schools may soon follow that model. Rather than take pride in the win–loss record of a school's athletic teams, perhaps the model will shift to pride in the total number of students who play sport at any level.

Community programs that emphasize participation sport will also grow as young athletes search for opportunities to exercise, be with their friends, and have fun outside of school. The reduced emphasis on competition will be attractive to kids and families who have no aspirations as athletes but simply want to play sports and enjoy them. The demands for hours of practice, year-round devotion, expensive

IN THE ARENA WITH . . .

No-Cut School Teams Work for Tennis

One of the most anxiety-ridden moments in the lives of young adolescents is the day they are cut from the team. It damages their fragile ego and self-esteem, upsets their parents, and robs them of a valuable peer experience outside of the classroom. If the goal of athletics is to teach kids skills they can use throughout life, then it makes little sense to eliminate them. That strategy is like ignoring the weaker readers in a class—just say to them "Sorry, you're not good enough." But it doesn't have to be that way. One sport, tennis, with the help of the United States Tennis Association (USTA), is helping to change the thinking that school sports are for the elite few. You see, the goal of the organization is to get more kids playing tennis and keep them playing for a lifetime of good health and fitness.

Nearly 3,000 high school tennis coaches have bought into the program. Here's how it works. Many no-cut schools have a varsity tennis team, a reserve squad and junior varsity, and a middle school team. A lack of court space for all those kids is solved by scheduling different times for each squad for practice and matches or using nearby courts at a public park. Coaching supervision is solved by adding part-time assistants (USTA even helps with grants to compensate them) or volunteer assistants or by requiring that the better players help coach the less experienced ones. Using Friday afternoons and weekends for sub-varsity team match play is normal. Booster clubs and local community tennis organizations or user fees can also help with the expense for equipment or coaching compensation (USTA 2010).

Brooke deLench, founder of the MomsTeam website for youth sport parents, believes no-cut rules for school teams below varsity level just make sense. "The present model of one small team might have made sense in 1924 when the size of teams was roughly equal to number who wanted to play, but it doesn't make sense today" says deLench. "We're trying to get kids to be more active, off the computer and away from the television but it's time to step up with real solutions" (deLench 2008).

The USTA recognizes no-cut high school programs publicly and provides clinics on models to follow, literature, and a network of coaches who can help. They know a "feeder" system of younger players coming up will invariably uncover some diamonds in the rough who will be stalwart varsity players. Just offering the chance to a hundred or so kids to be part of the school tennis team, whatever their skill level, really has no downside to it. Could you do a similar thing with a sport other than tennis?

coaching, and specialization in just one sport will be discarded for the opportunity to play for recreation.

Extreme sports will continue to grow, as will sport activities that are focused on the player, are informally organized, and are novel in skills and strategy. Newer sports like Ultimate Frisbee, paintball, rock climbing, mountain biking, cardio kickboxing, and snowboarding will take their place among more traditional recreational sports such as biking, hiking, and other natural outdoor activities.

Coed teams may also encourage sport participation. Sports like softball, volleyball, soccer, tennis, and golf are just a few of the sports that adapt well to coed teams. The natural interest among teenagers to spend time with the opposite sex creates a natural drawing card for participation sport.

Young people aren't the only ones participating in sport. As health costs continue to climb, health insurers and employers will explore the benefits of encouraging physical activity among employees to minimize health risks, loss of productive work days, and drain on health insurance programs. With older adults approaching 100 million of the total U.S. population of over 300 million, their influence on every facet of society is going to be felt. Sport provides regular exercise, social interaction, and enhanced self-image, all important contributors to healthy living for older adults.

As with performance sport, participation sport faces roadblocks as well. The first roadblock is simply lack of interest in sport on the part of those who played as children and dropped out. These adults need to be wooed back to sport with the offer of a different kind of experience. Leaders need to become more committed to increasing physical activity among young people, creating a change in consciousness among parents and kids through consistent marketing and waging publicity

ACTIVITY TIME-OUT

Invent Your Own Coed Sport Team

At the varsity sport level, the vast majority of teams are divided by gender. But what if you were to designate certain sports as coed, much as recreational programs have done for volleyball, softball, tennis, or golf? Take a sport of your choice and explain how the competition would work, some basic rules (such as minimum or maximum number of males and females at any time), and safety considerations. Develop a justification for a coed sport based on the benefits you believe it could bring to a sport program. If you are dead set against this potential innovation, you are welcome to present a well-reasoned argument in opposition to the proposal. Just make sure your position will stand up to scrutiny by your classmates.

campaigns on the value of sport programs based on participation rather than winning.

A second major roadblock is competition for money and facilities with traditional performance sport programs. Advocates of participation sport need to overcome this bias by enlisting the support of the masses, since they certainly outnumber those involved in performance sport. School programs, extracurricular programs, community programs, and park and recreation programs are all ultimately supported by tax dollars from all citizens. Why shouldn't those dollars be spent to benefit more kids rather than being concentrated on a small majority of elite athletes?

Most sport leaders were competitive athletes, and they tend to perpetuate similar programs. It will take a new breed of leaders who are dedicated to participation sport and are willing to change the status quo. They will also need patience, since it is not likely that change will happen quickly or without consistent pressure. They will also need to enlist the aid of some powerful allies such as physicians, health insurers, corporate leaders, and politicians.

Finally, activities other than sport will continue to compete for people's time. Entertainment via television or computers has become a powerful competitor. The lack of physical activity that results from submitting to the lure of spending hours in front of a screen may contribute to a national health crisis. Creative minds must work to educate people about the benefits of physical activity, and then it is up to sport organizers to make sport accessible, convenient, and fun for participants.

Effects of Social Changes

Significant social changes in the last 50 years have affected sport and will continue to do so. As discussed in chapter 11, the civil rights movement of

the 1960s opened up sport to minorities. African Americans have become dominant in football and basketball, and Latinos account for one-third of the players in MLB. As more minorities move into the middle class, their children will begin to explore other sports such as tennis, swimming, golf, or volleyball—all sports that were once the exclusive provenance of affluent whites. As these sports become more inclusive, positions of influence such as those held by coaches, organizers, and members of governing boards will include members of minority groups.

As discussed in chapter 12, the women's movement that ushered in Title IX in 1972 changed sport dramatically. The explosion in female participants has changed sport forever, but equity with male participants is still an elusive goal. Steady pressure to conform to the law will be required by women's rights advocates, and female athletes must continue to be assertive.

Girls face some unique issues in sport. Puberty arrives an average of two years earlier in girls, affecting their physical capacity and sometimes their interest in sport. Teenage girls drop out of sport just when many boys, fueled by new levels of testosterone, are consumed by competitive sport. A clear transition from performance sport to participation sport needs to be available for girls at a younger age before they drop out for good.

Older women, too, will continue to have a significant effect on sport. Those who loved performance sport will prolong their careers with expanded professional, semiprofessional, and community leagues that offer strong competition. By far, though, most women who don sneakers and active wear are looking for healthy workouts to maintain physical appearance, control body weight, socialize, have fun, and increase their energy for the demands of daily living. New sports or variations on traditional sports must be ready for an influx of females to recreational participation sport. The recent surge of female participation in yoga, tai chi, strength training, and similar physical disciplines is an example of the new trends.

As mentioned previously, the aging of our society may be the most influential trend of all in sport. Age-group competition for older adults will continue to grow as seniors seek the thrills of competitive sport and the challenge of testing themselves against others or the environment.

Other older adults are more interested in exercise simply to maximize good health, posture, and energy. Social interaction, fun, and release from stress are more important to these adults. Coaches and program leaders will need to continue to tinker with the formula for sport that meets the needs of these older athletes. More frequent but shorter workouts with less intensity seems to be the best schedule for older adults. Time to socialize during or after activity is a strong attraction and should be made available in a comfortable setting.

Sexual preference will continue to be a topic of controversy in the coming years. Historically, sport has not been kind to gays and lesbians, particularly performance sport. A few successful homosexual athletes have publicly announced their sexual preference, but most have quietly concealed it to avoid controversy.

The Gay Games and local gay athletic organizations have exploded around the world. The Gay Games were founded in 1982 in San Francisco and attracted 1,350 participants. Attendance steadily grew until the 1994 event in New York City registered over 10,000 athletes. Successive games in Amsterdam, Sydney, Chicago, and Cologne have all surpassed that number. Competitors from 70 nations competed in 35 different sports in Cologne in 2010 in front of an open-

ing ceremony crowd exceeding 25,000 that was entertained by music stars Agnes and Taylor Dayne. Unlike other world competitions, the Gay Games enables people from all walks of life to compete against each other regardless of skill level, age, or physical challenge. The Gay Games define winning as achieving one's best, and competitors are matched against others of similar skill.

Gays and lesbians join local athletic clubs to enjoy physical activity, meet new people, receive emotional support, and have fun without the pressure of dealing with the historically homophobic sport world. As public acceptance of gays and lesbians grows, more athletes will have the courage to announce their sexual preference and insist on equal opportunities. The sport world will become more accepting of athletes, coaches, and sport administrators who embrace the gay or lesbian lifestyle.

Finally, mental and physical disabilities have historically eliminated people from sport participation. With the advent of laws that prevent discrimination against people with disabilities, their sport participation has blossomed as well. The Special Olympics and the Paralympics have offered competitive and participation sport to people with disabilities at the national and international level. Local communities and schools have gradually sought to add sport programs for people with disabilities and wherever possible have sought to include these athletes in existing programs. Some sports have been modified and others invented that are appropriate for those with handicaps. Education, financial support, and coaches' training are keys to sustaining the growth in opportunities for these athletes.

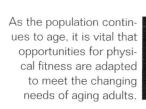

As the population continues to age, it is vital that opportunities for physical fitness are adapted to meet the changing needs of aging adults.

Effects of Spectatorship

Spectatorship has always been a double-edged sword for sport as a whole. Some marketing studies have shown increases in participation that are attributed to increases in spectators and the popularity of star athletes. Certainly Michael Jordan's amazing career and resulting popularity raised interest in basketball worldwide. Yet other sports such as soccer grew by leaps and bounds in the United States with virtually no heroes or stars until Mia Hamm and her teammates captivated fans with their remarkable international record. A sport does not necessarily need to have great players to become popular.

It is clear that access to sport will increase in the future as more television coverage of sport is offered. Pay-per-view channels will carry selected sport programs, and channels exclusively devoted to sports such as golf and tennis are already available. The Internet will likely revolutionize spectatorship in the future as people will be able to follow their college teams, high school teams, and even youth sport events like the Little League World Series from anywhere in the country.

The question is, will increased access create more sport fans, or will fans simply have more choices and spend more hours in front of the television or computer? If we believe that participation in sport will increase in the future, will spectatorship also increase?

Consider the average person who has time commitments to work, family, and the responsibilities of daily life. Carving time from that schedule for exercise and sport has proved to be the most perplexing barrier for most people. If they also increase the amount of time spent watching sport, something else will have to suffer; 10 hours of leisure time a week can be split only so many ways.

The power brokers in sport will mount a vigorous campaign to attract spectators in order to enhance their products. For them, participation is irrelevant; income from spectators, commercial sponsors, and media rights produces their revenue.

One potential strategy for power brokers is to press for legalized sport gambling to get fans more actively involved in their favorite teams and players. Pressure on local and state governments to legalize gambling on sport will mount as the next natural step following the legalization of gambling at Native American reservations and offshore locations. Inducements such as allocating a percentage of gambling revenues toward education, youth sport programs, or other popular social programs will provide a dilemma for taxpayers who are suspicious of gambling interests. Internet gambling that so far is legal will attract some scrutiny as it grows and prospers.

More politicians are also looking toward approving sport betting to combat mounting financial deficits in their states due to the economic issues in recent years. The first state to challenge prior bans on sport betting was Delaware, which wanted to open up sport betting in 2009. The National Collegiate Athletic Association and all professional sports joined together to resist the efforts, and eventually the courts ruled against the state of Delaware. But the stage is set, and it is likely the pressure to expand sport betting will continue and that the issue will continue to be debated and considered.

Effects of Technology

The relentless search for excellence in performance, combined with the quest for sales of new products, will continue to spur research and development of new sport equipment of every type. Field surfaces,

ACTIVITY TIME-OUT

Legalized Sport Betting

In chapter 18 on deviance, we investigated the issue of gambling on sports and reviewed the current status. The trends in the United States have clearly favored an expansion of legalized gambling in recent years, often driven by attempts to raise additional revenue by states suffering through an economic malaise. The roadblocks to legalized wagering on sport include organized and powerful opposition by both college and professional sport officials who fear that legalized sport wagering will corrupt sport, produce pressure on athletes to intentionally affect the outcome of games, and attract the involvement of organized crime. Based on the current trends and obvious power struggles, what is your prediction on legalized betting occurring in the next 10 to 15 years? Can you see any compromise that expands gambling but somehow limits it to pacify those who fear it will damage the public trust in sports results?

EXPERT'S VIEW

Biotechnology and Athletes

Robin Parisotto is a former researcher with the Australian Institute of Sport who has studied the Defense Advanced Research Project Agency (DARPA) located in the United States (Parisotto 2006). DARPA explores revolutionary research in biotechnology that could have dramatic effects on performance enhancement in sport—and all of it legal. Recent advances in technology in sport have included training in altitude chambers, cooling vests, drag-efficient swimsuits, and aerodynamically efficient bicycles. But the future promises even more astounding possibilities.

One of these technologies is to introduce a "pain vaccine" that stops the initial shock from injury and lasts for up to 30 days. This would eliminate the need for painkilling injections and needles before, during, or after competition. Wouldn't you like to be vaccinated now? Another such advancement is the use of laser technology to rapidly repair injured tissue such as skin, bone, cartilage, ligaments, and tendons. This innovation could eliminate a recovery time of weeks or months for typical sports injuries and could have athletes back in competition in a matter of days. One more intriguing concept is a project known as the Metabolically Dominant Soldier (MDS), in which researchers are aiming to increase the metabolic work rate of human cells to promote strength and endurance. The target is to increase the capacity of a person who now can execute 80 push-ups to executing more than 300 push-ups, or walk forever with a 150-pound backpack. The premise of this research is to reduce the amount of time soldiers have to dedicate to consuming calories in order to perform prolonged physical effort on the battlefield. It could be done by eliminating food (for up to a week) and letting the body use the nutrients it has already stored for emergencies. The application for athletes is that they could train even harder and simply use glucose drinks to subsist. No more energy bars, pasta, or snacks would be necessary, just a change to the body's physiological functions.

There will be those who believe these performance enhancements bear some similarity to the use of drugs and fear that sports will be compromised through artificial means. Yet we have seen so many advancements in training, equipment, and medical care in past decades; surely there will be increasing pressure to push forward to the limits of what our imagination and technology can yield.

court surfaces, and pool construction will continue to improve through technology. Likewise, items such as tennis rackets, golf clubs, vaulting poles, baseball bats, and footwear will continue to improve.

One positive effect of equipment advances will be the ease with which a beginning player can learn a new sport or an intermediate player can immediately improve. Consider that the larger heads of newer tennis rackets and golf clubs have added performance consistency to hundreds of thousands of weekend warriors' games. The story is much the same with adjustments in length and design of skis.

Similarly, for high-performance athletes, some technological advances will allow them to move faster, jump higher, hit harder, increase speed, and improve consistency. However, some of these advances may also come with increased risk to the body, which may not stand up to the increased forces of movement. Injury monitoring will become critical to prevent harm to elite athletes who

embrace new technology. A good example of this risk was seen in the rush to install synthetic turf on football fields 20 years ago. While athletes could run faster and jump higher, the rate of injuries exploded as joints simply could not withstand the force. Athletes and coaches forced a return to natural grass fields to protect their careers and their health.

Training methods based on scientific research will improve as we learn how to push the human body to the limit. Methods of strength and endurance training along with enhanced nutrition will equip athletes to perform better for longer periods of time. Along with improved performance will come better systems of training to prevent overuse injuries and strengthen traditional trouble spots. It will be possible to rehabilitate high ankle sprains and torn anterior cruciate ligaments in half the time it takes now (Van Riper 2009).

Drugs and other performance-enhancing substances will continue to be a hot topic. As drug-testing protocols become more accurate and routine, there will still be athletes who attempt to cheat. The question is whether the technology of sport organizers will be able to stay ahead of or at least even with those who seek to circumvent current testing methods.

Recovery from sport injuries will become quicker, and permanent disabilities will be fewer due to new procedures for joint and tissue repair and even replacement. Synthetic knees, hips, and ankles are becoming commonplace, and other joints will follow. Participation in activity or even professional careers will be prolonged by surgical interventions we cannot yet imagine.

Coaches will eventually have access from the sidelines to the physical state of athletes. Assessment of head injuries, lack of conditioning, or risk of injury will be available; coaches will no longer have to rely on how athletes say they feel, but instead will have scientific assessment to rely on, even in the midst of competition. The prevalence of head injuries in sports like football and soccer has recently gained widespread public attention. We've become more aware of the long-term effects of concussions that have resulted in many fine former athletes suffering for a lifetime once their playing career is over. More research, better equipment protection, and a more cautious protocol for treatment are likely to emerge in the next few years.

A final, far-reaching issue is that of genetic engineering to produce exceptional athletes. The moral, ethical, and legal issues will be hotly debated in the coming years as science forges ahead in exploring options to alter genetic makeup. Imagine parents choosing the genetic makeup of their children or adjusting it during childhood. For most of us, these questions are too complicated to even comprehend, and it is likely that the debate will rage for years.

Effects of the Electronic Media

In the last 25 years, the Internet has opened up possibilities that did not seem to exist just a few decades ago. Here are a few ideas of what may happen in the next 25 years.

As mentioned previously, fans will have a wider range of sports to watch on computers that will be hooked up to larger screens. The action will be on demand, meaning people do not have to plan their day around sport but can watch when it fits their mood and schedule. It is virtually certain that fewer fans will watch the traditional big games that

networks choose to feature, because they will now have access to all games. Anyone who supports a college team will be able to see that team in action on a given day. Fans of less popular sports will be able to watch their favorites rather than just what network television chooses to present. The trend in these directions has already begun, and consumers will gradually demand even more choices.

The wildly popular fantasy teams and leagues that provide interactive entertainment will continue to grow. Live games that only allow you to watch passively can be replaced with exciting fantasy games with you positioned as the coach. Internet games that simulate professional sport shift the role of the user from a spectator to a coach who can pick the players on the team, choose the defense or offense, and call plays.

Athletes will be more accessible to their fans through online chat rooms and discussions. Where athletes were once hidden by game uniforms and helmets and protected from contact with fans, the athlete of the future will need to learn to be more open, accessible, and personable. Coaches will be miked at halftime so fans can overhear their tactical adjustments for the second half, athletes will be miked during competition, and fans will have an inside view of the sport experience like never before.

ESPN has dominated sport coverage for the last few decades and now boasts 10 popular channels across the world, including ESPN, ESPN2, ESPN News, ESPN Classic, and ESPN College, and also attracts high traffic to ESPN.com, which delivers sport news 24 hours a day. ESPN has begun to explore the power of social media with more than a half million combined Facebook and Twitter followers. ESPN's credibility is established; athletes trust it to get their message out, and fans trust the reporting. But social networks may cut into its market soon.

Professional teams are now using their own digital channels to link fans of their team to each other and connect them to the team's brand. Through social media, Facebook and Twitter, and their own digital channels, teams can connect their sponsors to their fans, sell tickets, and generate profits. As stadium seats are priced out of reach for middle-class families (like the Yankees' $1,000 seats), social media can help link up fans with their teams even if they never attend a home game. If fans feel they are important to the team's success, can get inside information, and can share opinions with other fans, you've hooked them for life (Reed 2010).

Will Sport Change?

If you have any doubt whether sport will change in the future, look at the last 50 years. Since the 1950s, sport has expanded dramatically to become a huge corporate moneymaker. Professional football, basketball, baseball, ice hockey, tennis, and golf have made multimillionaires out of athletes and sustained the corporate organizations that regulate and control these sports. We once thought an athlete who earned $10,000 for a single season of play was amazingly rich. When Joe DiMaggio agreed in 1949 to the first $100,000 contract to play center field for the New York Yankees, we thought that was the zenith of sport compensation—yet today's superstars are signing contracts worth up to $10 million per year for up to seven years! Even taking inflation into account, athletes' salaries rose 10-fold over the last quarter century, while the median real hourly earnings of the average American worker went *down* by about 5% (Lambert 2001).

As discussed throughout this book, social changes have opened up opportunities for people of all races and ethnic groups, for women, and for athletes with disabilities. In spite of these significant changes, more are yet to come.

Who Will Lead the Way?

Those who follow functionalist theory would likely take the view that sport can be changed from the inside by improving the current sport culture through better marketing and promotion, presenting athletes as role models, making events more fan friendly, and trumpeting record-setting performances. This approach is the traditional conservative philosophy that holds to maintaining the status quo but improving it by producing more of what currently exists.

Reformists using functionalist theory are more likely to call for changes such as finally equalizing opportunities for females, minorities, and athletes with disabilities. They are likely to fight to control the use of performance-enhancing substances to ensure equal competition. Similarly, they may pressure collegiate athletics to pay athletes some modest wages in Division I programs while also limiting entry into the professional ranks until age 20 or so.

All of these types of proposals suggest that sport can be improved by tinkering with the current model and adjusting to trends while maintaining the essential integrity of the model.

Those who subscribe to more radical changes in sport may use conflict theory to present their case.

What changes can this young athlete expect to see in the next 10 years?

They may see a new model that opens sport as healthy recreation and cooperative physical activities to all citizens. They reject the current corporate structure, emphasis on winning, bottom-line mentality, and exploitation of athletes to benefit the power brokers who make millions from their performances.

Feminist theorists will push to improve the number of women in coaching, administration, media, and other key leadership positions and will press for equal pay for women in all aspects of sport.

Interactionist theorists see the changes in sport as coming from the bottom up. That is, athletes themselves will force change that better suits their needs.

377

Two groups of athletes stand out as potential agents of change: youth and older adults. The professional model for sport does not fit the majority of athletes in either age group. Instead these groups will emphasize participation, healthy living, cooperation rather than competition, and accommodation of all skill levels. If changes within traditional sport are not forthcoming, it seems likely both young and senior athletes will invent sport models of their own that better address their needs and interests. Extreme sports have already made a mark among young people, and perhaps similar changes will become popular with senior athletes.

Critical theorists might also affect youth and high school sport. If educators take the lead on the value and place of sport, the programs might look very different. Intramural sports that include all students have the potential to grow in high schools as they have in colleges with increased student demand for use of facilities for physical recreation rather than for a relatively few privileged athletes. Parents will have to insist on a new approach to youth sport that supports participation for every child regardless of economic level, ability, race, gender, or disability. Critical theorists will exert pressure to shift significant funding from performance sport to participation sport. The success of programs will be judged not by the win–loss record, but by the number of young people who participate and continue playing year after year.

Another significant change will be to establish standards of coaching at every level and avoid hiring coaches who are not appropriately certified. Public opinion could lead the way to this change to protect athletes who are directly affected by inadequate coaching. Parents are likely to insist on a level of coaching that reflects better education, a clear philosophy of coaching that parallels the goals of the specific program, and a more humanistic style of relating to athletes. Coaches who use outdated approaches and authoritarian methods of coaching will be more likely to struggle, especially in educational settings.

Critical theorists will also look at the current expenditure of public funds to support professional franchises and stadiums, as well as so-called sweetheart deals that entice wealthy franchise owners to move a team to a particular city. A reformist critical theorist would rather have that money spent on facilities or programs that directly benefit local citizens by offering opportunities to play sports rather than watch them. Compromises may be struck that allow some money to be spent on both participating

and spectating if it can be shown that one approach also benefits the other.

The question of leadership still has not been answered. History will show that very few athletes become agents of change, especially during their playing days. Why risk all they have worked for unless they have suffered badly within the present system? A retiring NFL player who admits he cannot read in spite of a college degree might have cause; but of those who are frustrated, few have the courage or ability to express their frustration.

Coaches are not likely to rebel against a system that has been their life. Owners of professional teams, leaders in major sport organizations, and athletic directors have all invested their lives in the sport establishment.

Who Will Fight for Change?

Will it be you—someone who has studied sport, thought about it, and developed some strong opinions? Will it be parents who want a better experience for their progeny? Maybe it will be independent sport institutes like the Center for the Study of Sport at Northeastern University, politicians who believe they can advance their career by taking up the mantle of sport change, academic leaders at universities, sports writers, or sport commentators.

Or will changes occur as a reflection of a society that continues to adjust its values, economics, and political philosophies? Perhaps large coalitions of citizens will find themselves on the same side of arguments and band together to accomplish change. It seems clear from an analysis of demographics that U.S. society is heading quickly toward a large population dominated by older adults. That group has money, time, and a keen interest in sport as part of a healthy lifestyle. Exercise for its own sake will never be able to compete with the joy of sport or the social interaction it encourages. The fitness gym offers physical training benefits but lacks the universal appeal of games and sport. In the near future, a large proportion of our population will look to sport for help in blazing a new trail of longer, healthier lives.

What do you think?

Chapter Summary

In this chapter we have examined the social trends that may affect the role of sport in our life. The major trends that were identified include aging of the population; protection for all people regardless

■ Who will lead changes in sport? Coaches? Athletes? Or you?

of age, race, gender, sexual preference, or disability; continued expansion of performance sport by corporate sport leaders; enhancement of coaching competency; and technological improvement that may enhance sport performance.

Conflicts between consumers and leaders of performance sport and those of participation sport were also considered. Those conflicts include struggles over fair shares of funding, use of facilities, public programs, and access for everyone.

We discussed the effect of opening sport participation to people of all ages, racial groups, and ethnic groups, as well as both genders, people with different sexual preferences, and those with disabilities. The demand for expanded programs and need for more financial support is a concern and likely to create a struggle among various advocacy groups.

Watching sport was considered both from a positive and negative point of view. While traditional performance sport will continue to try to grow its fan base and provide entertainment, we may find that a parallel growth in participation sport will conflict with these goals. Where spectatorship enhances

participation and vice versa, the two groups will benefit from the synergy of working cooperatively.

Technological advances will affect the ability of athletes to generate exceptional performances and will ease the way for beginning athletes to take up a new sport. Performance-enhancing substances will continue to be a knotty problem for sport administrators; and time, money, and effort will be allocated to ensure equal competition for everyone. Improved methods of sports medicine will enable better treatment and recovery from injuries and will include replacement of body parts that break down from overuse.

Finally, we looked at how sport might change in the future, who will lead those changes, and what those changes might focus on. History provides some instructive lessons on how changes have occurred in the past, but peering into the future is more challenging. In the final analysis, changes in sport will be dictated by changes in our society, our needs, our values, and perhaps outside influences. Perhaps you will be a catalyst for change in your community!

GLOSSARY

abuse—The willful infliction of injury, pain, mental anguish, intimidation, or punishment.

adult-organized sports—Sports that are organized by parents or other governing bodies. Activities are more structured than in other programs and are played according to a fixed set of rules.

amateurs—Those who play for the intrinsic satisfaction of improving fitness, enjoying the competition, refining physical skills, working as part of a team, or simply embracing the challenge and excitement of testing skills against nature or other competitors; participation in sport is the key rather than the outcome.

Amateur Sports Act of the United States—Act of the U.S. Congress that established the United States Olympic Committee (USOC) and outlined its responsibilities.

American Association of People with Disabilities (AAPD)—The largest national nonprofit cross-disability organization dedicated to the 56 million Americans with disabilities.

Americans with Disabilities Act (ADA)—Landmark national legislation that protects the rights of Americans with disabilities.

anabolic steroids—Synthetic steroid hormones used to increase the size of muscles temporarily; illegal and sometimes abused by athletes.

anorexia nervosa—Eating disorder characterized by self-starvation.

appreciate—To increase in value.

athlete-organized sports—Sports that are organized by athletes without adult supervision. Activities are less structured and rules are made up as play progresses.

bed tax—A $1 fee on hotel rooms that goes into a special fund to help finance public sport stadiums.

biomechanics—The study of the structure and function of biological systems using principles of physics applied to human motion.

biophysical domain—Academic discipline of study of physical activity that includes physiology, biomechanics, nutrition, and sports medicine.

bulimia nervosa—Eating disorder characterized by overeating (bingeing) followed by purging, usually through laxative use or self-induced vomiting.

burnout—Exhaustion of physical or emotional strength as a result of prolonged stress that causes athletes to discontinue competitive sport.

capital assets—Tangible property that cannot be easily converted into cash.

capitalism—An economic system that is based on the accumulation and investment of capital by individuals who then use it to produce goods or services.

compulsive exercise—Eating disorder characterized by too much exercise rather than altered food intake.

conflict theory—Theory based on the work of Karl Marx that sees sport as being built on the foundation of money and economic power.

content research—Type of research in which information or pictures are collected from articles, magazines, and TV programs and the data are assigned to categories around a particular theme.

conventional stage—The second level of moral reasoning; most adults and society at large fall into this category, in which behavior is guided by what is acceptable to others.

corporate sport—Another name for the business of professional sport.

critical theories—Theories that look critically at culture and determine the source of authority that one group has over another.

cultural capital—The skills and abilities people gain from education and life experiences. Cultural capital may include attitudes, expectations, and self-confidence.

depreciation—Decreased value over time of equipment, tools, or athletes (in sports).

deviant—Referring to behavior that differs from the accepted norms.

direct spectators—People who attend live sporting events at a stadium, an arena, or another venue.

disability—A condition of mental or physical impairment that limits capacity in life.

economic capital—The financial resources a person has or controls.

economic model—Model that emphasizes the financial profit to be made from any endeavor.

electronic media—Media that include television, radio, and the Internet.

ethnicity—The cultural heritage of a group of people that arises from social customs.

ethnography—Study of data collected by researchers who immerse themselves in an environment and keep recorded conversations or notes.

exercise physiology—The study of human systems to enhance strength, speed, and endurance in performance.

extrinsic rewards—Rewards such as money, fame, and power.

female athlete triad—Disorder that includes disordered eating, amenorrhea, and osteoporosis.

feminist theory—Social theory that investigates the effect of gender within society.

figurational theories—Theories proposing that we are all connected by networks of people who are interdependent on one another by nature, through education, and through socialization.

focus groups—Interviews with small groups of people.

functionalist theory—Theory that looks at sport as a social institution that reinforces the current value system in a society.

games—An aspect of play that shows more evidence of structure and is competitive. The goals for participating are clear: They are mental, physical, or a combination of both; they are governed by informal or formal rules; they involve competition; winning is determined by luck, strategy, or skill; and the result is an end product such as prestige or status.

gender verification—Used for 30 years by the Olympics to test female athletes to ensure fair competition; discontinued in 1999 as demeaning, unnecessary, and unreliable.

hazing—Any action that inflicts physical or mental harm or anxiety or that degrades a person, regardless of location, intent, or consent of participants.

hegemony theory—Critical theory that focuses on dominance, which is the power that one individual or group has over others.

high-performance athletes—Athletes of any age who aspire to the highest levels of performance and typically become professional athletes.

historical research—Research that looks at trends in sport over time.

hooliganism—Rowdy, violent, or destructive behavior; term often used to describe behavior of working-class men who disrupt soccer games with violence, excessive drinking, exchange of insults, destruction of property, and interruptions of the game.

indirect spectators—People who listen to or watch sports electronically by radio, television, or the Internet or who read about sports in newspapers or magazines.

interactionist theories—Theories that view society from the bottom up rather than the top down; they focus on the social interactions among people that are based on the reality people choose to accept.

interviews—Face-to-face personal questioning to elicit information, attitudes, or opinions.

intrinsic rewards—Rewards such as fun, health, self-satisfaction, and fitness.

lower class—Lowest level of the social class system; comprises unskilled laborers who essentially do work that is assigned and supervised by others.

masters—A classification in competitive sport for older athletes that usually starts at age 35 and is then divided into 5- or 10-year intervals.

middle class—Middle and largest level of the economic class system in the United States; includes skilled laborers, teachers, and people in the service industry.

minorities—Portions of the population that are different from others based on some criterion such as race.

motor learning and behavior—The study of relatively permanent changes in motor behavior that result from practice or experience.

naming rights—Rights to name an athletic stadium or facility (e.g., American Airlines Arena in Miami), purchased by corporations as a means of advertising.

nationalism—A spirit of loyalty and devotion to a nation; a strong characteristic of worldwide sport competition like the Olympic Games.

nutrition—The study of how food and drink affect performance.

Olympic Games—An international sporting event held every four years that provides competition in most summer and winter sports.

overconformity—Behavior that goes beyond what is generally accepted. In sport, such behavior includes altering food intake or using supplements to meet an ideal body image.

over-the-counter drugs—Nonprescription drugs that are designed to promote healing from sickness or injury or to mask pain.

pedagogy—The study of the art and science of teaching.

personal seat licenses (PSLs)—License that gives fans the right to buy season tickets for specific seats in a stadium.

philosophy of sport—The study of the definition, value, and meaning of sport.

play—Free activity that involves exploring our environment, self-expression, dreaming, and pretending. There are no firm rules, and the outcome of the activity is unimportant.

politics—The art and science of government, of influencing governmental policy, or of holding control over a government.

postconventional stage—The highest level of moral reasoning; an autonomous, principled stage of thinking in which people adopt certain moral principles and hold to that behavior regardless of social punishment or reward.

preconventional stage—Basic level of moral understanding; being right means following authority with the understanding that there will be punishment if the rules aren't followed.

prescription drugs—Drugs prescribed by a doctor that are designed to promote healing from sickness or injury or to mask pain.

print media—Media that include newspapers, magazines, and books.

private funds—Monies raised from owner contributions, league contributions, bank loans, loans from local businesses, and personal seat licenses.

professional athletes—Paid performers who perform work by training to hone their physical skills to the highest level for competition with other elite athletes.

psychosocial domain—Academic discipline of the study of physical activity that includes psychology, motor learning and behavior, and pedagogy.

public funds—Monies raised from public sources, such as sales taxes, proximity and beneficiary taxes, general obligation and revenue bonds, and tax increment financing.

public tax funds—Tax funds collected by local or state governments that provide services to citizens.

qualitative data—Data collected through interviews or observations of individuals or groups or through analysis of societal characteristics and trends.

quantifiable studies—Studies producing data that can be counted and analyzed statistically.

race—Attributes that are passed along genetically.

racism—A belief that race is the primary determinant of human traits and that racial differences produce an inherent superiority of a particular race.

religion—The belief in a god or supernatural force that influences human life.

revenue-producing sports—Intercollegiate sports such as football and basketball that typically produce more revenue than expense for the university.

revenue sharing—Sharing within leagues of income from television contracts and other sources to protect smaller markets where income might be less.

social capital—Capital that depends on family, friends, and associates and includes resources based on group memberships, relationships, and both social and business networks.

social class—A category of people who share similar positions in society based on their economic level, education, occupation, and social interaction.

socialization—The process of interacting with other people and learning social customs, morals, and values.

social media—Internet-based communication among people through such sites as Facebook, MySpace, Twitter, YouTube, and blogs.

social stratification—Class assignments based on levels of power, prestige, and wealth.

social theories—Theories about a society and social life based on systematic research and logic, providing frameworks from which we can evaluate our present situation and perhaps discover a need for change.

societal analysis—Use of social theories to examine life from a social point of view.

sociocultural domain—Academic discipline of the study of physical activity that includes history, philosophy, and sociology.

sociology—The study of a society, its institutions, and its relationships including social issues, social organization, and the potential for social change.

sport—Institutionalized competitive activity that involves physical skill and specialized facilities or equipment and is conducted according to an accepted set of rules to determine a winner.

sport announcers—Electronic media personalities who broadcast sports events.

sport history—The study of the tradition and practices of physical activity and sport over time and within different countries, cultures, and civilizations.

sporting behavior—A gender-neutral term for sportsmanship.

sport participation—Taking an active, participatory role in sports.

sport psychology—The study of human behavior in sport, including enhancing performance and treating disorders that affect optimal performance.

sport pyramid—A way of understanding sport; the pyramid contains the four elements of human activity—play, games, sport, and work.

sportsmanship—A behavior that is characterized by fair play and respect for others.

sports medicine—Branch of medicine that deals with the prevention, care, and rehabilitation of injuries caused by participation in physical activity and sport.

sport sociology—The study of sport and physical activity within the context of the social conditions and culture in which people live.

sport spectators—People who watch sports.

sports writers—Journalists in the print media who specialize in sports.

stacking—An unusual distribution of white and black athletes in certain positions in sports that cannot be explained by a random distribution.

stimulants—Class of drugs that produce a temporary increase in functional activity or efficiency.

survey research—Research conducted through questionnaires.

Title IX—Landmark legislation passed in 1972 requiring any institution receiving federal funding to provide equal opportunities for males and females.

total salary cap—The total financial commitment a team is allowed to make to all players on the roster in combined salary and benefits.

underconformity—Behavior that does not conform to generally acceptable behavior. In sport, such behavior includes rule breaking, hazing, and excessive drinking.

upper class—Highest level of the American economic class system; comprises the top 1% of households and controls approximately 35% of the nation's wealth.

upper-middle class—Second highest level of the social class system; comprises professionals such as physicians, attorneys, and managers who typically have significant amounts of discretionary income.

work—Purposeful activity that may include physical or mental effort to perform a task, accomplish something, overcome an obstacle, or achieve a desired outcome. Sport can take on the characteristics of work as it moves toward the professional level.

youth sport—Sport engaged in by children ages 6 to 12.

REFERENCES

Aaron, H. 1999. Time 100: Jackie Robinson. http://205.188.238.109/time/time100/heroes/profile/robinson01.html. Accessed August 15, 2010

AARP Magazine. 2008. 50 reasons to love being 50, September/October.

ABC News. 2004. BALCO chief on sports doping scandal. December 3. http://abcnews.go.com/2020/story?id=297995&page=1. Accessed May 22, 2005.

ABC News. 2010. Saints vs. Colts Super Bowl scores title of most watched telecast ever. http://abcnews.go.com/print?id=9780233. Accessed June 16, 2010.

Acosta, V., and Carpenter, L. 2009a. Are we there yet? *Academe Online*, July-August. www.acostacarpenter.org/AAUP_%20Are%20We%20There%20Yet.pdf. Accessed July 10, 2010.

Acosta, V., and Carpenter, L. 2009b. *Women in intercollegiate sport: A longitudinal study, 1977-2009*. Brooklyn, NY: Brooklyn College.

Acosta, V., and Carpenter, L. 2010. *Women in intercollegiate sport: A longitudinal, national study: Thirty three year update*. www.acostacarpenter.org. Accessed July 12, 2010.

Adherents. 2005. Largest religious groups in the United States of America. www.adherents.com/rel_USA.html. Accessed November 15, 2005.

Agassi, A. 2009. *Open: An autobiography*. New York: Knopf.

Al-Ahmed, A. 2008. Bar countries that ban women athletes. www.nytimes.com/2008/05/19/opinion/19iht-edahmed.3.13017836.html?_r=1&page. Accessed July 16, 2010.

Alfred University. 1999a. High school hazing: How many students are hazed? www.alfred.edu/hs_hazing/howmanystudents.cfm. Accessed October 16, 2010.

Alfred University. 1999b. National survey of sports teams: Who is most at risk? Where are hot spots? www.alfred.edu/hs_hazing/mostatrisk.cfm. Accessed October 16, 2010.

Amateur Athletic Foundation Olympic Primer. 2005. Issues of the Olympic Games. Olympic reports. www.aafla.org./6oic/primer_frmst.htm. Accessed October 17, 2010.

Ambrosius, R. 2010. Brand matters in an aging marketplace. *Journal on Active Aging*, May/June.

American Association of People with Disabilities. 2005. About AAPD. www.aapd.com/site/c.pvI1IkNWJqE/b.5555493/k.C88C/About_Us.htm. Accessed August 30, 2010.

Americans Disability Technical Assistance Centers. 2004. Historical context of the Americans with Disabilities Act. www.adata.org/whatsada-history.aspx.html. Accessed February 2, 2005.

American Gaming Association. 2009. Fact sheet: Sports wagering. www.americangaming.org/Industry/factsheets/issues_detail.cfv?id=16. Accessed July 27, 2010.

American Sport Education Program (ASEP). 2010. Overview. www.asep.com/overview.cfm. Accessed July 10, 2010.

American Sportscasters Association. 2009. ASA names "Top 15 Women Sportscasters," Visser voted no. 1. www.americansportscastersonline.com/top15womensportscasters.html. Accessed June 19, 2010.

American Sports Data, Inc. 2005. *American team sports: A status report*. Hartsdale, NY: SGMA.

Amr, H. 2008. The Muslim Olympics? www.brookings.edu/opinions/2008/0828_muslim_olympics.aspx?p=1. Accessed July 16, 2010.

Ankeny, J. 2009. The reality of fantasy sports. *Entrepreneur*. www.entrepreneur.com/article/printthis/203140.html. Accessed June 18, 2010.

Anspaugh, D.J., Hunter, S., and Dignan, M. 1996. Risk factors for cardiovascular disease among exercising versus nonexercising women. *American Journal of Health Promotion* 5 (10), 3.

Ariss, J. 2000. Sportsmanship. Reprint from *Touching Base Magazine*. www.slopitch.org/sportsmanship.htm. Accessed May 10, 2004.

Ashe, A. Jr. 1977. An open letter to Black parents: Send your children to the libraries. *New York Times*, February 6, sec. 5, p. 2.

Ashe, A. Jr. 1988. *A hard road to glory*. New York: Warner Books.

Assibey-Mensah, G. 1997. Role models and youth development: Evidence and lessons from the perceptions of African-American male youth. *Western Journal of Black Studies* 21 (4), 242.

Associated Press. 2006a. AP: Players could scrap new drug policy. May 9. http://mlb.mlb.com/NASApp/mlb/news/article.jsp?ymd=20060509&content_id=1445484&vkey=news_mlb&fext=.jsp&c_id=mlb. Accessed June 12, 2006.

Associated Press. 2006b. Mediation unsuccessful in Penn State bias lawsuit against coach. *USA Today*, May 15. www.usatoday.com/sports/college/womensbasketball/bigten/2006-05-15-psu-mediation_x.htm. Accessed June 1, 2006.

Associated Press. 2006c. Penn State coach accuses group of trying to exploit bias case. *USA Today*, May 18.

www.usatoday.com/sports/college/womensbasketball/bigten/2006-05-18-portland_x.htm. Accessed June 1, 2006.

Associated Press. 2009. Alcohol-related rowdiness spawns tests. http://sports.espn.go.com/ncf/news/story?id=4485528. Accessed October 26, 2009.

Association for Women in Sports Media (AWSM). 2000. Membership Directory. Farmington, CT http://awsmonline.org. Accessed October 10, 2010.

Association for Women in Sports Media (AWSM). 2009. AWSM updates. Quotable from Lesley Visser. http://awsmonline.org/. Accessed June 19, 2010.

August, H. 2004. Many Elis break from norm, lean right. *Yale Daily News*, November 11. www.yaledailynews.com/ article.asp?AID=27281. Accessed January 29, 2005.

Auman, G. 2004. Muslim basketball player quits USF team. *St. Petersburg Times*. http://pquasb.pqarchiver.com/sptimes/access/694207871.html?FMT+ABS&FMTS=ABS:F. Accessed January 24, 2005.

Bahri, C. 2005. Spearheading the empowerment of Muslim women. www.happynews.com/news/1172005/spearheading-the-empowerment.htm. Accessed May 24, 2006.

Baker, P., and Zeleny, J. 2009. For Obama, an unsuccessful campaign. *New York Times*, October 3. www.nytimes.com/2009/10/03/sports/03obama.html?_r=1&pagewanted=print. Accessed July 23, 2010.

Ball, D., and Loy, J. 1975. *Sport and social order: Contributions to the sociology of sport*. Reading, MA: Addison-Wesley.

Ballparks. 2006a. Bank of America Stadium. http://football.ballparks.com/NFL/CarolinaPanthers/index.htm. Accessed August 30, 2010.

Ballparks. 2006b. Gillette Stadium. http://football.ballparks.com/NFL/NewEnglandPatriots/newindex.htm. Accessed August 30, 2010.

Balyi, J., Way, R., Norris, S., Cardinal, C., and Higgs, C. 2005. Canadian sport for life: Long-term athlete development resource paper. Vancouver, BC: Canadian Sport Centres. www.canadiansportforlife.ca/default.aspx?PageID=1058&LangID=en. Accessed October 18, 2010.

Barber, B., Eccles, J., and Stone, M. 2001. Whatever happened to the jock, the brain, and the princess? Young adult pathways linked to adolescent activity involvement and social identity. *Journal of Adolescent Research* 16 (5), 429-455.

Basichis, G. 2010. Florida youth sports coaches to require background checks. http://dailyplanet.corragroup.com/2010/04/florida-youth-sports-coaches-to-require-background-checks. Accessed July 23, 2010.

BBC Sport. 2005. Miller "surprised" EPO is illegal. http://news.bbc.co.uk/sport2/hi/other_sports/winter_sports/4334612.stm. Accessed June 1, 2006.

BBC News. 2009. Tiger Woods in new sponsorship loss as AT&T drops deal. http://news.bbc.co.uk/2/hi/8436514.stm. Accessed June 15, 2010.

Beesley, S. 2009. WNBA salaries fall far short of their male counterparts. http://personalmoneystore.com/moneyblog/2009/04/09/wnba-salaries-fall-short-male-counterparts/. Accessed August 24, 2010.

Beijing. 2008. Record women's participation. http://en.beijing2008.cn/news/official/ioc/n214559789.shtml. Accessed July 16, 2010.

Beikoff, K. 2010a. Who watched the Vancouver Winter Olympics? www.suite101.com/content/who-watched-the-vancouver-winter-olympics-a210238. Accessed October 18, 2010.

Beikoff, K. 2010b. Will more tests at the London Olympics catch more sports cheats? *Paralympic Sport*, April 16. www.suite101.com/content/will-more-tests-at-the-london-olympics-catch-more-sports-cheats-a226300. Accessed August 27, 2010.

Bell, J. 2004. NFL tug-of-war over revenue. *USA Today*. July 6, 2004.

Beller, J., and Stoll, S. 1994. Sport participation and its effect on moral reasoning of high school student athletes and general students. *Research Quarterly for Exercise and Sport*, March, suppl. 65.

Benedict, J., and Yaeger, D. 1998. *Pros and cons: The criminals who play in the NFL*. New York: Warner Books.

Best, C. 1987. Experience and career length in professional football: The effects of positional segregation. *Sociology of Sport Journal* 7 (4), 410-420.

Bird, H. 2010. The future of USA soccer and what Bob Bradley could learn from Sir Alex. http://bleacher-report.com/articles/418524-the-future-of-usa-soccer-and-what-bob-bradley. Accessed August 1, 2010.

Birrell, S. 2004. Feminist theories for sport. In *Handbook of sports studies*, ed. J. Coakley and E. Dunning, 61-75. London: Sage.

Bissinger, H. 1990. *Friday night lights*. New York: Da Capo Press.

Bloom, J. 2000. *To show what an Indian can do: Sport at Native American boarding schools*. Minneapolis: University of Minnesota Press.

Bloomberg. 2009. U.S. newspapers decline in circulation accelerates. www.bloomberg.com/apps/news?pid=newsarchive&sid=aJfOZ0XN22jY. Accessed July 20, 2009.

Blumstein, A., and Benedict, J. 1999. Criminal violence of NFL players compared to the general population. *Chance* 12 (3), 12-15.

Booth, D., and Loy, J. 1999. Sport, status and style. *Sport History Review* 30 (1), 1-26.

Borzilleri, M.J. 2003. USOC targets positions, pay raises. *The Gazette* (Colorado Springs, CO), June 11.

Bowen, W., and Levin, S. 2003. *Reclaiming the game: College sports and educational values*. Princeton, NJ: Princeton University Press.

Bowles, W., and Jenson, M. 2001. Cultural capital. www.williambowles.info/mimo/refs/tece1ef.htm. Accessed January 1, 2006.

Brady, E., and Giler, R. 2004a. In a lot of cases, they have no other choice. *USA Today*, July 3.

Brady, E., and Giler, R. 2004b. To play sports, many U.S. students must pay. National Association of College Women Athletics Administrators. www.nacwaa.org/rc/rc_artilepr_paytoplay.php. Accessed January 1, 2005.

Brady, E., and Sylwester, M. 2004. Trends in girls sports. *USA Today*, June 17.

Brand, M. 2004. In athletics, level field must begin in classroom. *New York Times*, May 9.

Bredemeier, B., and Shields, D. 2006. Sports and character development. President's Council on Physical Fitness and Sports. *Research Digest*, March, Series 7, no. 1.

Brelje, B., and Kuhns, M. 2009. East Stroudsburg University field hockey team forfeits over hazing allegations. *Pocono Record*, October 30. www.poconorecord.com/apps/pbcs.dll/article?AID=/20091030/NEWS/910300344/www.poconorecord.com/apps/pbcs.dll/article?AID=/20091030/NEWS/910300344/. Accessed November 1, 2009.

Brennan, C. 2005. 25 years later, Olympic boycott gnaws at athletes. *USA Today*. www.usatoday.com/sports/columnist/brennan/2005-04-13-brennan_x.htm. Accessed July 23, 2010.

Brennan, C. 2006. Northwestern, Duke matters sign of larger problem. *USA Today*, May 18, C2.

Brennan, D. 2001. Sanctity of sport. www.tothenextlevel.org. Accessed October 30, 2004.

Brigham Young University Athletics. 2006. www.byucougars.com. Accessed June 7, 2006.

Brown, G. 2000. Beating the odds. *NCAA News*, December 18, 2000.

Brown, M. 2001. The shoe's on the other foot. http://healthlibrary.epnet.com/GetContent.aspx?token=af362d974f80-4453-a175-02cc6220. Accessed June 8, 2006.

Browne, D. 2004. *Amped: How big air, big dollars and a new generation took sports to the extreme*. New York: Bloomsbury.

Bruce, T. 2000. Never let the bastards see you cry. *Sociology of Sports Journal* 17 (1), 69-74.

Brylinsky, J. 2002. National standards for athletic coaches. ERIC clearinghouse on teaching and teacher education. Washington, DC. www.ericdigests.org/2004-1/coaches.htm. Accessed February 27, 2005.

Bunker, L. 1988. Lifelong benefits of youth sport participation for girls and women. Speech presented at the Sport Psychology Conference, University of Virginia, Charlottesville.

Bureau of Labor Statistics. 2010-2011. Occupational outlook handbook. Athletes, coaches, umpires, and related workers. www.bls.gov/oco/ocos251.htm. Accessed July 28, 2010.

Burnett, D. 2005. Sportsmanship checklist for kids. www.printablechecklists.com/checklist38.shtml. Accessed October 18, 2010.

Carlson, D., and Scott, L. 2005. What is the status of high school athletes 8 years after their senior year? *Statistics in brief: National Center for Education Statistics*, 1-19. Washington, DC: U.S. Department of Education.

Carpenter, L., and Acosta, R. 2005. *Title IX*. Champaign, IL: Human Kinetics.

Carpenter, C., and Stehr, M. 2009. Intended and unintended effects of youth bicycle helmet laws. www.gse.uci.edu/docs/Carpenter_Stehr%20Bicycle_Manuscript_50409.pdf. Accessed July 23, 2010.

Carter, R. 2005. Ashe's impact reached far beyond the court. SportsCentury biography. http://espn.go.com/classic/biography/s/Ashe_Arthur.html. Accessed August 15, 2010.

Cary, P. 2004. Fixing kids' sports: Rescuing children's games from crazed coaches and parents. *U.S. News and World Report*, June 7.

Cauchon, D. 2005. Childhood pastimes are increasingly moving indoors. *USA Today*, August 12.

Cauchon, D. 2009. Women gain as men lose jobs. *USA Today*, September 2.

CBS News. 2009. Delaware sports betting dealt legal blow. August 31. www.cbsnews.com/stories/2009/08/31/sportsline/main5277188.shtml. Accessed November 13, 2009.

CBS News. 2010. Super Bowl ad prices dip, but still pricey. www.cbsnews.com/stories/2010/01/11/sportsline/main6082591.shtml. Accessed May 27, 2010.

Centers for Disease Control and Prevention. 2000. Youth risk behavior survey 1999. www.cdc.gov/mmwr/preview/mmwrhtml/ss4905a1.htm. Accessed October 18, 2010.

Centers for Disease Control and Prevention. 2008. Fact sheet: Understanding school violence. www.cdc.gov/ncipc/dvp/YVP/SV_Factsheet.pdf. Accessed October 18, 2010.

Centers for Disease Control and Prevention. 2010. State indicator report on physical activity, 2010 national action guide. www.cdc.gov/physicalactivity/downloads/PA_State_Indicator_Report_2010_Action_Guide.pdf. Accessed October 18, 2010.

Chaddock, G. 2003. U.S. notches world's highest incarceration rate. *Christian Science Monitor*, August 18.

Cherner, R. 2005. If you billed it around faith, they will certainly come. *USA Today*, July 22.

Christianity Today. 2008. Greater than gold. www.christiantoday.com/article/greater.than.gold.witnessing.christ.in.beijing/21229.htm. Accessed October 18, 2010.

Citizenship Through Sports Alliance. 2005. 2005 Youth sports national report card. www.sportsmanship.org/News/1105%20Report%20Card-Fgrade.pdf. Accessed June 1, 2006.

CNN Sports Illustrated. 2001. Jury rules for NFL. http://sportsillustrated.cnn.com/. Accessed May 22, 2001.

Coakley, J. 2004. *Sports in society*. 8th ed. New York: McGraw Hill.

Coakley, J., and Donnelly, P., eds. 1999. *Inside sports*. London: Routledge.

Coakley, J., and Dunning, E., eds. 2004. *Handbook of sports studies*. London: Sage.

College Sports Information Directors of America (CoSIDA). 2001. Over 200 women sign up as members of Female Athletic Media Executives (FAME). *CoSIDA Digest*, April.

Colorado High School Activities Association (CHSAA). 2010. www.chsaa.org. Accessed July 11, 2010.

Condor, R. 2004. Living well: When coaches and parents put too much emphasis on winning, kids drop out. *Post-Intelligencer* (Seattle, WA), September 30.

Crain, W. 1985. *Theories of development*, 118-136. Englewood Cliffs, NJ: Prentice Hall.

Crosset, T. 1999. What do we know and what can we do about male athletes' violence against women: A critical assessment of the athletic affiliation and violence against women debate. *Quest*, August.

Crosset, T., Benedict, J., and McDonald, M. 1995. Male student-athletes reported for sexual assault: Survey of campus police departments and judicial affairs offices. *Journal of Sport and Social Issues* 19 (2), 126-140.

Cuban, M. 2004. My new hedge fund. The Mark Cuban weblog, November 27. www.blogmaverick.com/entry/1234000570021684/. Accessed June 26, 2006.

Cummings, D. 2009. Beijing's empty venues reveal heavy cost of Olympics. www.findingdulcinea.com/news/sports/2009/feb/Beijing-s-Empty-Venues-Reveal-Heavy-Cost-of-Olympics.html. Accessed October 18, 2010.

Curnutte, M. 2007. Financial gap widening between NFL's haves and have-nots. www.usatoday.com/cleanprint/?1276545969000. Accessed June 14, 2010.

Cycling News. 2005. More Armstrong allegations from L'Equipe! October 8. www.cyclingnews.com/features/?id=2005/nelson_lequipe. Accessed May 23, 2006.

Daily Mail. 2010. Caster Semenya finally proves she's woman enough to run after 11-month gender row. www.dailymail.co.uk/sport/othersports/article-1292473/Caster-Semenya-set-athletics-return-following-gender-row.html. Accessed August 10, 2010.

Deford, F. 1976. Religion in sport. *Sports Illustrated*, April 19, 92-99.

Deitsch, R. 2009. Dirtiest NFL player: Steelers' Ward. SI.com, November. http://sportsillustrated.cnn.com/2009/football/nfl/11/04/dirty/index.html. Accessed September 1, 2010.

Delaney, T., and Madigan, T. 2009. *The sociology of sports*, 160. Jefferson, NC: McFarland.

deLench, B. 2008. No-cut rule for teams below varsity makes sense. www.momsteam.com/print/406. Accessed July 30, 2010.

Didziulis, V. 2010. What does the future hold for U.S. soccer? www.poder360.com/article_detail.php?id_article=4439. Accessed August 1, 2010.

Dobie, M. 2000. Race and sports in high school. In *Best newspaper writing 2000*, ed. C. Scanlon, 319-387. St. Petersburg, FL: Poynter Institute for Media Studies.

Dodds, T. 2000. Opening minds no harder than opening doors. *American Editor*, January-February.

Donnelly, P. 2004. Interpretive approaches to the sociology of sport. In *Handbook of sports studies*, ed. J. Coakley and E. Dunning, 77-91. London: Sage.

Drake Group. 2009. The Drake Group proposals. www.thedrakegroup.org/proposals.html. Accessed August 15, 2010.

Dubner, S. 2007. NFL vs. MLB as a labor market: A freakonomics quorum. http://freakonomics.blogs.nytimes.com/2007/11/28/nfl-vs-mlb-as-a-labor-market-a-freako. Accessed June 14, 2010.

Dudley, C. 2010. Terrell Owens biography—played multiple sports in high school and college, courted controversy, set new records. http://biography.jrank.org/pages/2816/Owens-Terrell.html. Accessed July 9, 2010.

Duncan, M., and Messner, M. 2005. Gender in televised sports: News and highlights shows, 1989-2004. Amateur Athletic Foundation of Los Angeles. www.aafla.org/9arr/ResearchReports/tv2004.pdf. Accessed June 1, 2006.

Dunning, E. 1999. *Sport matters: Sociological studies of sport, violence, and civilization*. London: Routledge.

Dworkin, J., Larson, R., and Hansen, D. 2003. Adolescents' accounts of growth experiences in youth activities. *Journal of Youth and Adolescence* 32 (1), 17-36.

DW-World.de. 2005. Referee scandal threatens Germany's World Cup, January 24. www.dw-world.de/dw/article/0,1564,1467560,00.html. Accessed January 31, 2005.

Edwards, H. 1973. *Sociology of sports*, 63-69, appendix A. Homewood, IL: Dorsey Press.

Eitzen, S. 1992, December. Sports and ideological contradictions: Learning from the cultural framing of soviet values. *Journal of Sport and Social Issues* 16, 144-149.

Eitzen, S. 2003. *Fair or foul: Beyond the myths and paradoxes of sport*. 2nd ed. Lanham, MD: Rowman & Littlefield.

Eitzen, S. 2004. Social control in sport. In *Handbook of sports studies*, ed. J. Coakley and E. Dunning, 370-381. London: Sage.

Eitzen, S., and Sage, G. 1978. *Sociology of American sport*. Dubuque, IA: William C. Brown.

Eitzen, S., and Sage, G. 2002. *Sociology of North American sport*. 7th ed. Boston: McGraw-Hill.

Elias, N., and Dunning, E. 1986. *Quest for excitement: Sport and leisure in the civilising process*. Oxford: Blackwell.

Engwall, D., Hunter, R., and Steinberg, M. 2004, May-June. Gambling and other risky behaviors on university campuses. *Journal of American College Health* 52 (6), 245-255.

Entine, J. 2000. *Taboo: Why Black athletes dominate sports and why we're afraid to talk about it.* New York: Public Affairs.

Entine, J. 2004. Race and sport 1 and 2: The race to the swift—if the swift have the right ancestry. *Peak Performance.* www.pponline.co.uk/encyc/0657b.htm. Accessed December 16, 2004.

ESPN. 1999. Wilt spoke of regrets, women and meadowlark. ESPN.com, October 13.

http://espn.go.com/nba/news/1999/1012/110905.html. Accessed May 10, 2005.

ESPN. 2009. New Mexico player banned, apologizes. Sports.espn. http://sports.espn.go.com/ncaa/news/story?id=4629837. Accessed July 26, 2010.

ESPN. 2010a. 46 coaches on banned list. ESPN.com. http://sports.espn.go.com/oly/swimming/news/story?id=5220940. Accessed October 19, 2010.

ESPN. 2010b. Erin Andrews bio. ESPN.com. http://search.espn.go.com/erin-andrews-bio/. Accessed October 19, 2010.

ESPN. 2010c. Major League Baseball team salaries. http://espn.go.com/mlb/team/salaries/_/name/nyy/new-york-yankees. Accessed June 15, 2010.

ESPN. 2010d. Sport science: Home run derby. http://espn.go.com/video/clip?id=5373166. Accessed October 4, 2010.

ESPN Sports Business. 2009. Stadium naming rights. http://espn.go.com/sportsbusiness/s/stadiumnames.html. Accessed July 13, 2009.

Ewing, M., and Seefeldt, V. 1990. *American youth and sports participation.* Lansing: Youth Sports Institute at Michigan State University.

Fanbay.net. 2005. Women at the Olympics. www.fanbay.net/olympics/htm. Accessed September 25, 2005.

Farrey, T. 2002. Laws get a workout. ESPN.com, June 3. http://espn.go.com/otl/hazing/friday.html. Accessed September 5, 2005.

Fejgin, N. 1994. Participation in high school competitive sports: A subversion of school mission or contribution to academic goals? *Sociology of Sport Journal* 11 (3), 211-230.

Fellowship of Christian Athletes. 2008. About FCA. www.fca.org/AboutFCA/. Accessed August 30, 2010.

Fine, G. 1987. *With the boys: Little League baseball and pre-adolescent culture.* Chicago: University of Chicago Press.

First basket, The: A Jewish basketball documentary. 2008. www.thefirstbasket.com. Accessed October 2, 2010.

First Tee, The. 2010. The First Tee life skills experience. www.thefirsttee.org/club/scripts/view/view_insert.asp?IID=13105&NS=PUBLIC. Accessed July 11, 2010.

Fish, M. 2009a. Donaghy accused of probation violation. ESPN NBA. http:/sports.espn.go.com/nba/news/story?id=4420908. Accessed November 13, 2009.

Fish, M. 2009b. What is a college QB worth? ESPN.com. http://sports.espn.go.com/espn/otl/news/story?id=4733249. Accessed May 25, 2010.

Fleder, R. 2005. *Sports illustrated 50: The anniversary book.* New York: Time.

Forbes.com. 2009. The celebrity 100. www.forbes.com.lists/2009/53/celebrity-09_The-Celebrity-100_EarningsPrevYear. Accessed August 30, 2010.

Forbes.com. 2010. The business of baseball, #1 New York Yankees. www.forbes.com/lists/2010/33/baseball-valuations-10_New-York-Yankees_334613.html. Accessed October 19, 2010.

Fox News. 2010a. Mark McGwire's steroid use tarnishes home run record, January 12. www.foxnews.com/printer_friendly_story/0,3566,582858,00.html. Accessed July 27, 2010.

Fox News. 2010b. Elin Nordegren gets $750M, custody of kids in exchange for silence in Tiger Woods divorce. www.foxnews.com/entertainment/2010/06/30/elin-nordegren-gets-m-custody-kids-exchange-silence-tiger-woods-divorce/. Accessed October 16, 2010.

Fox News. 2010c. "Glee." www.fox.com/glee. Accessed October 1, 2010.

Fox Sports. 2006. Schools end use of slogan over drinking woes. Foxsports.com, May 16. http://msn.foxsports.com/cfb/story/5612364. Accessed May 22, 2006.

Frank, R. 2004. Challenging the myth: A review of the links among college athletic success, student quality and donations. Report to the Knight Commission on Intercollegiate Athletics. www.knightcommission.org/index.php?option=com_content&view=article&id=73&Itemid=4. Accessed October 19, 2010.

Frankel, D. 1998. Turner can't keep Murdoch from Dodgers. eonline.com, March 19. www.eonline.com/News/Items/0,1,2713,00.html. Accessed June 10, 2006.

Frey, W. 2010. Race and ethnicity. *State of metropolitan America: On the front lines of demographic transformation*, 50-63. Washington, DC: Brookings Metropolitan Policy Program. www.brookings.edu/metro/MetroAmericaChapters/race.aspx. Accessed October 18, 2010.

Frommer, F. 2009. Delaware sports betting dealt legal blow. Associated Press. www.cbsnews.com/stories/2009/08/31/sportsline/main5277188.shtml. Accessed November 13, 2009.

Fullerton, R. 2003. Watching the pros vs. playing the game: How sports coverage affects community-level athletes. www.cces.ca/pdfs/CCES-PAPERSum-Smith-Fullerton-E.pdf. Accessed June 1, 2006.

Gale Group. 1999. Muhammad Ali. www.galegroup.com/free_resources/bhm/bio/ali_m.htm. Accessed August 24, 2005.

Gallup Poll. 2005. Six in 10 Americans are pro football fans. www.gallup.com/poll/14812/Six-Americans-Pro-Football-Fans.aspx. Accessed June 13, 2009.

Game Face. 2002. From the locker room to the boardroom: A survey on sports in the lives of women business executives, February. Survey commissioned by Mass-Mutual Financial Group and Oppenheimer Funds. www.superednet.com/gameFace.html. Accessed May 15, 2005.

Garber, G. 2002. It's not all fun and games. ESPN.com, June 3. http://espn.go.com/otl/hazing/wednesday.html. Accessed September 5, 2005.

Garcia, C. 1994. Gender differences in young children's interactions when learning fundamental motor skills. *Research Quarterly for Exercise and Sport* 66 (3), 247-255.

Gaul, G. 2009. College sports, Inc. Washinton Post Investigations. http://voices.washingtonpost.com/washingtonpostinvestigations/2009/01/today_post_investigations_debu.html. Accessed July 14, 2009.

Gebicke, M. 1996. Director, military operations and capabilities issues. Letter to the honorable John McCain, Chairman, Subcommittee on Readiness Committee on Armed Services, United States Senate, June 14. GAO/NSIAD-96-189R DOD Olympic Support.

Genel, M. 2000. Gender verification no more? *Medscape Women's Health Journal*. http://ai.eecs.umich.edu/people/conway/TS/OlympicGenderTesting.html. Accessed October 19, 2010.

Gertz, S. 2004. Revisiting the pagan Olympic Games. *Christianity Today*, August 16. www.christianitytoday.com/ch/news/2004/aug19.html. Accessed October 19, 2010.

Gibbons, S. 2003. Sports news shortchanges female players, fans. Maynard Institute for Journalism, May 13. www.maynardije.org/columns/guests/030514_sportsnews. Accessed August 15, 2005.

Gibbons, S., Ebbeck, V., and Weiss, M. 1995. Fair play for kids: Effects on the moral development of children in physical education. *Research Quarterly for Exercise and Sport* 66, 247-255.

Girard, R. 2010. Is the YMCA's name and logo change a good idea? *Fort Worth Christianity and Culture Examiner*, July 13. www.examiner.com/christianity-culture-in-fort-worth/is-the-ymca-s-name-and-logo-change-a-good-idea-vote-here. Accessed July 22, 2010.

Girls in the Game. 2010. About us. www.girlsinthegame.org/content/index.asp?s=475&t=About-Us. Accessed October 19, 2010.

Gould, D. 1993. Intensive sport participation and the prepubescent athlete: Competitive stress and burnout. In *Intensive participation in children's sports*, ed. B.R. Cahill and A. Pearl, 19-38. Champaign, IL: Human Kinetics.

Griffin, P. 1998. *Strong women, deep closets: Lesbians and homophobia in sports*. Champaign, IL: Human Kinetics.

Gruneau, R. 1999. *Class sports and social development*. Champaign, IL: Human Kinetics.

Gumpel, E. 2009. For the love of the game. *Women Entrepreneur*. www.womenentrepreneur.com/2009/01/for-the-love-of-the-game.html. Accessed August 30, 2010.

Hackensmith, C. 1966. *History of physical education*. New York: Harper & Row.

Hadley, R. 2010. Another flock of NFL lambs could be headed to financial disaster in long term. www.standard.net/topics/sports/2010/04/28/another-flock-nfl-lambs-could-be-headed. Accessed April 20, 2010.

Hargreaves, J., and McDonald, I. 2004. Cultural studies and the sociology of sport. In *Handbook of sports studies*, ed. J. Coakley and E. Dunning, 48-60. London: Sage.

Harrell, E. 2009. South Africa slams Semenya's gender test. *Time*. www.time.com/time/printout/0,8816,1921847,00.html. Accessed September 24, 2009.

Harris, K. 2004. Pro athletes get in the political game. *Sun Sentinel* (Fort Lauderdale, FL), October 29.

Harris Interactive. 2001. Sports and women: Reaching this critical "casual fan." www.harrisinteractive.com/news/allnewsbydate.asp?NewsID=391. Accessed August 15, 2005.

Harris Interactive. 2004. Trends and tudes. Vol. 3, Issue 9, September. www.harrisinteractive.com/news/newsletters_k12.asp. Accessed June 1, 2006.

Harris Poll. 2004. Survey of Americans with disabilities. National Organization on Disability, Washington, DC. www.nod.org/research_publications/nod_harris_survey/. Accessed October 19, 2010.

Hawes, K. 1999. Women's sports enter NCAA arena. *NCAA News*, December 6. http://web1.ncaa.org/web_files/NCAANewsArchive/1999/19991206/active/3625n32.html. Accessed August 15, 2010.

Hawes, K. 2001. Grant carried on the "idea" long after AIAW fell. *NCAA News*, May 21. http://web1.ncaa.org/web_files/NCAANewsArchive/2001/Association-wide/grant%2Bcarried%2Bon%2Bthe%2B_idea_%2Blong%2Bafter%2Baiaw%2Bfell%2B-%2B5-21-01.html. Accessed August 15, 2010.

Hayes, G. 2008. Central Washington offers the ultimate act of sportsmanship. http://sports.espn.go.com/ncaa/columns/story?columnist=hays_graham&id=3372631. Accessed August 21, 2010.

Hechinger, F. 1980. About education. *New York Times*, February 19, 1980.

Hemery, D. 1986. *Sporting excellence, a study of sport's highest achievers*. London: Collins Sons.

Henry, B., and Yeomans, P. 1984. *History of the Olympic Games*. Sherman Oaks, CA: Alfred.

Hills, C. 2004. Cuban hedges bet on NBA. *Focus on Family*, December 16. www.family.org/cforum/fosi/gambling/nac/a0034646.cfm. Accessed June 1, 2006.

Hoch, P. 1972. The world of playtime, USA. *Daily World*, April 27, 12.

Hoffman, S.J. 1992. *Sport and religion*. Champaign, IL: Human Kinetics.

Hoffman, S. 2009. *Introduction to kinesiology*. 3rd ed. Champaign, IL: Human Kinetics.

Hoffstein, L. 2010. Katie at the Bat Team. www.katieatthebatteam.org/. Accessed July 25, 2010.

Hogan, H. 2008. This just in: Women watch the Olympics—and enjoy it. www.afterellen.com/blog/stuntdouble/this-just-in-women-watch-the-olympics-and-enjoy-it. Accessed October 12, 2010.

Holbrook, J.E., and Barr, J. 1997. *Contemporary coaching: Trends and issues*. Carmel, IN: Cooper.

Holmes, L. 2005. Study finds few college athletes with eating disorders. http://mentalhealth.about.com/cs/eat/a/athleteeat.htm?p=1. Accessed July 27, 2010.

Holway, L. 2005. A fight to the death: NCAA vs. AIAW. Unpublished. Bryn Mawr, PA: Bryn Mawr College.

Houston Chronicle. 2004. Marvelous messenger. www.chron.com/content/chronicle/sports/special/barriers/ashe.html. Accessed October 10, 2004.

Huff, D. 2005. Best by state: The top high school athletic programs in America. http://sportsillustrated.cnn.com/2005/magazine/05/11/top.high.map0516/. Accessed January 15, 2006.

Hughes, G. 2004. Managing black guys: Representation, corporate culture, and the NBA. *Sociology of Sport Journal* 21, 163-184.

Humphreys, J. and Plummer, M. 1996. The economic impact of hosting the 1996 Summer Olympics. www.selig.uga.edu/forcat/Olympics/OLYMTEXT.htm. Accessed November 11, 2005.

Huston, W. 2005. Sports is the opiate of the masses. *American Daily*, January 18. www.americandaily.com/2951. Accessed January 18, 2005.

Hutchinson, E. 2004. Hornung was honest about Black athletes, many universities aren't. AlterNet, April 7. www.alternet.org/columnists/story/18358/. Accessed December 16, 2004.

Huizinga, J. 1950. *Homo Ludens: A study of the play element in culture*. Boston: Beacon Press.

IMG Academies. 2010. Full-time tuition rates. www.imgacademies.com. Accessed July 11, 2010.

Indianapolis Chamber of Commerce. 2006. Amateur sports capital of the world. www.indychamber.com/sportRec.asp. Accessed May 22, 2006.

Inside Higher Ed. 2008. A (money) losing proposition. http://insidehighered.com/layout/set/print/news/2008/05/16/ncaa. Accessed June 15, 2010.

International Council on Active Aging. 2010. www.icaa.cc/. Accessed July 20, 2010.

International Olympic Committee. 2010. www.olympic.org. Accessed June 10, 2010.

International Sport. 2010. National Sportsmanship Day, Tuesday March 2, 2010. www.internationalsport.com/nsd/. Accessed July 9, 2010.

IPSOS World Monitor. 2002. Trend profiler II: Couch and field: Eight sports' global draw. First quarter, 2002. www.ipsos.ca/prod/wm/. Accessed October 21, 2004.

Issa, S. 2001. *Muslim girls' sports camp*. Los Angeles: Muslim Women's League.

Jacobson, D. 2007. The revenue model: Why baseball is booming. www.bnet.com/article/the-revenue-model-why-baseball-is-booming/210671. Accessed October 19, 2010.

Jenkins, B. 2004. Sportsline. *USA Today*, November 19.

Jenkins, C. 2000. Caught in gambling's web. *USA Today*, May 24.

Jenkins, S. 2010. On television, highlights of women's sports are running low. *Washington Post*, June 4. http://pqasb.pqarchiver.com/washingtonpost/access/2049347001.html?FMT=ABS&FMTS=ABS:FT&date=Jun+4%2C+2010&author=Sally+Jenkins&pub=The+Washington+Post&edition=&startpage=D.1&desc=On+television%2C+women%27s+sports+highlights+are+running+low. Accessed October 19, 2010.

Jensen, C. 2008. Fast tracks: Danica Patrick. www.forbes.com/2008/11/06/046_print.html. Accessed July 17, 2010.

Johnson, W. 1973a. And smile, smile, smile. *Sports Illustrated*, June 4, 38, 76-78.

Johnson, W. 1973b. Courting time in Peking. *Sports Illustrated*, 39, July 2, 12-15.

Johnson, W. 1973c. Sport in China. *Sports Illustrated*, 39, part 1, September 24, 82-100.

Jones, D. 2002. Many successful women say sports teaches valuable lessons. *USA Today*, Money Section, March 22.

Jones, T. 2010. Alabama governor avoids controversy by turning down gambling bet. www.casinogamblingweb.com/gambling-news/gambling-law/alabama_governor_avoids_controversy_by_turning_down_gambling_bet_53675.html. Accessed October 19, 2010.

Josephson, M. 2004. Character counts: Sportsmanship survey. Josephson Institute. www.charactercounts.org. Accessed December 8, 2004.

Josephson, M. 2007. Report reveals propensity of high school athletes to lie and cheat when the stakes are high. Josephson Institute. www.charactercounts.org. Accessed September 1, 2009.

Josephson, M. 2008. The ethics of American youth—2008 summary. http://charactercounts.org/programs/reportcard/index.html. Accessed September 9, 2009.

Journalism Jobs. 2002. 2002 RTNDA/Ball State University salary survey. www.journalismjobs.com/salaries.cfm. Accessed April 4, 2005.

Katz, S. 2005. Sub-mergent power: Struggles for equality under the AIAW/NCAA merger. Unpublished. Bryn Mawr, PA: Bryn Mawr College.

Kelber, M. 2009. God and football: The NFL's chaplains give advice. *Time*, October 30. www.time.com/time/printout/0,8816,1933406,00.html. Accessed July 22, 2010.

Kidd, B., and Donnelly, P. 2000. Human rights in sports. *International Review for the Sociology of Sport* 35 (2), 131-48.

King, C.R., and Fruehling, C. 2001. *Team spirits: The Native American mascots controversy*. Lincoln: University of Nebraska Press.

King, R. 2004. This is not an Indian. *Journal of Sport and Social Issues* 28 (1), 3-10.

Klafs, C., and Lyon, J. 1978. *The female athlete*. 2nd ed. St. Louis: Mosby.

Klayman, B. 2008. NFL average team value tops $1 billion: Forbes. www.reuters.com/assets/print?aid=USN1020214220080910. Accessed June 14, 2010.

Klein, Alan. 1991. Sport and culture as contested terrain: Americanization in the Caribbean. *Sociology of Sport Journal* 8:79-85.

Knight Commission on Intercollegiate Athletics. 2001. A call to action: Reconnecting college sports and higher education. www.knightcommission.org/images/pdfs/2001_knight_report.pdf. Accessed October 19, 2010.

Kosmin, B., and Keysar, A. 2009. American religious identification survey 2008. Trinity College, Hartford, CT, March. www.americanreligionsurvey-aris.org. Accessed October 15, 2009.

Kreit, A. 1998. Professional wrestling and its fans. www.solie.org/articlesw/pwandfans.html. Accessed July 19, 2010.

Kretchmar, R. S. 1994. *Practical philosophy of sport*. Champaign, IL: Human Kinetics.

Kvalsund, P. 2007. Introduction peace and reconciliation. Sport for Development and Peace International Working Group. http://www.toolkitsportdevelopment.org/html/topic_8C99D814-CFBC-494E-8BAD-8C51BCAEA5BE_6458A396-8CE6-4E87-BD61-6C626363A7AB_1.htm. Accessed September 10, 2010.

Lajis, R. 1996. The history of drug abuse in sports. www.prn2.usm.my/mainsite/bulletin/sun/1996/sun27.html. Accessed January 15, 2006.

Lambert, C. 2001. Has winning on the field become simply a corporate triumph? *Harvard Magazine*, September-October. www.harvard-magazine.com/online/09014.html. Accessed May 23, 2006.

Landau, E. 2009. College's too-fat-to-graduate rule under fire. CNN. www.cnn.com/2009/HEALTH/11/30/lincoln.fitness.overweight/index.html. Accessed October 19, 2010

Lapchick, R. 1999. Race, athletes and crime. Special issue, *Sports Business Journal* [Online]. http://web.bus.ucf.edu/sportbusiness/articles.aspx?y=2000. Accessed October 19, 2010.

Lapchick, R. 2001. Tennis opens up. http://web.bus.ucf.edu/sportbusiness/articles.aspx?y=2000. Accessed December 10, 2004.

Lapchick, R. 2003. Just do it: Asian American athletes. Asian-Nation: The landscape of Asian America. http://web.bus.ucf.edu/sportbusiness/articles.aspx?y=2000. Accessed December 10, 2004.

Lapchick, R. 2008. Racial and gender report card: College sports. www.tidesport.org/racialgenderreportcard.html. pp. 33-45. Accessed August 21, 2009.

Lapchick, R., Little, E., Mathew, R., and Zahn, J. 2008. The 2008 racial and gender report card of the Associated Press sports editors. University of Central Florida, DeVos Sport Business Management Program. www.tidesport.org/racialgenderreportcard.html. Accessed June 10, 2010.

Lapchick, R. 2008-2009. Racial and gender report card: Professional sports. www.tidesport.org/RGRC/2008/2008_RGRC.pdf. Accessed October 19, 2010.

Lapchick, R. 2009a. Press release: New study reveals marked improvements for the graduation rates for African-American student athletes. Research corner. www.tidesport.org/ncaagraduationrates.html. Accessed October 19, 2010.

Lapchick, R. 2009b. Racial and gender report card: College Sports. www.tidesport.org/RGRC/2009/2009_College_Sport_RGRC.pdf.

Lapchick, R. 2010a. TIDES: Institute for Diversity in Sports. 2010 racial and gender report card. Major League Baseball. www.tidesport.org/RGRC/2010/2010_MLB_RGRC_updated.pdf. Accessed October 19, 2010.

Lapchick, R. 2010b. TIDES: Institute for Diversity in Sports. 2010 racial and gender report card. Major League Soccer. www.tidesport.org/RGRC/2009/2009_MLS_RGRC.pdf. Accessed October 19, 2010.

Lapchick, R. 2010c. TIDES: Institute for Diversity in Sports. 2010 racial and gender report card: National Football League. www.tidesport.org/RGRC/2010/2010%20NFL%20Racial%20and%20Gender%20Report%20Card.pdf. Accessed October 10, 2010.

Lapchick, R. and K. Mathews. 1999. *Race and gender report card*. Boston: Northeastern University Center for Study of Sport in Society.

Lavigne, P. 2008. Pro sports figures more invested in this presidential campaign. ESPN.com, September 4. http://sports.espn.go.com/espn/otl/news/story?id=3565666. Accessed October 19, 2010.

Layden, T. 2004. Hanging from the BALCO-ny. SI Vault. http://sportsillustrated.cnn.com/vault/article/web/COM1038283/index.htm. Accessed August 15, 2010.

Leadership for Healthy Communities. 2010. Overweight and obesity Among African-American youths. Fact sheet. http://www.leadershipforhealthycommunities.org/images/stories/lhc_factsheet_africanamerican_rev_3.pdf. Accessed May 10, 2010.

Ledman, D. 2008. *A (Money) losing proposition* (Inside Higher Ed). Available: http://insidehighered.com/layout/set/print/news/2008/05/16/ncaa.

Lee, R., McAlexander, K., and Banda, J. 2011. *Reversing the obesogenic environment*. Champaign, IL: Human Kinetics.

Le Fevre, D. 2002. *Best new games*. Champaign, IL: Human Kinetics.

Leonard, L. 2000. The decline of the black athlete. ColorLines. www.arc.org/C_Lines/CLArchive/story3_1_03.html. Accessed December 4, 2005.

Leonard, W. 1980. *A sociological perspective of sport*. Minneapolis: Burgess.

Levin, J. 2007. What's wrong with *Sports Illustrated* and how to fix it. *Slate*, October 31. www.slate.com/toolbar.aspx?action=print&id=2177143. Accessed June 20, 2010.

Lin, Z., Jui-Chia, C., and Esposito, E. 2005. Successful leadership in sport. http://thesportdigest.com/article/successful-leadership-behavior-sport. Accessed October 19, 2010.

Lipsyte, R. 2003. Reform movements build in American college sports. *New York Times*, November 30.Little League. 2005. About our organization. www.littleleague.org. Accessed May 10, 2005.

Litsky, F and Branch, J. 2010. John Wooden, who built incomparable dynasty at U.C.L.A., dies at 99. *New York Times*. June 5. www.nytimes.com/2010/06/05/sports/ncaabasketball/05wooden.html?_r=2&adxnnl=. Accessed July 29, 2010.

LiveScience. 2008. Girls' most dangerous sport: Cheerleading. www.livescience.com/health/080811-cheerleading-injuries.html. Accessed July 25, 2010.

Lodriguss, J. 2005. Sports photography tips and techniques. www.astropix.com/SPORTSPIX/NSC/NOTES.HTM. Accessed May 10, 2005.

Lombardo, B. 1999. Coaching in the 21st century: Issues, concerns and solutions. *Sociology of Sport* [Online]. htpp://physed.otago.ac.nz/sosol/v2i1/v2ila4.htm. Accessed September 5, 2005.

Lopiano, D. 1994. Equity in women's sports: A health and fairness perspective. *The Athletic Woman* 13 (2), 281-296.

Lopiano, D. 2001. Gender equity and the Black female in sport. www.womenssportsfoundation.org/Content/Articles/Issues/Equity-Issues/G/Gender-Equity-and-the-Black-Female-in-Sport.aspx. Accessed October 19, 2010.

Lowitt, B. 1999. Terrorists turn '72 Munich Olympics into bloodbath. *St. Petersburg Times*, December 29. www.sptimes.com/News/122999/news_pf/Sports/Terrorists_turn__72_M.shtml. Accessed July 22, 2010.

Lowry, T., and Keating, T. 2007. The power players. SportsBusiness. www.businessweek.com/bwdaily/dnflash/content/sep2007/db20070925_346159.htm. Accessed October 19, 2010.

Loy, J., and Booth, D. 2004. Functionalism in sport and society. In *Handbook of sports studies*, ed. J. Coakley and E. Dunning, 8-25. London: Sage.

Lumpkin, A. 2010, October. Teachers and coaches as leaders demonstrating character and competence. *JOPERD* 81 (8), 49-52.

Luschen, G. 2000. Doping in sport as deviant behavior and its social control. In *Handbook of sports studies*, ed. J. Coakley and E. Dunning, 461-476. London: Sage.

MacLeod, C. 2007. Chinese sports schools feel an urgency to find gold. *USA Today*, June 14, 1A.

Maguire, J. 1999. *Global sport: Identities, societies, civilizations*. Cambridge, UK: Polity Press/Cambridge Press.

Maguire, J., Jarvie, G., Mansfield, L., and Bradley, J. 2002. *Sport worlds: A sociological perspective*. Champaign, IL: Human Kinetics.

Major League Baseball. 2010. Rosters showcase foreign-born players. http://mlb.mlb.com/news/print.jsp?ymd=20100406&content_id=9103912&vkey=news_ml. Accessed July 12, 2010.

Malina, R., and Cumming, S. 2003. Current status and issues in youth sports. In *Youth sports: Perspectives for a new century*, ed. R. Malina and M. Clark, 7-25. Monterey, CA: Coaches Choice.

Marikar, S. 2009. Tiger Woods plus four more sports stars to fall from grace. ABC News, December 4. http://abcnews.go.com/print?id=9240643. Accessed July 27, 2010.

Marta, S. 2008. Dallas Cowboys seat license holders hope for a big return. www.seasonticketrights.com/PressBox-Article.aspx?cid=9. Accessed June 15, 2010.

Martens, R., Flannery, T., and Roetert, P. 2002. The future of coaching education in America. www.nfhs.org/script-content/va_Custom/vimdisplays/ contentpagedisplay.cfm?content. Accessed January 9, 2006.

Martens, R., and Seefeldt, V., eds. 1979. *Guidelines for children's sports*. Reprint. Washington, DC: American Alliance for Health, Physical Education, Recreation and Dance.

Martin, B. 1996. Ten reasons to oppose all Olympic Games. *Freedom* 57 (15), 7.

Martzke, R. 2003. NBC keeps rights for Olympic broadcasts through 2012. *USA Today*, June 6. www.usatoday.com/sports/olympics/2003-06-06-nbc_x.htm. Accessed June 18, 2010.

Matus, R. 2004. USF controversy goes global. *St. Petersburg Times*, September 17. http://pqasb.pqarchiver.com/sptimes/access/694655171.html?FMT=ABS&FMTS=ABS:F. Accessed January 24, 2005.

McCarthy, M. 2004. NBC Universal's gamble on Olympics pays off. *USA Today*, August 29.

McCarthy, M. 2008. Marketers alter their pitches with more females tuning in. *USA Today*. www.usatoday.

com/sports/2008-09-17-women-marketing_N. htm?loc=interstitialskip. Accessed October 19, 2010.

McMurray, B. 2010. Texas high school record book. *Texas Football Magazine, Fort Worth Star-Telegram* archives. All-time highest attendance. www.txprepsfootball.com/ Recordbook.htm. Accessed July 2, 2010.

McNamara, T. 2000. You're a dumb broad—and that's progress. *Columbia Journalism Review* 38 (5), 43.

Menez, G., and Woo, A. 2005. Best high school athletic programs. *Sports Illustrated.* http://sportsillustrated. cnn.com/2005/magazine/05/11/top.high.school0516/. Accessed January 15, 2006.

Merriam-Webster's collegiate dictionary. 2001. 11th ed. Springfield, MA: Merriam-Webster.

Messner, M. 2002. *Taking the field: Women, men and sports.* Minneapolis: University of Minnesota Press.

Messner, M., and Cooky, C. 2010. Gender in televised sports, news and highlights shows, 1989-2009. Center for Feminist Research, University of Southern California, Los Angeles.

Michener, J. 1987. *Sports in America.* Greenwich, CT: Fawcett.

Miller, R., and Associates. 2005. Sports business market research handbook. www.rkma.com. Accessed November 10, 2005.

Mills, R. 1997. Tapping innate resilience in today's classrooms. Research/practice. Center for Applied Research and Educational Improvement. University of Minnesota. www.cehd.umn.edu/CAREI/Reports/Rpractice/ Spring97/tapping.html. Accessed October 19, 2010.

Miracle, A., and Rees, C. 1994. *Lessons of the locker room: The myth of school sports.* New York: Prometheus Books.

MSNBC. 2006. A look at the NHL's new rules. www. msnbc.msn.com/id/8672777/. Accessed January 2, 2006.

Muñoz, C. 2004. Dominican baseball. http://pegasus. cc.ucf.edu/~jtorres/domrep/baseball/. Accessed October 19, 2010.

Murphy, P., Sheard, K., and Waddington, I. 2004. Figurational sociology and its application to sport. In *Handbook of sports studies*, ed. J. Coakley and E. Dunning, 92-105. London: Sage.

Muse, W. 2000. Commentary: Who is responsible for learning in our society? *Auburn University News.* January 11, 2000. www.auburn.edu//administration/univrel/ news/archive/1_00news/1_00brooks.html. Accessed May 18, 2006.

National Association of Sport and Physical Education (NASPE). 2008. *National coaching report.* Reston, VA: AAHPERD.

National Association for Sport and Physical Education (NASPE). 2009. Quality coaches, quality sports: National standards for sport coaches, 2nd edition. www. aahperd.org/naspe/standards/nationalStandards/Sport-Coaches.cfm. Accessed November 13, 2009.

National Association of State Boards of Education. 2008. Fit, healthy and ready to learn: Chapter D—policies to encourage physical activity. www.nasbe.org/index. php/shs/78-model-policies/121-policies-to-encourage-physical-activity. Accessed August 2, 2010.

National Basketball Association. 2009. NBA players from around the world: 2008-2009 season. www.nba. com/players/int_players_0809.html. Accessed July 5, 2010.

National Collegiate Athletic Association. 2007a. Sports wagering. *NCAA News* release, March 16. http://web1.ncaa.org/web_files/PressArchive/ 2007/Miscellaneous/2007%2bNCAA%2bB. Backgrounder%2b--sports%2b.Wagering.html. Accessed July 27, 2010.

National Collegiate Athletic Association. 2007b. Native American mascot policy—status list. http://web1.ncaa. org/web_files/PressArchive/2007Announcements/ Native%2bAmerican%2bMascot%2bPolicy%2b-%2bstatus%2bList.html. Accessed July 13, 2010.

National Collegiate Athletic Association. 2008a. NCAA sports sponsorship and participation rates report: 1981-82–2007-08. www.ncaapublications.com/ p-4177-1981-82-2008-09-ncaa-sports-sponsorship-and-participation-rates-report.aspx. Accessed June 16, 2009.

National Collegiate Athletic Association. 2008b. Refined reporting shines brighter light on spending. *NCAA News*, April 17. http://web1.ncaa.org/web_files/NCAANews-Archive/2008/association-wide/refined%2breportin g%2bshines%2bbrighter%2blight%2bon%2bspendi ng%2b-2bo4-17-08%2bnews.html. Accessed August 20, 2009.

National Collegiate Athletic Association. 2008c. Gender equity report for 2005-2006. www.ncaapublications. com/productdownloads/GER06.pdf. Accessed July 4, 2010.

National Collegiate Athletic Association. 2009a. NCAA Division I manual, 2008-2009 constitution, operating bylaws, and administrative bylaws. www.ncaapublica-tions.com/p-4180-2010-2011-ncaa-division-i-manual. aspx. Accessed October 26, 2009.

National Collegiate Athletic Association. 2009b. NCAA holds first-ever Division II winter championships festival. *NCAA News* release, March 5. http://web1. ncaa.org/web_files/PressArchive/2009/Champion-ships/20090305_d2_winter_champ_fest_rls.html. Accessed August 20, 2009.

National Collegiate Athletic Association. 2009c. What's the difference between Divisions I, II and III? www.ncaa. org/wps/wcm/connect/public/ncaa/about+the+ncaa/ who+we+are/differences+among+the+divisions/ division+i. Accessed August 20, 2009.

National Collegiate Athletic Association. 2009d. Who is the NCAA? www.ncaa.org/wps/wcm/connect/public/ NCAA/About+the+NCAA/Who+We+Are/. Accessed July 2, 2010.

National Collegiate Athletic Association. 2010a. Estimated probability of competing in athletics beyond the high school interscholastic level. www.ncaa.org/wps/wcm/connect/public/ncaa/issues/recruiting/probability+of+going+pro. Accessed July 5, 2010.

National Collegiate Athletic Association. 2010b. Why student-athletes are not paid to play. www.ncaa.org/wps/wcm/connect/public/ncaa/issues/why+student-athletes+are+not+paid+to+play. Accessed July 27, 2010.

National Collegiate Athletic Association. 2010c. Sports wagering study shows progress in education. www.ncaaa.org/wps/wcm/connect/public/ncaa/resources/latest+news/2010+news+stories/june+news+stories/sportswagering+study+shows+progress+in+education?pageDesign=print+template. Accessed July 27, 2010.

National Council of Youth Sports (NCYS). 2010. www.ncys.org. Accessed June 28, 2010.

National Education Association. 2005. Issues in education, school safety. www.nea.org/schoolsafety/index.html. Accessed May 2, 2006.

National Federation of State High School Associations (NFSH). 2000. Sports medicine: National eating disorders screening program targets high school segment. www.nfhs.org/ScriptContent/VA_Custom/vimdisplays/contentpagedisplay.cfm?Content_ID=230&SearchWord=eating%20disorder. Accessed September 5, 2005.

National Federation of State High School Associations. 2004. The case for high school activities. www.nfhs.org/content.aspx?id=3287&terms=The+case+for+high+school+activities. Accessed October 19, 2010.

National Federation of State High School Associations. 2006. Sexual harassment and hazing: Your actions make a difference! www.nfhs.org/search.aspx?searchtext=Sexual%20harassment%20and%20hazing. Accessed October 19, 2010.

National Federation of State High School Associations. 2008-2009. Athletics participation survey. www.nfhs.org. Accessed June 27, 2010.

National Federation of State High School Associations. 2009a. *High School Today*. Pay to play sports. http://www.nfhs.org/search.aspx?searchtext=Pay%20to%20play%20sports. Accessed October 19, 2010.

National Federation of State High School Associations. 2009b. Press release. High school sports participation increases for 20th consecutive year. www.nfhs.org/content.aspx?id=3505. Accessed June 21, 2010.

National Federation of State High School Associations. 2009c. Press release. Three new coach education courses now available. www.nfhs.org/content.aspx?id=3531. Accessed November 13, 2009.

National Federation of State High School Associations. 2010. NFHS coaches code of ethics. www.misshsaa.com/coaches_code_of_ethicsathle.htm. Accessed July 29, 2010.

National Institutes of Health. 2008. Children's physical activity drops from age 9-15, NIH study indicates. http://newsinhealth.nih.gov/2008/September/capsules.htm. Accessed October 19, 2010.

National Senior Games Association. 2010. History of NSGA. www.nationalseniorgames.com/about-nsga/history-nsga. Accessed July 20, 2010.

National Sporting Goods Association. 2009. Women increase market clout in 2009 athletic footwear purchases. www.nsga.org/i4a/pages/index..cm?pageid=4302. Accessed July 16, 2010.

National Survey of Children's Health (NSCH). 2005. Overweight and physical activity among children: A portrait of states and the nation. http://hchb.hrsa.gov.overweight.into.htm. Accessed June 26, 2010.

National Women's Law Center. 2002. *The battle for gender equity in athletics: Title IX at thirty*. June. Washington, DC.

Native American Sports Council (NASC). 2009. Native American professional athletes and Olympic athletes. www.nascsports.org. Accessed September 16, 2009.

Neuman, R. 2005. Adventures in cybersound. www.acmi.net.au/AIC/ENC_BROADCASTING.html. Accessed November 10, 2005.

Newman, M. 2010. First lady announces "Let's Move!" campaign. Major League Baseball. www.mlb.com/news/print.jsp?ymd=20100719&content_id=12406930vkey=news. Accessed July 22, 2010.

NewsSmith. 1996. Post Olympics: What's next? www.smith.edu/newssmith/NSFall96/PostOlympics.html. Accessed May 10, 2006.

New York Daily News. 2010. Glee (TV Show). www.nydailynews.com/topics/Glee+(TV+Show). Accessed October 1, 2010.

New York Post. 2010. 700M watched World Cup final. www.nypost.com/f/print/entertainment/tv/watched_world_cup_final_tuIZvchzSI6hV. Accessed July 15, 2010.

New York Street Games. 2010. A crash course for the essential urban games. Book and DVD. www.newyorkstreetgames.com/home.html. Accessed October 10, 2010.

Nichols, K. 1997. What is the relationship between eating disorders and female athletes? www.vanderbilt.edu/AnS/psychology/health_psychology/sport.htm. Accessed September 5, 2005.

Nielsen Media Research. 2008. Beijing Games most-watched Olympics ever. http://blog.nielsen.com/nielsenwire/media_entertainment/beijing-games-most-watched-olympics-ever. Accessed July 6, 2010.

Nielsen Company. 2010. Viewers prefer Olympic-themed ads. www.marketingcharts.com/television/viewers-prefer-olympic-themed-ads-12116/. Accessed October 12, 2010.

Nielsen Media Research. 2010. 2010 World Cup reaches nearly 112 million U.S. viewers. http://blog.nielsen.com/nielsenwire/media_entertainment/2010-world-cup-reaches-nearly-112-million-u-s-viewers/. Accessed July 15, 2010.

Nixon, H. 2008. *Sport in a changing world*, 158-164. Champaign, IL: Human Kinetics.

O'Keefe, M., and Quinn, T. 2005. Yanks losing at money ball. *Daily News* (New York), December 4.

Olympic Charter. 2004. Fundamental principles of Olympism. #1. http://multimedia.olympic.org/pdf/en_report_122.pdf. Accessed October 14, 2004.

Olympics Fanhouse. 2010. Visnovsky reprimanded after doping test, February 22. http://olympics.fanhouse.com/2010/02/28/visnovsky-repreimanded-after-doping-test/. Accessed July 27, 2010.

Orlando Sentinel. 2010. Women are bigger viewers of the Kentucky Derby. http://blogs.orlandosentinel.com/sport-sentinel-sports-now/2010/04/30/kentucky-derby-w. Accessed July 15, 2010.

Orlick, T. 1974. The sports environment, a capacity to enhance, a capacity to destroy. Paper presented at the 6th Canadian Symposium of Sports Psychology, September, Halifax, Nova Scotia.

Osborne, B. 2010. NCAA on demand website breaks single day record. http://geek.com/articles/news/ncaa-on-demand-website-breaks-single-day-record-2010. Accessed June 18, 2010.

Outward Bound. 2010. About Outward Bound. www.outwardbound.org/index.cfm/do/exp.about. Accessed July 25, 2010.

Overman, S.J. 1997. *The influence of the Protestant ethic on sport and recreation*. Aldershot, UK: Avebury Press.

Page, R. 2009. Freedom Spirit senior women's softball team remains golden. *Saint Petersburg Times*. August 23. http://www.tampabay.com/sports/community/article1029623.ece. Accessed October 9, 2009.

Pappano, L., and Taylor, L. 2009. Acosta and Carpenter on why it's nonsense-talk that females want male coaches. WomenTalkSports.com. www.womentalksport.com/items/read/52/63191. Accessed July 15, 2010.

Parker, S. 2004. Few make money. *USA Today*, September 1.

Parisotto, R. 2006. Sport and bio-technology—the future is almost here. www.sportingo.com/sports/a966_sport-biotechnology-future-almost-here. Accessed October 16, 2010.

Payne, E., and Isaacs, L. 2008. *Human motor development*. 7th ed. New York: McGraw-Hill.

Payscale. 2010. Salary snapshot for sports anchor jobs. www.payscale.com/research/US/Job-Sports_Anchor/Salary. Accessed June 19, 2010.

Pennsylvania State University. 2010. Penn State University official athletic site—football. www.gopsusports.com/sports/mtt/paterno-joe00html. Accessed July 30, 2010.

Peretti-Watel, P., Guafliardo, V., Vergeris, P., Mignon, P., Pruvost, J., and Obadia, Y. 2004. Attitudes toward doping and recreational drug use among French elite student-athletes. *Sociology of Sport Journal* 21 (1).

PewInternet.org. 2009. Pew Research Center's Internet and American Life Project. Home broadband adoption. http://pewinternet.org/Reports/2009/10-Home-Adoption-2009.aspx. Accessed June 18, 2010.

Plotz, D. 2000. The god of the gridiron. *Slate*, February 4. www.slate.com/toolbar.aspx?action=print&id=74294. Accessed July 21, 2010.

Politi, S. 2010. St. Anthony coach Bob Hurley Sr. to be inducted into Naismith Basketball Hall of Fame. *Newark Star-Ledger*, April 2. http://blog.nj.com/njsports_impact/print.html?entry=/2010/04/st_anthony_coach_bob_hurley. Accessed July 30, 2010.

Potuto, J., and O'Hanlon, J. 2006. National study of student athletes regarding their experiences as college students. University of Nebraska–Lincoln and supported by grant from NCAA. http://findarticles.com/p/articles/mi_m0FCR/is_4_41/ai_n27484184/. Accessed January 10, 2010.

Powell, S. 2008. *Souled out: How blacks are winning and losing in sports*. Champaign, IL: Human Kinetics.

President's Council on Physical Fitness and Sports. 2010. Physical activity facts. www.fitness.gov/resources_factsheet.htm. Accessed May 24, 2010.

Pribut, S., and Richie, D. 2002: A sneaker odyssey. www.drpribut.com/sports/sneaker_odyssey.html. Accessed June 7, 2006.

Price, S.L. 1997, December. Is it in the genes? *Sports Illustrated*, 52 ff.

Publishers Weekly. 2005. http://reviews.publishersweekly.com/bd.aspx?isbn=0060758635&pub=pw. Accessed June 8, 2006.

Quest. 2006. www.pastornet.net.au/quest/mission.htm. Accessed June 7, 2006.

Quinn, E. 2005. Eating disorders in athletes: About health and fitness. www.sportsmedicine.about.com/cs/eating-disorders. Accessed September 5, 2005.

Quinn, L. 2007. Most popular sports around the world. http://ezinearticles.com/?Most-Popular-Sports-Around-The-World&id=551180&opt=print. Accessed June 4, 2009.

Quinn, K. 2009. *Sports and their fans*. Jefferson, NC: McFarland.

Quinn, T.J., and Fainaru-Wada, M. 2008. U.S. pro sports leagues still trail in drug-testing arms race, May 22. ESPN.com. http://sports.espn.go.com/espn/print?id=3408399&type=Columnist&imagesPrint=off. Accessed November 1, 2009.

Reed, F. 2010. Social media and the future of sports. Sports Marketing 2.0. www.marketingpilgrim.com/2010/01/social-media-and-the-future-of-sports.html. Accessed July 30, 2010.

Rees, C., and Miracle, A. 2004. Education and sport. In *Handbook of sports studies*, ed. J. Coakley and E. Dunning, 277-290. London: Sage.

Rhoden, W. 2007. *Third and a mile: From Fritz Pollard to Michael Vick—an oral history of the trials, tears and triumphs of the black quarterback*. New York. ESPN.

Rhoden, W. 2009. Stringer's long, rewarding trip to Hall of Fame. *New York Times*, September 10. www.nytimes.com/2009/09/10/sports/basketball/10rhoden.html?ref=c_vivian_stringer. Accessed July 30, 2010.

Rice, E., Hutchinson, J., and Lee, M. 1958. *A brief history of physical education*. New York: Ronald Press.

Rice, G. 1941. *Only the brave and other poems*. New York: Barnes.

Riemer, H., and Chelladurai, P. 1995. Leadership and satisfaction in athletics. *Journal of Sport and Exercise Psychology* 17, 276-293.

Rigauer, B. 2004. Marxist theories. In *Handbook of sports studies*, ed. J. Coakley and E. Dunning, 28-47. London: Sage.

Ritzer, G. 2004. *The globalization of nothing*. Thousand Oaks, CA: Pine Forge Press.

Rivers, C. 2003. Sports stars act like perks include abusing women. Women's eNews. http://womensenews.org/story/commentary/031008/sports-stars-act-perks-include-abusing-women. Accessed February 4, 2005.

Robinson, M. 2010. *Sport club management*. Champaign, IL: Human Kinetics.

Robinson, R. 1999. *Rockne of Notre Dame: The making of a legend*. New York: Oxford University Press.

Rubin, R. 2010. St. Anthony High School (Jersey City) coaching legend Bob Hurley voted into Basketball Hall of Fame. *New York Daily News*, April 6. www.nydailynews.com/fdcp?1280499055495. Accessed July 30, 2010.

Sabo, D., Miller, K., Melnick, M., and Heywood, L. 2004. *Her life depends on it: Sport, physical activity and the health and well-being of American girls*. East Meadow, NY: Women's Sports Foundation.

Sage, G. 1972. Value orientations of American college and high school coaches. *Proceedings of the 75th Annual NCPEA for Men*, 174-186.

Sage, G. 1973, October. Occupational socialization and value orientations of athletic coaches. *Research Quarterly* 44, 269-277.

Sage, G. 1998. *Power and ideology in American sport*. 2nd ed. Champaign, IL: Human Kinetics.

Sanchez, J. 2005. Latino Legends team announced. http://mlb.mlb.com/NASApp/mlb/news/article.jsp?ymd=20051026&content_id=1260107&vkey=news_mlb &fext=.jsp&c_id=mlb. Accessed December 4, 2005.

Sandomir, R. 1997. Murdoch bids for Dodgers simply to bolster a lineup. *New York Times*, May 16. http://marshallinside.usc.edu/mweinstein/teaching/fbe552/552secure/notes/dodgers-murdoch. Accessed June 10, 2006.

Sandomir, R. 2010. World cup ratings certify a TV winner. *New York Times*. www.nytimes.com/2010/06/29/sports/soccer/29sandomir.html?scp=1&sq=World cup ratings certify a TV winner&st=cse. Accessed October 9, 2010.

Santa Fe Independent School District vs. Doe, U.S. Supreme Court. 2000. Ontario Consultants on Religious Tolerance. www.religioustolerance.org. Accessed July 3, 2005.

Sappenfield, M. 2010. Bode Miller bronze: What a difference four years makes, February 15. www.csmonitor.com/layout/set/print/content/view/print/280409. Accessed July 27, 2010.

Scheiber, D. 2004. History of Olympic Games. *St. Petersburg Times* (St. Petersburg, FL), September 8.

Scheiber, D. 2005. Extreme evolution. *St. Petersburg Times* (St. Petersburg, FL), August 4, C1, C8.

Schrager, A. 2004. CU president testifying before Congress. www.9news.com/storyfull.aspx?storyid=25369. Accessed October 15, 2005.

Schultz, J. 2004. Discipline and push-up: Female bodies, femininity, and sexuality in popular representations of sports bras. *Sociology of Sport Journal* 21 (2).

Schwartz, A. 2009. Ex-N.F.L. executive sounds alarm on head injury. *New York Times*, October 28. www.nytimes.com/2009/10/28/sports/football/28football.html?_r=1&pagewanted=p. Accessed November 1, 2009.

Schwartz, L. 2005a. Billie Jean won for all women. www.espn.go.com/sportscentury/features/00016060.html. Accessed June 2, 2006.

Schwartz, L. 2005b. Jackie changed the face of sports. www.espn.go.com/sportscentury/features/00016431.html. Accessed August 13, 2005.

Seefeldt, V., Ewing, M., and Walk, S. 1992. *Overview of youth sports programs in the United States*. Washington, DC: Carnegie Council on Adolescent Development.

Sharp, D. 1994. The women who took the jounce out of jogging. *Health Magazine*, September 25.

Sheffer, M., and Schultz, B. 2007. Double standard: Why women have trouble getting jobs in local television sports. *Journal of Sports Media* 2, 77-101. http://muse.jhu.edu/login?uri=/journals/journal_of_sports_media/v002/2.sheffer.html. Accessed July 18, 2010.

Shelton, G. 2005. This is the week of hit man. *St. Petersburg Times* (St. Petersburg, FL), February 3, 1C.

Shields, D. 2002. Charles Barkley's head fake. *Slate*, November 22. www.slate.com/id/2074459/. Accessed March 15, 2004.

Shields, D. 2005. Bad behavior cited in youth sports study. *USA Today*, November 29, 13C.

Simmons, K. 2002. Sex crimes on campus often silent. *Atlanta Journal Constitution* (Atlanta, GA), February 17.

Slater, R. 2003. *Great Jews in sport*. Middle Village, NY: Jonathan David.

Sleek, S. 2004. Psychologists help debunk the myth of Michael Jordan. www.umich.edu/~paulball/webpage%20papers/Psychologists_Michael-Jordan.htm. Accessed December 16, 2004.

Smart, R. and Smart, M. 1982. Children: Development and relations. 4th ed. New York: MacMillan, 460-463.

Smit, B. 2008. *Sneaker wars*. New York: Harper Collins.

Smith, H. 2009. FAQs about me. http://ladyfigureskater.com/index.php?option=com_content&view=article&id=23&Itemid. Accessed July 17, 2010.

Smith, J. 2010. On cue, New York Yankees' Derek Jeter goes into acting mode. St. Petersburg Times at tampabay.com. www.tampabay.com/sports/baseball/rays/on-cue-new-york-yankees-derek-jeter-goes-into-acting-mode/1121913. Accessed October 12, 2010.

Smith, R. 1986. Toward a cognitive-affective model of athletic burnout. *Journal of Sport Behavior* 18 (1), 3-20.

Spears, B., and Swanson, R. 1978. *History of sport and physical activity in the United States*. Dubuque, IA: Brown.

Special Olympics. 2010. www.specialolympics.org. Accessed July 21, 2010.

Splitt, F. 2004. The faculty-driven movement to reform big-time college sports. Drake Group. www.thedrakegroup.org. Accessed January 20, 2005.

Sporting Goods Manufacturers Association. 2001. Youth sports in America: The parental perspective. www.sgma.com. Accessed February 20, 2005.

Sporting Goods Manufacturers Association (SGMA). 2004. Sports participation topline report. 2004 edition. www.sgma.com. Accessed March 10, 2004.

Sporting Goods Manufacturers Association. 2005a. Extreme-sports: Ranking high in popularity. Press release. May 31, 2005. www.sgma.com/press/2005/1117636042-19826.html. Accessed August 4, 2004.

Sporting Goods Manufacturers Association. 2005b. Team sport in a state of flux: The ups and downs. www.sgma.com. Accessed February 20, 2005.

Sporting Goods Manufacturers Association. 2008a. Extreme sports: An ever-popular attraction. www.sgma.com/press/2_Extreme-Sports:-An-Ever-Popular-Attraction. Accessed August 13, 2009.

Sporting Goods Manufacturers Association. 2008b. U.S. trend in team sports. 2008 edition. www.sgma.com/reports/233_US-Trends-In-Team-Sports-2008-Edition. Accessed June 29, 2009.

Sporting Goods Manufacturers Association. 2008c. Sports participation topline report. 2008 edition. www.sgma.com. Accessed July 10, 2009.

Sporting Goods Manufacturers Association. 2009a. SGMA's 2009 tracking the fitness movement. www.sgma.com. Accessed October 8, 2009.

Sporting Goods Manufacturers Association. 2009b. Peak age analysis reveals keys to growing team sports. www.sgma.com/press/145_Peak-Age-Analysis-Reveals-Keys-to-Growing-Team-Sp. Accessed October 12, 2009.

Sporting Goods Manufacturers Association. 2009c. Organized sport play dominates team sport market. www.sgma.com/press/153_Organized-Sport-Play-Dominates-Team-Sports-Market. Accessed October 12, 2009.

Sporting Goods Manufacturers Association. 2009d. Team sports participation affected by many outside factors. www.sgma.com/press/171_Team-Sports-Participation-Affected-By-Many-Outside-Factors. Accessed June 25, 2010.

Sporting Goods Manufacturers Association. 2010. Sports participation topline report. 2010 edition. www.sgma.com.

SportingNews. 2003a. Commission seeks fix for scandal-plagued U.S. Olympic Committee, June 19. www.sportingnews.com/soccer/articles/20030619/479205p.html. Accessed June 10, 2004.

SportsBusiness Daily. 2009. U.S. Open on pace for around $200 M in revenue, $110-115 M profit. www.sportsbusinessdaily.com/article/132960. Accessed June 15, 2010.

Sports Doctor, Inc. 2000. Women's issues. The female athlete. www.sportsdoctor.com/articles/female9.html. Accessed June 8, 2006.

Sports Illustrated for Women. 2000. Top 100 female athletes of the 20th century. http://sportsillustrated.cnn.com/siforwomen/top_100/1/. Accessed September 24, 2009.

Srakocic, K. 2010. NHL players' union approves ban on head shots. http://www.usatoday.com/sports/hockey/nhl/2010-03-25-head-shot-rule_N.htm. Accessed October 19, 2010

Streetplay. 2010. Stickball: Do you have what it takes? www.streetplay.com/stickball/equipment.shtml. Accessed October 10, 2010.

Steeves, B. 2003. Top 15 frequently asked questions about stadiums. www.leg.state.mn.us/docs/2004/other/040634/Stadium/www.stadium.state.mn.us/faq.pdf. Accessed October 19, 2010.

Stephen, E. 1994. For love, for money, for real money. www.wwu.edu/~stephan/webstuff/es.19thBB.html. Accessed Ocober 10, 2004

Stevens, T. 2005. Ted Stevens Olympic and Amateur Sports Act. http://videos.usoc.org/legal/TedStevens.pdf. Accessed October 19, 2010

Stevenson, C. 1997. Christian athletes and the culture of elite sport: Dilemmas and solutions. *Sociology of Sport Journal* 14, 241-262.

Stewart, C. 2005. Should boys and girls be coached the same way? www.coachesinfo.com/category/becoming_a_better_coach/13/. Accessed March 2, 2005.

Stoll, S., and Beller, J. 2005. Female student athletes' moral reasoning 1987-2005. Center for Ethics, University of Idaho. www.educ.uidaho.edu/center_for_ethics/index.htm. Accessed June 20, 2005.

StopHazing. 2009. Myths & facts about hazing. www.stophazing.org/mythsandfacts.html. Accessed November 2, 2009.

St. Petersburg Times. 2005. Always a diamond jubilee. February 9.

St. Petersburg Times. 2007. New York Yankee$$$. June 14, 2C.

Suggs, W. 2002. Title IX at 30: In the arena of women's college sports, the 1972 law created a legacy of debate. *Chronicle of Higher Education* 48 (14), A38-42.

Sundgot-Borgen, J., and Torstveit, M.K. 2004. Prevalence of eating disorders in elite athletes is higher than in the general population. http://journals.lww.com/cjsportsmed/Abstract/2004/01000/Prevalence_of_Eating_Disorders_in_Elite_Athletes.5.aspx. Accessed October 19, 2010.

Team Marketing Report. 2008. Fan cost index. www.teammarketing.com/fancost/. Accessed June 25, 2009.

Television Bureau of Advertising. 2005. Top 25 network telecasts (sports). www.tvb.org. Accessed January 15, 2006.

Texas University Interscholastic League. 1998. Benefits of extracurricular activities. www.uil.utexas.edu/admin/benefits.html. Accessed November 14, 2004.

Thamel, P. 2010. U.S. Basketball prodigy quits Israeli pro team. *New York Times.* www.nytimes.com/2010/03/20/sports/basketball/20tyler.html?_r=1&ref=jeremy_tyler. Accessed July 6, 2010.

Thibaut, A. 2009. Women as consumers of sport: Myth or reality? Presentation at 2009 Women and Sport Conference, London. www.nzc-consulting.com/assets/pdfs/articles/7.pdf. Accessed October 19, 2010.

TMZ. 2010. NFL star accused of beating pregnant girlfriend. January 28. www.tmz.com/2010/01/28/steven-jackson-pregnant-girlfriend-beating-police-report-statement-las-vegas-nf/. Accessed October 19, 2010.

Topkin, M. 2004. Provocative poses divide U.S. women. *St. Petersburg Times* (St. Petersburg, FL), August 25, 9C.

Tornoe, J. 2005. Olympic-style sporting tournament to showcase Hispanic athletes. http://juantornoe.blogs.com/hispanictrending/2005/11/olympicstyle_sp.html. Accessed December 4, 2005.

Tse, A. 2010. Tiger's scandal: A $30 million hit? *The Street,* June 16. www.thestreet.com/print/story/10787342.html. Accessed July 27, 2010.

Tsiokos, C. 2005. Sports as the opiate of the masses. Population Statistic, September 4. www.population-statistic.com/index.php?s=Sports+as+the+opiate+of+the+ masses&submit=search. Accessed May 15, 2006.

Tufts University. 2006. Athletic footwear: Industry analysis: www.docstoc.com/docs/7937512/Athletic-Footwear-Industries-Analysis. Accessed July 1, 2009.

Tuggle, C. 2003. Study shows ESPN still not paying much attention to women's sport. www.unc.edu/news/archives/aug03/tuggle080103.html. Accessed October 19, 2010.

Turco, D., and Ostrosky, T. 1997. Touchdowns and fumbles: Urban investments in NFL franchises. *Cyber-Journal of Sport Marketing.* www.ausport.gov.au/fulltext/1997/cjsm/v1n3/turco.htm. Accessed November 3, 2005.

United Cerebral Palsy. 2004. Americans with Disabilities Act. An overview. www.ucp.org/ucp_generaldoc.cfm/1/8/32/32-11218/3905. Accessed October 19, 2010.

United States Bureau of Labor Statistics. 2009. Occupational employment and wages, May 2009: 27-2021 athletes and sports competitors. www.bls.gov/oes/current/oes272021.htm. Accessed November 5, 2010.

United States Census Bureau. 2005-2007. Fact sheet. American Community Survey 3-year estimates. http://factfinder.census.gov?servletACSSAFFFacts?_submenuId=factsheet_0&_sse=on. Accessed June 24, 2009.

United States Census Bureau. 2006-2008 American Survey 3-Year Estimates. S2301 Employment Status. http://factfinder.census.gov/servlet/STTTable?_bm=y&-geo_id=01000US&-qr_name=AC. Accessed October 9, 2010.

United States Census Bureau. 2008a. An older and more diverse nation by midcentury. Press release. www.census.gov/Press-Release/wwwreleases/archives/population/012496.html. Accessed September 3, 2009.

United States Census Bureau. 2008b. Current population survey for 2008. www.ilr.cornell.edu/edi/disabilitystatistics/StatusReports/2008-PDF/2008-StatusReport_US.pdf?CFID=7053820&CFTOKEN=32757198&jsessionid=f03092faaaed6a432e68165f123586b4c6b7. Accessed October 19, 2010.

United States Census Bureau. 2008c. Income and Earnings Summary Measures by Selected Characteristics: 2009 and 2009. Table 1. www.census.gov/prod/2010pubs/p60-238pdf. Accessed October 14, 2010.

United States Census Bureau. 2008d. People and families in poverty by selected characteristics: 2008-2009. Table 4. www.census.gov/hhes/www/poverty/data/incpovhlth/2009/table4.pdf. Accessed October 14, 2010.

United States Census Bureau. 2009. Statistical abstract of the United States. Arts, recreation and leisure. Tables for 2007 and 2008. http://www.census.gov/prod/2007pubs/08abstract/arts.pdf. Accessed October 19, 2010.

United States Department of Health and Human Services. 1997. Shalala urges greater sports participation for girls; releases first government report showing physical, mental and social benefits of sports and physical activity for girls. Press release, March 28. www.girlpower.gov/press/research/sports.htm. Accessed May 14, 2006.

United States Department of Health and Human Services. 2001. Overweight and obesity threaten U.S. health gains; physical activity is critical. Press release. December 13. www.fitness.gov/sg_cta-obesity.htm. Accessed April 25, 2004.

United States Department of Health and Human Services. 2008. HHS announces physical activity guidelines for Americans. News release. www.hhs.gov/news/press/2008pres/10/20081007a.html. Accessed October 14, 2009.

United States Equestrian Team Foundation. 2010. www.uset.org/contact.php. Accessed July 19, 2010.

United States Lacrosse Association. 2009. Lacrosse participation in 2009. www.uslacrosse.org/LinkClick.aspx?fileticket=CleeYXUm2Js%3d&tabid=2907. Accessed July 10, 2010.

United States Olympic Committee. 2010, General Information. http://www.teamusa.org/about-usoc/usoc-general-information. Accessed October 22, 2010.

United States Paralympics. 2010. The Paralympics Games. http://usparalympics.org. Accessed October 19, 2010.

United States Tennis Association. 2004. USTA 2004 yearbook. Lynn, MA: H.O. Zimman.

United States Tennis Association. 2008. World's largest public tennis park—and home of the US Open—to be renamed USTA Billie Jean King National Tennis Center. www.usta.com/Active/News/USTA-News/Press-Releases/351958_USTA_To_Rename_National_Tennis_Center_To_Honor_Billie_Jean_King/. Accessed October 19, 2010.

United States Tennis Association. 2010. No-cut school tennis teams. www.usta.com/youth-Tennis/schools/highschool/. Accessed July 30, 2010.

Up2Us. Coach for America. An innovative coaching model. www.up2us.org/coach-for-america. Assessed December 10, 2009.

USA Coaching. 2010. United States Olympic Committee: Coaching ethics code. www.usacoaching.org/resources/Coaching%20Ethics%20Code_new.pdf. Accessed October 16, 2010.

USA Network. 2010. Coach. www.usanetwork.com/series/coach/. Accessed October 9, 2010.

USA Today. 2003. NBC keeps rights for Olympic broadcasts through 2012. http://usatoday.printthis.clickability.com/pt/cpt?action=cpt&title=USATODAY.com+-+N. Accessed June 18, 2010.

USA Today. 2009. NFL average ticket prices rise; thank the Dallas Cowboys. http://content.usatoday.com/communities/thehuddle/post/2009/09/nfl-average-ticket-prices-rise-thank-the-dallas-cowboys/1 Accessed October 6, 2009.

USA Today. 2010. A day to promote good sportsmanship across the USA. www.usatoday.com/sports/2010-02-27-sportsmanship-day_N.htm?loc=interstitialskip. Accessed September 25, 2010.

Vancouver Sun. 2010. NBC's Vancouver Olympic coverage ousts American Idol from TV ratings throne.

February 18. www.vancouversun.com/story_print.html?id=2581974&sponsor=. Accessed July 5, 2010.

VanderZwaag, H., and Sheehan, T. 1978. Introduction to sport studies. Dubuque, IA: Brown.

Van Riper, T. 2009. The future of sports. www.forbes.com/2009/03/04/nba-nhl-mlb-nfl-sports-business_future_sports.html. Accessed August 1, 2010.

Vare, R. 1974. Buckeye: A study of coach Woody Hayes and the Ohio State football machine. Harper Magazine Press, 38.

Voepel, M. 2008. "Bad girls" mind-set, Pierson and Parker a volatile mix. http://sports.espn.go.com/wnba/columns/story?columnist=voepel_mechelle&id=3502251. Accessed October 19, 2010.

Wacquant, L. 2004. Body and soul: Notebooks of an apprentice boxer. New York: Oxford University Press.

Waldron, J. 2000. Stress, overtraining and burnout associated with participation in sport. Unpublished thesis. Lansing: Institute for the Study of Youth Sports at Michigan State University.

Wall Street Journal. 2004a. National finances league. St. Petersburg Times, September 21, D-1.

Wall Street Journal. 2004b. Sole search: When the shoe doesn't fit. St. Petersburg Times, August 28. D-1.

Washington Post. 2005. UCI criticizes drug allegations against Armstrong, September 10. www.washingtonpost.com/wp-dyn/content/article/2005/09/AR2005090901949.html. Accessed December 3, 2005.

Watkins, B. 2009. Black Coaches Association happy with NCAA college football. Black voices. www.bvonsports.com/2009/12/28/black-coaches-association-122809/. Accessed July 15, 2010.

Watson, N., and Czech, D. 2005. The use of prayer in sport: Implications for sport psychology consulting. http://athleticinsight.com/Vol7Iss4/PrayerinSports.htm. Accessed October 19, 2010.

Weber, S. 1956, September. Krauss-Weber tests. Pennsylvania Journal of Health, Physical Education and Recreation, 14-15.

Webster's Sports Dictionary. 1976. Springfield, MA: Merriam.

Wechsler, H. 2005. Binge drinking on America's college campuses. Findings from the Harvard School of Public Health College Alcohol Study. Cambridge, Massachusetts. www.hsph.harvard.edu/cas/Documents/monograph_2000/cas_mono_2000.pdf. Accessed October 19, 2010.

Weekley, D. 2009. No denying Tiger's effect on television ratings. Charleston Gazette, April 11. www.wvgazette.com/Sports/DaveWeekely/200904110289. Accessed August 25, 2009.

Weinberg, R. 30: Tyson bites Holyfield's ear in rematch. ESPN.com. http://sports.espn.go.com/espn25/story?page=moments/30. Accessed July 26, 2010.

Weinberg, R., and Gould, D. 2005. *Foundations of sport and exercise psychology*. 4th ed. Champaign, IL: Human Kinetics.

Wendel, T. 2005. When smiles leave the game. *USA Today*, August 23, A-13.

Wilhelm, S. 2008. Public funding of sports stadiums. Policy perspectives. www.cppa.utah.edu/publications/finance_tax/Sports_Stadiums.pdf. Accessed October 19, 2010.

Willmsen, C. 2004. Felons found coaching amateur youth sports. Crimes revealed in Washington, Idaho; background checks considered nationally. *Seattle Times*. March 7. www.thefreelibrary.com/_/print/PrintArticle.aspx?id=113988706. Accessed July 23, 2010.

Wilson, S. 2010. AP Source: Backup samples positive for 5 Olympians. http://abcnews.go.com/print?id=8032799. Accessed October 19, 2010.

Wilt, P. 2010. 2020 vision of American soccer's future. Pitch invasion. http://pitchinvasion.net/blog/2010/05/05/2020-vision-of-american-soccers-future/. Accessed August 1, 2010.

Wojnarowski, A. 2005. *The miracle of St. Anthony*. New York: Gotham Books.

Women's Basketball Hall of Fame. 2010. C. Vivian Stringer. www.wbhof.com/stringer.html. Accessed July 30, 2010.

WomenSport International. 2006. Interesting media coverage facts. www.sportsbiz.bz/womensportinternational/archives/2003/040103_wsf_media.htm. Accessed June 12, 2006.

Women's Sports Foundation. 1989. *Minorities in sport: The effect of varsity sports participation on the social, educational and career mobility of minority students*. New York: Women's Sports Foundation.

Women's Sports Foundation. 1995. Media—images and words in women's sports: The foundation position. www.womenssportsfoundation.org/Content/Articles/Issues/Media-and-Publicity/M/Media--Images-and-Words-In-Womens-Sports-The-Foundation-Position.aspx. Accessed October 19, 2010.

Women's Sports Foundation. 1998. Research report: Sport and teen pregnancy. www.womenssportsfoundation.org/Content/Research-Reports/Research-Report-Sport-and-Teen-Pregnancy.aspx. Accessed October 19, 2010.

Women's Sports Foundation. 2001a. The female athlete triad. www.womenssportsfoundation.org/cgi-bin/iowa/issues/body/article.html?record=721. Accessed June 2, 2006.

Women's Sports Foundation. 2001b. Research report: Health risks and the teen athlete. www.womenssportsfoundation.org/Content/Research-Reports/Research-Report-Health-Risks-and-the-Teen-Athlete.aspx. Accessed October 19, 2010.

Women's Sports Foundation. 2007. Addressing the issue of verbal, physical and psychological abuse of athletes: The foundation position. www.womenssportsfounda-tion.org/Content/Articles/Issues/Coaching/A/Addressing-the-Issue-of-Verbal-Physical-and-Psychological-Abuse-of-Athletes--The-Foundation-Position.aspx. Accessed October 19, 2010.

Women's Sports Foundation. 2008. Go out and play: Youth sports in America. www.womenssportsfoundation.org/Content/Research-Reports/Go-Out-and-Play.aspx. Accessed June 28, 2010.

Women's Sports Foundation. 2009. Women's sports and fitness facts and statistics. www.womenssportsfoundation.org. Updated March 26, 2009. Accessed September 24, 2009.

Woods, R. 2004. *Coaching tennis successfully*. Champaign, IL: Human Kinetics

World Anti-Doping Agency. 2010. A brief history of anti-doping. www.wada-ama/org/en/About-WADA/History/A-Brief-History-of-Anti-Doping/. Accessed October 19, 2010.

World Health Organization. 2003. Health and development through physical activity and sport. www.goforyourlife.vic.gov.au/hav/admin.nsf/Images/WHO_statement_on_health_and_PA.pdf/$File/WHO_statement_on_health_and_PA.pdf. Accessed May 22, 2010.

World of Sport Science. 2009. Mature athletes. www.faqs.org/sports-science/Je-Mo/Mature-Athletes.html. Accessed October 19, 2010.

World Sports for All Congress. 2002. Sport for all and elite sport: Rivals or partners? http://multimedia.olympic.org/pdf/en_report_555.pdf. Accessed September 15, 2004.

World Team Tennis. 2010. Billie Jean King. www.wtt.com/page.aspx?article_id=1252. Accessed October 19, 2010.

Wottenberg, B.B. 2003. *It will be a smaller world after all*. Washington, DC: American Enterprise Institute.

Young, K. 2004. Sport and violence. In *Handbook of sports studies*, ed. J. Coakley and E. Dunning, 382-408. London: Sage.

YMCA. 2010. A brand new day: The YMCA unveils new brand strategy to further community impact. www.ymca.net/news-releases/20100712-brand-new-day.html. Accessed July 22, 2010.

Zarda, B. 2008. Double amputee sprinter cleared for olympic competition. *Popular Science*. www.popsci.com/score/article/2008-05/double-amputee-sprinter-cleared-olympic-competition. Accessed July 20, 2010.

Zegers, C. 2008. Brandon Jennings goes to Europe. About.com: Basketball. http://basketball.about.com/od/nbadraft/a/brandonjennings.htm. Accessed July 6, 2010.

Zimbalist, A. 2010. Is it worth it? *Finance & Development*, March. www.imf.org/external/pubs/ft/fandd/2010/03/pdf/zimbalist.pdf. Accessed June 15, 2010.

Zinser, L. 2010. U.S.C. sports receive harsh penalties. *New York Times*. www.nytimes.com/2010/06/11/sports/ncaafootball/11usc.html?_r=1&pagewanted=print. Accessed July 5, 2010.

Note: Page numbers followed by an italicized *f* or *t* refer to the figure or table on that page, respectively.

Courtesy of Ron Woods.

Ronald B. Woods, PhD, is an award-winning performance coach with Human Performance Institute and an adjunct professor at the University of Tampa and the University of South Florida. He received his PhD from Temple University. He has 40 years of experience as a teacher, coach, and administrator of sports.

Previously, he spent 20 years with the United States Tennis Association. He was named the first director of player development of a program that assisted in the development of top junior players into touring professional players—including Pete Sampras, Venus and Serena Williams, and Jennifer Capriati. In 1996, the International Tennis Hall of Fame awarded him the Educational Merit Award.

He was honored by the United States Professional Tennis Association as National Coach of the Year in 1982 and named a Master Professional in 1984. He is a member of the American Alliance for Health, Physical Education and Dance and was a member of the U.S. Olympic Coaching Committee for eight years.

*You'll find
other outstanding
sociology of sport resources at*

www.HumanKinetics.com

In the U.S. call

1-800-747-4457

Australia...08 8372 0999
Canada 1-800-465-7301
Europe..+44 (0) 113 255 5665
New Zealand...0800 222 062

HUMAN KINETICS
The Information Leader in Physical Activity & Health
P.O. Box 5076 • Champaign, IL 61825-5076 USA